Orchid Biology—Reviews and Perspectives, V

Orchid Biology

REVIEWS AND PERSPECTIVES, V

EDITED BY

JOSEPH ARDITTI

Department of Developmental and Cell Biology
University of California, Irvine

TIMBER PRESS
Portland, Oregon

© 1990 by Timber Press, Inc.
All rights reserved.

ISBN 0-88192-170-X
Printed in Hong Kong

TIMBER PRESS, INC.
9999 S.W. Wilshire
Portland, Oregon 97225

Dedicated by the editor to
Robert Ernst, Haruyuki Kamemoto, and Adisheshappa Nagaraja Rao
on their retirement

CONTENTS

ILLUSTRATIONS

BOARD OF EDITORS

AUTHORS

JOSEPH ARDITTI supported himself as an undergraduate student by working part-time for Roy M. Scott, an orchid grower in Bel Air, California. He received his Ph.D. from the University of Southern California in 1965 with a dissertation on vitamin metabolism in germinating orchid seeds. Dr. Arditti accepted a position with the University of California, Irvine, in 1966. His research centers on the biochemistry, development and physiology of orchids. Dr. Arditti spent many summers and his sabbatical leaves doing research on orchids at the Botany Department, National University of Singapore, and the Bogor Botanical Gardens in Indonesia.

LEONID VLADIMIROVICH AVERYANOV graduated from Leningrad State University in 1977 with a degree in botany. Since then he has specialized in the systematics of orchids from temperate Eurasia at the Komarov Botanical Institute of the USSR Academy of Sciences in Leningrad where he earned his doctorate in 1893. He has participated in numerous botanical expeditions within and outside the USSR. At present he is working on the systematics of Vietnamese orchids as part of a Soviet-Vietnamese Project entitled "Flora of Vietnam."

PAUL M. CATLING received his Ph.D. from the University of Toronto in 1980, after which he accepted the position he currently holds as research scientist with Agriculture Canada and Associate Curator of the Agriculture Canada herbarium (DAO). Dr. Catling's research involves taxonomy and ecology of aquatic plants, sedges and other monocot groups including the Orchidaceae. He has co-authored a book on the orchids of Ontario and has published many papers concerning ecology, pollination biology and taxonomy of temperate and neotropical orchids.

TATJANA MIKHAILOVNA CZEREVCZENKO graduated from the Biology Department of Kiev State University, Kiev, Central Republic, U.S.S.R. in 1970 with a Candidate dissertation entitled *Growth Regulators in Floriculture*. She earned her doctorate in 1985 from the same University with a dissertation on Biology and Culture of Tropical Orchids. During the last 13 years, Dr. Czerevczenko has been Chief of the Department of Tropical and Subtropical Plants at the Central Republic Botanical Garden in Kiev. She is also co-author with G. P. Kushnir of a Russian language book on orchids entitled *Orchidei v Kultura* (Orchids in Cultivation) which was published in Kiev in 1986 by the Naukova Dumka publishing house.

KINGSLEY WAYNE DIXON is currently a Research Officer at Kings Park Botanic Garden in Perth, Western Australia. Dr. Dixon obtained his undergraduate and doctoral degrees in the Botany Department of the University of Western Australia, where he also conducted much of the research reported in this volume (under a Postdoctoral Fellowship provided by the World Wildlife Fund). He has wide interests in the Western Australian flora, and, in addition to a number of research papers, has published a book entitled *Tuberous, Cormous and Bulbous Plants* co-authored by Professor J. S. Pate.

ROBERT M. HAMILTON, now retired, was Associate Professor at the School of Librarianship and Assistant Librarian for Collections at the University of British Columbia. He has compiled several reference books on Canada and a number of indexes to orchid illustrations as well as guides to the care of orchids.

IRENE V. KOSAKOVSKAYA graduated from the Biology Department, Kiev State University, Kiev, Central Republic, U.S.S.R. in 1980 with a Candidate dissertation on the *Biological Characteristics of Ribulose bis-Phosphate Carboxylase from Somatic Hybrids of Higher Plants.* Her studies centered on the molecular mechanisms of plant adaptation under different stress conditions. At present she is scientific secretary at the Central Republic Botanical Garden.

JOHN KUO is a lecturer in electron microscopy at the University of Western Australia. After graduating with a B.Sc. from the University of Taichung, Taiwan, he obtained his doctorate at Carlton University, Ottawa, Canada. Following that he accepted a postdoctoral position at Monash University, Melbourne, before taking up his present post in Western Australia. Dr. Kuo has wide ranging interests within the field of plant ultrastructure, including that of sea grasses, spikelets of wheat, pods and seeds of legumes, and storage reserves of seeds (the latter two topics in collaboration with Professor Pate).

MARTHA HOFFMAN LEWIS received an A.B. from the University of California, Berkeley, and her M.A. and Ph.D. in Latin and Greek from Bryn Mawr College. Dr. Lewis taught at the University of Illinois, Urbana and at Rockhurst College, Kansas City, Missouri. Her publication *The Official Priests of Rome under the Julio-Claudians: A Study of the Nobility from 44 B.C. to 68 A.D.* (1955, Papers and Monographs of The American Academy in Rome, vol. 16), is a scholarly book in the field of Roman history. She became interested in orchids while teaching a course on modern poetry. Dr Lewis is now retired.

JOHN STEWART PATE, a Fellow of the Australian Academy of Science and of the Royal Society (London), is currently Professor of Botany at the University of Western Australia. He is a graduate of Queens University, Belfast, Northern Ireland, where he held a personal chair in Plant Physiology from 1970–1973. Professor Pate has broad interests in plant nutrition and adaptation, working on both native and agricultural plants, especially grain legumes. He is the editor and co-author of a number of books and research publications, including several on the biology of Western Australian native plant species.

RUSSELL SINCLAIR is a lecturer in the Department of Botany, The University of Adelaide, South Australia. He received a B.Sc. Honors degree at the University of Sydney, majoring in physics, then moved into botany as a postgraduate student at the University of Adelaide where he received a Ph.D. for work on the energy balance of arid zone plants. Dr. Sinclair spent two years in the School of Biological Sciences, University of Malaya, where his interest in tropical vegetation began, before returning to Adelaide to work mainly on the water relations of arid sclerophyll vegetation. In 1978 he revisited Malaysia on sabbatical leave to carry out a study of the water relations of epiphytic ferns and orchids.

FRITS WARMOLT WENT received his Ph.D. from the University of Utrecht with a dissertation on the discovery of the first plant hormone—auxin. After receiving his Ph.D. in 1927, he accepted an appointment at the famed botanical gardens in Bogor (then Buitenzorg) Indonesia. He left Bogor at the end of 1932 to accept a position at the California Institute of Technology and arrived in Pasadena in January, 1933. While there, Prof. Went engaged in pioneering research in the plant sciences. He also trained many graduate students who went on to become well-known plant scientists in their own right. During his stay at CalTech, Prof. Went worked on orchids and was the co-formulator of the well-known Vacin and Went medium for orchid seed germination which is also used for tissue culture. Prof. Went left CalTech in 1958 to become Director of the Missouri Botanical Garden in St. Louis. He stayed in that position until 1965 when he moved to the University of Nevada, Reno, to become Director of the Desert Research Institute. After his retirement Dr. Went lived in Reno (where he wrote the opening chapter for this volume) as Professor Emeritus before moving to Oregon.

PREFACE

My aim as editor of *Orchid Biology Reviews and Perspectives* has always been, and still is, to present authoritative reviews on all aspects of the Orchidaceae. Since it is clearly impossible to accomplish this goal in one or even two volumes, *Orchid Biology Reviews and Perspectives* is a continuing series. I have also endeavored to include in each volume topics which will interest a large audience even if some chapters may have a wider appeal than others. The long term result of this approach will be a well-balanced repository of orchid knowledge. In line with this policy, the present volume of *Orchid Biology* contains chapters on topics not covered in the previous volumes (see pp. 406–407 for the contents of Vol. I–IV). Also in accordance with the established policy of this series, the chapters are written by authorities in each field and all save the first chapter were subjected to pre-publication review by at least two experts (one who knows orchids and the other a specialist in the subject), and myself.

In 1880 Charles Darwin and his son Francis suggested that a factor which diffuses from the tips of seedlings might influence phototropic responses. More than a quarter of a century later, in 1909, following research at the Bogor (then Buitenzorg) Botanical Garden in Indonesia (at that time the Netherlands Indies), the well-known German plant physiologist, Hans Fitting, proposed the term *Pollenhormon* to describe a substance in *Phalaenopsis* pollen which caused flower senescence. By doing so, Fitting became the first botanist to introduce the hormone concept, and the term itself, into plant physiology, but he did not discover the actual substance. That discovery was made by Frits W. Went as part of his dissertation research, and published in the *Proceedings of the Royal Dutch Academy of Science* (*Proceedings of Koninklijke Nederlanse Akademis van Wetenschappen* 30: 10–19, 1927). This—the discovery of the first plant hormone, the auxin indoleacetic acid—was a major advance at the time and still ranks as one of the most important discoveries in botany. It made possible the explanation and understanding of many aspects of plant physiology and development including phototropism, gravitropism and apical dominance. Tissue culture, micropropagation (mericloning), weed control, chemical root induction and many other widely used practical procedures depend upon and would be impossible without auxins.

The discovery of auxin led to the recognition of Prof. Went as one of the most eminent, and respected plant physiologists in history. Although not directly related to orchids, the discovery of auxin has had a decisive bearing on orchidology. In addition, Prof. Went made important direct contributions to the understanding of orchid flowering, carbon fixation, ecology and seed germination. In 1949 he and Emil Vacin published the now widely used Vacin and Went culture medium which was initially designed for seed germination, but is also suitable for tissue culture.

Prof. Went was invited to give a seminar at UCI in 1984 and stayed at our home. My wife, Tura, who is from Malaysia, cooked a Malayasian dinner to remind him of his days in Java (Indonesian and Malaysian food are similar), after which we hosted a party in his honor. While discussing orchids that evening and early next morning (Prof. Went is a very early riser) and looking at my orchid books, I asked him to write the chapter for this volume. He agreed and sent me a manuscript in about a month. To the best of my knowledge, some of the details regarding his dissertation research and other facts in his chapter have never been published before.

As a young boy interested in botany before coming to the U.S., later as an undergraduate at UCLA and graduate student at USC (my favorite school), I became acquainted with Prof. Went's discovery and was awed by it. However, I never believed that we would someday meet. But we did, for the first time about 1970, and he proved to be very kind and considerate. In 1973 one of his students and I collaborated on a paper dealing with vitamin metabolism in germinating orchid seeds. We met again during the Botanical Congress in Sydney, Australia and most recently in 1984 when he was a guest in our home. For all these reasons, scientific, historical, and personal I am very pleased that the first chapter in this volume is by Frits W. Went, the discoverer of the first plant hormone—auxin.

One of the most unusual orchids in the world is the subterranean *Rhizanthella gardneri* in Western Australia. I first became acquainted with this species in 1972 when Alex George (now executive editor of the *Flora of Australia* project) showed me a piece (in alcohol) of an accidentally discovered plant. The unique habitat and growth habit of this orchid raised many questions which could not be answered at the time. Kingley W. Dixon, John S. Pate and John Kuo now provide many answers and interesting details about this unusual orchid in their chapter.

Photosynthesis, respiration, mineral nutrition, metabolism, flowering and water relations are among the more fundamental topics treated in plant-related textbooks or courses. Of these, only the last was not covered in previous volumes of *Orchid Biology Reviews and Perspectives.* This was a significant shortcoming and on reading two very interesting articles about water relations in orchids by Dr. Russell Sinclair, I asked him to write a chapter for this volume. He agreed and on discovering that sufficient literature was not available in Australia, came to UCI for about a month to use my library and reprint collection and the interlibrary loan service in the University library to locate relevant literature. His chapter covers water relations in orchids from several perspectives.

Orchid pollination by animal vectors has attracted considerable attention due to the fascinating and sometimes unusual or even bizarre mechanisms associated with the process. Much less known, but equally interesting, is auto-pollination in orchids. Dr. Paul M. Catling, a perceptive student of this pollination mode describes the mechanisms in a thoroughly informative and interesting chapter.

As in the rest of Europe, the Russian nobility and wealthy middle class grew orchids as a hobby before the communist revolution. Books on orchids were published in Russia before the turn of the century. They include works by local authors as well as translations of important British books. All this came to an end with the revolution. Research on orchids may have come to a pause, but not a full stop. For many years the late Vera

Alexeevna Poddubnaya Arnoldi worked on orchid embryology at the botanical gardens in Moscow and published numerous interesting papers (all but one or two in Russian), and two very good general books (also in Russian). Her two books on plant embryology (in Russian) contain significant portions on orchids. Several orchid experts are presently active in the Soviet Union, but they publish virtually exclusively in Russian and are therefore not very well known in the West.

I was born in Bulgaria and fortunately left with my family in September 1944, just before the iron curtain descended between it and the west. Being 12 years old when we left I can no longer speak Bulgarian, but can still read some. Russian is very similar and therefore I can follow the orchid literature in that language with difficulty. The papers by Dr. Leonid V. Averyanov impressed me due to his multifaceted research on a single, but very large genus—*Dactylorhiza*, so I asked him to write a chapter about it. Despite many other commitments and extensive travel, Dr. Averyanov agreed and wrote a comprehensive treatment in English in a relatively short time. I think that his approach to the systematics and evolution of *Dactylorhiza* may well spur similar studies with other orchid genera, especially large ones such as *Dendrobium, Oncidium,* and *Epidendrum.*

Dactylorhiza was also studied for many years by my late friend Dr. Pieter Vermeulen, the well-known Dutch orchidologist. I first met him during an orchid conference and then visited him in Holland in 1974. He came to the U.S. the following year and again a few years later. In addition to *Dactylorhiza,* Dr. Vermeulen was interested in the rostellum and promised to write a chapter about it for *Orchid Biology Reviews and Perspectives,* but unfortunately passed away on 25 November 1981 in Heiloo, Holland at the age of 82 before being able to do so.

Orchid Biology Reviews and Perspectives, Vol. II includes a chapter by two important Chinese orchidologists, Chen Sing-chi and Tang Tsin. This was the first major review in the West on the orchids of China since the revolution and possibly longer. As far as I can determine, Chapters 5 and 7 in this volume are the first major reviews in the West on orchids by authors from the Soviet Union.

Orchids are mentioned in the more obscure as well as the most widely appreciated literature, art and music. The subject has fascinated me for years and I have written about it in a popular vein. A treatment of this topic in an appropriate scholarly manner requires expertise in these areas and that is what Dr. Martha W. Hoffman Lewis brings to her chapter. I enjoyed it immensely and think that it belongs in a series like *Orchid Biology Reviews and Perspectives* even if other opinions may hold that science and the arts should not mix. Why shouldn't they?

In the science fiction novel *Fountains of Paradise,* one of those associated with the construction of a space elevator is placed by the author and one of the great writers in this field, Arthur C. Clarke, near a flower of *Dendrobium macarthiae.* One could assume perhaps that some day the orchid would be placed in an elevator going up. Mr. Clarke, who authored a delightful story about orchids several years before *Fountains,* wrote me that he put the orchid into the story for my sake. Thus I may be responsible for the first fictional association between orchids and space. Unfortunately I could not put a real orchid in space because NASA did not agree with my suggestion that orchids are an excellent organism for the study of certain gravitropic responses. The first orchid in space was put there by scientists from the Soviet Union and I read about it in a newspaper report. Later I received reprints on the subject from those who carried out the research.

While Dr. Averyanov was writing his chapter on *Dactylorhiza,* he assisted me by inviting Dr. T. M. Czerevczenko to write a review about orchids in space. She agreed and together with T. V. Kosakovskaya wrote a very informative and intriguing chapter. I think that the Russian effort to make their stations more habitable by growing plants in general and orchids in particular in them is an indication of a genuine and serious commitment to space research and colonization. This is a clear indication of much better and more human planning than by NASA as well as a more astute selection of experimental organisms. It also suggests that the U.S.S.R. will be ahead of the U.S. in orchid space studies for years to come.

The appendices in *Orchid Biology Reviews and Perspectives* are intended to present more applied information than the chapters for the benefit of scientists and practical growers. In this volume Robert M. Hamilton, who indexed *Orchid Biology, Reviews and Perspectives* volumes II and III, presents a compilation of the flowering dates of a very large number of orchid species. Bert traveled widely and consulted periodicals in many libraries, including my own to compile this list. Since orchid nomenclature presents problems due to the numerous, constant, sometimes unnecessary and always vexing taxonomic changes, Mr. Hamilton has compiled a list of synonyms to accompanyhis flowering dates table. This list or some of its entries will not be acceptable to all systematists, but it facilitates use of the appendix and is therefore included here.

This volume is dedicated to three noted orchidologists who are also valued personal friends. Dr. Robert Ernst came to the U.S. at the start of World War II. Trained as an industrial chemist in Austria, he eventually established a successful chemical company near Los Angeles, California. Along the way he became interested in orchids and so combined his hobby, profession and scientific inclination in research on carbohydrate physiology and biochemistry.

We met in 1967 as a result of his research and have worked together ever since. Robert usually comes once a week to UCI where he not only engages in productive research, but also helps colleagues and guides students. He is my best friend and has stood by me in good times and bad, always ready to help emotionally, materially and in any other manner which would promise to do the most good. His generosity with time, resources, knowledge and affection are well known to all who are fortunate enough to know him. Following his retirement he enrolled as a graduate student at UCI where he earned his Ph.D. in 1979. As this is written, he is an Adjunct Associate Professor of the Department of Developmental and Cell Biology, UCI where he is carrying out more and better orchid research than ever. His scientific contributions to orchidology and chapters in *Orchid Biology Reviews and Perspectives,* Volumes II and III are outstanding.

One of my professors who was a teaching assistant at Cornell University when Dr. Haruyuki Kamemoto was a student there told me once that "Kami" never received a grade lower than an A. This would not surprise those who know him. He is generally acknowledged to be the "father" of modern orchid cytology both by virtue of his own research and through the training of many graduate students, post-doctoral fellows and research associates, (one of the best known of is Prof. Ryuso Tanaka of the University of Hiroshima, Japan). In addition to his work with orchids, Prof. Kamemoto works with *Anthurium* and other plants. His achievements with them are of major importance and he is, therefore, the recipient of numerous awards from orchid societies, horticultural groups and the University of Hawaii. Prof. Kamemoto retired in late 1986 or early 1987, but now in retirement he seems to be doing exactly what he did before: excellent research, teaching and breeding of orchids and anthuriums.

On my first visit to Singapore in 1969, I went to the Botany Department at the University of Singapore (then at the old Bukit Timah campus) to meet Prof. Adisheshappa

Nagaraja Rao (he usually signs as A. N. Rao and his friends call him Rao). I was then an Assistant Professor and new to orchid research. He was already highly regarded, a Professor in an English-style University and the occupant of the chair once held by R. E. Holttum. I was nervous, but should not have been for Rao proved to be down to earth, genial, kind and a great host. He made me feel comfortable immediately and introduced me first to Dr. Popuri Nageswara (Danny) Avadhani who also became a good friend and later to Dr. Chong Jin Goh (Goh Chong Jin).

Following this first visit I returned to the Botany Department, University of Singapore and later National University of Singapore (NUS) almost annually during summers and sabbatical leaves (I met my wife Tura, who is from Malaysia on such a visit in 1981). We engaged in joint research mostly on carbon fixation by orchids and also wrote chapters for *Orchid Biology Reviews and Perspectives* Volume II. The Botany Department at NUS became my second academic home and often wished it were the first, because Rao was easily the best Department Chairman I have ever worked with. His Department was superb. He also became a very good and loyal friend. Prof. Rao retired about 1986, but is still active in the Botany Department, NUS, doing research, writing, traveling and organizing symposia.

I consider myself fortunate to know Robert, Kami and Rao, to be their friend and to have had the opportunity to work with such exemplary human beings and scientists. Retirement! On paper all them have retired from one occupation or another; in fact all three are still very active in research, teaching and other scholarly activities.

Glossaries were appended to each chapter for the first time in *Orchid Biology Reviews and Perspectives,* Vol. IV. They are intended to facilitate reading of the chapters by those who may not be familiar with the terminology of a specific area. Comments about them have been positive, and I am continuing the practice in this volume.

Orchid Biology Reviews and Perspectives Vol. V was indexed with Indexer 1.0, a computer program written by Kevin J. Hackett, who was a student in my laboratory. Nothing can make indexing a book fun, but this program made the task tolerable and rapid.

I thank the authors, board of editors, my wife Tura, Robert Ernst, and Leslie Paul Nyman for their help. Les, who is now a faculty member at the Department of Biology, California Polytechnic University, Pomona, CA, was especially helpful by assuming some of the responsibilities at a time when I preferred not to have the burden. Working with Mr. Richard Abel and the staff at Timber Press has been a pleasure and I am grateful to them for a job well done.

Most of all I thank my son Jonathan for sitting on my lap or climbing on my back as I worked. Every now and then he gave me or wanted a hug and a kiss and assured me that he loves me despite my preoccupation with the "coputer" or "puter" when he would have preferred us to play with his toys. I could not have edited or indexed this volume without his help. Thank you Jonathan.

Joseph Arditti

Irvine, California   May 1989

Fig. 1-1. Frits Warmolt Went (b. 18 May 1903, Utrecht, Holland).

Orchids in My Life

FRITS W. WENT

It was not until Dr. Joseph Arditti asked me to write something about my acquaintance with orchids for this volume that I realized what an important role orchids have played in my life.

Let me start right at the beginning. One day in June 1912 an important event occurred at the botanical garden in Utrecht, Holland, of which my father, Prof. F.A.F.C. Went was director. That was the arrival of a Wardian Case from Java, Indonesia. A Wardian Case was an ordinary wooden case covered with a hipped glass-covered top in which living plants could be transported on the deck of a steamship. A sailor was assigned to water the plants regularly, and on deck the plants received the necessary light. This particular case contained about 100 plants of *Dendrobium crumenatum*, the "pidgeon orchid" from Java (and also common all over S.E. Asia), which had been sent a month and a half earlier from Bogor, Java. These plants were to be grown in the greenhouse at Utrecht, to determine if they would behave in a way similar to those in Bogor, Indonesia. There they exhibit the curious behavior of flowering, thousands of them, on exactly the same day with not a single one a day earlier or later[a]. Such a "flower-day" is quite spectacular since each plant bears dozens or hundreds of white, fragrant flowers along its stems.

In Bogor in 1912 a number of flower-days occurred, especially from May–October (the so-called dry season) but in the first year after moving the plants to Holland not a single *Dendrobium* flowered. On May 12, 1913 several plants in the Utrecht greenhouses flowered, and curiously enough some *Dendrobium crumenatum* plants in the greenhouses of the Universities in Bonn and Hamburg flowered on the same day, but this was accidental, since in the following years they never flowered simultaneously with those in Utrecht. But still, if one plant flowered in Utrecht, usually a number of other *Dendrobiums*

---

[a]This also occurs in Singapore and Malaysia. The phenomenon is called gregarious flowering.—Ed.

flowered on the same day. So the conclusion was that something in the immediate environment of the plants triggered the flower opening, but this was neither light nor temperature (Went 1898; Rutgers and Went 1915; Went and Rutgers 1915). It was not until some years later that Coster (1925) discovered the triggering mechanism. It was the sudden lowering of temperature after a heavy rain which started some buds to grow and flower nine days later. This conclusion was confirmed by some experiments in which *Dendrobium* plants were placed in refrigerators for one afternoon. They flowered exactly 9 days later, so it was not every rain which caused flowering, which was obvious since Bogor has 268 rainy days per year.

A somewhat similar behavior controls the simultaneous flowering of all coffee plants in a plantation. They also flower 9 days after a heavy rain, which usually is the first heavy rain at the end of the dry season. Then a whole coffee plantation is fragrant with the sweet smell of the coffee flowers. Dr. Greet Mes discovered, that in this case it was the wetting of the small flower buds which triggered their opening 9 days later. Simply submerging a whole coffee plant in a container of water causes it to flower 9 days later. We first used this trick in Pasadena before botanical meetings by dumping some of our potted coffee plants in water 9 days before the meeting. The dais for the speakers was always flanked by spectacularly fragrant coffee trees.

I mentioned the paper by Rutgers and Went. Let me tell you somewhat more about Rutgers. It is a story from "orchids to politics". As a student I knew little about him, although he was a student of my father's, but he was much older than I. He received his Ph.D under the guidance of my father in 1911 and soon afterwards went to Java, to become the director of an Experiment Station in Bogor, where in his free time he studied and wondered about the flowering behavior of *Dendrobium crumenatum*. As a director of an experiment station he developed executive skills and grew into an accomplished diplomat, at the expense of his botanical background. Upon his return to Holland Queen Wilhelmina first appointed him Secretary of the Colonies and later Governor of Surinam, at that time still a Dutch colony. In that way he closed a cycle of sorts for, as a student of my father, he became a successor of my father's father-in-law who was Governor of Surinam at the turn of the century, also appointed by Queen Wilhelmina. On his departure from Java and abandonment of Botany which occurred at the same time as my arrival there and entry into the botanical world, he donated his botanical reprints to me.

The following years when I was in high school and University, my contact with orchids was restricted to field trips and excursions. In the neighborhood of Utrecht, situated in the lowlands of Holland, the only orchids grew in marshy meadows, and were not very interesting or spectacular. Only on excursions which my father made yearly with botany students to the southernmost part of the Netherlands in a hilly country, were some interesting encounters with orchids to be had. In the small forests I occasionally saw *Neottia nidus avis,* an ivory-colored "saprophyte", which is nurtured by fungi in the surrounding humus as mycorrhiza, since the orchids lack chlorophyll so cannot photosynthesize (actually the orchid is parasitic on the fungus).

We found other orchids in southern Limburg including some very rare *Ophrys* species. It is curious that, although growing in very small numbers in oft-frequented meadows, they still persist. This is partly due to their "saprophytic" existence which keeps their persisting stems and roots underground. Thus, picking them does not destroy the living plant, which does not reproduce well by seed for although the seeds are very numerous they are exceedingly small and rarely germinate. The rarity in number of specimens of *Ophrys* orchids is probably due to the fact that only when the seeds happen to be joined at the same time and place with their mycorrhizal fungus can a new plant become established. This is true of every orchid since all of them depend for the first months or longer on the presence and activity of associated mycorrhizal fungus.

While I was working on my Ph.D. I did not depend on orchids, but on oats, the seedlings of which supplied me with my experimental material. It was known that oat seedlings are very sensitive to light and are a fine material for studying phototropism, which became my thesis problem. I had chosen this because my father's laboratory had become well known for the study of this subject. In the middle of my studies I was drafted for military service. I was allowed to choose the branch of service I wished so selected the chemical branch, because its training camp was located in my home town, Utrecht. I was not even required to live in the barracks, but could sleep and eat at home. Since this arrangement relieved me of the supervision of a sergeant, I (mis-) used the nights to work in the laboratory while surreptitiously sleeping during the service lectures. It was easy to remain undetected because when the lieutenant woke me up with a question, there turned out to be only one answer: "about 300 meters, lieutenant".

I became an accomplished military slacker and carried out experiments during the quiet nights in the laboratory. These experiments were not necessarily useful, and were sometimes just silly.

We students had many discussions about the mechanism of phototropism, which depended on a growth process. But, the problem was whether the phototrophically bending stem was retarded or accelerated on the lighted or the darkened side. I was convinced there was also a growth-accelerating substance involved which my fellow students did not want to accept, so I finally determined to convince them (and my father as well) that such a growth substance existed. After a number of preliminary experiments, I one night placed a number of oat seedling tips on a small block of gelatin in the belief that this unknown substance would permeate into it. After an hour I placed this block on one side of an oat seedling, simultaneously placing a similar block of pure gelatin on the opposite side. An hour later the seedling started to grow away from the treated gelatin block. Although I had hoped that this would happen, I was profoundly excited by this simple experiment. I ran to my parents home which was also located adjacent to the garden and woke up my father at 3 a.m., shouting, "Father, come and see, I have discovered the growth substance". I was sorely disappointed that he did not jump out of his bed, but replied: "Fine, then repeat the experiment tomorrow. If you are right it will work again" and went back to sleep. And indeed it worked the next day.

Then followed 2 exciting months, perhaps the most exciting in my life, when night after night this basic experiment was repeated and modified to find out more about this plant growth substance, later named auxin. I used this discovery of the first plant hormone as the basis for my Ph.D. thesis, which I completed in November 1927. My dissertation so excited the botanical world that 50 years later it had become one of the most cited papers in the botanical literature.

In the course of this work I was compelled to disprove a number of erroneous beliefs and prejudices. For example, some of my more esoterically inclined fellow students thought of growth as a sort of spirit and not a simple substance; so I had to establish the difference between a spirit and a substance. I was completely convinced that I was dealing with a substance. When I left agar blocks with auxin overnight in a warm laboratory room the auxin disappeared through bacterial action, whereas when I kept the agar blocks outside my window in the winter cold overnight the auxin remained active. The most conclusive evidence for the existence of a material growth-promoting substance came when I could establish that it had a molecular weight between 300 and 400. Who could conceive of a spirit having a molecular weight? And the students who believed that the phototropic curvature came about by destruction of a growth-promoting substance on the lighted side of an organ were answered when I could show that auxin was light and heat stable and was transported preferentially to the dark side (Went 1928).

During all these years of study, I lived in my parents' house next to the botanical garden so had the opportunity to meet a great number of botanists from around the world who visited my father and his laboratory, which at that time was one of the most advanced botanical institutes and a source of a new generation of botanists. Since Utrecht was not a tourist town, most of the scientists who visited also became house guests or at least came for dinner. They included David Fairchild, who wrote a number of botanical travel books including *The World was my Garden*; Karl von Goebel, who started the famous Botanical Garden in Munich; and Hans Fitting[b], who worked with orchids in the 1900s. He was a surprise to me for through his many lengthy articles on all sorts of plant-physiological problems I formed a mental picture of him as an old, somewhat bookish professor while in reality he was a tall, fine figure of a man.

After receiving my Ph.D. in November 1927, I was so lucky as to be immediately appointed as a botanist at the famous Botanic Garden in Bogor, Java, Indonesia. There were only a few jobs for botanists in Holland, whereas there were plenty in Dutch colonies especially at tropical experiment stations. I was free to work on any subject in which I was interested, and since epiphytes in the tropics were an interesting subject, I chose that. It was especially attractive because so little work had been done on it since A.F.W. Schimper's work in the previous century and also since most of the work would have to be done in the cool, tropical rainforest, above 1,500 m alt. in Tjibodas, which was the mountain garden associated with the garden in Bogor.

There were several ways in which one could study epiphytes:

1. Cut down the tree with all its epiphytes on its branches, but this is vadalism,
2. Climb each tree which would leave the smaller branches unexplored, and lead to the opposition of millions of ants and bees, which I had already met in South America on a trip with my father to the jungles of Surinam in 1923, or
3. Observe a whole tree with field glasses. I chose the third method, which after some training worked so very well that I could recognize most epiphytes, especially orchids, when in flower, except the smaller bulbophyllums. In this way I made epiphyte inventories of well over 100 different tree species. To my surprise, I found that virtually every tree species had its own special epiphytes so that after some time I could often identify the tree species by the orchids which were living on them. For instance, *Oberonia oxystophyllum* grew only on *Cestrum nocturnum* (an introduced small tree) and *Appendicula ramosa* only on *Saurauya* species. Although these trees grew with their branches intermixed, the orchids never made a mistake by growing on the wrong tree (Went 1940).

This fact was apparently known by native orchid collectors who climbed only specific trees to collect a particular orchid species. I tried to correlate their occurrence with light

[b]As a result of his work with *Phalaenopsis* pollen in Bogor, Fitting suggested a "pollen hormone" (the first use of the word "hormone" relative to plants), which was later shown to be auxin.—Ed.

intensity, or roughness of the tree bark or other physical properties of the host tree, but was unsuccessful. I therefore assumed that there were chemical differences between the trees, e.g., in tannin content, or differences in mycorrhizal flora. But I did not investigate this hypothesis since it seemed unlikely when I learned that in North America all orchids were grown on the same *Osmunda* fiber. In addition to my ecological studies with orchids, I did some physiological work with them.

I first did CO_2 studies in a glass-covered shed in the rainforest with *Schoenorchis juncifolia*, an orchid resembling *Tillandsia usneoides*. It hangs in long garlands from the branches of *Weinmannia blumei* or *Castanea javanica* as long, slender stems with slender, 10 cm-long, green, terete, gracefully bent leaves. To study their CO_2 exchange, I suspended a piece of stem with 3–4 leaves in a glass tube through which ordinary forest air was sucked. Such air has a low but constant CO_2 content, in the low light at the forest bottom there is not enough photosynthesis to remove appreciable amounts of CO_2 from the air. The CO_2 content of the air which had passed along the *Schoenorchis* was measured and remarkably enough the orchid took up CO_2 during night and gave it up during day, in the manner succulents have been found to do (Crassulacean Acid Metabolism or CAM)[c]. This behavior was not known to occur at that time in ordinary green plants, so I thought I had made a mistake. But it is now well known that CAM commonly occurs in all succulent plants including many orchids.

Daily weight change measurements were made with these *Schoenorchis* branches in the same glass-covered shed. Their daily CO_2 exchange was so slight that no weight changes due to photosynthesis could be expected. Their daily weight changes were entirely due to changes in their water content. Thus their daily weight loss was entirely due to transpiration while their weight gain during the night was due to water vapor uptake. These weight changes were recorded on self-built automatic balances which recorded hourly the weight of *Schoenorchis* branches of about 20 cm length suspended from thin, copper wires. Under the glass roof they were unable to take up rain water so the nightly weight increase was due to water vapor uptake only. These *Schoenorchis* branches lost weight in the long run especially when one of the older leaves died which proved that water vapor uptake was associated with life processes and was not a purely inorganic, osmotic vapor uptake. The latter could also be measured by osmotic measurements of leaves, which when alive had an osmotic potential above that of the osmotic concentration of their cell sap (60 atm. versus 19 atm. of their cell sap), which kept them in equilibrium with the 92–95% relative humidity of the forest atmosphere. The equilibrium was due to a negative turgor inside their cells which could be measured by the Ursprung and Blum method. It was also visible when a cell wall was slightly injured under the microscope while lying in paraffin oil which then was sucked in rapidly through a hole in the cell wall in the form of microscopic oil bubbles. A number of *Schoenorchis* branches in the glass house were still alive after 4 years having hung suspended from copper wires. But, no other orchids treated in this way survived for more than a year.

I also want to mention another curious orchid experience I had in the Far East; it had to do with the regrowth of the vegetation on the island of Krakatau, which was completely destroyed by hot ashes during the volcanic eruption of 1883. A whole new flora

[c]This is the first field study of carbon fixation by orchids. Another pioneer was Prof. Erich Nuernbergk at the Botanical Garden in Hamburg between ca 1950 and 1965. Prof. O. Warburg of Germany also a visitor to Bogor and one of the founders of the Hebrew University in Israel, published the first paper on the subject in 1886–1888 as a result of laboratory work.—Ed.

had become established on the island by 1928, when I visited it for the first time. During the first 10 years, only sea-borne and wind-blown seeds had arrived from the neighboring islands of Java and Sumatra establishing a coastal flora and an island vegetation consisting mostly of ferns and grasses. But by 1928 a secondary forest was established on the slopes of the island. Yet there were few epiphytes on the tree branches, and hardly any orchids. One of these was *Acriopsis javanica,* a common epiphyte in Java, where, in its hollow rhizomes, an ant (*Crematogaster*) lives symbiotically. A few years earlier Dr. Docters van Leeuwen, the director of the Botanical Garden of Bogor, had visited Krakatau and had seen the *Crematogaster* ants walking excitedly on tree limbs, apparently uneasy because of the absence of its common domicile, *Acriopsis.* But when I found that first specimen of *Acriopsis,* it was inhabited by *Crematogaster.* So the two members of this symbiosis had arrived independently on Krakatau, but upon meeting they had immediately re-established their relationship.

My epiphyte studies in Java were cut short by my acceptance of a position as an Assistant Professor at the newly founded California institute of Technology in Pasadena, California. The invitation was extended by Prof. Thoman H. Morgan when the plant physiologist there, my good friend Herman Dolk, was killed in an automobile accident just after completing a small laboratory for plant hormone investigations.

We arrived on January 23, 1933 in Pasadena by way of Hong Kong, Shanghai, Yokohama, Hawaii and San Francisco. I remained there for the next quarter of a century, first to study plant hormones and later environmental effects on plant growth including orchids.

This transition from my study of the internal factors of plant growth to the external ones has a curious history which I want to explain. Soon after my arrival in Pasadena I became acquainted with a most remarkable man, a retired physician, Dr. Henry O. Eversole, who until a short time before his death had a pronounced influence on my life. His career was most remarkable. He had studied medicine both in the U.S.A. and Vienna and was a successful tuberculosis specialist. His career took him to Paris where he became representative of the Rockefeller Foundation for eastern Europe. Upon retirement he settled on a hilltop in La Canada, close to Pasadena. Never a man to sit idly, he took up *Phalaenopsis* growing as a hobby, but as a result of a back injury suffered in an automobile accident in Siberia, he was unable to operate a greenhouse. Therefore, he approached the Carrier company and asked them to build an air conditioned greenhouse for him to house his *Phalaenopsis.* They refused, claiming that this was impossible since they had failed to build one in the eastern U.S. Undismayed by their refusal, he succeeded with the help of an engineer (Mr. A. J. Hess) and a physicist (Dr. L. Marshall) in building a functional air conditioned greenhouse next to his home which he operated successfully for a number of years. Being a humanitarian, Dr. Eversole wondered whether his air conditioned greenhouse could not be used by agriculturists to improve the growing of crops. So he began visiting the agricultural experiment stations in California. Finally he visited me one morning with the question whether I would be interested in having an air conditioned greenhouse. This offer came at an opportune moment since I had just decided that I wanted to change my field of research, which had been the study of plant hormones, the internal factors controlling plant growth. Dr. K. V. Thimann and I had just written the monograph *Phytohormones* summarizing all work done until 1937 in that field. So with the prospect of having the opportunity of studying the external factors controlling plant growth, I accepted Dr. Eversole's offer with one provision: Not to get *one* but *two* such greenhouses built so that one condition could be compared with another.

Miss L. Clark, Dr. Eversole's sister-in-law, provided the construction funds for the new greenhouses, and a triumvirate: Dr. Eversole, Dr. Marshall and Mr. Hess produced the plans for the greenhouses which were completed in 1939. The first problem was to find the right experimental material and a number of plants including cotton, tobacco, peas, corn, tomatoes and other agricultural crops were tested to find the best experimental material. It was important to find a plant which (1) responded immediately upon changing experimental treatments, (2) was easy to measure, (3) was easily obtainable, (4) was genetically well analyzed, (5) was an annual and (6) not too large to fit in the greenhouses. The choice finally fell upon the tomato which responds within a day to changing conditions, grows optimally under the daylight conditions of Pasadena, both in summer and in winter and is an ideal greenhouse crop. But my first experimental treatments, which tested the effects of the relative humidity of the air, was a failure because this factor had so little effect on tomatoes. Leaf size in tobacco was significantly changed by the relative humidity of the air in which it was grown, but tomatoes did not respond at all. The plants grew well, but they did not produce fruits; the first 100 plants produced a total of 4 fruits.

At that time it was thought that the C-N ratio controlled fruit production, so my various botanical and agricultural visitors suggested that I either gave my plants too much or insufficient nitrogen, or that I gave them too much or not enough light, but nothing helped. Then I decided to change the temperature in my greenhouses that had been kept for a year at 26°C since I had assumed that was the ideal temperature for heat-loving tomatoes. So I changed the temperature of one greenhouse to 17°C, while keeping the other at 26°C. This change produced immediate results: The tomatoes at 17°C set fruit immediately, whereas those at 26°C remained fruitless. Even more remarkable: Fruit set was restricted to the tomato plants which were kept at 17°C during the night only. It was best when the plants were maintained at 26°C during the day and at 17°C at night. This preference for a higher day temperature than night temperature turned out to be generally true for most other plants as well so that we started to talk about thermoperiodicity as a basic property of plants, like photoperiodism which had come to be accepted as a basic response of many plant species to day length. This became even clearer in subsequent experiments in which tomato plants were moved from the warm greenhouse to the cool one only during the night but kept in the light. They did not produce fruits so the low temperature worked only in darkness.

Soon such a large number of plants had to be tested under so many conditions that the first two Clark greenhouses were insufficient. I visited Dr. Robert Millikan, Chairman of the Board of Trustees (in practice President) of the California institute of Technology, to ask him whether he could find $200,000 for an expanded set of air conditioned greenhouses. This request was strongly supported by Dr. Eversole, and in due time Dr. Millikan found a donor. Unfortunately prices rose rapidly after the end of World War II, so that actually $407,000 was needed to construct the needed set of greenhouses, but a telegram from Dr. Millikan to Mr. Earhart, the prospective donor straightened out this difficulty and in June 1949 the new Earhart Plant Research laboratory could be dedicated and put into full use. The entire building had first to be sterilized with HCN, since I had decided to work under the strictest quarantine conditions, excluding all insects. These conditions were maintained successfully for the rest of the life of the greenhouses.

Before the final plans for the new greenhouses were made, Dr. Eversole took me east in his automobile to visit a number of botanical institutes so as to not overlook any pos-

sible innovations which might be included in the new plans. In this venture the experience of Dr. Eversole was invaluable. He had visited so many laboratories for the
Rockefeller Foundation that a short general impression sufficed for him to evaluate the
effectiveness of any set-up after he had queried me in minute detail about my impres-
sions. This was an invaluable education for me and I found only a few ways in which our
own plans could be improved.

This trip east with Dr. Eversole provided another valuable experience. He knew most
of the important orchid growers in the east and introduced me to them; in that way I
learned a good deal about orchid culture. In the course of the years I found more and
more space for orchids in the Earhart greenhouses. In the first place they turned out to be
excellent experimental material. As a by-product there were the flowers which turned
out to be very useful if distributed judiciously among the secretaries at Cal Tech; we
received marvelous cooperation from the various departments, especially from
Buildings and Grounds. From among the orchid growers in the vicinity of Pasadena, we
always could count on receiving the necessary orchid seedlings or even mature plants.
One of the first things I learned from orchids was that the growing medium we used for
crop plants, namely a mixture of vermiculite and gravel, watered with a Hoagland mixture of nutrient salts, was not ideal for a number of orchid species, for instance
Paphiopedilum did not grow properly in an inorganic medium, but needed leaf mold to
grow and flower. This was apparently true for other terrestrial orchids as well, since
Cymbidium also preferred an organic medium, whereas typical epiphytic orchids did
well in an inorganic medium (e.g., *Cattleya* and *Phalaenopsis*).

A great deal of work was carried out with *Cattleya*. While there are many species, all
from South America, only one, *C. trianae*, was investigated in the Earhart Laboratory in
great detail. It grew both at 17° and 30°C, but its growth was slow at the lower temperatures, however its outstanding response was to photoperiods. Flower primordia are
formed in both long and short days but develop into flowers only in short photoperiods,
such as 8 hour daylengths. Flower sheaths of plants kept at 16 hour photoperiods all
abort and the flower buds dry up. In another fairly extensive experiment, two large *C.
trianae* plants obtained from the Fred A. Stewart Nursery were broken into 2–3 bulb
plants and the divisions were kept under 16 hour photoperiods for a full year. Not a
single flower developed. The plants were divided into 3 subgroups kept for 1, 3 or 4
months under 8 hour days. The ones brought into the 8 hour days for 1 month did not
flower at all, but had green sheaths with aborted flower buds. When they had had 3
months of short days, all produced 1–2 flowers and after 4 short-day months there were
no open flowers but all had 2 flower buds. We produced a spectacular flowering plant
using one large 200 pseudobulb plant; after a 4-month period of long days, it was
brought into short days. Three months later the plant was covered with 250 flowers
simultaneously. This was a much admired demonstration of effective flower control.

We also did some experiments to learn whether *Cattleya* plants need a rest period
before they will flower. This turned out not to be the case. But any new shoot development completely inhibits flower formation, which apparently is a question of competition for carbohydrates. An orchid exposed to full daylight in long days excretes a great
deal of sugar as droplets on its stems and flower sheaths. This phenomenon of sugar
excretion can be observed in many other plant genera which have stopped growing for
one reason or another. For example, the lower leaf surfaces of *Populus* leaves exposed to
full sunlight in summer became sticky with excreted sugar.

The flowering of *Cymbidium* plants is very complicated. Mr. R. Casamajor whose specialty was the growing of *Cymbidium* had observed that only pseudobulbs with 10 or more adult leaves were capable of producing flower shoots. But old pseudobulbs which have lost their leaves seem to inhibit flower shoot formation, so a successful *Cymbidium* grower has to repot his plants every few years removing the old pseudobulbs which then can be replanted if desired. In 1950 I received 60 clone divisions of a *Cymbidium lowianum* from Mr. Hertrich of the Huntington Gardens. These were planted in leaf mold and placed in the different greenhouses of the Earhart Laboratory. In the course of about 2 years, these plants developed to flowering size. Using the same technique which Blaauw had used in his laboratory in Holland for the study of flower bulbs (weekly or monthly dissection of a number of pseudobulbs grown under well controlled conditions of temperature and moisture), a number of *Cybidium* pseudobulbs were dissected under a microscope. Such a pseudobulb has buds in each bract or leaf axil, but only 1 or 2 have more than 2 nodes and only 1 develops into a vegetative or flowering shoot. When this single shoot starts to grow, it forms first 15 nodes which develop into scales and are placed in 2 stichae (alternate or ½ phyllotaxis). If the bud remains vegetative, the new nodes continue to alternate and from the 16th node on will develop leaves. When the bud develops into an inflorescence, from the 16th node on the phyllotaxis becomes 2/5 and all these nodes develop bracts with a flower bud (Casamajor and Went, 1954; Casamajor, 1955). Thus the flowers in the inflorescence are placed in a spiral arrangement.

The conditions under which shoots will become inflorescences are very complicated. They must be maintained first under long day conditions at high temperatures, such as occur in summer. When moved to night temperature at 10°C, they immediately become generative. When *Cymbidium* plants are kept continuously in 16-hour photoperiods at 20°C day and 14°C night temperatures, all buds which are developing become inflorescences. Thus, we were able to keep a *Cymbidium* plant continuously in flower for a whole year. When plants come out of the long summer days and into autumn cool nights, they form flower shoots in a sufficiently warm winter and flower next spring, but not during the rest of the year. Southern California and areas in Australia have just the right climate for *Cymbidium* culture in open lathhouses, if the nights do not become too cold in winter, such as in Santa Barbara in California.

Phalaenopsis culture in a temperate climate is only possible in greenhouses, for they need temperatures of around 26°C during the day and 20°C at night, as Dr. Eversole had discovered in his greenhouse in La Canada and I could confirm in the Earhart Plant Research Laboratory. It is amazing that in his single greenhouse he could discover the fact of thermoperiodicity simply by observing the behavior of his plants and manipulating his thermostat. But he practically lived with his plants 24 hours a day, and observed them very carefully.

Orchids were only a sideline in the research which the special air-conditioned facilities enabled me to carry out. I have already mentioned that my main experimental plant was the tomato. Its almost immediated response to a change in the environment in the form of a change in its growth rate, made it possible to study its sugar metabolism, nutrient transport, photosynthesis, stomatal response, transpiration, hormonal control and temperature response in general, in addition to its thermoperiodism. To my surprise none of these processes ordinarily controlled the growth of tomato plants, and I was especially surprised—even chagrined—that it was not hormones which controlled their growth; on the contrary, it was growth which controlled their photosynthesis.

I believe the reasons that this surprise discovery was not made earlier were:

1. I was the first investigator to establish the optimal growing conditions for the tomato plant and
2. That I did not limit my study of the tomato plant to a single or just a few physiological processes, but tried to study the whole range of their physiology.

I later learned that not only tomatoes were thermoperiodic, but most other plants such as potatoes, peas, etc., were as well. The facilities of the Earhart Plant Research Laboratory enabled me also to study the autoecology of many wild plants, including desert annuals, *Yucca brevifolia, Veratrum viride,* etc. Thus I think that this laboratory has also contributed its share to the field of ecology.

But this article dealing mainly with orchids is not the place to praise the advantages of a Phytotron: This I tried to do in my book *The Experimental Control of Plant Growth* (1957). Now with so many phytotrons in existence, such promotion is no longer necessary.

In 1955 I was invited to visit Australia to assess the need for a phytotron there. On my way I toured New Zealand for two weeks, which covered the two Islands completely, from Auckland via Palmerston North and Christchurch to Dunedin. I was taken throughout Australia, to get a good idea of the botanical problems which a phytotron would help solve. I arrived in Sydney and was successively shown Canberra, Brisbane, the Darling Downs and surrounding country, Melbourne, Tasmania from Hobart to Queenstown, Adelaide, the central deserts as exemplified by Alice Springs and the Simpson Desert, and Western Australia and Perth from Albany to Broome. It all was botanically most interesting, for in almost every respect the flora differs from that of the rest of the world. Australia is a very old continent that was separated early from the other continents so its flora also developed largely without contact with that of the rest of the world. Most of the trees in Australia belong to only 2 genera: *Eucalyptus* and *Acacia.* There is a remarkable similarity in the shrubs throughout the continent, with Fabaceae (Lenguminosae), Proteaceae and Myrtaceae the dominating shrub families, while most orchids belong to genera different from those in Europe and America. Since there are only few areas with moist forests, there are few epiphytic orchids. And the few there are (*Dendrobium*) are mostly related to Asian genera. But of orchids there are many terrestrial genera, especially in Western Australia in its moister areas, practically all unknown in the rest of the world and with a different appeal as well. Since they are all ground orchids, I have never seen any of them in cultivation anywhere.

In April 1958 I received a very attractive offer for a new and very different job; director of the Missouri Botanical Garden in St. Louis. This was in a sense nothing new for me: I was born in a Botanical Garden (in Utrecht), my first job was as assistant in the Botanical Garden in Bogor, Java, and I was elected as president of the Board of Trustees of the newly created Los Angeles State and County Arboretum (LASCA) in Arcadia next to Pasadena, which position I held for 9 years. At the same time I was dissatisfied with my position at Cal Tech mainly due to personality clashes and I had more or less finished my work with the Earhart Plant Research Laboratory by writing a description of it and the results combined in *The Experimental Control of Plant Growth* published in 1957. I also was denied an application for a Guggenheim fellowship, which would have taken me away from Cal Tech. On the other hand, one of my first tasks in St. Louis would be a problem of greenhouse construction and as an added attraction I was given a generous travel budget. So I accepted the directorship with alacrity, taking a leave of absence from Cal Tech and moving to St. Louis in August 1958.

There, just 100 years earlier in 1859, a wealthy unmarried businessman, Henry Shaw had dedicated his garden and entire estate as the Missouri Botanical Garden, still locally known as Shaw's Garden. Originally it had started with an adequate endowment, but the trustees had been unable to keep it up, and despite being a public institution it received no financial assistance from the state or city. Furthermore, the director in the previous years had put the main strength of its plant collections in *Cattleya* orchids, which did not thrive in the polluted St. Louis air and so had to be moved out into the country to Gray's Summit, 30 miles west of St. Louis. So the main attraction of the Garden was gone. And, in addition, some of the greenhouses had deteriorated to the extent that they were unusable or unsafe and had to be abandoned.

My first task was to build a new main greenhouse to replace the old palm house, the monumental center of the garden. This the trustees, under leadership of their President, Robert Brookings Smith, had obligated themselves to do. Nor was the situation of the garden hopeless in other ways, since in the previous years drastic measures had been taken to clean the St. Louis polluted air to the point where the orchids could be brought back to the city.

The first order of activity was the renewal of the palm house. Just rebuilding the old house was out of the question, for part of the iron frame work was rusted out, and rebuilding it would have cost more than a completely new house. Besides, greenhouse construction had advanced over the last half century after air-conditioning had made its entry. With my experience in greenhouse building it seemed a proper job for me. But I soon realized that to air-condition a really large greenhouse would overstrain the available air conditioning equipment and require ducts of such dimensions that hardly any room would be left for plants.

After lengthy discussions with an architect, Mr. Eugene Mackey, I decided that instead of fighting the temperature inequality caused during the day by the sun's heating, I would use the daily heat absorption of a greenhouse by creating and maintaining a temperature *gradient* instead of a constant temperature. This would require a variable speed of ventilation in the greenhouse. It would be necessary to control the temperature of the incoming air by radiators and keep the outgoing air temperature constant by varying the rate of airspeed. The architect then suggested a geodesic dome for the shape of the greenhouse which would yield a temperature gradient from north to south that could be maintained during the day and one in the east-west direction during the night by utilizing the night cooling for maintaining a gradient. Thus two crosswise air streams during day and night would provide four temperature regimes in the various areas of the greenhouse:

1. a warm-day warm-night, hot tropics climate;
2. a warm-day cool-night, warm desert climate;
3. a cool-day warm-night, tropical islands climate and
4. a cool-day cool-night climate in tropical mountains

For the east-west airstream we used an underground walkway which existed under the old palmhouse to guide the heating pipes from the heating plant to the garden structures further east. This required only a slight addition to the duct system.

The geodesic dome was to be constructed entirely from aluminum pipe which was precut by an airplane manufacturer and shipped to St. Louis. The greenhouse cover was to be plastic, ½ inch thick polyethylene, as glass was considered too dangerous in the event of a hail storm. Construction started early in 1959 and it was hoped that the entire dome could be completed before winter to save the palms in the old palm house. Due to all manner of unexpected delays this was not possible and the old palms were lost, but in the spring of 1960 three trucks delivered to us a shipment of Florida-grown palms, mainly from the Fairchild Gardens near Miami. In early fall the geodesic dome, which we named Climatron, was practically completed and inaugurated with lectures by Dr. Detlev Bronk, president of Rockefeller University and Prof. Erwin Bunning from Germany. It was an impressive sight for the 3,000 who attended when the one hundred and twelve 1,000-watt lights were turned on at dusk in the Climatron.

The Climatron led to a revival of Shaw's Garden, and in the first year we collected $97,000 in admissions. We also had our share of difficulties, e.g., during the first bad cold spell the radiators which were to heat the incoming air froze and many plants at the lower level of the Climatron died.

To grow the sometimes tiny, epiphytic orchids of Costa Rica and other areas in the huge Climatron (where they would disappear as individuals) I had them grown on artificial trees, made of welded iron pipe covered with osmunda (cut-up tree fern stems). These artificial trees were placed in the appropriate climatic area of the Climatron and did very well for some time. But the gardeners in the course of time neglected to water them and they died after a few years. Neglect also killed most of Cal Dodson's splendid collection of Ecuadorian orchids, leaving a motley collection of cattleyas. Other non-spectacular orchids like *Phymatidium* also disappeared over the years.

I mentioned earlier that *Cattleya* orchids could not stand the air pollution which the inhabitants of St. Louis had to live with. After this air pollution had been reduced by banning the burning of high sulfur, strip-mined, soft coal in the city it was thought that the removal of SO_2 from the city air had done the job and our cattleyas could be brought back to Shaw's Garden. But this was not so, as we found out in our home. As director of Shaw's Garden, I had the privilege of using garden grown cattleyas for decoration of our dinner table at official dinners. Whereas cut *Cattleya* flowers normally stay in good condition for about a month, in our home they wilted within a few days. This was due to the fact that we cooked with gas, which produces ethylene and other toxic gases upon burning. So apparently it was not SO_2 which caused the dry-sepal disease of cattleyas, but ethylene.

This also elucidated another well-known but unexplained botanical laboratory problem: When experimenting with plants, lighting gas was not to be used in the laboratory. It was thought that slight leaks in the piping killed the plants but in reality their loss was due to the production of toxic gasses upon burning of the gas. In recent years it has been found that such toxic gases can be removed by catalytic afterburners. So I thought, and was supported in this opinion by lighting-gas producers, that with the use of catalyic afterburners, gas flames could be used for direct greenhouse heating. This would have two advantages; it would eliminate the heat losses in steam production for the conventional heating of greenhouses, and the CO_2 produced in the burning of gas inside the greenhouses would benefit photosynthesis by plants. So I had an open gas flame heater with a catalytic afterburner installed in an experimental greenhouse. I moved a number of sensitive plants into that greenhouse. But to my regret tomatoes were badly affected by ethylene, produced in spite of the afterburner. Then it dawned upon me that the afterburner is effective only when in continuous use and not when heating is only intermittent, as greenhouse heating usually is. That is also the case when gas heating is used in warehouse heating, even when employed in connection with catalytic devices. Thus this type of heating is not allowed in houses or other places occupied by humans, since the toxic gases create considerable air pollution.

I disappeared with the orchids. In a dispute with the trustees I resigned towards the end of 1963, but kept my professorship at Washington University, where I continued my studies on air-quality and air-pollution which I had never abandoned since my first studies in Pasadena and the Phytotron. In 1965 I accepted a research position at the Desert Research Institute in Reno, Nevada and remained there until my retirement.

In 1967 I was invited to join an expedition to the Amazon with the research vessel "Alpha Helix" of the Scripps Oceanographic Institute. This gave me an opportunity to study air-pollution in the tropics for my equipment, a gas chromatograph and a condensation nucleus recorder, required an electrical supply of 110 volt a.c., a current the Alpha Helix could supply even in the middle of the rain forest. I had not counted on the opposition (or just stupidity?) of the Brazilian Customs service which impounded my equipment for almost the whole time I was in the Amazon region. So I had to employ my time in a different way, building on my interest in the ecology of the rain forest, which dated back to my five years in Java.

With the microscopes on the Alpha Helix, I could study the root development of the rain forest *in situ* by placing a dissecting microscope on the ground and lying prone behind it. For illumination I used sunspots which occurred here and there between the dense foliage. It turned out that practically all tree roots were found in the upper few centimeters of the soil, where they seemed to be restricted to the humus layer formed by the fallen leaves and dead branches of the surrounding trees. The humus and the roots had formed an intricate net with fungal hyphae joining the roots to the dead leaves. The hyphae entered the roots as mycorrhiza. In contrast with a temperate forest there were no mushrooms on the ground. So apparently all food gathered by the hyphae (which in temperate forests goes at least partly to the fruiting bodies of the fungi) went here to the mycorrhizal roots. Almost the only mushrooms in these rainforests are found on tree stumps or above-ground branches where the food gathered by the fungal hyphae from the humus cannot disappear into the roots as in mycorrhiza. Other indications that mycorrhiza is a sink for the food gathered by hyphae is their necessity for the growth of so-called saprophytes which are actually parasites on the fungus because they cannot produce organic foods themselves due to the lack of chlorophyll, and therefore depend entirely on that supplied by the fungal hyphae. Mycorrhiza also plays another role for orchids. Fungi supply the organic food orchid seeds need in the absence of endosperm which is lacking in orchid seeds. Knudson was the first scientist to supply sugars in orchid seedling media making the first *in vitro* orchid seedling culture possible and Emil Vacin (who worked in my laboratory; Vacin and Went, 1949) formulated a universal medium for orchid seed culture[d] and also added tomato juice. The juice seems to contribute vitamin-like substances to the medium. Later the vitamin needs of orchid seedlings were studies specifically by J. A. Hijner (Hijner and Arditti, 1973) in my laboratory in 1950.

I have observed orchids growing in many parts of the world, from the near-arctic, *Cypripedium* in Alaska, to a red flowering *Dendrobium* at timberline in Java and New Guinea. The most exceptional orchid growing space I know is a spot a few square feet wide in the Joshua Tree National Monument in the California desert. In its Cottonwood Springs area is a little spring which runs the year around. It supports a number of mesquite shrubs and in their shade a little grass plot harbors a dozen *Epipactis gigantea*

---

[d]The Vacin and Went medium which has proven to be one of the best media for seed germination and tissue culture of many orchids.—Ed.

plants which reappear year after year in the spring. It is curious that it grows only in that one spot in Cottonwood Springs where once a single seed seems to have been blown in by wind.

In another case I found some orchids in a "loma" in Peru, surrounded by one of the driest deserts in the world, near the Atacama desert. Lomas are low hill areas near the coast of Peru where coastal fogs hang for a good part of the year and occasionally cause small amounts of precipitation so that they harbor a growth of small trees in their valleys. The trees are *Capparis prisca* and a *Caesalpinea* of which the branches are covered with thick moss cushions in which *Peperomia* and *Begonia* grow, and a few specimens of the orchid *Altensteinia*. The nearest other orchids grow on the east slopes of the Andes hundreds of miles away.

My most recent encounters with orchids were in the Sierra Nevada Mountains and in Austria. Just 40 km south of Reno is a research area, Little Valley, in which I worked for many summers after 1965. It has a fine Sierra Nevada vegetation with shady pine forests and sunny *Artemisia tridentata* fields. In a mountain valley grow thousands of *Spiranthes romanzoffiana* in late summer and *Habenaria* spp. along shady mountain streams. But the most interesting orchid is *Corallorhiza maculata* with its pink chlorophylless stems and flowers. Whereas the underground plant parts of *Neottia*, *Sarcodes* and *Pterospora* are densely packed roots, as the species name *Neottia nidus avis* indicates, the underground parts of *Corallorhiza* are red mycorrhizal stems or rhizomes, whose stem tips grow out into flower shoots. Their underground stems should actually be called mycorrhizomes.

I had another encounter with orchids in Austria. I was invited to teach in Vienna after retiring in Reno. I spent the spring semester 1975 at the Plant Physiological Institute in Vienna, in the place where Wiesner and Molisch taught and worked. This caused me more effort than I had expected, for I had promised that my lectures would be in German, but in half a century I had forgotten my German.

At the end of my stay in Vienna, the botanists arranged for a number of excursions which I was invited to attend. One of the last was to the east, very close to the Czechoslovakian border. We walked up the Hainburger Mountain where I found *Neottia nidus avis* and was shown a purple plant, which they claimed to be a dicot but I recognized as the orchid, *Limodorum,* also a "saprophyte" like *Neottia*. It is very rare in Holland but seems to be common in Eastern Europe.

Most of the orchid people I have known have just one overriding interest, and that is orchids, no matter what their professional specialties, whether university faculty, such as Knudson;[e] businessmen or women; or professional people, especially physicians. All spend practically all their free time in their greenhouses. In the pre-war years, the orchid-growing business was so profitable that many amateurs expanded their hobbies into commercial orchid growing.

Among the professionals I met was Oakes Ames, a professor at Harvard. When on a tour around the world, he visited the Botanic Gardens of Bogor. I guided them through the gardens, particularly pointing out all the orchids, in which we were not specialized. But those we had were all grown on small *Plumeria* trees at breast height in a special section of the garden. The orchid specialist of the garden, J. J. Smith,[f] was exclusively inter-

---

[e]Prof. Knudson was also interested in other aspects of plant biology including single cell culture and enzymes. In addition, he was very successful in the stock market.—Ed.

[f]A monument to Smith was erected and still exists at the Bogor Botanical Gardens.—Ed.

ested in describing herbarium specimens and practically never looked at living plants. When once every five years he took his year's leave of absence, he spent it in Holland, where from the first of October until the last day of March he stayed indoors because he was afraid of the winter climate.

In Bogor I also met Prof. Hans Burgeff, who spent a year and a half in Java to study orchids in the wild. He also studied orchids in his laboratory in Wurzburg, where he discovered so much about their symbiosis with fungi.

Docters van Leeuwen, the director of the Bogor Garden, was the exact opposite of Smith. He was an outdoors man, interested in both plants and animals, and was my Cicerone who introduced me to the tropical flora. The first year he took me every morning for an hour or longer on his daily inspection of the garden.[g] As a result I knew almost as many tropical plants as the taxonomists who worked on the flora of Indonesia at the herbarium of the garden, who often specialized in only one or two families of plants, and even then only recognizing herbarium material. One of them even went so far as to tell his assistant to press a plant before he could name it.

A very curious character among the botanists who worked for many years at the Bogor Botanical Garden was Backer. He was a primary school teacher in Java and as a botanist an entirely self-made man. He knew the plants growing in Java including orchids perhaps better than any professional botanist, so was appointed at the herbarium of the garden to write a flora of Java. He had a very critical mind and an even more critical attitude towards people. He wrote a critical review of *Flora of Java* written by his colleague Dr. Koorders. Backer published this review himself, because he could not find a publisher who would print such a scathing criticism. He sent copies to many people, including the Governor General of the Netherlands East Indies who became so incensed over the abusive language, that he provided Koorders with a 1,000 guilders subsidy to publish a rebuttal, because "no book could be so bad as Backer had made it out". After Backer left the employ of the garden, he wrote another book, damningly critical of the work of his former director, Docters van Leeuwen, on the revegetation of the flora of Krakatau, which Backer mistakenly claimed had never been destroyed by the eruption of 1883. A particularly extraordinary example of his negative attitude toward people occurred when he once complained to me that his daughter had passed a critical exam (I think it was for her MD) so he was now forced to write her a letter of congratulations.

There were so many curious or even vicious characters among the botanists of the botanical garden in Bogor that my mother cried a whole day when I was appointed a botanist there.

But let me close with a mention my good friend, the late Dr. C. G. G. J. van Steenis, who died in 1988 and whose career for the first 20 years of our conscious lives paralleled mine almost to the day. We were in the same class in high school and both made a herbarium of plants from Holland. We both studied Botany at the University of Utrecht, obtaining our Ph.D. only weeks apart, became botanists at the Bogor Botanical Garden at the same time, and in Java mounted many excursions together. He stayed in Java after I left, but we received honorary degrees in Montreal only a day apart. He was the editor of the monumental *Flora Malesiana* in many volumes and has written other botanical books. While van Steenis is not an orchid specialist, his book *The Mountain Flora of Java* contains

[g]During my visits to Bogor I always took similar walks in the afternoon at the end of the work day. I saw and learned something new on every walk. These walks are among my most pleasant experiences.—Ed.

a number of beautiful paintings of orchids by M. Toha,[h] a superb Indonesian botanical illustrator who still lives in Bogor. Whenever I returned to Holland, I visited him to discuss old times and argue about Botany in general. A story told about van Steenis while he was interned in Indonesia by the Japanese during World War II is that an officer demanded his pocket knife. The officer would neither take it by force nor ask for it politely and van Steenis refused to accede to his demand. As a result he was put in solitary confinement for a punishingly long time. After his release, the Japanese approached him asking politely "May I please have your knife?" van Steenis handed it over saying "Why didn't you say so before?"[i] Such was his spirit.

Literature Cited

Casamajor, R. 1955. Factors governing the flowering of Cymbidiums. Cymbidium Soc. News 10: 8–12.

Casamajor, R. and F. W. Went 1954. Cypripediums at Earhart Laboratory. Cymbidium Soc. News 9: 2–3.

Coster, Ch. 1925. Periodische Blüteerscheinungen in den Tropen. Ann. Jard. Bot. Buitenzorg 35: 125–162, Tab XVIXXI.

Hijner, J. A. and J. Arditti 1973. Orchid mycorrhiza: Vitamin production and requirements by the symbionts. Amer. J. Bot. 60: 829–835.

Rutgers, A. A. L. and F. A. F. C. Went, 1915. Periodische Erscheinungen bei den Blüten des *Dendrobium crumenatum* Lindl. Ann. Jard. Bot. Buitenzorg. 14: 129–160.

Vacin, E. F., and F. W. Went. 1949a. Some pH changes in nutrient solutions. Bot. Gaz. 110: 605–613.

Went, F. A. F. C. 1898. Die Periodicität des Blühens von *Dendrobium crumenatum* Lindl. Ann. Jard. Bot. Buitenzorg (Suppl. II), pp. 73–77.

Went, F. A. F. C. and Rutgers, A. A. L. 1915. On the influence of external conditions on the flowering of *Dendrobium crumenatum* Lindl. Proc. Kon. Akad, Wetnesch. Amsterdam 18: 526–530.

Went, F. W. 1928. Wuchsstoff und Wachstum. Rec. Trav. Bot. Neerl. 25: 1–116.

Went, F. W. 1940. Soziologie der Epiphyten eines tropischen Urwaldes. Ann. Jard. Bot. Buitenzorg 50: 1–98

[h]Toha is now painting Indonesian orchids for a book by N. Soediono and myself to be published by Timber Press.—Ed.

[i]van Steenis provided me with copies of the well known photograph of Hugo de Vries (who was a relatively short man) standing next to an inflorescence of *Amorphophallus titanum* which was taller than him. The "price" requested by van Steenis for the photographs was two reprints of the paper (*Ann. Bot.* 51:269–278) which I duly sent him.—Ed.

2

The Western Australian Fully Subterranean Orchid *Rhizanthella gardneri**

KINGSLEY W. DIXON, JOHN S. PATE, and JOHN KUO

*The literature survey pertaining to this chapter was concluded in January 1986. The chapter was submitted in January 1986, and the revised version was received in April 1987.

Introduction

Many terrestrial orchids spend at least the early part of their existence as saprophytic protocorms buried a few centimeters down in leaf litter, soil or rotting wood (Dressler, 1981). Depending on the species this phase of growth may last from only a few to many months, after which the plants of some but not all species become photoautotrophic. Fully achlorophyllous species, on the other hand, retain a dominant subterranean phase for their entire life span and continue to rely on fungal associations of a saprophytic, parasitic or epiparasitic nature for their supply of carbohydrates and other organic and inorganic nutrients.

The majority of achlorophyllous orchids develop an above-ground phase which functions in flowering and seed dispersal (e.g. members of the genera *Epipogium*, *Didymoplexis* and *Gastrodia*). However the Australian genus *Rhizanthella* remains below ground, or, at least, below the litter layer, even when forming flowers and seeds. This cryptic behavior has continued to confound observers since accidental discoveries of the orchids half a century ago. Even at present the eastern Australian species *R. slateri* (Rupp) M. Clements and Cribb has been seen once in flower in the wild in the past decade, while its western counterpart, *R. gardneri* R. Rogers, has only recently been rediscovered (George, 1980; Dixon, 1982; Dixon and Pate, 1984). Although known in several locations, *R. gardneri* still requires considerable effort to locate specimens nondestructively in its native habitat, even where it is currently known to be prolific.

History

By the time of the first properly documented discovery of *Rhizanthella gardneri* by a farmer, John Trott, at Corrigin in 1928 (Fig. 2-1, Table 2-1), the known orchids of Western Australia comprised 22 genera and 109 species. Presently the orchid flora stands at 145 species in 28 genera, and among these are two achlorophyllous genera (*Rhizanthella* and *Gastrodia*) from the mediterranean-type ecosystems of the southwest, and the genera *Dipodium* and *Didymoplexis* from tropical northern regions of the state.

As a result of its subterranean habit, the early accidental discoveries of *Rhizanthella* were all made during land clearing operations associated with the establishment of cereal farming in what is now termed the wheatbelt of Western Australia. These early locations, including the type of locality, are now devoid of native vegetation, and, as arable farm land, no longer support the orchid. Within a month of the initial discovery in May 1928, two additional locations for the orchid were found, one at Shackleton, the other at Goomalling (Fig. 2-1). These three discoveries were unrelated, but coincided with an era of particularly active land clearance in this region of the wheatbelt. R. S. Rogers in his description of *Rhizanthella* in 1928 commented: "In each instance, the orchid appears to have been turned up by the plough or cultivator." Additional specimens found by the keen sighted Trott made possible a study of the morphology of the orchid by Rogers (1928), and of its fungal symbiont by Pittman (1929). Of the 39 specimens purported to have been collected by Trott, only six now remain in herbaria (George, 1980), all still bearing evidence of the damage inflicted during their accidental excavation.

Early discoveries of this mysterious, fully subterranean plant roused great excitement among the local public and scientific fraternity of the day, and, within six months of its discovery, wax models of the plant had been placed on exhibition at scientific meetings and museums in Western Australia.

It may well be that Trott's collections were not in fact the first true sightings of *Rhizanthella.* As early as 1914 an unusual subterranean flower was sighted during farm clearing near Wubin, a wheatbelt town some 300 km north of Corrigin. The original descriptions of the plant and its habitat would now lead us to suggest that it was *Rhizanthella,* but no herbarium voucher specimen survives to validate this view. However, there have been several cases of plants thought to be *Rhizanthella* turning out to be other species. For instance, *Rhizanthella* has been commonly confused with frutifications of the stink-horn fungus *Clathrus* spp., the earth-star fungus *Geastrum* spp., and especially with flowers of the holoparasitic broomrape (*Orobanche minor* Smith, Orobanchaceae).

In the period 1929–1959 the orchid was seen only very sporadically (Fig. 2-1, Table 2-1), and always in association with the initial stages of clearing of bushland. These finds encompassed a number of locations within the wheatbelt, but the orchid was always found in intimate association with the root system of the multistemmed shrub *Melaleuca uncinata* R.Br., *Myrtaceae* the broom honeymyrtle (Fig. 2-2, Plate 2-1a-c)—one of the 120 species of this genus found in Western Australia. Recent studies have confirmed the regular association of the fungus with living *M. uncinata* (Warcup, 1985), and its invariable occurrence in leached grey or white sand inordinately low in organic matter. In the latter respect it contrasts with *R. slateri* of eastern Australia, a species occurring in soils rich in leaf litter and organic matter.

After a lapse of twenty years, the orchid was rediscovered in 1979 when a farmer kicked over a small stump when climbing through a fence and noticed a *Rhizanthella* below. This time the location, 300 km southeast of any previous principal locality, was (Fig. 2-1) on new farming land near the south coast town of Munglinup. With this discovery it became possible for the first time to examine intact plants in only partly disturbed vegetation, albeit on private land already mostly deployed in farming.

With the publicity attending the 1979 rediscovery, the authors visited the site at Munglinup to acquaint themselves with the appearance and habitat of the orchid. We then decided to search for it by the simple but laborious technique of gently lifting the surface litter around plants of *M. uncinata.* We concentrated first on stands of mature vegetation close to the original sites of discovery in the Corrigin-Shackleton-Babakin area, but later ventured more widely throughout the wheatbelt. Our first discovery of one plant in May 1980 on a reserve at Babakin (Fig. 2-1), spurred the World Wildlife Fund of Australia, the Australian Orchid Foundation and government agencies to finance further searches for the orchid over the next four years. The successful findings of the orchids and the general location of these finds are summarized in Table 2-1, together with information on the numbers of flowering specimens discovered in each year of study. The principal aims of the projects were to:

1. survey relic native vegetation in the vicinity of all earlier recorded localities of *Rhizanthella,* and to extend more general surveys to the remainder of the wheatbelt;
2. develop non-destructive, widescale methods of surveying vegetation for *R. gardneri* and for assessing in greater detail its abundance in localities where it was eventually discovered;
3. investigate the autecological requirements of the species as a basis for its management on reserves;

4. recommend to appropriate authorities the acquisition of a number of suitably-sized reserves to preserve effectively as many as possible of the known localities of *Rhizanthella;*

5. attempt artificial propagation of the species with a view to replenishment of existing colonies depleted in the wild.

The supposed extreme rarity of the species placed obvious limitations on the nature of the research, precluding, in particular, any experimental studies requiring the taking of numerous specimens.

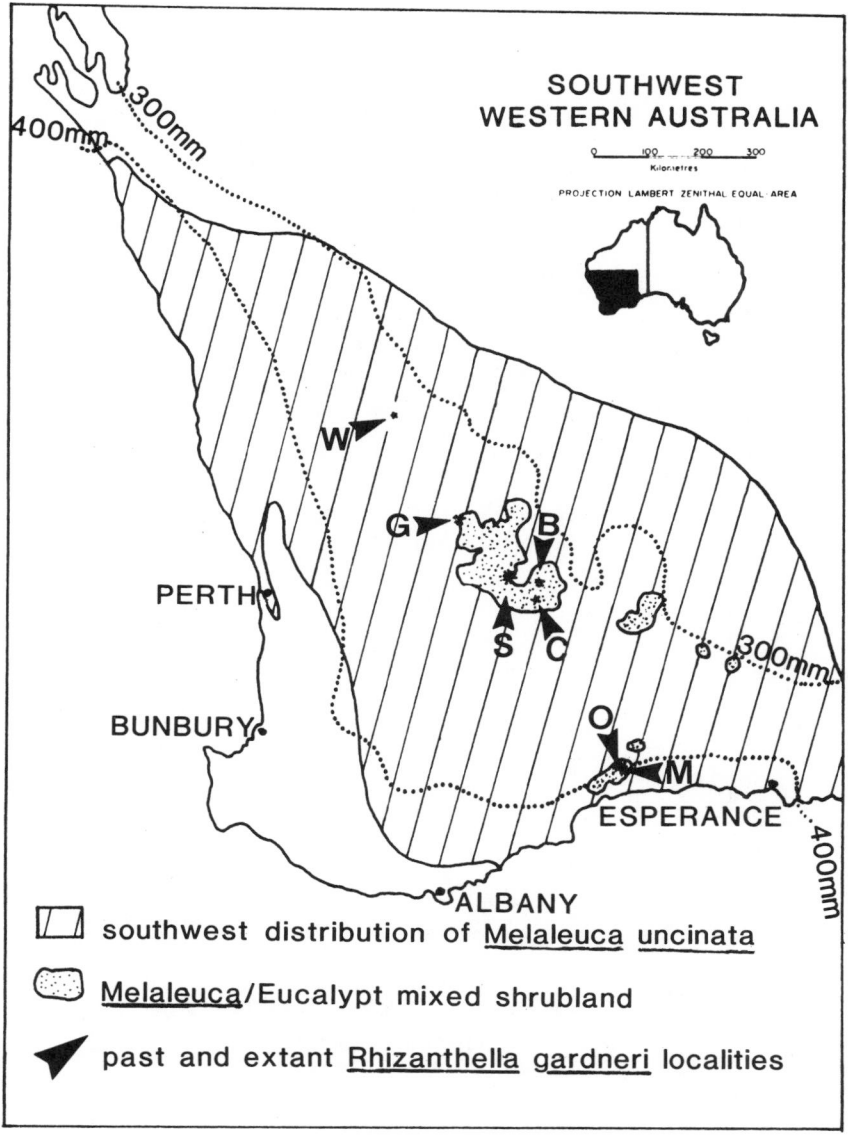

Fig. 2-1. Map of the study region within South West Australia showing overall distribution of broom honey-myrtle (*Melaleuca uncinata*), host shrub to the underground orchid *Rhizanthella gardneri.* Past and present locations of the orchid are arrowed and all but one (the initial discovery site at Wubin) are seen to occur within *Melaleuca*/eucalypt mixed shrubland (as defined and mapped by Beard, 1981); 300 mm and 400 mm isohyets are indicated. W: Wubin, G: Goomalling, S: Shackleton (includes Moonigin), B: Babakin (includes West Babkin), C: Corrigin, O: Oldfield River (includes Cheadanup), M: Munglinup.

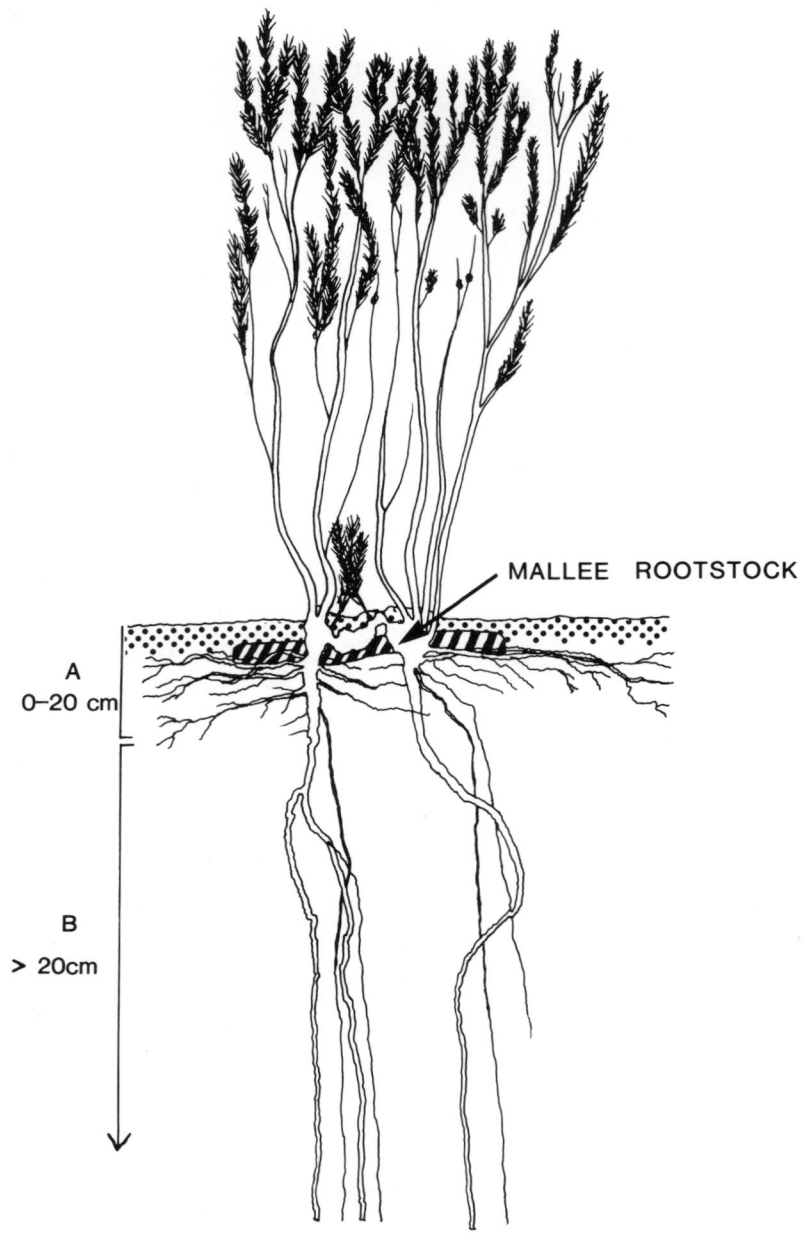

MALLEE   ROOTSTOCK

A
0–20 cm

B
> 20cm

Zones of typical occurrence of
Rhizanthella gardneri

Fig. 2-2. Schematic drawing of the occupancy zone of *Rhizanthella gardneri* and its lignotuberous, multistemmed (mallee type) host *Melaleuca uncinata.* Note fine fibrous feeding roots and deeply penetrating tap roots of the myrtle.

Plate 2-1. **A.** Typical stand of broom honey myrtle (*Melaleuca uncinata*) where one might find the underground orchid *Rhizanthella gardneri*. **B.** Partial excavation of an inflorescence (capitulum) and daughter tubers of a plant of *Rhizanthella gardneri*. Note depth-seeking dropper to one of the daughter tubers. The withered bracts of another capitulum is seen towards the rear of the photograph ($\times \frac{1}{3}$). **C.** Photograph of partly-exposed capitulum after removal of surface litter. Note reflexed bracts and proximity of inflorescence to stem base of the host plant (*Melaleuca uncinata*).

Table 2-1. Discovery of *Rhizanthella gardneri.*

Date	Month	Discovery Site[a]	Method of[b] Discovery	Number of Inflorenscences Collected/Sighted
1914	?	Wubin[c]	A	1[d]
1928	May	Corrigin[c]—(Type)	A	39
1928	June	Goomalling[c]	A	(1) +[d]
1928	June	Shackleton[c]	A	(1) +[d]
1938	June	Moonigin[c]	A	1
1938	Aug	Corrigin[c]	A	1
1940	?	Corrigin[c]	A	(1) +[d]
1959	May	Babakin[c]	A	1
1979	May	Munglinup[c]	A	11
1980	May	Munglinup[e]	D(R)	15
1980	May	Babakin[e]	D	1
1981	Jun–Aug	Babakin[e]	D	38
1981	Jun	West Babakin[e]	D	2
1981	Jul–Oct	Cheadanup[e]	D	6
1981	Aug–Sep	Oldfield River[e]	D	5
1982	May–Jun	Babakin[e]	D(R)	110
1982	May	West Babakin[e]	D(R)	4
1982	Aug	Cheadanup[e]	D(R)	
1982	May	West Babakin[e]	D(R)	4
1982	Aug	Cheadanup[e]	D(R)	4
1982	Jun	Oldfield River[e]	D(R)	4
1983	May	Babakin[e]	D(R)	5
1984	May	Babakin[e]	D(R)	16

[a]Location of township or reserves as shown in Fig. 2-1.
[b]A—accidental discovery during clearing of bush for agriculture; D—deliberate non destructive searching by scraping litter in stands of *Melaleuca uncinata*; D(R)—deliberate, site revisited.
[c]George (1980)
[d]One or more specimens allegedly discovered, but no material retained for examination and verification.
[e]Dixon and Pate (1984)

Deliberate Searches for *Rhizanthella gardneri*

On the basis of discoveries prior to 1980, the surveys in 1980–1984 were restricted almost entirely to dense stands of broom honeymyrtle (*Melaleuca uncinata,* Plate 2-1a, Fig. 2-2) albeit from a wide range of soil types and ecosystems. Attention was devoted to examining existing conservation areas or unvested, uncleared government-owned land within the rainfall zone of 300–400 mm of annual precipitation (Fig 2-1).

Using LANDSAT satellite images, some indication was obtained of the type and condition of the vegetation, in some cases even to the extent of detecting the presence of extensive stands of *M. uncinata* (as subsequently verified by ground-based expeditions, Dixon and Pate, 1984). From this initial survey, apparently suitable locations were selected and visited systematically to test whether further detailed searching was justified. In general, habitats were selected only if *M. uncinata* was the dominant upper stratum, or the major understory element within a particular thicket, scrub or mallee formation (Muir 1977).

The search procedure involved very careful surface scraping of the litter and superficial soil layers within and adjacent to the base of each plant of *M. uncinata,* to look for emerging or open inflorescences (Plates 2-1b, 2-3a). The tool employed was a hand fork with curved tines, not unlike the classic European "truffle rake". Where flowering heads were present, the only damage observed to the orchid through litter scraping was the

Plate 2-2. **A.** Detail of capitulum nearing pollinia-producing stage. Note relfexed bracts (Br) and crowding of the non-resupinate flowers (Fl) within the capitulum (×3). **B.** Ethanol-preserved specimen of *Rhizanthella gardneri* showing terminal capitulum (Ca), parent tubers (PT) and current season young daughter tubers (DT × ⅔; specimen loaned courtesy of Mr. Alex George, then of W. A. Herbarium, Perth). **C.** Recently exposed capitulum of *Rhizanthella gardneri* showing two termites already present inside. Note yellow pollinia on the lower termite in the photograph, and the spirally-arranged flowers (× 2.5).

Plate 2-3. **A.** Capitula of different ages (youngest 1, oldest 3) adjacent to each other, found well below the soil surface. Also note the progressive coloration and reflexing of bracts with age. (×1.3; photograph courtesy Mr. Andrew Brown). **B.** Partly-withered bracts on already-fertilized capitulum containing developing seed capsules. This capitulum was only just beneath the litter, some of which is retained in natural position to the right of the photograph. Note dark maroon colouration of bracts at this stage (× 1.3). **C.** Inside view of the ripe capitulum showing withered and dry bracts, fertilized ovaries turned into fleshy fruits (FR) and unfertilized and unpollinated flowers towards the middle of the capitulum (×2.5). **D.** Section through a fleshy fruit showing color dimorphism of ripe seeds. The yellow or light coloured seeds (arrows) germinate more easily *in vitro* (× 15).

very occasional loss of the tips of the involucral bracts—a happening shown not to affect materially the subsequent ripening of seeds within the capitulum (Plate 2-3c, d). All litter was restored as far as possible to its original position at a study site, whether or not an orchid had been discovered. Some orchid plants were tagged discretely to facilitate future observations, which included analysis of adjacent soil, examinations for soil biota, especially fungi, and records of the number of flowers and mature seed capsules developed on each inflorescence.

The search totalled over 3,000 man hours of effort, greatly aided by the voluntary help of members of the Western Australian Native Orchid Study and Conservation Group (Plate 2-1a, c). Less than 4% of the areas searched produced positive results, despite a number of apparently suitable sites being revisited several times during the study program. Searches were restricted to the winter–spring months (May–October)—the only period when *Rhizanthella* capitula are recognizable. It would have been impractical, and thoroughly reprehensible on conservation grounds, to attempt to locate the deeply buried (8–10 cm) tubers by excavation of the species outside this period.

Comprehensive records were made of all fauna and flora encountered at sites proving positive for *Rhizanthella* (Dixon and Pate 1984). Apart from identifying biota possibly of significance to the reproduction and survival of the orchid, the discovery in a study area of other rare or endangered species (Marchant and Keighery, 1979; Rye, 1982) would obviously strengthen any case being made for a locality to be afforded the highest possible conservation status.

Presently-known Localities for *Rhizanthella gardneri*

The 1980–1984 survey resulted in the discovery and tagging of approximately 180 plants from four previously unknown locations for the species (see Table 2-1). The present distribution (Fig. 2-1), including the 1979 Munglinup location, suggests two nodes of occurrence, one in the central wheatbelt, the other near the south coast. These may represent relics of what was once a much larger, possibly continuous distribution range.

Soils of the past and present *Rhizanthella* sites are usually of duplex character, consisting generally of sandy-clays to sandy-loams, frequently with a gritty texture (Plates 2-1b, 2-3a, b). The presence of an underlying clay base at 20 cm or more depth appears important, possibly in optimizing seasonal water relations for the plants. The soils studied contained less than 2% (by weight) of organic matter, high levels of iron and sodium ions, but abnormally low levels of potassium, nitrogen, phosphorus, zinc, and copper ions (Dixon, 1982).

There was some evidence (Dixon and Pate, 1984) that periodicity and intensity of falls of rain might have considerable impact on the timing and overall success of flowering in a particular season. *Rhizanthella* initiates inflorescences and may even reach anthesis before the start of the new season rains in May (Fig. 2-3). Therefore one might expect that rainfall of the preceding summer, or even that for the whole previous year might be a major determinant of flowering performance. The data for the Babakin site (Dixon and Pate, 1984) lent some support to this suggestion.

In every instance in which *Rhizanthella* was encountered in undisturbed vegetation, its capitula were found within 20 cm of a plant of *M. uncinata* (Plate 2-1a, c). Also all specimens at a site were invariably associated with stands of the host species with densi-

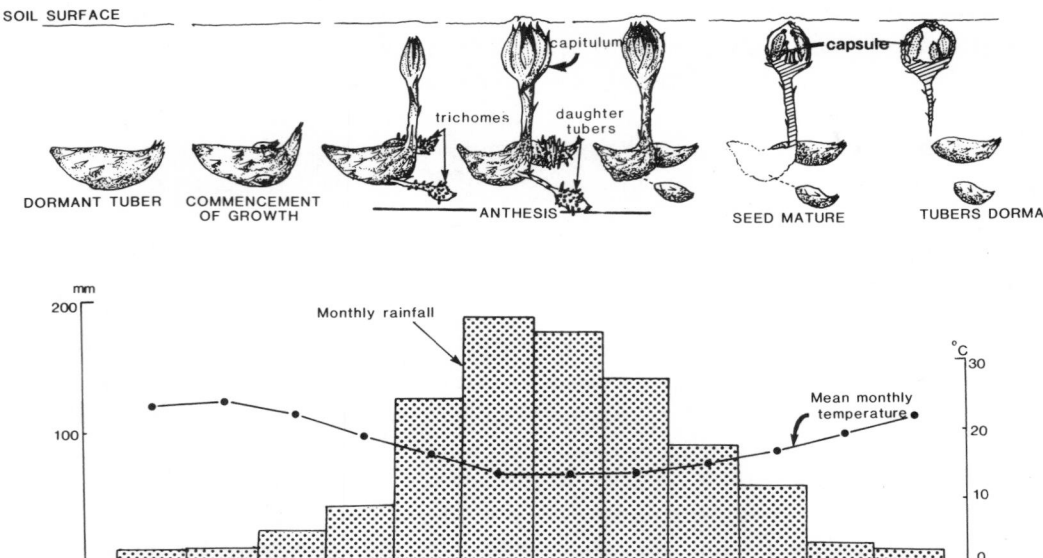

Fig. 2-3. Phenological scheme for the underground orchid *Rhizanthella gardneri* in relation to rainfall and temperature experiences over a typical season of growth. Note terminal inflorescence, lateral production of daughter tubers, complete annual replacement of parent tuber and long period of maturation of fruits in capitulum.

ties of 60–240 plants/100 m² (Plate 2-1a). Significantly, no single plant species other than *Melaleuca uncinata* was consistently present as near neighbor to the orchid. However, frequent inhabitants of the vicinity of *Rhizanthella* sites were various mallee-type species of *Eucalyptus,* the myrtle *Melaleuca scabra* R.Br., and the monocotyledons *Gahnia ancistrophylla* Benth., *Lepidosperma longitudinale* Labill., and one as yet unidentified member of the Restionaceae (aff. *Loxocarya*). All of the above species, however, were also generally associated with *Melaleuca uncinata* thickets, even where the orchid had not been observed.

Viewed more generally, all known sites occur within those parts of the species range of *Melaleuca uncinata* listed by Beard (1981) as *Melaleuca/Eucalyptus* mixed shrubland. This vegetation type encompasses only a small fraction of the total area of occurrence of *M. uncinata* in southwestern Australia (Fig. 2-1). However, not all *Melaleuca/Eucalyptus* mixed shrubland sites have been surveyed exhaustively, so it is possible that further sites for the orchid remain to be discovered.

Biology and Morphology of *Rhizanthella* and its Presumed Host *Melaleuca uncinata*

All *Rhizanthella* plants discovered in undisturbed vegetation were associated with mature (1.5–2.3 m tall) thickets of *Melaleuca uncinata,* each myrtle plant with 3–8 erect stems arising from a swollen lignotuber, 15–30 cm wide and buried just below the soil surface (Fig. 2-2). Association of *Rhizanthella* with these roots was so intimate that inflorescences of the orchid were sometimes seen to emerge from between convolutions of the lignotuber and its shoot bases.

Growth of the root stock of *Melaleuca uncinata* is clearly seasonal. A vertical root system extends many meters in well drained situations, and it probably increases in length and diameter only during the wet season (Fig. 2-3). Annual regrowth of fine feeding, mycorrhizal roots commences with the onset of the winter rains, but these roots remain alive and active only so long as soil moisture remains high in the surface soil layers. The region 3–15 cm below the soil surface is where these ephemeral feeding roots of *Melaleuca uncinata* are located. That is also where the tubers of the orchid typically occur (Fig. 2-2), and presumably where the orchid derives maximum benefit from any mycorrhizal associate which it might share with the myrtle. Indeed, partial excavations close to the tubers of *Rhizanthella* (Plate 2-1b) revealed extensive mycorrhizal growth investing both the fine roots of the associated myrtle (Plate 2-4a, b) and the orchid. However, it was impracticable to observe direct connections between myrtle and orchid *via* a continuous mycelial component without resorting to isotopic methods (Bjorkman, 1960).

Permission was granted to the authors by the Western Australian Wildlife Authority to excavate and remove specimens of *Rhizanthella*. The accounts below of tuber anatomy, endophyte relationships, and reproductive morphology and structure derive largely from these specimens, and information recorded from others who had already had access to excavated specimens (Rogers 1928, George 1980, George and Cooke, 1981). Additionally, using seeds and endophyte isolates from the specimen, successful attempts were made at *in vitro* culture of *Rhizanthella,* with and without its associate myrtle both in our laboratory (K. W. Dixon and J. S. Pate unpublished) and in the Waite Institute in South Australia (Warcup 1985). This made it possible to obtain further information about morphology of the plant, and may prove a promising system for future physiological studies.

The stem tubers of *Rhizanthella* (Pate and Dixon 1982) are thick, cylindrical (1–2 cm diameter), fleshy structures up to 5 cm in length (Plate 2-2b), and covered with a thick mantle of trichomes (Plate 2-4c, d) which are interspersed with closely adhering, triangular leaf scales (Plate 2-2b). As far as is known, tuber development during a new season is accompanied by senescence of tubers which had formed during the previous season (Rogers 1928). Inflorescences form terminally on tubers toward the end of the growing season (Plate 2-2b). As a result production of daughter tubers is axillary (Plates 2-1b, 2-2b) and growth essentially sympodial. Depth adjustment by daughter tubers is accomplished by dropperlike extensions (Plate 2-1b), though plant growth is normally maintained in a horizontal plane 10–15 cm below the soil surface. The phenology of the species is summarized in Fig. 2-3, together with data on rainfall and mean monthly temperatures.

The solitary, terminal inflorescence of *Rhizanthella* (Plates 2-1b, 2-2b, Fig. 2-3) is attached to a tapering peduncle, itself sheathed in elongated scale leaves whose margins curl inward with age. The possession of a capitulum by *Rhizanthella* is unusual but not unique among the Orchidaceae. The capitulum varies in width from 2-5 cm and in unexcavated plants is entirely enclosed by two rows of 6–19 bracts, each 2–5 cm long (Plates 2-1b, 2-2a, 2-3a). In some instances the bracts enlarge and open to such an extent as to force their way through the litter (Plate 2-3b). This opens a channel into the capitulum through which insects might enter. Most capitula, however, remain fully subterranean, indicating that pollination by flying insects may be rare, if occurring at all.

Observations by George (1980) and George and Cooke (1981) using a small muslin tent placed over the orifice above a bloom showed removal of pollinia by a small fly in

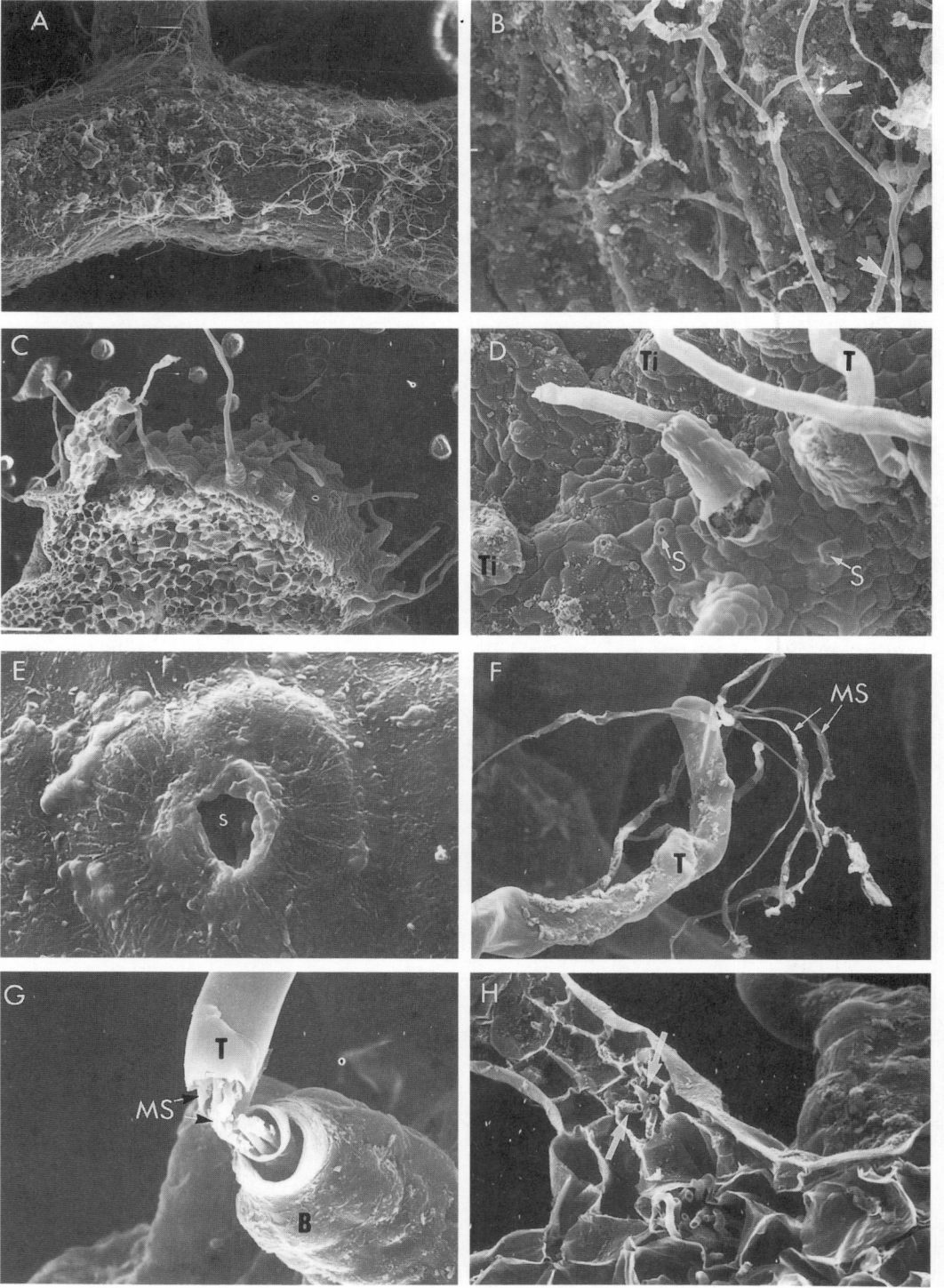

the genus *Megaselia* (Phoridae). Insects in this group are thought to feed on decaying fungal matter, such as basidiocarps. Similar observations by Dixon (1982) showed a fungus gnat (family Cecidomyiidae) and a wasp (Bracomidae, sub family Alysinae) to be also capable of removing pollinia. The more likely pollinating agents, however, are termites of the genus *Drepanotermes* which were observed systematically to visit flowers (Plate 2-2c) within the capitulum, and may effect transfer of pollen massulae between blossoms. If this proves to be widespread, inbreeding is likely to be frequent, as in other achlorophyllous orchids (Dressler, 1981). Whether termites stumble accidentally into, or are specifically lured to the capitulum is uncertain, but their involvement as pollinators may well prove to be unique among orchids, 60% of the species of which are pollinated by bees or wasps (van der Pijl and Dodson, 1966). Peakall (1984), however, has recently reported pollination of *Leporella fimbriata* by winged male ants (*Myrmecia* sp) and Jones (1975) have recorded ant pollination in *Microtis*.

George (1980) reports the emission of a formalin-like scent from cut surfaces of the flowering structure.

Observations on naturally occurring unexposed capitula indicated that pollination and seed set were normally very low (less than 5%). In specimens whose flowers were hand pollinated (using toothpicks to collect and deposit pollen) seed set was increased substantially, with up to 40% of the flowers forming fruits and viable seed. Small numbers of seeds from such plants were collected for studies on germination and establishment of fungal symbiosis in our laboratory and donated for similar purposes to the Australian National Botanic Garden, Canberra (M Clements) and the Waite Institute, South Australia (J Warcup).

The 40–120 flowers within a capitulum are arranged in 8–12 spirally arranged rows (Plates 2-2a, c, 3c). Anthesis occurs over a week or so, starting with the outer whorls and finishing incompletely in flowers near the center of the capitulum (Plates 2-2c, 2-3c). Observations in the Babakin population showed that with approaching anthesis each flower bud swells into a crozierlike configuration and intensifies in color from pink to red or maroon (Plate 2-2a). The perianth then straightens and its galea-like tube opens towards the center of the capitulum (Plate 2-2a) in a non-resupinate fashion (George 1980). The labellum is fleshy and conduplicate, protruding only slightly and resting on the raised sinus formed by fusion of the anterior margins of the lateral sepals (Plate 2-2a).

The young ovary is succulent and not ribbed, 5–6 mm long and continuous with the perianth. After pollination it enlarges to 10–15 mm and becomes globoid in shape (Plate 2-3c). Unlike the situation in other geophilous orchids such as *Corybas* and *Chiloglottis*, the peduncle does not elongate. Each fleshy fruit within the capitulum contains 50–150

Plate 2-4. **A.** Scanning electron micrograph (SEM) of mycorrhiza-infected root of *Melaleuca uncinata* ($\times$ 44). **B.** Detail of mycorrhizal infection shown in A. Note clamp connections (arrow) indicating the fungus is a Basidiomycete ($\times$ 440). **C.** SEM (side view) of thick slice of tuber of *Rhizanthella gardneri*, showing broad cortical zone inside tuber and trichomes on epidermal surface of tuber ($\times$ 14). **D.** SEM of tuber surface of *R. gardneri* near the tuber growing point showing stomata (St) and robust nature of trichomes (Tr). Two trichome initials are evident (Ti), neither yet with an expanded trichome ($\times$ 54). **E.** SEM of stoma (St) of *R. gardneri* showing lack of subsidiary cells ($\times$ 860). **F.** SEM of terminal portion of trichome (Tr) already infected with mycorrhiza and showing a number of mycelial strands (MS) extending outwards from its tip ($\times$ 110). **G.** SEM of broken proximal region of trichome (Tr) showing multicellular, wart-like base (Ba) and a number of mycelial strands (MS) running through the trichome ($\times$ 220). **H.** SEM of Transverse section of tuber of *R. gardneri* through base of trichome. Note multicellular nature of base of trichome and presence of coils of hyphae (arrows) in some of the cells ($\times$ 220).

seeds (Plate 2-3d), usually dark brown in color, but occasionally light brown or cream colored. Seed development takes some 6–7 months, compared to 6–8 weeks for other orchid species sympatric with *R. gardneri*. By mid summer (January) the fruit wall has become hard and brittle, as have the surrounding involucral bracts. Parts of the peduncle and tuber, however, remain fleshy until the next season (April/May) when the capitulum is likely to have collapsed and become infiltrated with soil and debris. Termites have been observed to consume dried parts of the capitulum, but not the dried fruits.

Laboratory studies by ourselves (unpublished data) have shown that intact and viable seeds are voided in faeces of small marsupials such as hopping mice (*Notomys* spp) following voluntary feeding on ripe capitula. Whether such animals effect dispersal in nature is debatable (George, 1980). Similarly, the role of termites in dispersal is not understood, although they might be considered as the most likely candidate in view of their subterranean habits and known ability to transfer organic materials over great distances. In any event, the hard dry seeds of *Rhizanthella* are likely to be unpalatable to ants or termites, which is unlike the situation with the ant-dispersed genera *Dendrochilum* and *Acriopsis* whose seeds contain superficial oil bodies (Dressler, 1981).

Seed germination and seedling establishment have yet to be observed in the wild.

Anatomy and Ultrastructure of the Tuber and its Endophyte

Examination of the tuber surface of *Rhizanthella* by scanning electron microscopy (Plate 2-4c, d) demonstrates the robust nature of the trichomes and the multicellular, wart-like trichome base (Plate 2-4d, g), as originally described by Pittman (1929). In external morphology the trichomes resemble those of the genera *Corybas, Yoania* and *Gastrodia* (Campbell 1963, 1972) and certain southwestern Australian orchids studied by Dixon and Ramsay (1984). The extended apical cell of each trichome is vacuolate and free of inclusions, but carries a number (3–6) of hyphal strands (Plate 2-4f, g) which presumably connect internally with other parts of the endophyte (Plate 2-4h) and externally *via* the soil interface with adjacent mycorrhizal components of the host (Plate 2-4a, b). Stomata are visible at moderately high density on the tuber surface (Plate 2-4d). They lack subsidiary cells (Plate 2-4e), and no hyphae of the endophyte were observed to enter (or exit) from the tuber *via* stomata.

Plate 2-5. **A.** SEM view of outer cortex of tuber of *Rhizanthella gardneri* showing four infected cells with bunched coils of intracellular mycorrhizal hyphae surrounding an uninfected cell (× 240). **B.** Light micrograph of transverse section of tuber of *R. gardneri* showing vascular bundle (VB) and cells infected with mycorrhizal hyphae (arrows) in tuber cortex. (Tissue embedded in glycol methacrylate and stained with toluidine blue; × 50). **C.** Light micrograph of tuber cell infected with hyphae, from same preparation as photographed in B. (× 450). **D.** Transmission electron micrograph (TEM) of intracellular hyphae (Hy) in tuber, showing thick wall of fungus (Wa) and apparently healthy state of host cytoplasm, as evidenced by intact mitochondria (Mi; × 3600).

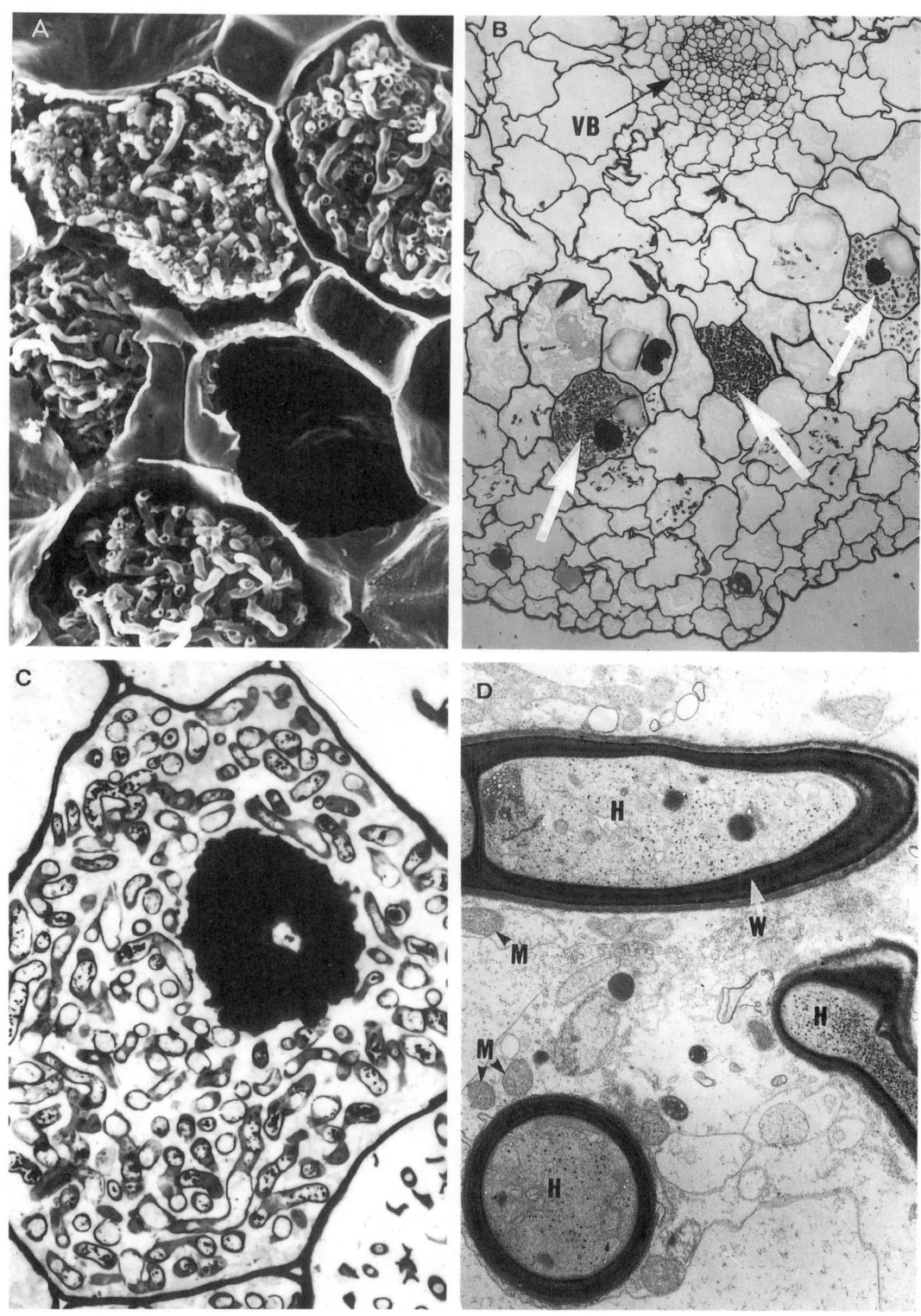

Transverse sections of tubers, observed with a scanning electron microscope or a light microscope show vascular bundles (Plate 2-5b) scattered throughout a ground tissue consisting of large vacuolate cells. A high proportion of these in the outer and inner cortical layers are infected with the endophyte (Plate 2-5a, d). The coiled configuration of the live endophyte can be seen with the scanning electron microscope (Plate 2-5a). As in the case of *Gastrodia* (Campbell 1972), there is no evidence of sclerenchyma or other specialized supporting tissues in the tuber (Plate 2-5b). There is also no evidence of substantial deposits of starch or wall reserves as is commonly found in root tubers of many chlorophyllous orchids (Pate and Dixon, 1982).

According to Hadley (1982) achlorophyllous orchids usually exhibit particularly intense fungal infection, a feature held to be related to their dependence on the fungal partner for carbon. In agreement with this, mature parts of tubers of *Rhizanthella* are uniformly infected up to six to ten cell layers in from the epidermis. Infection of new parts of the tuber appears to occur rapidly and progressively (Fig. 2-3). Profuse intracellular branching occurs early and follows infection of the young tuber cells (Plate 2-5a), resulting in characteristic hyphal coils or pelotons. During this state biotrophic exchanges across the living interface of host cell and endophyte are likely, as in other tolypophagous orchids. There is no evidence of breakdown of hyphae as they enter cells, as is the case with ptyophagous species such as *Gastrodia sesamoides* (Hadley 1982), although necrotrophic benefit to the host may occur much later when the intracellular hyphae are digested (Plate 2-5b). This may not take place until the tuber tissues are much older, probably after several months of nutrient transfer *via* healthy intact hyphae. Old parts of tuber tissue where fungal digestion is prominent, contain yellowing zones of cells.

The Endophyte and Nutrition of *Rhizanthella gardneri*

The endophyte of *Rhizanthella* was originally described by Pittman (1928) as being "*Rhizoctonia*-like" and recent work by Warcup (1985) has confirmed that at least two strains of the form genus *Rhizoctonia* may be involved in symbiosis with the orchid and its host *Melaleuca uncinata*. The endophyte resembles the basidiomycete genus *Thanatephorus,* a known symbiont of orchids (Warcup 1981; Hadley 1982).

It is widely held that holomycotrophic orchids derive carbon from their fungal partner which breaks down the organic matter of surrounding litter or humus. Alternatively or additionally they may engage in a three-way epiparasitic relationship with an autotrophic tree or shrub species. In the latter case, carbon passes from roots of the woody species to a shared mycorrhizal partner and thence becomes available to the orchid. Relationships predominantly of an epiparasitic kind have been suggested for the following genera: *Gastrodia*—unnamed fungus—*Leptospermum* Myrtaceae (Campbell, 1963); *Gastrodia*—*Armillaria*—*Nothofagus* Fagaceae (Campbell 1962, 1980); *Yoania*—*Lycoperdon*—*Beilschmeidia* Lauraceae (Campbell 1970), and, outside the Orchidaceae, in certain achlorophyllous representatives of the sub family Monotropoideae of the Ericaceae (*Pterospora, Sarcodes* and *Monotropa:* Robertson and Robertson, 1982).

However, with few exceptions, (Bjorkman, 1960) definitive tracer studies of nutrient flow from woody host to epiparasitic partner are lacking, and since the surrounding soil is rich in organic matter, a significant saprophytic element in nutrition of orchid or monotropoid is highly likely.

As stated previously, *R. gardneri* inhabits soils extremely deficient in organic matter, implying that a purely or predominantly organic matter-dependent nutritional base for the orchid would be extremely doubtful. The recent success of Warcup (1985) and ourselves in cultivating the orchid from a seed in an artificial *Melaleuca-Rhizoctonia-Rhizanthella* system corroborates this view, at least to the extent of demonstrating a highly effective epiparasitism by the orchid when organic matter is absent or at very low level in the medium.

Seed Morphology and Structure, Germination, and Early Establishment of Symbiosis with a Fungal Partner

The large size (75 μg) and unusual shape (Plate 2-6a) and color polymorphism (Plate 2-3d) of the seeds of *Rhizanthella* set this orchid apart from the more usual microspermous members of the family. The essentially spheroid seeds have a prominent circular ridge at one end corresponding to the hilum (Plate 2-6a, b), and point of attachment of the ovule to the placenta. Elaborate files of elongate cells with strongly birefringent (Plate 2-6c, d) inner tangential and radial thickenings radiate out from this ridged area.

Like other orchid seeds, the embryo bears little evidence of differentiation (Plate 2-6b, c, d, f), although it exhibits polarization to the extent that the shoot apex eventually forms distally to the hilum. Each of the 200 or so cells of the embryo contains rich reserves of lipids and protein bodies (Plate 2-6e, f) but no starch (Plate 2-6c). Crystalline inclusions in the protein bodies are presumed reserves of mineral elements (Plate 2-6e).

Germination of seeds in laboratory culture occurs more readily in light than dark colored seeds. It is preceded by swelling of the embryo and cracking of the seed coat (Fig. 2-4). The hilum corresponds to the point of entry of the endophyte into the seed, and adjacent cells of the embryo eventually show intracellular proliferation of the fungus. By three months after germination, the body of the protocorm is already some 2–3 times the size of the seed. Radiating from it are a number of trichomes (Fig. 2-4), each a possible entry site for fungal hyphae. After five months the elongated shape of the mature tuber is clearly apparent and the growing shoot apex clearly demarcated and flanked by trichome primordia (Fig. 2-4).

Seedlings germinated in mineral agar in the presence of the fungus are ready for transplanting into the rooting medium of soil grown *Rhizoctonia*-inoculated *Melaleuca uncinata* plants 3–4 months after germination. Our observations on seedling growth through a perspex window in the side of the potted host plant show rapid tuber growth over the ensuing 9 months. First flowering was recorded by Warcup (1985) in 15month old plants.

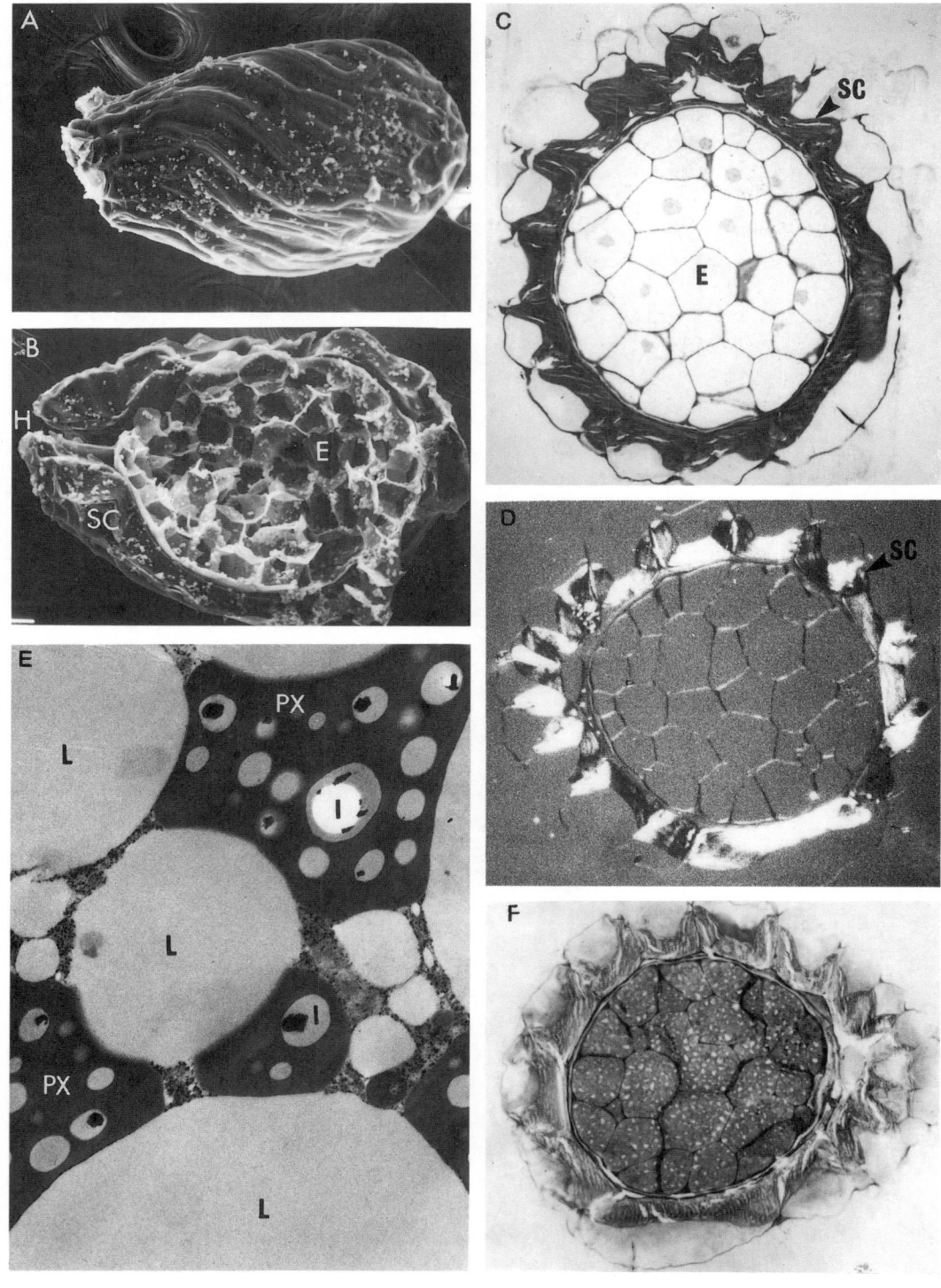

Plate 2-6. **A.** SEM of seed of *Rhizanthella gardneri* showing spiral striations on outer surface. The hilum end of the seed is to the left (×110). **B.** SEM showing inner face of a split seed, showing large-celled supposedly undifferentiated embryo (Em), thick seed coat (SC) and hilum (H) (× 110). **C.** Light micrograph of TS of glycol methacrylate-embedded seed, stained with periodic acid Schiff's reagent (PAS) and toluidine blue. Note strong staining reaction of inner tangential and radial wall thickenings of cell layer of seed coat (SC) and light staining of cytoplasm of cells of embryo (Em). Nuclei are visible in some cells. The negative reaction of the embryo to PAS indicated absence of starch (× 160). **D.** Transverse section of seed viewed under a polarizing microscope showing strong birefringence of wall thickenings on seed coat (SC) (×160). **E.** TEM of reserves of embryo showing large oil droplets (Li) surrounding a dense protein matrix (PX) in which are embedded crystalline globoid-type inclusions (I), presumed site of storage of phytate and associated mineral elements (× 12000). **F.** Light micrograph of transverse section of seed following staining with amido black. Note strong reaction of embryo, indicating presence of dense protein deposits (× 160).

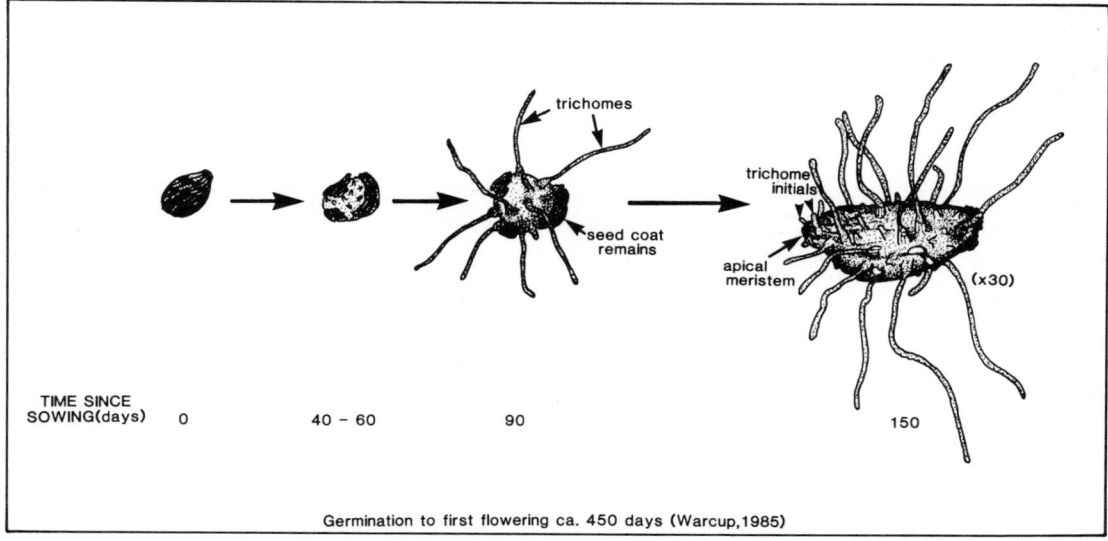

Fig. 2-4. Germination and early protocorm development of *Rhizanthella gardneri* from seeds germinated on nutrient agar in the presence of the mycorrhizal fungus. Note elongated trichomes, each a potential site of invasion by the fungus.

Taxonomic Affinities of *Rhizanthella* and Comparisons with Other Australian Achlorophyllous Orchids

Rhizanthella gardneri possesses several characters considered primitive for the Orchidaceae (Dressler, 1981). These include spiral arrangement of leaves, a terminal inflorescence, nonreuspinate flowers, fleshy fruits, large hard seeds, low seed number, an 'endosperm-like' embryo, mealy pollen, and stomata lacking subsidiary cells. On the other hand, by virtue of its totally underground habit and ability to survive aphotosynthetically in soils extremely low in organic matter, it may well be considered to represent the ultimate in specialization among orchids.

Early evolutionists considered Australian orchids to be dominated by exotic elements which arrived *via* the Malay Peninsula or New Guinea (Rogers, 1922). However, it is now believed that many terrestrial orchid genera probably have origins within Australia, as is likely the case for several other angiosperm groups (Melville, 1973; Blake et al., 1974; Barlow, 1981). Specifically in relation to *Rhizanthella,* one might suggest an origin from a subterranean or semi-subterranean saprophytic progenitor, which originated in shaded or densely-forested habitats in relatively fertile soils, possibly with a pronounced litter layer. With the onset of arid conditions (Bowler 1982), replacement of forest by sclerophyllous shrubs, and progressive deterioration of soil nutrient and organic matter status, species such as *Rhizanthella* with a well developed capacity for epiparasitism and other specializations for a fully subterranean existence would have survived comparatively unaltered.

When speculating on the possible evolution of aclorophyllous forms from autotrohpic progenitors it is of interest to record that achlorophyllous mutants are occasionally encountered in several normally chlorophyllous Australasian species, like *Pterostylis dilatata* A. S. George, (K. W. Dixon, unpublished) and *P. vittata* Lindley (observations by the Western Australian Native Orchid Study and Conservation Group) in Western Australia, and in *Calochilus robertsonii* Benth, in Eastern Australia (Nicholls, 1951).

Currently *Rhizanthella* is included in the subtribe Rhizanthellinae of the Gastrodieae. Clements and Cribb (1984) reduced the monotypic genus *Cryptanthemis* to be synonomous with *Rhizanthella* on the basis of a number of characters, including a hinged labellum, partially fused perianth parts, and a capitulum.

Among recent treatments, Dressler (1981) has agreed to placement of the underground orchids within the tribe Gastrodieae, while other authors have suggested affinity with the Neottieae (Balogh 1982), or with the predominantly Australasian Diuridae (W. Barthlott personal communication)—a tribe of 460 species of which the only geophilous, achlorophyllous member is *Corybas cryptanthus* from New Zealand (Campbell, 1972). Below tribal level *Rhizanthella* has been linked with *Prasophyllum* by virtue of the hinged labellum, similar column details and the possession of large numbers of nonresupinate flowers (Clements and Cribb, 1984).

The information given in Table 2-2 attempts to summarize some of the principal characters of *R. gardneri, R. slateri* and other Australasian achlorophyllous genera. Despite absence of information on several characters, especially for *R. slateri,* it is clear that the two fully underground species are much more similar to one another than to the bulk of other achlorophyllous genera. Earlier workers, considered achlorophylly alone to be sufficient grounds for grouping the genera together. However, we believe that these genera possess sufficient morphological and ecological diversity to require much further investigation, hopefully bringing to bear the modern tools of taxonomy, such as DNA typing, isoenzyme characterization and ultrastructural features of the vegetative and reproductive organs. Only then can one comment comprehensively on taxonomic status.

Table 2-2. Comparison of *Rhizanthella gardneri* with other Australasian predominantly holomycotrophic orchids.

CHARACTER	*RHIZANTHELLA GARDNERI*	*RHIZANTHELLA SLATERI*	OTHER HOLOMYCOTROPHIC GENERA
Storage organ morphology	Fleshy stem tuber.	Fleshy elongated rhizome.	Fleshy, mostly rhizomatous, abbreviated rhizome with fleshy roots in *Galeola, Eulophia* and *Dipodium*.
Roots	Absent, but trichomes cover tuber surface.	Absent	Most genera with tuberous or fine roots; *Galeola* has aerial roots on inflorescence; some species arhizal but with trichomes.
Storage organ seasonality	Complete annual tuber replacement.	Not known	Annual additions of rhizome segments and/or roots. Some species complete annual replacement of tubers.
Endophyte type: type of digestion by host.	*Rhizoctonia* (perfect stage probably *Thanatephorus cucumeris*: tolypophagous digestion	Not known	*Rhizoctonia* in *Dipodium* and *Gastrodia*: ptyophagy in *Gastrodia*.
Vegetative multiplication	1–3 daughter tubers per plant after flowering.	Not known	Mostly non-clonal.
Inflorescence type	Bract-encased, concave capitulum.	Bract-surrounded, convex capitulum.	Terminal or axillary raceme, rarely single flowered, bracts scale-like.
Breeding pattern: pollinating agents.	Autogamy or outbreeding unlikely: pollinators gnats, wasps or termite.	Pollination unknown.	Mostly outbreeding, but autogamy in *Aphyllorchis* and *Epipogium*: pollinators bees, wasps; gnat pollination in fungus-like species.
Labellum sensitivity	Once or twice irritable.	Mobile, irritable(?)	Hinged, movable, but not irritable.
Fruit development	No post-fertilization elongation of peduncle. Capsule fleshy indehiscent; 6–7 months maturation time.	Some post-fertilization elongation; capsule somewhat fleshy. Dehiscence pattern and maturation time unknown.	Post-fertilization elongation in *Gastrodia queenslandica*, capsules dehiscent, maturation times from less than 1 week to several months.
Seed characteristics	Large globular (0.5mm diameter, 75μg F. wt), spiral structures on thick seed coat, colour polymorphism.	Not known.	Extremely small dust-like elongate seeds; seed coats ornamented in *Gastrodia*, with wavy straiations in *Galeola*.
Possible seed dispersal agents	Termites, small mammals.	Not known.	Wind dispersal; seeds of *Galeola* winged.
Habitat vegetation type	Shrublands with mallee *Eucalyptus*; invariable association with *Melaleuca uncinata*.	Dense to open *Eucalyptus* forest.	Grassland (*Dipodium*), rain forest margins (*Aphyllorchis*) and rain forest (*Galeola*).
Annual rainfall Soil type	300–500 mm Sandy-clay to sandy loam, podzolic; often on duplex soils, 1–3% (W/W) organic matter litter layer nil–1 mm deep.	1300 mm Loamy-clay, sometimes rocky and podzolic; organic matter 20–30% leaf litter 10–15 mm deep.	500–2000 mm Highly variable soil types, but generally thick litter layer and high humus content; some species only in rotting wood or deep-litter layer.

Source References: Authors observations on *Rhizanthella, Gastrodia, Dipodium, Galeola*; further observations on *Rhizanthella* and on *Cryptanthemis* from Rogers 1928, Rupp 1932, Campbell 1980, George 1980, George and Cooke 1981, Clements and Cribb 1984, and D. Blaxell (pers. comm.). For other Australasian holomycotrophic orchids source data from Nicholls 1951, Dockrill 1969, Warcup 1981.

Conservation and Management

As far as we know *Rhizanthella gardneri* is an extremely rare species which unfortunately occurs primarily in areas suitable for cereal cultivation. On these grounds it would appear that all but less than 10% of the habitats where it may have once occurred are now under agriculture. Worse still, applications for release of new lands for agriculture in potential *Rhizanthella* habitats continue to outstrip survey efforts to locate the orchid.

The enormous difficulty in locating *Rhizanthella,* let alone the problem of effectively monitoring the vigor of existing populations, present great obstacles in management of the species. Clearly the best policy is to direct conservation and management policies towards maintaining adequate healthy stands of the host species *Melaleuca uncinata,* in the hope that they will provide large and varied resource of habitats in which the orchid may well still be present, or into which it might be introduced were the species to be deemed greatly endangered.

Too frequent fires, invasion of habitats by weeds and exotic animals, deliberate or accidental human interference of known habitats of the orchid, and the general deterioration of native bush caused by aerial drift or surface water leaching of agricultural fertilizers, are all potent deleterious influences (Dixon and Pate, 1984). A further, more subtle cause for concern, is the possibility that the few remaining populations will degenerate through elimination of pollinating agents, native mammals which might distribute seeds, or merely by genetic deterioration of the species due to lack of input by sexually derived genotypes. As shown here, natural seed set in our study locations is extremely poor in present populations, but can be increased many fold by hand pollination. This may indicate that current maintenance of the species is largely by vegetative multiplication through formation of daughter tubers, giving little potential for long-distance spread within a habitat.

As described earlier, the methodology currently exists for establishing the *Rhizanthella-Rhizoctonia-Melaleuca* association in glasshouse culture, therby giving the opportunity for replenishing stands of the orchid in existing habitats or even for establishing the species in areas where it currently does not exist. Considerable thought must be given before proceeding with such a venture, but the fact that this type of approach is available for conservation of the species must surely offer considerable reassurance.

Acknowledgments

We thank the World Wildlife Fund Australia, the Western Australian Department of Conservation and Land Management, and the Australian Orchid Foundation for financial support of the research described here. We are also indebted to members of the W. A. Native Orchid Study and Conservation Group (Inc.), whose members devoted many hours to searches for the orchid.

Literature Cited

Barlow, B A. 1981. The Australian flora: its origin and evolution. In *Flora of Australia*. Vol. 1. Aust. Gov. Publishing Service, Canberra. pp. 25–77.

Balogh, P. 1982. *Rhizanthella* R. S. Rogers, a misunderstood genus (Orchidaceae). *Selbyana*: 27–33.

Beard, J. S. 1981. *Vegetation Survey of Western Australia*. 1:1,000,000 Series. Swan. University of Western Australia Press, Nedlands.

Bjorkman, E. 1960. *Monotropa hypopitys* L.—an epiparasite on tree roots, *Physiologia Plantarum*. 13: 308–327.

Blake, S. T. B., G. Briggs, N. T. Burbidge, H. Clifford, R. Hoogland, L. A. Johnson, R. Melville, R. Schodde, and R. L. Specht. 1974. Primitive seed plants inthe Australian flora. In *Conservation of Papua New Guinea*, eds R. L. Specht, E. H. Roe and V. H. Boughton. *Aust. J. Bot.* Suppl. No. 7.

Bowler, J. M. 1982. Aridity in the late Tertiary and Quarternary of Australia. In *Evolution of the flora and fauna of arid Australia* eds. W. R. Barker and P. J. M. Greenslade, Peacock Publ. Adelaide.

Campbell, E. O. 1962. The mycorrhiza of *Gastrodia cunninghamii* Hook. f. *Trans. Roy. Soc. N.Z.* 1: 290–6.

Campbell, E. O. 1963. *Gastrodia minor* Petrie, an epiparasite of Manuka *Trans. Roy. Soc. N.Z.* 2: 73–81.

Campbell, E. O. 1970. The fungal association of *Yoania australis*. Trans. R. Soc. N.Z., Biol. Sc. 12: 12.

Campbell, E. O. 1972. The morphology of the fungal association of *Corybas cryptanthus*. *J. Roy. Soc. N.Z.* 2: 43–47.

Campbell, E. O. 1980. Non-green orchids of New Zealand. *Orchids in New Zealand*. 6: 49–51.

Clements, M. and P. Cribb. 1984. The underground orchids of Australia. *Kew Magazine*. 11: 84–91.

Dixon, K. W. 1982. *Rhizanthella* in 1981. *The Orchadian* 7: 99–100.

Dixon, K. W. and J. S. Pate. 1984. Biology and distributional status of *Rhizanthella gardneri* Rogers. The Western Australian Underground Orchid. *Kings Park Research Notes* No. 9, 54 pp.

Dixon, K. W. and R. R. Ramsay. 1984. Mycorrhiza of Western Australia orchids. *The Orchadian* 8: 22–23.

Dockrill, A. W. 1969. *Australian indigenous orchids*. Vol. 1. The epiphytes, the tropical terrestrial species. The Society for Growing Australian Plants. Sydney.

Dressler, R. L. 1981. *The orchids—natural history and classification*. Harvard University Press, Cambridge, Mass., U.S.A.

George, A. S. 1980. *Rhizanthella gardneri* R. S. Rogers—the underground orchid of Western Australia. *Amer. Orchid Soc. Bull.* 49: 631–644.

George, A. S. and J. Cooke. 1981. *Rhizanthella*—the underground orchid of Western Australia. *Proc. Orchid. Symp. 13th Int. Bot. Congress*, Sydney, Australia. 74–75, 77–78.

Hadley, G. 1982. Orchid mycorrhiza. *In Orchid biology reviews and perspectives II*, ed. J. Arditti. Cornell University Press, U.S.A.

Jones, D. L. 1975. Pollination of *Microtis parviflora*. *Annals of Botany* 39: 585–589.

Marchant, N. G. and G. J. Keighery. 1979. Poorly collected and presumably rare vascular plants of Western Australia. *Kings Park Research Notes* No. 5.

Melville, R. 1973. Relict plants in the Australian flora and their conservation. In *Nature conservation in the Pacific.* eds A. B. Costin and R. H. Groves. Aust. Nat. University Press, Canberra. pp. 83–90

Muir, B. G. (1977). Biological survey of the Western Australian wheat belt. Part 2: vegetation and habitat of bendering reserve. Records of the Western Australian Museum, supplement 3.

Nicolls, W. H. 1951. *Orchids of Australia.* Georgian House, Melbourne, Australia.

Pate, J. S. and K. W. Dixon. 1982. *Tuberous, cormous and bulbous plants—biology of an adaptive strategy.* University of Western Australia Press, Nedlands, 6009. 268 pp.

Peakall, R. 1984. Observations on the pollination of *Leporella fimbriata* (Lindl.) A. S. George. *The Orchadian* 8: 44–45.

van der Pijl, L. and C. H. Dodson. 1966. *Orchid flowers: their pollination and evolution.* Coral Gables: University of Miami Press.

Pittman, H. A. 1929. Note on the morphology and endophytic mycorrhiza of *Rhizanthella gardneri* Rogers and certain other Western Australian Orchids. *J. Roy. Soc. West. Aust.* 15: 71–79.

Robertson, D.C. and J. A. Robertson. 1982. Ultrastructure of *Pterospora andromedea* Nuttall and *Sarcodes sanguinea* Torry mycorrhizas. *New Phytol.* 92: 539–551.

Rogers, R. S. 1922. Some developments in orchidology. *Report of the Australian and New Zealand association for the advancement of science.* 21: 330–365.

Rogers, R. S. 1928. A new genus of Australian Orchid. *J. Roy. Soc. West. Aust.* 15: 1–8.

Rupp, H. M. R. 1932. Notes on New South Wales orchids. *Proc. Linn. Soc. New South Wales.* 57: 57–61.

Rye, B. L. 1982. Geographically restricted plants of Southern Western Australia. *Dept. of Fisheries and Wildlife Report* No. 49. (Western Australian Government Publication).

Warcup, J. H. 1981. The mycorrhizal relationships of Australian orchids. *New Phytol.* 87: 371–381.

Warcup, J. H. 1985. *Rhizanthella gardneri* (Orchidaceae), its Rhizoctonia endophyte and close association with *Melaleuca uncinata* (Myrtaceae) in Western Australia. *New Phytol.* 99: 273–286.

PHYSIOLOGY

3

Water Relations in Orchids*

RUSSELL SINCLAIR

*The literature survey pertaining to this chapter was concluded in December 1986; the chapter was submitted in March 1987, and the revised version was received in September 1987.

Introduction

The huge family of Orchidaceae may be divided into two broad groups, epiphytes and terrestrials. The water relations of the two groups are very different. Epiphytes, growing without soil contact, have limited access to water other than that stored in their own tissues. Their above-ground habitat increases exposure to drying winds, high radiation and low humidity. Even after rain, drainage may be rapid so that the time during which water is accessible to the plant is limited. Water supply is intermittent and the onset of drought may be sudden and severe, if not always long-lasting. Consequently, the epiphytic habit is potentially one of the most stressful in the plant kingdom and it is not surprising that epiphytes reach their greatest diversity only in the humid tropics. The effective uptake of water, its storage within the plant, and control of losses in the face of these external stresses are the dominant themes in the study of epiphytic orchid water relations. Epiphytes are intrinsically interesting because they may face in extreme forms the problems of desiccation resistance common to all land plants. Terrestrial orchids on the other hand, occupy habitats in common with many other geophytes and little information has been published specifically on their water relations. Many occur in reasonably dry climates where they are drought avoiders (Levitt, 1980), the above-ground parts dying back at the onset of the dry season while the underground tuber or rhizome lies quiescent until the next rains. Other species inhabit boggy or marshy sites, where excess water may be the problem.

In this review the emphasis is predominantly on epiphytes, as these have attracted by far the most attention from plant anatomists, physiologists and ecologists. The first section deals with plant structures in relation to uptake, storage and the control of loss of water. There is a voluminous literature on orchid anatomy which is pertinent here. Measurements of water status in orchids are summarized next. This is followed by a survey of the surprisingly limited number of studies of orchid transpiration. Crassulacean Acid Metabolism (CAM), a highly effective biochemical adaptation to water stress, is discussed briefly.[a] The importance of water availability as a factor controlling orchid distribution patterns is examined. Finally, several special cases of unusual or extreme adaptations involving water relations conclude the chapter.

Structure and Function

Roots

The water balance of terrestrial plants depends on absorption through the roots, this being the major if not the only pathway by which water may enter. One of the most striking characteristics of many epiphytic orchids is the development of extensive aerial roots, growing either along the surface of the substratum or freely in the air out of contact with any surface. Two questions immediately arise in relation to water in the plant:

Are these aerial roots functional—can they absorb water and if so how?

Can water loss from these roots be controlled or prevented? In some cases the area of root exposed to the air is a significant proportion of the total surface area of the plant, yet typical roots do not have stomata and hence are poorly designed for controlling water loss. Are these aerial roots any different?

[a]See chapter on CAM in Orchid Biology II.—Ed.

The extensive literature on the morphology, anatomy and physiology of aerial roots of orchids has been reviewed by Pridgeon (1987) in Volume IV of this series. This review will not be duplicated here, but the main conclusions will be summarized as the topic is one of the most important themes in the study of orchid water relations.

The typical aerial root consists of a specialized outer epidermis of one, or often several cell layers, called the velamen. These cells are dead and filled with air at maturity. Beneath lies the cortex, its outermost layer specialized into the exodermis, whereas the innermost forms the endodermis as in most angiosperm roots. Within the endodermis, the central stele contains the vascular tissues. The outer layers, the velamen and exodermis, are particularly important in the study of root water relations.

Many detailed studies of velamen anatomy have been published (Pridgeon, 1987). The number of cell layers may vary between taxa from one to 24, though the most common numbers are two, three, four and five. Secondary wall thickenings of various kinds are usually present. Perforations in the walls between these allow free passage of air or water through the tissue. The thickenings probably provide support and prevent collapse after the degeneration of the protoplasts as the cells mature. Root hairs may form from the surface layer of young, living velamen cells, especially on the side of the root touching a surface.

When the root is wetted, most of the velamen takes up water very rapidly (like a sponge or blotting-paper) and the root changes from whitish or silvery to green. However, wedge-shaped masses of cells are water repellent and remain air-filled, forming columns as permanent gaseous passageways from the root surface to the under-lying exodermis (Fig. 3-1A). These structures have been named pneumathodes. In some cases the inner walls of exodermal cells at the base of a pneumathode break down where they adjoin an air space. This provides a direct pathway for gas exchange between the inner cortical cells and the atmosphere even when the velamen is wet with water.

The exodermis typically consists of long and short cells. The long cells, generally dead and empty at maturity, have walls that are suberized and thickened in various patterns, and often heavily lignified. These cells form a water impermeable barrier. Distributed among them are thin-walled short cells, called passage cells. These are alive and densely cytoplasmic, providing a pathway to the underlying cortex for water and nutrients. Hence passage cells play a key part in controlling water exchange between the inner living root tissues and the atmosphere.

Within the velamen immediately above passage cells, spongy masses of branching or intersecting fibers have often been observed. The fibers may consist of cellulose only or may be lignified and suberized. These fibrous bodies have been named tilosomes (Pridgeon et al., 1983). An early suggestion (Haberlandt, 1914), was that tilosomes might increase the absorption of water by condensing water vapor from the air in velamen cells and allowing it to be transferred to the passage cells beneath. An alterna-tive hypothesis (Leitgeb, 1865; Benzing et al., 1982) is that the tilosome fibers increase the diffusion pathway and slow down the loss of vapor from the living passage cells when the velamen is dry, while not impeding rapid liquid water uptake when velamen tissue is wetted. The tilosome could act like a one-way plug. A third possible role for the tilosome is to block the penetration of pathogenic bacteria or fungi into the passage cells (Pridgeon, 1987). Cyanobacteria, green algae and fungi are commonly found in velamen cells.

Many authors have reported that roots develop differently depending on whether they are fully exposed, in contact with a surface, or embedded in the soil. When aerial

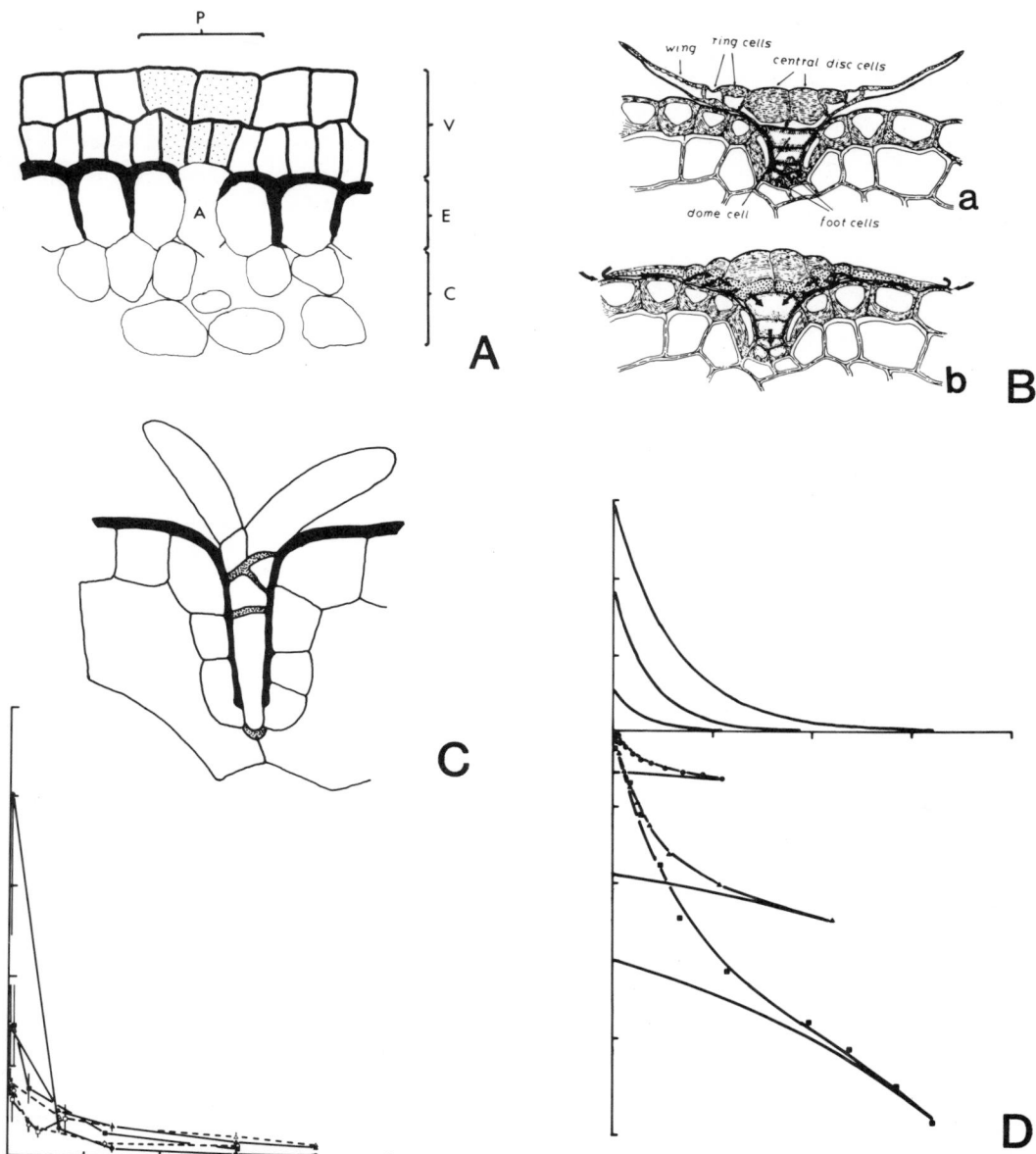

Fig. 3-1. **A.** Idealized transverse section of an aerial orchid root, showing a pneumathode. A. Thin-walled aeration-cell, empty and air-filled. P. pneumathode area stippled. V. velamen. E. exodermis. C. cortex. **B.** Foliar trichome of a xeric tillandsioid bromeliad in the dry (a) and wet, (b) state. Arrows indicate the pathway of water movement. From Benzing *et al.* (1976). **C.** Foliar trichome of the orchid *Eria ornata.* Stalk cells, with lignified cross-walls are sunk in a heavily cutinized pit in the epidermis, but there is a break in the cutin layer at the base. Redrawn from Raciborski (1898). **D.** Höfler diagrams showing the relationship between total water potential ψ, pressure potential ψ_p, osmotic potential ψ_π, and relative water content R. ■ *Eucalyptus cladocalyx,* ▲ *Populus nigra* (Sinclair and Venables 1983), ● *Dendrobium crumenatum* (Sinclair, 1983a). Water potential ψ values, measured by pressure chamber, are shown by symbols. Fitted curves, and the calculated curves for pressure potential ψ_p above the *x*-axis and osmotic potential ψ_π below were derived by the method of Sinclair and Venables (1983). **E.** Rates of water loss (% fresh weight per day) from orchids exposed to natural conditions but subjected to drought and sheltered from rain. Bogor, Java. ● *Dendrobium pandaneti* ○ *D. secundum* ▲ *D. crumenatum* △ *Eria ornata* ■ *Rhynchostylis retusa* □ *Aerides virens* Data are means calculated from tables in Kamerling (1912). Vertical bars represent standard deviations.

roots touch a surface, root hairs often develop on the ventral side, together with smaller velamen cells and thin-walled passage cells. On the dorsal side passage cells become more lignified or suberized, this surface evidently being modified for protection and reducing water loss. In some species pneumathodes only develop on the ventral or lateral surfaces, and the velamen, in some cases, may be reduced or sloughed off entirely on the dorsal surface. In these cases the thick walled exodermis protects the underlying tissues. Dorsi-ventral differentiation may be partly induced by environmental conditions but there is evidence that it is also partly innate. Terrestrial roots of many but not all species also have a well-developed velamen (Pridgeon, 1987).

Pridgeon summarized the consensus of early opinion on some of the functions of the velamen-exodermis system as follows:

1. The long, suberized/lignified cells of the exodermis protect the underlying cortex from dehydration.
2. Thin-walled, living short cells are conduits for nutrients from velamen to cortex.
3. Velamen protects underlying tissues from mechanical injury.
4. Velamen prevents desiccation by increasing the boundary layer around the root.

The more contentious question was whether the velamen also, and primarily, acted to condense water vapor and other gases from the atmosphere, or to absorb liquid water and solutes. Both views were proposed, and rejected, in the early literature. Additional early references on absorption of water vapor include Kerner and Oliver (1894) and von Sachs (1887). Giles and Agnihotri (1968) found that cellulose extracted from aerial roots had remarkably high absorptive capacity for water vapor, three to four times that of cotton cellulose, but the significance of this property *in vivo* was not pursued.

More recent work has found little evidence for the absorption of water vapor by aerial roots, and attention has been concentrated on the question of liquid water uptake.

Dycus and Knudson (1957)[b] concluded that aerial roots which were not in contact with a substrate could only absorb water and nutrients at the apex where velamen cells were still alive. Otherwise the surface was impermeable and the velamen acted mainly for protection and prevention of water loss; hence the aerial root was seen as a "liability" to the plant. Water absorption occurred, however, if the velamen was damaged, or if the root became attached to a substrate. This work has been largely superceded by studies (reviewed by Pridgeon, 1987), which show that intact aerial roots can absorb both liquid water and nutrients.

Sanford and Adanlawo (1973) showed correlations between the number of velamen cell layers, the thickness of exodermal walls, and tolerance of dry habitats, which suggest the importance of the protection and water conservation roles of the velamen. It has also been pointed out (Went, 1940), that when rain begins the first water to flow along a stem or drip through a canopy will have the highest nutrient content. Thus, by trapping this water and holding it in contact with the inner absorptive tissue of the root, the velamen adds significantly to the effectiveness of nutrient uptake. This effect may be very important in the nutrient-poor habitat which many epiphytes occupy.

Pridgeon (1987) concluded that attached aerial roots are absorptive, and that absorption is promoted by a thin-walled exodermis, root hairs, and a thick velamen which prolongs contact with moisture. The extent to which strictly aerial roots are absorptive is

---

[b]This is Knudson's last paper published a year before his death. Some have suggested that he was not as strict a supervisor then as during his earlier days.—Ed.

not as clear. Some absorption does occur, but more study is needed to determine its importance under natural conditions.

The velamen greatly increases the capacity of the epiphytic orchid to make use of intermittent rainfalls by extending the time during which living cortical tissues are in contact with a water (and nutrient) supply. This is especially important for plants which have no other means of external water storage such as the tanks of some bromeliads or the humus collected in the center of ferns such as *Asplenium* (see also Benzing, 1986).

Some orchids e.g., *Ansellia, Catasetum* and *Graphorkis* produce dense clusters of fine, negatively geotropic roots. Johansson (1974) suggested that these may function by condensing water vapor at night which is then transferred to living tissues, allowing such species to survive in dry habitats. However, Barthlott and Capesius (1975) detected no uptake of tritiated water by these, in contrast to the thicker aerial roots of several other species.

Dew on plant surfaces may be an important source of water in some plant communities such as cloud-forest. However, the importance of aerial roots in the absorption of dew is not yet clearly known.

Leaves

Leaves are the main site of photosynthesis in any plant which has them (some orchids do not). Consequently they must allow adequate gas exchange with the surrounding air, and this inevitably involves water loss. Any plants subjected to periodic drought would be expected to evolve modifications in leaf structure.

Adaptations of leaves of orchids for drought tolerance include:

1. Reduction of transpiration.
2. Water storage.
3. Retention of rain or condensed water.
4. Absorption of water as liquid or vapor.

The first two categories are well documented. The latter two are more controversial, and much less evidence is available to support them.

Among the copious nineteenth century plant anatomical literature, there are numerous studies which identify xerophytic features of orchid leaves (Trécul, 1855a and b; Chatin, 1858; Krüger, 1883; Dixon, 1894; Hering, 1900.) Haberlandt, (1914) discussed many aspects of orchid anatomy in relation to function and habitat. Solereder and Meyer, (1930) dealt with orchids in their Systematic Anatomy of the Monocotyledons. Gessner, (1956) covered water relations of epiphytes and lianas, and Withner et al. (1974) summarized many relevant aspects of orchid leaf anatomy.

Leaf characters which may reduce water loss include size, shape, the thickness of the cuticle, structure, density and distribution of stomata, presence and structure of surface hairs, and deciduousness.

Withner et al. (1974)[c] distinguished two distinct categories of orchid leaves, the ribbed or plicate and the leathery, which was sub-divided into soft, hard and fleshy types. The ribbed leaves are thin, membranous and sometimes deciduous, have little water-storage capacity and seldom bear hairs or trichomes. Common examples include leaves of *Coelogyne barbata, Calanthe furcata* and most *Catasetum* species. Cuticle thick-

[c]This review has been criticized by several orchid anatomists.—Ed.

ness varies with habitat and exposure, and may sometimes be thicker on the upper surface.

Leathery-leaved orchids are a more diverse group. In general the leaves are more rigid, thicker and lack prominent veins. Cuticle is thicker and waxier. Of the three sub-groups the soft leathery leaved type includes terrestrials such as *Paphiopedilum* and some epiphytes like *Phalaenopsis*. Leaves are stiffened by the cutin layer and thickened epidermal cell walls, but there is no extensive internal lignification. Cuticles are often thicker on the upper surface. Mesophyll cells usually contain fewer chloroplasts than those of the thin plicate leaves, and in some species some may be enlarged for water storage. In the second sub-group, the hard leathery leaved type, the cuticle is usually thick and heavy and epidermal cells may have distinctly thickened outer walls. Also, extensive lignified fiber bundles are present traversing the mesophyll tissue or forming layers near the leaf surface. These greatly strengthen the leaf and appear to form protective barriers between mesophyll tissue and the outside environment. The leaves are often elongated with a pronounced conduplicate, v-shaped formation. Most species with this leaf form are epiphytes. Water storage mesophyll may be found in this form also, but is most extensively developed in the third sub-group, the fleshy leaved orchids. These have thick cuticles and thick-walled epidermal cells, but less lignification in the mesophyll, some of which is modified into water storage tissue.

Dressler (1981) states that the thin, plicate leaf is thought to be the more primitive type, and Withner et al. (1974) claim it is best suited to moist relatively humid habitats where water stress is normally never severe. The other leaf forms are seen as having evolved in response to increasing water deficits. Soft leathery and fleshy leaves may store significant quantities of water, but are not usually found in the driest sites. The hard leathery leaf type is the most drought resistant. The very thick cuticles and thick walled epidermis together with extensive lignification offer excellent protection against desiccation and support for the leaf during periods of drought.

This scheme of Withner et al. (1974) correlating leaf form with increasing exposure to water stress seems plausible but there is very little experimental evidence to support it. Very few quantitative studies have simultaneously considered form, function and microclimate in orchid leaf water relations. Cuticle thickness increases generally in response to increasing exposure though it may also be partly genetically determined. Pridgeon (1982), for example, found in subtribe Pleurothallidinae that one group had moderate (6–14 μ) to very thick (up to 22.4 μ) cuticle. In another group the cuticle was thin (less than 3 μ), or of variable thickness. Whether the extra thickness is required for waterproofing the leaf has not been demonstrated experimentally, probable though this seems.

Epidermal wall thickness also appears at first sight to contribute to the resistance of leaves to water loss. However unless the cell walls are impermeable, such thickening in itself does not impede water movement. It is also difficult to see how the stiffening of the hard leaves by lignified fiber bundles could appreciably impede water loss. The relationship between sclerophylly and drought resistance needs further careful study.

The distinction between thin and thick leaves does have physiological significance, however, as in nearly all cases thick leaves (thickness greater than 1 mm) have Crassulacean Acid Metablosim (CAM), a very important adaptation to water stress which is discussed below. All thin orchid leaves examined show C_3 photosynthesis (Neales and Hew, 1975; Wong and Hew, 1973; McWilliams, 1970).

Small and narrow leaves are better adapted to exposed sites than larger ones, because they lose heat more efficiently by convection and therefore do not heat as readily in full sun (Sinclair, 1970; Grace and Wilson, 1976; Grace et al., 1980). However, thick leaves also absorb more solar radiation than thin ones, so the thickness of xerophytic orchid leaves of the hard leathery type appears to lead to a less favorable energy balance in an epiphyte in an exposed position. However Madison (1977), suggested that the water storage tissue of thick leaves might actually improve the energy balance by dampening temperature fluctuations as the leaf is periodically exposed to sunflecks. No experimental investigations of this idea have been published. The study of energy budgets of epiphytes in relation to micro-habitats in a tree canopy would be fascinating, though difficult to carry out in the field.

Stomata provide the primary control over water loss from the leaf. In many species stomata are sunken to varying depths below the epidermal surface. Where the cuticle is thick, cuticular ridges may form a chamber over the guard cells. Haberlandt (1914), and many others since then have pointed out that these hyperstomatic cavities reduce transpiration by increasing the pathway along which water vapor must diffuse to leave the leaf, and by trapping stagnant, humid air outside the stomatal pore. Orchid stomata are not always sunken; they may lie flush with the epidermal surface or even protrude above it. However, sunken stomata and the development of cuticular ridges do appear to predominate in dry habitats.

The number of stomata per unit area, or stomatal density might be thought of as a useful character to relate to the drought resistance of a species, but this character is quite variable, both in a single plant and between plants (Metcalfe and Chalk, 1979; Stace, 1965). One reason for this variability is that a leaf developing under water stress may have smaller epidermal cells but a total number similar to that in a more mesic leaf of the same species. As a result, stomatal density actually increases in the stressed leaf. A preferred taxonomic character is the Stomatal Index I:

$$I = \frac{S}{E + S} \times 100$$

where S = number of stomata, and E = number of epidermal cells. In many plant groups this index is relatively constant within a species, though interestingly, still influenced by the atmospheric humidity under which plants were grown. Few measurements of stomatal index have been published for orchids. Some are given in Table 3-1, together with values for dicotyledons from various habitats, but there are insufficient data to draw conclusions. There are values of stomatal density in the literature, but in view of the variability of this character they are of doubtful value as they are not usually related to habitat characteristics.

In any case, it is the resistance of the leaf surface to water vapor diffusion that is important, rather than the number of stomata per unit area. When stomata are closed completely this resistance is largely a property of the cuticle and when open, the resistance depends not only on numbers of stomata but also on their dimensions and aperture. Stomatal aperture varies in complex ways with changes in light, temperature, humidity and CO_2 concentration, and the anatomy of the epidermis only partially explains the capacity of a plant to regulate water loss.

Leaf hairs may help conserve water by increasing the boundary layer thickness of air around the leaf and lengthening the diffusion pathway. However, hairs are not a dominant feature of orchid leaves. Some of the thin leaf group have hairs usually on the

Table 3-1. Values of stomatal index.[a]

Plant	Habitat	Stomatal Index Range	Reference
Orchids			
7 species	epiphytic	2.0–17.0	Singh and Singh (1974)
11 species	terrestrial	2.5–30.3	Borsos (1980)
Dicotyledons			
5 species	Aquatic	4.0–14.4	Salisbury (1928)
13 species	Woodlands	10.7–27.4	
2 species	Alpine/Arctic	17.2–19.2	
6 species	Water stressed sites	12.8–34.5	

[a]Stomatal Index $\qquad I = \dfrac{S}{E + S} \times 100$

where S = number of stomata, E = number of epidermal cells

lower surface, but these are often secretory and do not form a dense mat. The thicker leathery leaves are often glabrous. The possibility of hairs acting as water absorbing organs is discussed below.

Deciduousness is another adaptation to periodic drought which reduces water loss. Some thin leaved orchids, which grow in seasonally dry areas, avoid water stress during the dry season by shedding their leaves and entering a period of dormancy. Water may be stored in pseudobulbs or other parts of the plant. Deciduous leaves are found among the sympodial orchids but not monopodials, though the character is not universal by any means within the group. For example, within the genus *Polystachya* some species have deciduous leaves (e.g., *P. puberula*) while others (*P. tenuissima* for example) retain foliage through a dry season (Johansson, 1974). Permanently leafless orchids are discussed later.

The second type of adaptation of leaves for drought tolerance is water storage. Water-storage tissue is found in many orchid leaves and has already been mentioned as a characteristic of the thick, leathery-leaved group. One form of water storage tissue consists of living, thin-walled parenchyma cells, roughly isodiametric, with a thin layer of cytoplasm and a very large vacuole usually filled with water but occasionally with slimy mucilage. This tissue is often just below the adaxial epidermis and may vary from one or two cells thick to many times the thickness of the photosynthetic tissue (Haberlandt, 1914; Gessner, 1956; Madison, 1977; Pridgeon, 1982). Such a development of the parenchyma, if it originates from the ground tissue, is termed the hypodermis.

Early experiments (Schimper, 1888; Haberlandt, 1914, quoted in Madison, 1977) showed that when detached leaves dehydrated over a period of days, the hypodermis shrank while the photosynthetic tissue remained turgid, demonstrating that the hypodermis is a water storage tissue. In other cases, all mesophyll cells are enlarged and assume a water storage role while retaining some chloroplasts. Within hypodermal tissue, a second type of water storage cell is often found. These are nonliving cells, the spirally-thickened or tracheoidal idioblasts (Foster, 1956) which are discussed below. It is interesting that in most cases the hypodermal water-storage tissue is formed on the adaxial side of the leaf, so that light must penetrate this layer to reach the photosynthetic mesophyll beneath. Presumably intercellular airspaces and substomatal cavities must be maintained on the side of the leaf where stomata occur and gas exchange takes place, whereas the water storage cells may be tightly packed beneath the impermeable upper surface. Being water-filled and relatively transparent, they would not seriously reduce light penetration. Withner et al. (1974) mention some species, e.g., *Eria pannea* in which the water storage tissue has been internalized. During leaf development the abaxial surface grows entirely around the adaxial tissue, forming the whole outer surface of a leaf which finally becomes terete. The photosynthetic mesophyll forms a ring, in transverse section, inside which are a circle of vascular bundles and then a central core of water storage cells. This arrangement of photosynthetic and colorless water storage tissue is reminiscent of succulents such as the Cactaceae, but is unusual in orchids.

The third possible leaf modification to improve water relations in the plant is the arrangement of leaves in such a way that rain water is channelled to the base of the plant, to increase the supply to the root system or even to be stored in spaces between the leaf bases. Water storage in containers formed by swollen leaf bases is highly developed among the Bromeliaceae, the so-called tank bromeliads making up a large part of the epiphytic biomass of the new world tropics (Benzing, 1970; 1973). The tanks collect not only rainwater but also litter and other sources of nutrients and may supply all requirements of the plants for water and minerals. The epidermis of the leaf bases is also modified to allow absorption directly from the tank, so that the function of the root system is almost entirely reduced to that of anchoring the plant to its host. Although this strategy works well in habitats with a fairly even distribution of rainfall, it is not effective unless the tanks remain water-filled for much of the year. As a result, tank bromeliads do not occur where annual rainfall is less than 1,000 to 1,500 mm (Benzing, 1973).

The rosette form, so highly developed in the Bromeliaceae, is also found in Neotropical epiphytic genera of the Araceae, Commelinaceae, Agavaceae, and Gesneriaceae, but, surprisingly, is rarely found among epiphytes of other tropical areas (Madison, 1977). The birds-nest ferns (*Asplenium* spp.) and a few Liliaceae are among the few rosette shaped humus collectors of the old world tropics. Some orchids, e.g. *Grammatophylum* and *Coryanthes,* do collect debris among their stems and roots, forming "baskets" which may store water. However, the Orchidaceae very rarely seem to have developed their leaves as water or humus collectors, even though the tuft of closely spaced leaves arising form a pseudo-bulb in many species seems to be potentially easily adaptable for this purpose. Raciborski (1898) reported one example of an orchid that may trap water in a similar way to the bromeliads. He described an *Eria ornata* which grows high in the crowns of trees in Java, with prominent pseudobulbs topped by three or four large leaves which form a funnel. Early in the morning dew collects in the funnel, but by the afternoon its bottom is coated with a very water absorbent slime secreted by leaf hair cells. Raciborski claimed not only that water was collected by the funnel, but that it was also absorbed through the leaf surfaces.

Direct absorption of water is the fourth possible leaf adaptation. The idea that orchid leaves might contribute to the water budget of the plant in such a way, has appeared in the literature from time to time. In general if this occurs at all it certainly is not common. For example, Krause (1935) measured water absorption by leaves of ten orchid species. Detached leaves were allowed to dehydrate until they lost approximately 15% of their fresh weight, which sometimes required several days. They were then immersed in water and weight gains were measured periodically. The amount of water taken up was negligible, the thick cuticle and low stomatal density of the leaves apparently forming a very effective barrier to water movement.

Uptake of water through leaves is important and well documented in the Bromeliaceae. The tank bromeliads have already been mentioned, but the capacity to absorb water is most striking in the sub family Tillandsioideae, which includes the so-called atmospheric bromeliads which do not have tanks, but succulent leaves thickly covered with trichomes, and a greatly reduced root system. Water absorption by these specialized trichomes was first described by Schimper (1888) and has been studied extensively since then. The mechanism is outlined by Benzing and his associates (1976, 1986), and Rundel (1982; Fig. 3-1B). A trichome consists of a non-living shield or disk, one cell thick. At the center empty, thick-walled cells are connected to a column of three to five living stalk cells arising from a pit in the epidermal surface. The outer surfaces of shield and stalk cells are cutinized. When the leaf surface is wetted, the empty shield cells fill rapidly through their lower surface. The cells flex as they fill, bending the outer edges of the shield downward onto the leaf surface and creating a small cavity beneath. Water is drawn into this cavity under the shield by capillarity and down into the living stalk cells by osmosis, whence it reaches internal leaf tissue. When the leaf surface dries the shield cells empty, flexing the edges of the disk upwards. The central disk shrinks and lowers to its former position, sealing down tightly and preventing water loss from the living stalk cells or underlying mesophyll. Thus the shield operates as an efficient one-way valve.

Raciborski (1898) described rather similar though less elaborate trichomes on the leaves of the *Eria ornata* (Fig. 3-1C: see also Uphof, 1962). These consist of a basal cell and several intermediate stalk cells deeply sunk in a pit formed by heavily cutinized epidermal cells. A tuft of one to seven elongated cells extends above the surrounding epidermis. These secrete mucilage. The basal and intermediate stalk cells have lignified cross-walls, but there is a thin-walled region at the base of the hair corresponding to a break in the cuticle on the adjacent epidermis. Tests with eosin and $FeSO_4$ indicated that water was taken up rapidly by the exposed tuft and appeared to be able to move down to the base of the hair and hence through into the adjacent epidermal cells. It appeared that the younger trichomes secrete water absorbent mucilage, while the older ones absorb water caught in the funnel formed by the leaves. Similar hairs were observed in *Pholidota*, though here the leaf funnel is not as well formed. There was no direct evidence that the whole plant gains significant amounts of water by this process, though the anatomy is certainly suggestive.

More recently Pridgeon (1981) described and discussed in detail the trichomes on leaves of the Pleurothallidinae, a large neotropical sympodial sub-tribe of Orchidaceae containing over 3,000 species. He examined 120 species in 18 genera, and all had glandular trichomes on both leaf surfaces (Figures 3-2A, 3-2B). In young leaves these usually consist of a large, globose, thinwalled apical cell with dense cytoplasm, and a stalk cell which becomes heavily cutinized on the lateral walls, sunk in a crypt in the epidermis. The walls adjacent to the apical cell above and the hypodermal tissue below remain uncutinized, so that a water-proof tube is formed from the surface down to the underlying tissue. At this stage of development, the leaf blade has not yet unfolded nor have stomatal guard cells formed. Before this occurs, the apical cells of all the trichomes rupture and a brown opaque residue covers the exposed surface of the stalk cell.

The similarity between these trichomes and the more elaborate tillandsioid structure suggested that they might play a similar role in water absorption by leaves. Eosin dye was taken up by the apical cells and moved inward via the stalk to the hypodermal cells. The dye moved into the leaf even through stalk cells whose apical cell had collapsed, though the adjacent epidermis remained impervious. Sunken leaf hairs similar to those described by Pridgeon (1981) were reported by Solereder and Meyer (1930) in 58 orchid genera. Hence it might be expected on anatomical grounds that water uptake by leaves would occur in many epiphytic orchids, with a strong correlation between the

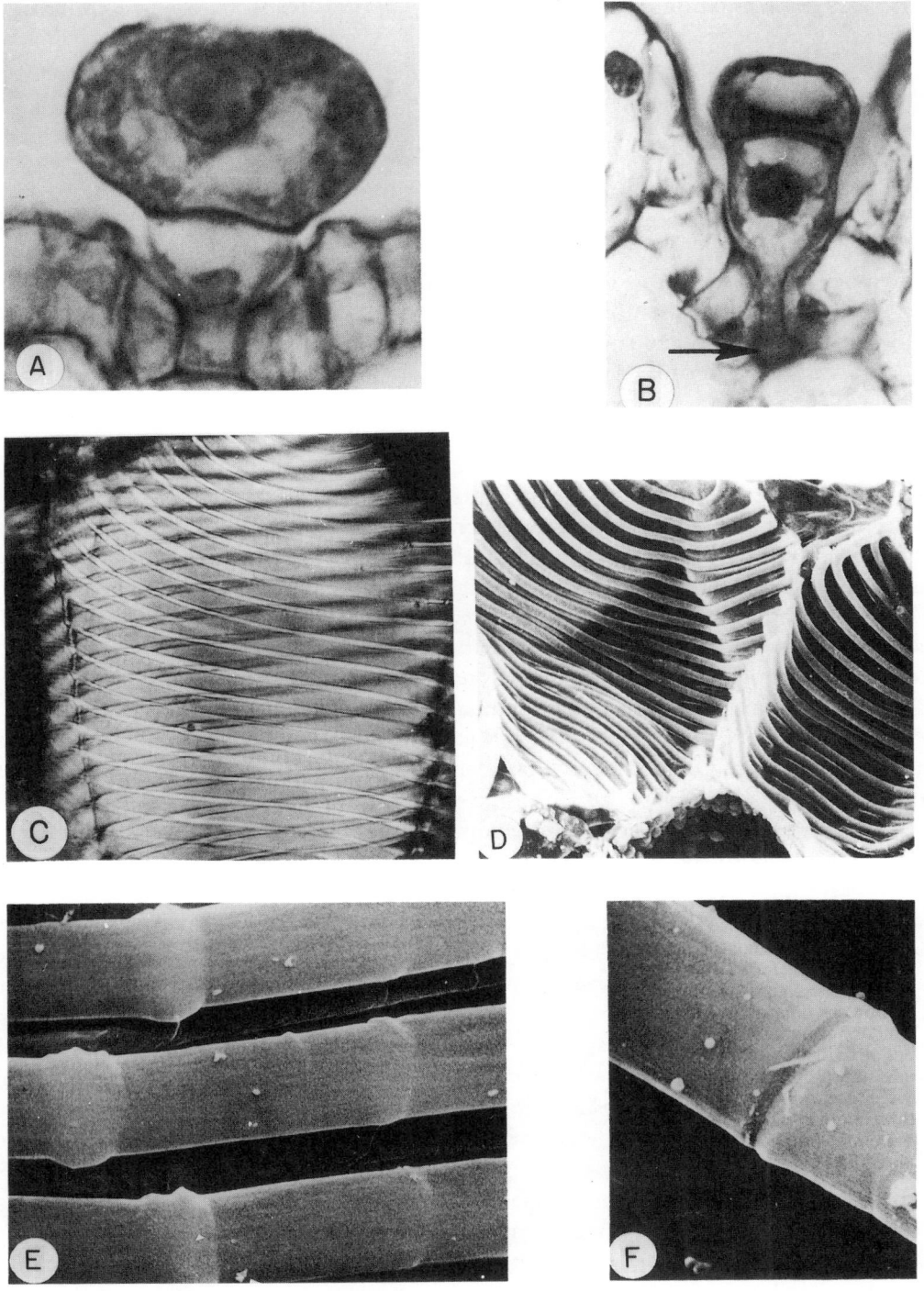

Fig. 3-2. Foliar trichomes in pleurothallid orchids. **A.** *Restrepiella ophiocephala,* **B.** *Pleurothallis mystax,* showing apical cell, stalk cell and smaller basal cell. From Pridgeon (1981). Spirally thickened idioblasts. **C.** *Cryptophoranthus cymbula* Luer. Abaxial hypodermal cell of leaf in transection ×975. **D.** *Pleurothallis circumplexa* Lindl. Mesophyll cells in transection ×240. From Pridgeon (1982). Articulations in the helical thickenings. **E.** Abaxial hypodermal cell of *Cryptophoranthus cymbula,* viewed externally ×3,800. **F.** Internal view of thickening of a mesophyll idioblast, *Pleurothallis circumplexa* with grooved inner face ×6,350. From Pridgeon (1982).

presence of these trichomes and the development of water storage tissue either in the leaf or pseudobulb.

However, recent experimental work does not support the idea. Benzing and Pridgeon (1983) measured uptake of water and ions, using radioisotopes ^{45}Ca, ^{35}S and ^{32}P by leaves of nine pleurothallid orchids, four non-pleurothallids and five tillandsioid bromeliads. For the water uptake experiments, excised leaves with cut ends sealed were allowed to decrease in fresh weight by 15–30%, transferred to a saturated atmosphere for 24 hours, and then exposed to mist for an equal period. They found that the bromeliads took up significant amounts of ions, with absorption greater in three atmospheric species than in two tank bromeliads. Uptake by the pleurothallid orchids on the other hand was significantly less, in several cases with no significant difference between pleurothallid and nonpleurothallid, glabrous orchids. The bromeliads tested took up water rapidly and rehydrated completely under mist, while orchid leaf weight gain was scarcely significant. Neither group gained weight in the saturated atmosphere, which is additional evidence against the hypothesis that plants may rehydrate by absorbing water vapor.

The conclusion from these experiments was that these orchid trichomes, though anatomically similar to the tillandsioid trichomes, did not function in the same way to take up water and nutrients. Benzing and Pridgeon (1983) suggested two reasons why this might be expected. Firstly, the epiphytic environment is harsh; it is patchy, subject to disturbance and water stress, and nutrient-poor. Hence there is need for frequent recruitment of new individuals, but accumulation of dry matter and nutrients is slow. In these conditions, it may be advantageous to reduce the vegetative plant body as much as possible and maximize resources devoted to reproduction. Tillandsioid bromeliads have done this by reducing the root-system greatly, with leaves taking over their absorbing function. Orchids have highly efficient root systems, hence it would not be expected that adaptations for absorption would develop in leaves as well. In fact as discussed below, some orchids have reduced the size of their shoot system and roots have taken over the photosynthetic function.

Secondly, it is advantageous for an epiphyte to have a mechanism for prolonging the contact between the absorbing tissues and the transient supplies of water and nutrients (Benzing, 1986). Bromeliad trichomes can do this with their overlapping shield discs forming a mat on the leaf surface. The comparable structure in orchids is the root velamen-exodermis formation, the passage cells being analagous to the bromeliad trichome stalk cells. In both cases, water is trapped rapidly in a layer of non-living cells which allows more time for the slower process of absorption into living tissue. Orchid leaves do not have this matted layer above the trichomes so that surface water tends to run off the leaf. While some absorption may occur, the primary function of these trichomes must be something else.

Pridgeon (1982) returned to the idea that secretion might be the primary function. As the trichomes do not persist intact in mature leaves, they may act by secreting mucilage and hence reduce transpiration in young leaves before the cuticle is fully developed and hardened. Raciborski (1898) also mentioned a secretory role for *Eria* trichomes, though he assumed that the mucilage produced might act as an absorber of water, rather than a waterproofing agent. Further study on the function of these orchid hairs appears warranted.

Orchid growers have been concerned about the effectiveness of foliar application of nutrients, which has prompted study of nutrient uptake through leaves. Sheehan et al.

(1967) found that ^{32}P could be taken up by leaves of *Cattleya* var. Trimos, (see also Poole and Sheehan, 1982) and Benzing, (1973) found some nutrient uptake by leaves of *Epidendrum tampense, (Encyclia tampensis)* but in this case the rate was less than one-eighth the rate of accumulation by roots. It seems probable that under natural conditions the absorption of water or nutrients by leaves is rarely significant.

Flowers

Flowers are temporary structures, but in many orchids the inflorescence, while it is present, may make up an appreciable portion of the total plant mass. Consequently the presence of flowers might have an effect on the water relations of the plant as a whole. There are only scattered references to aspects of floral anatomy relevant to water relations in the literature. Hering (1900) mentioned the occurrence of spirally thickened idioblasts in the flowering stem of *Listrostachys odoratissima*. Hsiang (1951) did not find any stomata in the epidermis of the perianth of *Cattleya labiata*, whereas Hew et al. (1980) found stomata present in flowers of ten species, but at very low frequency, typically 1/60 to 1/70 that of the lower leaf epidermis, and apparently non-functional. Some studies of water relations of flowers will be mentioned in later sections.

Pseudobulbs

Another possible water storage structure of many orchids is the swollen stem known as a pseudobulb, a term first used by Lindley in 1837 (Curtis, C. H., 1943).

The great majority of the epiphytic sympodial orchids develop pseudobulbs, in a wide range of shapes and sizes, from the size of a child's head (*Peristeria elata* Hook.) to a diameter of 3 mm or less (*Bulbophyllum minutissimum* F.v.M., Pfitzer, 1884; 1889). Pfitzer claimed that pseudobulbs serve as storage organs for water and organic substances, and, in species growing in reasonably dry climates, may comprise the bulk of the plant during the dry season when leaves are shed.

One example of pseudobulb structure is given by Chiang and Chen (1968) for *Pleione formosana*. In this case the conical, glossy pseudobulb has a one cell layer epidermis covered by a cuticle but with no stomata. A green chlorenchyma layer lies directly beneath the epidermis. Below is storage parenchyma, with cells of two types—smaller ones, clustered around the vascular tissue containing some chloroplasts and many starch filled plastids, and larger cells lacking starch. There are no air spaces between the cells. The authors concluded that (1) the pseudobulb served as both a carbohydrate store and a water store, (2) although it contained some chloroplasts the net photosynthesis rate would be negligible, due to lack of stomata or intercellular air spaces, (3) the chloroplasts may simply recycle CO_2 produced by respiration, (4) stored starch was moved into the cells clustered around the vascular tissue from other parts of the plant, and (5) the large colorless parenchyma cells functioned as the water store.

Curtis (1917) also noted that the pseudobulb tissue of two *Bulbophyllum* species consisted of two cell types; thin walled cells with numerous chloroplasts and larger water-storing elements, and epidermis which was thick-walled or protected by heavy cuticle. Stomata were not mentioned.

Wiebe and Al-Saadi (1976) measured the matric bound water in storage tissue of a number of succulents, including pseudobulbs of two orchids, *Coelogyne cristata* and *Bulbophyllum pictoratum*. Osmotic potential of expressed sap was also determined. In all cases the bound water amounted to only 1–11% of total water content, the values for orchids being 2% and 3%. Orchid osmotic potentials were also very small, −3.2 and −3.0 bar (Table 3-2). They concluded that in all such succulent tissue the water holding capacity was considerable, but this did not depend on generation of a steep water potential gradient by strong matric forces or concentrated cell ssp. Instead, flexible cells with low modulus of elasticity could take in copious water when it was available aided by a total structure which allowed expansion, for example the pleated, concertina-like ridges of many cactus stems. Many orchid pseudobulbs, but not all, show the same ridged structure as a cactus stem. Once stored, water is efficiently retained by means of an impermeable cuticle and daytime stomatal closure in CAM plants.

The expansion and contraction of storage organs with fluctuations in water content raises interesting mechanical problems, (Wiebe and Al-Saadi, 1976). An unusual cell type occurs widely in many orchid genera, in regions of pseudobulbs, aerial roots, stems and leaves which appear to be involved in water storage. These are the parenchyma cells with spiral thickenings, often referred to as tracheoidal idioblasts, though Pridgeon (1982) prefers to describe them simply as spirally thickened idioblasts. The significance of these cells is the subject of the next section.

Spirally Thickened Idioblasts

Reports and drawings of spirally thickened idioblasts occur in the earliest anatomical descriptions of orchids. Link (1849) described "Spiralzellen" in the tissue of aerial roots of *Stanhopea eburnea*. He did not know their function, but speculated that they might hold open channels through the root tissue to allow for absorption of atmospheric moisture. Their similarity to the tracheae of insects was noted. Trécul (1855b) discussed the formation of spiral thickenings in cells of orchid leaves, but did not comment on their function. Hering (1900) found idioblasts in various monopodial orchids, including *Aerides*, *Saccolabium giganteum*, and large numbers in the flowering stem of *Listrostachys odoratissima*. Raciborski (1898) mentioned "water-collecting tracheids" occupying ⅔ of the cortex of aerial roots of *Aerides virens*. Curtis (1917) noted thin-walled cells densely covered with spiral bands in the parenchyma of pseudobulbs of New Zealand *Bulbophyllum* spp., and the root cortex of *Sarcochilus adversus*. Other early reports cited by Olatunji and Nengim (1980) include those of Leitgeb (1865), Krüger (1883), Möbius (1887), Tominski (1905) and Metzler (1924). Hofmann (1930) reported the presence of such cells in leaves of *Oncidium ascendens*.

Pirwitz (1931) discussed examples of what had been termed "storage tracheids" or "water cells" in a number of plant families, including Orchidaceae. Some were living cells, but others contained no living cytoplasm when mature. There had been discussion about whether such cells filled with air when the plant lost water, and whether the spiral thickenings prevented their collapse. Pirwitz confirmed earlier findings (Krüger, 1883; Tominski, 1905) that in *Liparis* and *Oncidium* the spiral cells did contain gas when the plant was water stressed, but in other species, even after severe dehydration, they still contained liquid. In some cases the wall thickenings were seen to kink and form a zig-zag pattern under water stress, thereby allowing a greater volume change. Such shrinkage would allow the release of considerable water to surrounding tissue, whereas if cells retained a rigid shape little water could leave them unless air was admitted. Foster (1956) introduced the term tracheoid idioblasts, but stated that their role was very poorly understood, though water storage was often assumed. The nature of the relationship between tracheoid idioblasts, enlarged terminal tracheids and the spirally thickened cells which may form layers in seed coats or fruits deserves further study.

A much more detailed study of these spirally thickened idioblasts was reported by Olatunji and Nengim (1980). They examined 88 species of West African orchids for their presence in root, stem, pseudobulb or leaf. Forty-three species (49%), all of them epiphytes, contained idioblasts. None of the twelve terrestrial and only one epilithic/terrestrial species examined contained them. In the epiphytes the elements occurred in aerial roots (21 spp.), stem/pseudobulb (17) and leaf (23). The idioblasts were never associated with vascular tissues but were located in root or stem cortex, or leaf mesophyll.

Olatunji and Nengim (1980) also suggested that the idioblasts might provide mechanical support for surrounding parenchymatous tissue, preventing undue collapse during dry seasons. In some species like *Ansellia africana* and *Bulbophyllum*, they were aggregated in a mantle or sheath, which may make an efficient strengthening tissue. An elaboration of this idea, suggested earlier by Preston (1901), is that the cells actually function as mechanical springs, shrinking during desiccation but expanding on rehydration so enabling tissues and organs to regain their shape and turgidity. These elements are common in plants found in dry environments (not only epiphytic orchids but also members of several other families), but not all epiphytes have them. Evidently different plants, or different organs in the same plant, may be modified to similar environments in different ways.

Pridgeon (1982) investigated the vegetative anatomy of 200 species in 22 genera of the Pleurothallidinae, which lack pseudobulbs. Spirally thickened cells were found in hypodermal tissue or mesophyll in most taxa (Figure 3-2C, D). The cells generally lacked cytoplasm at maturity and the wall thickenings were primarily cellulose. Tests for lignin and suberin were negative, whereas Olatungi and Nengim (1980) found lignin in the idioblsats of the African genera they examined. Pridgeon confirmed Pirwitz's observations that the thickenings were articulated (Fig. 3-2E, F) allowing them to flex and permit considerable expansion or contraction of the cells as hydration changed. This strongly supported the idea that the cells function as water storage reservoirs and also provide mechanical support for surrounding tissue. Hypodermal tissue in genera lacking the spiral thickenings was frequently seen to be distorted, infolded or collapsed under water stress. Pridgeon avoided Foster's term tracheoidal idioblast, as the cell thickenings had very little lignification and the articulations are quite different from the secondary thickening patterns of xylem elements.

Benzing et al. (1983) observed the spirally thickened cells in the root cortex of ten orchids including several leafless species. These were not lignified or suberized. They noted that the thickenings often abutted adjacent intercellular spaces. According to them the thickenings provide support for the cells as they give up water and shrink during water stress, and also prevent the penetration of air into the cells from adjacent intercellular air spaces. When water potential of the tissue is very low, cavitation in these cells would release water to adjacent living cells, but if air then entered, the reservoirs would be very difficult to refill when the tissue rehydrated. Benzing (1986) developed this idea further, that one function of the thickenings is to prevent the intrusions of large amounts of air when the cell water contents cavitate under water stress.

As yet there are no experimental measurements of cavitation in spirally thickened idioblasts, though some of the early observers did report that the cells were sometimes filled with air (Pirwitz, 1931). Methods for detecting cavitation of water columns in xylem have now been developed (Milburn and Johnson, 1966; Milburn and Crombie, 1984; Tyree et al., 1984) and it would be most interesting to apply these techniques to a detailed study of the behavior of spirally thickened idioblasts in storage tissue under water stress.

Water Relations of Tissues

One of the most useful parameters in any study of the response of plants to an imposed water stress is the water potential of the tissues. Water potential is a measure of the energy status of water in any system. Formally related to chemical potential, it may be defined in terms of the work done moving unit quantity of water from a reference pool at zero potential to the point under consideration. A fully hydrated tissue is taken to have a water potential of zero and as the tissue dehydrates water potential becomes increasingly negative. In plant tissue water potential (ψ) has two major components, osmotic or solute potential (ψ_π) and pressure potential (ψ_p) or turgor pressure. At any time, $\psi = \psi_\pi + \psi_p$. In a fully hydrated tissue the pressure potential is equal and opposite to the osmotic potential. When the tissue loses enough water to reach wilting or turgor loss point, the osmotic potential equals the total water potential. Hence osmotic potential is also a useful parameter, because it sets the range of water potentials between full turgor and wilting point. Many plants from dry habitats, tolerant of severe water stress, have very negative osmotic potentials, i.e., very concentrated cell sap. Hence osmotic potential may have considerable ecological significance.

Water potential has the same dimension as pressure, and preferred units are megapascals (MPa) or bars. Osmotic potential is always negative and water potential usually so in plant tissue. In the older literature different definitions were often used, for example suction force (*Saugkraft*), and diffusion pressure deficit, with different units, frequently atmospheres, and different sign conventions. For ease of comparison, all data quoted have been expressed in bars or atmospheres and signs changed where necessary to conform to standard current usage. 1 MPa = 10 bar = 9.87 atmospheres = 145 p.s.i.

A few early studies of the osmotic potential ψ_π of epiphytic orchids have been reported (Table 3-2). Among the most extensive are those of Harris (1918, 1934) who expressed sap from plant tissue and measured osmotic potential by the depression of freezing point. He compared four families of vascular epiphytes from southern Florida and Jamaica (Table 3-3). The sap was extremely dilute, in all four families and in both areas. For the families represented in both areas, the Jamaican specimens had more dilute sap than those from Florida. In Jamaica also the epiphytes had more dilute sap than herbaceous terrestrial plants growing in the same area, by 3 to 5 atmospheres, and the osmotic potential was only one half to one third that of leaves of the trees on which they were growing.

Table 3-2. Osmotic potentials of orchid plant parts.

Species	Plant part	Osmotic potential ψ_π[a]	Units	Comments	Reference
Lepanthes ovalis	leaves	4.2	atm	measured by	Harris (1918)
L. divaricata	leaves	2.4	atm	freezing point	
Octadesmia montana	leaves	5.3	atm	depression	
Pleurothallis racemiflora	leaves	2.6	atm		
Stelis micrantha	leaves	2.6	atm		
S. ophioglossoides	leaves	2.7	atm		
Anacheilium cochleatum	leaves	5.2	atm		
Auliza nocturna	leaves	5.0	atm		
Encyclia tampensis	leaves	5.8	atm		
Macradenia lutescens	leaves	6.1	atm		
Polystachya minuta	leaves	6.0	atm		
Spathiger rigidus	leaves	4.5	atm		
Vanilla eggersii	stem	2.9	atm		
Epidendrum verrucosum	leaf	6.1–6.6	atm	terrestrial	
Prescottia stachyoides	leaf	6.3	atm	terrestrial	
Phaius tankervilleae	upper epidermis, leaf.	11.1	atm	measured by incipient plasmolysis. terrestrial. Bogor, Indonesia.	Blum (1933)
	mesophyll	23.4	atm		
Coelogyne asperata	upper epidermis	8.1	atm	terrestrial	
	mesophyll	23.4	atm	terrestrial	
Vanilla planifolia	mesophyll	10.4	atm	terrestrial	
Argostophyllum tenue	upper epidermis	11.1	atm	epiphytic	
	mesophyll	32.1	atm	epiphytic	
Coelogyne swaniana	upper epidermis	13.5	atm	epiphytic	
	mesophyll	16.9/12.7	atm	epiphytic	
	upper epidermis	11.9	atm	epiphytic	
	mesophyll	16.9	atm	epiphytic	
Liparis sp.	upper epidermis	6.0	atm	epiphytic	
	mesophyll	10.4	atm	epiphytic	
Eria cymbidiformis	upper epidermis	6.7	atm	epiphytic	
	mesophyll	7.4	atm	epiphytic	
Cymbidium atropurpureum	upper epidermis	10.4	atm	epiphytic	
	mesophyll	12.7/18.4	atm	epiphytic	
Dendrobium carnosum	upper epidermis	7.4	atm	epiphytic	
D. purpureum	upper epidermis	11.1	atm	epiphytic	
D. erectifolium	upper epidermis	16.0	atm	epiphytic	
	mesophyll	24.5	atm	epiphytic	
D. luxurians	upper epidermis	8.1	atm	epiphytic	
Xiphidium coeruleum	upper epidermis	7.4	atm	epiphytic	
	mesophyll	17.8	atm	epiphytic	
Grammatophyllum speciosum	upper epidermis	14.3	atm	epiphytic	
	mesophyll	17.8	atm	epiphytic	
Sarcanthus javanicus	upper epidermis	8.9	atm	epiphytic	
	mesophyll	9.6	atm	epiphytic	
Thrixspermum calceolus	upper epidermis	7.4	atm	epiphytic	
	mesophyll	8.1	atm	epiphytic	
Coelogyne asperata	upper epidermis	2.4	atm	flower, labellum	
	mesophyll	8.1	atm		

[a]All values are negative

Table 3-2. Continued.

Species	Plant part	Osmotic potential ψ_π[a]	Units	Comments	Reference
Grammatophyllum speciosum	upper epidermis	15.2	atm	flower, perianth	
	mesophyll	11.1	atm		
Taeniophyllum sp.	mesophyll	10.4	atm	measured *in situ* in rainforest, Cibodas.	
Dendrobium montanum	upper epidermis	6.7	atm		
	mesophyll	21.5	atm		
Dendrochilum pallideflavens	upper epidermis	16.0	atm		
	mesophyll	19.6/39.8	atm		
Schoenorchis juncifolia	upper epidermis	10.4	atm		
	mesophyll	14.3	atm		
Schoenorchis juncifolia	upper epidermis	6.7/12.7	atm		
	mesophyll	5.3/12.7	atm		
Ridleyella paniculata	upper epidermis	10.4	atm		
	lower epidermis	17.6	atm		
	palisade,	65.8			
	spongy parenchyma	19.6/29.7	atm		
Epidendrum cochleatum	leaves	5.3	atm	Florida freezing point depression	Harris (1934)
	pseudobulb	4.4	atm		
	leaves	5.0	atm		
	pseudobulb	3.4/5.1/5.4	atm		
	leaves	5.2	atm		
	leaves	5.3/5.0/5.2 atm 5.5/5.9			
	pseudobulb	4.4/3.4	atm		
E. conopseum		6.3/6.3/6.5 7.7	atm		
E. nocturnum		5.5/4.5/4.8 4.6/3.5/5.7 6.3/5.3/6.2 4.6	atm		
Epidendrum tampense (*Encyclia tempensis*)	leaves	4.8/6.4	atm		
	pseudobulb	3.0/6.0	atm		
E. (Spathiger) rigidum		3.5/5.7	atm		
E. imbricatum		3.6	atm	Jamaica	
E. verrucosum		6.2–7.0	atm		
Generalization: Orchidaceae of Florida hammocks average		4.88	atm		
Orchidaceae of Jamaican rainforest, average		3.34	atm		
Myrmecodia platytyrea	tuber (Knolle)	0.5–3	atm	*not* orchids— epiphytic	Spanner (1939)
	upper epid/leaf	2.4–5	atm	Rubiaceae— "ant-plants"	
	lower epid/leaf	5.2–7.8	atm	incipient plasmolysis	
M. echinala	tuber	0.5–2.5	atm	or freezing point	
	upper epid/leaf	2.2–5	atm	depression	
	lower epid/leaf	5 –7.8	atm		
Hydnophytum formicarium	tuber	2.2–5	atm		
	upper epid/leaf	4.8–8	atm		
	lower epid/leaf	8.2–11	atm		

Species	Plant part	Osmotic potential $\psi_\pi{}^a$	Units	Comments	Reference
Phalaenopsis	epid/fleshy leaf	5.8	atm	data from Senn (1913)	
Dendrobium crumenatum	pseudobulb/epid	10.1	atm	data from Senn (1913)	
D. luxurians	thick leaf; upper epidermis	8.0	atm	data from Blum (1933)	
Coelogyne swaniana	pseudobulb; upper epidermis	11.9	atm	data from Blum (1933)	
Dendrobium erectifolium	thin leaf; upper epidermis	16.0	atm	data from Blum (1933)	
Pleurothallis racemiflora	?	2.6	atm	method not stated	Curtis J. T. (1946)
Cattleya labiata	flower:				
	control column	5.99/5.76	atm	determinations made	Hsiang (1951)
	pollinated column	6.80/6.34	atm	115 hrs. after treatments	
	control perianth	5.22/5.93	atm		
	pollinated perianth	6.49	atm		
	IAA perianth	6.82	atm		
Cattleya bowringiana	flower:				
	control column	5.91/4.43	atm		
	pollinated column	6.37	atm		
	NAA column	5.16	atm		
	control perianth	4.33/5.40	atm		
	pollinated perianth	5.37	atm		
	NAA perianth	6.29			
Bulbophyllum pechei	pseudobulb	1.33	atm	freezing point depression	Gessner (1956)
Bulbophyllum pechei	leaf	4.34	atm		
Coelogyne wettsteiniana	pseudobulb	0.96	atm		
Coelogyne wettsteiniana	leaf	8.19	atm		
Schoenorchis juncifolia	leaf cells	20	atm	plasmolysis	Went & Sheps (1969)
Orchids with "tubers"	leaves	3.1	atm	species and method not given	Walter (1971)
(pseudobulbs?)	"tubers"	2.0	atm	Amari, E. Africa	
Orchids without "tubers",		4.3			
large aerial roots, no		6.1			
thickened stems		6.6			
Coelogyne cristata	pseudobulb	3.2 ± 0.5	bar	psychrometric method,	Wiebe & Al-Saadi
Bulbophyllum pictoratum	pseudobulb	3.0 ± 0.4	bar	sap extracted from frozen, thawed and crushed tissue.	(1976)
Eria velutina	leafy shoot	3.9/3.3	bar	calculated from pressure-volume curves	Sinclair (1983a,b)
Dendrobium tortile	leafy shoot	7.0/6.9	bar	measured by pressure chamber	
D. crumenatum	leafy shoot	5.4/4.9			

Table 3-3. Comparison of osmotic potential ψ_π of sap from Jamaican and Floridean epiphytes.[a]

Family	Jamaica		Florida	
	No. Species	Mean ψ_π	No. Species	Mean ψ_π
Bromeliaceae	3	−4.00 atm	10	−5.57 atm
Orchidaceae	7	−3.32	7	−5.06
Piperaceae	5	−4.34	1	−4.58
Gesneriaceae	1	−4.33	—	—

[a] Data from Harris (1918)

Blum (1933) made a detailed study of osmotic potential ψ_π and water potential ψ (*Saugkraft* or "suction force" in his terminology) in the tropical vegetation of the Botanic Gardens at Buitenzorg (now Bogor) and Tjibodas (now Cibodas), Java. He measured water potential ψ using an isopiestic method and osmotic potential ψ_π by incipient plasmolysis. This allowed separate determinations to be made of several different tissue types within the one organ.

Osmotic potentials of 16 orchids growing in the Bogor Gardens are listed in Table 3-2. In all cases the ψ_π of the mesophyll was more negative than that of the epidermis, and some values were surprisingly large. ψ_π of three terrestrial orchids was not significantly different from that of the epiphytes, and there was no correlation between osmotic potential and presence or absence of water storage tissue. A few measurements of flower tissue gave values in the same range as leaves.

Osmotic potential of five more species of orchid growing on the edge of the forest at the higher altitude of Cibodas, were among the least negative of any plants studied. Blum commented that drought resistance did not appear to be correlated with a very negative ψ_π, for instance *Schoenorchis juncifolia* was among the most drought resistant species but had a relatively small ψ_π. There was no explanation for the surprisingly large value for the mesophyll of *Ridleyella paniculata*.

Went and Sheps (1969) also reported ψ_π for *S. juncifolia,* in this case one of the more negative (−20 atm.). Both readings may have been taken from the same plant, as in each paper the orchid is described as suspended from wires beneath a glass roof in the forest so that only gaseous exchange was allowed. Blum recorded that the plant continued to produce flowers after more than a year, while Went's measurements were made after four years.

Wiebe and Al-Saadi (1976) found extremely dilute sap in pseudobulbs of two species. Hsiang (1951) reported low values for orchid flower tissue and Sinclair (1983a,b) found dilute sap in three species, *Eria velutina, Dendrobium tortile* and *D. crumenatum* using the pressure-volume curve method.

Gessner (1956) quoted from Blum, Senn and Spanner, and reported some values of his own for two species in which ψ_π of the pseudobulbs was significantly less negative than that of the leaves. He suggested that this may be important in postponing water loss from storage tissue under water stress, but also pointed out that some of the measurements might be inaccurate. Pseudobulbs may be very rich in mucilage, and values of ψ_π measured cryoscopically on expressed sap may not necessarily be the same as those existing in intact cells in undisturbed tissue. All measurements of ψ_π of sap extracted from plant tissue necessarily include an unknown degree of error due to this unavoidable alteration of the composition of the sap on extraction, so that many early measurements must be treated with caution. The incipient plasmolysis method or the "pressure-volume curve" method are not subject to the same criticism. For a discussion of methods of measuring components of water potential in plants, see Barrs (1968) or Kramer (1983).

Schwarz (1936), quoted by Gessner (1956), measured changes in osmotic potential in epiphytes as the concentration of the nutrient solution was varied. Whereas large adjustments were recorded in species of Araceae and Bromeliaceae, an orchid (*Phalaenopsis hybrida*) changed very little.

The clear conclusion from all these data, rather surprising at first sight, is that epiphytic orchids have very dilute sap. This can be seen in Table 3-4, from Blum (1933), which summarizes his measurements on a wide range of vegetation types. The osmotic potentials of the orchids are the smallest of any of the groups.

Water potential ψ is a less satisfactory parameter to record for comparative purposes, as it may vary widely diurnally and seasonally. Hence single readings, unless accompanied by details of the conditions at the time and the previous history of the plant, may be misleading. Table 3-5 contains some values of water potential with brief comments on the conditions, where stated, and Table 3-4 as well as values of ψ_π also contains Blum's summary of water potential measurements on the numerous vegetation types he examined, including the ranges, which are really more useful. Note that some of Blum's data in Table 3-5 were quoted by Gessner (1956) as being osmotic potential measurements. However, the original paper makes it clear that these were water potentials measured by the isopiestic method.

These data show that just as the osmotic potentials of orchids are small, so too the water potentials are never found to be very negative, in comparison with typical values for other plant groups.

Sinclair (1983b) carried out detailed studies of three orchid species in Kuala Lumpur, Malaysia; *Eria velutina*, *Dendrobium tortile* and *D. crumenatum*. The plants were suspended under shelter from rain but exposed to ambient air and indirect light. Initially well watered, they were subjected to drought for one month, with regular measurements of water potential ψ, relative water content (see below) and leaf diffusive resistance. After an initial fall of 3 to 4 bars ψ declined very gradually, and although the period of stress

Table 3-4. Mean osmotic ψ_π and water potentials ψ for different groups of tropical plants cultivated in Java, Indonesia[a,b].

	OSMOTIC POTENTIAL ψ_π			WATER POTENTIAL ψ		
	Upper epidermis	Mesophyll	Lower epidermis	Mean	Least negative	Most negative
Aquatic Ferns	—	—	—	− 8.0	− 4.0	−11.9
Terrestrial Ferns	−18.0	−30.4	—	−21.6	−11.9	−34.6
Epiphytic Ferns	−10.7	−30.1	—	−11.2	− 4.0	−25.5
Conifers	—	—	—	−19.2	−12.7	−23.4
Cycads	—	—	—	−21.9	− 9.6	−34.6
Palms	−27.9	−50.3	−25.1	−22.8	− 6.7	ca−73.9
Araceae	−10.8	—	—	− 8.3	− 5.3	− 9.6
Scitamineae	−12.4	—	—	−12.6	− 3.3	−22.5
Bromeliaceae	−12.8	—	—	− 7.5	− 5.3	− 8.9
Dicot. trees	−19.1	−60.8	−17.6	−14.8	− 4.7	−32.1
Herbs and Shrubs	−11.1	−31.9	−15.9	− 9.4	− 5.4	−17.8
Lianas	−14.3	—	−19.6	−24.0	−10.4	−39.8
Terrestrial orchids	− 9.6	−19.1	—	− 8.1	− 6.7	−13.5
Epiphytic orchids	−10.0	−16.7	−12.0	− 9.7	− 1.3	−32.1

[a]Units are atmospheres
[b]From Blum, 1933

was much longer than those species would normally experience in their native habitat the final values were surprisingly high (i.e. close to zero). To appreciate the significance of the data for epiphytic orchids it is helpful to consider tissue water relations in terms of the so-called Höfler diagram, in which the components of water potential are plotted

Table 3-5. Water potentials ψ of orchids.

Species	Plant part	ψ	Units	Comments	Reference
Coelogyne swaniana	leaf	−8 to −12	atm	diurnal range, 2 days	Blum (1933)
Phaius tankervilliae	leaf	−5 to −11	atm	diurnal range, 2 days	
Terrestrials				Bogor Gardens;	
Coelogyne asperata	leaf	−6.7	atm	measured by the	
	labellum	−6.7	atm	isopiestic method:	
Trichoglottis retusa	leaf	−13.5	atm	change in length of tissue	
	perianth	−5.3	atm	strips in a range of sucrose solutions.	
Epiphytes					
Agrostophyllum tenue	leaf	−24.5	atm		
Coelogyne swaniana	perianth	−9.6	atm		
Liparis sp.	leaf	−6.0	atm		
Eria cymbiformis	leaf	−4.7	atm		
Cymbidium atropurpureum	leaf	−8.1	atm		
Dendrobium carnosum	leaf	−1.3	atm		
D. purpureum	leaf	−5.3	atm		
D. erectifolium	leaf	−19.6	atm		
D. luxurians	leaf	−5.3	atm		
Xiphidium coeruleum	leaf tip	−3.3	atm		
	leaf base	−5.3	atm		
Grammatophyllum speciosum	leaf	−32.1	atm		
	perianth	−8.9	atm		
		−7.4	atm		
	leaf tip	−14.3	atm		
	leaf base	−8.1	atm		
Sarcanthus javanicus	leaf	−5.3	atm		
Thrixspermum calceolus	leaf	−2.3	atm		
Taeniophyllum sp.	root parenchyma	−4.0	atm	open site, measured *in situ* in rainforest, Cibodas, 1.5m above ground.	
Dendrobium montanum	leaf parenchyma	−5.3	atm	open, shady site	
Dendrochilum pallideflavens	leaf parenchyma	−9.6	atm	open, shady site	
Ridleyella paniculata	leaf parenchyma	−14.3	atm	open, shady site	
Liparis sp.	leaf parenchyma	−8.9	atm	shady forest, 2m	
Schoenorchis juncifolia	leaf parenchyma	−6.0 −10.4	atm atm	open site, 2m	
Epidendrum radicans	leaf	−3.0	bar	measured as part of leaf air-space determination	Smith & Heuer (1981)
Aranda Deborah	flowers	−4.49 −3.43	bar bar	08.00am 16.00pm	Goh (1983)
Eria velutina	shoot	−0.6 −5.6	bar bar	measured by pressure chamber	Sinclair (1983b)
Dendrobium tortile	shoot	−0.0 −8.3	bar bar	well-watered stressed 1 month	
D. crumenatum	shoot	−0.0 −7.2	bar bar	well-watered stressed 1 month	

against the relative water content R of the tissue, where R is defined as

$$R = \frac{\text{Fresh Weight} - \text{Dry Weight}}{\text{Fully Turgid Weight} - \text{Dry Weight}}$$

R is a number less than one, which approaches one as tissue becomes fully hydrated.

Fig. 3-1D shows Höfler diagrams for an epiphytic orchid, *Dendrobium crumenatum*, a deciduous tree (*Populus nigra*) and an evergreen sclerophyll tree (*Eucalyptus cladocalyx*). Because of its dilute sap, the turgor pressure ψ_p of the orchid is never high even at its maximum, and it falls to zero for a small decrease in relative water content. This turgor loss point is approximately the point at which stomatal closure is induced; a relatively small loss of water or decrease in water potential brings the epiphyte to this point.

A plant such as the *Eucalyptus* growing in a dry climate where long periods of drought and slowly drying soil must be endured, has the capacity to tolerate very concentrated cell sap and very negative water potentials before turgor is lost. This allows the tree to extend the period of stomatal opening, and hence gas exchange and carbon gain. By contrast, the epiphytic orchid lives in a regime of rather short but severe droughts, and with very limited access to any external source of water during dry periods. It would gain little advantage from generating very negative internal water potentials. The external water potential is likely to be either close to zero (during rain) or to fall rapidly to extremely low levels (between rains). In this situation, the epiphyte relies on an efficient means of sensing the onset of water stress and responding by curtailing gas exchange to lie quiescent until water again becomes available. See also Benzing (1986).

Transpiration

Very few measurements of orchid transpiration rates have been published. This is surprising, since the xerophytic adaptations that have been described or postulated in orchids presumably evolved in response to the intermittent drought typical of the epiphytic habitat. If so, it would be expected that one effect of these adaptations would be to restrict water loss under drought conditions. Any study of orchid or other epiphyte adaptation should include measurements of rates of water loss, with comparisons between epiphytes and other types of vegetation. Yet such studies are very rare, and none appears to have been attempted recently.

There are some reasons for this lack of data. Firstly, in the past techniques have been inadequate. Until fairly recently, most methods of measuring transpiration involved weighing. Potted plants are easily weighed and lysimeters allow the weighing of larger blocks of soil with the vegetation they support, but large trees and epiphytes still attached to tree branches cannot be dealt with by this means. Still, transpiration of many epiphytic orchids could easily be measured by weighing. Orchids may be grown on artificial substrates—sections of branches, hanging baskets or pieces of board, which could be suspended between weighings in a tree canopy in a close approximation to natural conditions. Some measurements of this type have been made, but surprisingly few (Kamerling, 1912; Walter, 1971). Another common method of measuring transpiration involves the rapid weighing of cut leaves or shoots. The rate of weight loss so measured is extrapolated to give an estimate of the rate for intact leaves on the plant. Several objections to this method have been raised (Barrs, 1968; Slavik, 1974), but for lack of a better one it has been widely used and some data for orchids by this method are available (Schimper, 1935; Gessner, 1956; Johansson, 1974; Sanford, 1978).

More recently transpiration has been measured routinely in gas-exchange chambers by infra-red gas analysis or psychrometers which monitor changes in vapor concentration. These methods appear to have been applied only to orchid flowers, (Hew et al., 1980). They are more difficult to use in the field than in the laboratory, particularly in a tropical rainforest canopy.

This raises the second reason for lack of transpiration data for epiphytes. The most drought-tolerant species usually are found high in the upper canopy, sometimes on small branches, all but inaccessible even for observation, let alone being reached with complex equipment. Much work on forest canopies has been done from towers, instrumented masts, ladders and catwalks, but such expensive methods have not yet been available for studies of epiphytes.

The other sense in which epiphytes are inaccessible is geographic. Most epiphytic orchids are native to the humid tropics, while most plant physiologists and most funding agencies are based in temperate zones. This lack of resources for biological research in the tropics has drastically restricted our knowledge of some of the most complex, and most rapidly disappearing ecosystems of the world.

Yet another factor which limits the value of such transpiration data as are available, is that a measurement is almost meaningless unless the conditions under which it was made are also stated. Transpiration is influenced greatly by air temperature, humidity, wind-speed and light intensity, as well as by the stomatal conductance of the leaves. Therefore unless a set of results was obtained under carefully specified conditions, they cannot be easily compared with other data. Isolated readings (Tables 3-6 and 3-7) are of limited value except for broad generalizations.

Table 3-6. Orchid transpiration rates, expressed as a percentage of fresh weight.

Species	Wt loss/day % F.W. 1st day	Wt loss/day % F.W. after 3 mths	Total wt loss % F.W. after 8 days	Total wt loss % F.W. after 3 mths	Comments	Reference
Aerides virens	1.2	—	10.6	—	Measured at Bogor.	Kamerling
Dendrobium	1.4	0.28	7.8	29	Whole plants	(1912)
secundum	2.9	0.24	22.6	67	suspended under	
D. crumenatum	1.6	0.30	16.3	63	shelter, exposed to	
Eria ornata	2.9	0.20	16.5	42	outside air.	
Rhynchostylis retusa	8.0	0.055	29.9	45	Means of 3 to 5 sets	
Dendrobium pandaneti					of measurements.	
Coelogyne	3.3				Cut leaves in	Gessner
hüttneriana					glasshouse	(1956)
Bulbophyllum sp.	2.5		20		Measured at	Walter
3 unidentified spp.	8.3				Amani, E. Africa by	(1971)
lacking	7.7		20–25%		Walter, 1934.	
pseudobulbos.	7.1				Plants suspended under shelter; rates calculated from published diagram.	
Calyptrochilum christyanum						
(long, narrow leaves)			40.9 ± 4.9		Cut leaf weighing; leaves hung for	Sanford (1978)
(short, broad leaves)			40.5 ± 6.6		38–48 days in laboratory.	
C. emarginatum			37 ± 11			

Table 3-7. Orchid transpiration rates, expressed as weight loss per hour, either as % fresh weight or absolute weights.

Species	Rates Wt. loss/hr., % F.W.	g dm^{-2}hr^{-1}	Comments	Reference
Grammatophyllum speciosum		0.07	av. over a 12hr. day, plant in shade	Haberlandt, quoted in Schimper (1935) p. 222.
Cattleya labiata	0.15–0.55		cut flowers	Hsiang (1951)
Cymbidium bicolor		0.0029– 0.0066		Gessner (1956)
Graphorchis lurida	11.2	0.14	weight loss of cut leaves over 3 min.; measured in daylight, 2–4pm	Johansson (1974)
Angraecum subulatum	2.3			
A. distichum	1.5			
A. podochiloides	0.7			
Bulbophyllum linderi	0.5/0.72	0.08		
B. winkleri	0.4	0.05		
B. saltatorium	0.4			
B. bufo	0.4			
Polystachya dalzielii	20.0			
P. puberula	11.2			
P. leonensis	8.6			
P. affinis	4.9			
P. rhodoptera	2.8			
P. laxiflora	1.4			
Ancistrochilus rothschildianus	5.5			
Brachycorythis kalbreyeri	6.3			
Cyrtorchis arcuata	0.8/0.56	0.02		
Diaphananthe pellucida	0.7	0.03		
D. bidens	0.6			
Bolusiella talbotii	0.3			
Chamaeangis vesicata	0.3			
Nephrangis filiformis	0.3			
Calyptrochilum christyanum	0.3			
C. emarginatum	0.36	0.04		
Tridactyle tridactylites	3.7			
T. anthomaniaca	0.6			
Plectrelminthus caudatus	2.9			
Habenaria leonensis	1.0			
Aranda 'Wendy Scott'		0.015 ± 0.0004	Flowers, in light	Hew *et al.* (1980)
		0.015 ± 0.0004	Flowers, in darkness	
Vanda 'Tan Chay Yan'		0.017 ± 0.0006	Flowers, in light	
		0.017 ± 0.0002	Flowers, in darkness	
Oncidium 'Golden Shower'		0.119 ± 0.0028	Leaves, in light	
		0.015 ± 0.0002	Leaves, in darkness	
Vanda 'Tan Chay Yan'		0.020 ± 0.0004	Leaves, in light	
		0.041 ± 0.0007	Leaves, in darkness	
Dendrobium bigibbum		0.017 ± 0.0004	Flowers, various conditions of light, humidity, [CO_2] and ABA	

As pointed out by Gessner (1956), it is less important to know a transpiration rate under conditions of plentiful water supply than to determine the way in which this rate is restricted by the plant as water availability is reduced during a drought. The capacity to restrict transpiration in the face of developing water stress is one important adaptation of xerophytes. There are few data showing this for orchids.

There is a problem with units as well. Transpiration has been expressed in terms of weight loss as percentage of fresh weight of the plant, weight loss for a whole plant or per unit leaf area. The time intervals may range from seconds to days or even weeks. Short-term values may be valuable in some applications but they are not easily integrated to give longer term averages. They may be misleading, for example, if measured during the day in a CAM plant which has its stomata open at night, or is following a diurnal rhythm significantly different from that of a C_3 plant.

In studying epiphytes such as orchids which have little or no external water storage (i.e. no access to soil or a humus accumulation), transpiration during a drought could usefully be expressed as a percentage of the initial water content of the plant, thus showing the relationship between the rate of water loss and the storage still available. I know of no data expressed in this way.

A brief survey of published transpiration data follows:

The Botanic Gardens and associated laboratory at Bogor (formerly Buitenzorg), Indonesia, have been a focus for much work on orchid biology including physiology. Here Kamerling (1912) carried out some of the early measurements of orchid transpiration. Five species were grown on two-decimeter-square boards, which allowed entire plants to be suspended beneath shelter from rain but otherwise exposed to ambient conditions similar to their native habitat. Weight loss was followed during periods without water ranging from seven days to three months. Results were given as absolute weight loss or as percent fresh weight of the plant. Species studied included the sympodial orchids (with pseudobulbs): *Dendrobium secundum, D. crumenatum, D. pandaneti, Eria ornata*, and the monopodial *Aerides virens, Rhynchostylis retusa* and *Phalaenopsis amabilis*. Rates of water loss expressed as percent fresh weight per day (% F.W. day $^{-1}$) have been plotted from Kamerling's data (Figure 3-1E) and total weight loss after three months is shown in Table 3-6.

Three months of drought was rather longer than the plants would normally experience. Kamerling's rainfall data for northern Java show a dry season of about six months, but only in one year of the four recorded was there a calendar month with no rain at all. All the orchids survived, but some were in better condition than others. Kamerling points out that in determining the drought tolerance of species, three factors should be considered:

1. The normal rate of transpiration at the start of experiments.
2. The control of transpiration.
3. The water reserves of the plant.

On this basis *Dendrobium secundum* showed the greatest tolerance, with a relatively low initial transpiration rate, but rapid restriction of water loss, leading to the smallest percentage weight loss at the end of the experiment. At the other extreme was *Dendrobium pandaneti* with very rapid initial transpiration leading to exhaustion of water reserves, shedding of nearly all leaves and a very low final transpiration rate. Although the plants survived, they took several years to recover fully. *Dendrobium crumenatum* and *Eria ornata*, although losing over 60% of initial fresh weight, nevertheless appeared healthy and even flowered toward the end of the drought period. Total water contents of the plants were not measured, but were estimated to be about 50% of original weight for *Dendrobium pandaneti,* 80% for *Dendrobium crumenatum,* 75% for *Eria ornata* and 55–60% for *Rhynchostylis retusa.*

Walter (1971) obtained some transpiration data at a Biological Research Station at Amani, in the Usambara Mountains, East Africa, in 1934, using the same method as Kamerling. Rates of water loss have been calculated from the published graph and expressed in the same units in Table 3-6. The *Bulbophyllum* lost weight at a steady rate for 9 days. Lacking pseudobulbs, each of the other three species had initially much higher rates, but these declined to much lower levels after 9 days. After that time all plants had lost between 20% and 25% of their original weight, a more rapid loss than most of the Javanese orchids. The African orchids began to show signs of damage after 10–12 days, but in their native habitat they were wetted almost daily and would not normally experience even this short drought. It was found that if aerial roots were dipped in water for an hour, the plant could gain about 15% of its fresh weight: i.e. several days' water loss was rapidly replaced.

Schimper (1935) quotes figues measured by Haberlandt at Bogor during the rainy season, for individual leaves of a number of species, including one orchid, *Grammatophyllum speciosum* (Table 3-7). The original data were in grams $dm^{-2}.day^{-1}$, and an estimate of the hourly rate has been inserted in the table for comparison with other values. There was a wide range, the average of 17 species being 1.14 ± 0.81 g $dm^{-2}.day^{-1}$, while the orchid was 0.89 g $dm^{-2}.day^{-1}$, or below the mean. All measurements were in shade, and were much lower than those for tree species measured in Holland, though the conditions under which the latter measurements were made were not stated.

Richards (1957) quotes some further measurements made at Bogor by Stocker (1935) on three trees and three herbs, using the leaf weighing technique. No orchids were measured, but the data are useful for comparison. The maximum rate for the trees was 1–1.3 g $dm^{-2}.hr^{-1}$ (recalculated in compatible units), for herbs 0.2 g $dm^{-2}.hr^{-1}$. Hence transpiration of trees was an order of magnitude higher than that for the orchid measured by Haberlandt, and even the rates for shade herbs were higher.

Gessner (1956) found a wide range of transpiration rates for epiphytes under "optimum conditions for evaporation"; the one orchid in the list, *Cymbidium bicolor,* had the lowest rate (Table 3-7). Gessner emphasizes, as did Kamerling, that the capacity to restrict transpiration when water is not available is more important for epiphytes than the rate of water loss under well watered conditions. Some data are given of weight loss as percent fresh weight, for cut leaves from plants grown in a Münich glasshouse, hung in 40% relative humidity at 18°C for 6 days. Epiphytes lost water as slowly as succulents and much more slowly than mesophytes and hydrophytes. The orchid *Coelogyne hüttneriana,* after an initial steep drop, averaged 3.3% F.W. day^{-1} (Table 3-6).

Johansson (1974) measured transpiration by the leaf weighing method for 41 West African epiphytes, including 28 orchids. This work was part of a study of epiphytes in the Nimba region of northern Liberia, an area with a pronounced monsoonal climate, and a 4–5 month dry season (Table 3-7). Measurements were made at a vapor pressure deficit of 20–25 mb, in daylight between 1400–1600 hr. The weight loss was measured over only the first three minutes, and rates in % F.W. $hr.^{-1}$ calculated from these initial rates. This may explain why some of Johansson's rates are much higher than those of Kamerling or Walter. As Johansson points out, the leaf weighing method has many shortcomings, but may be useful for comparing a number of species under the same conditions. Of the species he examined, three had very high water loss rates, more than 10% F.W. hr^{-1}. Of these three *Polystachya dalzielli,* with the highest rate, grows in the highest cool mist-swept parts of the mountains, *Polystachya puberula* also occurs in humid habitats with thin leaves and no obvious adaptations to withstanding desiccation. The high rate for *Graphorchis lurida* was surprising, as this species occurs in very exposed habitats, but it was suggested that its unusual root system growth, with a dense mat of upward growing, thin-walled aerial roots, may contribute to its water economy by trapping condensing dew during the night. However, no evidence was given for this.

Three orchids, *Polystachya leonensis, Brachycorythis kalbreyeri* and *Ancistrochilus rothschildianus* were among the group with rates of 5–10% F.W. hr^{-1}. These all come from moist habitats.

The species with the lowest rates, below 1% F.W. hr^{-1}, were all orchids, and many of these were monopodial, with tough leaves which are retained on the plant during the dry season.

Sanford (1978) determined water loss from two W. African species by the cut-leaf weighing method, but in this case leaves were suspended in the laboratory, in diffuse light, at 22–23.6°C, 64–85% R.H. for periods of 38–48 days (Table 3-6). Two forms of *Calyptrochilum christyanum* and one of *Calyptrochilum emarginatum* were tested. *Calyptrochilum* is the most widespread genus of epiphytic orchids in W. Africa, with evidently a wide range of tolerance and the capacity to withstand the 3–6 month dry season. The long narrow leaf form of *Calyptrochilum christyanum* occurs in the wetter parts of its range. All leaves showed initial rapid weight loss, with diurnal fluctuations indicating stomatal activity. Then followed a decline in rate of loss such that leaves were not showing permanent damage at the end of the drought period. Final % weight losses were not significantly different between the three taxa, but the *Calyptrochilum christyanum* from wetter sites had a significantly more rapid rate of initial weight loss. Unfortunately data were presented graphically in such a way that initial rates cannot be calculated.

Hsiang (1951) measured transpiration from individual cut flowers of *Cattleya labiata.* Both pollination and auxin treatment stimulated transpiration over an 11 day period, and as no stomata were found on the perianth epidermis, the rates of water loss represented purely cuticular transpiration. Interestingly, these rates are similar to the lowest rates measured by Johansson, but the conditions of the experiment were not recorded.

Hew, Lee and Wong (1980) studied the morphology and physiology of stomata of several orchid flowers. Among other measurements they recorded transpiration of flowers and leaves under a range of conditions. Differential thermistor psychrometers were used in an open gas system, with regulated humidity, temperature and light intensity. Their transpiration data are summarized in Table 3-7, converted to units consistent with earlier measurements. Conditions were 28°C, 55–65% R.H. and light intensity $1.4 \times 10^2 \mu$E m^{-2}s^{-1}, except for *Dendrobium bigibbum* where a range of conditions was used. The flowers had stomata, unlike those of Hsiang, but flower transpiration rates did not differ from light to darkness, and both were comparable to leaf rates when the stomata were closed. The *Oncidium* was thin-leaved hence a C$_3$ plant, whereas the *Vanda* had thick leaves, hence was a CAM plant and opened its stomata in the dark (see below). Flowers of *Dendrobium bigibbum* were exposed to a range of light intensities, water vapor deficits, CO$_2$ concentrations and ABA concentrations, none of which had a significant effect on transpiration. The stomata in these flowers appeared to be completely non-functional.

The total surface area of many small orchids must increase significantly when they flower, so if the flowers were to transpire at the same rate as the leaves, this could greatly increase the drain on stored water. However, the above reports suggest that flower transpiration is cuticular and hence low, though not negligible. It would be interesting to see more extensive surveys of floral transpiration.

From the limited data available it can be concluded that epiphytic orchids usually transpire slowly, possibly much more slowly than the trees on which they grow. Some which inhabit cool, moist sites may transpire rapidly when water is freely available and respond to the onset of drought by shedding leaves. Others restrict water loss rapidly as soon as water availability begins to decline, and may persist for very long periods, losing water very slowly. Still others appear to have low daily transpiration rates at all times.

The most important plant characteristic affecting transpiration is stomatal behavior. Most of the early studies do not mention this, and until the development of modern diffusion porometers the study of stomatal movement was often laborious and difficult, especially in the field. It is now known, however, that a large number of epiphytic orchids share with Cactaceae and other succulents the carbon fixation pathway Crassulacean Acid Metabolism (CAM), which is highly effective in conserving water. This will be reviewed briefly in the next section.

Crassulacean Acid Metabolism in Orchids

CAM occurs widely in the Orchidaceae and has been recorded in 69 species or cultivars compared with 33 which show C_3 photosynthesis or at least no evidence of CAM. (Avadhani et al., 1982). In a survey of Australian vascular epiphytes and related species Winter et al. (1983) found 53 species of orchids showing evidence of CAM, while 41 did not. All C_3 orchids have thin leaves. Those showing CAM have thick leaves, usually greater than 0.9 mm. (Neales and Hew, 1975; Wong and Hew, 1973, 1975; McWilliams, 1970; Ando, 1982), although no evidence of CAM was found in a thick-leaved *Paphiopedilum parishii* (Donovan et al, 1984). Other characters of CAM orchids include cell succulence, diurnal fluctuations in titratable acidity and malic acid content, ratio of ^{13}C to ^{12}C similar to C_4 plants rather than C_3, and a reversed diurnal stomatal rhythm, with stomata open at night and closed during the day (Avadhani et al, 1982; Arditti, 1979).

It is this reversal of the normal stomatal rhythm which enables CAM plants to be drought tolerant. CO_2 diffuses into the leaves and is fixed into organic acids during the night, when temperatures are low and humidity high, hence minimizing the loss of water by transpiration. Stomata may be closed for much if not all of the day, greatly restricting water loss during the time when the vapor pressure gradient from internal tissues of leaves to the outside air is greatest. Photosynthesis proceeds via the normal Calvin-Benson pathway (Bidwell, 1979), using CO_2 released internally by the breakdown of organic acids stored during the night. For the process to be effective in conserving water, the leaf must have a very high diffusive resistance when stomata are closed. Avadhani et al. (1982) listed data showing that cuticle thickness for a number of thick-leaf CAM orchids is much greater than for thin-leaf C_3 species.

A few reports have been published of the performance of CAM orchids under water stress. Fu and Hew (1982) imposed short-term water stress, up to 9 days, on seedlings and adults of *Aranda* 'Christine 9' and *Dendrobium taurinium*, by watering plants with polyethylene glycol at an osmotic potential of -18 bars. The diurnal fluctuation of titratable acidity in leaves was reduced, the peak declining by about 50%. Relative water content of leaves also dropped significantly. After the stress was removed, relative water content recovered within 3 days but acidity cycling was slower to respond. Well watered plants began positive CO_2 uptake at 1500 hours, indicating that stomata opened by mid afternoon, a common pattern for CAM plants. By the third day day-time CO_2 uptake had ceased, and the night uptake rate progressively declined, with the peak shifting from 2200 hours to 0200 hours. Watering caused the original pattern to reestablish. Similar responses have been observed in CAM plants from other families (Ting, 1985).

Sinclair (1984) found the typical CAM pattern of fluctuating leaf acidity and nocturnal stomatal opening in *Dendrobium tortile, Dendrobium crumenatum* and *Eria velutina*. The plants were subjected to drought for 3 weeks by withholding water. The amplitude of the leaf acidity cycle remained about the same for *Eria velutina* and *Dendrobium tortile*, but declined by about 50% in *Dendrobium crumenatum*. In each case the stomatal behavior changed. Under maximum hydration, *Eria velutina* stomata remained open during both the day and night. The other species showed maximum stomatal aperture soon after dawn, with a steady decline during the morning, followed by an opening movement beginning about sunset (*Dendrobium crumenatum*) or later in the evening (*Dendrobium tortile*). As water stress developed, the maximum stomatal aperture decreased and the extent of the daytime closure increased until there was virtually no stomatal opening by day. The night-time opening, though much reduced, was not eliminated completely as has been reported for *Opuntia basilaris* (Cactaceae; Szarek and Ting, 1977). This progressive restriction of stomatal opening was very effective in controlling water loss. Over the drought period leaf water potential fell by between 4 and 7.3 bars in the orchids. Relative water content decreased to between 65% and 80%. By comparison the epiphytic fern *Pyrrosia angustata* (Polypodiaceae) given the same treatment, suffered a decline in water potential of 11.8 bars and in relative water content to 40% after only 8 days (Sinclair, 1983b).

Clearly the CAM mode of photosynthesis allows considerable flexibility in the response of stomata to stress. Under conditions of abundant water stomata may be open for much of the day as well as the night, allowing a long period for gas exchange. As water stress develops, the length of time they are open is progressively shortened. Also, the time of opening is steadily restricted to the night hours when water loss by transpiration is minimal. Cockburn et al. (1979) showed that stomata of CAM plants respond to the internal concentration CO_2 in the leaf, as is true for plants generally (Kramer, 1983). Daytime closure is due to internal CO_2 release from breakdown of malate prior to photosynthetic fixation. Opening commences as the CO_2 level falls late in the day. However, under severe water stress this opening response is overridden.

The interaction between CAM activity, internal CO_2 concentration and stomatal aperture was used as a convenient explanation for the behavior of stomata in young leaves of the hybrid, *Arachnis* 'Maggie Oei' (Goh et al, 1984). Both young and old leaves showed fluctuating diurnal acidity rhythms, but the amplitude in the young leaves was only half that of mature ones. Stomata in young leaves opened from late morning to about 3 p.m. but stayed closed throughout the night. Those of mature leaves had a typical CAM rhythm, opening gradually in the afternoon, remaining open all night and closing about 8 a.m. Mature leaves showed a large net influx of CO_2 by night, and a small gain during the day. Clearly CAM activity was not fully developed in the young leaves. Stomatal behavior may have been a result of the fact that during the night internal CO_2 concentration was not reduced enough for stomata to open. By day, C_3 photosynthesis could reduce it sufficiently to allow normal opening. Some acid was fixed in the dark but not enough for its breakdown to outrun photosynthesis, as occurs in nature CAM leaves.

As indicated above CAM, though widely distributed among the orchids, is by no means universal. Both pathways may be found in different species within the same genus, e.g. *Dendrobium, Bulbophyllum, Cymbidium, Coelogyne, Vanda.* Ando (1982) found that 30 "nobile-type" *Dendrobium* cultivars showed C_3 photosynthesis while 28 "phalaenopsis-cane-type" *Dendrobium* varieties showed CAM. This may have some significance for the organization of orchids in glasshouses for commercial cultivation. However, the ecological significance is that broadly, CAM has evolved in species that have adapted to very dry sites. This will be discussed in more detail below.

Although CAM activity has most frequently been demonstrated in orchid leaves, other organs have occasionally been studied also. Goh (1983) measured fluctuations in acidity typical of CAM in the flowers of five orchid hybrids shown to have this pathway in their leaves. The flowers of a C_3 species showed no such fluctuations. However, the amplitude of acid fluctuations in flowers was much lower than that of the leaves. There was actually a net release of CO_2 from the flowers both by night and by day, despite a demonstrated fixation of $^{14}CO_2$ in darkness as well as light. Although stomatal resistance was not measured the data suggested that the flowers had stomata which remained partly open continuously, allowing some CO_2 exchange (and hence, water vapor loss) both day and night. Hew et al. (1980; Table 3-7) concluded that transpiration rates of flowers were cuticular and that their stomata were non-functional. Their data could also be explained by partly open, but immobile stomata. In either case, gas exchange between flowers and the atmosphere is low and not under diurnal stomatal control.

Aerial roots of epiphytic orchids have also been tested for CAM activity. Hew et al. (1984) examined the hybrids *Arachnis* 'Maggie Oei' and *Aranthera* 'James Storie'. Titratable acidity fluctuated in aerial roots in typical CAM fashion though the amplitude was lower than in leaves. No variation was found in terrestrial roots. ^{14}C fixation was demonstrated both in the light and dark, the rate being four times greater under illumination. Net exchange of CO_2 was negative in the dark, and close to zero in the light. Consequently there was a net loss of CO_2 from the roots over 24 hours. The roots clearly showed CAM activity, but not sufficient for a net carbon gain. The photosynthetic activity would have recycled a significant part of the CO_2 produced by root respiration and hence reduced the drain by the root system on leaf photosynthesis, but the measured rates of CO_2 exchange also demonstrated that there was a significant diffusion pathway for water vapor loss from these roots to the atmosphere.

Very similar results were reported for *Arachnis* 'Maggie Oei' and *Aranda* 'Deborah' by Goh et al. (1983). The aerial roots fix some carbon but not enough to be completely autotrophic.

The details of gas exchange from roots become most interesting in the case of the extraordinary leafless orchids, in which leaves are almost completely absent and all photosynthesis takes place in the aerial roots. The water relations puzzles posed by these plants are the subject of a later section.

Epiphyte Distribution Patterns

European interest in the conditions under which epiphytic orchids grow in the wild developed during the nineteenth century with a great upsurge of enthusiasm for growing such exotic plants in glasshouses. Many of these efforts were highly unsuccessful. Large consignments of orchids were collected in tropical Africa or America and shipped to Europe at great expense, only to die in hothouses due to ignorance of the necessary conditions for successful growth. An early paper by Lindley (1835) on the distribution of orchids in relation to climatic conditions, was written specifically with this problem in mind. Lindley surveyed the climatic conditions in numerous areas where orchids grow prolifically, and pointed out to horticulturists that successful cultivation of tropical epiphytes requires not only heat but also high humidity.

As ecological studies progressed in the twentieth century, the distribution of epiphytes in relation to the availability of water became a recurring theme. However, epiphytes as a group are very difficult to study *in situ*. So many of the diverse populations occur in relatively remote areas and so many of the orchids in particular grow high in the canopies of tall forest trees. It is not surprising that ecological studies of orchid epiphytes are not numerous.

Relatively broad-scale descriptions of regional distribution patterns have been published for several areas in the humid tropics. In Africa, Lebrun (1937) worked in the Belgian Congo, now Zaire, Sanford (1967; 1969) in Southern Nigeria, Morris (1968; 1970) in Malawi, Piers (1968) in East Africa and Stewart and Campbell (1970) in East and Central Africa. Studies in the Himalayas were reported by Vij et al. (1983) and Mehra and Vij (1974). In the New World tropics, Dunn (1941) described the habitats of orchids of Panama, Curtis (1947) worked in Haiti and Sugden and Robins (1979) in Colombia. Southeast Asian studies on orchid distribution include work by Schlechter early this century in what was then German New Guinea, and is now Papua New Guinea (published in translation 1982), Holttum (1960) largely in the Malay peninsula, and in the Philippines Valmayor and Baldovino (1984). Hosokawa (1943) studied the epiphyte flora of Micronesia.

On a smaller scale, the distrubition of epiphytes and epiphyte communities on single trees was reported in detail in the classic paper by Went (1940) on the Cibodas forest near Bogor, Indonesia. Most observations were made by telescope or binoculars. A more recent wide-ranging study of orchid ecology was carried out by Johansson (1974) in the Nimba Mountains, Northern Liberia.

From studies such as these, the most important environmental variables controlling orchid distribution patterns are found to be light, temperature, the nature of the host plant and the availability of water and nutrients, (Sanford, 1974; Pridgeon, 1987).

As Sanford and Pridgeon point out, water may occur in four forms:

1. Liquid films on plant and substrate surfaces.
2. Fine droplets in the air (mist, cloud).
3. Fine droplets condensed on surfaces (dew).
4. Water vapor in the air.

The debate about absorption of water vapor by leaves or roots has been mentioned above. The general consensus, on both empirical and theoretical grounds, is that water vapor is not likely to be a significant source of water for plants under most conditions. Dew forms from saturated air only on surfaces that are cooler than the surrounding air.

This may occur at night for leaves of plants in open clearings or in the outer tree canopy, but night temperatures inside a forest are usually too uniform for significant dew to form (Sanford, 1974). Hence the main influence of high humidity is to slow down transpiration and thereby delay the onset of water stress.

Airborne water droplets however do usually condense and form water films on plant surfaces, fog drip from leaves etc. Uptake of water from this source is possible, and can be especially rapid through plant surfaces which are (1) not waterproof, such as the leaves of bryophytes or filmy ferns, or (2) adapted for water uptake, like the velamen-covered aerial roots of orchids.

The climatic requirements for epiphytes may be quite different from those of terrestrial plants. For example, a foggy climate with little precipitation may supply very little moisture to terrestrial plants relying on soil water recharge. On the other hand epiphytes may be supplied quite adequately by water films maintained by condensing fog. Conversely high rainfall, if it occurs as heavy showers interspersed with long dry spells, may support luxuriant terrestrial vegetation but few epiphytes.

Grubb and Whitmore (1966) carried out a detailed study of climate and microclimate at two sites in Ecuador, one in Lowland Rainforest at 380 m, the second on the slopes of the Andes at 1710 m, in Lower Montane Rainforest. The dominant feature of the Montane site was the frequent occurrence of fog-bound days, when temperature and light intensity were reduced, and vegetation wetted continually by condensation. Fog-free days were rather similar to typical lowland days, where fog never occurred. The montane area had much more abundant bryophytes, lichens, filmy ferns and shade-tolerant vascular epiphytes than the lowland site, whereas there was only a small difference in numbers of vascular shade-intolerant epiphytes in the two forests. They stressed that the montane site was more favorable for epiphytes both because conditions favoring water loss are decreased and because opportunities for water uptake are increased. They claimed the latter point had received too little emphasis in the literature. Although high humidity does reduce transpiration, periods of desiccation do occur, and it is the regular re-wetting of foliage by the liquid water films from condensation of fog that provides the vital water supply for many epiphytes, particularly among the lower plant groups. Among groups such as the orchids with thick cuticle and other xeromorphic features, the absorption of water from these liquid films may be less important.

However a relationship between orchids and mist or cloud is found repeatedly in the regional studies referred to above. Curtis (1947) found by far the greatest number of orchids and orchid species in the cloud forests of Haiti between 2,500–8,000 ft. (760–2,400 m) where constant clouds borne in by the prevailing winds kept the canopy wet throughout the year. Mehra and Vij (1974) and Vij. et al. (1983) found the largest numbers of orchid species in the altitude range 750 to 1,500 m.

Schlechter (1982) in New Guinea, and Valmayor and Baldovino (1984) in the Philippines become quite lyrical about the profusion of orchid genera and species in the mossy mist forests above about 1,000 m, where temperatures are cool, humidity high, light intensity low and mist almost continuous. Morris (1968) also reported the greatest proliferation of species and numbers in the "mist zone" between 4,500 and 5,000 ft. (1,400–1,500 m). Interestingly, in this region of Malawi, the vegetation type in the mist zone was not Montane rainforest but savannah. Sanford (1967) discussed the influence of land form and topography on microclimate, and hence orchid distribution in Nigeria. He noted that during the dry season morning mists occurred very regularly in certain areas, and sharp changes in the density of epiphytic orchids correlated with these areas to the extent that "it would be possible to determine orchid population density by charting the mist patterns at dawn during the dry season." Such smallscale variations in micro-climate are masked in regional data, and may be difficult to detect. In fact, Sanford (1969) suggested that it may often be possible to deduce features of the local micro-climate such as length of dry seasons, degree of humidity, and frequency of condensation during the night and early morning from the distribution of epiphytic orchids.

Sanford, (1968) reported a quantitative study of orchid species diversity in relation to gradients of moisture availability in Southern Nigeria, using counts of plants from felled trees in logging areas plus binocular surveys of nearby standing trees. Species diversity did decrease from the area with most favorable moisture regime to the driest site. There were also changes in the distribution patterns of closely related species. These occurred together most frequently in the moister sites, but rarely did so in the driest.

Another common observation (Holttum, 1960; Johansson, 1974) is that epiphytic orchids may grow profusely in riverine forest, even though further away from the stream, the forest may be relatively dry and support few epiphytes. Schlechter (1982) described such stream-side forests in New Guinea as a "real El Dorado for orchid hunters." Piers, (1968) observed similar conditions in East Africa. Rivers allow a break in the canopy which lets more light down to lower levels, and creates a microclimate of high and constant humidity. This humidity, while unlikely to contribute significantly to water uptake by orchids, may reduce transpiration enough to allow many more species to thrive than in the drier, adjacent forest. The effect may be quite localized. In Tanzania, Johansson (1974) recorded that 60% of the trees in riparian forest had epiphytes, compared with only 8.3% of those in wooded grassland 50 m away from the river bank.

The characteristics and age of the host tree affect epiphyte distribution, and water may be one of the important factors here also. Few if any epiphytes are confined to a single host species, but some trees regularly carry a much heavier epiphyte load than others. A widespread generalization is that trees with rough bark, and older trees carry the most epiphytes (Went, 1940; Eggeling, 1947; Johansson, 1974; Vij et al., 1983). Sanford (1974) discusses the epiphyte-host relationship and states that it tends to become more specific near the edge of the range of an orchid. In very moist areas orchids may grow almost anywhere, whereas in drier areas they are confined to rough-barked trees (see also Vij et al., 1983). The greater moisture-holding capacity of rough bark seems an obvious reason for this preference, but few quantitative measurements appear to have been made (Johansson, 1974). The increase in epiphytes with tree age may simply be a result of the time it takes for them to become established, or for tree limbs to grow to suitable positions in the forest canopy, but it may also be due to increasing roughness in the bark of older trees.

Environmental variation may occur on many scales. As well as the regional or local variations discussed above, there may be large differences in microclimate between the base and the canopy of a single tree. Significant gradients may occur within the canopy itself, e.g. between upper and lower surfaces of branches. Mehra and Vij (1974) distinguished four categories of epiphytic orchid in their Eastern Himalayan study region:

1. Foot epiphytes, growing at the base of trees, protected from sharply fluctuating conditions, with high humidity and low light.
2. Branch epiphytes, growing on branches but protected by outer canopy from long direct exposure.

3. Tree-top epiphytes exposed to most extreme conditions. Only a few species occurred here, and all were deciduous in the dry season.
4. Moss-forest epiphytes, growing in the dense bryophyte mats of stunted vegetation on exposed ridge-tops.

Johansson, (1974) used a five zone scheme to describe epiphyte distribution on a single tree:

1. Trunk base
2. Trunk up to first branch
3. Basal
4. Middle and
5. Outer branch zone of the canopy.

In general each zone was characterized by a particular group or groups of epiphytes, in response to a complex of environmental gradients. Any one species may have quite narrow limits of tolerance for a number of microclimatic variables. Johansson proposed a theoretical model of the distribution patterns across the three canopy zones (where most orchids occurred) in terms of increasing and decreasing gradients. Factors increasing toward the outer canopy included temperature, light intensity and wind velocity. Decreasing factors were roughness of substrate, humus deposits, nutrient content of substrate, moisture in substrate and air humidity. Among the species recorded in the trees studied six different distribution patterns were identified which were related to these hypothetical gradients. This approach appears potentially very productive, and emphasizes the need to take account of a complex of interacting factors, not simply a single one such as humidity or evaporating power of the air. To carry such studies further, microclimatic measurements are needed in the canopy to relate directly to the distribution patterns observed. Clearly this poses even more formidable logistic and instrumental problems than the quantitative observation and measurement of the epiphytes themselves, itself a most difficult task.

Although detailed micrometeorological studies have not been published, some physiological measurements on the orchids themselves have been related to variations in habitat. Reference has already been made to the osmotic potential measurements of Harris (1918; 1934). Cell sap was found to be more concentrated in orchids from drier sites. Sanford and Adanlawo (1973) found a correlation between dryness of habitat and number of velamen layers in the aerial roots of West African orchids. Johansson (1974) measured transpiration from detached leaves under constant conditions and found a reasonable correlation between rate of water loss and habitat, with many of the high transpiration rates occurring in species from cool, mist-swept sites. Three of the highest rates did occur in plants from seasonally dry habitats. However, these three are all deciduous during the dry season. Sanford (1978) did a similar study on *Calyprochilum emarginatum* and two forms of *Calyprochilum christyanum* in West Africa, and found the most rapid rate of water loss from the plants from more mesic sites.

Benzing et al. (1982) measured transpiration and photosynthesis of *Catasetum integerrimum* and *Encyclia tampensis* which may occur on the same host tree in Florida. The first is a humus epiphyte, with C_3 photosynthesis, rapid transpiration and deciduous leaves. The root system also dies back each dry season but persists to anchor the plant and accumulate humus. This plant is a drought avoider. *Encyclia tampensis* on the other hand which grows on small exposed twigs, is a CAM plant with low transpiration rate.

The fact that two such different epiphytes may be found on the same host shows that very steep gradients in micro-climate should be expected within the canopy of host trees. Identifying the water use requirements of species might allow the mapping of tree crowns into zones of water availability, as suggested on a larger scale by Sanford, and this in turn could lead to further study of the factors creating the zones.

Mapping of this nature was attempted by Winter et al. (1983) as part of their survey of a wide range of Australian epiphytes, for crassulacean acid metabolism. A clear relationship between habitat and CAM emerged. All six terrestrial orchids examined were C_3 plants; of the lithophytes, the two CAM species occurred on exposed rocks, the others in well-shaded localities. Of the epiphytes 62% from relatively open forest areas showed CAM, while only 24% of species from wet lowland and montane rainforests were CAM plants. Four species occurred in both vegetation types, and showed more strongly developed symptoms of CAM at the drier sites. The distribution of CAM among the epiphytes of a single tree is shown in Figure 3-3 which demonstrates the increasing frequency of the adaptation toward the more exposed outer branches of the upper canopy. This gradient is similar in general to the environmental gradient proposed by Johansson for the upper canopy.

Despite the difficulties of access, there is scope for a great deal of fascinating environmental physiology in further exploring these relationships between microhabitat and a range of physiological adaptations in the complex mosaic of the epiphyte habitats of the upper rainforest and montane forest canopy.

Special Cases

Paphiopedilum—Guard Cells without Chloroplasts

The genus *Paphiopedilum* has aroused great interest among plant physiologists since it was discovered (Nelson and Mayo, 1975) that its stomata are almost unique in the plant kingdom, in that the guard cells lack chlorophyll. Nine species have now been examined (Rutter and Willmer, 1979; Zeiger et al., 1985): *P. acmodontum, P. aureum hyeanum, P. barbatum, P. ballosum, P. harrisianum, P. insigne, P. leeanum, P. philippinense* and *P. venustrum*, using fluorescence microscopy, and in all cases no chloroplasts were found in the guard cells. Unusual colorless, spindle-shaped plastids were present, also prominent oil droplets and abundant mitochondria.

Nevertheless the stomata are functional. Nelson and Mayo found that the stomata opened rapidly in light, with a sensitivity to quite low intensities and a greater response to blue than to red light. High CO_2 concentration caused closure in light of either color.

This discovery was of great interest to physiologists as it demonstrated that guard cell chlorophyll was not essential for stomatal functioning, not even for the CO_2 independent bluelight opening response. A number of other aspects of stomatal physiology have since been investigated in *Paphiopedilum* which has become a useful genus for testing hypotheses about the complex interacting processes of stomatal control.

In all other species examined, potassium ion uptake into guard cells accompanies stomatal opening (Willmer, 1983). This a major generator of the decreasing osmotic potential that causes the swelling of the guard cells. However, in *Paphiopedilum* Nelson

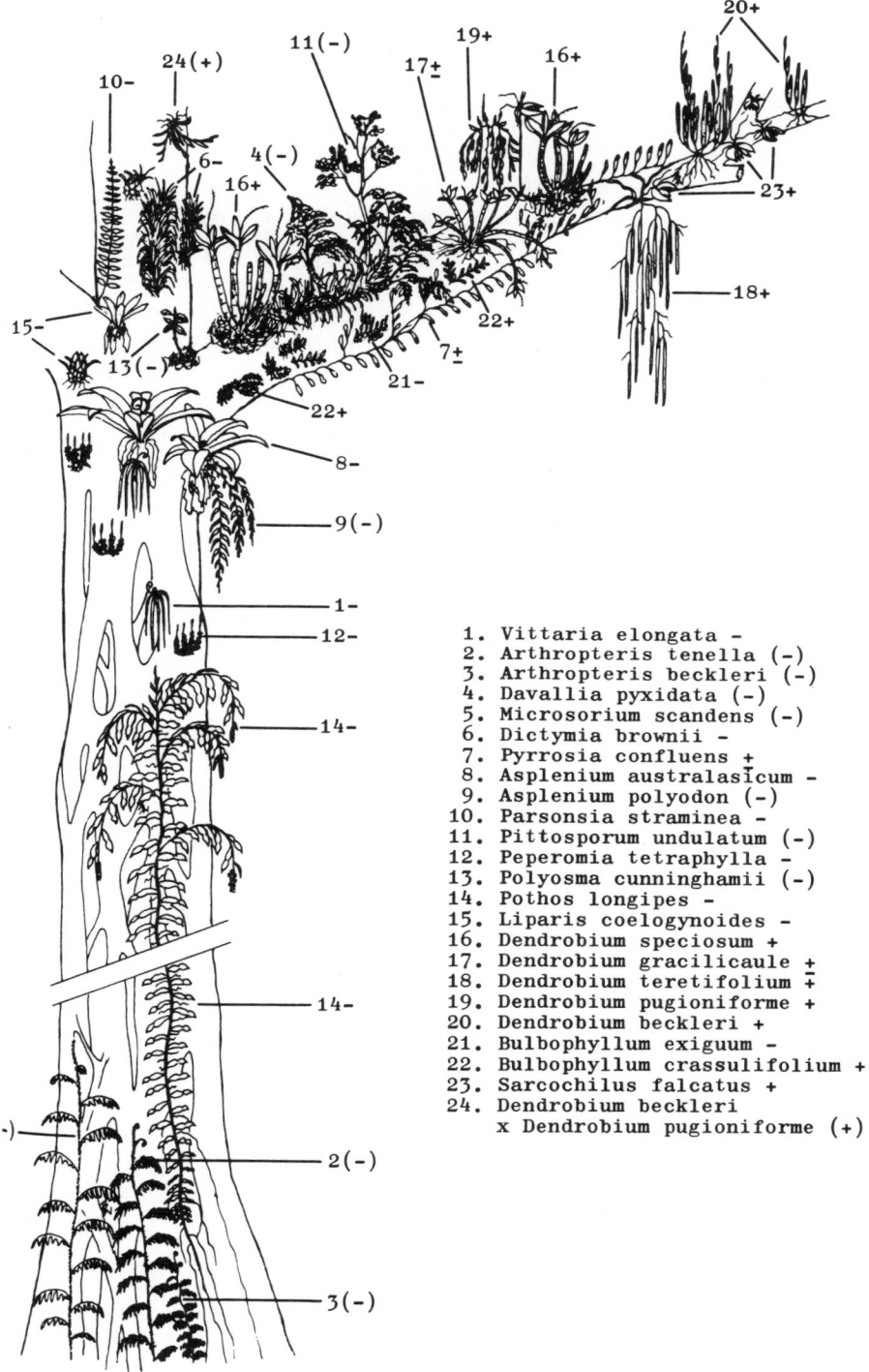

1. Vittaria elongata -
2. Arthropteris tenella (-)
3. Arthropteris beckleri (-)
4. Davallia pyxidata (-)
5. Microsorium scandens (-)
6. Dictymia brownii -
7. Pyrrosia confluens +
8. Asplenium australasicum -
9. Asplenium polyodon (-)
10. Parsonsia straminea -
11. Pittosporum undulatum (-)
12. Peperomia tetraphylla -
13. Polyosma cunninghamii (-)
14. Pothos longipes -
15. Liparis coelogynoides -
16. Dendrobium speciosum +
17. Dendrobium gracilicaule ±
18. Dendrobium teretifolium ±
19. Dendrobium pugioniforme +
20. Dendrobium beckleri +
21. Bulbophyllum exiguum -
22. Bulbophyllum crassulifolium +
23. Sarcochilus falcatus +
24. Dendrobium beckleri
    x Dendrobium pugioniforme (+)

Fig. 3-3. Semischematic summary of distribution of epiphytes on a 40m emergent *Ficus watkinsiana* in Subtropical Rainforest, Dorrigo National Park, N.S.W. with respect to microhabitat zone and photosynthetic pathway. The +sign indicates pronounced CAM, the ±sign indicates weak CAM and the −sign indicates C_3 photosynthetic CO_2 fixation. Signs in parenthesis indicate suspected conditions on the basis of leaf succulence. From Winter *et al.* (1983).

and Mayo (1977) and Outlaw et al. (1982) could find no evidence for K^+ accumulation in guard cells on opening, though Schnabl and Raschke (1980) and Willmer (1983) claimed that this ion did accumulate. Nelson and Mayo found that K^+ appeared to be almost excluded from the entire epidermis. They suggested that this might be linked with the lack of guard cell chlorophyll, as potassium deficiency affects the pathway of chlorophyll synthesis.

Responses of the stomata to light were further investigated by Zeiger et al. (1983). They found an opening response in guard cells in isolated epidermal strips in blue but not red light. They suggested that earlier reports of a response to red light in intact leaves may have been an indirect effect due to a reduction of CO_2 concentration in leaf air spaces by mesophyll photosynthesis. The isolated guard cells did open somewhat wider in CO_2-free air, but with no significant light-CO_2 interaction. The response of the stomata to blue but not red light was confirmed by Zeiger et al. (1985).

Williams et al. (1983) measured gas exchange and stomatal conductance of intact *Paphiopedilum* plants under a range of white light and relative humidity conditions. They found that the stomata opened in response to light but that maximum conductance was low and rates of photosynthesis were also low, as is typical of shade plants. The stomata were quite sensitive to humidity and conductance declined rapidly as the air became drier. They concluded that *Paphiopedilum* has adapted to dim light, low nutrient habitats in which small stomatal aperture and low rates of photosynthesis are appropriate. Under these conditions, the lack of guard cell chloroplasts is not physiologically important. Guard cell chloroplasts are necessary to generate wide stomatal apertures and high conductances in bright light, but for the *Paphiopedilum* species in their natural habitats such high conductances are neither necessary nor desirable. Zeiger et al. (1985) reported that there is a range of guard cell chlorophyll concentrations in the Orchidaceae, with *Paphiopedilum* at one extreme adapted to slow growth rates and low stomatal conductance with no guard cell chlorophyll at all. Whether the lack of chlorpolasts is a positive advantage is not known, though it could possibly prevent high stomatal conductances under bright light when net photosynthesis is already saturated at low light levels.

These remarkable chloroplast-free stomata provide a most valuable experimental system for the study of guard-cell functioning. The mechanism of action of CO_2 on guard cells is still not understood (Assman and Zeiger, 1985). The weak response of *Paphiopedilum* stomata to CO_2 may aid the study of this aspect, as well as their ability to open without the benefit of the energy supply from photophosphorylation which normal chloroplasts might provide. The ecological significance of the unusual stomata would also repay further study.

Shootless Orchids

One of the bizarre adaptations of the family is to be found in the so-called shootless orchids. These epiphytic plants consist almost entirely of a root system arising from a very shortened stem which usually bears only tiny vestigial leaves, though in some species larger leaves may form briefly before the plant flowers. A few hundred species of shootless orchid are known, distributed among about a dozen genera of the sub-tribe Sarcanthinae (Benzing and Ott, 1981). They occur in tropical areas in the Americas, Asia and Africa (Rolfe, 1914; Teuscher, 1972).

The shootless orchids raise fascinating problems of water relations. In fact they raise in extreme form the problem posed by the aerial roots of the leafy epiphytes, namely how can water loss be regulated from an organ with no stomata? The roots of leafless species contain chlorophyll and it has long been known that they are the photosynthetic organs of the plants, i.e. that the plants are autotrophic rather than parasitic (Müller, 1885; Pfitzer, 1889). Early studies of *Taeniophyllum zollingeri* (Wiesner, 1897) showed that its roots grew extremely slowly, but the rate increased with light intensity up to about ⅛ full daylight. At higher intensities the rate declined, but no growth occurred in the absence of light.

As pointed out by Benzing et al. (1983), the roots of shootless orchids have three conflicting roles. They must:

1. absorb liquid water and nutrients when they are available.
2. minimize water vapor loss by transpiration.
3. carry out photosynthesis, hence allowing adequate gas exchange for this purpose.

As early as 1914, Rolfe suggested that the development of shootlessness was an extreme adaptation against drought. He postulated that it was an extension of the habit of shedding leaves during the dry season. As the deciduous character developed, persistent roots containing chlorophyll gradually took over the photosynthetic role entirely, leaf development being dispensed with. However, no evidence was given to support this sequence of events. Other authors have stated that although shootless orchids are found in the outer canopy they usually occur in relatively moist habitats such as along river banks, in swamp vegetation or in rather dense and therefore shady forest, or areas of high rainfall (Johansson, 1974; Benzing and Ott, 1981; Benzing et al., 1983). Teuscher (1972) in a discussion of the cultivation of leafless orchids, states also that they usually occur in sites such as upright stems free from moss, with high humidity but not very frequent wetting. They do not thrive in cultivation if watered too frequently but need high humidity.

If shootless orchids were adapted to extreme drought, their roots would be expected to be very resistant to water loss. This in turn would suggest a thick velamen layer. Sanford and Adanlawo (1973) showed that the number of cell layers in this tissue was positively correlated with the aridity of the habitat for leafy epiphytes, but the velamen of the leafless orchids is quite thin, typically two layers (Benzing and Ott, 1981).

Benzing et al. (1983) measured rates of desiccation of excised roots from ten orchids including four shootless species. There was a wide range of values, but the shootless species as a group were not significantly different from the leafy species.

Several recent studies of gas exchange of shootless orchids have been reported (Benzing and Ott, 1981; Benzing et al., 1983; Cockburn et al., 1985; Winter et al., 1985). All species examined showed typical CAM fluctuations in titratable acidity. This has also been found in the aerial roots of leafy orchids (see above). However, the roots of leafy orchids showed a net loss of carbon over a 24-hour period; although some carbon fixation did occur, it was not sufficient to balance the net loss of respiratory CO_2 from the roots.

If this were true for the roots of shootless species also they clearly could not survive as autotrophs, but in fact it was found that shootless species could maintain carbon gain in their roots over a 24-hour period. Winter et al. (1985) described the pattern of CO_2 exchange in *Campylocentrum tyrridion* as resembling in great detail that of classical CAM plants, despite the lack of stomata or any means of regulating gas exchange from the root.

Benzing et al. (1983) described a possible mechanism for regulating gas exchange in roots of *Harrisella porrecta* (Fig. 3-4A). Changes in the turgor of cortical cells as a root lost water might cause the closing together of cells adjacent to the aeration cells in the exodermis, restricting gas exchange and loss of water vapor. This would explain control of water loss from a root during periods of desiccation, but it could not provide the diurnal control of gas exchange which stomata give in a normal CAM plant. Furthermore, neither Cockburn et al. (1985) nor Winter et al. (1985) found any evidence for anatomical features which could regulate CO_2 or water fluxes in the shootless species they studied.

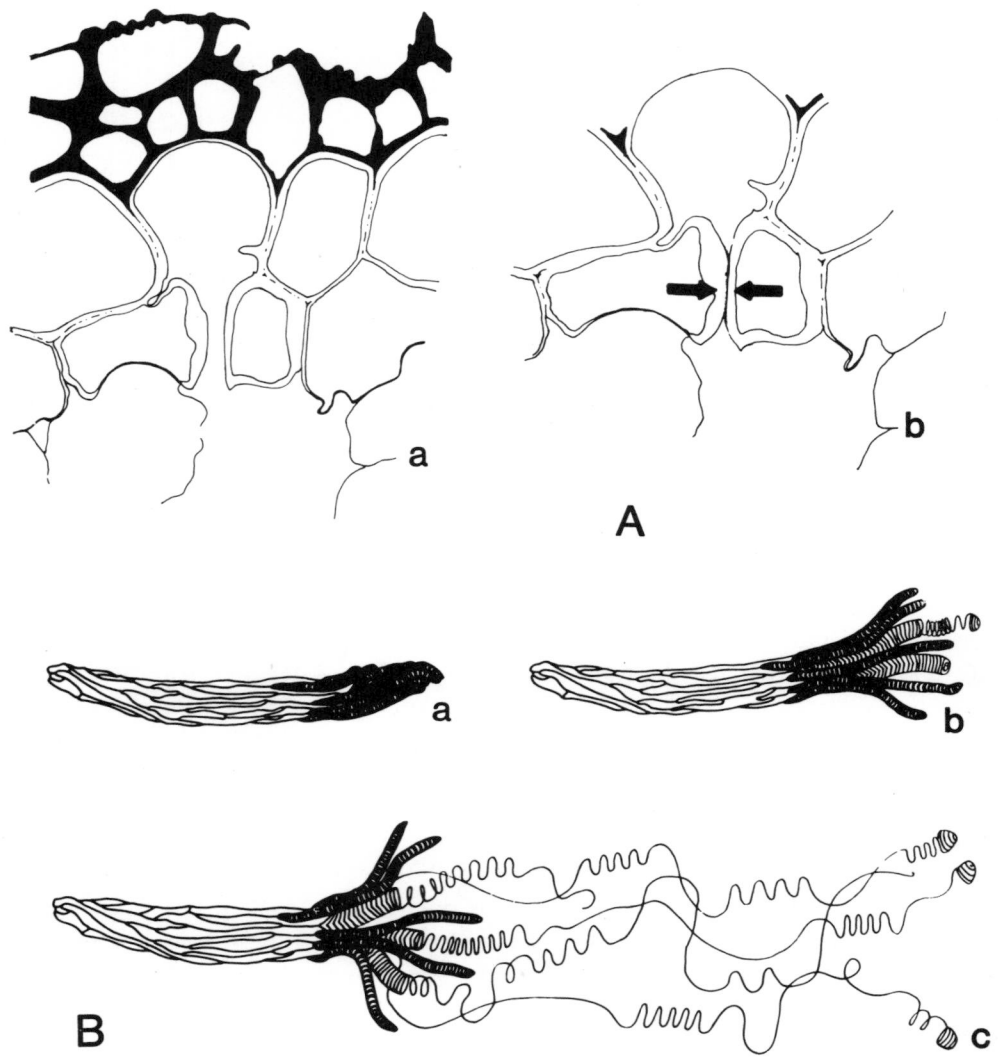

Fig. 3-4 **A.** A possible mechanism for the regulation of gas exchange in the root of *Harrisella porrecta*. Changes in the turgor of thickened cortical components beneath the aeration cell or shrinkage of the root core as a whole may effect movement in the direction indicated by arrows. a. turgid. b. flaccid. From Benzing et al. (1983). **B.** Seed of *Chiloschista lunifera*. (a) Dry seed, showing thick helical spiral thickening in the E-cells towards the micropylar end. (b) Ten seconds after contact with water. E-cells have begun to spread, and the fine helical threads of F-cells have begun to unravel. (c) After 15 minutes in water. E-cells have spread wider, F-cell threads have stretched up to 4 mm. From Barthlott and Ziegler (1980).

This lack of any analogue of stomatal control seems contrary to the whole concept of CAM as a water-conserving mechanism, and it raises two problems. How can a net positive carbon gain be achieved in the absence of stomatal control, and why is CAM operating if it is not a drought resistance mechanism? Three suggestions have been made which all depend on the root having a rather high resistance to diffusion of gases at all times.

Firstly, the dark fixation of CO_2 to malate is an efficient means of recapturing CO_2 released by respiration and so preventing loss by night.

Secondly during the day, Cockburn et al. (1985) estimated the internal CO_2 concentration to be close to atmospheric. If the release of CO_2 from malate was regulated in such a way that the concentration in the internal air spaces never rose above atmospheric then there would never be significant outward (or inward) diffusion during the day. The biochemical basis for such control is however not yet known.

Thirdly, both Benzing et al. (1983) and Winter et al. (1985) suggested that CAM prevents damage to the chloroplasts, by maintaining a high internal CO_2 concentration during the day. Without CAM, damage might occur if the resistance to inward diffusion allowed CO_2 levels to fall too low.

Essentially these roots harvest CO_2 slowly at night across a significant diffusion barrier. They prevent its loss across the same resistance by day by regulating deacidification in such a way that a significant concentration gradient never develops. CAM is therefore not directly related to water conservation in these species but is a carbon conserving mechanism. Cockburn et al. even suggested this should be given a distinct term "astomatal CAM" to distinguish it from the more usual situation.

A second suggestion for the reason shootlessness developed is that these plants are in fact partial parasites via mycorrhizal fungi, which provide both inorganic nutrients and some carbon from the living tissues of the host tree. Dressler (1981) and Ruinen (1953) discussed this idea for leafy orchids. Johansson (1977) gave some circumstantial evidence that the leafless species *Microcoelia exilis* does reduce the vigor of the shoots on which it grows, but alternative possible reasons for this type of host behavior were offered by Benzing (1979).

The third suggestion as to why shootlessness developed was argued in detail by Benzing (1979), Benzing and Ott (1981) and Benzing et al. (1983). They claimed that the habitats of extreme epiphytes are stressful both because of lack of nutrients and periodic drought, and also because of their patchiness in space and time. Consequently there is strong selection pressure favoring high efficiency in utilizing nutrients and in maximizing reproductive output. Reduction of leaf biomass in orchids allows the allocation of more resources to reproduction. A similar reduction occurred in the Bromeliaceae inhabiting the most exposed sites, but in that case it was roots which were reduced until in *Tillandsia* their function has been entirely taken over by leaves.

The Role of Water in Seed Germination

The habitat of epiphytic orchids is typically patchy, infertile and subject to considerable stress. It is also unpredictably disturbed, as bark is shed, tree branches fall carrying their load of epiphytes with them, or occasionally winds may break loose part or all of a community growing in the outer canopy (Benzing, 1986). In order to colonize such a habitat, there has been strong selection pressure toward production of large numbers of very small seed, and approximately 80% of epiphytes have wind-dispersed seed (Madison, 1977). It is well known that orchid seed is among the smallest of any Angiosperm family, so small that for a very long time the "dust" contained in fruit capsules was not recognized as seed at all (Arditti, 1967, 1979). Many terrestrial orchids also inhabit infertile and intermittently disturbed sites, such as acid bogs, porous or infertile soils (Benzing, 1981) and hence may be subject to similar selection pressures. The lightest seed recorded by Harper et al. (1970) was *Goodyera repens* at 0.2 µg.

The typical orchid seed consists of a small spherical embryo suspended within a membranous, often transparent testa made up of dead, empty cells which vary a great deal in shape and size. The membranous testa has a "balloon-like" effect (van der Pijl, 1982) and greatly increases the chances of the seed being dispersed by wind. The outer surface of the testa may feature intricate patterns of ridges and sculpturing, beautifully shown in scanning electron microscope photographs (Rauh et al., 1975; Arditti, 1979). This sculpturing makes the surface very resistant to wetting, so that the seed floats readily and may be carried long distances by flowing water. Arditti (1967) reported that 10–15 minutes of vigorous shaking was required to sink orchid seed. Burgeff (1936) studied seed wettability in great detail.

The very characteristics which make these tiny seeds so readily dispersed by wind and water, do appear to pose problems for the successful establishment of seedlings. Three questions may be posed:

1. How does the seed become attached or anchored to a suitable site?
2. How does water penetrate the highly repellent surface to initiate germination?
3. How does the very young seedling survive long enough to become established in a site subject to intermittent severe water stress?

Harper et al. (1970) give many examples of the subtle effects which such seed characteristics as hairs, hygroscopically flexing awns, surface shapes etc. have on the success rate of germination of seeds on different kinds of surface. They make the point that to be successful seeds not only must disperse effectively but also must land at a suitable site in such a way that germination can take place readily. No mention was made of orchids in this study of the seed as a landing device, but the ideas clearly apply to plants which colonize such difficult sites as tree branches. The water repellent seed coat would seem to pose a serious threat that seed, having reached a suitable site by wind dispersal, could be washed away again by the next rain.

One fascinating solution to this problem has been reported by Barthlott and Ziegler (1980) for *Chiloschista lunifera*, a leafless epiphyte occurring in Northern India, Burma, Thailand and Indonesia. The embryo is surrounded by a very light yet strong seed coat 0.6 mm long, with cells reinforced by spiral thickenings of two types near the micropylar end. One type of cell (the E-cell) has a particularly thick helical spiral, resembling tracheoid cells. The second type (F-cell) has thinner walls and very fine thread-like helical thickening [Fig. 3-4B(a)].

The seed is disseminated by wind in the usual way. When it lands on a wet surface, such as a water drop or water film it is initially unwettable, but the apical region is more hydrophobic than the basal, micropylar end. The seeds orient themselves obliquely on the water surface with only the helically thickened cells touching. Within a few seconds, the E-cells begin to spread and elongate [Fig. 3-4B(b)]. At the same time the F-cells rupture and the fine helical threads spread out over the water surface, reaching a length of up to 4 mm after 15–20 minutes. By this time the seeds have a long "comet-like" tail of threads [Fig. 3-4B(c)].

As the water film evaporates, the threads bind the seed tightly to the substrate. The binding is so effective that seeds will adhere firmly even to smooth glass surfaces and no extra mounting was necessary in preparing specimens for examination under the scanning electron microscope.

This extraordinary adaptation is clearly a very effective mechanism for binding the seeds to the smooth bark of the trees on which they grow. However, other species growing in similar habitats appear not to share the adaptation. Spirally thickened cells have long been known to occur in the outer envelope of some orchid seed (Link, 1849), but among 1,100 species in 210 genera examined by Barthlott and Ziegler *Chiloschista lunifera* was the only species to release spiral threads in this way on contact with water. This may be one of the most complex attachment mechanisms to be found anywhere among angiosperm seeds.

It is possible that other types of seed simply lodge eventually in cracks and crevices in the substrate, perhaps after several displacements by wind or water. This is surely one of the reasons for the generalization mentioned above that roughbarked trees tend to carry more epiphytes, although other factors affecting the growth of the plants would also contribute.

Little information seems to be available on the second question, namely how water eventually penetrates an initially water repellent testa. Mechanical or microbial breakdown may be involved, but this is a difficult question to study in the field. Barthlott (1981) stated that the sculpturing of seed surfaces may increase non-wettability and also reduce contamination by pathogenic micro-organisms. In the case of orchids, which rely on infection by mycorrhizal fungi for successful germination, this raises a further problem.

Once germination has begun the seedling would appear to be in a much more precarious situation, as actively growing tissue is much less resistant to water stress than dry dormant seed embryos (Levitt, 1980). Yet the development of the young seedling is slow, and in the absence of infection by mycorrhizal fungi stops at the early protocorm stage, as the cells have no endosperm and lack the capacity to metabolize any available nutrients. When seedlings are grown in culture, care is taken never to expose them to low humidity or water stress (Boyd, 1963; Arditti, 1967, 1979). How do young seedlings survive in the wild?

It is obvious that seedlings do survive, although the mortality rate must be very high among the millions of seed released, and it has been suggested that seeds, or young seedlings, may survive further dispersal by wind after germination and mycorrhizal infection have begun. Ames (1922) suggested that the orchids which re-invaded Krakatau within a few years of the island's catastrophic eruption in 1883, probably arrived carrying their symbiotic mycorrhizal fungi with them, as the correct fungi were unlikely to be present in the sterilized landscape. Ames suggests (see also Johansson, 1974) that seed may often lodge initially close to a parent plant where the mycorrhizal fungus is common. Because growth is slow even after inoculation, the young seedling at the early protocorm stage could easily become detached and redispersed. The slow development is an advantage if it allows this inoculation and subsequent dispersion, but there must be sufficient tolerance of desiccation by the developing seedling to survive the journey.

J. T. Curtis (1943) observed the slow development of protocorms and young seedlings in five species of the terrestrial *Cypripedium*, which did not produce an exposed green leaf until the third year. The point was made in this study that conditions must remain suitable for growth for a long time while the seedling is vulnerable, and in particular the soil must not dry out. Around the edges of favorable sites for these orchids which inhabit damp boggy areas, intermittent dry spells were considered a severe hazard for the survival of seedlings. In epiphytic species the young seedlings must tolerate much more extreme conditions, but there appears to be very little if any information about their degree of water stress tolerance. Madison (1977) suggested that the protocorm of the young seedling, like initial succulent structures produced by some other epiphyte seedlings, may act as an immediate water storage to carry the young plant through intermittent drought. However, there is no experimental evidence for this, and unless a sufficiently waterproof cuticle surrounded the protocorm to prevent water loss the small size of the structure would allow rapid dehydration.

Most of the extensive literature on orchid seed germination deals with horticultural practice and artificial propagation. Much less work has been done on seedling ecology, especially of epiphytes. This is another area where careful research would be rewarding, though it will be made difficult by the extreme smallness of the seed, the slow rate of growth of seedlings, the inaccessibility of many natural habitats, and the complication of the fungal symbiosis.

Movement

To conclude this review, brief mention will be made of the movement of plant parts caused by rapid turgor changes. The best known and most carefully studied turgor-operated movement is undoubtedly the diurnal opening and closing of stomatal pores by the guard cells, but a number of others are also well known. These include diurnal opening and closing of some flower petals, of leaflets, especially in legumes, and such touch-sensitive movements as the folding of the leaves of the sensitive plant *Mimosa pudica* or the closing of the Venus fly-trap, *Dionaea muscipula*.

Touch-sensitive movement occurs in the flowers of several orchid genera, in each case as part of the adaptation that ensures pollination. Perhaps the best known example is the terrestrial genus *Pterostylis* which is found in Australia, New Zealand, New Guinea and New Caledonia. The movement in *Pterostylis* flowers has been described by a number of authors (Cheesman, 1872; Fitzgerald, 1875; Haberlandt, 1914; Rupp, 1930; Northen, 1972).

The *Pterostylis* flower has a hood formed by tightly overlapping petals and dorsal sepal (Figure 3-5). Fused lateral sepals may block entrance to the flower except by way of the labellum. In the species in which the movement occurs, the labellum consists of a narrow limb attached to a claw, with a brush-like appendage sprouting from the point where the limb joins the claw. This claw is the motile tissue and the brush is probably the sensor, though this has not been confirmed. The column has broad wings arising from the upper portion, forming a partial tunnel around the stigma.

When a small insect lands on the limb the claw suddenly curves inward, throwing the limb against the column and trapping the insect inside the flower. The only way of escape is via the tunnel at the top of the column, past the stigmatic surface and pollinia, hence forcing the insect into the role of pollinator.

The initial movement may take less than a second, and the claw gradually relaxes over a period of between thirty minutes and three hours, after which the trap is reset and will

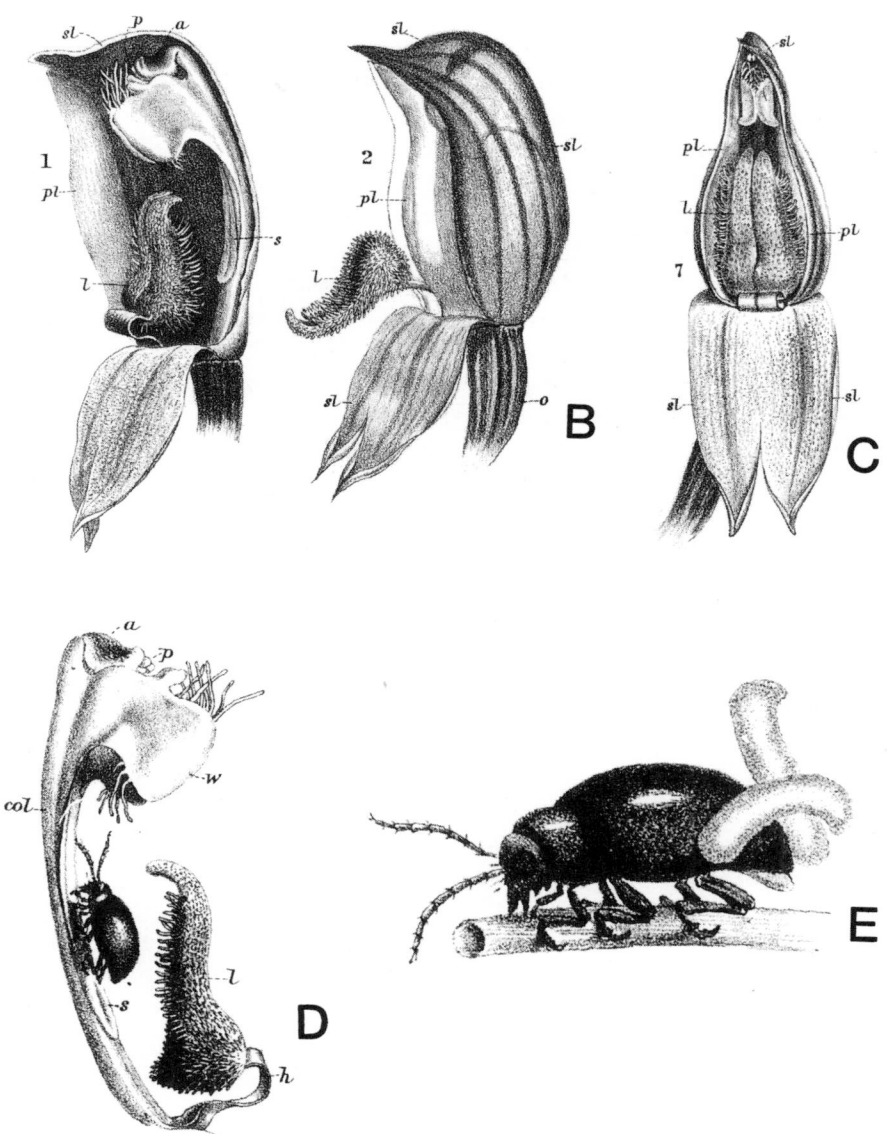

Fig. 3-5. Touch-sensitive movement in flower of *Pterostylis longifolia.* **A.** and **C.** view of partly cut-away flower, showing labellum raised after stimulation. **B.** Intact flower, with labellum extended before stimulation. **D.** Small beetle crawling up column, having been trapped inside flower by sudden movement of labellum. **E.** beetle carrying pollinia after escaping from flower. Drawings reproduced from Fitzgerald (1875). This beetle is probably not the normal pollinator but was used to demonstrate the mechanism. Explanation of symbols:

a anther	*h* hinge	*o* ovary	*pl* petal	*sl* sepal
col column	*l* labellum	*p* pollen	*s* stigma	*w* wing

respond to another touch. The time required for reopening is temperature sensitive.

Another elaboration of this pollinator trap has been pointed out by R. Bates (pers. comm.). In many *Pterostylis* flowers the perianth parts forming the hood have translucent panels, allowing light to shine through into the inside cavity. This "light at the end of the tunnel" is an added inducement to the insects to crawl upwards, and hence past the waiting stigma.

A very similar process occurs in the South American genus *Porroglossum*, endemic to the Andes of Colombia, Ecuador and Venezuela. The movement of the labellum in these flowers was first observed at Kew in 1877 and described by Oliver (1888) in *Porroglossum echidnum*, at that time named *Masdevallia mucosa*. The labellum closed in about one second, and reopened in about twenty minutes. Sweet (1972) described this movement for six species of *Porroglossum*. Holttum (1955) reported that flowers of the genus *Plocoglottis* have a sensitive lip, though in some species the movement is a once-only reaction and the lip cannot be reset once it has been triggered. *Acostaea* is another genus reported to have actively movable flower parts (Dressler, 1981). *Drakaea* and *Spiculaea*, terrestrial genera endemic to Western Australia, have also been listed as having an actively movable labellum (Dressler, 1981; Sweet, 1972). However, this is incorrect. The labellum is hinged, but the pollination mechanism is a case of pseudo-copulation. Wasps are attracted to the flower by scent and the shape of the labellum which approximates the wingless female. The male clasps the labellum and attempts to fly away with it. The hinge then allows the labellum to swing over bringing the insect into contact with the column and the pollinia (Hoffman and Brown, 1984). So in this case the movement is caused by the insect, not the flower.

The physiology of the touch-sensitive movement apparently has not been studied in detail, but it is probably similar to that which occurs in *Mimosa pudica* where turgor changes in the pulvinus caused by massive fluxes of potassium ions cause the rapid movements of leaflets or leaves. In orchid flowers such reversible turgor changes would be expected in the claw at the base of the labellum. In the case of *Porroglossum* a diurnal rhythm has also been reported (Oliver, 1888; Sweet, 1972), the lip closing about one hour after sunset and re-opening before sunrise. Hence phytochrome may possibly also be involved.

Catasetum displays a rapid movement as part of the pollination process, but this is probably not directly caused by changes in turgor pressure (Dressler, 1981). The stipe is stretched over a knob formed by the column. As the flower matures, tension builds up in the elastic stipe. When it is fully mature the slightest touch causes the viscidium to be released, and the entire pollinaria are thrown out with considerable force, to strike and adhere to the body of the disturbing insect. This mechanism is similar to the release of a stretched spring or rubber band.

Detailed physiological studies have been made of a touch-sensitive movement in flowers of another mainly Australian family, Stylidiaceae, the trigger-plants (Findlay, 1982). Here the column formed by fusion of stamens and style is sensitive; when a foraging insect probes into the flower and touches its base, the column flips rapidly over (in 15–20 milliseconds) depositing pollen on the insect's back, or receiving it from there. Findlay measured biophysical aspects of this rapid movement in great detail, and similar study of the touch-sensitive orchid flowers would be most interesting.

Conclusion

Much more has been published on orchid morphology and anatomy than on physiology, and many intriguing questions relating to water relations remain unanswered. As indicated throughout this review, there are many areas where the available information is limited and much valuable and absorbing work could still be done. Much of this work, though not all, must be carried out in field situations on plants in their natural habitat. The difficulty this imposes is surely one reason why so much interesting work remains to be done.

The importance for the plant of water uptake by aerial roots not attached to a substrate needs further study, particularly in cloud forests, where actual rates of condensation and weight gain by plants could be measured.

Many studies linking leaf form, transpiration rate and plant microclimate would be possible. For example, what is the significance of the lignification and development of fibre bundles in hard leathery leaves, and do these leaves really transpire more slowly than other types? Energy balance studies of leaves *in situ* could reveal the significance of leaf shapes and orientations on the branch, the temperature response of succulent leaves to sun-flecks, and the whole pattern of variability of the energy input to the microsites throughout a tree canopy.

The behavior of spirally thickened idioblasts in orchid tissue subject to water stress would repay further study. Does the water cavitate within them as dehydration proceeds? Does air then penetrate and if so, how easily do the cells refill? Do they really help prevent the collapse of whole tissues under stress?

More modern methods could be used to check and extend the early measurements of osmotic potential and water potential, some of which are suspect. The generalization that orchid sap is very dilute seems valid, but more studies of the dynamics of water potential changes as epiphytes are subject to drought and rehydration would build on this knowledge. Similarly, measurements of stomatal behavior and transpiration rates of plants growing in natural conditions would test the generalizations that are made about drought tolerance based largely on plant structures and anatomy.

Detailed study of epiphyte distribution patterns would be most rewarding if it could be linked to measurements of the small-scale micro-climate, and to physiological parameters, such as photosynthetic rates, transpiration rates, water potentials and the responses of these to wetting and drying. Of course for this kind of physiological ecology, the challenges of instrumentation and logistics are enormous.

Stomatal physiologists will no doubt continue to make use of the unique chloroplast-free guard cells of *Paphiopedilum* in studying the mechanisms of stomatal function, while the regulation of gas exchange (without stomata) in the photosynthetic roots of the shootless orchids is another problem not completely understood.

Then there is the whole question of mechanisms of seed attachment to suitable sites and the growth and survival of protocorms and young seedlings in the face of the fluctuating water stress of an epiphytic habitat.

Finally the biophysics of the movement of the labellum in flowers such as *Pterostylis* would provide a rather esoteric, but interesting project.

J. T. Curtis (1952) gave a very comprehensive list of suggested "ecological life history studies" for vascular epiphytes, together with references to work already done in each area. Many of the suggestions made above repeat or extend items on this list. It is surprising how many of Curtis' references were old when the paper was written; in some cases little more information has been added since then. There is scope for much more rewarding study of orchid water relations provided that the threatened habitats in which so many occur can be saved from destruction.

Acknowledgments

I thank Joseph Arditti for making available his extensive literature collection; David Benzing for useful conversations, and Kees Elferinck and Marisela Pando for translations of Dutch and Portuguese papers. The visit to Dr. Arditti's laboratory was partly supported by a study leave grant from the University of Adelaide. I am also very grateful to Anthony Fox for reproducing figures, and for the patience of typists Carol Robinson, Bronwyn Burns and Pam Jowitt.

Glossary

Words marked with an asterisk are used as defined by Esau (1977).

Abaxial.* Directed away from the axis. Opposite of adaxial.

Adaxial.* Directed towards the axis. Opposite of abaxial.

Angiosperms. A major division of the plant kingdom, commonly called flowering plants. Reproductive organs are in flowers, seed is borne within a closed ovary.

Anticlinal.* Perpendicular to the nearest surface.

Articulated. Jointed. Capable of bending easily at certain points.

Atmosphere. Average atmospheric pressure at sea level. Equal to 14.7 p.s.i. or 1.013 bar.

Bar. Pressure of 10^5 Pascal (pa) $= 0.1$ MPa $= 0.987$ atmospheres $= 14.5$ p.s.i.

CAM. See Crassulacean acid metabolism.

Canopy. The outer layers of foliage of a tree or shrub. The uppermost leafy layers of a forest.

Cavitation. The sudden development of a gas bubble in water under tension in an enclosed container.

Chlorenchyma.* Parenchyma tissue containing chloroplasts.

Cortex. The tissue between the vascular cylinder and epidermis of a stem or root.

Crassulacean acid metabolism. Fixation of carbon dioxide in the dark into organic acids which are used in photosynthesis by day.

Crypt. Simple tube or cavity.

Cuticle.* A layer of fatty material, cutin, rather impervious to water, located on the outer walls of epidermal cells.

Cutin.* A complex fatty substance considerably impervious to water; present as an impregnation of epidermal walls and as a separate layer, the cuticle, on the outer surface of the epidermis.

Cytoplasm. Groundmass of cell contents which encloses the nucleus and all other components.

Decimeter. One tenth of a meter; dm.

Depression of freezing point. The lowering of freezing point caused by dissolved solutes. May be measured in order to determine concentration or osmotic potential.

Diffusion porometer. Instrument for measuring stomatal resistance or conductance of a leaf by sensing the rate at which water vapor diffuses out of the leaf.

Diffusion pressure deficit. An old term, equivalent to water potential but with opposite sign. The pressure with which water would diffuse into a cell if it were placed in pure water.

Dorsal.* Situated on the upper surface.

Dorsiventral.* Possessing distinct upper and lower sides.

Drought avoider. Plant which can maintain a high water content and water potential when exposed to an extermal water stress.

Endodermis.* Innermost layer of cortex in roots and stems; forms a sheath around the vascular region, with suberin deposited in the anticlinal walls.

Eosin. Red acidic dye.

Epidermis. The outermost cell layer of primary origin of the plant, sometimes comprising more than one layer.

Epilithic. Growing on or attached to rocks.

Exodermis.* The outermost layer or layers of cells of the cortex of some roots, with walls which may be suberized and/or lignified.

F.W. Fresh weight.

Geophyte. Plant with underground parts (rhizome, bulb or tuber) which go dormant and store food over winter when above-ground parts die back.

Geotropic. Capable of growth in a direction determined by gravity.

Glabrous. Devoid of hairs.

Glandular trichome.* A trichome or hair having a unicellular or multicellular head composed of secretory cells.

Globose. = Globular, rounded like a globe or sphere.

Herbaceous. Non-woody.

Höfler diagram. Graph of total water potential and its components plotted against relative water content of a cell or tissue.

Hypodermis.* A layer or layers of cells beneath the epidermis distinct from the underlying ground tissue cells.

Idioblast.* A cell in a tissue that differs markedly in form, size or contents from other cells in the same tissue.

Isodiametric.* Regular in form, with all diameters equally long.

Isopiestic solution. A solution of a non-penetrating solute of such concentration that no net exchange of water occurs between an immersed tissue sample and the solution; hence the osmotic potential of the solution equals the water potential of the tissue.

Leaf diffusive resistance. Resistance to loss of water vapor by diffusion through leaf surface.

Lignified.* Impregnated with lignin.

Lignin.* Organic substance or mixture of substances derived from phenylpropane, imparting strength to many secondarily thickened cell walls.

Lithophyte. Plant which grows on exposed rock.

Lysimeter. Large, soil-filled container sunk in the ground and mounted on weighing device, for measuring evapotranspiration.

Megapascal (MPa). Unit of pressure. See Bar.

Mesophyll.* The photosynthetic parenchyma of a leaf blade located between the two epidermal layers.

Microclimate. The set of environmental variables (temperature, radiation, humidity, etc.) which influence conditions on a small scale such as within a vegetation canopy.

Micropyle.* The opening in the integuments of an ovule through which the pollen tube usually enters the embryo sac.

Mucilage. Carbohydrate polymer, capable of absorbing water, swelling and forming a slimy gel.

Neotropics. New world tropics; the tropical areas of North, Central and South America.

Osmotic potential, ψ_π. The component of water potential due to the presence of dissolved solutes. See water potential.

Parenchyma. A ground tissue of living, thin-walled, non-specialized cells which may vary in structure and function.

Passage cell.* Cell in exodermis or endodermis that remains thin-walled when the associated cells develop thick secondary walls.

Perianth.* Petals and sepals of a flower considered together.

Pericycle.* That portion of the ground tissue of the stele between the conducting tissues and endodermis.

Photophosphorylation. The formation of ATP using energy from light during photosynthesis.

Plastid.* A cytoplasmic organelle; may be concerned with photosynthesis, starch storage, or contain various pigments.

Plicate. Pleated; folded like a fan.

Pneumathode. In velamen, a group of cells, usually with spiral thickenings, which remain air-filled when velamen is saturated with water, enabling gas exchange.

Pressure potential, ψ_p. The component of water potential due to hydrostatic pressure or tension. See water potential.

Protoplast.* Protoplasm of a plant cell without the cell wall.

Pseudobulb. A thickened stem internode for storage of water and food reserves.

P.s.i. Pounds per square inch.

Psychrometer. Instrument for measuring water vapor concentration or humidity.

Relative water content, R. Water content of tissue expressed as a fraction or percentage of the fully turgid water content.

Rhizome. Thick, horizontal, usually underground stem.

Riparian. Growing on the banks of streams or rivers.

Riverine. = Riparian.

Sclerophyllous. Hard-leaved; leaves having thick cuticle, much lignified tissue and reduced intercellular spaces.

Solute potential. = osmotic potential.

Spirally thickened idioblast. Idioblast with pronounced spiral thickenings of the cell wall, but not part of the vascular tissue.

Stele.* Central cylinder of plant axis, consisting of the vascular system and associated ground tissue.

Stomata.* Openings in the epidermis of leaves and stems bordered by pairs of guard cells and serving in gas exchange.

Stomatal conductance. Measure of the ability of stomata to permit gas exchange; reciprocal of stomatal resistance.

Suberin.* Waxy substance deposited in some cell walls (e.g. in cork cells) and rendering them impermeable to water.

Suberized. Impregnated with suberin.

Terete. Slender-cylindrical.

Thermistor. Semi-conductor device for sensing temperature; used in some designs of psychrometer.

Tilosome. A fibrous excrescence from the cell walls of the innermost velamen layer, adjacent to passage cells of the root exodermis.

Tracheid. A water conducting xylem cell that has no perforations.

Tracheoidal. Having secondarily thickened, lignified cell walls resembling a tracheid.

Trichome. A plant hair or epidermal outgrowth.

Tritiated water. Water in which some molecules have one hydrogen atom replaced by the radioactive isotope tritium.

Transpiration. Evaporation of water from a plant surface, mainly through stomata.

Tuber. Swollen part of an underground stem or root, acting as a reservoir for food and/or water.

Turgor pressure. Hydrostatic pressure within a cell, due to vacuolar contents pressing against the cell wall.

Vacuole. A cavity in the cytoplasm containing an aqueous solution and bounded by a membrane.

Velamen. A multiple root epidermis consisting of dead cells at maturity, and bordered internally by an exodermis.

Ventral. Situated on the lower surface.

Water potential, ψ. The potential energy of water in a system; may be composed of a hydrostatic component (pressure potential, usually positive in living cells but negative in xylem) and an osmotic component (osmotic potential, always negative). Water always tends to move from a region of higher to lower water potential.

Water stress. Stress caused by lack of water, or low (negative) water potential.

Xerophyte.* Plant adapted to a dry habitat.

Xeric. Characterized by a meagre supply of water.

μm. Micro-meter, 10^{-6} meter.

ψ Water potential (which see).

ψ_π Osmotic potential. The component of water potential due to the presence of dissolved solutes; always negative. See water potential.

ψ_p Pressure potential or turgor pressure. The component of water potential due to hydrostatic pressure or tension; usually positive in living cells but negative in xylem. See water potential.

Literature Cited

Ames, O. 1922. Observations on the capacity of orchids to survive in the struggle for existence. *Orchid Rev.* 30: 229–234.

Ando, T. 1982. Occurrence of two different modes of photosynthesis in *Dendrobium* cultivars. *Scientia Horticulturae.* 17: 169–175.

Arditti, J. 1967. Factors affecting the germination of orchid seeds. *Bot. Rev.* 33: 1–97.

Arditti, J. 1979. Aspects of the physiology of orchids. *In* H. W. Woolhouse (ed.), *Advances in Botanical Research.* 7: 421–655. Acad. Press, New York.

Assmann, S. M. and E. Zeiger. 1985. Stomatal responses to CO_2 in *Paphiopedilum* and *Phragmipedium.* Role of the guard cell chloroplast. *Plant Physiol.* 77: 461–464.

Avadhani, P. N., C. J. Goh, A. N. Rao, and J. Arditti. 1982. Carbon fixation in orchids. *In* J. Arditti (ed.), *Orchid Biology: Reviews and Perspectives II.* Cornell Univ. Press, Ithaca, New York, pp. 173–193.

Barrs, H. D. 1968. Determination of water deficits in plant tissues. *In* T. T. Kozlowski (ed.), *Water deficits and Plant Growth.* Vol. I. Academic Press, New York, pp. 235–368.

Barthlott, W. 1981. Epidermal and seed surface characters of plants: systematic applicability and some evolutionary aspects. *Nordic J. Bot.* 1(3): 345–355.

Barthlott, W., and I. Capesius. 1975. Mikromorphologische und funktionelle Untersuchungen am Velamen radicum der Orchideen. *Ber. Deutsch. Bot. Ges.* 88: 379–390.

Barthlott, W. and B. Ziegler. 1980. Über ausziehbare helicale Zellwandverdickungen als Haft–Apparat der Samenschalen von *Chiloschista lunifera* (Orchidaceae). *Ber. Deutsch. Bot. Ges.* 93: 391–403.

Benzing, D. H. 1970. Foliar permeability and the absorption of minerals and organic nitrogen by certain tank bromeliads. *Bot. Gaz.* 131: 23–31.

Benzing, D. H. 1973. The monocotyledons: their evolution and comparative biology. I. Mineral nutrition and related phenomena in Bromeliaceae and Orchidaceae. *Quart. Rev. Biol.* 48(2): 277–290.

Benzing, D. H. 1979. Alternative interpretations for the evidence that certain orchids and bromeliads act as shoot parasites. *Selbyana* 5: 135–144.

Benzing, D. H. 1981. Why is Orchidaceae so large, its seeds so small, and its seedlings mycotrophic? *Selbyana* 5: 241–242.

Benzing, D. H. 1986. The vegetative basis of vascular epiphytism. *Selbyana* 9: 23–43.

Benzing, D. H., A. Bent, D. Moscow, G. Peterson, and A. Renfrow. 1982. Functional correlates of deciduousness in *Catasetum integerrimum* (Orchidaceae). *Selbyana* 7: 1–9.

Benzing, D. H., W. E. Friedman, G. Peterson, and A. Renfrow. 1983. Shootlessness, velamentous roots, and the preeminence of Orchidaceae in the epiphytic biotope. *Amer. J. Bot.* 70(11): 121–133.

Benzing, D. H., K. Henderson, B. Kessel, and J. Sulak. 1976. The absorptive capacities of bromeliad trichomes. *Amer. J. Bot.* 63: 1009–1014.

Benzing, D. H., and D. W. Ott. 1981. Vegetative reduction in epiphytic Bromeliaceae and Orchidaceae: its origins and significance. *Biotropica* 13: 131–140.

Benzing, D. H., D. W. Ott, and W. E. Friedman. 1982. Roots of *Sobralia macrantha* (Orchidaceae): Structure and function of the velamen-exodermis complex. *Amer. J. Bot.* 69: 608–614.

Benzing, D. H. and A. M. Pridgeon. 1983. Foliar trichomes of Pleurothallidinae (Orchidaceae): functional significance. *Amer. J. Bot.* 70: 173–180.

Bidwell, R. G. S. 1979. *Plant Physiology.* Second Edition. Macmillan Publishing Co. New York.

Blum, G. 1933. Osmotische Untersuchungen in Java. I. *Ber. Schweiz. Bot. Ges.* 42: 550–680.

Borsos, O. 1980. Anatomy of wild orchids in Hungary. I. Tissue structure of leaf and floral axis. *Acta Agronomica Acad. Sci. Hung.* 29: 369–389.

Boyd, H. 1963. The Goldsmith Technique. *Aust. Orch. Rev.* 28(1): 37.

Burgeff, H. 1936. *Samenkeimung der Orchideen.* G. Fischer Verlag, Jena. 312 pp.

Chatin, M. Ad. 1858. Anatomie du rhizome, de la tige et des feuilles. *Mem. Soc. Sci. Nat. Cherbourg.* 6: 33–69.

Cheeseman, T. F. 1872. On the fertilization of the New Zealand species of *Pterostylis. Trans. & Proc. New Zealand Institute* 5: 352–357.

Chiang, Y.-L and Y.-R. Chen. 1968. Observations on *Pleione formosana* Hayata. *Taiwania* 14: 271–302.

Cockburn, W., I. P. Ting, and L. O. Sternberg. 1979. Relationships between stomatal behavior and internal carbon dioxide concentration in crassulacean acid metabolism plants. *Plant Physiol.* 63: 1029–1032.

Cockburn, W., C. J. Goh, and P. N. Avadhani. 1985. Photosynthetic carbon assimilation in a shootless orchid, *Chiloschista usneoides* (Don) Ldl. A variant on Crassulacean Acid Metabolism. *Plant Physiol.* 77: 83–86.

Curtis, C. H. 1943. Pseudobulbs. *Orchid Rev.* 51:137.

Curtis, J. T. 1943. Germination and seedling development in five species of *Cypripedium* L. *Amer. J. Bot.* 30: 199–206.

Curtis, J. T. 1946. Nutrient supply of epiphytic orchids in the mountains of Haiti. *Ecology* 27: 264–66.

Curtis, J. T. 1947. Ecological observations on the orchids of Haiti. *Amer. Orchid Soc. Bull.* 16: 262–269.

Curtis, J. T. 1952. Outline for ecological life history studies of vascular epiphytic plants. *Ecology* 33: 550–558.

Curtis, K. M. 1917. The anatomy of the six epiphytic species of the New Zealand Orchidaceae. *Ann. Bot.* 31: 133–149.

Dixon, H. H. 1894. On the vegetative organs of *Vanda teres. Proc. Royal Irish Acad.* 3: 441–458.

Donovan, R. D., J. Arditti, and I. P. Ting. 1984. Carbon fixation by *Paphiopedilum insigne* and *Paphiopedilum parishii* (Orchidaceae). *Annals of Bot.* 54: 583–586.

Dressler, R. L. 1981. *The Orchids: Natural history and Classification.* Harvard University Press, Cambridge.

Dunn, H. A. 1941. The major orchids of Panama. The physiography of their habitats. *Amer. Orch. Soc. Bull.* 9: 251–267.

Dycus, A. M., and L. Knudson. 1957. The role of the velamen of the aerial roots of orchids. *Bot. Gaz.* 119: 78–87.

Eggeling, W. J. 1947. Observations on the ecology of the Budongo rain forest, Uganda. *J. Ecol.* 34: 20–87.

Esau, K. 1977. *Anatomy of Seed Plants.* 2nd Edition. John Wiley and Sons, New York.

Findlay, G. P. 1982. Generation of torque by the column of *Stylidium. Aust. J. Plant Physiol.* 9: 271–286.

Fitzgerald, R. D. 1875. *Australian Orchids.* Vol. I. Part I. Government Printer, Sydney.

Foster, A. S. 1956. Plant idioblsats: remarkable examples of cell specialization. *Protoplasma* 46: 184–193.

Fu, C. F., and C. S. Hew. 1982. Crassulacean acid metabolism in orchids under water stress. *Bot. Gaz.* 143: 294–297.

Gessner, F. 1956. Der Wasserhaushalt der Epiphyten und Lianen. *In* W. Ruhland (ed.), *Handbuch der Pflanzenphysiol.* Vol. 3. Springer Verlag, Berlin, pp. 915–950.

Giles, C. H., and V. G. Agnihotri. 1968. Water vapor absorption by aerial roots: a new type of high specific surface cellulose. *Chem. & Industry:* 1192–1194.

Goh, C. J. 1983. Rhythms of acidity and CO_2 Production in Orchid Flowers. *New Phytol.* 93: 25–32.

Goh, C. J., J. Arditti, and P. N. Avadhani. 1983. Carbon fixation in orchid aerial roots. *New Phytol.* 95: 367–374.

Goh, G. J., O. Wara-Aswapati, and P. N. Avadhani. 1984. Crassulacean Acid Metabolism in young orchid leaves. *New Phytol.* 96: 519–526.

Grace, J., F. E. Fasehun, and M. Dixon. 1980. Boundary layer conductance of the leaves of some tropical timber trees. *Plant, Cell & Environ.* 3: 443–450.

Grace, J., and J. Wilson. 1976. The boundary layer over a *Populus* leaf. *J. Expt. Bot.* 27: 231–241.

Grubb, P. J., and T. C. Whitmore. 1966. A comparison of montane and lowland rain forest in Ecuador. II. The climate and its effects on the distribution and physiognomy of the forests. *J. Ecol.* 54: 303–333.

Haberlandt, G. 1914. *Physiological Plant Anatomy.* Trans. from 4th German Ed. by M. Drummond. Macmillan, London.

Harper, J. L., P. H. Lovell, and K. G. Moore. 1970. The shapes and sizes of seeds. *Ann. Rev. Ecology & Systematics.* 1: 327–356.

Harris, J. A. 1918. On the osmotic concentration of the tissue fluids of phanerogamic epiphytes. *Amer. J. Bot.* 5: 490–506.

Harris, J. A. 1934. *The physico chemical properties of plant saps in relation to phytogeography.* Univ. Minn. Press.

Hering, L. 1900. Zur Anatomie der monopodialen Orchideen. *Botanisches Centra-blatt* 84: 1–11; 35–45; 72–82; 113–122; 145–152; 177–184.

Hew, C. S., G. L. Lee, and S. C. Wong. 1980. Occurrence of non-functional stomata in the flowers of tropical orchids. *Ann. Bot.* 46: 195–201.

Hew, C. S., Y. W. Ng, S. C. Wong, H. H. Yeoh, and K. K. Ho. 1984. Carbon dioxide fixation in orchid aerial roots. *Physiol. Plant.* 60: 154–158.

Hofmann, E. 1930. Über die Anatomie des Blattes von *Oncidium ascendens* Lindl. *Akad. Wiss. Wien. Sitzungsber. Math-Naturwiss. Klasse.* 139: 189–193.

Hoffman, N., and A. Brown. 1984. *Orchids of Southwest Australia.* University of Western Australia Press.

Holttum, R. E. 1955. Notes on pollination of orchids of the genus *Plocoglottis. Malayan Nature Journal* 9: 111–115.

Holttum, R. E. 1960. The ecology of tropical epiphytic orchids. *In* P. M. Synge (ed.), *Proc. Third World Orchid Conf.,* Royal Hort. Soc. London. pp. 196–203.

Hosokawa, T. 1943. Studies on the life-forms of vascular epiphytes and the epiphyte flora of Ponape, Micronesia. *Trans. Nat. Hist. Soc. Taiwan.* 33: 35–55; 71–89; 113–141.

Hsiang, T.-H. T. 1951. Physiological and biochemical changes accompanying pollination in orchid flowers. I. General observations and water relations. *Plant Physiol.* 26: 441–455.

Johansson, D. 1974. Ecology of vascular epiphytes in West African rain forest. *Acta Phytogeogr. Suec.* 59: 1–129.

Johansson, D. R. 1977. Epiphytic orchids as parasites of their host trees. *Amer. Orchid Soc. Bull.* 46: 703–707.

Kamerling, Z. 1912. De Verdamping van epiphyte Orchideën. *Natuurkund. Tijdschr. Ned. Ind.* 71: 54–72.

Kerner, (initials not given) and Oliver (initials not given). 1894. Orchid Roots. In *The Gardeners' Chronicle* 15: 748.

Kramer, P. J. 1983. *Water Relations of Plants.* Academic Press, New York.

Krause, H. 1935. Beiträge zur Kenntnis der Wasseraufnahme der oberirdische Pflanzenorgane. *Österr. Botan. Zeitschrift.* 84: 257–258.

Krüger, P. 1883. Die oberirdischen Vegetationsorgane der Orchideen in ihren Beziehungen zu Clima und Standort. *Flora* 66: 435–443; 451–459; 467–477; 499–510; 515–524.

Lebrun, J. 1937. Observations sur les épiphytes de la forêt équatoriale congolaise. *Soc. Sci. Bruxelles.* 57: 31–38.

Leitgeb, H. 1865. Die Luftwurzeln der Orchideen. *Denk. Wien Acad. Math. Naturw. Klasse.* 24: 179–222.

Levitt, J. 1980. *Water Deficits and Plant Growth.* 2nd Ed. Acadamic Press, New York.

Lindley, J. 1835. Upon the cultivation of epiphytes of the orchis tribe. *Trans. Hort. Soc. London,* 2nd Ser. 1: 42–50.

Link, H. 1849. Bermerkungen über den Bau der Orchideen. Zweite Abh. 117–127 + plates. *Physikalische Abhandlungen der Königliche Akademie der Wissenschaften zu Berlin.*

McWilliams, E. L. 1970. Comparative rates of dark CO_2 uptake and acidification in the Bromeliaceae, Orchidaceae and Euphorbiaceae. *Bot. Gaz.* 131: 285–290.

Madison, M. 1977. Vascular epiphytes: their systematic occurrence and salient features. *Selbyana.* 2: 1–13.

Mehra, P. N., and S. P. Vij. 1974. Some observations on the ecological adaptions and distribution pattern of the East Himalayan orchids. *Amer. Orchid Soc. Bull.* 43: 301–315.

Metcalfe, C. R., and L. Chalk. 1979. *Anatomy of the Dicotyledons.* Vol. I. 2nd Ed. Clarendon Press, Oxford.

Metzler, von W. 1924. Beiträge zur vergleichenden Anatomie blattsukkulenter Pflanzen. *Bot. Archiv* 6: 50–83.

Milburn, J. A., and D. S. Crombie. 1984. Sounds made by plants. A novel application of acoustic emission analysis. *Bull. Aust. Acoustic Soc.* 12: 1–15.

Milburn, J. A., and R. P. C. Johnson. 1966. The conduction of sap. II. Detection of vibrations produced by sap cavitation in *Ricinus* xylem. *Planta* 69: 43–52.

Möbius, M. 1887. Über den anatomischen Bau der Orchideenblätter und dessen Bedeutung für das System dieser Familie. *Jabrb. Wiss. Bot.* 18: 530–607.

Morris, B. 1968. The epiphytic orchids of the Shire Highlands, Malawi. *Proc. Linn. Soc.* 179: 51–66.

Morris, B. 1970. *The Epiphytic Orchids of Malawi.* The Society of Malawi.

Müller, F. 1885. Wurzeln als Stellvertreter der Blätter. *Zeitschr. für die gesamte Kosmos* 17:443.

Neales, T. F., and C. S. Hew. 1975. Two types of carbon fixation in tropical orchids. *Planta* 123: 303–306.

Nelson, S. D., and J. M. Mayo. 1975. The occurrence of functional non-chlorophyllous guard cells in *Paphiopedilum* spp. *Canad. J. Bot.* 53: 1–7.

Nelson, S. D., and J. M. Mayo. 1977. Low K^+ in *Paphiopedilum leeanum* leaf epidermis: implications for stomatal functioning. *Canad. J. Bot.* 55: 489–495.

Northen, R. T. 1972. *Pterostylis* and its sensitive gnat trap. *Amer. Orch. Soc. Bull.* 41: 801–806.

Olatunji, O. A., and R. O. Nengim. 1980. Occurrence and distribution of tracheoidal elements in the Orchidaceae. *Bot. J. Linn. Soc.* 80: 357–370.

Oliver, F. W. 1888. On the sensitive labellum of *Masdevallia mucosa* Rchb.f. *Ann. Bot.* 1: 237–253.

Outlaw, W. H., J. Manchester, and V. E. Zenger. 1982. Potassium involvement not demonstrated in stomatal movements of *Paphiopedilum.* Qualified confirmation of the Nelson-Mayo report. *Canad. J. Bot.* 60: 240–244.

Pfitzer, E. 1884. Zwergartige Bulbophyllen mit Assimilationshohlen im Innern der Knollen. *Ber. d. Deutsch. Bot. Ges.* 2: 472–480.

Pfitzer, E. 1889. Orchidaceae. *In* A. Engler and K. Prantl (eds), *Die natürlichen Pflanzenfamilien nebst ihren Gattungen und wichtigeren Arten.* II (6) pp. 52–224.

Piers, F. 1968. *Orchids of East Africa.* 2nd Ed. J. Cramer, Lehre.

Pirwitz, K. 1931. Physiologische und anatomische Untersuchungen an Speichertracheiden und Velamina. *Planta* 14: 19–76.

Poole, H. A., and T. J. Sheehan. 1982. Mineral nutrition of orchids. *In* J. Arditti (ed.), *Orchid Biology: Reviews and Perspectives, II* Ch. 6. Cornell Univ. Press. Ithaca, New York, pp. 195–212.

Preston, C. E. 1901. Structural studies on Southwestern Cactaceae. *Bot. Gaz.* 32: 348–351.

Pridgeon, A. M. 1981. Absorbing trichomes in the Pleurothallidinae (Orchidaceae). *Amer. J. Bot.* 68: 64–71.

Pridgeon, A. M. 1982. Diagnostic anatomical characters in the Pleurothallidinae (Orchidaceae). *Amer. J. Bot.* 69: 921–938.

Pridgeon, A. M. 1987. The velamen and exodermis of orchid roots. *In* J. Arditti (ed.), *Orchid Biology: Reviews and Perspectives IV* Cornell Univ. Press, Ithaca, New York, pp. 139–192.

Pridgeon, A. M., W. L. Stern, and D. H. Benzing. 1983. Tilosomes in roots of Orchidaceae: Morphology and systematic occurrence. *Amer. J. Bot.* 70: 1365–1377.

Raciborski, M. 1898. Biologische Mittheilungen aus Java. *Flora* 85: 325–361.

Rauh, W., W. Barthlott, and N. Ehler. 1975. Morphologie und Funktion der Testa staubförmiger Flugsamen. *Bot. Jahrb. Syst.* 96: 353–374.

Richards, P. W. 1957. *The Tropical Rain Forest.* Cambridge Univ. Press.

Rolfe, R. A. 1914. Leafless orchids. *Orchid Rev.* 22: 73–75.

Ruinen, J. 1953. Epiphytosis. A second view on epiphytism. *Annales Bogoriensis* 1(2): 101–157.

Rundel, P. W. 1982. Foliar uptake of water in vascular plants. *In* O. L. Lange, P. S. Nobel, C. B. Osmond & H. Ziegler (eds.), *Encyclopedia of Plant Physiology.* New Series Vol. 12B. Springer Verlag, Berlin. Ch. 4. Water uptake by organs other than roots. pp. 114–119.

Rupp, H. M. R. 1930. *Guide to the Orchids of New South Wales.* Angus & Robertson, Sydney.

Rutter, J. C., and C. M. Willmer. 1979. A light and electron microscopy study of the epidermis of *Paphiopedilum* spp. with emphasis on stomatal ultra structure. *Plant, Cell & Environ.* 2: 211–219.

Salisbury, E. J. 1928. On the causes and ecological significance of stomatal frequency, with special reference to the woodland flora. *Phil. Trans. R. Soc. Lond.,* Ser. B, 216: 1–65.

Sanford, W. W. 1967. Orchids of West Africa. *Amer. Orch. Soc. Bull.* 36: 963–969.

Sanford, W. W. 1968. Distribution of epiphytic orchids in semi-deciduous tropical forest in Southern Nigeria. *J. Ecol.* 56: 697–705.

Sanford, W. W. 1969. The distribution of epiphytic orchids in Nigeria in relation to each other and to geographic location and climate, type of vegetation and tree species. *Biol. J. Linn. Soc.* 1: 247–285.

Sanford, W. W. 1974. The ecology of orchids, *In* C. L. Withner (ed.) *The Orchids, Scientific Studies.* Wiley-Interscience, New York. pp. 1–100.

Sanford, W. W. 1978. Weight loss from detached orchid leaves: *Calyptrochilum christyanum* and *C. emarginatum. Amer. Orchid Soc. Bull.* 47: 217–223.

Sanford, W. W., and I. Adanlawo. 1973. Velamen and exodermis characters of West African epiphytic orchids in relation to taxonomic grouping and habitat tolerance. *Bot. J. Linn. Soc.* 66: 307–321.

Schimper, A. F. W. 1888. Die epiphytische Vegetation Amerikas. *Bot. Mitt. Trop.* 2: Gustav Fischer, Jena. 162. pp.

Schimper, A. F. W. 1935. *Pflanzengeographie auf physiologischer Grundlage.* 3rd ed. Gustav Fischer: Jena.

Schlechter, R. 1982. *The Orchidaceae of German New Guinea.* (Trans. by R. S. Rogers, H. J. Katz, and J. T. Simmons) Aust. Orchid Foundation, Melboune.

Schnabl, H., and K. Raschke. 1980. Potassium chloride as stomatal osmoticum in *Allium cepa* L., a species devoid of starch in guard cells. *Plant Physiol.* 65: 88–93.

Schwarz, K. 1936. *Enährungsphysiologische Untersuchungen an Epiphyten* Diss. Würzburg.

Senn, G. 1913. Der osmotische Druck einiger Epiphyten und Parasiten. *Verhandl. Naturforsch. Ges. Basel* 24: 179–183.

Sheehan, T. J., J. N. Joiner, and J. K. Cowart. 1967. Absorption of ^{32}P by *Cattleya* 'Trimos' from foliar and root applications. *Florida State Hort. Soc.* 80: 400–404.

Sinclair, R. 1970. Convective heat transfer from narrow leaves. *Aust. J. Biol. Sci.* 23: 309–321.

Sinclair, R. 1983a. Water relations of Tropical Epiphytes. I. Relationships between stomatal resistance, relative water content and the components of water potential. *J. Exp. Bot.* 34: 1652–1663.

Sinclair, R. 1983b. Water Relations of Tropical epiphytes. II. Performance during droughting. *J. Exp. bot.* 34: 1664–1675.

Sinclair, R. 1984. Water Relations of Tropical epiphytes. III. Evidence for Crassulacean Acid Metabolism. *J. Exp. Bot.* 35: 1–7.

Sinclair, R., and W. N. Venables. 1983. An alternative method for analyzing pressure-volume curves produced with the pressure chamber. *Plant, Cell and Environ.* 6: 211–217.

Singh, V., and H. Singh. 1974. Organization of stomatal complex in some Orchidaceae. *Curr. Sci.* 43(15): 490–491.

Slavik, B. 1974. *Methods of studying plant water relations.* Springer-Verlag, Berlin & New York.

Smith, J. A. C., and S. Heuer. 1981. Determination of the volume of intercellular spaces in leaves and some values for CAM plants. *Ann. Bot.* 48: 915–17.

Solereder, H., and F. J. Meyer. 1930. *Systematische Anatomie der Monokotyledonen.* VI. Microspermae. Borntraeger, Berlin.

Spanner, L. 1939. Untersuchungen über den Wärme und Wasserhaushalt von *Myrmecodia* und *Hydnophytum. Jb. wiss. Bot.* 88: 243–283.

Stace, C. A. 1965. Cuticular studies as an aid to plant taxonomy. *Bull. Brit. Museum (Nat. Hist.) Botany Ser.* 4: 1–78.

Stewart, J., and B. Campbell. 1970. *Orchids of Tropical Africa.* Allen & Co., London.

Stocker, O. 1935. Transpiration und Wasserhaushalt in verschiedenen Klimazonen. III. Ein Beitrag zur Transpirationsgrösse in javanischen Urwald. *Jb. wiss. Bot.* 81: 464–496.

Sugden, A. M., and R. J. Robins. 1979. Aspects of the ecology of vascular epiphytes in Columbian cloud forests. I. The distribution of the epiphytic flora. *Biotropica* 11: 173–188.

Sweet, H. R. 1972. The genus *Porroglossum. Amer. Orch. Soc. Bull.* 41: 513–524.

Szarek, S. R., and I. P. Ting. 1977. The occurrence of Crassulacean acid metabolism among plants. *Photosynthetica* 11: 330–342.

Teuscher, H. 1972. *Microcoelia guyoniana* and other leafless epiphytic orchids. *Amer. Orch. Soc. Bull.* 41: 497–501.

Ting, I. P. 1985. Crassulacean Acid Metabolism. *Ann. Rev. Plant Physiol.* 36: 595–622.

Tominski (initials not given). 1905. *Die Anatomie des Orchideenblattes in ihrer Abhängigkeit von Klima und Standort.* Diss. Berlin.

Trécul, M. A. 1855a. Observations sur la structure des feuilles des orchidées, et sur une glande cryptiode que présentent plusieurs d'entre elles. *Bulletin de la Soc. Bot. de France.* 2: 445–452.

Trécul, M. A. 1855b. Formations spirales dans des cellules que referment les feuilles de certaines orchidées. *Bull. de la Soc. Bot. de France.* 2: 153–158.

Tyree, M. T., M. A. Dixon, and R. G. Thompson. 1984. Ultrasonic acoustic emissions from the sapwood of *Thuja occidentalis* measured inside a pressure bomb. *Plant Physiol.* 74: 1046–1049.

Uphof, J. C. T. 1962. Plant Hairs. *In* W. Zimmerman and P. G. Ozenda (eds), *Encyclopedia of Plant Anatomy.* Vol. 4 Pt. 5. Borntraeger, Berlin.

Valmayor, H. L., and D. Baldovino. 1984. *Orchidiana Philippiniana.* Vol. I. Eugenio Lopez Foundation, Manila.

Van der Pijl, L. 1982. *Principles of dispersal in higher plants.* 3rd Ed. Springer Verlag, Berlin.

Vij, S. P., N. Shekhar, S. K. Kashyap, and A. K. Garg. 1983. Observations on the orchids of Nainital and adjacent hills in the central Himalayas (Ecology and distribution). *Research Bull. (Science) Panjab Univ.* 34: 63–76.

von Sachs, J. 1887. *Lectures on the Physiology of Plants.* (Translated by H. M. Ward) Clarendon Press, Oxford.

Walter, H. 1971. *Ecology of Tropical and Sub-tropical Vegetation.* (Translated by D. Mueller-Dombois.) Oliver and Boyd, Edinburgh.

Went, F. W. 1940. Soziologie der Epiphyten eines tropischen Urwaldes. *Ann. Jard. Bot. Buitenzorg* 50 1–98.

Went, F. W., and L. O. Sheps. 1969. Environmental Factors in regulation of growth and development: ecological factors. *In* F. C. Steward (ed.), *Plant Physiology: a Treatise.* Vol. Va Acadamic Press, New York. pp. 299–406.

Wiebe, H. H., and H. A. Al-Saadi. 1976. Matric bound water of water tissue from Succulents. *Physiol. Plant.* 36: 47–51.

Wiesner, J. 1897. Pflanzenphysiologische Mittheilungen aus Buitenzorg (VI). *Akad. Wiss. Wien. Sitzungsber. Math.-Naturwiss Klasse.* 56: 77–98.

Williams, W. E., C. Grivet, and E. Zeiger. 1983. Gas exchange in *Paphiopedilum.* Lack of chloroplasts in guard cells correlates with low stomatal conductance. *Plant Physiol.* 72: 906–908.

Willmer, C. M. 1983. *Stomata.* Longman, London.

Winter, K., E. Medina, V. Garcia, M. L. Mayoral, and R. Muniz. 1985. Crassulacean Acid Metabolism in roots of a leafless orchid, *Campylocentrum tyrridion* Garay & Dunsterv. *J. Plant Physiol.* 118: 73–78.

Winter, K., B. J. Wallace, G. C. Stocker, and Z. Roksandic. 1983. Crassulacean acid metabolism in Australian vascular epiphytes and some related species. *Oecologia* 57: 129–141.

Withner, C. L., P. K. Nelson, and P. J. Wejksnora. 1974. The anatomy of orchids. *In* C. L. Withner (ed.), *The Orchids—Scientific Studies.* John Wiley & Sons, Inc., New York, p. 267–347.

Wong, S. C., and C. S. Hew. 1973. Photosynthesis and photorespiration in some thin-leaved orchid species. *J. Singapore Nat. Acad. Sci.* 3: 150–157.

Wong, S. C., and C. S. Hew. 1975. Do orchid leaves photorespire? *Amer. Orch. Soc. Bull.* 44: 902–906.

Zeiger, E., S. M. Assmann, and H. Meidner. 1983. The photobiology of *Paphiopedilum* stomata: opening under blue but not red light. *Photochem. and Photobiol.* 38: 627–630.

Zeiger, E., C. Grivet, S. M. Assmann, G. F. Deitzer, and M. W. Hannegan. 1985. Stomatal limitation to carbon gain in *Paphiopedilum* sp. (Orchidaceae) and its reversal by blue light. *Plant Physiol.* 77: 456–460.

4

Auto-pollination in the Orchidaceae

PAUL M. CATLING

Introduction

The whole case is perplexing in an unparalleled degree, for we have in the same flower elaborate contrivances for directly opposed objects. (Darwin, 1877, p. 57 regarding self-pollination in *Ophrys apifera*.)

Many orchids possess remarkable adaptations to ensure cross-pollination, including amazing methods of attracting and controlling pollinators. Through a combination of odor, color and texture, the flower of the bee orchid (*Ophrys apifera*) mimics a female bee. Males are attracted and copulate with the flowers. In spite of the evolution of such impressive and even bizarre adaptations, many orchids have become secondarily modified in such a way as to ensure self-pollination without the aid of pollinators. This is auto-pollination, and in most cases it is followed by self-fertilization and the abundant production of apparently viable seed. Auto-pollination in the bee orchid was first described by Brown in 1833, and his is probably the earliest reference to auto-pollination in an orchid. Darwin provided information on 23 auto-pollinating orchids, but he found it difficult to rationalize, for his careful experiments had suggested to him that "nature . . . abhors perpetual selfpollination." His classic work, "On the various contrivances by which orchids are fertilized by insects", made orchids the classic example of preventing continual self-pollination.

The next great pollination biologist to devote much thought to auto-pollination was Müller. In his remarkable book, *The Fertilization of Flowers* (1883), which was much praised by Darwin[a], Müller attended more closely than Darwin had to the many contrivances for auto-pollination. His commentary on self-and cross-fertilization may be one of the best ever written. He noted that "cross-fertilization is better for a plant than self-fertilization, but . . . self-fertilization is infinitely better than no fertilization at all and consequent sterility."

Of course there were many other ideas on the significance of auto-pollination and ensuing self-fertilization. Some claimed that it represented sophistication, while others suggested that the most successful species were those that avoided it completely, or that it was trivial and accidental. Although Müller's early statements are the most sustainable in the light of current knowledge, it was apparently Darwin's strong statement that precipitated much of the early documentation of self-pollination in orchids. Not long after Darwin's publication, Forbes (1884) published his contribution, "On the contrivances for ensuring self-fertilization in some tropical orchids". A few years earlier Moore (1877) had described auto-pollination of orchids in bud. In 1888 Ridley produced a valuable summary of all existing information on auto-pollination in orchids. It soon became clear that auto-pollination was much more widespread than Darwin realized. Authors of regional orchid floras began to remark on the auto-pollinating species that occurred in the area with which they were concerned. King and Pantling (1898) found auto-pollination to be widespread among the orchids of Sikkim. Reiche (1910) stated that "the sexual reproduction of Chilean orchids extensively is based on autogamy, and apparently only secondarily on xenogamy". Schlechter (1914) found autopollination to be "much more common than normally expected" in the orchid flora of New Guinea. Interestingly, all of these are mountainous regions (see Geographic Aspects). Nevertheless, the number of auto-pollinating species increased far beyond 23,

[a]Darwin also corresponded extensively with Müller's brother, Fritz, who lived in Hanau, Brazil.Ed.

and there was evidence of regional significance. All this and other new information was reviewed in a classic paper by Kirchner in 1922, who also discussed mechanisms and consequences. Kirchner referred to *ca.* 140 species which are more or less characterized by auto-pollination. Martens (1926) provided additional observations of auto-pollinations in orchids. Smith (1928, 1929) discussed auto-pollination in East Indian orchids under several headings relating to the mechanism and degree of commitment.

For a period of almost 50 years there were no substantial additions, with the exception of Hagerup's (1952) work. He described the phenomenon of auto-pollination in the bud stage of northern European orchids and suggested that half of the orchids of Denmark were auto-pollinating. Pijl and Dodson (1966) devoted relatively little space to auto-pollination in their excellent work on orchid pollination. The apparent lack of interest in auto-pollination during this period may be attributed to the fact that it was downstaged by the fascinating new aspects of cross-pollination in orchids which were being elucidated at the time, and which made Darwinian concepts increasingly compelling. Also, some of the articles on auto-pollination in plants and in orchids specifically (e.g. Martens, 1926) presented a particularly anti-Darwinian view, and seem to have made the subject distasteful.

In the last 15 years there has been renewed interest in pollination biology. The significance of auto-pollination has been considered by several evolutionary biologists and more than 30 articles have documented the phenomenon in orchids from different parts of the world.

Recognition of Self-pollination and the Use of Terms

There are three kinds of pollination. In cross-pollination pollen from a different plant is deposited on the stigma. Geitonogamous pollination occurs where the stigma receives pollen from a different flower on the same plant. Self-pollination occurs where pollen from the same flower reaches the stigma. Pollinators provide an opportunity for outbreeding, but their activity can also result in inbreeding. Self-pollination, which always results in inbreeding, can occur either as a result of visitation by a pollinator, or without the intervention of a vector as a result of flower characteristics that promote it. Wherever the term "auto-pollination" is used, it means automatic (i.e., vectorless) self-pollination. "Pollinator-dependent" refers to species not capable of auto-pollination.

Although auto-pollination has been frequently called "autogamy", this is a rather loose application of the latter term which actually refers to self-fertilization (autogamy = self-marriage). It should be noted however, that in all cases of auto-pollinating orchids that have been studied in detail, self-fertilization and seed development have followed autopollination. The term "spontaneous self-pollination" is appropriate but cumbersome. Since auto-fertility has long been used to describe the outcome of automatic self-pollination, and "auto" is consistent with "autogamy", the term "auto-pollination" allows precision and avoids confusion.

It may seem easy at first to recognize auto-pollinating species, but the only way to prove that the mechanism is operative is with careful observation and/or experimentation. Sometimes it is assumed that all open flowers are cross-pollinated, whereas those that are closed or never open are auto-pollinated. Fertilization in open flowers is called "chasmogamy" (= open marriage). The term for fertilization in closed flowers is "cleistogamy" (= closed marriage). In fact, many open flowers auto-pollinate and some closed flowers are either cross-pollinated (like tropical Musaceae and Marantaceae) or produce seeds vegetatively without pollination (i.e., through apomixis or more specifically agamospermy, see Catling, 1982, 1986 for examples in Orchidaceae). Not surprisingly the subterranean orchids of Australia (*Rhizanthella gardneri* and *R. slateri*) were thought to be auto-pollinating but recent studies provide evidence of pollination by small flies (Clements and Cribb, 1984).

When flowers are securely covered with cloth bags to prevent pollinator visits and they still produce seed, either auto-pollination or agamospermy is operating. If anthers are removed from the bagged flowers at an early stage (emasculation) and seeds still develop, then agamospermy has taken place. However, if no seeds result when pollinia are removed from bagged flowers which otherwise produced seed there are two possibilities: auto-pollination and subsequent fertilization (i.e., autogamy) or agamospermy induced by auto-pollination. The distinction may be made through anatomical study or by correlative seed morphology (e.g., Catling, 1986). Agamospermy is apparently rare in vascular plants and in the Orchidaceae (Catling, 1985c, 1986). Some cases of auto-pollination included here may actually be examples of pollination-induced agamospermy. However, on the basis of present knowledge, this is probably true of relatively few.

The distinction between pollinator-dependence and auto-pollination is also sometimes difficult to make. In many cases below I will refer to "auto-pollinated" taxa, but it should be remembered that in some of these there may also be opportunities for pollination by pollinators. Most orchids are not capable of auto-pollination and the presence or absence of this capability is usually structurally apparent. For example, auto-pollination can sometimes be detected in the older flowers on ripened capsules by the fact that the pollinia remain partly in the anther cells, but contact and germinate on the distal portion of the stigmatic surface. This has permitted detection in dried herbarium specimens (Catling, 1985b).

Characteristics of Auto-pollinating Orchids

It has been shown that auto-pollinating plants frequently differ from their pollinator-dependent relatives in a number of predictable characters (Ornduff, 1969). There have been few detailed comparisons in the Orchidaceae (Mehrhoff, 1983), but most of the character differences that have been suggested have a very broad application. These character differences are not only of biological and taxonomic significance, but they also aid in the detection of auto-pollination. Some of them seem to occur frequently in orchids (Table 4-1).

Many of these character differences involve reduced attractiveness of the auto-pollinating species. For example, the self-pollinating *Isotria medeoloides* has smaller flowers on shorter stalks than the pollinator-dependent *Isotria verticillata* (Mehrhoff, 1983). A nectar-containing mentum is readily apparent in the larger flowers of pollinator-dependent plants of *Corallorhiza odontorhiza* but practically absent in the smaller flowers of cleistogamous plants (Catling, 1983a). Fringed petals are well developed in the pollinator-dependent *Corybas fimbriata* and so is the hood-like dorsal sepal. In the auto-pollinating *Corybas despectans*, the lip is only slightly ragged and the dorsal sepal is not fully developed into a hood (Fig. 4-6). A contrasting floral color pattern is lacking or at least reduced in most auto-pollinating orchids. In the auto-

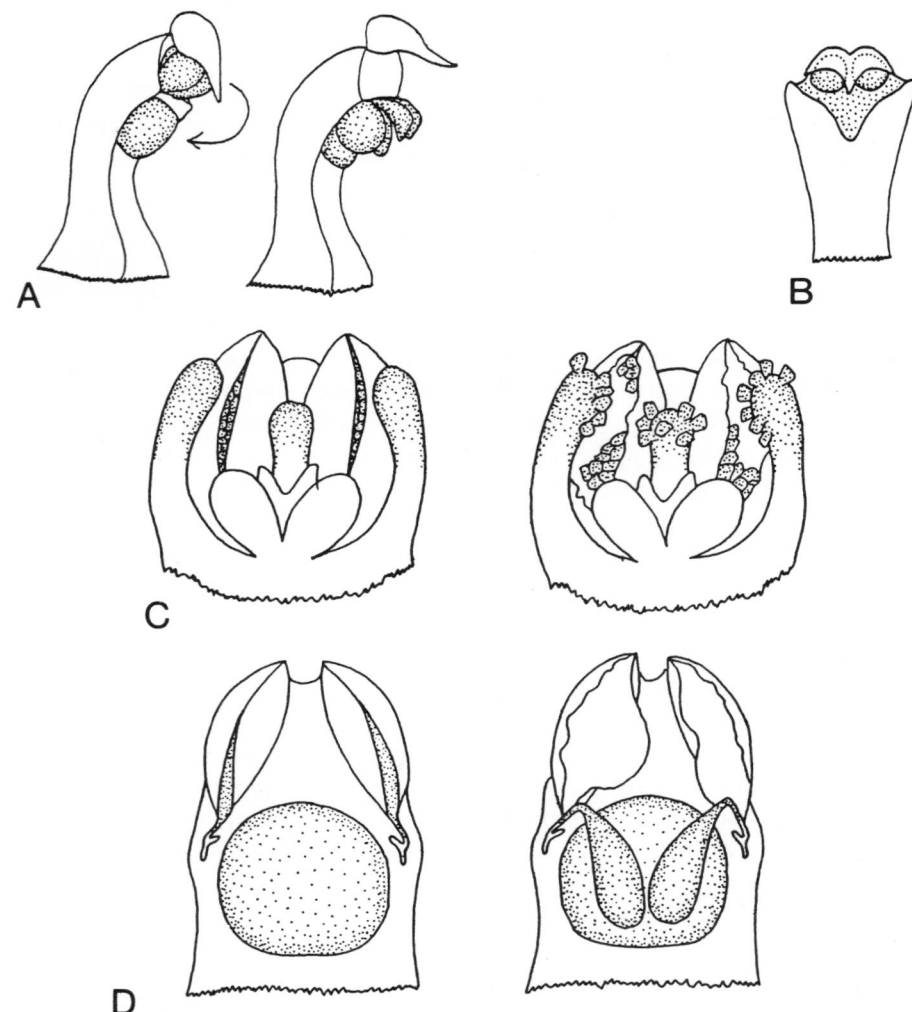

Fig. 4-1. Examples of auto-pollination in the Orchidaceae. A, Rotation of pollinia onto the stigmatic surface in *Corallorhiza maculata*; B, Absence of rostellum in the cleistogamous *Corallorhiza odontorhiza*; C, Falling of massulae onto 3 stigmatic lobes in *Platanthera clavellata*; D, Bending of the caudicle which brings the pollinia onto the stigmatic surface in *Platanthera hyberborea*. Drawings by P. M. Catling from fresh material collected in northeastern North America.

Table 4-1. List of frequent character differences between auto-pollinating orchids and their pollinator-dependent relatives.

Character	Pollinator-dependent	Auto-pollinated
Flower stalk	Long	Short
Sepals, petals and lip	Large	Small
Spur, mentum or nectary	Present	Absent or reduced
Lip and/or petals	Lobed, fringed or emarginate	Entire
Floral color pattern	Contrasting	Little or no contrast
Nectar guides	Present	Absent
Flowers	Widely opening	Semi-closed or entirely closed
	Scented	Scentless
Rostellum	Separating anther and stigma	Absent or reduced or position altered
Pollen grains	Many	Fewer
Ovules per flower	Many	Fewer
Fruits	Some not maturing	All maturing

pollinating *Encyclia cochleata* var. *triandra* the contrast of dark and light lines is reduced both in intensity and area, in comparison with the pollinator-dependent *Encyclia cochleata* var. *cochleata* (Fig. 4-3). The reduced attractiveness of flowers of some auto-pollinating plants may result from a lack of selection for attractiveness (Ornduff, 1969). However, it has also been suggested that reduced attractiveness could be positively selected for to reduce interference with auto-pollination (Mehrhoff, 1983).

Other characters (Table 4-1) are associated with the process of auto-pollination, or with the result. Of these, the relatively high fecundity (i.e., the tendency for all or most of the ovaries to ripen and produce seed) is a particularly useful character in the detection of auto-pollination. Often with pollinator-dependent orchids, many flowers in the inflorescence or in a colony are not visited, and consequently many ovaries do not expand with seed. In a colony of the auto-pollinating *Cypripedium passerinum*, all flowers give rise to ovaries with seed. The development of ripe capsules is often less than 10% in colonies of other North American lady's-slipper orchids, which are pollinator-dependent.

Methods of Auto-pollination

With regard to methods, it is possible to discuss only the physical and developmental characteristics of auto-pollination in orchids. These are reflected in gross morphology. The chemical and anatomical aspects have not been investigated.

The "method" of auto-pollination may be determined by considering the way in which a particular auto-pollinating flower differs from its pollinator-dependent relatives. Various methods in orchid flowers have been elaborated by various authors (Ridley, 1888; Smith, 1928, 1929; Kirchner, 1922; Pijl and Dodson, 1966; Catling, 1983a, 1985a). In fact the situation is more complicated than any of these authors imagined. Frequently one or more methods are combined and in most cases they are poorly documented and little understood. There has been a tendency for observers to notice a single phenomenon associated with auto-pollination (for example, sliding of pollinia onto the stigmatic surface) and to emphasize it without regard to other phenomena which are involved (e.g., early opening of the anther to release the pollinia, reduction in the size of the rostellum, and oversecretion of the stigma).

It is helpful to consider five major categories of auto-pollinating phenomena. These will be discussed briefly with examples. Within some major categories, a number of separate methods are recognized (Table 4-2), and as far as possible, these methods are assigned numerically to species in Table 4-3.

In general the most common methods of auto-pollination involve the lack of a rostellum or the falling of friable pollinia onto the stigmatic surfaces. Auto-pollination as a consequence of a bending caudicle is common in Orchideae and in the Vandoideae. In the Cypripedoideae, auto-pollination results exclusively from structural modification.

Table 4-2. Summary of methods of auto-pollination in the Orchidaceae.

1. Oversecretion of the stigma.
2. Movement of the perianth.
3. Movement of the stigma.
   (a) movement of the stigmatic arms.
   (b) involution or proliferation of tissue.
4. Movement of anther or pollinia.
   (a) falling of friable pollen.
   (b) falling or sliding of entire pollinia.
   (c) rotation of pollinia.
   (d) bending of caudicle, stalklet or pollen mass.
5. Structural modification.
   (a) rostellum and/or clinandrium absent or dissolving.
   (b) rostellum is stigmatic and/or other specialized stigmatic tissues develop.
   (c) additional anthers contact stigma.
   (d) pollinia and stigma develop in contact due to curvature changes and changes in length of stigmatic branch.

Table 4-3. List of auto-pollinating orchids including taxonomic status, pollination methods[a], location and references [using the classification of Dressler (1981)].

SUBFAMILY/TRIBE/Subtribe Species	Pollination Method	Location	Reference
SUBFAMILY—CYPRIPEDIOIDEAE			
CYPRIPEDIOIDEAE			
Cypripedium dickinsonianum	5d	Chiapas, Mexico	Hagsater, 1984
Cypripedium passerinum var. *passerinum*	5d	Alb., Ont., Yuk., Canada	Catling, 1983
Paphiopedilum lowii	5d	Asia	Day, 1972
Paphiopedilum mastersianum	5d	Asia	Day, 1972
Phragmipedium lindenii	5c	Columbia, Ecuador, Peru	Dodson, 1966
SUBFAMILY—SPIRANTHOIDEAE			
ERYTHRODEAE			
Goodyerinae			
Anoectochilus longicalcaratus		Sumatra	Smith, 1928
Cystorchis aphylla	?5a, 5b	Java	Smith, 1907, 1928
Goodyera carnea	5a	Sikkim, India	King & Pantling, 1898
Goodyera procera	1		Forbes, 1884
Goodyera repens var. *repens*	?4a	Denmark	Hagerup, 1952
Goodyera striata	4d	Mexico	Greenwood, pers. comm.
Goodyera triandra	5c	New Guinea	Smith, 1928
Kuhlhasseltia papuana	5a	New Guinea	Smith, 1928
Lepidogyne longifolia	5c	New Guinea	Smith, 1928
CRANICHIDEAE			
Spiranthinae			
Beloglottis ecallosa			Hamer, 1981
Brachystele unilateralis (*Spiranthes diuretica*)	2		Reiche, 1910
Cyclopogon prasophyllum	5a	Chiapas, Mexico	Salazar, pers. comm.
Cyclopogon sp.	5a	S. Vera Cruz, Mexico	Salazar, pers. comm.
Cyclopogon stenoglossa			Garay, pers. comm.
Discyphus scopulariae			Burns-Balogh, 1984, and pers. comm.
Eurystyles cotyledon			Dodson, pers. comm.
Hapalorchis lineatis (*Sauroglossum tenue*)		Brazil	Garay, pers. comm.
Helonoma (*Spiranthes*) *bifida*		Venezuela	Garay, pers. comm.
Pelexia sp.			Burns-Balogh, 1984, and pers. comm.

[a]See Table 4-2.

SUBFAMILY/TRIBE/Subtribe Species	Pollination Method	Location	Reference
Sarcoglottis sp.			Burns-Balogh, 1984, and pers. comm.
Sacoila (Stenorrhynchos) hassleri			Burns-Balogh, pers. comm.
Sacoila lanceolata var. *paludicola*	5a	S. Florida, U.S.A.	Catling, 1986
Schiedeella sp.	5a	Mexico	Greenwood, pers. comm.
Spiranthes australis			Ridley, 1888
Spiranthes ovalis var. *erostellata*	5a	Eastern U.S.A.	Catling, 1982, 1983
Spiranthes prasophylla var. *cleistogama*		Guatemala	Ames & Correll, 1952
Spiranthes sinensis (*S. australis*)	5a	Australia	Ridley, 1888; Bates, 1978; Bates, pers. comm.
Spiranthes sinensis var. *novae-zealandiae*		New Zealand	Garay, pers. comm.
Spiranthes spiralis	4a, ?5b	Denmark	Hagerup, 1952
Cranichidinae			
Cranichis fertilis		Venezuela	Garay, pers. comm.
Cranichis muscosa		Puerto Rico	Ackerman, pers. comm.
Prescottia cf. *stachyodes*		S. Vera Cruz, Mexico	Salazar, pers. comm.
Cryptostylidinae			
Cryptostylis arachnites			Forbes, 1884
Cryptostylis fulva		New Guinea	Schlechter *fide* Smith, 1928

SUBFAMILY—ORCHIDOIDEAE
NEOTTIEAE
Limodorinae

Cephalanthera damasonianum			Darwin, 1904
Cephalanthera longifolia			Darwin, 1904
Cephalanthera grandiflora (?=*C. alba*)	4a, 5a	England	Darwin, 1862, 1877
Cephalanthera rubra	4a, ?5b	Denmark	Hagerup, 1952
Eburophyton austinae	4a	California, U.S.A.	Kipping, 1971
Epipactis gigantea		California, U.S.A.	Merritt, 1897
Epipactis helleborine (*E. latifolia*)	4a, ?5b	Demark	Hagerup, 1952
	4c	Europe	Martens, 1926

(The capacity of the pollinia to pivot around the rostellum is described, but auto-pollination was not actually observed.)

Epipactis leptochila	4a	Norway	Nannfeldt, 1946
Epipactis microphylla	4a	Bavaria	Müller, 1868; Kirchner, 1922b
Epipactis palustris	4a	Europe	Kirchner, 1922a; Hagerup, 1952
Epipactis persica			Hagerup, 1952
Epipactis purpurea	4a, ?5b	Denmark	Hagerup, 1952
Epipactis viridiflora			Müller, 1868; Darwin, 1869
Limodorum abortivum	?5a	Europe	Pedicino, 1874; Freyhold, 1877; Kirchner, 1900, 1922a

Listerinae

Listera ovata	4a	Europe	Kirchner, 1922

(auto-pollination disputed by Nilsson (1981a,b), who suspected that 1.3% of his experimental plants that auto-pollinated, did so through the aid of minute insects (thrips) which infested the flowers. Darwin (1869) earlier suggested that thrips may play a significant role in auto-pollination, possibly making this a case of insect-aided auto-pollination.)

Neottia nidus-avis	5	England	Darwin, 1869; Resvoll, 1911; Kirchner, 1922a

Table 4-3. Continued.

SUBFAMILY/TRIBE/Subtribe Species	Pollination Method	Location	Reference
DIURIDEAE			
Chloraeinae			
Bipinnula sp.	2	Chile	Reiche, 1910
Chloraea falklandica			Kirchner, 1922a
Chloraea fonchii		Chile	Reiche, 1910
Chloraea inconspicum	?5a		Kranzlin, 1897–1903
Chloraea philippi		Chile	Reiche, 1910
Gavilea (Asarca) araucana		Chile	Reiche, 1910
Gavilea lutea (Asarca commersonii)		Chile	Reiche, 1910
Caladeniinae			
Caladenia bicalliata		SW. Australia	Bates, pers. comm.
Caladenia catenata var. *minor*		SW. Australia	Bates, 1978
Caladenia latifolia		SW. Australia	Bates, 1978
Caladenia pusilla		SW. Australia	Bates, pers. comm.
Chiloglottis cornuta	5	New Zealand	Thomson, 1879, 1880; Stoutamire, 1975
Chiloglottis diphylla		Australia	Fitzgerald, 1876; Ridley, 1888
Paracaleana minor		SW. Australia	Bates, 1978
Pterostylidinae			
Pterostylis aphylla		SW. Australia	Bates, 1978
Pterostylis foliata		SW. Australia	Bates, 1978
Acianthinae			
Corybas despectans		SW. Australia	Bates, 1978
Corybas sp.		New Zealand	Holland, 1961
Stigmatodactylus (*Pantlingia*) *paradoxa*	5a	Sikkim, India	King & Pantling, 1898
Diuridinae			
Calochilus campestris		Australia	Cady, 1972
Calochilus holtzei (?=*C. inberbes*)		Australia	Jones & Gray, 1974
Calochilus paludosus		SW. Australia	Bates, 1978
Calochilus robertsonii		SW. Australia	Bates, 1978; Stoutamire, 1983
Orthoceras strictum		Australia	Fitzgerald, 1888; Rogers, 1913
Thelymitra carnea var. *carnea*	4a	SW. Australia	Bates, 1978; Fitzgerald, 1876
Thelymitra carnea var. *rubra*		SW. Australia	Bates, 1978
Thelymitra circumsepta		Australia	Thomson, 1880; Fitzgerald, 1888
Thelymitra decora		SW. Australia	Bates, 1978
Thelymitra flexuosa		Australia	Rogers, 1913
Thelymitra fusco-lutea		SW. Australia	Rogers, 1913; Bates, 1978
Thelymitra ixioides		SW. Australia	Bates, 1978
Thelymitra javanica	4a	Java	Smith, 1928
Thelymitra longifolia		Australia, New Zealand	Fitzgerald, 1876 Thomson, 1879
Thelymitra luteocilium		SW. Australia	Bates, 1978
Thelymitra matthewsii		SW. Australia	Bates, 1978
Thelymitra media		Australia	Bates, pers. comm.
Thelymitra mucida		SW. Australia	Bates, 1978
Thelymitra nuda		Australia	Thomson, 1880; Fitzgerald, 1888
Thelymitra pauciflora (including var. *holmesii*)		SW. Australia	Bates, 1978
Thelymitra retecta		Australia	Bates, pers. comm.
Thelymitra sp. nov.		Australia	Beardsell, unpub.
Thelymitra venosa (probably wind-assisted)	4a	SW. Australia	Rogers, 1913; Jones, 1971; Bates, 1978

SUBFAMILY/TRIBE/Subtribe Species	Pollination Method	Location	Reference
Prasophyllinae			
Microtis parviflora	3b	Australia	Jones, 1975
Microtis unifolia sub M. *porrifolia*	3b	New Zealand, Australia	Thomson, 1879; Bates, 1984
Prasophyllum beaugleholei	?3b ?4a, ?5a	Australia	Jones, 1972a
Prasophyllum colensoi		New Zealand	Thomson, 1879
Prasophyllum gracile (?=*P. goldsackii*)		SW. Australia	Bates, 1978
Prasophyllum fitzgeraldii		SW. Australia	Bates, 1978
Prasophyllum fuscum		SW. Australia	Bates, 1978
Prasophyllum pallidum		SW. Australia	Bates, 1978
ORCHIDEAE			
Orchidinae			
Dactylorhiza maculata	4d	Europe	Martens, 1926; Dressler, 1981; Catling, 1983
Coeloglossum viride var. *viride*	?4a	Faroes	Hagerup, 1952
Neotinea intacta	4a	Europe	illustrated by Reichenbach, 1865; Darwin, 1869
Ophrys apifera	4d	England and continental Europe	Darwin, 1862, 1877;
(wind-assisted, see Darwin, 1877, p. 54; Martens, 1926; illustrated by Pijl & Dodson, 1966 and Davies & Davies, 1985)			
Ophrys botteroni	4d	Bavaria	Chodat, 1913; Kirchner, 1922a

Ophrys scolopax
   (*O. fuciflora, O. arachnites* var.
   pseudoscolopax-fecundans in part)
		France	Moggridge, 1865

Orchis latifolia	4d	Belgium	Martens, 1926
Orchis morio	4d	Belgium	Martens, 1926
Platanthera albida var. *albida* (*Leucorchis albida*)	4a	Faroes	Hagerup, 1952
Platanthera clavellata (& all or some combination of 5a & 5b)	4a	NE. U.S.A.; Ont. Nova Scotia, Canada	Gray, 1862; Darwin, 1869; Catling, 1983
Platanthera chorisiana	5a	Queen Charlotte & Vancouver Is., B.C., Canada	Catling, 1985b
Platanthera hyperborea	4a, 4b 4d	Greenland NE. North America	Hagerup, 1952 Gray, 1862; Darwin, 1869; Catling, 1983
Serapias lingua	4a	Spain	Pais, 1969
Serapias parviflora (*S. oculata*)		Europe	Kirchner, 1922a
Habenariinae			
Habenaria mesodactyla	4a	Belize	Catling, unpub.
Habenaria rodeiensis		Belize	Catling, unpub.
Herminium monorchis	?4b	Europe	Kirchner, 1922a
Peristylis grandis	4a	Java	Smith, 1928
Stenoglottis fimbriata	3a	S. Africa	Schelpe, 1970
Stenoglottis woodii	3a	S. Africa	Schelpe, 1970
DISEAE			
Disinae			
Disa macrantha		S. Africa	Darwin, 1877
Disa stolzii (*D. erubescens* ssp. *carsonii*)		S. Malawi, Africa	Gassner, 1982
Monadenia bracteata		S. Africa	H. Kurzweil, pers. comm.

Table 4-3. Continued.

SUBFAMILY/TRIBE/Subtribe Species	Pollination Method	Location	Reference
Corycinnae			
Pterygodium newdigatae			Kranzlin, 1910b
TRIPHOREAE			
Psilochilus physurifolius			Dressler, 1981
WULLSCHLAEGELIEAE			
Wullschlaegelia aphylla		Puerto Rico	Ackerman, pers. comm.
Wullschlaegelia sp.		Mexico	Greenwood, pers. comm.
SUBFAMILY—EPIDENDROIDEAE VANILLEAE **Lecanorchidinae**			
Lecanorchis javanica		Java	Smith, 1928
Pogoniinae *Codonorchis tetraphylla* (*Pogonia lessonii*)		Chile	Reiche, 1910
Isotria medeoloides	4b, 5a	E. North America	Mehrhoff, 1983
GASTRODIEAE **Gastrodiinae**			
Didymoplexis cornuta	5c		Smith, 1928
Gastrodia sp.		SW. Australia	Bates, 1978
EPIPOGIEAE			
Epipogium mutans	5a	Sikkim, India	King & Pantling, 1898
Epipogium roseum			Smith, 1928
	5	Java	Leeuwen, 1937
(expansion of the stigma and retraction of anther flaps allowing the pollinia and stigma to come into contact)			
		Australia	Jones, 1985
ARETHUSEAE **Bletiinae**			
Arundina (Dilochia) pentandra		Asia	Garay, pers. comm.
Arundina speciosa	3, ?5a		Forbes, 1884
Basiphyllaea angustifolia		Puerto Rico	Ackerman, pers. comm.
Basiphyllaea corallicola	5a	S. Florida, U.S.A.	Luer, 1972
Bletia purpurea	5a	S. Florida, U.S.A.	Luer, 1972; pers. comm.
Bletia (Crybe) rosea (*B. purpurata*)	5a	Mexico, Guatemala	Greenwood, pers. obs.
Bletia campanulata		Mexico	Dressler, 1968
Bletia macristhmochila		Mexico	Dressler, 1968
Bletia urbana		Mexico	Dressler, 1968
Calanthe aureifolia		Sumatra	Smith, 1928; Dressler, 1968
Calanthe inaperta (*Phaius villosus*)	?5a		Moore, 1876
Calanthe manii	5a	Sikkim-Himilaya	King & Pantling, 1898
Calanthe papuana		New Guinea	Smith, 1928
Calanthe veratrifolia var. *cleistogama*	?5a	New Guinea	Schlechter, 1914
Calanthe vestita var. *sumatrana*	?5a	Sumatra	Smith, 1928
Calanthe sp.	1, 5a		Scott, 1865; Schlechter, 1914
Chysis laevis	5a		Kirchner, 1922a
Dilochia wallichii	5c	Java, Sumatra	Smith, 1928
Hexalectris nitida		Mexico	Greenwood, pers. comm.
Phaius amboinensis	5a		Forbes, 1884; Smith, 1928

SUBFAMILY/TRIBE/Subtribe Species	Pollination Method	Location	Reference
Phaius albescens			Forbes, 1884
Phaius australis (*P. grandiflorus*)		Queensland, Australia	Rogers, 1921
Phaius australis var. *bernaysii* (*P. bernaysii*)		Queensland, Australis	Rogers, 1921
Phaius blumei			Forbes, 1884; Knuth, 1898–1905
Phaius maculatus	4b (wind- assisted)		Ridley, 1888
Phaius pictus	?3a, 3b, ?5a	Australia	Jones, 1976
Phaius tankervilliae	5a, 5c	Java	Smith, 1928
(discussion of post-pollination phenomena in Gandawidjaja & Arditti, 1982)			
Plocoglottis glaucescens		New Guinea	Schlechter, 1914
Spathoglottis microchilina	5a	Java	Smith, 1928
Spathoglottis paulinae	4d		Ridley, 1888
Spathoglottis plicata	5a	Malaysia, Puerto Rico	Forbes, 1884; Smith, 1928; Dressler, 1981; Ackerman, pers. comm.
Spathoglottis sp.		New Guinea	Schlechter, 1914
Tainia penangiana	5a	Ambon, Java	Smith, 1905, 1928

COELOGYNEAE
Coelogyninae

Entomophobia kinabaluensis			Vogel, 1984
Otochilus sp.		India	Garay, pers. comm.
Pholidota sp.		India	Garay, pers. comm.

MALAXIDEAE

Liparis caespitosa	5a		Schlechter, 1914
Liparis cleistogama	?5a	Ambon	Smith, 1905
(but Smith (1929) reported cleistoflory)			
Liparis longipies	4b, 5a		Schlechter, 1922a
Liparis loeselii	4c	Ont., Canada; N.Y., Wis., U.S.A.	Catling, 1980
	4c	Bavaria	Kirchner, 1922b
Malaxis sp.		Mexico	Greenwood, pers. comm.
Microstylis histionantha	?4b		Ridley, 1888
Microstylis maximowicziana	5a	Sikkim, India	King & Pantling, 1898; Kranzlin, 1911
Microstylis soleiformis		Java	Smith, 1928
Microstylis nephroglossa		New Guinea	Schlechter, 1914
Oberonia cleistogama		New Guinea	Schlechter, 1914; Smith, 1928
Oberonia linearis	5a	New Guinea	Smith, 1928

EPIDENDREAE
Eriinae

Eria albotomentosa			Forbes, 1884
Eria bifalcis		New Guinea	Schlechter *fide* Smith, 1928
Eria clausa		Sikkim	King & Pantling, 1898
Eria cleistogama		New Guinea	Smith, 1928
Eria excavata		Sikkim	King & Pantling, 1898
Eria falcata		Java	Smith, 1928
Eria inamoena	5a	New Guinea	Schlechter, 1914
Eria isochila			Smith, 1928
Eria aff. *javensis*	4d		Forbes, 1884; Smith, 1928
Eria stenophylla		New Guinea	Schlechter *fide* Smith, 1928
Eria teysmannii (*Trichotosia dajakorum*)		Borneo	Smith, 1928

Table 4-3. Continued.

SUBFAMILY/TRIBE/Subtribe Species	Pollination Method	Location	Reference
Podochilinae			
Agrostophyllum crassicaule	1, 5a	New Guinea	Schlechter, 1914
Agrostophyllum compressum	1, 5a	New Guinea	Schlechter, 1914
Agrostophyllum denbergeri		Krakatau	Smith, 1928
Agrostophyllum dichorense	1, 5a	New Guinea	Schlechter, 1914
Agrostophyllum graminifolium	1, 5a	New Guinea	Schlechter, 1914
Agrostophyllum montanum	1, 5a	New Guinea	Schlechter, 1914
Agrostophyllum pelorioides	1, 5a	New Guinea	Schlechter, 1914; Smith, 1928
Agrostophyllum stenophyllum	1, 5a	New Guinea	Schlechter, 1914; Smith, 1928
Agrostophyllum superpositum	1, 5a	New Guinea	Schlechter, 1914
Agrostophyllum verriciforum	1, 5a	New Guinea	Schlechter, 1914
Appendicula biumbonata		New Guinea	Schlechter, 1914
Appendicula bracteata	5a	New Guinea	Schlechter, 1914; Smith, 1928
Appendicula carinifera	5a	New Guinea	Schlechter 1914; Smith, 1928
Appendicula cleistogama		New Guinea	Schlechter, 1914
Appendicula concava	5a	New Guinea	Schlecter, 1914; Smith, 1928
Appendicula cryptostigma		New Guinea	Schlechter, 1914
Appendicula diamuensis		New Guinea	Schlechter, 1914
Appendicula flaccida		New Guinea	Schlechter, 1914
Appendicula isologlossa		New Guinea	Schlechter, 1914; Smith, 1928
Appendicula kaniensis	5a	New Guinea	Schlechter, 1914; Smith, 1928
Appendicula lobogyne		New Guinea	Schlechter, 1914
Appendicula lutea	5a	New Guinea	Schlechter, 1914; Smith, 1928
Appendicula oblonga	5a	New Guinea	Schlechter, 1914; Smith, 1928
Appendicula pseudopendula		New Guinea	Schlechter, 1914
Appendicula torricelliana		New Guinea	Schlechter, 1914
Cyphochilus sp.		New Guinea	Schlechter, 1914
Thelasiinae			
Oxyanthera abbreviata	5a	New Guinea	Schlechter, 1914
Oxyanthera papuana	5a	New Guinea	Schlechter, 1914
Phreatia coelonychia	5a	New Guinea	Schlechter, 1914; Smith, 1928
Phreatia densiflora			Kranzlin, 1911
Phreatia gracilis	5a	New Guinea	Schlechter, 1914; Smith, 1928
Phreatia microphyton		New Guinea	Smith, 1928
Phreatia oreogena	5a	New Guinea	Schlechter, 1914; Smith, 1928
Phreatia trilobulata	5a	New Guinea	Schlechter, 1914; Smith, 1928
Thelasis capitata		Padang Uplands	Smith, 1928
Thelasis carinata		Cape York Peninsula, Australia	Jones, 1985b
Thelasis compacta	5a	New Guinea	Schlechter, 1914
Thelasis papuana		New Guinea	Smith, 1928
Laeliinae			
Broughtonia sanguinea		Jamaica	Sauleda & Adams, 1984
Cattleya aurantiaca	5a		Knudson, 1956
Cattleya crispa (*Laelia crispa*)	?5a		Darwin, 1862, 1877
Cattleya patinii			Dressler, 1981
Cattleya sp.	1	Trinidad	Cruger, 1865

SUBFAMILY/TRIBE/Subtribe Species	Pollination Method	Location	Reference
Cattleya sp.	?5a		Moore, 1877
Caularthron bilamellatum	5a	Belize	Catling, unpub.; Dressler, 1981
Dimerandra emarginata		Nicaragua	Hamer, 1984a
Encyclia boothiana var. *erythonoides*	5c	S. Florida, U.S.A.	Luer, 1971, 1972; Dressler, 1981
Encyclia bradfordii		Trinidad	Withner, 1970
Encyclia chacaoensis		Mexico	Dressler & Pollard, 1976
Encyclia cochleata var. *triandra*	5c	S. Florida, Cuba, Hispaniola Puerto Rico	Luer, 1971, 1972; Dressler, 1981 Ackerman, pers. comm.
Encyclia cretacea		Mexico	Dressler & Pollard, 1976
Encyclia gravida		Mexico	Dressler & Pollard, 1976 Withner, 1970
Encyclia isochila var. *tridens* (*Epidendrum belvederense*)		Dominican Republic	Withner, 1970
Encyclia monitcolum		Hispaniola, Jamaica	Withner, 1970
Encyclia ochracea		Mexico	Dressler & Pollard, 1976
Encyclia pygmaea		Puerto Rico	Ackerman, pers. comm.
Encyclia sintenisii		Puerto Rico	Ackerman, pers. comm.; Withner, 1970
Epidendrum eustirum		Mexico	Hagsater, pers. comm.
Epidendrum funkii		Ecuador	Hagsater, pers. comm.
Epidendrum latifolium		Puerto Rico	Ackerman, pers. comm.; Dressler, 1981
Epidendrum nocturnum	?5a	S. Florida, U.S.A. Puerto Rico Brazil	Luer, 1972 Ackerman, pers. comm. Stort & Pavanelli, 1985
Epidendrum pallens		N. Costa Rica	Catling, unpub.; Hagsater, pers. comm.
Epidendrum phragmites		Nicaragua	Hamer, 1982
Epidendrum rigidum		S. Florida, U.S.A. Mexico	Catling, unpub. Hagsater, pers. comm.
Epidendrum variegatum	?5a		Hart, 1886
Epidendrum sp.	1, 5a	Trinidad	Cruger, 1865; Moore, 188??
Epidendrum sp.	5c	S. Brazil	Freyhold, 1877
Epidendrum sp.	5c	Brazil	Darwin, 1862, 1877
Epidendrum sp.		Ecuador	Hagsater, pers. comm.
Hexadesmia fasciculata	5a	N. Costa Rica	Catling, unpub.
Jacquiniella globosa		Belize	Catling, unpub.
Jacquiniella sp.		Guatemala, Mexico	Hagsater, pers. comm.
Laelia cinnabarina (perhaps artifically induced)			Darwin, 1862, 1877
Oerstedella aberrans		Guatemala	Hagsater, pers. comm.
Oerstedella centradenia		Costa Rica, Panama	Hagsater, pers. comm.
Oerstedella thurstonorum		Ecuador	Hagsater, pers. comm.
Schomburgkia lyonsii			Fowlie, 1963

Table 4-3. Continued.

SUBFAMILY/TRIBE/Subtribe Species	Pollination Method	Location	Reference
Schomburgkia marginata			Jones, 1968
Schomburgkia undulata			Jones, 1968
Schomburgkia sp.	1	Trinidad	Cruger, 1865
Pleurothallidinae			
Physosiphon loddigesii (but produced empty seed)	?4b		Kirchner, 1922a
Pleurothallis carioi		Belize	Catling, unpub.
Pleurothallis corniculata		Nicaragua	Hamer, 1984a
Pleurothallis ghiesbreghtiana var. *cleistogama*		Guatemala	Ames & Correll, 1952
Pleurothallis quadrifida		Nicaragua	Hamer, 1984a
Pleurothallis ruscifolia	4b		Kirchner, 1922a
Pleurothallis sempergemmata			Luer, 1977
Restrepiopsis clausa			Luer, 1978
Stelis cleistogama		Guatemala	Ames & Correll, 1952
Dendrobiinae			
Dendrobium aqueum			Kranzlin, 1910
Dendrobium atavus			Smith, 1928
Dendrobium brymerianum var. *histrionicum*			Kranzlin, 1910
Dendrobium chrysanthum (related to *D. denneanum*)			Darwin, 1862
Dendrobium chryseum	4b, 5a		Ridley, 1888
Dendrobium cleistogamum	5a		Kranzlin, 1910
Dendrobium crepidatum		Sikkim	King & Pantling, 1898
Dendrobium clausum	5a	New Guinea	Schlechter, 1914
Dendrobium cretaceum	5a		Darwin, 1869, 1877; Moore, 1877
Dendrobium dendrocolloides	5a	New Guinea	Smith, 1928
Dendrobium densiflorum (possibly based on *D. galliceanum*)			Kranzlin, 1910
Dendrobium excavatum		Borneo	Smith, 1928
Dendrobium finisterrae		New Guinea	Smith, 1928
Dendrobium gemellum		Java	Smith, 1928
Dendrobium giulianettii			Kranzlin, 1910
Dendrobium homoglossum		New Guinea	Smith, 1928
Dendrobium hosei	5c	Malay Peninsula	Smith, 1928
Dendrobium isomerum		Sumatra	Smith, 1928
Dendrobium mastersianum (related to *D. anosum*)	4b		Kranzlin, 1910
Dendrobium noesae		Java	Smith, 1928
Dendrobium normale			Smith, 1928
Dendrobium obcuneatum	5a		Kranzlin, 1910
Dendrobium pachystele		New Guinea	Schlechter *fide* Smith, 1928
Dendrobium pandaneti	5c	Java, Sumatra, Bangka, Malay Peninsula	Smith, 1928
Dendrobium paucilaciniatum	5c	Ternate, Indonesia	Smith, 1928
Dendrobium polycarpum			Kranzlin, 1910
Dendrobium quadriferum		New Guinea	Smith, 1928
Dendrobium sarcopodioides		New Guinea	Smith, 1928
Dendrobium suberectum (*Sarcopodium suberectum*)	5c	Borneo	Smith, 1928
Dendrobium tetrodon		Java	Smith, 1928; Comber, 1983
Dendrobium tetrodon var. *vanvuurenii*		Celebes	Smith, 1928
Dendrobium tetraedre			Smith, 1928
Dendrobium triviale			Kranzlin, 1910
Dendrobium sect. *gastidium*		New Guinea	Schlechter, 1914
Bulbophyllinae			
Bulbophyllum aphanopetalum			Schlechter, 1911

Table 4-3. Continued.

SUBFAMILY/TRIBE/Subtribe Species	Pollination Method	Location	Reference
Bulbophyllum cleistogamum		Riau, Indonesia	Smith, 1928
Bulbophyllum dasyphyllum	5a	New Guinea	Schlechter, 1914; Smith, 1928
Bulbophyllum dischidiifolium	5a		Smith, 1907b
Bulbophyllum nieuwenhuisii		Borneo	Smith, 1928
Bulbophyllum scrobiculilabre	5a	New Guinea	Smith, 1928
Bulbophyllum triandrum	5c	New Guinea	Smith, 1928
Bulbophyllum verruciferum var. *carinatisepalum*	5c		Schlechter, 1914

SUBFAMILY—VANDOIDEAE
POLYSTACHYEAE

Polystachya concreta (*P. luteola*)		Virgin Islands, West Indies	Ackerman, pers. comm.; Eggers, 1881
Polystachya foliosa		Puerto Rico	Ackerman, pers. comm.
Polystachya furiformis	?5a	S. Africa	Schelpe, 1970
Polystachya singaporensis	5a	Singapore	Smith, 1928
Polystachya zeylandica	?5a	Mascarene	Moore, 1876

VANDEAE
Sarcanthinae

Cleisostoma (*Sarcanthus*) *parishii*			Darwin, 1877
Mystacidium inapertum	5a	Madagascar	Ridley, 1885
Papilionantha (*Aerides*) *longicornu* (wind-assisted)		Sikkim, India	King & Pantling, 1898
Schoenorchis paniculata		Malaysia	Smith, 1928
Taeniophyllum hasseltii	4a	Java	Smith, 1928
Thrixspermum spp.		Malaysia	Schlechter, 1914

MAXILLARIEAE
Corallorhizinae

Aplectrum hyemale	?4c	Illinois, U.S.A.	Hogan, 1983
Corallorhiza maculata var. *maculata*	4c	Ont., Canada	Catling, 1983
Corallorhiza maculata var. *occidentalis*	4c	California, U.S.A.	Kipping, 1971
Corallorhiza odontorhiza	5a	E. North America	Case, 1964; Luer, 1975; Catling, 1983
Corallorhiza trifida var. *trifida* (*C. innata*)		Bavaria	Kirchner, 1922a
	4c	Ont., Canada	Catling, 1983
Corallorhiza sp.	4c	Mexico	Greenwood, pers. comm.
Govenia sp.		Mexico	Greenwood, pers. comm.
Govenia sp.		Ecuador	Greenwood, pers. comm.

Zygopetalinae

Cochleanthes flabelliformis		Puerto Rico	Ackerman, pers. comm.

Maxillariinae

Maxillaria rufescens var. *cryptogama*			Reichenbach fil., 1877
Maxillaria rufescens		Puerto Rico	Ackerman, pers. comm.

Dichaeinae

Dichaea hystricina		Puerto Rico	Ackerman, pers. comm.

CYMBIDIEAE
Cyrtopodiinae

Chrysoglossum sp.	5a		Forbes, 1884

Table 4-3. Continued.

SUBFAMILY/TRIBE/Subtribe Species	Pollination Method	Location	Reference
Cymbidium ensifolium (C. sundaicum)			Smith, 1928
Eulophia acutilabra	5a	Zambia, South Africa	Williamson, 1984
Eulophia alta		Puerto Rico	Ackerman, pers. comm.
	4d	Vera Cruz, Mexico	Salazar, pers. comm.
Eulophia ecalcarata		Zambia, South Africa	Williamson, 1984
Eulophia falcata		Zambia, South Africa	Williamson, 1984
Eulophia katangensis		Zambia, South Africa	Williamson, 1984
Eulophia macaulayae	5a	Zambia, South Africa	Williamson, 1984
Eulophia nyassae		Zambia, South Africa	Williamson, 1984
Eulophia penduliflora	5a	Zambia, South Africa	Williamson, 1984
Eulophia saxicola		Zambia, South Africa	Williamson, 1984
Oeceoclades maculata (Eulophidium maculatum)	4d		Ridley, 1888
	4d	S. Florida, U.S.A.	McCartney, 1985
	4d	Puerto Rico	Gonzalez & Ackerman, 19??
Stanhopeinae			
Acineta dalessandroi		Ecuador	Dodson, pers. comm.
Oncidiinae			
Oncidium oestlundianum		W. Mexico	Dodson, pers. comm.
Oncidium pollardii		Mexico	Salazar, pers. comm.
Psygmorchis gnomus			Dodson & Dressler, 1972
Psygmorchis zamorensis (Oncidium glossomystax)	4d	Ecuador	Dodson, pers. comm.
Trichopilia fragrans	?4d		Ridley, 1888
Trizeuxis falcata	4d		Kirchner, 1922a

1. Oversecretion of the stigma

In this case, excess stigmatic fluid contacts the pollinia and pollen tubes develop and enter the stigma. Examples include *Thelymitra circumsepta* (Fitzgerald, 1875–76) and *Phaius blumei* (Forbes, 1884). Oversecretion of the stigma does not, by itself, result in auto-pollination. It is usually associated with other changes. In fact there are no well-documented cases of auto-pollination in the absence of either abnormal (with regard to related pollinator-dependent taxa) movements or structure. Oversecretion may be an important component of auto-pollination in many species, especially in cases of cleistogamy [*Agrostophyllum* spp. for example, (Schlechter, 1914)], but is not readily apparent and thus is easily overlooked.

2. Movement of the perianth

During the process of floral senescence, perianth segments (sepals and/or petals and/or lip) curve in a manner that brings the pollinia and the stigma into contact. Examples include *Chiloglottis diphylla* (Fitzgerald, 1876; Ridley, 1888) and *Bipinnula* sp. (Reiche, 1910).

3. Movement of the stigma

In *Stenoglottis fimbriata*, stigmatic "arms" bend inward (Fig. 4-2) and contact pollen masses falling out of the anther (Schelpe, 1970). Rapid proliferation and involution of the margins of the stigma bring about contact with the pollinia in *Microtis uniflorus* (Bates, 1984) and *Phaius pictus* (Jones, 1976). In *Thelymitra longifolia* and *Arundina speciosa*, the involution of the stigmatic margin is accompanied by a down-curving of the pollen mass (Forbes, 1884).

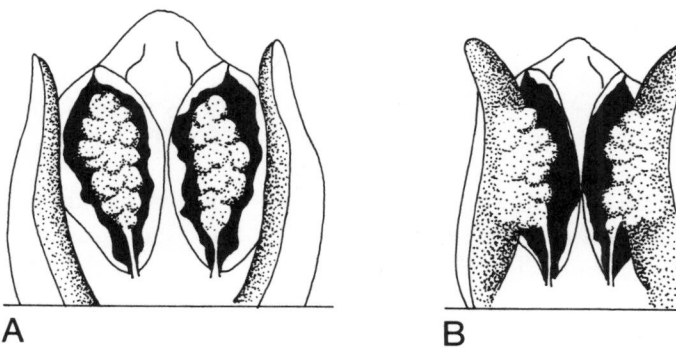

A **B**

Fig. 4-2. Auto-pollination in *Stenoglottis fimbriata* showing the column from below when the flower first opens (A) and a few days later when the stigmatic arms have bent inwards and caught falling pollen masses (B). Redrawn from drawings provided by Dr. E. A Schelpe made from living material in South Africa.

4. Movement of anther or pollinia

There are many cases of friable pollen, tetrads, or massulae, falling directly onto the stigmatic surface. Examples include *Cephalanthera grandiflora* (Darwin, 1877), *Cephalanthera rubra* (Hagerup, 1952), *Serapias lingua* (Pais, 1969), and *Plantanthera clavellata* (Fig. 4-1c; Gray, 1862; Catling, 1983). In such cases the anthers must open and the strands (composed of viscin, elastoviscin or sporopollenin) and/or sticky substances which hold the pollinia together must either not develop or they decay. Also the stigmatic surface or surfaces must be directly below the anthers.

In *Pleurothallis ruscifolia* and *Physosiphon loddigesii*, the whole anther falls onto the stigmatic surface (Kirchner, 1922a), whereas in *Herminium monorchis* (Kirchner, 1922a), *Dendrobium chryseum* (Ridley, 1888) and *Isotria medeoloides* (Mehrhoff, 1983), the entire pollinia slide onto the stigmatic surface.

Falling or sliding can occur only if there are no obstructions and when the stigma is below the anther. In some cases the absence of the rostellum facilitates this, as in *Isotria medeoloides* (Mehrhoff, 1983).

Rotation of the pollinia onto the stigmatic surface differs from falling or sliding since they must remain attached to the column and turn around the corner (i.e., the edge of the rostellum) until they reach the stigmatic surface which is behind or beside the anther, rather than below it. Examples include *Spathoglottis paulinae* (Fitzgerald, 1876; Ridley, 1888), *Corallorhiza maculata* and *C. trifida* (Fig. 4-1a and Catling, 1983), and *Liparis loeselii* (Catling, 1980).

In many orchids there is a release of the pollinia from the anther, but they remain basally attached to the column in the region of the viscidium (i.e., the viscidium remains inside the bursicle). A bending of the caudicle, stalklet or pollen mass brings the pollinia into contact with the stigmatic surface. Examples include *Platanthera hyperborea* (Fig. 4-1d and Catling, 1983), *Ophrys apifera* (Darwin, 1877, p. 53; van der Pijl and Dodson, 1966, Fig. 87), *Oncidium glossomystax* (van der Pijl and Dodson, 1966, Fig. 88). In *Microtis uniflorus*, a contraction of the caudicle has been reported (Bates, 1984).

An interesting case of bending of the anther-bearing branches of the column is described by Day (1972) in races of *Paphiopedilum lowii* and *P. mastersianum*. Self-pollination involving bending of the stipe or rotation may be significantly enhanced by the action of rain striking the flowers. This has been demonstrated for *Liparis loeselii* (Cattling, 1980) and *Oecoclades maculata* (Gonzalez and Ackerman, 1985).

5. Structural modifications

In most auto-pollinating orchids, the rostellum either does not develop, develops incompletely, or in a few cases disintegrates during flowering, allowing the pollinia and stigma to come in contact. The flowers may remain tightly closed (cleistogamy) as in *Corallorhiza odontorhiza* (Fig. 4-1b and Catling, 1983); open a very little like some races of *Bletia purpurea* (Luer, 1972; Catling, unpublished) or open normally as in *Spiranthes ovalis* var. *erostellata* (Catling, 1983), *Sacoila lanceolata* var. *paludicola* (Catling, 1985c), and some *Cattleya aurantiaca* (Knudson, 1956).

In *Calanthe manii*, the bottom of the clinandrium (or androclinium—the portion of the column around or under the anther) develops incompletely or disintegrates resulting in contact between stigma and pollinia (King and Pantling, 1898; Kirchner, 1922a). This may be of wider occurrence and could accompany some cases of an incomplete or disintegrating rostellum, but is less readily observed. It is reported also in *Microstylis maximowicziana* (King and Pantling, 1898; Kranzlin, 1911) and *Pantlingia paradoxa* (King and Pantling, 1898).

Another kind of structural modification involves a rostellum which assumes the primitive condition of a functional stigmatic lobe. This lobe is either in contact with the pollinia or positioned in a manner which allows it to receive falling pollen. Examples include *Platanthera clavellata* (Fig. 4-1c and Catling, 1983) and *Cyrtorchis aphylla* (Smith, 1907).

Both *Platanthera clavellata* (Fig. 4-1c) and *Stenoglottis fimbriata* (Fig. 4-3) have lateral stigmatic arms. These may represent the partly arrested development of an early primitive condition in tissue development. They may also be newly evolved structures, but the former seems more likely. The stigmatic processes in *Habenaria mesodactyla* (Fig. 4-10) apparently represent a similar development.

If additional stigmatic surfaces could be developed and could facilitate auto-pollination, additional anthers can also be expected. A typical example is *Phragmipedium lindenii* (Dodson, 1966), but this has occurred in a few other taxa including *Encyclia cochleata* var. *triandra* (Fig. 4-3) and *Encyclia boothiana* var. *erythronoides* (Luer, 1971, 1972; Dressler, 1981; Catling, unpublished).

Finally there are some cases where column structure, including especially the positions of the stigmatic surface and the anther, is such that the pollinia and the stigma develop in contact. This may be achieved in part by a shortening of the stigmatic branch as seems to be the case in *Cypripedium passerinum* (Catling, 1983) and *Cypripedium dickinsonianum* (Hagsater, 1984).

Fig. 4-3. Auto-pollinating *Encyclia cochleata* var. *triandra* (left) from the Big Cypress (*Catling s.n.,* DAO) in south Florida, and cross-pollinating *Encyclia cochleata* var. *cochleata* (right) from Belize (*Catling and Brownell B25.1,* AMES). Photographs by P. M. Catling.

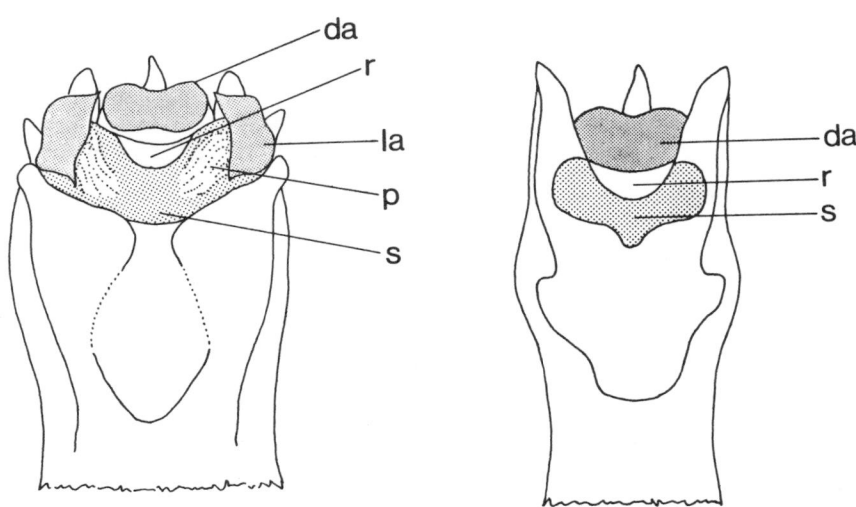

Fig. 4-4. Columns viewed from below of auto-pollinating *Encyclia cochleata* var. *triandra* (left) from the Big Cypress in south Florida, and cross-pollinating *Encyclia cochleata* var. *cochleata* (right) from Belize. da = dorsal anther, la = lateral anther, p = pollen tubes entering stigmatic tissue, r = rostellar flap, s = stigmatic surface. Drawings by P. M. Catling.

6. Classification of methods

The lack of detailed information on methods makes it undesirable at this point to try to classify them as more or less advanced from an evolutionary viewpoint. Until there is a more complete understanding of tissue development and chemical aspects allowing an understanding of how a caudicle bends, how a rostellum is reduced and how difficult it is to develop auxiliary stigmatic tissue etc., classification of this type is to be avoided. Furthermore, since certain methods of auto-pollination do not seem to give rise to others (i.e., there does not seem to be a sequence of methods), it is not appropriate to consider primitive and advanced states.

Degrees of Auto-pollination

In many cases, one of two closely related taxa auto-pollinates, and the other is pollinator-dependent. In addition, both auto-pollination and pollinator-dependence can be found within species and even within individuals.

For individual plants, the classic example is the seasonal cleistogamy in north temperate violets (*Viola* spp., Violaceae). A specific plant may produce open pollinator-dependent flowers in the spring and auto-pollinated cleistogamous blossoms during the summer. This is found in a number of plant families, but interestingly there are no known cases of seasonal cleistogamy or seasonal auto-pollination in the Orchidaceae.

In many instances, an auto-pollinating orchid plant can be cross-pollinated or contribute to cross-pollination. This can occur because auto-pollination often takes place late in flowering or at least after the flower has been open for a few days. In the absence of pollination by a vector (an insect or bird), auto-pollination can take place. This faculative outbreeding in auto-pollinating orchids is not well documented. Examples include: *Sacoila lancolata* var. *paludicola* (Catling, 1985c); *Microtis parviflora* (Jones, 1975); *Liparis loeselii* (Catling, 1980); *Corallorhiza maculata* (Catling, 1983a); and *Thelymitra pauciflora* (Bates, 1978). Even some species in which auto-pollination begins before the bud opens, as in races of *Cattleya aurantiaca* (Knudson, 1956), may be cross-pollinated and cross-fertilized if foreign pollen tubes grow more rapidly than those of the same flower.

There are undoubtedly many more examples of faculative outbreeding in auto-pollinating orchid flowers, but there are also numerous instances where there is absolutely no opportunity for outbreeding because the flowers remain tightly closed. Closed flowers do not prevent cross-pollination in some tropical plants, but there is no evidence for cross-pollination in the cleistogamous flowers of orchids (Table 4-3). Cleistogamy is generally less common than spontaneous selfing in open flowers (Lord, 1981), and the same seems to be true in the Orchidaceae. There are at least 40 orchid taxa in which some level of cleistogamy has been reported.

Some of the orchids with essentially closed flowers open their flowers very briefly under especially favorable environmental conditions. This has been called "ecological cleistogamy". It occurs in an auto-pollinating race of the West Indian *Bletia purpurea*. The flowers on a single plant open in some years, but not in others, apparently depending on the weather (Catling, unpublished). A plant of *Dendrobium crepidatum* from Thailand which produced only cleistogamous flowers for several years, suddenly had both normal and cleistogamous flowers (E. A. Schelpe, personal communication). Eggers (1881) noted that plants of the West Indian *Polystachya luteola* produce cleistogamous flowers in dry spells and open blossoms during moist periods. *Liparis cleistogama* is said to be cleistogamous in the wet and misty rainforest, but produces open flowers in drier air outside the forest. It has been assumed that this reflects the response of a single plant, but in fact Smith (1905) did not refer to any experiment and was comparing plants of different regions on the basis of communication from Schlechter. Smith's (1928) extensive experience with Indonesian orchids pointed "more toward a great fixity in the production of certain forms of flower than toward variability for reasons of external influence". As it stands, there are few well-documented examples of ecological cleistogamy in orchids.

In some cases, auto-pollinating morphs have been accorded formal taxonomic rank and in other cases they have not. Thus it is more convenient to consider genetically closely related groups rather than taxonomic ranks, such as species *per se*. Most, if not all, auto-pollinating orchids have close pollinator-dependent relatives, and thus there are many examples of different amounts of auto-pollination within genetically closely related groups. An example in *Thelymitra* is of particular interest.

Thelymitra pauciflora var. *holmesii* of South Australia (Fig. 4-5) includes two different kinds of plants. One opens very briefly under optimal conditions of heat, sunshine and humidity (Fig. 4-5a). This permits cross-pollination, but if it does not occur, then auto-pollination proceeds. The other kind produces flowers which never open, despite weather conditions, but auto-pollinate in bud (Fig. 4-5b). The ovaries swell with ripe seed gradually, and the flower buds begin to turn brown. In terms of breeding system the plants with flowers which open only briefly are apparently the intermediates in a group of closely related genotypes. The outbreeding, open-flowered extreme is referred to another species called *Thelymitra nuda*.

Fig. 4-5. Auto-pollinating *Thelymitra pauciflora* var. *holmesii*. A plant which has opened its flowers (left) allowing cross-pollination and/or pollinia removal, but nevertheless retains the fertility insurance of auto-pollination. Another plant with permanently closed, cleistogamous flowers (right) which auto-pollinate. Photographs by R. Bates.

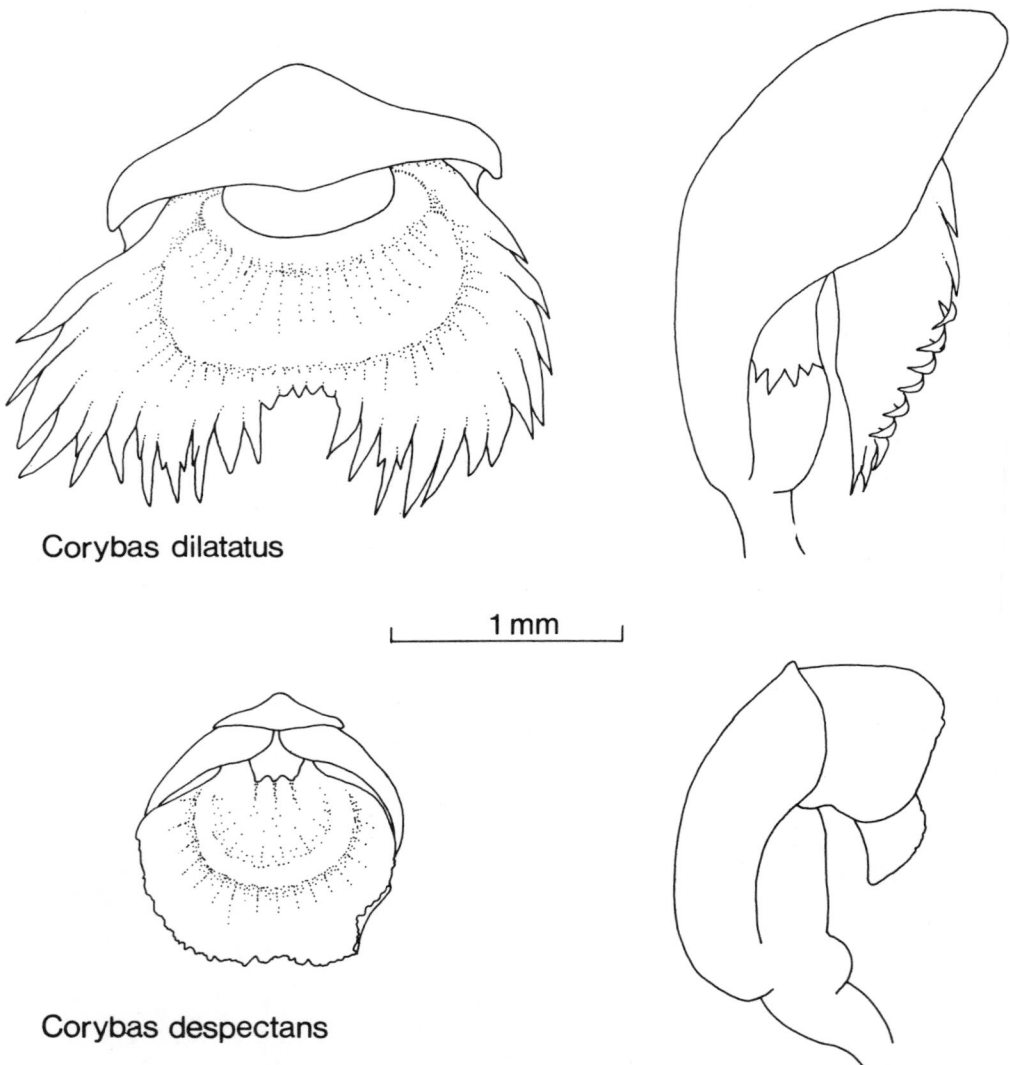

Fig. 4-6. Frontal and lateral views of the flowers of the cross-pollinated *Corybas fimbriata* (above) and the auto-pollinated *Corybas despectans* (below). Drawings by P. M. Catling from colour slides provided by R. Bates.

Phenotypic and Genotypic Control

Environmental control of auto-pollination in closed flowers (which has usually been referred to as cleistogamy), has been well documented in some vascular plant species. Uphof (1938) in his major review used the orchids *Liparis caespitosa*, *Appendicula cleistogama* and *Oberonia cleistogama* as examples of "ecological cleistogamy" (i.e., caused by various factors of the environment), based on Schlechter's (1914) observations in New Guinea and Sumatra. *Liparis caespitosa* was found to have cleistogamous flowers at high elevations but plants at lower elevations developed normal, open, pollinator-dependent blossoms. Schlechter and Uphof apparently believed these cleistogamous flowers to be a direct response to high atmospheric moisture. Cleistogamy in other plant families has also been associated directly with wet weather (Davis and Heywood, 1965, p. 367). An association between high atmospheric moisture and cleistogamy may exist in the orchids of New Guinea (and in other plants elsewhere). However, there is no proof that this is a direct environmental effect, rather than an inherited one or at least a consequence of genotype-environmental interaction (see Degrees of Auto-pollination). Furthermore, it is quite possible that the open-flowered plants Schlechter noted were also auto-pollinating like the closed ones. The known cases of temporal variation in flower opening (e.g., *Bletia purpurea* and others, see above) do not represent a turning on and off of auto-pollination, which occurs regardless, but rather a turning on or off of the opportunity for cross-fertilization.

Auto-pollination in orchids is much more than just a case of flowers not opening. The various structural and developmental modifications suggest a genetic basis, as does the fact that auto-pollinating races frequently have discrete geographic distributions and are often abundant where they occur. Furthermore some auto-pollinating races are found to be the same year after year under natural circumstances and in cultivation. This is true, for example, of cleistogamous *Corallorhiza odontorhiza* and *Spiranthes ovalis* var. *erostellata*. Thus it appears that in most, if not all cases, auto-pollination in orchids has a genetic basis with little environmental control. However, the possibility of genotype-environmental interactions remains to be adequately explored.

Occurrence in the Orchid Family

Auto-pollination is found in each of the six subfamilies and most of the tribes and subtribes of the Orchidaceae. There are a number of tribes, including a few large ones, where it is presently unknown, but until a more extensive survey is available, it seems undesirable to attach any significance to the lack of evidence. It is clear that auto-pollination is widespread in the family. The phenomenon is not associated with any particular evolutionary lines or levels, but rather it seems to have evolved independently many times.

At the present time auto-pollination is known in 350 species (Table 4-3), but it is suspected on the basis of high fecundity and floral features (Table 4-1) in many other species. C. H. Dodson (personal communication) suspects that 20% (i.e., 600) of the Ecuadorian orchids self-pollinate. If there was adequate information on all of the orchids of Ecuador alone, it would more than double the present list! Based on all the very "sketchy" information available, it seems likely that autopollination occurs in two to several thousand orchid species, that is 5–20% of the largest family of vascular plants. This is rather remarkable considering that the family is characterized by some of the most sophisticated cross-pollination mechanisms known.

Auto-pollination may be more common among terrestrials than epiphytes. Approximately 75% of the reported auto-pollinators (Table 4-3) are found among the 25% of the orchids (Dressler, 1981) which are strictly terrestrial. This may be a result of the relative lack of information from tropical areas where epiphytes occur, but that is not the only explanation. Terrestrials have probably been more often exposed to new environments and newly available territory on a grand scale, for example, following deglaciation. Under such circumstances, auto-pollination may be a selected advantage. In the largely tropical and subtropical regions, where environments have been more stable (except with regard to the recent past), auto-pollination may be much less of an advantage and consequently not as frequent. Some geographic patterns and evolutionary concepts lend support to this view (see below).

Geographic Aspects

The auto-pollinating members of a closely related group tend to occur at higher latitudes and/or are more widespread geographically. For example, the auto-pollinating *Cypripedium passerinum* occurs in relatively colder climates and at higher latitudes than most other North American *Cypripedium* species. It also has a broader geographic distribution than other *Cypripedium* species (Catling, 1983a). Likewise the auto-pollinating *Spiranthes ovalis* var. *erostellata* is widespread in the eastern United States whereas the pollinator-dependent *Spiranthes ovalis* var. *ovalis* is restricted to the extreme southeast (Catling, 1983c). *Spiranthes sinensis* in Australia is also exemplary, with the auto-pollinating form (Fig. 4-7, 4-8) being confined to colder areas in the south (Fig. 4-9) and at higher elevation. In South America the auto-pollinating *Phragmipedium lindenii* is found in Ecuador, Columbia and Venezuela, whereas the related pollinator-dependent *Phragmipedium wallisii* occurs only in southern Ecuador (Garay, 1979). There are exceptions, however, such as the auto-pollinating, North American *Isotria medeoloides,* which is rare and localized in comparison to its chasmogamous relative, *Isotria verticillata,* which is a more common taxon with a wider distribution (Mehrhoff, 1983). However, in this latter case, quite different things are being compared. Perhaps an outbreeding race of *Isotria medeoloides* should be searched for.

Fig. 4-7. Pollinator-dependent (left) and auto-pollinating (right) races of Australian *Spiranthes sinensis.* Photographs by R. Bates.

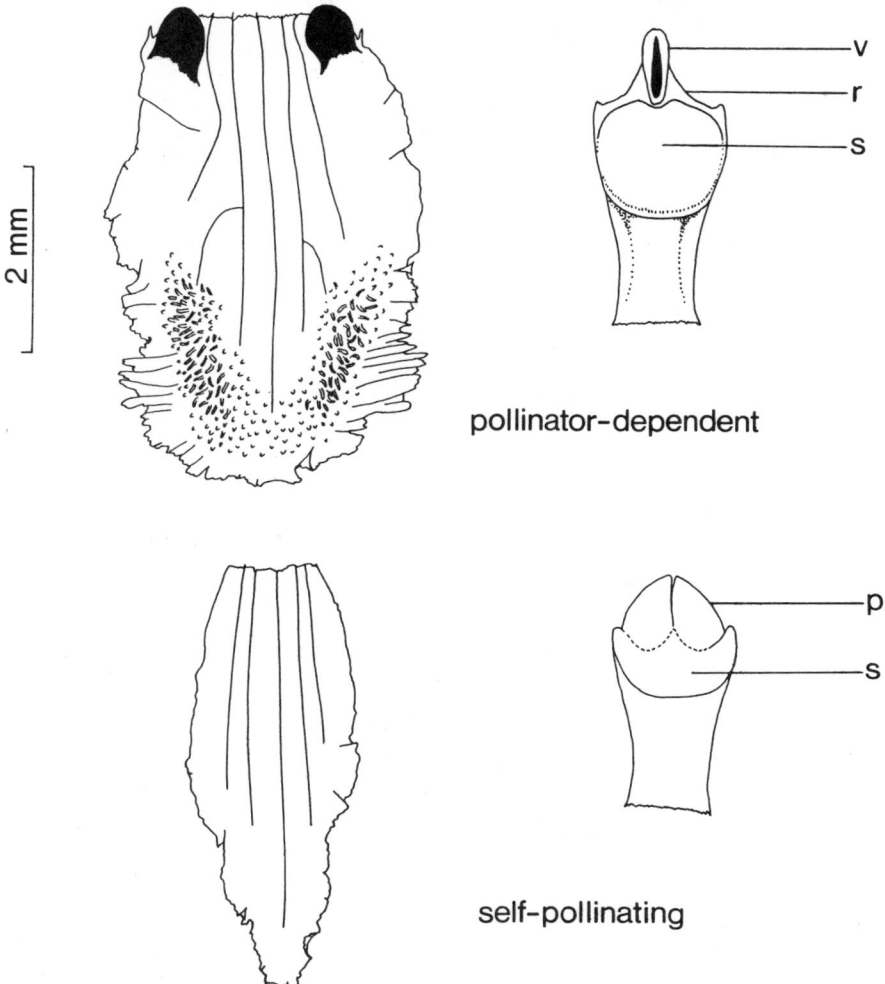

pollinator-dependent

self-pollinating

Fig. 4-8. Camera lucida drawings of the lips (left) and columns (right) of; the pollinator-dependent race of *Spiranthes sinensis* (above) and the auto-pollinating race (below). Drawing by P. M. Catling from material from south Australia (*Bates 3245* and *3248* respectively, DAO).

In boreal regions of the northern hemisphere, where only terrestrials occur and the number of species is usually less than 40, the incidence of auto-pollination may be 50% (Hagerup, 1952; Catling, 1985a). A relatively high percentage of auto-pollinating species is also characteristic of higher elevations. In the mountainous portion of south-eastern Australia, 25% of orchid taxa are auto-pollinating, which is higher than in Australia as a whole (Bates, 1978). Likewise in mountainous regions of Sikkim (King and Pantling, 1898), New Guinea (Schlechter, 1914) and Chile (Reiche, 1910), there is a relatively high incidence of auto-pollination among orchids. In contrast, auto-pollination in tropical and subtropical lowlands is not pronounced and often noticeable primarily along the coasts and on islands (Catling, unpublished).

The tendency for auto-pollination to be relatively prominent in geographically isolated situations may be exemplified in the isolated tropical orchid flora of south Florida, U.S.A. (Catling, 1986). Eight of the tropical orchid taxa present here are auto-pollinating, but all are pollinator-dependent somewhere in their tropical range. In some of the

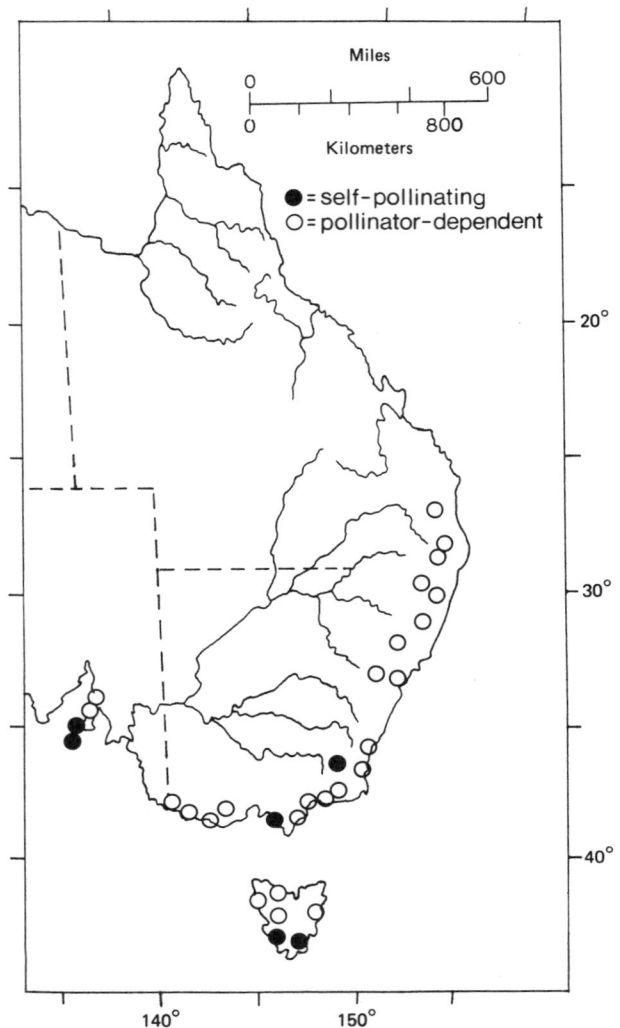

Fig. 4-9. Distribution of auto- and cross-pollinated races of *Spiranthes sinensis* in Australia based on field studies of R. Bates.

Malaysian *Dendrobium* spp., it appears that auto-pollination occurs at range limits, for example in *D. crepidatum* at the ends of its range in western Sikkim and southeastern Thailand.

Evolutionary Implications

Auto-pollination has a genetic basis, occurs throughout the orchid family, and has apparently evolved independently on many occasions. Therefore it must be a selected advantage under certain circumstances. This view is supported further by the abundance and extensive range of many auto-pollinating taxa. It is also a widely held view with regard to flowering plants in general. Several authors have provided evidence that auto-pollination is derived from outcrossing and serves as an adaptation which secures survival (Arroyo, 1973).

A major disadvantage of auto-pollination has been presumed to be the loss of genetic variability resulting in reduced adaptation capability. However, auto-pollinating groups have in some cases outlasted their pollinator-dependent relatives (Stebbins, 1957), and genetic variability may persist in inbreeding populations (Allard et al., 1968). The fact that some auto-pollinating orchid taxa are often geographically more widespread than their outcrossing relatives, suggests that their level of variability is not a short term disadvantage. In addition, some auto-pollinating orchids occupy a very broad spectrum of habitats suggesting genetic heterozygosity (Mehrhoff, 1983). Variability in auto-pollinating orchids is apparent in other ways. For example, the auto-pollinating *Thelymitra pauciflora* shows the greatest floral variation of any *Thelymitra* taxon in Australasia (Willis, 1970). This observation may have been promoted by the more marked interpopulation variation in auto-pollinators due to genetic drift. In fact most studies have shown greater genetic variability in pollinator-dependent species (Hamrick et al., 1979), and it is this extra variability, along with its widespread distribution among populations, that is generally thought to confer long-term advantage.

Another disadvantage of inbreeding is "inbreeding depression", involving reduced vigor and competitive ability (Charlesworth and Charlesworth, 1979). However, Arroyo (1973) speculated that there often is no competition with outcrossing conspecific genotypes at the time of initial establishment. Once plants are established and past the most competitive developmental stage, inbreeding depression may be a less serious disadvantage. However, inbreeding depression may be absent in many selfing taxa (Jain, 1976).

The circumstances under which auto-pollination is advantageous can be adduced from several correlations. For example, the majority of the successful flowering plant colonizers are auto-pollinating species (Allard, 1965). Many of the successful orchid colonizers are also auto-pollinators. Roadsides and abandoned gravel and sand quarries in northeastern North America are soon occupied by *Platanthera hyperborea*, *Platanthera clavellata* and *Liparis loeselii* which are all auto-pollinating (and by *Spiranthes cernua* and *Spiranthes casei* which are agamospermic). In Australia, exotic pine plantations (*Pinus radiata*) are occupied predominantly by auto-pollinating species (R. Bates, personal communication). Orchids were among the first plants to appear and establish on the volcanic island of Krakatau after the eruption of 1883, and those that appeared first were species that are known to have auto-pollinating races [(including *Arundina speciosa*, *Phaius tankervilleae*, and *Spathoglottis plicata* (van Leeuwen, 1936)]. Allard (1965) notes that the genetic systems of autopollinators "may be regarded as optimum both for opportunistic settlement and enduring occupation of diverse and complex habits."

A relatively high frequency of autogamous flowering plants generally has been noted in some isolated and/or arctic and subarctic situations (Hagerup, 1950,1951; Rick, 1966; Swales, 1979), and the same phenomenon has been noted within the Orchidaceae (see Geographic Aspects). The reason suggested for relatively high levels of auto-pollination in these new and temporary, isolated, and boreal situations is fertility insurance in a pollinator-depauperate environment. However, some environments previously considered to be pollinator-depauperate, such as the Arctic, are not pollinator-depauperate (Kevan, 1972). Insects are present and many plants depend on them. Thus, an absence of pollinators may not always provide the explanation. Questioning the concept of auto-pollination and autogamy arising as a consequence of pollinator-paucity, Levin (1972) alluded to the orchid floras of the tropics "where autogamous derivatives of auto-incompatible species grow in areas sustaining a multitude of self-incompatible zoophilous species and a rich pollinator fauna".

In unsaturated environments, the average fitness of the progeny of self-fertilization is higher than that of the progeny of crossings (Stebbins, 1970). According to the "infective principle", the progeny of auto-pollination have an advantage in a particular environment due to their close genetic similarity with the already adapted parent, whereas some of the new combinations in crossings may not be adaptive. There is no evidence for this however (Lloyd, 1978), and various authors have provided good arguments that autogamy probably does not arise through the genetic effects of auto-pollination (Arroyo, 1973). Even some of the classic examples such as mine populations of *Armeria maritima* have been rejected (Lefebvre, 1970).

Harper (1977) suggested that auto-pollination may function to protect adaptive patterns of variability which may otherwise be lost due to outbreeding. Although such long-term benefits are a possibility, the evolution of various levels of auto-pollination in plants can be explained by individual selection (Lloyd, 1979).

The fertility insurance argument seems to be the most reasonable one, but the advantage may operate in ways other than pollination in a pollinator-depauperate environment. For example, auto-pollination may arise through competition for pollinator service (Levin, 1972; Motten, 1982). This possibility may also help to explain the existence of auto-pollination in areas where pollinators are abundant. Lloyd (1978) suggested that the advantages of auto-pollination are best seen in considering two extreme situations. First, when the average fitness of cross-fertilized seeds is much higher than that of self-fertilized seeds, but cross-pollination is insufficient or unreliable. Second, when the environment is unsaturated and the average fitness of cross- and self-fertilized zygotes is similar, but the number of propagules produced is particularly important.

Unreliable cross-pollination and an unsaturated environment may often occur together, making auto-pollination especially advantageous. The periodically dry, fire-prone and severely disturbed "Miombo" woodlands of Zambia appear to present such a situation. The species of *Eulophia* in these woodlands auto-pollinate, whereas those in the wet grasslands and "dambo" (bogs), or in areas of higher atmospheric humidity are pollinator-dependent (Williamson, 1984).

Many instances of auto-pollination in orchids are partial or facultative (i.e., occurring later in the flowering period so that crossing is possible). Auto-pollinators are apparently capable of adjusting their variability systems rapidly by virtue of ready modification of the levels of outcrossing, crossover rates, and other factors which govern recombination rates (Allard, 1965). Local differences in selfing rates could develop in response to different selection pressures, and auto-pollination would tend to restrict gene flow and contribute to modification of floral characters (Levin, 1971). Such trends would reinforce ethological isolating mechanisms resulting in speciation. It has been suggested that populations with no absolute barriers to selfing, and with intermediate levels of self-fertilization, appear to be the most likely starting point for the evolution of outbreeding mechanisms (Charlesworth and Charlesworth, 1979).

A number of orchid groups contain many very closely related and more or less auto-pollinating taxa. It does not seem unreasonable to consider such groups to be in the early stages of speciation, with auto-pollination acting as an important isolating factor. In the Australian genus *Thelymitra*, some taxa are obligate auto-pollinators whereas others are pollinator-dependent, and the remainder occupy various intermediate positions. Other examples include European *Epipactis* spp. and *Orchis* spp. (Proctor and Yeo, 1973, p. 252; Richards, 1981) and *Habenaria* in tropical America.

In some instances structures which may have evolved to facilitate auto-pollination are present in both the pollinator-dependent and auto-pollinating taxa, and they may characterize an evolutionary line. The stigmatic process in the genus *Habenaria* (*sensu stricto*) provide a good example (Fig. 4-10). They function to trap falling massulae (pollen packets), thus permitting auto-pollination (Catling, unpublished). If the stigma was located on the underside of the column, as is the case in most orchids, the falling massulae would not reach it. Thus, a rather unusual pollen-trapping structure is necessary.

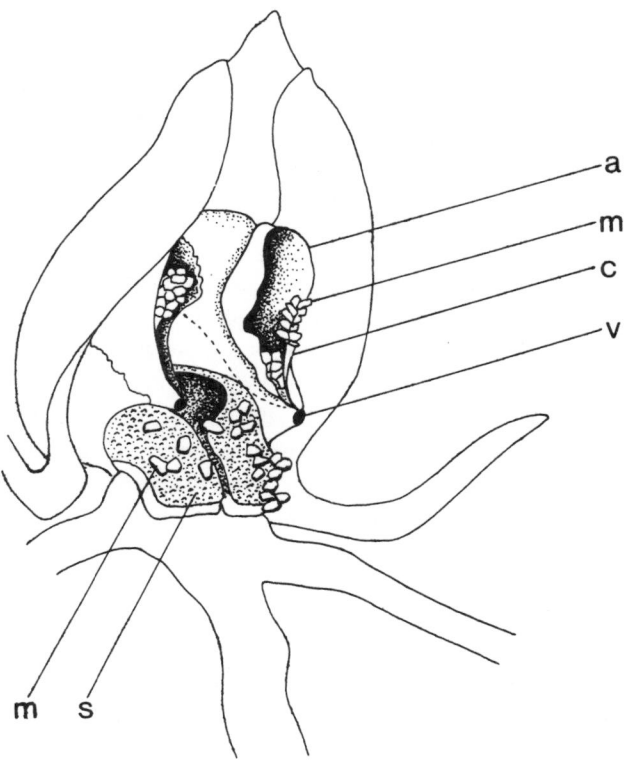

Fig. 4-10. Auto-pollination of *Habenaria mesodactyla*, the massulae falling onto the prominent stigmatic process. Drawing by P. M. Catling from material collected in the Mountain Pine Ridge of central Belize (*Catling and Brownell B38*, AMES). a = anther, c = caudicle, m = pollen massulae, s = stigmatic process, v = viscidium.

Taxonomic Implications

The main taxonomic "problem" with autogamy resides in its effect on the taxonomist's estimate of relationship. Note that the evolution of auto-pollination in distantly related taxa is convergent with regard to various morphological traits [e.g., small, obscure, barely open flowers (Table 4-1); Ornduff, 1969]. Ornduff and Crovello (1968) found that in a numerical analysis of Limnanthaceae which emphasized floral characters, unrelated autogamous taxa were placed together. The best phylogenetic arrangement was obtained by using characters unassociated with the breeding system. Floral morphology is especially important in the classification of the Orchidaceae, but the above example illustrates how easy it would be to deviate from a phylogenetic classification if this were to be considered in isolation.

Arising from the problems of relationship are the problems of rank. The uniquely modified median petal in the Orchidaceae (the lip) is a family trait and the features of the column are significant in characterizing genera and species. Auto-pollinating orchids sometimes have a lip that is barely differentiated from the other petals and a column that is very unlike that of their close relatives. Such deviations may suggest a different genus. However, a new genus cannot always be created if a phylogenetic classification is the object.

Some auto-pollinating orchids were assumed to represent a new genus (or their potential divergence has been emphasized at the expense of true relationship). For example, the self-pollinating race of *Epipactis latifolia* (i.e., *Epipactis latifolia* var. *viridiflora*) was described as a new species in a new genus *Parapactis*. The closed-flowered auto-pollinating race of *Cryptostylis arachnites* was described as a new species in a newly created genus *Chlorosa*, and some peloric self-pollinating *Spathoglottis* were described as new species in the new genus *Paxtonia*. These new genera were established regardless of the fact that the only differences were in floral structure associated with auto-pollination. Some outstanding orchid taxonomists have been misled by phenomena associated with auto-pollination. Lindley described *Crybe rosea* on the basis of its soft pollinia, which are in fact a modification associated with auto-pollination in a plant belonging to the genus *Bletia* (i.e. *Bletia purpurata*). Ames (1922) discredited Schlechter's (1920) circumscription of *Spiranthes* on the basis of the anomalous *Spiranthes novaezealandiae*. Ames thought that the absence of a rostellum in this species cast serious doubt on the value of the bifid rostellum in characterizing a group to which it obviously belonged. Now the absence of a rostellum is understood as simply a modification for self-pollination probably resulting from strong selection for colonizing ability in a species extending its range into an isolated area (the island of New Zealand). The group to which it belongs is in fact well characterized by a bifid rostellum and Schlechter's circumscription has been largely accepted.

Since there is little evidence that new evolutionary lines arise from an extreme (structural) adaptation to auto-pollination, it seems entirely unjustified to create a new genus for the sole purpose of accommodating a difference in column structure. Most auto-pollinating orchids (including the cases of extreme modification in floral structure involving cleistogamy and peloria) can be related to a "normal" taxon or are at least reliably placed in a genus on the basis of vegetative features. Thus auto-pollinating taxa belong to existing genera or species, unless a number of other characters distinguish them. Fortunately in most cases of discrete auto-pollination morphology, an ancestor (or at least relative) has been identified and the auto-pollinating taxon is accorded specific or intraspecific rank (the latter usually as a variety). Many auto-pollinating orchids are characterized by minor structural modifications that have a geographic pattern. Most modifications involving auto-pollination are considered to be "minor" because they involve either the loss of a structure or the reinstatement of a primitive condition. This is in contrast to "major" modifications which involve the creation of an entirely new structure. Since the varietal concept, when logically applied (Catling and Lucas, 1987) involves minor and few, yet discontinuous morphological characters that have discrete distributions, it seems particularly appropriate for the recognition of auto-pollinating orchids. In the rare cases where auto-pollination occurs without any structural modification and/or associated discrete characters, there is no reason to attempt to recognize it in the classification.

The extreme floral modification of an auto-pollinating taxon has caused it to be regarded as a genus on the one hand, and as a misunderstood monstrosity on the other. *Phragmipedium lindenii,* an auto-pollinating taxon with a strap-like lip and a third stamen pressed against the stigma, was at one time considered a monstrous form of *Phragmipedium caudatum.* It is, however, a widespread, abundant and distinctive taxon. The eventual discovery of a *Phragmipedium lindenii* plant with a normal lip but all other features of *Phragmipedium lindenii* (a "normal abnormality"), suggested as ancestry of the peloric plant and this ancestor was apparently not *Phragmipedium caudatum,* at least not directly (Dodson, 1966). To complete the story, it was subsequently found that the "normal" *Phragmipedium lindenii* was actually referrable to *Phragmipedium wallisii* described in 1873 (Garay, 1979).

Considering the preceding discussion, it seems remarkable that Lewis (1963) argued that autogamy had little relevance to taxonomic problems. It should be remembered that autogamy is part of a syndrome involving adaptation to new and disturbed habitats, and other aspects of the syndrome such as polyploidy and hybridization contribute their share to the difficulty of the taxonomic decision. Yet morphological features are the basis for higher plant classification, and auto-pollination in the Orchidaceae does have some compelling morphological aspects. Lewis (1963) may be correct with regard to some groups, like *Gayophytum,* where there is a good deal of supplementary evidence available upon which to base a decision, but many taxonomic decisions regarding the Orchidaceae have to be based on relatively little supplementary information.

The case of the North American *Corallorhiza odontorhiza* is a perplexing example. There are two very different kinds of plants. One has open flowers that are insect-pollinated and the other has closed, auto-pollinating blossoms (Catling, 1983a). There are differences in perianth and column morphology as well as in ovary and seeds. Unfortunately there is no difference in geographic distribution or ecology between the two morphs. An uneasiness about this paucity of geographical and ecological distinction and a lack of information on casual factors has led to a reluctance on the part of taxonomists to formally recognize the cleistogamous morph. It has recently been found that a particular morph produces true to its type each year (pers. obs.), but it is still not known whether the seeds from either morph can give rise to both kinds of plants.

Conclusions

Auto-pollination is widespread in the orchid family, having been reported in 350 species representing each of the six subfamilies and most of the tribes and subtribes. Many auto-pollinating orchids differ from their pollinator-dependent relatives in 1) smaller flower size, 2) paler and less contrasting colors, 3) more limited development of specialized structures, and 4) reduced overall attractiveness. It apparently has a genetic basis, although in a few auto-pollinating species there are indications of environmental control of flower-opening (which provides an opportunity for cross-pollination). It appears to have evolved independently many times and is accomplished in different ways by different species.

Auto-pollination appears to be more common among terrestrial orchids than among epiphytes, and is frequently associated with higher altitudes and latitudes, distributional limits, geographically isolated situations and newly available habitats. The advantage of auto-pollination seems to be in situations where pollination by animals is unreliable and/or where the environment is unsaturated (i.e., under colonizing circumstances). Facultative auto-pollination may have played a significant role in orchid evolution, by allowing reproductive isolation. The structural modifications associated with auto-pollination have sometimes led to the establishment of new genera resulting in a classification that does not reflect true relationship. Despite features that differ at the level of genera or above, most auto-pollinating taxa can, and should, be related to pollinator-dependent ancestors, and recognized at the level of species, subspecies, varieties or forms.

Acknowledgments

Ideas and significant information were contributed by the following: L. A. Garay of the Oakes Ames Orchid Herbarium of Harvard University; R. Bates and D. J. Jones, both of south Australia; C. H. Dodson of the Missouri Botanical Garden; J. D. Ackerman of the University of Puerto Rico; the late E. A. Schelpe of the University of Cape Town, South Africa; E. Hagsater and G. A. Salazar Chavez, both of Asociacion Mexicana de Orquedeologia A. C.; and E. W. Greenwood of Oaxaca, Mexico. Mr. R. Bates kindly provided photographs of auto-pollinating *Thelymitra pauciflora* var. *holmesii* and auto-pollinating and pollinator-dependent morphs of *Spiranthes sinensis,* as well as distributional information. Valuable criticsms of early drafts of the manuscript were provided by D. G. Lloyd of the University of Canterbury, Cristchurch, New Zealand; S. C. H. Barrett of the University of Toronto, Canada; B. J. D. Meeuse of Washington; and N. H. Williams of the Florida State Museum. Editorial help was kindly provided by J. Arditti.

Literature Cited

Allard, R. W. 1965. Genetic systems associated with colonizing ability in predominantly self-pollinated species. pp. 49–76. *In* Baker, H. G., Stebbins, G. L. Jr. (eds.), *The genetics of colonizing species.* New York-London Academic Press.

Allard, R. W., S. K. Jain and P. L. Workman. 1968. The genetics of inbreeding species. *Advances Genet.* 14: 55–131.

Ames, O. 1922. *Orchidaceae* 7: 127–129.

Ames, O. and D. S. Correll. 1952. Orchids of Guatemala. *Fieldiana* 26(1 & 2): 1–727.

Arroyo, M. T. Kalin. 1973. Chiasma frequency evidence on the evolution of autogamy in *Limnanthes floccosa* (Limnanthaceae). *Evolution* 27: 679–688.

Baker, H. G. 1955. Self-compatibility and establishment after "long-distance" dispersal. *Evolution* 9: 347–348.

———. 1967. Support for Baker's Law—as a rule. *Evolution* 21: 853–856.

Bates, R. 1978. Pollination of orchids—Part 9. *J. Native Orchid Soc. S. Austral.* 2(8): 7–8.

———. 1984. The genus *Microtis* R.Br. (Orchidaceae): a taxonomic revision with notes on biology. *Adelaide Botanical Garden* 7(1): 45–89.

Beardsell, D. V. and P. Bernhardt. 1983. Pollination biology of Australian terrestrial orchids. pp. 166–179. *In* Williams, E. G., Knox, R. B., Gilbert, J. H., and P. Bernhardt (eds.). *Pollination '82.* University of Melbourne Press. Parkville, Vic.

Brown, R. 1833. On the organs and mode of fecundation in Orchidaceae and Asclepiadaceae. *Trans. Linn. Soc. London* XVI: 683–746.

Burns-Balogh, P. 1984. Evolution of the monandrous Orchidaceae. II. Evolution of characters and pollination in Spiranthoideae. *The Canadian Orchid Journal* 2(2): 27–31.

Cady, L. 1972. Notes on the pollination of *Calochilus campestris* R.Br. *Orchadian* 4:52.

Catling, P. M. 1980. Rain-assisted autogamy in *Liparis loeselii* (L.) L. C. Rich. (Orchidaceae). *Bull. Torrey Bot. Club.* 107(4): 525–529.

———. 1982. Breeding systems of northeastern North American *Spiranthes* (Orchidaceae). *Canad. J. Bot.* 60(12): 3017–3039.

_____ . 1983a. Autogamy in eastern Canadian Orchidaceae: a review of current knowledge and some new observations. *Naturaliste Canad.* 110: 37–53.

_____ . 1983b. Pollination in northeastern North American *Spiranthes* (Orchidaceae). *Canad. J. Bot.* 61(4): 1080–1093.

_____ . 1983c. *Spiranthes ovalis* var. *erostellata* (Orchidaceae), a new autogamous variety from the eastern United States. *Brittonia* 35(2): 120–125.

_____ . 1985a. Canadian orchids: distribution and pollination biology. pp. 121–135 *in:* K. W. Tan ed. *Proc. 11th World Orchid Conf.* Miami.

_____ . 1985b. Self-pollination and probable autogamy in Chamisso's Orchid, *Platanthera chorisiana*. *Naturaliste Canad.* 111(4): 451–453.

_____ . 1986. Breeding systems of *Sacoila lanceolata* (Aubl.) Garay *sensu lato* in south Florida. *Ann. Missouri Bot. Gard.* 74: 58–68.

Catling, P. M. and Z. Lucas. 1987. The status of *Calopogon tuberosus* var. *latifolius* with comments on the application of varietal rank. *Rhodora* 89: 401–413.

Charlesworth, D. and B. Charlesworth. 1979. The evolutionary genetics of sexual systems in flowering plants. *Proc. Roy. Soc. London, Ser. B, Biol. Sci.* 205: 513–530.

Chodat, R. 1913. *Ophrys botteroni. Bull. Soc. Bot. Geneve* 5:18.

Clements, M. and P. Cribb. 1984. The underground orchids of Australia. *Kew Mag.* 1(2): 84–91.

Comber, J. B. 1983. *Dendrobium tetrodon* Rchb. f. *Malayan Orchid Rev.* 17: 16–18.

Cruger, H. 1865. A few notes on the fecundation of orchids, and their morphology. *J. Linn. Soc., Bot.* 8(31): 127.

Darwin, C. 1869. XVI—Notes on the fertilization of orchids. *Ann. Mag. Nat. Hist.,* 4th series 4(21): 143–159.

_____ . 1862, first edition. 1877, second edition, expanded and revised. 1904, third edition. *The various contrivances by which orchids are fertilized by insects.* John Murray, London.

Davies, P. H. and J. A. Davies. 1985. The genus *Ophrys*—part 1. *Amer. Orchid Soc. Bull.* 54(2): 132–141.

Davis, P. H. and V. H. Heywood. 1965. *Principles of angiosperm taxonomy.* D. Van Nostrand Inc., New York.

Day, C. Jr. 1972. Observations of self-pollination in *Paphiopedilum* species. *Amer. Orchid Soc. Bull.* 41(7): 592.

Dodson, C. H. 1966. Studies in orchid pollination. *Cypripedium, Phragmopedium* and allied genera. *Amer. Orchid Soc. Bull.* 35: 125–128.

Dodson, C. H. and R. L. Dressler. 1972. Two undescribed genera in the Orchidaceae—Oncidiinae. *Phytologia* 24(4): 286–292.

Dressler, R. L. 1968. Notes on *Bletia* (Orchidaceae). *Brittonia* 20: 182–190.

_____ . 1981. *The orchids, natural history and classification.* Harvard University Press, Cambridge, Mass.

Dressler, R. L. and G. E. Pollard. 1976. The genus *Encyclia* in Mexico. *Asociacion Mexicana de Orquideologia,* Mexico.

Eggers, B. E. 1881. Kleistogamie einiger westindischer Pflanzen. *Bot. Centralbl.* VIII: 57–59.

Fitzgerald, R. D. 1875–76. *Australian orchids.* (parts 1 and II respectively). Sydney, New South Wales.

Forbes, H. O. 1884. On the contrivances for ensuring self-fertilization in some tropical orchids. *J. Linn. Soc., Bot.* 21: 538–550.

Fowlie, J. A. 1963. Ecology notes: *Schomburgkia lyonsii. Amer. Orch. Soc. Bull.* 32: 31–33.

Freyhold, E. von. 1877. Uber bestaubung and das Auftreten mehrerer Antheren bei *Limodorum abortivum* Sw. *Verh. Bot. Vereins Prov. Brandenburg.* 23–28.

Gandawidjaja, D. and J. Arditti. 1982. Post-pollination phenomena in orchid flowers. XI. Autogamy in *Phajus tankervilliae* (Aiton) Bl., Orchidaceae. *Amer. J. Bot.* 69(3): 335–338.

Garay, L. A. 1979. The genus *Phragmipedium. Orchid Digest* 43: 133–148.

Gassner, A. 1982. Observations on the pollination of *Disa stolzii* in southern Malawi. *Orchid Rev.* 90:230.

Gonzalez, N. and J. D. Ackerman. 1985. Pollination biology of *Oecoclades maculata* (Orchidaceae): Rain assisted autogamy. Abstr. 441. *Amer. J. Bot.* :954–955.

Gray, A. 1862. Fertilization of orchids through the agency of insects. *Amer. J. Sci., Series 2,* 34: 420–429.

Hamer, F. 1981. *Las Orquideas de el Salvador.* Volume 3. The Marie Selby Botanical Gardens, Sarasota, Florida.

_____ . 1982. Orchids of Nicaragua. Part 2. *Icones Plantaruum Tropicarum,* Fascicle 8. Marie Selby Botanical Gardens, Sarasota, Florida.

_____ . 1984a. Orchicds of Nicaragua. Part 4. *Icones Plantaruum Tropicarum,* Fascicle 11. Marie Selby Botanical Gardens, Sarasota, Florida.

_____ . 1984b. Orchids of Nicaragua. Part 5. *Icones Plantaruum Tropicarum,* Fascicle 12. Marie Selby Botanical Gardens, Sarasota, Florida.

Hagerup, O. 1941. Bestovningen hos *Liparis* og *Malaxis. Bot. Tidskr.* 45: 396–402.

_____ . 1952. Bud autogamy in some southern orchids. *Phytomorphology* 2: 51–60.

Hagsater, E. 1984. *Cypripedium dickinsonianum* Hagsater: A new species from Chiapas, Mexico. *Orquidea* (Méx.) 9(2): 209–212.

Hamrick, J. L., Y. B. Linhart and J. B. Mitton. 1979. Relationships between life history characteristics and electrophoretically detectable genetic variation in plants. *Ann. Rev. Ecol. Syst.* 10: 173–200.

Harper, J. L. 1977. *Population biology of plants.* Academic Press. London.

Hart, J. H. 1886. Self-fertilization of *Epidendrum variegatum* Hook. *Gard. Cron.*, n.s. 26:11.

Hogan, K. P. 1983. The pollination biology and breeding system of *Aplectrum hyemale* (Orchidaceae). *Canad. J. Bot.* 61: 1906–1910.

Holland, D. 1961. Native orchids of New Zealand. *Ameri. Orch. Soc. Bull.* 30: 372–373.

Jones, D. L. 1971. A study of the self-pollination of *Thelymitra venosa* R.Br. and some notes on its implications. *Victoria Naturalist* 88: 217–219.

———. 1972a. The self-pollination of *Prasophyllum beaugleholei* W. H. Nichols. *Orchadian* 4(2): 16, 18–19.

———. 1972b. The self-pollination of *Prasophyllum beaugleholei* W. H. Nicholls. *Victoria Naturalist* 89(5): 144–146.

———. 1975. The pollination of *Microtis parviflora* R.Br. *Ann. Bot.* (London) (new series) 39: 585–589.

———. 1976. The self-pollination of *Phaius pictus* T. E. Hunt. *Austral. Orchid Rev.* December. 210–213.

———. 1985a. The self-pollination of *Epipogium roseum* (D. Don) Lindley. *Orchadian:* (in press).

———. 1985b. Amendments to the description of *Thelasis carinata* Bl. *Orchadian:* (in press).

Jones, D. L. and B. Gray. 1974. The pollination of *Calochilus holtzei* F. Muell. *Amer. Orchid Soc. Bull.* 43: 604–606.

Jones, H. G. 1968. A note on *Schomburgkia* in Trinidad. *Lloydia* 3(3): 268–271.

Kevan, P. G. 1972. Insect pollination of high arctic flowers. *J. Ecol.* 60: 831–847.

King, G. and R. Pantling. 1898. The orchids of Sikkim-Himalaya. *Ann. Roy. Bot. Gard.* Calcutta 8: 1–342.

Kipping, J. L. 1971. *Pollination studies of native orchids.* M. A. Thesis. San Francisco State College.

Kirchner, O. von. 1900. Mitteilungen uber die Bestaubungseinrichtungen der Bluten. *Jahresh Vereins vaterl.* Naturk. Wurtt. Emberg. 348–384.

———. 1922a. Uber Selbstbestaubung bei den Orchidaceen. *Flora* 115: 103–129.

———. 1922b. Zur Selbstbestaubung der Orchidaceen. *Ber. Deutsch. Bot. Ges.* 40: 317–321.

Knudson, L. 1956. Self-pollination in *Cattleya aurantiaca* (Batem.) P. N. Don. *Amer. Orchid Soc. Bull.* 25: 528–532.

Kranzlin, F. 1898–1905. Orchidearum genera et species. *Chloraceae.* Berlin.

———. 1910. Orchidaceae-Monandrae-Dendrobiinae part I in Engler's *Das Pflanzenreich* 45(IV:50): 1–358.

———. 1911. *Dendrobieae II.* Thelasinae Daselbst, Leipzig.

Leeuwen, W. W. Docters van. 1936. Krakatau, 1883 to 1933. *Ann. Jard. Bot.* Buitenzorg 46: 1–506, 47: 1–186.

Levin, D. A. 1971. The origin of reproductive isolating mechanisms in flowering plants. *Amer. Naturalist* 113: 67–79.

———. 1972. Competition for pollinator service: a stimulus for the evolution of autogamy. *Evolution* 26: 668–669.

Lewis, H. 1963. The taxonomic problem of inbreeders. *Regnum Vegetabile* 27: 37–44.

Lloyd, D. G. 1978. Demographic factors and self-fertilization in plants, pp. 67–88. *In* O. T. Solbrig, ed. *Demography and the dynamics of plant populations.* Blackwell, Oxford.

———. 1979. Some reproductive factors affecting the selection of self-fertilization in plants. *Amer. Naturalist* 113(1): 67–79.

Lord, E. M. 1981. Cleistogamy, a tool for the study of floral morphogenesis, function and evolution. *Bot. Rev.* 47: 421–449.

Luer, C. A. 1971. Abnormal development of the anther—A report of two cases. *Florida Orchidist.* 14: 26–29.

———. 1977. Icones Pleurothallidinarum, (Orchidaceae)—Miscellaneous species in the Pleurothallidinae. *Selbyana* 3(3,4): 203–412.

———. 1978. A new genus in the Pleurothallidinae (Orchidaceae). *Selbyana* 2(2,3): 199–204.

Martens, P. 1926. L'autogamie chez l'*Orchis* et chez quelques autres Orchidees. *Bull. Soc. Roy. Bot. Belgique* 59(1): 69–88.

McCartney, C. 1985. Orchids of Florida. The orchids of Everglades National Park—1. *Amer. Orchid Soc. Bull.* 54(3): 265–276.

Merritt, A. J. 1897. Notes on the pollination of some California mountain flowers. *Erythrea* 5: 56–59.

Mehrhoff, L. A. III. 1983. Pollination in the genus *Isotria* (Orchidaceae). *Amer. J. Bot.* 70(10): 1444–1453.

Moggridge, J. T. 1865. Observations on some orchids of the south of France. *J. Linn. Soc., Bot.* 8: 256–228.

Moore, S. 1876. Mascarene orchidology. *J. Bot.*, n.s. 5: 289–292.

———. 1877. Bud-fertilization in orchids. *J. Bot.* 15: 85–86.

Muller, H. 1868. Beobachtungen an westfalischen Orchideen. *Verh. Naturh. Vereines. Preuss. Rheinl.* XXV. 3 Folge, 5: 7–36.

_____ . 1883. *The fertilization of flowers*. (transl. by D. W. Thompson). Macmillan and Co, London.

Nannfeldt, J. A. 1946. Tre for Norden nya *Epipactis*-arter. *Bot. Not.* 1946: 1–28.

Nilsson, L. A. 1981a. The pollination ecology of *Listera ovata* (Orchidaceae). *Nordic J. Bot.* 1: 461–480.

_____ . 1981b. *Pollination ecology and evolutionary processes in six species of orchids*. Abstract of Ph. D. Thesis. Uppsala University.

Ornduff, R. 1969. Reproductive biology in relation to systematics. *Taxon* 18: 121–133.

Ornduff, R. and T. J. Crovello. 1968. Numerical taxonomy of Limnanthaceae. *Amer. J. Bot.* 55: 173–182.

Pais, M.S. S. 1969. L'autogamie chez *Serapias lingua* L. (Orchidees). *Portugaliae Acta Biol.* Ser. B, Sist. 11 (3–4): 297–300.

Pedicino, N. 1874. Sul processo d'impollinazione e su qualche altro fatto nel *Limodorum abortivum*. *Rendiconti Reale Accad. Sci. Fis.*

Pijl, L. van der and C. H. Dodson. 1966. *Ordhid flowers— their pollination and evolution*. Univ. of Miami Press, Coral Gables.

Proctor, M. and P. Yeo. 1973. *The pollination of flowers*. New Naturalist Series, Collins, London.

Reiche, C. 1910. Orchidaceae Chilensis. *Ann. Mus. Nac. Chile. sect. Bot.* 18: 1–84.

Reichenbach, H. G. 1865. *Neotinea intacta,* the new Irish Orchid. *J. Bot.* 3: 1–5.

_____ . 1877. Bud-fertilization in orchids. *J. Bot.* 15:85.

Resvoll, T. R. 1911. Sidt om blomstens bygning og bestovning hos *Neottia nidus-avis. Biol. Arbejder tilegnede Eug. Warming. Kopenhagen.* 159–165.

Richards, A. J. 1981. The influence of minor structural changes in the flower on breeding systems and speciation in *Epipactis* (Orchidaceae). *Abstract in Proc. Int. Bot. Congr.* 13:102.

Ridley, H. N. 1885. The orchids of Madagascar. *J. Linn. Soc., Bot.* 21.

Ridley, H. N. 1888. Notes on self-fertilization and cleistogamy in orchids. *J. Linn. Soc., Bot.* 24: 389–395.

Rogers, R. S. 1913. Mechanisms of pollination in certain Australian orchids. *Trans. & Proc. Roy. Soc. South Australia* 37: 48–64.

_____ . 1921. Notes on the gynostemium in the genus *Diuris* and on the pollinary mechanism in *Phajus. Trans. & Proc. Roy. Soc. South Australia* 45: 264–269.

Sauleda, R. P. and R. M. Adams. 1984. A reappraisal of the orchid genera *Broughtonia* R.Br., *Cattleyopsis* Lem. and *Laeliopsis* Lindl. *Rhodora* 86: 445–467.

Schelpe, E. A. 1970. Self-pollination, cleistogamy and apomixis among South African orchids. *S. African Orchid J.* March: 9–10.

Schlechter, R. 1907. *Bot. Jahrb. Syst.* 39:56.

_____ . 1911. *Bot. Jahrb. Syst.* 45:36.

_____ . 1914. Die Orchidaceen von Deutsch-Neu-Guinea. *Repertorium specierum novarum regni vegetabilis,* herausg. von F. Fedde. Beihefte, Bd. I, Dahlem. (a 1982 translation by R. Katz and J. D. Simmons produced by the Australian Orchid Foundation, Melbourne).

_____ . 1920. Versuch einer systematischen Neuordnung der Spiranthinae. *Beih. Bot. Centralbl.* 37: 317–454.

Scott, J. 1865. On the individual sterility and cross-impregnation of certain species of *Oncidium. J. Linn. Soc., Bot.* 8: 162–167.

Smith, J. J. 1905. *Die Orchideen von Ambon.* Batavia. 1905.

_____ . 1907. Die Orchideen von Java. *Bull. Dep. Agric. Indes Neerl.* 8.

_____ . 1907b. Die Orchideen von Nova Guinea. *Bull. Dep. Agric. Indes Neerl.* 13.

_____ . 1928. Zelfbevruchting bij Orchideen. *Natuurk. Tijdschr. Ned.-Indie* 88: 122–140.

_____ . 1929. Autogamy in Orchidaceae. *Orchid Rev.* 37: 75–78.

Solbrig, O. T. 1977. On the relative advantages of cross-and self-fertilization. *Ann. Missouri Bot. Gard.* 63: 262–276.

Stort, M. N. S. and E. A. dos Santos Pavanelli. 1985. Formation of multiple or adventive embryos in *Epidendrum nocturnum* Jacq. (Orchidaceae). *Ann. Bot.* 55: 331–336.

Stoutamire, W. P. 1975. Pseudocopulation in Australian terestrial orchids. *Amer. Orchid Soc. Bull.* 44: 226–233.

_____ . 1983. Orchids and wasps. *Swans* 13: 8–9.

Swales, D. E. 1979. Nectaries of certain arctic and sub-arctic plants with notes on pollination. *Rhodora* 81: 363–407.

Thomson, G. M. 1879. On the methods of fertilization of some New Zealand orchids. *Trans. & Proc. New Zealand Inst.* 11: 418–424.

_____ . 1880. Fertilization of New Zealand flowering plants. *Trans. & Proc. New Zealand Inst.* 13: 241–288.

Uphof, J. C. T. 1968. Cleistogamic flowers. *Bot. Rev.* 4: 21–49.

Vogel, E. F. de. 1984. Percursor to a revision of the genera [*Entomophobia* (gen nov.], *Geesinkorchis* (gen nov.), *Nabuluia* and *Chelonistele* (Orchidaceae–Coelogyniane). *Blumea* 30: 197–205.

Willimason, G. 1984. Observations of a mechanism by which self-pollination may occur in *Eulophia*

(Orchidaceae). *J. S. African Bot.* 50(4): 417–423.

Willis, J. H. 1970. *A handbook of plants in Victoria.* Vol. 1, 2nd ed. Melbourne Univ. Press.

Withner, C. L. 1970. Die kleistogamen Epiendrum-Arrten der Sektion Encyclia. *Die Orchidae* 21: 4–7.

Glossary

Agamospermy: Apomixis in which embryos and seeds are formed asexually.

Androclinium: Portion of the column around or under the anther. (see also Clinandrium)

Apomixis: Reproduction without fertilization, in which meiosis and fusion of gametes are partially or totally suppressed.

Autogamy: The process of self-fertilization.

Bursicle: A sacklike covering over the viscidium or caudicle in some orchids.

Caudicle: The slender stalklike appendage of the pollen masses in orchids.

Chasmogamy: Pollination occurring after the opening of a flower.

Cleistogamy: The condition of having flowers, often small and inconspicuous, which remain unopened and within which self-pollination takes place.

Cleistogamous: Refers to flowers which automatically self-pollinate without opening; a form of autogamy.

Clinandrium: A cavity or area in which the anther is situated on the column in flowers of the Orchidaceae.

Colonizer: An organism, usually with a high reproductive rate, which invades and colonizes a new habitat or territory.

Conspecific: Belonging to the same species.

Elastoviscin: A clear, very elastic substance found in pollinia and especially in caudicles.

Ethological: Pertaining to behavior.

Fecundity: The potential reproductive capacity of an organism or population, measured by the number of gametes or asexual propagules.

Mentum: A sac-like projection in some orchid flowers formed by the lateral sepals and the base of the column.

Morph: A form; any individuals of a polymorphic group; any phenotypic or genetic variant; any local population of a polymorphic species exhibiting distinctive morphology or behavior.

Peloria: An abnormal often hereditary regularity of structure occurring in normally irregular flowers. An abnormality in which the lip is like the other petals in form, or vice versa; a radially symmetrical mutant of a species which normally has bilaterally symmetrical flowers.

Sporopollenin: The substance which makes up the exine of pollen grains (oxidative polymers of carotenoids and/or carotenoid esters).

Unsaturated environment: An environment capable of containing a greater number of organisms.

Viscidium: A viscid (sticky) part of the rostellum which is clearly defined and removed with the pollinia as a unit, and serves to attach the pollinia to an insect or other agent.

Viscin: See Elastoviscin.

Zoophilous: Pollinated by animals; having an affinity for animals.

5

A Review of the Genus *Dactylorhiza**

LEONID V. AVERYANOV

*The literature survey pertaining to this chapter was concluded in March 1986; the chapter was submitted in December 1986, and the revised version was received in September 1987.

Introduction

The genus *Dactylorhiza*[a], which at one time was combined with *Orchis*, the type genus of the family Orchidaceae, belongs to the subtribe Orchidinae, tribe Orchideae, subfamily Orchidoideae (Dressler, 1981). This is the largest genus in the group of genera, which forms the so-called "*Dactylorhiza*-alliance". From the evolutionary point of view it represents an intermediate stage in one of the geophytic directions in the evolution of orchids starting with hypothetical primitive *Cephalanthera*-like ancestors and extending to such highly specialized terrestrial genera from the ancient Mediterranean area as *Orchis, Ophrys, Serapias, Himantoglossum, Steveniella*, etc. The study of dactylorchids is therefore very important for an understanding of the adaptations of orchids to terrestrial habitats under conditions of pronounced seasonal changes. Two previous works were devoted to the study of the genus *Dactylorhiza* (Klinge, 1898; Vermeulen, 1947). Questions of nomenclature were dealt with by a number of contributors (Soó, 1962; Hunt and Summerhayes, 1965; Averyanov, 1986). Species of dactylorchids which occur in Europe (Soó, 1980), Asia (Renz, 1978; Renz and Taubenheim, 1984) and the Soviet Union (Averyanov, 1982, 1983a, b) were studied during the last decade. More extensive reviews of dactylorchids are available in a number of monographs (Sundermann, 1975; Nelson, 1976, 1979; Fuller, 1983; Averyanov, 1983c).

Anatomy and Morphology of Dactylorchids

All species of the genus *Dactylorhiza* are perennial herbs with an unbranched erect stem, a spiral arrangement of leaves and terminal spicate inflorescence. They are similar to tuber-forming geophytes.

The evolutionary appearance and development of the tuberoid, also known as the "sinker" (Dressler, 1981), are undoubtedly due to the seasonal climatic changes, which necessitate nutrient storage for the following year's growth. Formation of the tuberoid probably evolved as a consequence of the thickening of the root base. This resulted at first in the formation of finger-like tuberoids which occur in relatively primitive dactylorchids (aggr. *D. fuchsii*, aggr. *D. incarnata*). Further evolution proceeded along lines of greater specialization and resulted in a cylindrical tuberoid structure in more advanced species of *Dactylorhiza* (aggr. *D. sambucina*, aggr. *D. sulphurea*) and in the closely related genus *Orchis* (Fig. 5-1e; Averyanov, 1983a, c). This structure is often polystelic, that is, it includes several vascular cylinders, as though several roots have grown together (Ogura, 1953; Dressler, 1981).

Evolutionary changes in the stems of specialized forms of the genus consisted mainly in reduction of the number of nodes (for example, in high mountain and northern species; Fig. 5-1c). The formation of subterranean creeping shoots in *D. iberica* (Fig. 5-1f) is a unique modification of the stem. This character is, apparently, an evolutionary adaptation which compensates for limited seed production by the species and prevents extinction (Averyanov, 1983a).

Anatomically the stems of all species in the genus are very similar. They are formed by an apical meristem and have no intercalary meristems in their nodes. The mature stem is

---

[a]The name of the genus (and the common name for all its species—dactylorchid) is derived from the Ancient Greek δαχτθλοζ (finger) and reflects the characteristic form of the tubers of these plants.

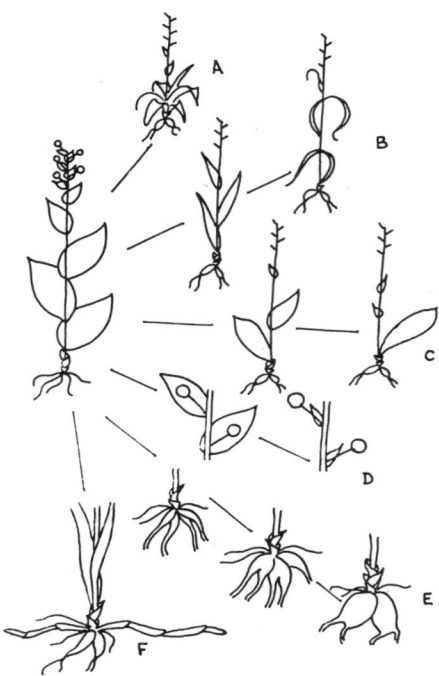

Fig. 5-1. The evolutionary trends of vegetative organs in the genus *Dactylorhiza* (Averyanov, 1983c).

covered by a layer of epidermal cells enveloped by an external cuticle. Next to the epidermis is a 3–6 layered chlorenchyma consisting of rounded cells with many chloroplasts and numerous large intercellular spaces. A 3–5 layered cylinder of sclerenchyma cells, usually more or less lignified, is located inside the chlorenchyma. As a rule, the sclerenchyma also surrounds the vascular bundles. The central part of the stem consists of parenchyma which disappears as the plant matures and is replaced by a cavity. Appearance during ontogenesis and the size of this cavity is an important systematic character for the genus (Borsos, 1980).

The leaves of dactylorchids are formed by an intercalary meristem, situated at their bases. At the end of its activity this meristem widens, surrounds the stem and forms a leaf sheath.

The stomata, situated on the lower surface of the leaf and on the stem are anomocytic. However, their development can be either agenous or hemimesogenous, and the former is always dominant. The hemiperigenous and hemimesoperigenous type of stomatal development has also been observed, but occurs very rarely. The ratio of developmental types of stomata varies even in closely related species of the genus *Dactylorhiza* (Rasmussen, 1981).

Ancestors of dactylorchids probably had a large number of wide leaves attached at approximately equal distances on the shoot as occurs in most primitive species of the genus. In more recently evolved species the leaves vary from almost rounded to linear. Specialization in this case proceeded from wide ovate leaves to narrow-lanceolate and linear ones (Fig 5-1b). The most specialized are the linear, longitudinally folded, curved leaves of a number of northern and mountain species. Specialization of bracts tends mainly toward reduction (Fig 5-1d). The rosettelike arrangement of leaves at the stem base (Fig. 5-1a) in some high mountain and arid species (Averyanov, 1983a) is a more advanced specialization within the genus.

The edges of the leaves and bracts in species of the genus consist of epidermal cells which bear papillae covered with large numbers of cuticular folds. The size of the papillae and the character of the cuticular folds vary considerably among species (Fig 5-2). This and other vegetative characters can be used taxonomically within *Dactylorhiza* and for the delimitation of the genus itself.

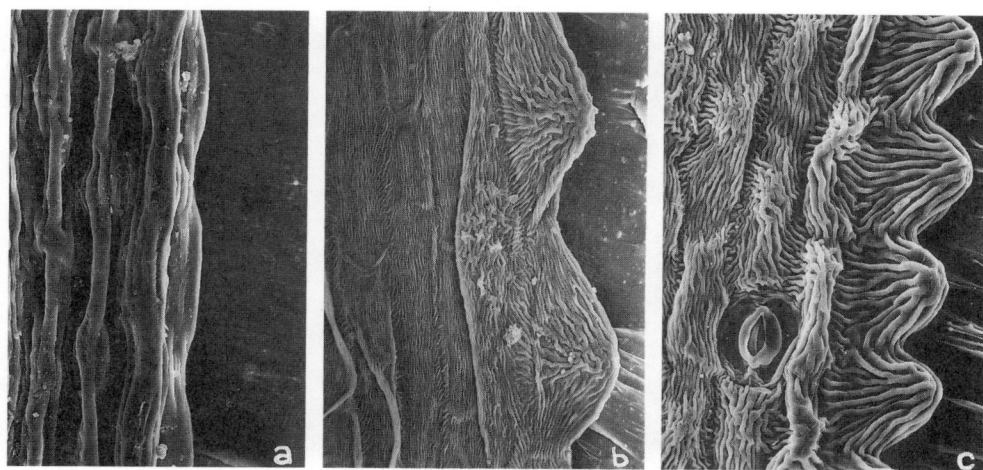

Fig. 5-2. Micromorphology of the leaf edge in different species of the genus *Dactylorhiza* (Averyanov, 1983c). Explanation of symbols: **a**, *D. incarnata.* × 275; **b**, *D. sambucina.* × 275; **c**, *D. salina.* × 275.

Flowers

Flowers of dactylorchids are highly zygomorphic and have six free perianth segments. Segments of the outer and inner whorls (except the labellum) are similar in form and size. The well developed lip is of different form and extends at the base to form a cylindrical spur. Stamens of the inner whorl are completely reduced. Only one (the median stamen of the outer whorl) functions normally. The other two are modified into barely visible staminodes situated on the sides of the anther. Columns are rather small and the sessile stigma consists of three lobes situated at the base of the anther above the entrance to the spur (Vermeulen, 1947; Averyanov, 1983; Fig. 5-3.).

The pollen grains of dactylorchids occur in polyades (Kuprianova and Alioschina, 1967) or massulae (Caspers and Caspers, 1976) within a two-celled anther. Polyades are connected to each other with mucilaginous strands of a polysaccharide and form clavate pollinia. The central sterile axis of the pollinium is extended into a more or less elongated caudicle which terminates in a retinaculum or viscidium (Fig. 5-3). These structures play an important part in the pollination process. In the flower of dactylorchids, the two pollinaria are completely divided. Pollinia are completely hidden within the anther cells and the caudicles lie freely in tissue folds of the anther base where they are separated by a small rostellum. In the base of the anther, the caudicles are combined and their retinacula or viscidia are covered by a small bilocular operculum which is located over the stigma itself (Fig. 5-3). The operculum opens easily when the insect-pollinator contacts it and tries to penetrate into the spur. In this case, the viscidia become exposed and on touching the body of the insect-pollinator become attached to it (usually to its anterior part or head).

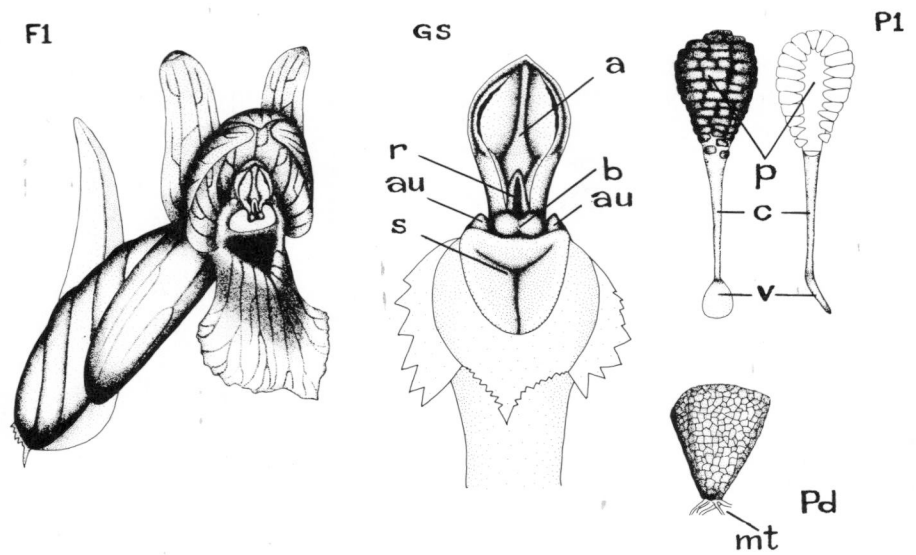

Fig. 5-3. Structure of the dactylorchid flower (Averyanov, 1983c). a, anther; au, auricle; b, bursicle; c, caudicle; Fl, flower (*D. incarnata*). Explanation of symbols: GS, gynostemium or column; mt, mucilaginous threads; p, pollinium; Pd, polyade; Pl, pollinarium; r, rostellum; s, stigma; v, viscidium.

The pollinaria can be pulled easily from the anther cells and carried away by pollinators. In the air the caudicle of the pollinium dries very quickly and bends in a specific manner positioning the pollinium so that during a subsequent visit of the insect to another flower of the same species of dactylorchids, it touches the stigma. Some portion or the entire pollinium remains on the sticky surface of the stigma.

Flowers of dactylorchids are entirely lacking in nectar and no other attractants have been discovered to date (Darwin, 1877; Faegri and van der Pijl, 1979). Specific pollinators are unknown. The flowers of all species are pollinated by bumblebees (Nilsson, 1980, 1981), bees and flies (Faegri and van der Pijl, 1979). Some of the pollinators (*Apis mellifera*, *Bombus lapidarius* and *B. terrestris*) probably exploit the stigmatic exudate of the flowers (*Dactylorhiza fuchsii*) which contains glucose and amino acids (Dafni and Woodel, 1986). Food deception has been shown to exist in *D. sambucina* (Nilsson, 1980, 1981).

The most primitive flower in the genus *Dactylorhiza* is small, faintly colored and has a small lip with a short saccate spur (*D. incarnata*). Evolution of this organ has proceeded in the direction of enlargement and strengthening of the zygomorphy. The increasing level of zygomorphy of the flower consists mainly of 1) enlargement and elaboration of the lip, 2) lengthening of the spur (*D. umbrosa*), 3) increasing proximity of perianth segments (except the lip), 4) formation of a helmet (*D. iberica*), and 5) the appearance of awn-shaped tips in the petals of the inner and outer whorl (*D. aristata*). In more advanced dactylorchids, the lip differs sharply from other perianth segments and often consists of three lobes. Its surface is covered with epidermal papillae which are externally similar to those on the edges of the leaves and bracts. They are usually 50–60 μm long, but sometimes may reach 120–150 μm (*D. iberica*). Their width is 20–30 μm (Averyanov, 1983c).

Flower color has changed during the evolution of the genus from relatively pale pink and yellowish flowers in relatively primitive species to bright-lilac (*D. traunsteineri, D. euxina, D. umbrosa*) and dark-violet ones (*D. cordigera*) in more advanced dactylorchids. The selective forces of this evolutionary trend are still unclear.

Ovaries in all species are tricarpelate, inferior, twisted and consist of one chamber with parietal placentation. Flowers are sessile.

Pollen

Like most orchids, all species of the genus *Dactylorhiza* have highly specialized pollen grains. They occur in tetrahedral polyades 140–300 μm long and 80–200 μm wide in pollinia that are typical for the tribe Orchideae. The polyade usually contains a large number of pollen grains with greatly reduced walls. No typical pollen structure is common to the various species. A distinct exine exists only on the outward side of peripheral pollen grains in the polyade. The attachment between peripheral pollen grains is so intimate that they are often almost indistinguishable. Fused outward walls of peripheral pollen cells result in a rigid "exine" polyade envelope. The structure of this envelope in orchids and especially in members of the tribe Orchideae is very variable and therefore useful in taxonomy (Caspers and Caspers, 1976; Schill and Pfeiffer, 1977; Dressler, 1981).

In dactylorchids the pollen cells which form the surface of tetrahedral polyades are polygonal in shape. They are usually slightly elongated along the edges and sides of the polyade. At the base of polyade, they are elongated along the pollinium axis. Cell size varies from 10–14 μm in length and 10–20 μm in width. Sculpturing on the surface of the pollen grains is of three types, established in the Orchidaceae (Schill and Pfeiffer, 1977).

Type I ("laevigat-scabros"—Schill and Pfeiffer, 1977) the surface is slightly rough with the surface of the exine covered with small torulae (Fig. 5-4a). This type is characteristic for most species of the genus *Dactylorhiza* in the sections of *Dactylorhiza, Sambucinae* and *Aristatae*.

Type II ("verrucos-hamulat"—Schill and Pfeiffer, 1977) possesses a very variable exine surface, which is formed by short, curved semicylinder-like excrescences (Fig. 5-4b). These excrescences can fuse fully with each other and form either a finely perforated or a finely reticulate surface texture. This type occur in some of species of the section *Dactylorhiza*.

Type III ("reticulat-fragmentimurat"—Schill and Pfeiffer, 1977) has a surface formed by irregular torulose excrescences which are fused in a pectinaceus structure which covers the exine with a continuous net (Fig. 5-4c). This type is characteristic only of the monotypic section *Iberanthus*.

Exine structures in the genus *Dactylorhiza* are shown in Fig. 5-5. The morphological variations in exine structure have no clear adaptive value.

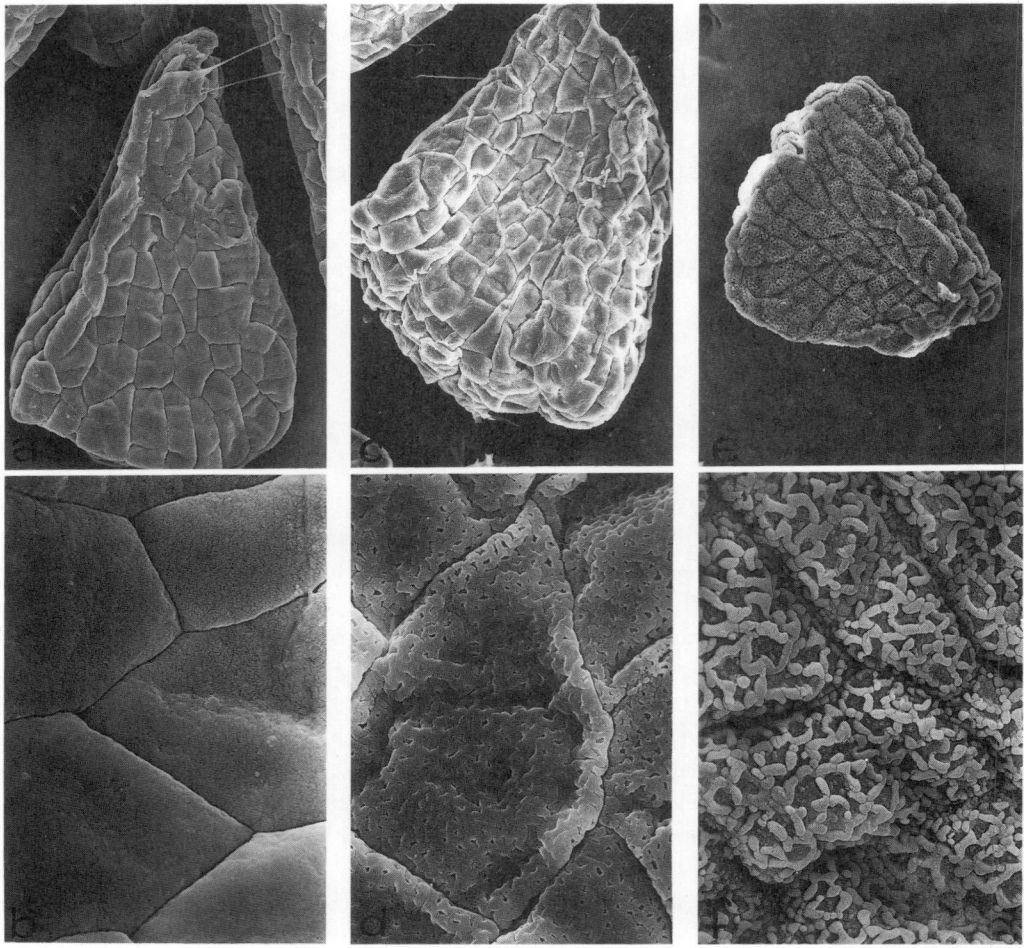

Fig. 5-4. Different surface types of pollen grains in the genus *Dactylorhiza.* **a,b,** type 1 (*D. flavescens*). × 250, × 1700; **c,d,** type 2 (*D. majalis*). × 250, × 1700; **e, f,** type 3 (*D. iberica*). × 250, × 1700 (Averyanov, 1983c).

Seeds

Species of the genus *Dactylorhiza* have seeds similar to those of most orchids. Their number is large and can reach (in *D. maculata* for example) 6,000 seeds per capsule (Darwin, 1877). A considerable reduction, which is typical for orchid seeds, exists in combination with specialized structures that enable them to float in the air. In dactylorchids and related genera, such a highly specialized tissue is the seed coat or testa. When mature it is a thin membrane that surrounds the embryo and contains a considerable volume of air. This allows the seed to float in the air for long periods, and "fly" to cover large distances. It has an important adaptive value.

The testa in orchids is extremely variable (Arditti et al., 1979, 1980a, b; Barthlott and Ziegler, 1981). In dactylorchids it is spindle-like, widest in the middle where the embryo

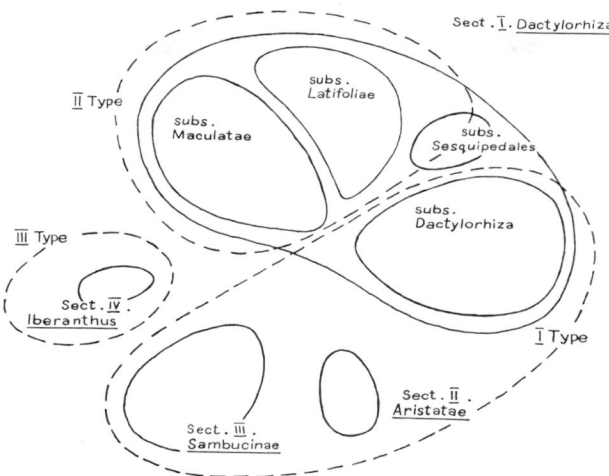

Fig. 5-5. Occurence of different pollen grains surface types in the genus *Dactylorhiza*. Explanation of symbols: Solid line indicates the toxonomic affiliations within the genus; the occurence of different pollen grain surface types is marked by the dotted line.

is located. The size of testae varies from 350 to 1100 μm in length and from 150 to 300 μm in width. The smallest seeds are those of *D. aristata* (350–500 × 200–250 μm) and the largest are produced by *D. urvilleana* (900–1100 × 150–250 μm) (Averyanov, 1983c).

Cells of the testa are polygonal in shape, bounded by thickened lignified anticlinal walls. In most species of *Dactylorhiza* they are elongated along the seed axes. The length of the testa cells is almost equal to their width in *D. incarnata* and *D. aristata,* the species with the smallest seeds (Averyanov, 1983c). Their shape as well as the ratio of their number on the transverse and longitudinal axes, is an important diagnostic character that permits the separation of the closely related *Dactylorhiza* and *Orchis* (Fig. 5-6; Tohda, 1983). The direction of specialization is from seeds with a relatively multicellular testa in *Dactylorhiza* to an extremely simplified seed coat consisting of a very small number of cells in *Orchis.*

In dactylorchids anticlynal cell walls in the testa are closely attached to each other. There are no intercellular spaces. The walls of the seed coat are very thin, membranous and stretched (like in drum skin) along thickened and lignified anticlinal cell walls. As seeds mature, cells of the one-layered testa lose their cytoplasm and the periclinal walls fuse with one another, at least in the center.

The surface structure of periclinal walls of the testa in dactylorchids is very variable. In one group of species the surfaces of the periclinal walls are not sculptured, in others sculpturing is present. Sculpturing of the periclinal walls in geographically variable in some species (Tohda, 1983). The form and presence of trabeculae is the basis of the classification of the structure of periclinal walls of testa cells of the genus into 4 types.

Type I (*D. incarnata*-type). The absence of trabeculae on periclinal walls of testa cells is typical for this class (Fig. 5-7a).

Type II (*D. maculata*-type). Periclinal walls of testa cells have transverse, sometimes dichotomously branching trabeculae which extend at right angles from the anticlinal cell walls (Fig. 5-7b).

Type II (*D. romana*-type). Trabeculae exhibit curved branching and anastomose with each other. Some do not join the anticlinal wall, become thinner and disappear on the

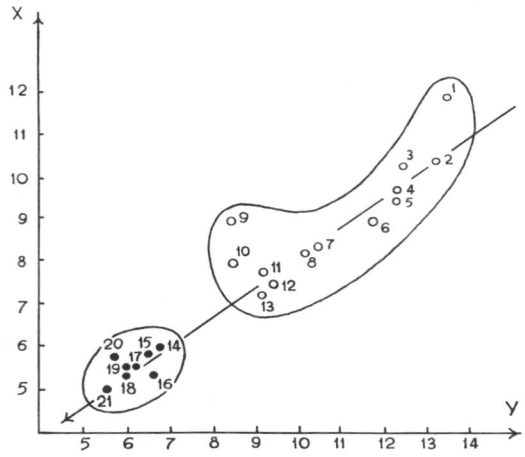

Fig. 5-6. Relation between cell numbers at the longest and widest axes of the testa in different dactylorchid species and *Orchis* species (Tohda, 1983). X — number of testa cells at the widest axis; Y — number of testa cells at the longest axis; the direction of testa specialization is shown by the arrow. Key: 1, *Dactylorhiza sphagnicola;* 2, *D. sambucina;* 3, *D. incarnata;* 4, *D. integrata;* 5, *D. sp.;* 6, *D. majalis;* 7, *D. pur-purella;* 8, *D. traunsteineri;* 9, *D. foliosa;* 10, *D. aristata;* 11, *D. maculata;* 12, *D. ericetorum;* 13, *D. fuchsii;* 14, *Orchis morio;* 15, *O. simia;* 16, *O. laxiflora;* 17, *O. coriophora;* 18, *O. picta;* 19, *O. mascula;* 20, *O. longicruris;* 21, *O. purpurea.*

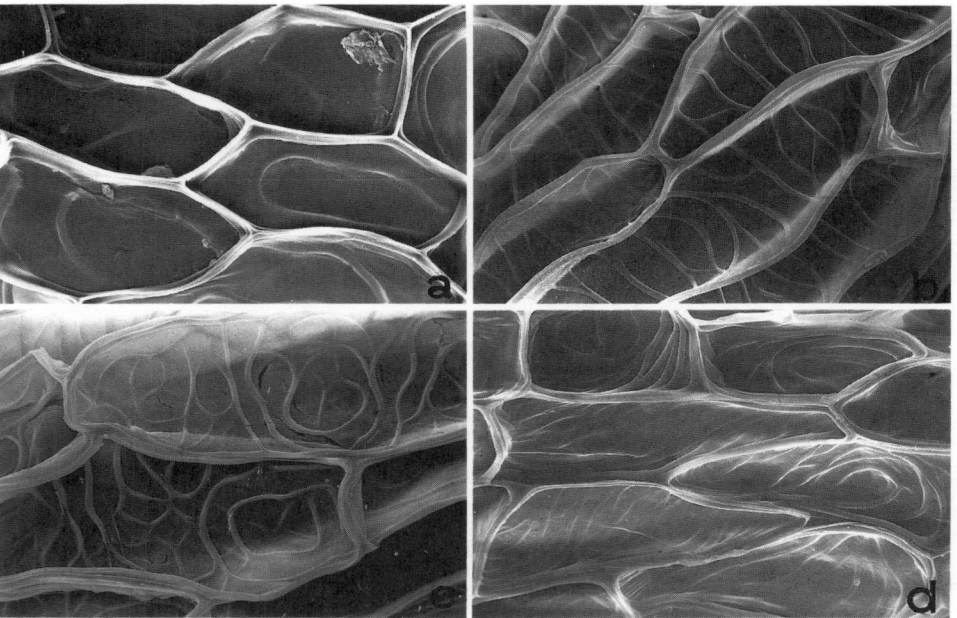

Fig. 5-7. Different morphological types of periclinal testa walls in seeds of *Dactylorhiza* species (Averyanov, 1983c). **a,** type 1 (*D. incarnata*). × 400; **b,** type 2 (*D. maculata*). × 400; **c,** type 3 (*D. romana*). × 400; **d,** type 4 (*D. aristata*). × 400.

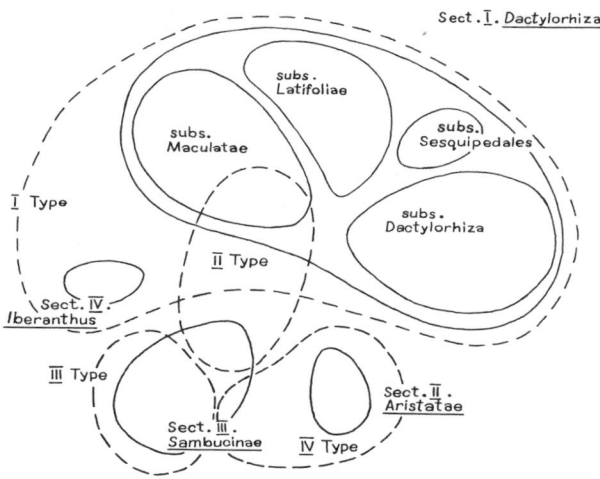

Fig. 5-8. Occurence of different morphological types of periclinal testa walls in seeds of the genus *Dactylorhiza*. Explanation of symbols: The solid line indicates the taxonomic groups within the genus; the occurrence of different types of periclinal testa walls in seeds is marked by the dotted line.

periclinal membrane (Fig. 5-7c).

Type IV (*D. aristata*-type). The trabeculae are "concentric" and arch-shaped. They extend at a sharp angle from the anticlinal walls and anastomose with each other in a pattern similar to the outline of the cell (Fig. 5-7d).

Schematically, the occurrence of these types in the genus *Dactylorhiza* is shown in Fig. 5-8. These types are, on the whole, similar to each other and therefore intermediate morphological variants can occur in a number of cases. The form of the trabeculae has no clear adaptive value.

The embryo in dactylorchids seeds is very small and essentially undifferentiated. In longitudinal sections it has a slightly bipolar structure because of larger cells which form one of its poles.

Chromosomes

The basic chromosome number for species of the tribe Orchideae as well as for the genus *Dactylorhiza* is 2n=40. This chromosome number is found in most members of this tribe (Duncan, 1959; Feodorov, 1969). Specimens of this tribe are polyploids (but diploids in their function) in comparison with the most primitive orchid karyotype (2n=20 in *Cypripedium* for example). The basic chromosome number for orchids as an evolutionary group is x=10.

Morphologically similar metacentric chromosomes with very short arms are typical for *Dactylorhiza* and most members of the subtribe Orchidinae. On metaphase plates of root meristems, they appear as rounded or oval bodies which stain well with Heidenhein's ferrous hematoxylin or Schiff's reactive. Their length in species of the genus *Dactylorhiza* is within 1–2 (2,5) μm. The primary constriction is hard to see. There are no B-chromosomes (Averyanov, 1983c).

Autopolyploidy, aneupolyploidy and allopolyploidy were involved in the evolution of the karyotype of dactylorchids (Fig. 5-9). Karyotypes of the primary kind (2n=40) are

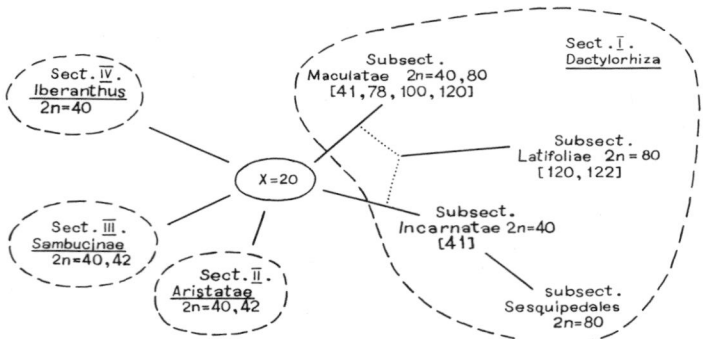

Fig. 5-9. Diagram of karyotype evolution in the genus *Dactylorhiza* from a basic chromosome number X = 20 (Averyanov, 1983c).

present in the only species of the monotypic section *Iberanthus* and in some of species of the section *Dactylorhiza*. The evolution of species in the subsection *Dactylorhiza* of the type section (sect. *Dactylorhiza*) proceeded at the diploid level. The primary chromosome number (2n=40) is also typical for many species in the subsection *Maculatae*. Tetraploid species of this subsection with 2n=80 arose by autopolyploidy (or allopolyploidy). The same process in species of the subsection *Dactylorhiza* led to tetraploids in the subsection *Sesquipedales*. Alloploid stabilization of hybrids between species of the subsections *Dactylorhiza* and *Maculatae* resulted in tetraploids among primary species of the hybridogenic subsection *Latifoliae* (Heslop-Harrison, 1954, 1957). Aneuploid change of the karyotype (2n=40 → 42) is typical for species of the section *Sambucinae* and *Aristatae*. This rearrangement is still evolving and in many species of these sections the norm is two chromosome numbers 2n=40 and 2n=42.

Polyploid plants with 2n=100, 120, 122 sometimes occur in populations of *D. maculata* and *D. russowii* (Vermeulen, 1938; Kliphuis, 1963; Averyanov, 1979b). Aneuploid forms with 2n=41, 78 can be found in *D. merovensis, D. hebridensis, D. psychrophila* and *D. maculata* (Averyanov et al., 1982a, b, 1985). Plants with such karyotypic anomalies are very rare. Morphologically and taxonomically they are similar to the parental species. In Fig. 5-9 and Table 5-1 they are presented in square brackets.

Somatic polyploidy was observed in several species of dactylorchids, when in a karyologically normal plants some tissues (or part of a tissue) have an anomalous chromosome number (Perring, 1968; Averyanov et al, 1982b).

Triploid hybrids (2n=60) are formed as a result of frequent hybridization between diploid and tetraploid species of dactylorchids. Sometimes they are very numerous and found in nature in large groups. Usually they are completely sterile. In a number of instances they can form up to 4% of normal seeds (Heslop-Harrison, 1957). Such seeds are formed either by parthenogensis (Heslop-Harrison, 1959) or through the fusion of gametes produced by anomalous meiosis. This leads to further degradation of the karyotype in the progeny and to the appearance of plants with 2n=44, 48, 52, 72 etc. (Lord and Richards, 1977). As a rule this is associated with anthropogenic influence on populations, which probably disturb existing isolation mechanisms among existing species.

In the subsection *Maculatae* some diploid and tetraploid species are morphologically very similar. This is particularly true for *D. fuchsii* (2n=40) and *D. maculata* (2n=80); *D.*

hebridensis (2n=40) and *D. elodes* (2n=80) as well as *D. psychrophila* (2n=40) and *D. sudetica* (2n=80). Most anatomical and morphological characters of these species correlate somewhat poorly with the ploidy level (Averyanov, 1979a). However, tetraploid and diploid species in this group prefer soils of different acidity and podzolization and they have not been observed to coexist in nature (Averyanov, 1982; Averyanov et al., 1982a, b). Although their triploid hybrids are sterile, all of these species are sometimes considered belonging to *D. maculata* s.l.

Relatively frequent changes of the ploidy level in progeny of one plant have been shown to occur in diploid and tetraploid species of *D. maculata* s.l. (Hagerup, 1944). The cases of haploidy (2n=40 → 2n=20 and 2n=80 → 2n=40) can be explained by the development of an embryo from an unfertilized egg or another haploid cell in the embryo sac (Hagerup, 1944). This has been shown to also occur in other orchids related to dactylorchid genera (Hageup, 1947; Heslop-Harrison, 1959).

Polyploidy can be explained by fertilization of unreduced eggs (2n=40 → 2n=60[b] and 2n–80 → 2n=120) and by autopolyploidization at an earlier stage of ontogenesis (2n=40 → 2n=80; Averyanov, 1979a). On the whole, development and fusion of the overwhelming majority of gametes proceeds normally. In the hypothetical scheme (Fig. 5-10) this is marked with boldface arrows. All plants with unusual chromosome numbers are sterile and relatively rare in nature; in Fig. 5-10 they are marked with an asterisk[c].

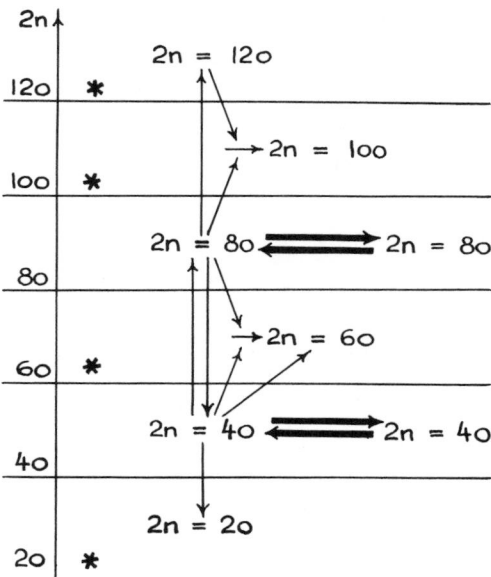

Fig. 5-10. Chart of possible spontaneous variations of the ploidy level in populations of *Dactylorhiza maculata* s.l. (Averyanov, 1979a).

[b]In most cases triploids result from hybridization of diploid and tetraploid plants.

[c]*D. maculata* s.l. with 2n=20 is known only in the embryo stage. Adult plants with such a chromosome number have not been observed in nature.

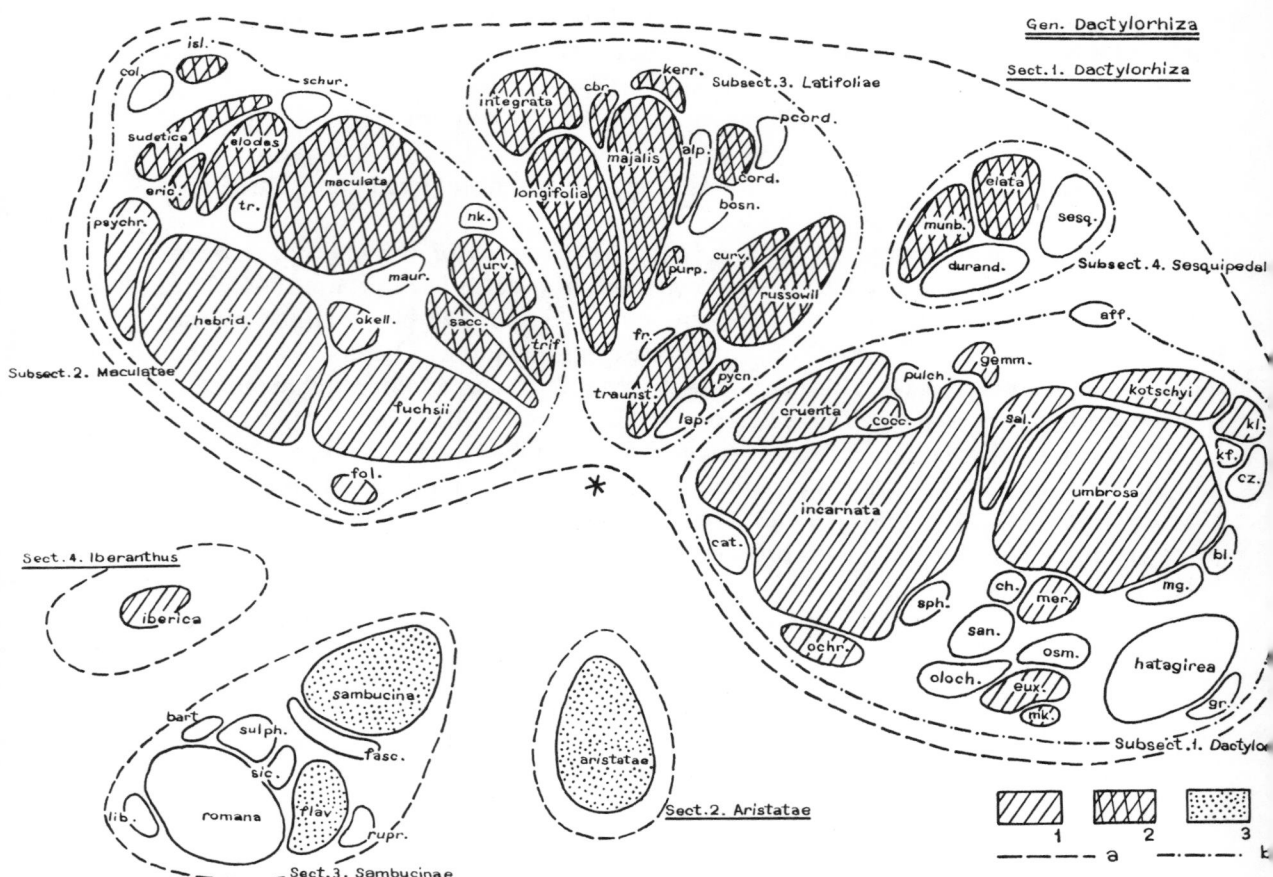

Fig. 5-11. Diagram of phylogenetic interrelations in *Dactylorhiza* species. Explanation of symbols: Distances between zones which designate species are an approximation of their affinity and their areas represent the relative extent of their distribution in combination with the polymorphism and the magnitude of the general species population. The approximate position of the ancestral complex is marked with an asterisk, and the distance from it is indicative of degree of evolutionary advancement (specialization) of taxa. Differences in species karyotypes are marked with shading: 1, 2n=40; 2, 2n=80; 3, 2n=40, 42, bodies designating karyologically unstudied species are not shaded. Sections limits are marked by line "a"; subsections limits—by line "b".

Abbreviations of species names in the diagram:

Sect. 1. *Dactylorhiza*
Subsect. 1. *Dactylorhiza*
1. *D. incarnata* incarnata
2. *D. cataonica* cat.
3. *D. ochroleuca* ochr.
4. *D. cruenta* cruenta
5. *D. coccinea* cocc.
6. *D. pulchella* pulch.
7. *D. sphagnicola* sph.
8. *D. gemmana* gemm.
9. *D. olocheilos* oloch.
10. *D. osmanica* osm.
11. *D. euxina* eux.
12. *D. markowitschii* mk.
13. *D. sanasunitensis* san.
14. *D. merovensis* mer.
15. *D. chuhensis* ch.
16. *D. salina* sal.
17. *D. umbrosa* umbrosa
18. *D. kotschyi* kotschyi
19. *D. magna* mg.

20. *D. baldshuanica* bl.
21. *D. czerniakowskae* cz.
22. *D. kafiriana* kf.
23. *D. kulikalonica* kl.
24. *D. hatagirea* hatagirea
25. *D. graggeriana* gr.
26. *D. affinis* aff.
Subsect. 2. *Maculatae*
27. *D. triphylla* trif.
28. *D. urvilleana* urv.
29. *D. nieschalkiorum* nk.
30. *D. saccifera* sacc.
31. *D. foliosa* fol.
32. *D. fuchsii* fuchsii
33. *D. okellyi* okell.
34. *D. hebridensis* hebrid.
35. *D. psychrophila* psychr.
36. *D. maculata* maculata
37. *D. maurusia* maur.
38. *D. elodes* elodes
39. *D. schurii* schur.

40. *D. transsilvanica* tr.
41. *D. ericetorum* eric.
42. *D. sudetica* sudetica
43. *D. colaënsis* col.
44. *D. islandica* isl.
Subsect. 3. *Latifoliae*
45. *D. majalis* majalis
46. *D. kerryensis* kerr.
47. *D. cambrensis* cbr.
48. *D. purpurella* purp.
49. *D. alpestris* alp.
50. *D. integrata* integrata
51. *D. longifolia* longifolia
52. *D. bosniaca* bosn.
53. *D. cordigera* cord.
54. *D. pseudocordigera* pcord.
55. *D. traunsteineri* traunst.
56. *D. francis-drucei* fr.
57. *D. russowii* russowii
58. *D. curvifolia* curv.
59. *D. pycnantha* pycn.

60. *D. lapponica* lap.
Subset. 4. *Sesquipedales*
61. *D. durandii* durand.
62. *D. munbyana* munb.
63. *D. elata* elata
64. *D. sesquipedalis* sesq.
Sect. 2. *Aristatae*
65. *D. aristata* aristata
Sect. 3. *Sambucinae*
66. *D. sambucina* sambucin
67. *D. fasciculata* fasc.
68. *D. sulphurea* sulph.
69. *D. sicula* sic.
70. *D. bartonii* bart.
71. *D. flavescens* flav.
72. *D. ruprechtii* rupr.
73. *D. romana* romana
74. *D. libanotica* lib.
Sect. 4. *Iberanthus*
75. *D. iberica* iberica

As indicated in the scheme, diploid and tetraploid plants can exchange genetic information irrespective of the sterility of their hybrids. This fact probably has a great adaptive value for *D. maculata* s.l. The genotype of diploids (similarly as it takes place in haploids) can change much faster than that of tetraploids under selection pressure. However, intensification of strong selection pressure can result in a considerable impoverishment of the gene pool of diploid populations and even put them on the verge of extinction. Therefore, it is possible that the flow of genetic information into such populations from closely related tetraploid species can avert extinction of the diploid species. Such interrelations may exist, for example, among *D. fuschii* and *D. maculata; D. hebridensis* and *D. maculata* and *D. elodes; D. psychrophila* and *D. sudetica.* On the other hand, useful and new genes can flow from diploids into tetraploids. In such cases, the tetraploid species can function as a reservoir and repository of genotypic variations which are constantly expressed and "tested" in diploids. Thus, hypothetically, related diploid and tetraploid species, which form the group"*D. maculata* s.l.", maintain their integrity and mutually determine the success of evolution (Averyanov, 1979a, 1983c).

Data on the karyology of *Dactylorhiza* species are brought together in Fig. 5-11 and Table 5-1.

Table 5-1. The taxonomy of dactylorchids.

Genus   *Dactylorhiza* Necker ex Nevski, 1937, *Tr. Bot. Inst. Ac. Sci. USSR,* Ser. 1,4:332.
Lectotype: *D. incarnata* (L.) Soó (*Orchis incarnata* L.)[a]
Section 1. *Dactylorhiza.*
Subsection 1. *Dactylorhiza.*
1-8. Aggregate *D. incarnata.*
1. *D. incarnata* (L.) Soó, 1962, *Nom. Nov. Gen. Dactylorh.:* 3
   Basionym: *Orchis incarnata* L., 1755, *Fl. Suec.,* ed. 2:312.
   Syn.: *Orchis impudica* Haller, 1769, in Crantz, *Stirp. Austr.* 2, 6:497.
       Orchis divaricata Rich., 1812, *Mer. Fl. Par.* 2:94.
       Orchis latifolia L. var. *angustifolia* Lois., 1828, *Fl. Gall.* 2:267.
       Orchis angustifolia Lois. ex Wimm. et Grabowski, 1829, *Fl. Siles.* 2, 2:252.
       Orchis lanceata Dietri, 1833, *Fl. Boruss.* 5.
       Orchis angustifolia Reichenb. var. *haussknechtii* Klinge, 1893, *Revis. Orch. cord. Orch. angustif.:* 70.
   2n = 40. Europe, W. Asia Minor, Crimea, N. Caucasus, Siberia, N. Central Asia, N. China, Mongolia.
2. *D. cataonica* (Fleischm.) Holub, 1964, *Preslia,* 36,3:252.
   Basionym: *Orchis cataonica* Fleischm., 1914, *Ann. Naturh. Mus. (Wien)* 28:34.
   Asia Minor, Transcaucasia.
3. *D. ochroleuca* (Wüstn. ex Boll.) Holub, 1974, *Folia Geobot. Phyt. Tax.* 9,3:272.
   Basionym: *Orchis incarnata* L. var. *ochroleuca* Wüstn. ex Boll., 1860, *Arch. Ver. Fr. Nat. Macklenb.* 14:307.
   Syn.: *Orchis incarnata* L. var. *straminea* Reichenb. f. ex Soó, 1933, in Keller et Schlechter, *Monogr. Icon. Orch. Europ. Mittelmeer.* 2,6–7:209.
   2n = 40. Central and N. Europe.
4. *D. cruenta* (O. F. Müll.) Soó, 1962, *Nom. Nov. Gen. Dactylorh.:* 4.
   Basionym: *Orchis cruenta* O. F. Müll., 1782, *Fl. Dan.* 5,15:4.
   Syn.: *Orchis haematodes* Reichenb., 1830, *Fl. Germ. Exc.:* 126.
       Orchis cruentiformis Neuman, 1909, *Bot. Not. (Lund)* 1909: 243.
       Orchis incarnata L. var. *hyphaematodes* Neuman, 1909, *Bot. Not. (Lund)* 1909:244.
       Orchis incarnata L. ssp. *guttata* Ugrinsky, 1911, *Tr. Obsch. Ispit. Prir. Chark. Univ.* 44:295.
   2n = 40. Central and N. Europe, Siberia.
5. *D. coccinea* (Pugsley) Aver., 1984, *Bot. J.* 69:875.
   Basionym: *Orchis latifolia* L. var. *coccinea* Pugsley, 1935, *J. Linn. Soc. London* (Bot.) 49,332:579.
   2n = 40. British Islands.
6. *D. pulchella* (Druce) Aver., 1984, *Bot. J.* 69:875.
   Basionym: *Orchis incarnata* L. var. *pulchella* Druce, 1918, *Rep. Bot. Exch. Club Brit. Isl.* 1918:167.
   British Islands.

[a]The term *Dactylorhiza,* introduced by Sergei Arsenievich Nevski (1908–1938) in 1937 as a generic name, was based on specimens of dactylorchids occuring in Europe (Necker, 1790). Therfore *Orchis incarnata* should be considered as the lectotype of the genus (Vermeulen, 1947; Smolyaninova, 1976), and not *Orchis umbrosa* (Farr, Leussink, Stafleu, 1979) which was the first dactylorchid known under the generic name *Dactylorhiza* (*Dactylorhiza umbrosa* Nevski, 1937).

Table 5-1. Continued.

7. *D. sphagnicola* (Höppn. ex Soó) Soó, 1962, *Nom. Nov. Gen. Dactylorh.*: 6.
    Basionym: *Orchis sphagnicola* Höppn. ex Soó, 1933, in Keller et Schlechter, *Monogr. Icon. Orch. Europ. Mittelmeer.* 2,6–7:259.
    W. Europe.
8. *D. gemmana* (Pugsley) Aver., 1984, *Bot. J.* 69:875.
    Basionym: *Orchis latifolia* L. var. *gemmana* Pugsley, 1935, *Journ. Linn. Soc. London (Bot.)* 49,332:578.
    2n = 40. British Islands.
9–12. Aggregate *D. olocheilos.*
9. *D. olocheilos* (Boiss.) Aver., 1984, *Bot. J.* 69:875.
    Basionym: *Orchis incarnata* L. var. *olocheilos* Boiss., 1884, *Fl. Orient.* 5:71.
    Syn.: *Orchis orientalis* Klinge ssp. *cilicica* Klinge, 1898, *Dactylorch. Monogr. Prodr.*: 41.
    Asia Minor.
10. *D. osmanica* (Klinge) Soó, 1962, *Nom. Nov. Gen. Dactylorh.*: 4.
    Basionym: *Orchis orientalis* Klinge ssp. *osmanica* Klinge, *Dactylorch. Monogr. Prodr.*: 42.
    Asia Minor.
11. *D. euxina* (Nevski) Czer., 1981, *Sosud. Rast. USSR*: 308.
    Basionym: *Orchis euxina* Nevski, 1935, *Fl. USSR* 4:709.
    Syn.: *Orchis cordigera* Fries var. *caucasica* Klinge ex Lipsky, 1897, *Acta Horti Petropol.* 14,10:306, nom. nud.
        Orchis monticola Klinge ssp. *caucasica* Klinge, 1898, *Dactylorch. Monogr. Prodr.*: 35.
        Orchis caucasica (Klinge) Medwedev, 1919, *Tr. Tiflissk. Bot. Gard.* 18, 2:476, non Regel, 1869.
    2n = 40. Caucasus, Transcaucasia.
12. *D. markowitschii* (Soó) Aver., 1983, *Bot. J.* 68:893.
    Basionym: *Orchis caucasica* (Klinge) Medwedev var. *markowitschii* Soó, 1926, *Notizbl. Bot. Gart. Berlin* 9,89:909.
    Syn.: *Orchis caucasica* (Klinge) Medwedev var. *alpina* Schlechter, 1927, in Keller et Schlechter, *Monogr. Orch. Europ. Mittelmeer.* 1:173.
    2n = 40. Caucasus, Transcaucasia.
13–15. Aggregate *D. sanasunitensis.*
13. *D. sanasunitensis* (Fleischm.) Soó, 1962, *Nom. Nov. Gen. Dactylorh.*: 4.
    Basionym: *Orchis sanasunitensis* Fleischm., 1914, *Ann. Naturh. Mus.* (Wien) 28:35.
    Asia Minor.
14. *D. merovensis* (Grosheim) Aver., 1983, *Bot. J.* 68:894.
    Basionym: *Orchis merovensis* Grosheim, 1928, *Beih. Bot. Centralbl.* 44:207.
    Syn.: *Dactylorhiza umbrosa* (Kar. et Kir.) Nevski var. *longibracteata* Renz, 1978, *Fl. Iran.* 126:131.
    2n = 40 [41]. Transcaucasia, N.-E. Turkey, N. Iran.
15. *D. chuhensis* Renz et Taub., 1984, *Fl. Turkey* 8:564.
    Syn.: *Dactylorhiza renzii* Aver., 1983, *Bot. J.* 68:893, non H. Baumann et Künkele, 1981.
    Transcaucasia, E. Turkey.
16–23. Aggregate *D. salina.*
16. *D. salina* (Turcz. ex lindl.) Soó, 1962, *Nom. Nov. Gen. Dactylorh.*: 4.
    Basionym: *Orchis salina* Turcz. ex Lindl., 1835, *Gen. Sp. Orch. Pl.*: 259.
    Syn.: *Orchis incarnata* L. var. *rhombeilabia acroglossa* Reichenb. f., 1851, *Icon. Fl. Germ.* 13–14:53.
    2n = 40. E. Caucasus, E. Transcaucasia, N. Central Asia, S. Siberia, N. China, Mongolia.
17. *D. umbrosa* (Kar. et Kir.) Nevski, 1937, *Tr. Bot. Inst. Ac. Sci. USSR*, Ser. 1,4:332.
    Basionym: *Orchis umbrosa* Kar. et Kir., 1842, *Bull. Soc. Nat. Moscou* 15:504.
    Syn.: *Orchis incarnata* L. var. *sesquipedalis altaica* Reichenb. f., 1851, *Icon. Fl. Germ.* 13–14:53.
        Orchis orientalis Klinge ssp. *turcestanica* Klinge, 1898, *Dactylorch. Monogr. Prodr.*: 37.
        Orchis persica Schlechter, 1918, *Feddes Repert.* 15:290.
        Orchis hatagirea Don var. *afganica* Soó, *J. Bot.* (London) 66:17.
        Orchis altaica (Reichenb. f.) Soó, 1933, in Keller et Schlechter, *Monogr. Icon. Orch. Europ. Mittelmeer.* 2, 6–7:214.
    2n = 40. Iran, Afghanistan, Pakistan, Central Asia, S. Siberia, N. China, Mongolia.
18. *D. kotschyi* (Reichenb. f.) Soó, 1962, *Nom. Nov. Gen. Dactylorh.*: 4.
    Basionym: *Orchis incarnata* L. var. *kotschyi* Reichenb. f., 1851, *Icon. Fl. Germ.* 13–14:53.
    Syn.: *Orchis incarnata* L. var. *knorringiana* Kraenzl., 1931, *Feddes Repert. (Beih.)* 65:34.
    2n = 40. Iran, Afghanistan, Pakistan, Central Asia, S. Siberia, N.-W. China, Mongolia.
19. *D. magna* (Czerniak.) Iconn., 1972, *Nov. Syst. Visch. Rast.* 9:303.
    Basionym: *Orchis magna* Czerniak., 1941, *Fl. Uzbek.* 1:528, 546.
    Afghanistan, Pakistan, Central Asia.
20. *D. baldshuanica* Czerniak. ex Aver., 1983, *Bot. J.* 68:534.
    Tadjikistan.
21. *D. czerniakowskae* Aver., 1983, *Bot. J.* 68:536.
    N.-E. Afghanistan, N. Pakistan, S.-E. USSR (Middle Asia), N.-W. China.
22. *D. kafiriana* Renz, 1978, *Fl. Iran.* 126:125.
    N.-E. Afghanistan, N. Pakistan.
23. *D. kulikalonica* Czerniak. ex Aver., 1983, *Bot. J.* 68:535.
    2n = 40. N.-E. Afghanistan, N. Pakistan, S.-E. USSR (Middle Asia), N.-W. China.
24–25. Aggregate *D. hatagirea.*

24. *D. hatagirea* (Don) Soó, 1962, *Nom. Nov. Gen. Dactylorh.*: 4.
    Basionym: *Orchis hatagirea* Don, 1825, *Prodr. Fl. Nepal.*: 23.
    Syn.: *Orchis latifolia* L. var. *indica* Lindl., 1835, *Gen. Sp. Orch. Pl.*: 260.
    E. Pakistan, N. India, Nepal, S.-W. China, Bhutan.
25. *D. graggeriana* (Soó) Soó, 1962, *Nom. Nov. Gen. Dactylorh.*: 4.
    Basionym: *Orchis graggeriana* Soó, 1928, *J. Bot.* (London) 66:15.
    N. India.
26. *D. affinis* (C. Koch) Aver., 1983, *Bot. J.* 68:895.
    Basionym: *Orchis affinis* C. Koch, 1849, *Linnaea* 22:284.
    Asia Minor, Transcaucasia.
Subsection 2. *Maculatae* (Parl.) Aver., 1983, *Bot. J.* 68:1160.
    Type:*D. maculata* (L.) Soó (*Orchis maculata* L.).
27–30. Aggregate *D. saccifera*.
27. *D. triphylla* (C. Koch) Czer., 1981, *Sosud. Rast. USSR*: 309.
    Basionym: *Orchis triphylla* C. Koch, 1849, *Linnaea* 22:283.
    Syn.: *Orchis basilica* L. ssp. *cartaliniae* Klinge, 1898, *Dactylorch. Monogr. Prodr.*: 50, p.p.
        Orchis amblyoloba Nevski, 1935, *Fl. USSR* 4:707.
    2n = 80. Asia Minor, Caucasus, Transcaucasia.
28. *D. urvilleana* (Steudel) Baumann et Kuenkele, 1981, *Mitt. Bl. Arbeitskr. Heim. Orch. Baden-Württ.* 13:240.
    Basionym: *Orchis urvilleana* Steudel, 1841, *Nomencl.* 2ed., 2:225.
    Syn.: *Orchis saccata* d'Urv., 1822, *Pl. Ins. Ponti Eus.*: 119, non Ten., 1811.
        Orchis lancibracteata C. Koch, 1849, *Linnaea* 22:284.
        Orchis basilica L. ssp. *cartaliniae* Klinge, 1898, *Dactylorch. Monogr. Prodr.*: 50, p.p.
        Orchis maculata L. var. *brotheri* Somm. et Lev. 1900, *Acta Horti Petropol.* 16:419.
        Orchis pontica Fleischm. et Handel-Mazzetti, 1909, *Ann. Naturh. Mus.* (Wien) 23, 1–2:208.
    2n = 80. Asia Minor, Iran, Caucasus, Transcaucasia.
29. *D. nieschalkiorum* H. Baumann et Kuenkele, 1981, *Mitt. Bl. Arbeitskr. Heim. Orch. Baden-Württ.* 13:259.
    N.-W. Turkey.
30. *D. saccifera* (Brongn.) Soó, 1962, *Nom. Nov. Gen. Dactylorh.*: 8.
    Basionym: *Orchis saccifera* Brongn., 1832, in Bory, *Exp. Scient. Moree* 3,2:259.
    Syn.: *Orchis tetragona* Heuffel, 1933, *Fl. Oder Allgem. Bot. Zeit.* 23:363.
        Orchis macedonica Griseb., 1841, *Reise Rumel.* 2:219, 302, nom. nud.
        Orchis macrostachys Tineo, 1846, *Pl. Rar. Sic.*: 7.
        Orchis maculata L. var. *cartalinoides* Klinge ex Fleischm., 1908, *Mitt. Nat. Ver. Steierm.* 45:176.
    2n = 40, 80 [42]. S. Europe, Asia Minor, Syria, Lebanon.
31. *D. foliosa* (Soland.) Soó, 1962, *Nom. Nov. Gen. Dactylorh.*: 7.
    Basionym: *Orchis foliosa* Soland., 1831, in Lowe, *Trans. Cambr. Phil. Soc.* 4:13.
    2n = 40. Madeira Islands.
32–35. Aggregate *D. fuchsii*.
32. *D. fuchsii* (Druce) Soó, 1962, *Nom. Nov. Gen. Dactylorh.*: 8.
    Basionym: *Orchis fuchsii* Druce, 1914, *Rep. Bot. Exch. Club Brit. Isl.* 4:105.
    Syn.: *Orchis maculata* L. var. *obscura* Neuman, 1909, *Bot. Not.* (Lund) 1909:152.
    2n = 40. Europe, Siberia, N.-W. China, Mongolia.
33. *D. okellyi* (Druce) Aver., 1984, *Bot. J.* 69:875.
    Basionym: *Orchis maculata* L. var. *Okellyi* Druce, 1909, *Irish Natur.*: 221.
    2n = 40. British Islands.
34. *D. hebridensis* (Wilmott) Aver., 1986, *Bot. J.* 71:92.
    Basionym: *Orchis hebridensis* Wilmott, 1939, *J. Bot.* (London) 77:192.
    Syn.: *Orchis maculata* L. var. *meyeri* Reichenb. f., 1851, *Icon. Fl. Germ.* 13–14:67.
        Orchis fuchsii Druce ssp. *rhoumensis* H.-Harrison f., 1949, *Trans. Proc. Bot. Soc. Edinburg* 35,1:53.
    2n = 40 [41, 80]. Europe, Siberia, Mongolia.
35. *D. psychrophila* (Schlechter) Aver., 1982, *Bot. J.* 67:308.
    Basionym: *Orchis maculata* L. var. *psychrophila* Schlechter, 1927, in Keller et Schlechter, *Monogr. Icon. Orch. Europ. Mittelmeer.* 1:183.
    2n = 40 [41]. N. Europe, Siberia (mountains).
36–44. Aggregate *D. maculata*.
36. *D. maculata* (L.) Soó, 1962, *Nom. Nov. Gen. Dactylorh.*: 7.
    Basionym:*Orchis maculata* L., 1753, *Sp. Pl.*: 942.
    Syn.: *Orchis candidissima* Krocker, 1814, *Fl. Siles.*: 16.
        Orchis angustifolia Krocker, 1814, *Fl. Siles.*: 16.
    2n = 80 [78, 100, 120]. Europe, W. Siberia.
37. *D. maurusia* (Emberger et Maire) Holub, 1973, *Folia Geobot. Phyt. Tax.* 8, 2:176.
    Basionym: *Orchis maurusia* Emberger et Maire, 1931, *Bull. Soc. Sci. Natur. Maroc.* 11, 4–6:109.
    Syn.: *Orchis maculata* L. ssp. *baborica* Maire et Weiller., 1959, in Maire, *Fl. Afr. Nord.* 6:309.
    N. Africa (Atlas Mountains).
38. *D. elodes* (Griseb.) Aver., 1982, *Bot. J.* 67:309.
    Basionym: *Orchis elodes* Griseb., 1846, *Über Bildung Torfs*: 25.
    2n = 80 [40]. Europe.

Table 5-1. Continued.

39. *D. schurii* (Klinge) Aver., 1984, *Bot. J.* 69:875.
   Basionym: *Orchis angustifolia* Reichenb. var. *recurva* Klinge f. *schurii* Klinge, 1893, *Revis. Orch. cord. Orch. angustif.*: 83.
   E. Europe (Carpathian Mountains).
40. *D. transsilvanica* (Schur) Aver., 1982, *Bot. J.* 67:309.
   Basionym: *Orchis transsilvanica* Schur, 1866, *Enum. Pl. Transsilv.*: 643.
   E. Europe (Carpathian Mountains).
41. *D. ericetorum* (Linton) Aver., 1982, *Bot. J.* 67:309.
   Basionym: *Orchis maculata* L. ssp. *ericetorum* Linton, 1900, *Fl. Bournemouth*: 208.
   2n = 80. Central and N. Europe.
42. *D. sudetica* (Poch ex Reichenb. f.) Aver., 1982, *Bot. J.* 67:310.
   Basionym: *Orchis maculata* L. var. *sudetica* Poch ex Reichenb. f., 1851, *Icon. Fl. Germ.* 13–14:66.
   Syn.: *Orchis maculata* L. var. *praecox* Webster, 1886, *Brit. Orch.*: 54.
      Orchis maculata L. var. *pumila* Neuman, 1909, *Bot. Not.* (Lund) 1909:245.
   2n = 80. Central and N. Europe, N.-W. Siberia.
43. *D. kolaënsis* (Montell) Aver., 1984, *Bot. J.* 69:875.
   Basionym: *Orchis maculata* L. var. *kolaënsis* Montell, 1947, *Mem. Soc. Fauna Fl. Fenn.* 23:166.
   Syn.: *Dactylorchis maculata* (L.) Vermeulen ssp. *montellii* Vermeulen, 1947, *Stud. Dactylorch.*: 141.
   N. Europe.
44. *D. islandica* (A. Löve et D. Löve) Aver., 1984, *Bot. J.* 69:875.
   Basionym: *Dactylorchis maculata* (L.) Vermeulen ssp. *islandica* A. Löve et D. Löve, 1948, *Chrom. numb. North. Pl. Sp.*: 106.
   2n = 80. Iceland.
Subsection 3. *Latifoliae* (Reichenb. f.) Aver., 1983, *Bot. J.* 68:1162.
   Type: *D. majalis* (Reichenb.) P. F. Hunt et Summerhayes (*Orchis majalis* Reichenb.).
45–49. Aggregate *D. majalis*.
45. *D. majalis* (Reichenb.) P. F. Hunt et Summerhayes, 1965, *Watsonia* 6,2:130.
   Basionym: *Orchis majalis* Reichenb., 1828, *Icon. Bot. Pl. Crit.*, 6,7:7.
   Syn.: *Orchis latifolia* L., 1753, *Sp. Pl.*: 941, p.p., nom. confus.
      Orchis comosa Scop., 1772, *Fl. Carn.* 2:198, nom. illeg.
      Orchis fistulosa Moench, 1794, *Meth. Pl. Horti Marburg.*: 713, nom. illeg.
   2n = 80. Central and N. Europe.
46. *D. kerryensis* (Wilmott) P. F. Hunt et Summerhayes, 1965, *Watsonia* 6,2:131.
   Basionym: *Orchis kerryensis* Wilmott, 1936, *Proc. Linn. Soc. London* 148:126.
   Syn.: *Orchis majalis* Reichenb. var. *occidentalis* Pugsley, 1935, *Journ. Linn. Soc. London (Bot.)* 49, 332:586.
   2n = 80. British Islands.
47. *D. cambrensis* (Roberts) Aver., 1984, *Bot. J.* 69:875.
   Basionym: *Dactylorchis majalis* (Reichenb.) Vermeulen ssp. *cambrensis* Roberts, 1961, *Watsonia* 5,1:41.
   2n = 80. British Islands.
48. *D. purpurella* (T. Stephenson et T. A. Stephenson) Soó, 1962, *Nom. Nov. Gen. Dactylorh.*: 5.
   Basionym: *Orchis purpurella* T. Stephenson et T. A. Stephenson, 1920, *J. Bot.* (London) 58:164.
   Syn.: *Orchis praetermissa* Druce var. *pulchella* Druce, 1920, *Rep. Bot. Exch. Club Brit. Isl.* 5:577.
   2n = 80. N.-W. Europe.
49. *D. alpestris* (Pugsley) Aver., 1983, *Bot. J.* 68:1164.
   Basionym: *Orchis alpestris* Pugsley, 1935, *J. Linn. Soc. London (Bot.)* 49, 332:587.
   Syn.: *Orchis cordigera* Fries ssp. *siculorum* Soó, 1927, *Feddes Repert.* 24:31.
      Dactylorchis majalis (Reichenb.) Vermeulen var. *alpestroides* Vermeulen, 1949, *Nederl. Kruidk. Arch.* 56:215.
   Europe.
50–51. Aggregate *D. integrata*.
50. *D. integrata* (E. G. Camus) Aver., 1984, *Bot. J.* 69:875.
   Basionym: *Orchis incarnata* L. var. *integrata* E. G. Camus, 1891, in Fourcy, *Vadem. Herb. Paris* ed. 6:325.
   Syn.: *Orchis integrata* (E. G. Camus) E. G. Camus, 1892, *Monogr. Orch. Fr.*: 48.
      Orchis praetermissa Druce, 1913, *Rep. Bot. Exch. Club Brit. Isl.* 3:341.
   2n = 80. N.-W. Europe.
51. *D. longifolia* (Neuman) Aver., 1984, *Bot. J.* 69:875.
   Basionym: *Orchis longifolia* Neuman, 1909, *Bot. Not.* (Lund) 1909:241.
   Syn.: *Orchis latifolia* L. var. *dunensis* Reichenb. f., 1851, *Icon. Fl. Germ.* 13–14:59, non Druce, 1917.
      Orchis latifolia L. ssp. *baltica* Klinge, 1898, *Dactylorch. Monogr. Prodr.*: 24.
   2n = 80. Central and N. Europe, Siberia, N. Central Asia, N.-W. China.
52–54. Aggregate *D. cordigera*.
52. *D. bosniaca* (G. Beck) Aver., 1984, *Bot. J.* 69:875.
   Basionym: *Orchis bosniaca* G. Beck, 1887, *Ann. Naturh. Mus.* (Wien) 2:53.
   Syn.: *Orchis latifolia* L. var. *lagotis* Reichenb. f., 1851, *Icon. Fl. Germ.* 13–14:58.
      Orchis latifolia L. var. *rochelii* Grisebach et Schenk, 1852, *Arch. Naturg.* (Berlin) 18,1:355.
   S.-E. Europe(Carpathian and Balkan Mountains).
53. *D. cordigera* (Fries) Soó, 1962, *Nom. Nov. Gen. Dactylorh.*: 5.
   Basionym: *Orchis cordigera* Fries, 1842, *Nov. Fl. Suec.* 3:130.
   Syn.: *Orchis latifolia* L. var. *conica* Lindl., 1935, *Gen. Sp. Orch. Pl.* :260.
      Orchis rivularis Heuff. ex Schur., 1866, *Enum. Pl. Transsilv.*: 642.
   2n = 80. E. Europe (Carpathian Mountains).

54. *D. pseudocordigera* (Neuman) Soó, 1962, *Nom. Nov. Gen. Dactylorh.*: 4.
 Basionym: *Orchis pseudocordigera* Neuman, 1909, *Bot. Not.* (Lund) 1909:236.
 Syn.: *Orchis latifolia* L. var. *conica Blyttii* Reichenb. f., 1851, *Icon. Fl. Germ.* 13–14:60.
 N. Europe (Scandinavian Peninsula).
55–60. Aggregate *D. traunsteineri.*
55. *D. traunsteineri* (Saut.) Soó, *Nom. Nov. Gen. Dactylorh.*: 5.
 Basionym: *Orchis traunsteineri* Saut., 1837, *Fl. Regensb.* 20, 1 *Beibl.* 3:36.
 Syn.: *Orchis angustifolia* Lois. ex Reichenb., 1831, *Icon. Bot. Pl. Crit.* 9:17, non *Bieb.*, 1808, nec Wimm. et
  Grab., 1829.
   Orchis latifolia L. var. *eborensis* Godfery, 1933, *Monogr. Icon. Nat. Brit. Orch.*: 166, 219.
   Orchis majalis Reichenb. ssp. *traunsteinerioides* Pugsley, 1936, *Proc. Linn. Soc. London* 148:124.
 2n = 80. Central and N. Europe, Urals.
56. *D. francis-drucei* (Wilmott) Aver., 1984, *Bot. J.* 69:875.
 Basionym: *Orchis francis-drucei* Wilmott, 1936, *Proc. Linn. Soc. London* 148:128.
 Scotland, Hebrides.
57. *D. russowii* (Klinge) Holub, 1964, *Preslia* 36,3:253.
 Basionym: *Orchis angustifolia* Lois. ex Reichenb. var. *russowii* Klinge, 1893, *Revis. Orch. cord. Orch.*
  angustif.: 84.
 Syn.: *Dactylorchis deweveri* Vermeulen, 1949, *Nederl. Kruidk. Arch.* 56:227.
 2n = 80 [120, 122]. Central and N. Europe, Siberia.
58. *D. curvifolia* (Nyl.) Czer., 1981, *Sosud. Rast. USSR*: 307.
 Basionym: *Orchis curvifolia* Nyl., 1844, *Spicil. Pl. Fenn.* 2:12.
 Syn.: *Orchis recurva* Nyl. ex Fries, 1846, *Summa Veget. Scand.* 1:61, nom. nud.
   Orchis angustifolia Lois. ex Reichenb. var. *recurva* Klinge, 1893, *Revis. Orch. cord. Orch. angustif.*:
    82.
 2n = 80. Central and N. Europe.
59. *D. pycnantha* (Neuman) Aver., 1983, *Bot. J.* 68:1163.
 Basionym: *Orchis angustifolia* Lois. ex Reichenb. ssp. *pycnantha* Neuman, 1909, *Bot. Not.* (Lund)
  1909:232.
 Syn.: *Orchis angustifolia* Lois. ex Reichenb. var. *Blyttii* Klinge, 1893, *Revis. Orch. cord. Orch. angustif.*: 79.
 2n = 80. N. Europe.
60. *D. lapponica* (Laest.) Soó, 1962, *Nom. Nov. Gen. Dactylorh.*: 5.
 Basionym: *Orchis angustifolia* Krocker var. *lapponica* Laest., 1843, in Hartm., *Skand. Fl.* 4:281.
 Syn.: *Orchis latifolia* L. var. *lapponica* Laest. ex Reichenb. f., 1851, *Icon. Fl. Germ.* 13–14:58.
   Orchis angustifolia Lois. var. *pusilla* Neuman, 1909, *Bot. Not.* (Lund) 1909:233.
 N. Europe.
Subsection 4. *Sesquipedales* (Vermeulen) Aver., 1983, *Bot. J.* 68:895.
 Type: *D. elata* (Poir.) Soó (*Orchis elata* Poir.).
61–64. Aggregate *D. elata.*
61. *D. durandii* (Boiss. et Reut.) M. Lainz., 1971, *Aport. Conocim. Fl. Gallega* 7:31.
 Basionym: *Orchis durandii* Boiss. et Reut., 1852, *Pugill. Pl. Nov.*: 111.
 Syn.: *Orchis orientalis* Klinge ssp. *africana* Klinge, 1898, *Dactylorch. Monogr. Prodr.*: 40.
 S.-W. Europe, N.-W. Africa.
62. *D. munbyana* (Boiss. et Reut.) Holub, 1981, *Folia Geobot. Phytotax* 19, 2:214.
 Basionym: *Orchis munbyana* Boiss. et Reut., 1852, *Pugill. Pl. Nov.*: 112.
 Syn.: *Orchis incarnata* L. var. *foliosa* Reichenb. f., 1851, *Icon. Fl. Germ.* 13–14:52.
 2n = 80. S.-W. Europe, N.-W. Africa.
63. *D. elata* (Poir.) Soó, 1962, *Nom. Nov. Gen. Dactylorh.*: 7.
 Basionym: *Orchis elata* Poir., 1789, *Voy. Barb.* 2:248.
 Syn.: *Orchis incarnata* L. var. *sesquipedalis algerica* Reichenb. f., 1851, *Icon. Fl. Germ.* 13–14:53.
   Orchis latifolia L. var. *elatior* Afz. ex Batt. et Trab., 1884, *Fl. Alger.*: 196.
   Orchis sesquipedalis Willd. var. *algerica* Briq., 1910, *Prodr. Fl. Corse* 1:169.
 2n = 80. N. Africa, Sicily.
64. *D. sesquipedalis* (Willd.) M. Lainz, 1971, *Aport. Conocim. Fl. Gallega* 7:31.
 Basionym: *Orchis sesquipedalis* Willd., 1805, *Sp. Pl.* 4:30.
 Syn.: *Orchis lusitanica* Steudel, 1841, *Nomencl. Bot.* 2ed. 2:224.
   Orchis incarnata L. var. *sesquipedalis genuina* Reichenb. f., 1851, *Icon. Fl. Germ.* 13–14:53.
   Orchis latifolia L. var. *corsica* Reverchom ex E. G. Camus, 1892, *Monogr. Orch. Fr.*: 158.
   Orchis elata Poir. ssp. *ambigua* Mart.-Donos ex Soó, 1927, *Feddes Repert.* 24:31.
 S.-W. Europe.
Section 2. *Aristate* Aver., 1983, *Bot. J.* 68:895.
65. *D. aristata* (Fisch. ex Lindl.) Soó, *Nom. Nov. Gen. Dactylorh.*: 5.
 Basionym: *Orchis aristata* Fisch. ex Lindl., 1835. *Gen. Sp. Orch. Pl.*: 262.
 Syn.: *Orchis latifolia* L. var. *beeringiana* Chamisso, 1828, in Chamisso et Schlechter, *Linnaea* 3:26.
 2n = 40,42. Korea, Japan, Kuril and Aleutian Islands, S. Sakhalin, S. Kamchatka, W. Alaska.
Section 3. *Sambucinae* (Parl.) Smoljian., 1976, *Fl. Europ. Czasti USSR* 2:52.
 Type: *D. sambucina* (L.) Soó (*Orchis sambucina* L.).
66–67. Aggregate *D. sambucina.*
66. *D. sambucina* (L.) Soó, 1962, *Nom. Nov. Gen. Dactylorh.*: 3.
 Basionym: *Orchis sambucina* L., 1755, *Fl. Suec.* 2ed.:312.
 2n = 40,42. Central Europe.

Table 5-1. Continued.

---

67. *D. fasciculata* (Tin. in Guss.) Aver., 1984, *Bot. J.* 69:875.
    Basionym: *Orchis fasciculata* Tin. in Guss., 1844, *Fl. Siculae Synops.* 2,2:875.
    Syn.: *Orchis insularis* Sommier, 1895, *Bull. Soc. Bot. Ital.:* 247.
    S. Europe.
68–74. Aggregate *D. sulphurea*.
68. *D. sulphurea* (Link) Franko, 1978, *J. Linn. Soc. London (Bot.)* 76,4:366.
    Basionym: *Orchis sulphurea* Link, 1806, in Schrader, *Neues Journ. Bot. (Schrad.)* 1,3:132.
    S.-W. Europe.
69. *D. sicula* (Tin. ex Reichenb. f.) Aver., 1984, *Bot. J.* 69:875.
    Basionym: *Orchis sicula* Tin. ex Reichenb. f., 1851, *Icon. Fl. Germ.* 13–14:63.
    Syn.: *Orchis markusii* Tin. ex Reichenb. f., 1851, *Icon. Fl. Germ.* 13–14:63.
        Orchis mediterranea Klinge ssp. *siciliensis* Klinge, 1898, *Dactylorch. Monogr. Prodr.:* 19.
    S. Europe.
70. *D. bartonii* (Huxley et P. F. Hunt) Aver., 1984, *Bot. J.* 69:876.
    Basionym: *Dactylorhiza romana* (Seb.) Soó ssp. *bartonii* Huxley et P. F. Hunt, 1967, *J. Roy. Hort. Soc.* (London) 92,7:309.
    E. Spain.
71. *D. flavescens* (C. Koch) Holub, 1976, *Folia Geobot. Phytotax.* 11,1:83.
    Basionym: *Orchis flavescens* C. Koch, 1849, *Linnaea,* 22:281.
    Syn.: *Orchis tenuifolia* C. Koch, 1849, *Linnaea,* 22:281.
        Orchis mediterranea Klinge ssp. *georgica* Klinge, 1898, *Dactylorch. Monogr. Prodr.:* 20.
    2n = 42. E. Asia Minor, Caucasus, Transcaucasia, Iran, E. Central Asia (Kopetdag Mountains).
72. *D. ruprechtii* Aver., 1983, *Bot. J.* 68:537.
    Caucasus, Transcaucasia.
73. *D. romana* (Seb.) Soó, 1962, *Nom. Nov. Gen. Dactylorh.:* 3.
    Basionym: *Orchis romana* Seb., 1813, *Pl. Rom.* 1:12.
    Syn. *Orchis pseudosambucina* Ten., 1815, *Syn. Nov. Pl.* 1ed:72.
    S. Europe, Crimea, W. Asia Minor, Syria, Lebanon, Cyprus.
74. *D. libanotica* (Mouterde) Aver., 1984, *Bot. J.* 69:876.
    Basionym: *Orchis romana* Seb. ssp. *libanotica* Mouterde, 1966, *Nouv. Fl. Liban,* Syrie 1:342.
Section 4. *Iberanthus* (Schlechter) Smoljian., 1976, *Fl. Europ. Czasti USSR* 2:51.
75. *D. iberica* (Bieb. ex Willd.) Soó, 1962, *Nom. Nov. Gen. Dactylorh.:* 3.
    Basionym: *Orchis iberica* Bieb. ex Willd., 1805, *Sp. Pl.* 4:25.
    Syn.: *Orchis angustifolia* Bieb., 1808, *Fl. Taur. Cauc.* 2:368.
        Gymnadenia angustifolia Spreng., 1826, *Syst. Veg.* 3:693.
        Orchis leptophylla C. Koch, 1849, *Linnaea* 22:282.
        Orchis natolica Fisch. et Mey., 1854, *Ann. Sci. Nat.* (Paris) Ser. 4, 1:30.
    2n = 40. S.-E. Europe, Asia Minor, Lebanon, Syria, Crimea, Caucasus, Transcaucasia.

Taxonomy of the Genus *Dactylorhiza*

The name *Dactylorhiza* for dactylorchids was introduced in 1790 by N. J. Necker, but its use as a generic term for *Dactylorhiza* was established formally much later by S. A. Nevski (1937). Several elements of the dactylorchid taxonomy were established during the last 150 years by a number of authors (Reichenbach fil, 1851; Parlatore, 1858; Schlechter, 1927). This taxonomy system was augmented subsequently by additional authors (Nevski, 1935; Pugsley, 1935; Vermeulen, 1947; Heslop-Harrison, 1954; Soó, 1960; Nelson, 1976, 1979; Smolyaninova, 1976). The latest classification of the genus *Dactylorhiza* was formulated by Averyanov (1983a, b; Table 5-1). Groups of closely related species are combined in so-called "species-aggregates", the use of which was proposed by Heywood (Heywood, 1963). Modern data on karyology and distribution of species are given in Table 5-1.

In Fig. 5-11 a philogenetic scheme of the genus *Dactylorhiza* is shown. It represents a cross-section of "the genealogical tree" at the modern stage (Averyanov, 1983b, c). Differences in karyotypes of species are shown with different shading.

Hypothetical historical interrelations of the main taxa of the genus are given in Fig. 5-12. The thickness of the trunks, which designate taxa, reflects the number of presently existing species (their number is indicated over the cuts of the corresponding trunks made at the modern stage of evolution of the genus).

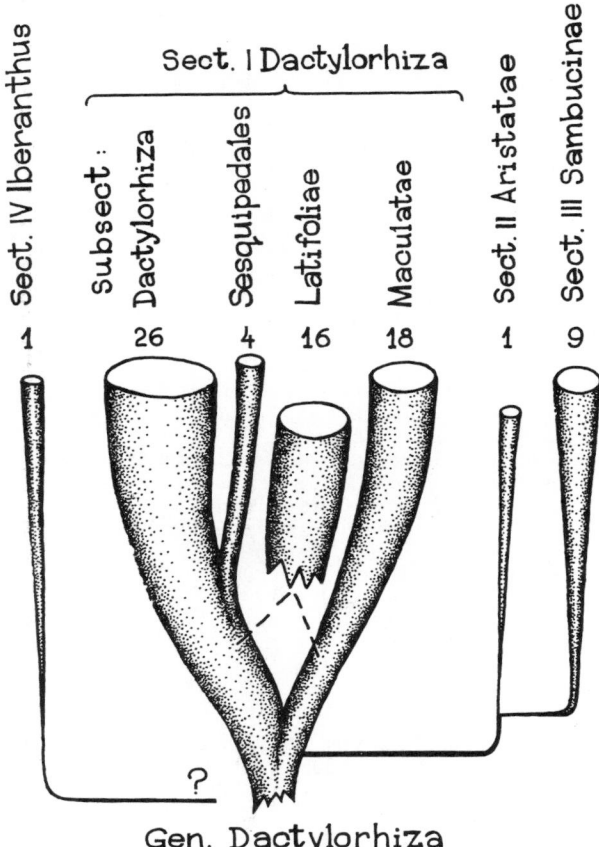

Fig. 5-12. Diagram of presumed historical interrelations of the main taxa of the genus *Dactylorhiza.* Thickness of the trunks designating taxa reflects their species richness (the number of presently existing species is marked above the cuts of the corresponding trunks).

Hybridization

Interspecific hybridization takes place very often in the genus *Dactylorhiza.* The data concerning hybrids among species of dactylorchids are given in numerous papers and several extensive reviews (Schlechter, 1927; Camus and Camus, 1928; Soó, 1933a, 1960, 1962; Dandy, 1958; Sundermann, 1975). According to some reports, hybrids may sometimes arise from more than two parent species[d]. Many of the hybrids known at present have binominal names.

Hybrids among species of the type section (sect. *Dactylorhiza*) of the genus *Dactylorhiza* are most common. This section contains 141 pairs of species which hybridize relatively often with each other in nature. Hybrids which have binominal names are listed in Table 5-2. Hybridization among species of this section is outlined in Fig. 4-13.

Hybrids are often also observed within the section *Sambucinae.* Most species of this section are sympatric and form a large area of intogression. Known hybrids of these species are indicated in Table 5-3. Only one of them has a binominal name.

[d]Under cultivation, triple hybrids of the kind *D. foliosa* × *D. maculata* × *D. majalis* (=*D. hepburnii* (Druce) Soó) are known (Soó, 1960). In nature formation of such "triple" hybrids is possible only between closely related species which produce relatively fertile progeny.

Table 5-2. Natural interspecific hybrid names of dactylorchids in section *Dactylorhiza.*

D. incarnata × *D. cruenta* (= *D.* × *krylowii*(Soó) Soó).
D. incarnata × *D. saccifera* (= *D.* × *serbica* (Fleischm.) Soó).
D. incarnata × *D. nieschalkiorum* (= *D.* × *renzii* H. Baumann et Kuenkele).
D. incarnata × *D. fuchsii* (= *D.* × *kerneriorum* (Soó) Soó).
D. incarnata × *D. maculata* (= *D.* × *ambigua* (Kerner) Sundermann). Morphologically derived types: *D.* × *beckeriana* (Höppner) Soó; *D.* × *elatior* (Afz.) Soó; *D.* × *gracilis* (Höppner) Soó; *D.* × *hoeppneri* (A. Fuchs) Soó; *D.* × *koningweniana* (A. Fuchs) Soó; *D.* × *rhenana* (Höppner) Soó; *D.* × *rigida* (Höppner) Soó; *D.* × *ruthei* (Schulze) Soó; *D.* × *steegeri* (Höppner) Soó; *D.* × *surensis* (Gsell) Soó; *D.* × *wirtgenii* (Höppner) Soó.[a]
D. incarnata × *D. elodes* (= *D.* × *carnea* (E. G. Camus) Soó).
D. incarnata × *D. schurii* (= *D.* × *claudiopolitana* (Simk.) Soó).
D. incarnata × *D. majalis* (= *D.* × *aschersoniana* (Hausskn.) Soó). Morphologically derived types: *D.* × *bavarica* (A. Fuchs) Soó; *D.* × *gennachiensis* (A. Fuchs) Soó; *D.* × *mulignensis* (Gsell) Soó; *D.* × *pseudotraunsteineri* (A. Fuchs) Soó; *D.* × *suevica* (A. Fuchs) Soó.
D. incarnata × *D. purpurella* (= *D.* × *latirella* (Hall) Soó).
D. incarnata × *D. alpestris* (= *D.* × *hochreutinerana* (Hellmayr) Aver.).
D. incarnata × *D. intergrata* (= *D.* × *wintoni* (Druce) Soó).
D. incarnata × *D. longifolia* (= *D.* × *ishorica* Aver.).
D. incarnata × *D. traunsteineri* (= *D.* × *stenostachys* (J. Murr.) Rauschert). Morphologically derived types: *D.* × *flixensis* (Gsell) Soó; *D.* × *thellungiana* (Br.-Bl.) Soó.
D. incarnata × *D. russowii* (= *D.* × *lehmannii* (Klinge) Soó).
D. incarnata × *D. sesquipedalis* (= *D.* × *dubreuilhi* (Keller et Jeanjean) Soó).
D. ochroleuca × *D. majalis* (= *D.* × *templinensis* Potucek).
D. cruenta × *D. salina* (= *D.* × *baicalica* Aver.).
D. cruenta × *D. maculata* (= *D.* × *samnaunensis* (Gsell) Soó).
D. cruenta × *D. majalis* (= *D.* × *predaensis* (Gsell) Soó).
D. cruenta × *D. traunsteineri* (= *D.* × *engadinensis* (Ciferri et Giacomini) Soó).
D. coccinea × *D. hebridensis* (= *D.* × *variabilis* (Heslop-Harrison f.) Soó).
D. osmanica × *D. urvilleana* (= *D.* × *breviceras* Renz et Taub.).
D. osmanica × *D. umbrosa* (= *D.* × *nevskii* H. Baumann et Kuenkele).
D. euxina × *D. umbrosa* (= *D.* × *bayburtiana* H. Baumann).
D. euxina × *D. urvilleana* (= *D.* × *rizeana* Renz et Taub.).
D. umbrosa × *D. urvilleana* (= *D.* × *sivasiana* H. Baumann et Keuenkele).
D. nieschalkiorum × *D. saccifera* (= *D.* × *boluiana* H. Baumann).
D. fuchsii × *D. maculata* (= *D.* × *transiens* (Druce) Soó).
D. fuchsii × *D. majalis* (= *D.* × *braunii* (Halacsy) Borsos et Soó).
D. fuchsii × *D. purpurella* (= *D.* × *venusta* (T. Stephenson et T. A. Stephenson) Soó).
D. fuchsii × *D. integrata* (= *D.* × *mortonii* (Druce) Soó).
D. fuchsii × *D. traunsteineri* (= *D.* × *kelleriana* (Ciferri et Giacomini) Soó).
D. fuchsii × *D. russowii* (= *D.* × *megapolitana* (Bisse) Soó).
D. hebridensis × *D. maculata* (= *D.* × *komiensis* Aver.).
D. hebridensis × *D. ericetorum* (= *D.* × *corylensis* (Heslop-Harrison f.) Soó).
D. hebridensis × *D. purpurella* (= *D.* × *hebridella* (Wilmott) Soó).
D. maculata × *D. majalis* (= *D.* × *vermeuleniana* Soó). Morphologically derived type: *D.* × *eifliaca* (A. Fuchs) Soó
D. maculata × *D. alpestris* (= *D.* × *czatoi* (Soó) Soó).
D. maculata × *D. integrata* (= *D.* × *batavica* Soó).
D. maculata × *D. traunsteineri* (= *D.* × *jenensis* (Brand-Soó).
D. maculata × *D. sesquipedalis* (= *D.* × *delamainii* (Keller et Stephenson) Soó).
D. elodes × *D. majalis* (= *D.* × *nummiana* (P. Fournier) Soó. Morphologically derived types: *Orchis* × *danguyi* P. Fournier; *Orchis* × *guffroyi* P. Fournier.
D. elodes × *D. integrata* (= *D.* × *hallii* (Druce) Soó).
D. elodes × *D. durandii* (= *D.* × *stephensonii* Soó).
D. schurii × *D. cordigera* (= *D.* × *szaboiana* (Soó) Soó).
D. ericetorum × *D. majalis* (= *D.* × *townsendiana* (Rouy) Soó).
D. ericetorum × *D. kerryensis* (= *D.* × *dinglensis* (Wilmott) Soó).
D. ericetorum × *D. purpurella* (= *D.* × *formosa* (T. Stephenson et T. A. Stephenson) Soó).
D. ericetorum × *D. traunsteineri* (= *D.* × *robertsii* Aver.).
D. majalis × *D. integrata* (= *D.* × *godferyana* Soó).
D. majalis × *D. traunsteineri* (= *D.* × *dufftiana* (Schulze) Soó).
D. purpurella × *D. integrata* (= *D.* × *insignis* (T. Stephenson et T. A. Stephenson) Soó).
D. integrata × *D. longifolia* Morphologically derived type: *D.* × *pardalina* (Pugsley) Aver.

[a]It is possible that *D. majalis* also took part in the formation of these derivative types.

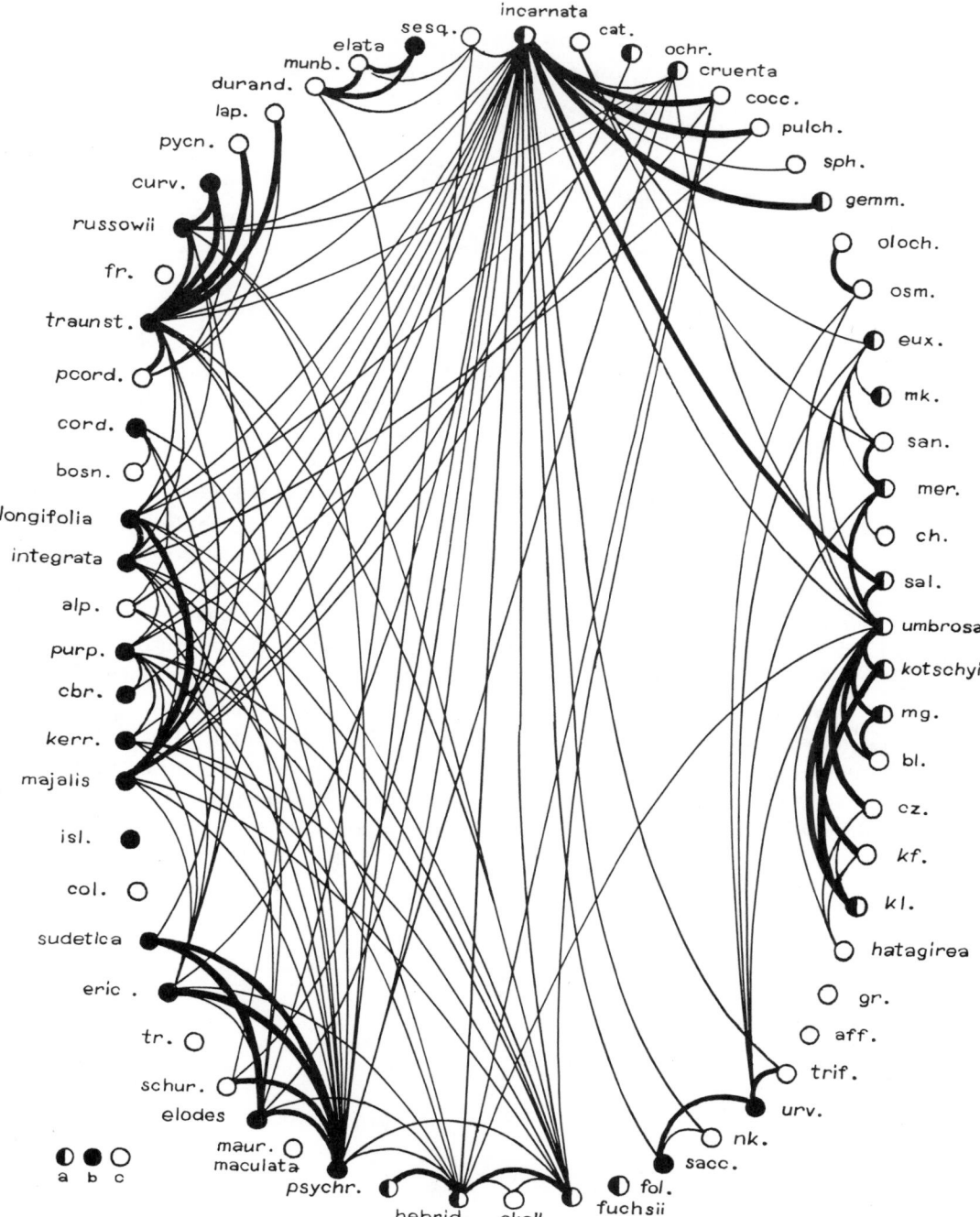

Fig. 5-13. Diagram of hybridization among species of the genus *Dactylorhiza*, section *Dactylorhiza*. Explanation of symbols: Species forming hybrids in nature are connected by lines (thin line, hybrids rare and sporadic; thick line, hybrids are numerous, sometimes form an introgression zone); a-diploid species (2n=40); b-tetraploid species (2n=80); c-species, the chromosome number of which is not yet known. Abbreviations of species names as in Fig. 5-11.

Intersectional hybrids of dactylorchids are considerably rarer and known only between species of sect. *Dactylorhiza* and those of the sections *Sambucinae* and *Iberanthus*. They occur in Europe and Asia Minor. All known hybrids of this type are listed in Table 5-4.

The formation of hybrids among several species of dactylorchids with very different genomes like *D. sambucina* (2n=40, 42) × *D. maculata* (2n=80) × *D. majalis* (2n=80) (=*D* × *gabretana* (A. Fuchs)Soó, suggested by Soó (Soó, 1960, 1962), is highly unlikely in nature. Their presumed complex nature may have arisen due to morphologically different hybrid individuals produced by a cross between only two species of dactylorchids.

In nature dactylorchids hybridize relatively easily with species of related genera of the subtribe Orchidinae. Such hybrids have been reported often (Klinge, 1898; Fuchs, 1921; Stephenson and Stephenson, 1922; Soó, 1933a, b; Dahl, 1941; Dandy, 1958; Malmgren and Segelberg, 1965; Hylander, 1966; Garay and Sweet, 1966; Soó and Borsos, 1966; Danielsson, 1970; Schmid et al., 1974; Sundermann, 1975; Wennerberg, 1978; Ericsson, 1980; Schmid, 1980; Savelsberg, 1981). All known intergeneric hybrids of dactylorchids have generic names (Hunt and Summerhayes, 1965; Garay and Sweet, 1966, 1969; Soó and Borsos, 1966). The interbreeding of dactylorchids with closely related genera is presented in Fig. 5-14. Dactylorchids form the largest number of intergeneric hybrids with *Gymnadenia conopsea* (15 hybrids), considerably fewer—with *Coeloglossum viride* (5) and *Platanthera bifolia* (5), all of whose flowers have nectar. Dactylorchids hybridize relatively often with *Orchis* species which have similar ecology and may coexist with them in one habitat, specifically *O. laxiflora* (5), *O. palustris* (6) and *O. morio* (4). Hybrids with other genera are considerably rarer. Among the dactylorchids, the largest number of intergeneric hybrids involve the most widely distributed and common species, *D. maculata* (10). Hybrids involving other species include, *D. majalis* (9), *D. incarnata* (7) and the now endangered species *D. sambucina* (9). All known intergeneric hybrids of dactylorchids and their binominals are listed in Table 5-5.

Table 5-3. Natural interspecific hybrids of dactylorchids in the section *Sambucinae.*

D. sambucina × D. fasciculata
D. sambucina × D. sulphurea
D. romana × D. flavescens
D. flavescens × D. ruprechtii
D. sambucina × D. romana (= D. × rombucina (Ciferri et Giacomini) Soó).

Table 5-4. Natural intrasectional hybrids of dactylorchids.

D. sambucina × D. incarnata (= D. × guillaumeae B. Christian).
D. sambucina × D. fuchsii (= D. × influenza (Sennholz) Soó).
D. sambucina × D. maculata (= D. × altobracensis (Coste) Soó).
D. sambucina × D. majalis (= D. × rupperii (Schulze) Soó).
D. romana × D. maculata (= D. × maculana (Ciferri et Giacomini) Soó).
D. iberica × D. incarnata (= D. × vogtiana H. Baumann).
D. iberica × D. nieschalkiorum (= D. × abantiana H. Baumann et Kuenkele).
D. iberica × D. osmanica.
D. iberica × D. saccifera (= D. × sultandagi Renz et Taub.; D. × gustavssonii H. Baumann).
D. iberica × D. umbrosa (= D. × kopdagiana H. Baumann).
D. iberica × D. urvilleana (= D. × balabiana H. Baumann).

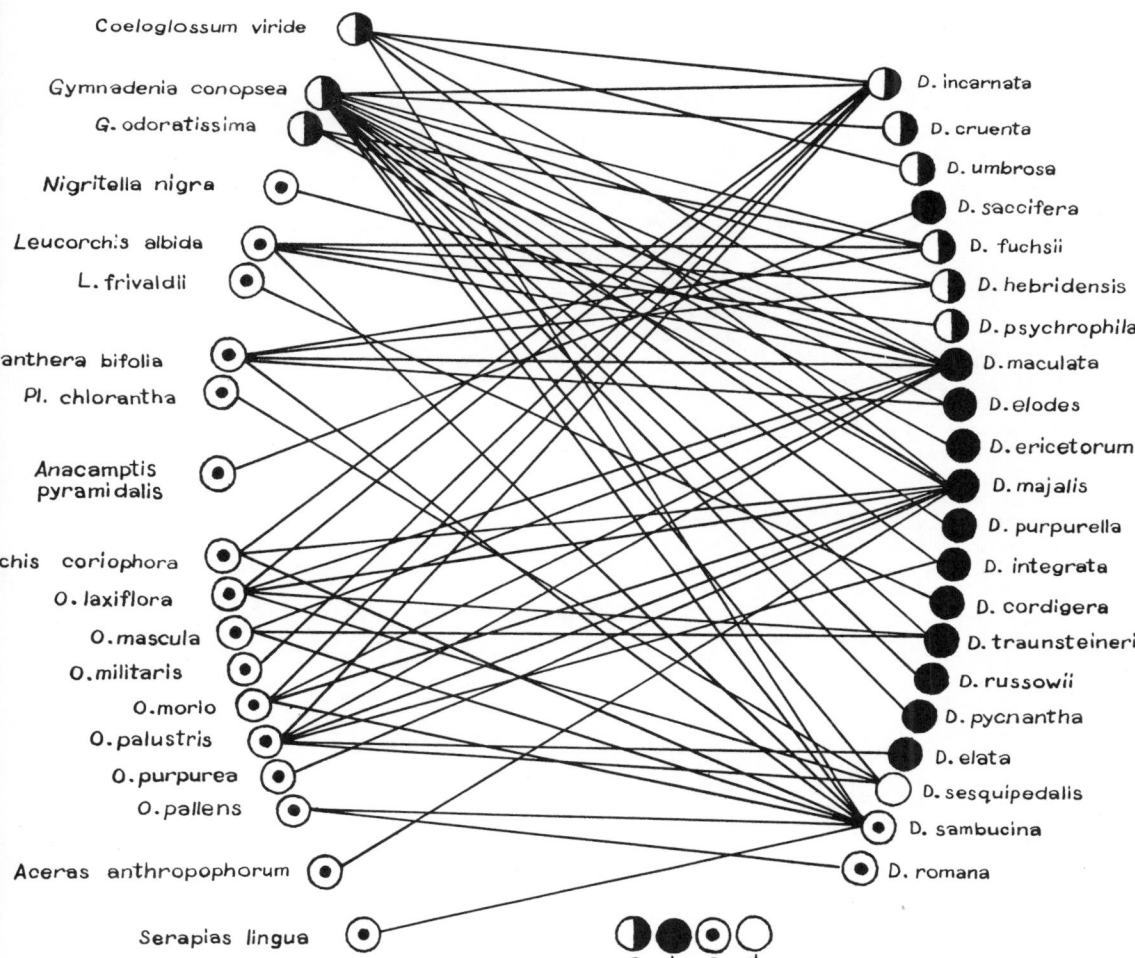

Fig. 5-14. Diagram of hybridization of dactylorchids with species of phylogenetically related orchid genera. Explanation of symbols: Species forming hybrids in nature are connected by lines; a, diploid species (2n=40); b, tetraploid species (2n=80); c, aneuploid species (2n=36–42); d, species, the chromosome number of which is not yet known.

Table 5-5. Natural intergeneric hybrids of dactylorchids.

Dactylorhiza × *Coeloglossum* C. Hartm. (= × *Dactyloglossum* P. F. Hunt et Summerhayes).
Dactylorhiza incarnata × *Coeloglossum viride* (L.) C. Hartm. (= ×*Dactyloglossum guilhotii* (E. G. Camus) Soó.
D. umbrosa × *C. viride* (= × *D. turcestanicum* (C. Keller et Soó) Soó).
D. maculata × *C. viride* (= × *D. conigerum* (Norman) Rauschert).
D. majalis × *C. viride* (= × *D. drucei* (E. G. Camus) Soó).
D. sambucina × *C. viride* (= × *D. erdingeri* (Kerner) Janchen).
Dactylorhiza × *Gymnadenia* R. Br. (= × *Dactylodenia* Garay et Sweet).
Dactylorhiza incarnata × *Gymnadenia conopsea* (L.) R. Br. (= × *Dactylodenia vollmannii* (Schulze) Aver.).
D. cruenta × *G. conopsea* (= × *D. raetica* (Paroz et Reinhard) Peitz).
D. fuchsii × *G. conopsea* (= × *D. gracilis* (A. Camus) Aver.).
D. fuchsii × *G. odoratissima* (L.) Rich. (= × *D. lawalree* Dalforge et Tyteca).
D. hebridensis × *G. conopsea*.
D. maculata × *G. conopsea* (= ×*D. heinzeliana* (Reichardt) Aver.). Morphologically derived type: × *D. st. quintinii* (Godfery) Aver.
D. maculata × *G. odoratissima* (= × *D. regeliana* (Bruegger) Peitz).
D. elodes × *G. conopsea* (= × *D. souppensis* (E. G. Camus) Aver.).

Table 5-5. Continued.

D. *ericetorum* × *G. conopsea* (= × *D. evansii* (Druce ex T. Stephenson et T. A. Stephenson) Aver.).
D. *majalis* × *G. conopsea* (= x *D. comigera* (Reichenb.) Aver.).
D. *majalis* × *G. odoratissima.*
D. *purpurella* × *G. conopsea* (= × *D. varia* (T. Stephenson et T. A. Stephenson) Aver.).
D. *integrata* × *G. conopsea* (= × *D. wintonii* (Druce) Aver.).
D. *traunsteineri* × *G. conopsea* (= × *D. fuchsii* (G. Keller et Soó) Aver.).
D. *russowii* × *G. conopsea* (= × *D. klingeana* (Aschers. et Graebn.) Aver.).
D. *pycnantha* × *G. conopsea.*
D. *sesquipedalis* × *G. conopsea* (= × *D. jeanjeanii* (G. Keller) Aver.).
D. *sambucina* × *G. conopsea* (= × *D. zollikoferi* (Stojan.) Peitz).
    Dactylorhiza × *Nigritella* Rich. (= × *Dactylitella* P. F. Hunt et Summerhayes).
Dactylorhiza maculata × *Nigritella nigra* (L.) Rich. (= × *Dactylitella tourensis* (Godfery) Janchen).
    Dactylorhiza × *Leucorchis* E. Mey. (= × *Dactyleucorchis* Soó).
Dactylorhiza fuchsii × *Leucorchis albida* (L.) E. Mey. (= × *Dactyleucorchis nieschalkii* Senghas).
D. *psychrophila* × *L. albida* (= × *D. nieschalkii* var. *minor* (Potucek) Kumpel).
D. *maculata* × *L. albida* (= × *D. bruniana* (Bruegger) Soó).
D. *cordigera* × *L. frivaldii* (Hampe ex Griseb.) Schlechter (= × *D. illyrica* Jahn et Kumpel).
D. *sambucina* × *L. albida* (= × *D. albucina* (Ciferri et Giacomini) Aver.).
    Dactylorhiza × *Platanthera* Rich. (= × *Rhizanthera* P. F. Hunt et Summerhayes).
Dactylorhiza fuchsii × *Platanthera bifolia* (L.) Rich.
D. *hebridensis* × *Pl. bifolia.*
D. *maculata* × *Pl. bifolia* (= × *Rh. somersetiensis* (A. Camus) Soó).
D. *elodes* × *Pl. bifolia* (= × *Rh. chevallieriana* (E. G. Camus) Soó).
D. *sesquipedalis* × *Pl. chlorantha* (Cust.) Reichenb. (= × *Rh. thilensis* (G. Keller et Jeanjean) Aver.).
D. *sambucina* × *Pl. bifolia* (= × *Rh. fournieri* (Royer) Soó).
    Dactylorhiza × *Anacamptis* Rich. (= × *Dactylocamptis* P. F. Hunt et Summerhayes).
Dactylorhiza saccifera × *Anacamptis pyramidalis* (L.) Rich. (= × *Dactylocamptis weberi* (Schulze) Soó).
    Dactylorhiza × *Orchis* L. (= × *Orchidactyla* P. F. Hunt et Summerhayes).
Dactylorhiza incarnata × *Orchis coriophora* L. (= × *Orchidactyla drucei* (Schulze) Borsos et Soó).
D. *incarnata* × *O. laxiflora* Lam. (= × *O. legueri* (E. G. Camus) Borsos et Soó).
D. *incarnata* × *O. militaris* L. (= × *O. jeanpertii* (E. G. Camus et Luis) Borsos et Soó).
D. *incarnata* × *O. morio* L. (= × *O. arbostii* (E. G. Camus) Borsos et Soó).
D. *incarnata* × *O. palustris* Jacq. (= × *O. uechtritziana* (Hausskn.) Borsos et Soó).
D. *maculata* × *O. laxiflora* (= × *O. valoni* (E. G. Camus) Borsos et Soó).
D. *maculata* × *O. mascula* L. (= × *O. pentecostalis* (Wettst. et Sennholz) Borsos et Soó).
D. *maculata* × *O. morio* (= × *O. timbaliana* (E. G. Camus) Borsos et Soó).
D. *maculata* × *O. palustris* (= × *O. neglecta* (E. G. Camus) Borsos et Soó).
D. *majalis* × *O. coriophora* (= × *O. sauzaiana* (E. G. Camus) Rauschert).
D. *majalis* × *O. laxiflora* (= × *O. chassagnei* (Alleizette) Borsos et Soó).
D. *majalis* × *O. morio* (= × *O. boudieri* (E. G. Camus) Borsos et Soó).
D. *majalis* × *O. palustris* (= × *O. rouyana* (E. G. Camus) Borsos et Soó).
D. *majalis* × *O. purpurea* Huds. (= × *O. questphalica* (Richter) Borsos et Soó).
D. *integrata* × *O. palustris* (= × *O. luizetiana* (E. G. Camus) Borsos et Soó).
D. *traunsteineri* × *O. laxiflora.*
D. *traunsteineri* × *O. mascula* (= × *O. masteineri* (Ciferri et Giacomini) Aver.).
D. *elata* × *O. palustris* (= × *O. kabyliensis* (G. Keller) Aver.).
D. *sesquipedalis* × *O. laxiflora* (= × *O. aquitaniensis* (G. Keller et Jeanjean) Aver.).
D. *sesquipedalis* × *O. palustris* (= × *O. lamarquei* (G. Keller et Jeanjean) Aver.).
D. *sambucina* × *O. coriophora* (= × *O. carpetana* (Willk.) Borsos et Soó).
D. *sambucina* × *O. mascula* (= × *O. speciosissima* (Wettst. et Sennholz) Soó).
D. *sambucina* × *O. morio* (= × *O. luciae* (Royer) Borsos et Soó).
D. *sambucina* × *O. pallens* L. (= × *O. chenevardii* (Schulze) Borsos et Soó).
D. *romana* × *O. pallens* (= × *O. romanallens* (Ciferri et Giacomini) Aver.).
    Dactylorhiza × *Aceras* R. Br. (= × *Dactyloceras* Garay et Sweet).
Dactylorhiza majalis × *Aceras anthropophorum* (L.) R. Br. (= × *Dactyloceras helveticum* (Ciferri et Giacomini) Garay et Sweet).
    Dactylorhiza × *Serapias* L. (= × *Serapirhiza* Potucek).
Dactylorhiza sambucina × *Serapias lingua* L. (= × *Serapirhiza sambucino-lingua* (Barla) Garay et Sweet).

Fig. 5-15. The Kainozoic era subdivisions (Harland *et al.,* 1982). The principal events of this era mentioned in the text are marked with asterisks (the time is indicated very roughly): a, the existence of the ancient heat-loving flora (Poltava flora) which included in its composition the dactylorchids ancestors; b, Great Tertiary or Alpine earth-movements (Alpine orogenesis) which resulted in the elevation of most of the major mountain chains of the world, such as the Alps, Himalayas, Rockies and Andes; c, period of origin of the primary ancient dactylorchids species (it was in the Miocene period that the geography of Europe and Northern Asia began to assume its present day form); d, a period of intense coolings usually known as the Glacial period or the Great Ice age.

Natural History of the Genus *Dactylorchiza* and Its Species

It is supposed that the ancestors of dactylorchids were not very specialized terrestrial heat-loving orchids of the Poltava flora, which were widely distributed in the Paleogene. Their thickened specialized roots were not evolved yet and in outward appearance the plants resembled primitive species of *Epipactis* and *Cephalanthera* (Dressler and Dodson, 1960). Formation of primary dactylorchid species and related tuber forming orchids is associated with powerful mountain raisings (Alpine orogenesis) in what is modern Europe at the end of the Paleogene or early Neogene. The more severe climate of relatively high mountains and especially the increased seasonal fluctuations and the cooler temperatures lead to the formations of subterranean storage organs in the ancestral forms which were located in the plains. As a result of the cooling at the end of Neogene and in the Pleistocene, the climatic conditions in the plains became similar to the climate of the ancient high mountains. Under these conditions, early species of dactylorchids could occupy plains areas where the degradation of thermophilic tertiary flora was proceeding. Most dactylorchids and the related genera *Gymnadenia, Leucorchis* and *Coeloglossum* as well as their Paleogene ancestors remained primarily hydrophilous plants. All of them have relatively primitive palmate (finger-like) tubers. The formation of such tubers was a "preadaptation" to existence in drier and arid conditions. The adaptation to arid climate proved to be an evolutionary response to development of such conditions in the territories of the ancient Mediterranean basin and has resulted in the evolution of a number of highly specialized genera (*Orchis, Ophrys, Himantoglossum, Aceras, Anacamptis, Comperia, Serapias, Steveniella* and *Traunsteinera;* Averyanov, 1983a, c).

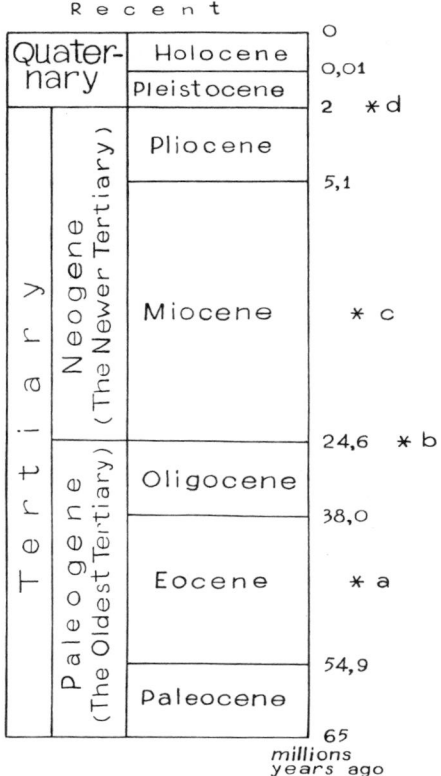

The direct ancestors of the genus *Dactylorhiza* were in existence toward the end of Paleogene and inhabited a vast area. Growth of mountains during the Alpine orogenensis in Eurasia led to the simultaneous formation of dactylorchids in a large area. Formation of the primary species of this genus occurred in the large mountain regions of modern Europe, Asia Minor, the Caucasus, Middle and Central Asia and, possibly, also those of North Africa (Fig. 5-16).

Later, as a result of Pleistocene cooling of the climate, a mass occupation of the plains of Europe and subsequently also of temperate Asia by species of dactylorchids took place. These species were formed originally in mountain ranges. The climatic changes during the Pleistocene are responsible for migrations of *Dactylorhiza* species and this contributed to hybridization and speciation. Periodically the most hydrophilous species of the genus (Sect. *Dactylorhiza*) expanded their territories considerably and after the disappearance of the glaciers they occupied habitats which were most similar to the habitats of the high mountains (Fig. 5-16). However, during the xerothermic maxima of the interglacial periods, their territories diminished to some extent. Extinction took place in regions subjected to especially severe aridization in the south of Siberia and north of Middle Asia. These facts can explain the disjunctions in the distribution of some present species. Several species, however, could adapt to life under the rather arid conditions of the ancient Mediterranean basin (Sect. *Sambucinae* and *Iberanthus*) owing to the formation of more specialized cylindrical, scarcely palmate tubers.

At present the genus *Dactylorhiza* comprises 75 species.

Section 1. *Dectylorizha.*

The largest section contains 64 of the most primitive species, which were originally hydrophilous. This section covers the largest geographical area coinciding in general with the present distribution of the genus (Fig. 5-17).

Subsection I. *Dactylorhiza.*

This subsection includes 26 species. Its distribution coincides with that of the type section (except for North Africa and the region beyond the polar circle). All species are of mountainous origins. Some authors (Nelson, 1976, 1979) separate them in two series—Ser. *Dactylorhiza* (=Ser. *Septentrionales* Nelson nom.invalid[e].) and Ser. *Orientales* Nelson.

1–8. Aggregate *D. incarnata.*

The species of this aggregate, particularly *D. incarnata* and *D. cataonoca* have many characters which make them the most primitive in the genus.

The main species of the aggregate, *D. incarnata,* originated in Europe and is now found throughout this continent, Siberia, Crimea, the Northern Caucasus, Northern Central Asia, China and Mongolia. A number of its southern populations (Crimea, North Caucasus etc.) are presently isolated from the main distribution area.

Closely related to *D. incarnata* (and as ancient) is *D. cataonica.* This species occurs in Eastern Asia Minor and in Transcaucasia. It has not migrated extensively.

Unlike the overwhelming majority of species in the genus, *D. ochroleuca* has yellowish-white flowers[f] and is endemic to Central and Western Europe reaching

[e]This taxon includes the type of the genus (*D. incarnata*) and according to nomenclature rules its name should be repeated in the name of the genus.

[f]Such plants should be distinguished from albino forms which occur from time to time in all species of the genus and have purely white flowers.

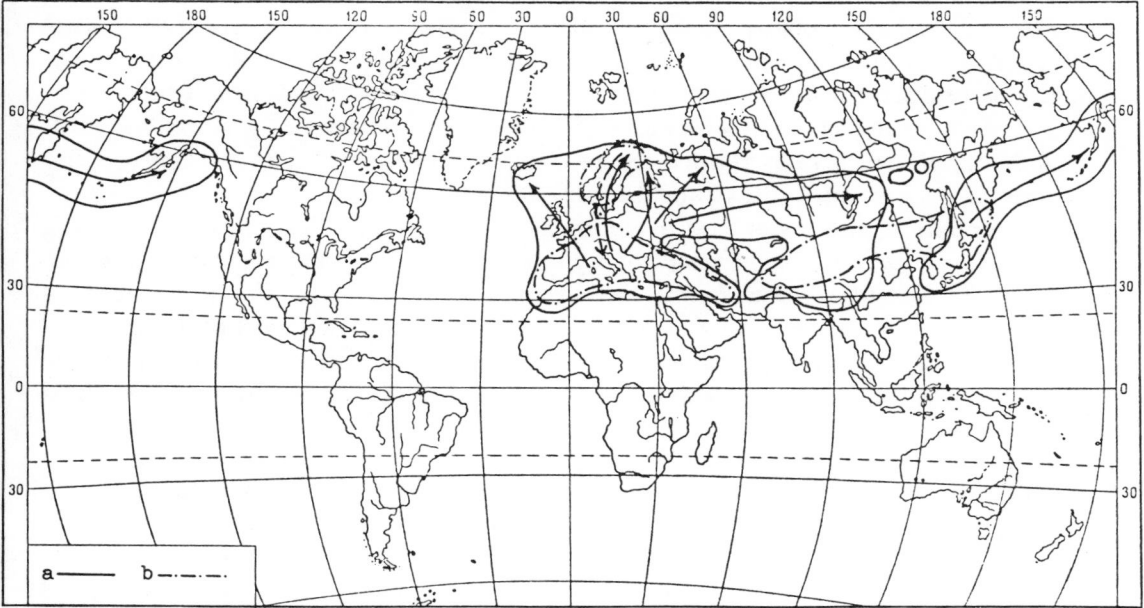

Fig. 5-16. Regions of formation of *Dactylorhiza* species and main paths of their migrations. Explanation of symbols: a, boundary of the present area of the genus; b, boundary of presumed primary area of the genus (arrows indicate the main paths of migrations of the species; broken line, the early quaternary migrations; solid line, quaternary and Holocene migrations) (Averyanov, 1983c).

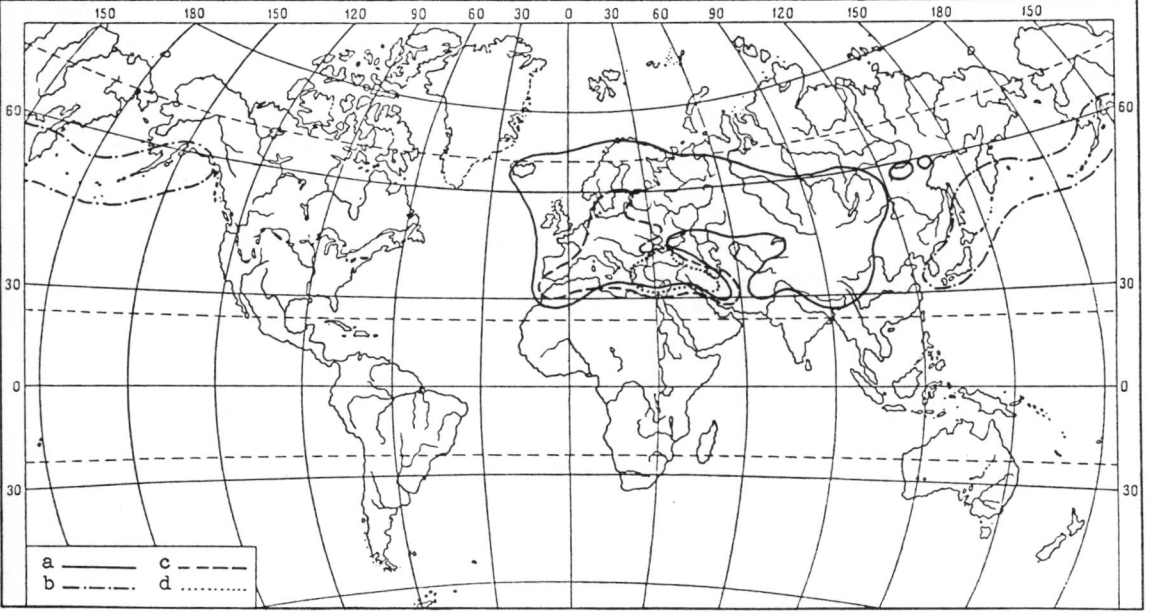

Fig. 5-17. Distribution of the genus *Dactylorhiza* sections. **a,** Sect. *Dactylorhiza;* **b,** Sect. *Aristatae;* **c,** Sect. *Sambucinae;* **d,** Sect. *Iberanthus* (Averyanov, 1983c).

Saarema island (Estonia, USSR) on the east. Ecologically it prefers carbonate fens.

The distribution of *D. cruenta* is very similar to that of *D. incarnata* but this species is not found in the mountains of the Crimea, the Caucasus and Middle Asia. Probably the migration of *D. cruenta* occurred somewhat later than that of *D. incarnata.* To the east it almost reaches the Sea of Okhotsk together with *D. incarnata,* and in the south it extends to Mongolia. *D. cruenta* has spotted leaves, a character found only in *D. chuhensis* and sometimes in *D. euxina* in this subsection.

The remaining species of aggr. *D. incarnata* are stenoendemics in West Europe. *D. coccinea, D. pulchella* and *D. gemmana* occur in the British Isles and adjacent islands. *D. sphagnicola* is found in Belgium, the Netherlands, West Germany and in the north of France. These species are usually associated with *D. incarnata* by introgressive hybridization. All of these are the youngest species of aggr. *D. incarnata* and their origin reflects the general process of the formation and development of the European flora after the most powerful glaciations.

9–12. Aggregate *D. olocheilos.*

All species of this group originated in the mountains of Asia Minor and the Caucasus. They have not migrated extensively during their evolution. *D. olocheilos* is endemic to the mountains of Southern Turkey. In the north (Pontic Ridge), it is replaced by *D. osmanica.* Both of these species in Transcaucasia and in the mountains of the Caucasus are replaced by *D. euxina* and its alpine derivate *D. markowitschii.*

13–15. Aggregate *D. sanasunitensis.*

Species of this group are close to aggr. *D. olocheilos* but differ from them by a longer spur which is also found in species aggr. *D. salina.* All of them evolved within regions of their origin without apparent migrations. *D. sanasunitensis* is found in the mountains of Asia Minor. In the east, in Iran and the Transcaucasia mountains, it is replaced by *D. merovensis. D. chuhensis* is a rare species, endemic to Armenia.

16–23. Aggregate *D. salina.*

The main distribution area of this aggregate includes the Middle and Central Asia mountains, Southern Siberia, Western China and Mongolia. *D. umbrosa* is the most widely distributed and most ancient species of this group. This species was formed simultaneously with the European and Asia Minor species of the genus, but, apparently, separately from them in the Tethys isles. Its present distribution includes Middle and Central Asia, Southern Siberia, Western China, Pakistan, Afghanistan and Iran. During the periodic coolings of the Pleistocene *D. umbrosa* repeatedly migrated north of its present distribution. The traces of these migrations can be seen at present as isolated populations in the territory of modern Kazakhstan (USSR) in the Turgai depression. In the western boundary of its distribution, in Iran, *D. umbrosa* comes into introgressive contact with *D. merovensis,* and in the mountains of Kun-Lun and Nanshan in China hybridizes with *D. hatagirea.*

In the north of its distribution area, *D. umbrosa* reaches in introgressive contact with *D. incarnata* s.str. and this has resulted in the polytopic formation of a hybridogenic species, *D. salina.* Its distribution at present includes southern Siberia, northern Middle Asia, Mongolia and Northern China. An isolated population is found in the Caucasus and in eastern Transcaucasia. Ecologically it prefers weakly saline meadows.

The remaining species of aggr. *D. salina* are relatively young derivates of *D. umbrosa.* The altitudinal zone differentiation of *D. umbrosa* gave rise to the formation of *D. kotschyi* and *D. magna.* Their distribution areas are similar to those of the parent species.

D. baldshuanica, D. kulikalonica and *D. kafiriana* are stenoendemic mountain species.

The first two are endemic to the mountains of Tajikistan (USSR). *D. kafiriana* occurs only in the north of Hindu-Kush (N. E. Afghanistan and N. Pakistan).

More widespread is *D. czerniakowskae* which occurs in the mountains of Middle Asia, Afghanistan, Pakistan and Northwestern China. All species of this aggregate hybridize easily with each other when they come in contact and rarer species can sometimes be fully "absorbed" by the more common one as a result of introgressive hybridization.

24–25. Aggregate *D. hatagirea*.

Species of this aggregate represent the Himalayan center of development of dactylorchids. *D. hatagirea* occur in Pakistan, northern India, Nepal, Butan and in the mountains of China near these countries. This species and *D. umbrosa* hybridize freely when the two come into contact. *D. graggeriana* is endemic to Kashmir.

D. affinis, a rather taxonomically isolated rare species, is found in eastern Turkey and Transcaucasia.

Subsection II. *Maculatae.*

This subsection includes 18 species of mountain origin. Its distribution area coincides with that of section *Dactylorhiza* except in the easternmost part.

27–30. Aggregate *D. saccifera*.

The central species of this group, *D. saccifera*, evolved in the mountains of Europe. The last cooling diminished its distribution and at present it can be found only in the mountains of Southern Europe and in the North of Asia Minor. In the eastern part of its distribution in Turkey, it is gradually replaced by two related species, *D. urvilleana* and *D. triphylla* which are also found in Iran and the Caucasus. The very large-flowered stenoendemic species *D. nieschalkiorum* which has been recorded only in Central Turkey adjoins this group. *D. foliosa*, a species endemic to the Madeira Isles, has no evident affinity with other members of the subsection. This species is cultivated in Europe as a horticultural plant (Regel, 1866) and freely hybridizes with other dactylorchids (Soó, 1960).

32–35. Aggregate *D. fuchsii*.

36–44. Aggregate *D. maculata*.

Species in these groups have evolved adaptations to the most rigorous conditions of high mountains, and this gave obvious advantages during Pleistocene glaciations. These aggregates were undergoing intensive development and differentiation at that time. This was accompanied by extensive migrations of some species throughout Europe, Siberia and North Africa. Their areas of distribution assumed the modern outlines in the Holocene.

Aggr. *D. fuchsii* includes diploid ($2n=40$) species, aggr. *D. maculata* has tetraploid ($2n=80$) species and taxa whose chromosome numbers are unknown. Both aggregates exhibit parallel variations, but they are seldom sympatric since their soil requirements differ.

The most primitive species of aggr. *D. fuchsii* is *D. fuchsii* s.str., which is widely distributed in Europe and Siberia. This species prefers rich, high pH soils. A more northern derivative of this species found in eutrophic peatlands is *D. hebridensis*. An alpine derivative of this aggregate occurring also in the north and in the Arctic is *D. psychrophilla*. This cryophilic species grew extensively in the periglacial zone of Pleistocene glaciers and migrated together with them. At present it occurs in the mountains of Europe, Northern Europe and in Southern Sibera (Altai, Sajan ridge). The calciphilous species *D. okellyi* which occurs throughout the British Isles and represents young European endemism adjoins this aggregate.

Tetraploid species of aggr. *D. maculata* were evolved from diploid species of aggr. *D. fuchsii*. Most of these species replace aggr. *D. fuchsii* species in swampy habitats with different levels of soil acidity. Active spreading of these species started rather recently when podzolization and oligotrophic soil swamping in Europe became fairly frequent after the last glaciation. Areas occupied by these species are apparently expanding at present. The most widespread species of this aggregate is *D. maculata*. Its area extends through Central and Northern Europe, and Western Siberia. During the intense cold periods of the Quaternary, *D. maculata* was found in Southern Europe. It also reached Northern Africa, where in the Atlas Mountains the related species *D. maurusia* evolved. This species is now endemic to the Atlas Mountains and completely isolated from *D. maculata*.

D. ericetorum and *D. elodes* are endemic to Europe. Both are found especially in poor soils. The former occurs in Central and Northern Europe and the latter reaches the Urals and grows in sphagnum upland bogs.

D. schurii and *D. transsilvanica* are endemic to the Carpathian Mountains, *D. islandica* occurs only in the south of Iceland and *D. colaënsis* is found in the north of Europe. These species represent young endemism in the European flora.

D. sudetica and the related species *D. psychrophila* (aggr. *D. fuchsii*) occur in the high mountains of Europe, in the European north, and in northern Siberia. Both species grow further north than other dactylorchids and reach the extreme north of Scandinavia. As usual all species of the aggregates are interrelated by introgressive hybridization. Hybrids between species of different aggregates are sterile.

Subsection III. *Latifoliae.*

This subsection numbers 16 species which evolved under mountainous or plains conditions through alloploid stabilization of hybrids between species of the subsection *Dactylorhiza* and *Maculatae*. Most are of European origin. Some authors assign the rank of a section (Smolyaninova, 1976) or a series (Nelson, 1976, 1979) to all species of this subsection.

45–49. Aggregate *D. majalis.*

The central species of the aggregate *D. majalis* was originally a plains species which is presently distributed in Western Europe. *D. kerryensis* and *D. cambrensis* in the British Isles are closely related to it. These species do not occur on the continent. They were formed as a result of relatively recent isolation of separate populations of *D. majalis*. Both hybridize easily with other species of the subsection (with *D. integrata*, *D. purpurella* and *D. traunsteineri*), but they do not exhibit a trend toward full absorption by more common species. *D. alpestris* was formed as a result of hybridization between *D. majalis* and *D. cordigera*. Distribution of this species throughout Europe clearly shows the paths of Holocene migrations of *D. cordigera* which is now extinct in most areas and can be found only in the Carpathians.

50–51. Aggregate *D. integrata.*

Both species of this aggregate evolved in European plains. *D. integrata* occurs in the Atlantic countries of Western Europe. On the other hand, *D. longifolia*, having evolved in the Baltic countries, migrated eastward. At present it is distributed widely in Eastern Europe and in the south of the Ural Mountains. An isolated part of its area includes the southern portion of Eastern Siberia, the north of Middle Asia and Mongolia. In Europe both species are associated through introgressive hybridization with each other and *D. majalis*.

52–54. Aggregate *D. cordigera*.

D. bosniaca and *D. cordigera* are mountain species and at present limited to the mountains of the Balkan Peninsula and the Carpathians. During the climatic pulsations of the Pleistocene, *D. cordigera* often migrated from its mountain habitats to the plains of Europe. This reached Scandinavia during its most intensive expansion where, in the mountains, the closely related endemic species *D. pseudocordigera* evolved. At present all three species of of aggregate *D. cordigera* have very limited distributions.

55–60. Aggregate *D. traunsteineri*.

This aggregate unites a group of very closely related species, all which originated in the European mountains. Some of them have very local distributions. *D. francis-drucei* is endemic to Scotland. *D. lapponica* and *D. pycnantha* occur only in Northern Europe. *D. traunsteineri* s.str. and *D. curvifolia* have wider distributions in practically the entire area of Central and Northern Europe. In the east both are gradually being replaced by the more active species *D. russowii* which in the past often migrated to the east reaching to the Baikal lake. At present the area of *D. russowii* is disjunctive and consists of a number of isolated populations. All species of this group are often interrelated by introgressive hybridization in areas where they come in contact with each other.

Subsection IV. *Sesquipedales*.

This subsection includes 4 species which are distributed in southern Europe and northern Africa. Nelson (1976, 1979) combined them as the series *Meridionales* Nelson.

61–64. Aggregate. *D. sesquipedalis*.

Species of this group evolved from an ancestor which was isolated as far back as the Neogene. This ancestral form was subject to increasing drought conditions for a long period. It gave rise to four modern species, *D. durandii* and *D. munbyana* which occur in the western Atlas mountains and in the south of the Pyrenees; *D. elata* which is distributed through the Atlas mountains and reaches the mountains of Sicily; and *D. sesquipedalis* which occurs in the south of Western Europe and in Corsica. In contact zones, these species show introgressive hybridization. They did not migrate extensively while evolving.

Section 2. *Aristatae*.

The only species of this monotypic section evolved from primary dactylorchids found in the thermophilic forest flora of Northern Eurasia during the early Neogene. As a result of general cooling and drying of the climate in the late Neogene, the distribution of primary dactylorchids became limited to the western and easter parts of its original general area. At present the climate in the area of this disjunction is sharply continental (Tolmaczov, 1954, 1974). The extinction of dactylorchid ancestors in the south of Eastern Siberia has isolated the ancestors of *D. aristata* from the main area of the genus a long time ago. Later it migrated to the east and became established in the Aleutian Isles and Western Alaska (Fig. 5-16). At present the distribution of this species has a marked oceanic nature (Fig. 5-17).

Section 3. *Sambucinae.*

This section includes 9 evolutionarily advanced species. Its distribution at present includes mostly the mountain regions of the Ancient Mediterranean (Fig. 5-17). Floral color dimorphism is typical of all species in this section.

66–67. Aggregate *D. sambucina.*

The most primitive species in the section is *D. sambucina.* It evolved in Europe and had its widest distribution during the Atlantic period of the Holocene. At present its distribution is more limited and it is found primarily in the Baltic Sea regions of Central Europe. The species is primary hydrophilous. In the south of Western Europe it is replaced by closely related species *D. fasciculata.*

68–74. Aggregate *D. sulphurea.*

All species of this group evolved from *D. sambucina*-like ancestors by adapting to relatively dry and arid habitats. Their life cycle is similar to that of ephemeroids. These species did not migrate extensively during their evolution. *D. sulphurea* occurs in the Pyrenees Mountains; *D. sicula* is found in the south of Italy, Sicily and Sardinia; *D. bartonii* is a stenoendemic of the Eastern Pyrenees; *D. libanotica* was evolved in what is now Lebanon. *D. romana* is the most widely distributed species of this aggregate. It occurs in low mountains in countries adjacent to the Mediterranean, and also in Asia Minor and the Crimea. It is related to all species of this aggregate through introgressive hybridization. In Turkey and further to the East, this species is completely replaced by *D. flavescens* which extends to the Caucasus, Iran and western Turkmenia (Kopet-dag mountains). A related alpine species in the mountains of Asia Minor and in the Caucasus is the *D. rupprechtii.* These species did not substantially change their distribution areas during the Quaternary.

Section 4. *Iberanthus.*

The single, ancient and very isolated species of this section, *D. iberica* is distributed in the mountains of the eastern Mediterranean basin in the Crimea, Transcaucasia, Asia Minor and Iran (Fig. 5-17). The habitats of the species apparently did not change during the Quaternary and its present distribution reflects the region of origin and formation of *D. iberica.*

A schematic map of species frequency in *Dactylorhiza* populated area is given in Fig. 5-18. The largest concentration of *Dactylorhiza* species is found in Western Europe (W. European center). There are from 13 to 18 species of dactylorchids in some sections of this region. Species that are equally widely distributed are *D. incarnata, D. cruenta, D. fuchsii, D. hebridensis, D. maculata, D. elodes, D. traunsteineri, D. russowii.* Stenoendemic species also occur in this center (*D. ericetorum, D. majalis, D. alpestris, D. purpurella, D. integrata, D. sambucina*). Areas of these species define the boundaries of the center. Moreover, the specific character of some regions of this center is defined by local endemic races. For the British Isles these are: *D. coccinea, D. pulchella, D. gemmana, D. okellyi, D. kerryensis, D. cambrensis, D. francis-drucei.* In the continental part of Western Europe the species is *D. sphagnicola.* For Scandinavia they are *D. pseudocordigera, D. pycnantha, D. lapponica.* Their evolution is associated closely with the last glaciation and occupation of the European territories which became free of ice in the early Holocene.

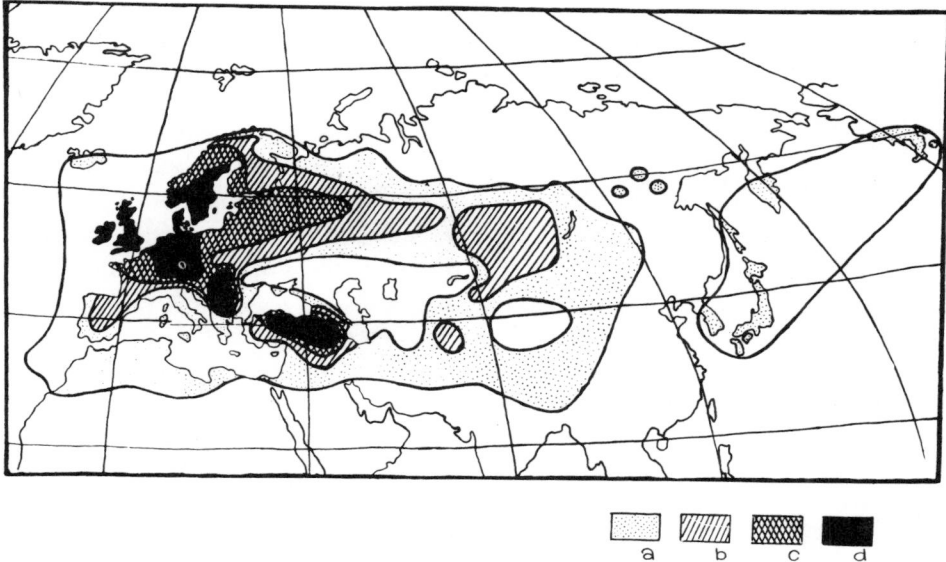

a b c d

Fig. 5-18. A schematic map of dactylorchids species concentration in the general distribution area of the genus *Dactylorhiza.* Explanation of symbols: Territories where different numbers of species occur are indicated with shading; **a**, 1–5; **b**, 6–9; **c**, 10–12; **d**, more than 12 species. Species of the genus do not occur in unshaded territories (Averyanov, 1983c).

On the whole, young endemism is typical for this center.

The influence of the Western European center of the genus on the abundance of species is very significant and pronounced especially toward the north and east. Owing to Gulf Stream influence *D. maculata, D. elodes, D. sudetica, D. hebridensis, D. psychrophila, D. colaënsis, D. pycnantha* and *D. lapponica* extend from the center into the far north of Scandinavia.

A considerable number of species radiates from the center eastwards. Only some of the species (*D. ochroleuca, D. ericetorum, D. majalis, D. pycnantha, D. lapponica, D. sambucina*) disappear just beyond the boundary of the center. Such species as *D. maculata, D. elodes, D. traunsteineri* and *D. curvifolia* reach almost to the Ural Mountains. *D. longifolia* and *D. russowii* extend practically to the Baikal region. Species of European origin such as *D. incarnata, D. cruenta, D. fuchsii* and *D. hebridensis* extend considerably eastwards.

In the southern direction the influence of the Western European center of dactylorchids on the abundance of species is not clearly marked. There are substantial differences between the Southern European flora of dactylorchids and that of Northern Africa. *D. maurusia* (aggr. *D. maculata*) is the only African species to show close affinity with European dactylorchids. The character of this part of the distribution of the genus is determined by the species aggr. *D. sesquipedalis* and aggr. *D. sulphurea*. In the extreme southwest of the area populated by the genus, the sole representative is *D. foliosa* (Madeira Isles).

The Carpathian-Balcan center of species abundance for the genus adjoins the Western European center from the southeast. Both of them are related in their species composition. *D. ochroleuca, D. sudetica, D. saccifera, D. majalis, D. alpestris, D. sambucina* and also more widespread dactylorchids species are common to both centers. Specificity of the Carpathian-Balcan center is defined by the species which are endemic to it: *D. schurii, D. transsilvanica, D. cordigera* and *D. bosniaca.*

A more isolated and third center of species abundance for dactylorchids is in Asia Minor (Asia Minor center). This center has only one common species (*D. iberica*) with the dactylorchid European flora. *D. triphylla, D. urvilleana, D. nieschalkiorum, D. cataonica, D. olocheilos, D. osmanica, D. sanasunitensis, D. merovensis, D. chuhensis, D. affinis, D. flavescens* and *D. ruprechtii* occur only here. Two additional species, *D. euxina* and *D. markowitschii* join the ones listed above in the Caucasus and Transcaucasia.

The second, and especially the third center of the species abundance of dactylorchids represent more ancient endemism of the genus *Dactylorhiza*. Species in these centers have undergone no substantial migrations in comparison with those of the Western European center of species abundance for the genus.

Considerable abundance of dactylorchids species in the Hindu-Kush and Pamir Mountains is defined by the widespread and common *D. umbrosa, D. salina, D. kotschyi, D. magna, D. czerniakowskae,* and the stenoendemic species *D. baldschuanica, D. kafiriana* and *D. kulikalonica.*

The genus is represented only by *D. hatagirea* and *D. graggeriana* in the Himalayas. In Southern Siberia a rather high level of dactylorchid species abundance is caused by penetration into the region of both European (*D. incarnata, D. fuchsii, D. hebridensis, D. russowii* and *D. longifolia*) and Central Asian species (*D. salina, D. umbrosa* and *D. kotschyi*). The eastern isolated part of the genus territory is represented by a single species, *D. aristata.*

On the whole the existence of the many still insufficiently studied, young, morphologically rather poorly defined, often stenoendemic species is characteristic of the genus *Dactylorhiza.* This is indirect evidence that intensive species radiation of the genus is proceeding at its present stage of development.

Literature Cited

Arditti, J., J. D. Michaud, and P. L. Healey. 1979. Morphometry of orchid seeds. I. *Paphiopedilum* and native California and related species of *Cypripedium. Amer. J. Bot.* 66: 1128–1137.

———. 1980a. Morphometry of orchid seeds. II. Native California and related species of *Calypso, Cephalanthera, Corallorhiza* and *Epipactis. Amer. J. Bot.* 67: 347–360.

———. 1980b. Morphometry of orchid seeds. III. Native California and related species of *Goodyera, Piperia, Platanthera* and *Spiranthes. Amer. J. Bot.* 67: 508–518.

Averyanov, L. V. 1979a. On the intraspecific structure of the taxon *Dactylorhiza maculata* (L.)'Soó s.l. (Orchidaceae). *Bot. J.* 64: 572–582 (in Russian).

———. 1979b. Chromosome numbers of some species of Orchidaceae family from the northwestern part of the USSR. *Bot. J.* 64: 863–877 (in Russian).

———. 1982. *Dactylorhiza maculata* s.l. (Orchidaceae) in the USSR. *Bot. J.* 67: 303–312 (in Russian).

———. 1983a. The genus *Dactylorhiza* (Orchidaceae) in the USSR. I. *Bot. J.* 68: 889–895 (in Russian).

———. 1983b. The genus *Dactylorhiza* (Orchidaceae) in the USSR. *Bot. J.* 68: 1160–1167 (in Russian).

———. 1983c. *Genus Dactylorhiza Nevski (Orchidaceae) in the USSR.* Dissertation. Bot. Inst. Ac. Sci. USSR. Leningrad (in Russian).

———. 1984. Taxonomic and nomenclature variations in the genus *Dactylorhiza* (Orchidaceae). *Bot. J.* 69: 875–876 (in Russian).

———. 1986. Taxonomic and nomenclature variations in the genus *Dactylorhiza* (Orchidaceae). *Bot. J.* 71: 92–93 (in Russian).

Averyanov, L. V., E. L. Averyanova, and A. N. Lavrenko. 1982a. The caryosystematic study of the orchids (Orchidaceae) of the Pechoro-Ilyshsky reservation. *Bot. J.* 67: 945–951 (in Russian).

———. 1982b. The caryosystematic study of orchids (Orchidaceae) on the territory of the Komi ASSR. *Bot. J.* 67: 1491–1499 (in Russian).

Averyanov, L. V., N. A. Medvedeva, and V. P. Serov. 1985. Chromosome numbers in the representatives of the family Orchidaceae from the Caucasus. *Bot. J.* 70: 999–1000 (in Russian).

Barthlott, W., and B. Ziegler. 1981. Mikromorphologie der Samenschalen als systemetisches Merkmal bei Orchideen. *Ber. Dtsch. Bot. Ges.* 94: 267–273.

Borsos, O. 1980. Anatomy of wild orchids in Hungary. I. Tissue structure of leaf and floral axis. *Acta Bot. Ac. Sci. Hung.* 29: 369–389.

Camus, E. G., and A. Camus. 1928. *Iconographie des Orchidées D'Europe.* 1–2. P. Lechevalier Ed., Paris.

Caspers, N., and L. Caspers. 1976. Zur oberflaechenskulpturierung der pollinien Mediterraner *Orchids-* und *Ophrys-* arten. *Pollen et Spores* 18: 203–215.

Dafni, A., and S. R. J. Woodel. 1986. Stigmatic Exudate and the Pollination of *Dactylorhiza fuchsii* (Druce)Soó. *Flora* 178: 343–350.

Dahl, E. 1941. *Gymnadenia conopsea* × *Orchis Traunsteineri* i Norge. *Nytt Mag. Nat.* 82: 103–104.

Dandy, J. E. 1958. *List of British vascular plants.* London Cat. Brit. Pl., London.

Danielsson, B. 1970. *Dactylorhiza Traunsteineri* × *Gymnadenia conopsea* funnen i norra Jämtland. *Svensk, Bot. Tidskr.* 64: 192–193.

Darwin, Ch. 1877. *The various contrivances by which orchids are fertilized by insects.* 2nd ed. revised. John Murray, London.

Dressler, R. 1981. *The orchids, natural history and classification.* Harvard Univ. Press, Cambridge, Massachusetts, London.

Dressler, R., and C. Dodson. 1960. Classification and phylogeny in the Orchidaceae. *Ann. Missouri Bot. Gard.* 47: 25–68.

Duncan, R. E. 1959. Orchids and cytology. In C. L. Withner (ed.), The Orchids. A Scientific Survey. Ronald, New York.

Ericsson, B.C. 1980. *Dactylorhiza fuchsii* × *Gymnadenia odoratissima* pa Omberg. *Svensk. Bot. Tidskr.* 74: 13–18.

Faegri, K., and L. Pijl. 1979. *The Principles of Pollination Ecology.* Pergamon Press, Oxford, New York, Toronto, Sydney, Paris, Frankfurt. 3rd ed.

Farr, E. R., J. A. Leussink, and F. A. Stafleu. 1979. *Index nominum Genericorum* (plantarum). I. Bohn, Scheltema & Holkema, Utrecht.

Fedrov, An. A. (Ed.). 1969. *Chromosome numbers of flowering plants.* Nauka, Leningrad (in Russian).

Fuchs, A. 1921. *Gymnadenia conopsea* R.Br. × *Orchis Traunsteineri* Saut. nov. hybrid. *Mitt. Bayer Bot. Ges. Erforsch. Heim. Fl.* 3,30: 529–530.

Füller, F. 1983. *Die Gattungen Orchis und Dactylorhiza.* A. Ziemsen Verlag, Wittenberg.

Garay, L, A., and H. R. Sweet. 1966. Natural and artificial hybrid generic names of orchids. *Bot. Mus. Leafl. Harv. Univ.* 21,6: 141–212.

_____. 1969. Natural and artificial hybrid generic names of orchids. Supplement 1. *Bot. Mus. Leafl. Harv. Univ.* 22,8: 273–296.

Hagerup, O. 1944. On fertilization, polyploidy and haploidy in *Orchis maculatus* L. sen. lat. *Dansk. Bot. Ark.* 11,5: 1–26.

_____. 1947. The spontaneous formation of haploid, polyploid and aneuploid embryos in some orchids. *Det. Kgl. Dansk. Sels. Biol. Meddelser.* 20,9: 1–22.

Harland, W. B., A. V. Cox, P. G. Llewellyn, C. A. G. Pickton, A. G. Smith, and R. Walters. 1982. *A geologic time scale.* Cambridge University Press, Cambridge.

Heslop-Harrison, J. 1954. A synopsis of the dactylorchids of the British Isles. *Ber. Geobot. Forschungsinst.* 1954: 53–82.

_____. 1957. On the hybridization of the common spotted orchid *Dactylorchis fuchsii* (Druce)Vermln., with the marsh orchids *D. praetermissa* (Druce)Vermln., and *D. purpurella* (T. and T. A. Steph.)Vermln. *Proc. Linn. Soc. London* 167: 176–185.

_____. 1959. Apomictic potentialities in Dactylorchids. *Proc. Linn. Soc. London* 170: 174–178.

Heywood, V. H. 1963. The species "aggregate" in theory and practice. *Reg. Veg.* 27: 26–37.

Hunt, P. F., and V. S. Summerhayes. 1965. *Dactylorhiza* Nevski the correct genera name of the dactylorchids. *Watsonia* 6: 128–133.

Hylander, N. 1966. *Nordisk kärlväxtflora* 2. Almqvist a.Wiksell, Stockholm.

Klinge, J. 1898. Dactylorchidis, orchidis subgeneris, Monographiae prodromus. *Acta Horti Petropol.* 17,1 (ed. seorsum expressa) :1–56.

_____. 1899. Zur Orientierung der *Orchis*—Bastarte und zur Polymorphie der *Dactylorchis*—Arten. *Acta Horti Petropol.* 17,2: 1–65.

Kliphuis, E. 1963. Cytological observations in relation to the taxonomy of the orchids of the Netherlands. *Acta Bot. Neerland.* 12: 172–194.

Kuprianova, L. A., and L. A. Alioschina. 1967. *Palinological Terminology of the Angiospermae Plants.* Nauka. Leningrad (in Russian).

Lord, R. M., and A. G. Richards. 1977. A hybrid swarm between the diploid *Dactylorhiza fuchsii* (Druce) Soó and the tetraploid *D. purpurella* (T. et T. A. Steph.) Soó in Durham. *Watsonia* 11: 205–210.

Malmgren, S., and I. Segelberg. 1965. *Dactylorchis fuchsii* × *Gymnadenia conopsea* pa Kinnekulle. *Svensk Bot. Tidskr.* 59: 168–169.

Necker, N.J. 1790. *Elementa Botanica* 3. Neowed. Rhenum ap. Soc. Typogr., Neowedae.

Nelson, E. 1976. *Monographie und Iconographie der Orchidaceen—gattung Dactylorhiza.* Georges und Antoine Claraz-Schenkung; Jubilämus stiftung der Schweizerischen Bankgesellschaft; Volkart-Stiftung Winterthur, Zürich.

———. 1979. Nachtrag zu E. Nelson Monographie und Ikonographie der Orchidaceengattung *Dactylorhiza. Taxon* 28: 592–593.

Nevski, S. A. 1935. Fam. 36. The orchids—Orchidaceae Lindl.: 589–730. In Komarov, V. L. (Ed.), *Fl. USSR* 4. Publ. Acad. Sci. USSR, Leningrad (in Russian).

———. 1937. Contributions to the Kugitang Mountains flora. *Fl. Syst. High. Pl.* 1,4: 199–346 (in Russian).

Nilsson, L. A. 1980. The pollination ecology of *Dactylorhiza sambucina* (Orchidaceae). *Bot. Notis.* 133: 367–385.

———. 1981. Pollination ecology and evolutionary processes in six species of orchids. *Acta Univ. Upss. Abstr. Upss. Diss. Fac. Sci.* 593: 1–40.

Ogura, T. 1953. Anatomy and morphology of the subterranean organs in some Orchidaceae. *Journ. Fac. Sci. Univ. Tokyo Bot.* 6: 135–157.

Parlatore, F. 1858. *Flora Italiana* 3. Typogr.le Monnier, Firenze.

Perring, F. H. 1968. *Critical supplement to the Atlas of the British flora.* Publ. Bot. Soc. Brit. Isl., London.

Pugsley, H. W. 1935. On some Marsh Orchids. *J. Linn. Soc. London (Bot.)* 49: 553–592.

Rasmussen, H. 1981. The university of stomatal development in Orchidaceae subfamily Orchidoideae. *Bot. J. Linn. Soc.* 82: 381–393.

Regel, E. 1866. Big leafing orchid. *Orchis foliosa* Soland. *Vestn. Ross. Horticult. Soc. St. Petersburg* 1866: 266–267 (in Russian).

Reichenbach, H. G. (fil.). 1851. *Iconographia Botanica Flora Germanica* 13–14 Orchideae. Sumptibus Fridr. Hofmeister, Lipsiae.

Renz, J. 1978. Orchidaceae. In Rechinger, K. H. (Ed.) *Fl. Iranica* 126. Akademische Druck Verlag., Graz.

Renz, J., and G. Taubenheim. 1984. 23. *Dactylorhiza* Necker ex Nevski: 535–551. In Davis, P. H. (Ed.) *Fl. Turkey* 8. Edinburgh Univ. Press., Edinburgh.

Savelsbergh, E. 1981. *Gymnadenia conopsea* (L.)R.Br. × *Dactylorhiza praetermissa* (Druce)Soó, eine intergenerische Hybride im Dunendistrikt von Voorne (Holland). *Orchidee* 32: 195–196.

Schill, R., and W. Pfeiffer. 1977. Untersuchungen an Orchideenpollinien unter besonderer Boruecksichtigung ihrer feinskulpturen. *Pollen et Spores* 19,1: 1–118.

Schlechter, R. 1928. *Monographie und Iconographie der Orchideen Europas und des Mittelmeergebietes* 1. Verlag Repertoriums, Dahlem.

Schmid, W. 1980. Ein Beitrag zur Kenntnis von *Dactylorhiza maculata* (L.)Soó, s.l. × *Gymnadenia odoratissima* (L.) Rich. = × *Dactylodenia regeliana* (Bruegg.)Peitz. *Mitteilung. Arbeitskr. Heim. Orch. Baden-Wurttemb.* 12: 27–37.

Schmid, W., H. R. Reinhard, and P. Gölz. 1974. *Coeloglossum viride* (L.)Hartm. × *Dactylorhiza maculata* (L.)Soó s.l. Erstfund in der Schweiz. *Orchidee* 25,2: 69–74.

Smolyaninova, L. A. 1976. Fam. 176. Orchidaceae Juss.—The orchids. :10–59. In Fedorov, An. A. (Ed.), *Fl. Europ. part of the USSR* 2. Nauka, Leningrad (in Russian).

Soó, R. 1933a. *Monographie und Iconographie der Orchideen Europas und des Mittelmeergebietes.* 2,6–7. Verlag Repertoriums, Dahlem.

———. 1933b. Sur les Dactylorchidees de l'Afrique septentrionale. *Bull. Soc. Hist. Nat. Afr. Nord.* 24: 167–175.

———. 1960. Synopsis generis *Dactylorhiza (Dactylorchis). Ann. Univ. Sci. Budapest. Biol.* 3: 335–357.

———. 1962. *Nomina nova generis Dactylorhiza.* Typogr. Ann. Univ. Sci. Budapest., Budapest.

———. 1980. *Dactylorhiza* Nevski :333–337. In Tutin, T. G., and al. (Ed.), *Fl. Europaea* 5. Cambridge Univ. Press, Cambridge, London, New York, New Rochelle, Melbourne, Sydney.

Soó, R., and O. Borsos. 1966. Geobotanische Monographie der Orchideen der Pannonischen und Karpatischen Flora.9. *Ann. Univ. Sci. Budapest. Biol.* 8: 315–336.

Stephenson, T., and T. A. Stephenson. 1922. Hybrids of *Orchis purpurella. J. Bot.* 60: 33–35.

Sundermann, H. 1975. *Europäische und mediterrane Orchideen.* Brücke-Verlag Kurt Schmersow, Hildesheim. 2nd Ed.

Tohda, H. 1983. Seed morphology in Orchidaceae. I. *Dactylorchis, Orchis, Ponerorchis, Chondradenia* and *Galeorchis. Sci. Rep. Tohoku Univ.* 4,38: 253–268.

Tolmaczov, A. I. 1954. *A Contribution the Evolving and Development of the Boreal Coniferous Forest.* Publ. Acad. Sci. USSR, Moskva, Leningrad (in Russian).

———. 1974. *An introduction to the plant geography.* Publ. Leningrad Univ., Leningrad (in Russian).

Vermeulen, P. 1938. Chromosomes in *Orchis. Chronica Bot.* 4,2: 107–108.

———. 1947. *Studies on Dactylorchids.* Drukkerij Fa Schotanus and Jens, Utrecht. Ph. D. Dissertation.

Wennerberg, A. 1978. Ett fynd av *Coeloglossum viride* × *Dactylorhiza maculata. Svensk Bot. Tidskr.* 78: 101–102.

Additional Literature

Adcock, E. M., E. Gorton, and G. P. Morries. 1983. A study of some *Dactylorhiza* populations in Greater Manchester. *Watsonia* 14: 377–389.

Afzelius, A. 1916. Zur Embriosackentwicklung der Orchideen. *Svensk Bot. Tidskr.* 10: 183–227.

Afzelius, K. 1958. En engendomling form av *Orchis maculata* L. Sen. lat. *Svensk Bot. Tidskr.* 52: 18–22.

Alleizette, C. 1936. Un nouvel hybride d'Orchis (*Orchis latifolia* × *laxiflora*) = × *Orchis chassagnei* Nob. *Bull. Soc. Bot. France* 83: 290–292.

_____. 1966. Etude sur les variations des orchidees du groupe *Dactylorchis* des prairies du sud-ouest de la France. *Bull. Soc. Bot. France* 113: 344–350.

Allen, D. E. 1971. *Dactylorhiza fuchsii* subsp. *okellyi* (Druce)Soó behavior and characters in the Isle of Man. *Watsonia* 8: 401–402.

Andersen, S. 1951. *Orchis praetermissa* Druce, en for Norden ny Gogeurt, fundet i Jylland. *Bot. Tidskr.* 48: 439–441.

Anon. 1976. *Dactylorhiza sambucina* (L.)Soó. *Orchideën* 38:170.

Averyanov, L. V. 1977a. On the intraspecific polymorphism of the *Dactylorhiza maculata* (L.)Soó. *Vestn. Leningrad Univ.9,Biol.,* 2:127 (in Russian).

_____. 1977b. Chromosome numbers of some species Orchidaceae family in Leningrad and Vologda district. *Bot. J.* 62: 547–553 (in Russian).

_____. 1983a. Main directions of the evolution of the genus *Dactylorhiza* Nevski and its system. :8–9. In *Abstr. Rep. 7 Congress All union Bot. Soc.* Nauka, Leningrad (in Russian).

_____. 1983b. New species of the genus *Dactylorhiza* (Orchidaceae) from Central Asia and Caucasus. *Bot. J.* 68: 534–539 (in Russian).

_____. 1983c. Origin and evolution of the genus *Dactylorhiza* Nevski (Orchidaceae Juss.). :24–26. In *Abstr. Rep. Conf. Orchid Conserv. and Cultivation.* Publ. Acad. Sci. Ukr. SSR, Kiev (in Russian).

_____. 1983d. Natural history of the genus *Dactylorhiza* Nevski (Orchidaceae) and perspectives of the preservation of its species. :6–8. In *Abstr. Rep. Conf. Conserv. Living Nature.* Publ. Agricult. Ministr. USSR, Moscow (in Russian).

_____. 1983e. Biological principles of the preservation of the species of the genus *Dactylorhiza* Nevski (Orchidaceae). :118. In *Abstr. Rep. Conf. Rational Use and Conserv. Soil and Plant Resources.* Publ. Baschk. branch Acad. Sci. USSR, Ufa (in Russian).

_____. 1983f. Chromosome numbers. Orchidaceae. *Bot. J.* 68:1682 (in Russian).

_____. 1984. A karyosystematic study of some species of orchids (Orchidaceae) in the middle-asian flora. *Bot. J.* 69: 245–247 (in Russian).

Averyanov, L. V., E. L. Averyanova, and A. N. Lavrenko. 1980. Caryosystematic characterization of the genus *Dactylorhiza* (Orchidaceae) in the Middle Tyman. *Bot. J.* 65: 983–989 (in Russian).

Averyanov, L. V., and T. E. Tepliakova. 1984. A karyosystematic study of orchids (Orchidaceae Juss.) in the northeast Altai. *Vestn. Leningrad Univ.* 21, *Biol.,* 4: 82–84 (in Russian).

Bär, A. 1976. Allganer Orchideen—Streiflicht: *Orchis maculata.* *Mitt. Naturwiss. Arbeitskr. Kempton* 20: 9–16.

Bateman, R. M. 1977. *Dactylorhiza fuchsii*—the common spotted orchid. *J. Orchid Soc. Gr. Brit.* 26:30.

_____. 1981. *Dactylorhiza incarnata:* early marsh orchid. *J. Orchid Soc. Gr. Brit.* 30: 3–5.

Bateman, R. M., and I. Denholm. 1983a. A reapparisal of the British and Irish dactylorchids, 1. The tetraploid marsh orchids. *Watsonia* 14: 347–376.

_____. 1983b. *Dactylorhiza incarnata* (L.)Soó subsp. *ochroleuca* (Boll)P. F. Hunt et Summerhayes. *Watsonia* 14: 410–411.

Baumann, H. 1983. Die balkanisch—orientalischen *Dactylorhiza*—Arten—ein Vergleich. *Mitt. Bl. Arbeitskr. Heim. Orch. Baden-Württ.* 5: 43–108.

Baumann, H., and S. Künkele. 1981a. Beiträge zur Taxonomic orientalischer *Dactylorhiza* Arten. *Mitt. Bl. Arbeitskr. Heim. Orch. Baden-Württ.* 13: 220–266.

_____. 1981b. Beiträge zur Nomenklatur und Verbreitung der mediterranean *Dactylorhiza*—Arten der Section *Sambucinae. Mitt. Bl. Arbeitskr. Heim. Orch. BAden-Württ.* 13: 455–478.

Beck, C. A. 1980. Orchid species at Waltham Abbey. *B. S.Bl. News* 24:26.

Beisenherz, W. 1973. Zur Verbreitung von *Dactylorhiza cruenta* und *D. pseudocordigera* in Skandinavien. *Orchidee* 24: 119–120.

Belikov, A. C. 1961. *Orchis maculata* L. :672–675. In Zizin, N. V. (Ed.) *Atlas Medicinal Plants USSR.* Publ. Med. Lit., Moscow (in Russian).

Bergstedt, L. 1980. Sumpnycklar, *Dactylorhiza traunsteineri,* ny för Bohuslän. *Svensk Bot. Tidskr.* 74: 307–310.

Bernard, C. 1983. Description de deux hybrides nouveaux d'Orichdées découverts dans la région des Grands Causses cevenois. *Bull. Soc. Bot. Fr. Lett. Bot.* 130: 153–156.

Birkedal, S., and J. Danielson. 1981. Första fyndet av mossnycklar (*Dactylorhiza sphagnicola*) i Skane. *Svensk Bot. Tidskr.* 75: 313–314.

Bodegom, J. 1976. Orchideën in Spanje:5. *Dactylorhiza. Orchideën* 38: 201–203.

Borsos, O. 1959. *Dactylorchis fuchsii* Druce et son affinite dans les flores Hongroise et Carpatique. *Acta Bot. Ac. Sci. Hung.* 5: 321–326.

_____. 1961. Geobotanische Monographie der Orchideen der Pannonischen und Karpatischen. Flora. V. *Ann. Univ. Sci. Budapest. Biol.* 4: 51–82.

Breiner, E., and R. Breiner. 1980. *Dactylorhiza incarnata* (L.) Soó var. *hyphaematodes* (Neum.) Vermeulen. *Mitt. Arb. Heim. Orch. Baden.-Württ.* 12: 105–109.

Bruggen, H. W. E. 1978. De orchideën van Europa:8. *Dactylorhiza iberica* (Bieb.) Soó. *Orchideën* 40: 102–104.

_____. 1980. *Dactylorhiza praetermissa* (Druce) Soó op het Belgische deel van St. Pietersberg. *Orchideën* 42:197.

Catling, P. M. 1982. New combinations for forms and varieties of some North American orchids. *Natur. Can.* 109: 277–278.

Ciferri, R., and V. Giacomini. 1950. *Nomenclator Florae Italicae.* Pars prima. Typ. Busca, Ticini.

Crackles, F. E. 1986. *Dactylorhiza majalis* (Reichb.) P. F. Hunt & Summerhayes subsp. *cambrensis* (R. H. Roberts) R. H. Roberts in S. E. Yorkshire. *Watsonia* 16: 78–80.

Curtis, T. G. F. 1980. *Dactylorhiza maculata* (L.) Soó x *D. traunsteineri* (Saut. ex Reichenb.) Soó (*D. ×jenensis* (Brand) Soó) in Ireland. *Irish Natur. J.* 20,4: 163.

Delforge, P., and D. Tyteca. 1982. Quelques orchidées rares on critiques d'Europe occidentale. *Bull. Soc. Roy. Belg.* 115: 271–288.

Doll, R. 1978. Neue Pflanzen-Sippen aus Mecklenburg. *Fedes Repert.* 89: 345–351.

Domin, K. 1926. O variabilite vstavace uzkolisteho (*Orchis Traunsteineri* Saut.) na novem ceskem nalezisti. *Vestn. Kralov. Cesk. Spol. Nauk* 1926: 1–9.

Dostal, L. 1981. *Dactylorhiza incarnata* var. *haematodes* v Popradskéy kotline. *Zpravy Cesk. Bot. Spol. CSAV* 16: 17–18.

Downie, D. G. 1959. The micorrhiza of *Orchis purpurella. Trans. Bot. Soc. Edinb.* 38: 16–29.

Druce, C. G. 1910. Short notes on *O. maculata* var. *O'kellyi. J. Bot.* 48: 22–23.

_____. 1924. *Orchis fuchsii* Druce. *J. Bot.* 62: 198–201.

Ekman, J. 1985. Mossnycklar och ofläskade sumpnycklar funna i Roslagen. *Svensk Bot. Tidskr.* 79: 85–91.

Ericsson, B. 1982. Mossnycklar och skogsfree växer pa Öland. *Svensk Bot. Tidskr.* 76: 1–4.

Ernst, K. 1908. *Orchis maculata* als Topfpflanze. *Möller's dt. Gärtn. Ztg.* 23: 1–266.

Fournier, P. 1931. *Orchis nummiana* P. Fournier (*O. elodes* × *latifolia* P. Fournier). *Bull. Soc. Bot. France* 78: 432–434.

Franco, A. 1978. *Dactylorhiza sulphurea* (Link) Franco, comb. nov. *Bot. J. Linn. Soc.* 76: 366–367.

Fröhner, S. 1977a. Fragen zur taxomischen Rangstufle von *Dactylorhiza fuchsii* (Druce) Soó. *Ber. Arbeitsgen. Sächs. Bot.*n.f. 11: 13–28.

_____. 1977b. Eine neue *Dactylorhiza*—Art aus dem Erzgebirge. *Ber. Arbeitsgem. Sächs. Bot.*n.f. 11: 29–34.

Fuchs, A., and H. Ziegenspeck. 1922. Aus der Monographie der *Orchis Traunsteineri* Saut. *Bot. Arch.* 2: 238–248.

_____. 1923. Aus der Monographie der *Orchis Traunsteineri* Sauter. II. Teil:Mycorhiza und Boden. *Bot. Arch.* 3: 238–261.

_____. 1924a. Aus der Monographie der *Orchis Traunsteineri* Saut. III. Entwicklungsgeschichte einiger deutscher Orchideen. *Bot. Arch.* 5: 120–132.

_____. 1924b. Aus der Monographie der *Orchis Traunsteineri* Saut. IV. Chromosomen einiger Orchideen. *Bot. Arch.* 5: 457–470.

_____. 1924c. *Orchis Traunsteineri* Sauter. II Teil. *Ber. Naturw. Ver. Schwaben Neuburg* 43: 1–118.

_____. 1927a. Die Dactylorchisgruppe der Ophridineen. *Bot. Arch.* 19: 163–274.

_____. 1927b. Entwicklung, Axen und Blatter einheimischer Orchideen, IV. Teil. *Bot. Arch.* 20,56:276–423.

Godfery, M. J. 1919. The probleme of the british Marsh Orchids. *J. Bot.* 57: 137–142.

_____. 1921. *Orchis elodes* Grisebach. *J. Bot.* 59: 305–308.

_____. 1923. *Orchis fuchsii* Druce. *J. Bot.* 61: 306–309.

_____. 1924. *Orchis latifolia* L., a historical study. *J. Bot.* 62: 35–41.

Godfery, M. J., T. Stephenson, and T. A. Stephenson. 1924. The British Dactylorchids. *J. Bot.* 62: 175–178.

Groll, M. 1965. Fruchtansatz, Bustäubung und Merkmalsanalyse bei diploiden und poliploiden sippen von *Dactylorchis* (*Orchis*) und *Gymnadenia conopsea. Osterr. Bot. Z.* 112: 675–700.

Gsell, R. 1943. Ueber *Orchis maculata* L. *Boissiera* 7: 333–345.

Gupta, R. 1966. *Orchis latifolia* Linn.—a little known economic plant of Northwest Himalayas. *Indian Forest.* 92: 701–703.

Haas, H. F. 1977. Asymbiotische Vermehrung europäischer Erdorchideen. I.*Dactylorhiza sambucina* (L.) Soó. *Die Orchidee* 28: 27–31.

Hadley, G., and G. Harvais. 1968. The effect of certain growth substances on asymbiotic germination and development of *Orchis purpurella*. *New Phytol.* 67: 441–445.

Hagerup, O. 1938a. A peculiar asymetrical mitosis in the microspora of *orchis*. *Hereditas* 24: 94–96.

——— . 1938b. Studies on the significance of polyploidy 2 *Orchis*. *Hereditas* 24: 258–264.

Hakon, R. 1941. Norske finnesteder for *Orchis sambucina*. *Nytt Mag. Naturvidens.* 81: 43–45.

Hartman, C. J. 1846. Undersökning om Linnes *Orchis latifolia* och *incarnata*. *Bot. Notis.* 1846: 145–150.

Harvais, G. 1972. The development and growth requirement of *Dactylorhiza purpurella* in asymbiotic cultures. *Canad. J. Bot.* 50: 1223–1229.

Harvais, G., and G. Hadley. 1967a. The relation between host and endophyte in orchid micorrhiza. *New Phytol.* 66: 205–215.

——— . 1967b. The development of *Orchis purpurella* in asymbiotic and inoculated cultures. *New Phytol.* 66: 217–230.

Hautzinger, L. 1972. *Dactylorhiza cruenta* (O. F. Mueller)Soó × *D. maculata* (L.)Soó ssp. *maculata*, ein neuer interspezifischer Bastard. *Bot. Gesellsch. Wien* 112: 115–117.

——— . 1980. Familie Orchidaceae-Libyen: *Orchis melchifafii*, sp.nova, und *Dactylorhiza cyrenaica*, comb.nova. *Ann. Naturhistor. Mus. Wien* 83: 475–478.

Havlickova, J., and J. Rydlo. 1982. Ohrozena lokalita *Dactylorhiza incarnata* ve strednim Polabi. *Zpr. Cs. Bot. Spolec.* 17: 142–144.

Heidemann, H. 1971. Eine wenig bekannte Form von *Dactylorhiza cruenta* (O. F. Müll.)Soó in den Alpen. *Orchidee* 22: 259–260.

Heinrich, D. 1980. *Dactylorhiza × templinensis* Potucêk-ein neuer Orchideenbastard aus Mecklenburg. *Naturschutzarb. Mecklenburg* 23: 30–31.

Hemke, E. 1980. Beobachtungen an Orchideen in der Tongrube Blankensee. *Bot. Rundbr. Bez. Neubrand.* 10: 87–89.

Heslop-Harrison, J. 1949. Field studies in *Orchis* L.1. The structure of dactylorchid population on certain islands in the Inner and Outer Hebrides. *Trans. Bot. Soc. Edinb.* 35: 26–66.

——— . 1950. *Orchis cruenta* Müll. in the British Islands. *Watsonia* 1: 366–375.

——— . 1951. A comparison of the some Swedish and British form of *Orchis maculata* L.s.l. *Svensk Bot. Tidskr.* 45:608–635.

——— . 1953a. Studies in Orchis L.2. *Orchis traunsteineri* Saut. in the British Isles. *Watsonia* 2: 371–391.

——— . 1953b. Microsporogenesis in some triploid hybrids. *Ann. Bot. Now.* ser. 17,68: 539–549.

——— . 1956. Some observations on *Dactylorchis incarnata* (L.)Verm. in the British Isles. *Proc. Linn. Soc. London* 166: 51–82.

——— . 1957. The physiology of reproduction in *Dactylorchis* I.Auxin and the control of meiosis, ovule formation and ovary growth. *Bot. Notis.* 110: 28–48.

——— . 1968. Genetic system and ecological habit as factors in Dactylorchid variation. *Jahresb. Naturw. Ver. Wuppertal.* 21–22: 20–27.

Holmen, K., and P. Kaad. 1956. Über *Dactylorchis traunsteineri* auf der Insel Läsö. *Bot. Tidskr.* 53: 35–48.

Holzfuss, E. 1925. Deutung zweier Bastardformen zwischen *Orchis incarnatus* und *latifolius*. *Abhandl. Ber. Pommersch. Naturf. Ges. St.* 6: 107–108.

Hossain, A. B. M., and E. A. Enayet. 1986. A note on *Orchis cyrenaica* (Orchidaceae). *Willdenowia* 16: 87–88.

Hunt, P. F., and V. S. Summerhayes. 1967. The genus *Dactylorhiza* in Britain. *Proc. Bot. Soc. Brit. Isl.* 6: 372–375.

——— . 1968. Die Gattung *Dactylorhiza* auf den Britischen Inseln. *Jahresb. Naturw. Ver. Wuppertal* 21–22: 119–122.

Huxley, A. J., and P. F. Hunt. 1967. A New orchid from Spain. *J. Roy. Hort. Soc.* (London) 92: 308–309.

Jagiello, M. 1986a. Stanowiska *Dactylorhiza cordigera* (Fries)Soó (Orchidaceae) w Polsce. *Fragm. Florist. et Geobot.* 30,3: 185–193.

——— . 1986b. A new name for *Dactylorhiza fuchsii* (Druce)Soó (Orchidaceae)? *Fragm. Florist. et Geobot.* 30,3: 213–216.

Jaros, V. 1975. Vorläufige Mitteilung über *Dactylorhiza latifolia* (L.)Soó östlich von Prag. *Cas. Nar. Mus.(Prague)* 142: 51–55.

Jonsell, B. 1982. Angsnycklar och sumpnycklar i nordligaste Uppland. *Svensk Bot. Tidskr.* 76: 103–111.

Kalopissis, J., and V. Kalopissis. 1978. Discovering a new orchid. *Hellenic Soc. Protect. Nat.* 14:40.

Kare, A. L. 1977. *Dactylorhiza × formosa* i Noreg. *Blyttia* 35: 19–22.

Keller, G., and R. Schlechter. 1938. *Monographie und Inconographie der Orchideen Europas und des Mittelmeergebietes*. 4. Selbslverlag, Berlin.

Kenneth, A. G. 1971. An orchid new to Scotland. *Glasgow Nat.* 18:589.

Kenneth, A. G., and D. J. Tennant. 1984. *Dactylorhiza incarnata* (L.)Soó subsp. *cruenta* (O. F. Mueller)P. D. Sell in Scotland. *Watsonia* 15: 11–14.

Klinge, J. 1893. *Revisio Orchis cordigera Fries und Orchis angustifolia Rchb.* Druck C. Mattiesen, Jurjew.

_____. 1894. Revisio *Orchis cordigera* Fries und *Orchis angustifolia* Rchb. *Arch. Naturk. Liv. Ehst. Kurlands, Ser. 2, Biol. Naturk.* 10: 257–359.

_____. 1899a. Dactylorchidis, orchidis subgeneris, Monographiae prodromus. *Acta Horti Petropol.* 17,1: 147–202.

_____. 1899b. Die homo- und polyphyletischen Formenkreise der *Dactylorchis*—Arten. *Acta Horti Petropol.* 17,2: 67–146.

_____. 1899c. Zur geographischen Verbreitung und Entstehung der *Dactylorchis*—Arten. *Acta Horti Petropol.* 17,2: 147–250.

Kreutz, C. A. J. 1979. *Dactylorhiza elata* (Poir)Soó var. *sesquipedalis* (Willd.)Landw. (*Orchis sesquipedalis* Willd.; *Dactylorchis sesquipedalis* (Willd.)Vermeulen) in Nederland. *Natuurh. Maandbl.* 68: 200–202.

Krey, W. D. 1977a. Ubekannter intergenerischer *Dactylorhiza cordigera* Bastard in Südjugoslawien. *Orchidee* 28: 144–145.

_____. 1977b. *Dactylorhiza russowii* (Klinge)Holub in Mecklenburg. *Orchidee* 28: 145–146.

Kümpel, H., and H. Jahn. 1979. Die Hybriden der Gattung × *Dactyleucorchis* Soó. *Feddes Repert.* 90: 401–406.

Kuusk, V. 1981. Balti sormkapp (*Dactylorhiza baltica*). *Eesti Loodus* 24:103.

_____. 1983. *Dactylorhiza baltica* (Klinge)Orlova. 29–31. In *Abstr. Rep. Conf. Orchid Conserv. and Cultivation.* Publ. Acad. Sci. Ukr. SSR, Kiev (in Russian).

Laanelaid, A. 1978. About *Orchis incarnata* with yellowish-white flowers. *Eesti Loodus* 21: 377–378.

Lacey, W. S. 1955. *Orchis traunsteineri* Saut. in Wales. *Proc. Bot. Soc. Brit. Isl.* 1: 297–300.

Lacey, W. S., and R. H. Roberts. 1958. Further notes on *Dactylorchis traunsteineri* (Saut.)Vermeul. in Wales. *Proc. Bot. Soc. Brit. Isl.* 3: 22–27.

Landwehr, J. 1975. Het geslacht *Dactylorhiza*: een aantal nieuwe vormen en aanvullingen van de nomenclatuur. *Orchideeën* 37: 76–80.

_____. 1979. De orchideeën van Europa: 10.*Dactylorhiza elata* (Poir.)Soó—Grote Rietorchis. *Orchideeën* 41: 24–26.

Lindley, J. 1830–1840. *The genera and species of orchidaceous plants.* W. Nicol, London.

Lojtnant, B. 1978. Nomenclatural notes upon Scandinavian orchids. *Feddes Repert.* 89: 13–18.

_____. 1979. *Dactylorhiza purpurella* ssp. *majaliformis* Nelson ex Lojtnant. *Bot. Tidskr.* 74: 175–176.

Löve, A., and D. Löve. 1961. Some nomenclatural changes in the European flora.1. Species and supraspecific categories. *Bot. Notis.* 114: 33–47.

Luer, C. A., and G. M. Luer. 1972. Variations in *Dactylorhiza aristata* in Alaska. *Amer. Orch. Soc. Bull.* 41: 205–207.

Lye, K. A. 1977. *Dactylorhiza × formosa* i Noreg. *Blyttia* 35: 19–22.

Mattfeld, J. 1922. *Orchis Uechtritziana* Hausskn. (*O. incarnata* L. × *O. palustris* Jack.) neu für die Mark. *Ver. Bot. Ver. Prov. Brandenb.* 63: 52–54.

Mazzola, P., R. Lidberg, and F. Raimondo. 1980. Critical notes on the Sicilian flora: the genus *Dactylorhiza* Necker ex Nevski sect. *Dactylorhiza*. *Anal. Jard. Bot. Madrid* 37,2: 661–676.

Meadows, G. E. M. 1981. Variation on an old theme. A journey into Spain: part. *Orchis spitzeli* and *Dactylorhiza insularis*. *Quart. Bull. Alp. Gard. Soc.* 49: 143–156.

Mika, J. 1980. Neobuykly vyskyt *Dactylorhiza majalis*. *Zpravy Cask. Bot. Spol. CSAV* 15:128.

Montell, J. 1921. *Orchis lapponicus* Laest, en länge förbisedd art. *Meddel. Soc. pro Fauna Fl. Fennica* 47: 55–57.

_____. 1947. *Orchis maculatus* L. var. *kolaënsis* mihi, nova var. *Mem. Soc. Fauna Fl. Fenn.* 23: 166–167.

Moore, D. M. 1978. *Flora Europea Notulae Systematicae ad Floram Europaeam Spectantes. Bot. J. Linn. Soc.* 76:367.

Nieschalk, A., and C. Nieschalk. 1971. Ein Vorkommen von *Dactylorhiza romana* (Seb.u Maur.)Soó ssp. *siciliensis* (Klinge)Soó (=Orchis mediterranea Klinge ssp. *siciliensis* Klinge) in Spanien. *Orchidee* 22: 110–114.

_____. 1972. Kritische Bemerkungen zur Taxonomie und verbreitung von *Dactylorhiza elata* (Poir.)Soó. *Philippia* 1: 139–148.

_____. 1975. Orientalische *Dactylorhiza*-Arten (Knabenkräuter, Orchideengewächse) in der Türkei: *Dactylorhiza cilicica* (Klinge)Soó, *Dactylorhiza osmanica* (Klinge)Soó und *Dactylorhiza umbrosa* (Kar. et Kir.)Nevski. *Philippia* 2: 221–235.

_____. 1978. Einige weitere Mitteilungen zur Kenntnis der Orchideen-flora in Spanien. *Orchidee* 29: 78–86.

Nordhagen, R. 1972. *Dactylorhiza praetermissa* (Druce)Hunt et Summerhayes, a marsh orchid new to Norway and adjacent part of North Europe. *Norw. J. Bot.* 19: 48–50.

Pagani, F. 1976. Fitocostituenti di orchidaceae. Nota 1. Componenti della *Orchis sambucina* L., *Orchis morio* L. *Boll. Chim. Farm.* 115: 407–412.

Palmgren, A. 1921. *Orchis maculata × sambucina* fran Aland. *Meddel. Soc. Pro Fauna Fl. Fennica* 46:2.

_____. 1925. *Orchis Traunsteineri* Saut. für Aland new. *Meddel. Soc. Pro Fauna Fl. Fennica* 49: 151–152.

Petit, J. 1980. Chronique de la Montagne Saint-Pierre:5. *Dactylorhiza praetermissa* (Druce) Soó a Lanaye. *Rev. Verv. Hist. Nat.* 37: 89–95.

_____. 1981. Chronique de la Montagne Saint-Pierre:7. Un hybride *Dactylorhiza praetermissa* ×*D. maculata meyeri* a Lanaye. *Rev. Verv. Hist. Nat.* 38: 64–66.

Petterson, B. 1947. On some hybrids population of *Orchis incarnata* × *maculata* in Gotland. *Svensk Bot. Tidskr.* 41: 115–140.

Potucek, O. 1975. Eine neue Orchideenhybride in der DDR-*Dactylorhiza* × *templinensis* Potucek. *Gleditschia* 3: 29–33.

Prete, C. 1979. Contributi alla conoscenza delle Orchidaceae d'Italia.4. *Dactylorhiza* × *maculatiformis* (Rouy) Borsos et Soó nuova per la flora italiana. *Webbia* 33: 217–219.

_____. 1981. Contributi alla conoscenza delle Orchidaceae d'Italia:3. Note sistematiche e corologiche sul genere *Dactylorhiza* Necker ex Nevski. *Excerpta Bot., A* 36:169.

Prochazka, F. 1979a. Okruh prstnatce plamateho (*Dactylorhiza maculata* aggr.) v Ceskoslovensku. *Spravy Cesk. Bot. Spol. CSAV* 14: 9–12.

_____. 1979b. Prstnatec Russowuy (*Dactylorhiza russowii*)—nove rozeznany a vyhynuly druh ceskoslovenske Kveteny. *Preslia* 51: 247–254.

_____. 1982. *Dactylorhiza majalis* subsp. *turfosa*, nove plemeno prstnatcemajoveho. *Preslia* 54: 289–295.

Prochazka, F., and O. Potucek. 1973. *Dactylorhiza incarnata* var. *haematodes* (Reichenb.fil.) Soó—novy taxon ceskoslovenske flory. *Preslia* 45: 90–93.

Pugsley, H. W. 1936. New British marsh Orchids. *Proc. Linn. Soc. London* 148: 121–125.

_____. 1939. Recent work on Dactylorchids. *J. Bot.* 77: 50–56.

_____. 1940. Further notes on British Dactylorchids. *J. Bot.* 78: 177–181.

Rajchel, R. 1964. *Orchis incarnata* L. subsp. *ochroleuca* (Wüstnei) O. Schwarz in Poland. *Fragm. Flor. Geobot.* 10: 193–197.

Ramin, I. 1979. *Dactylorhiza maculata*—das gefleckte Knabenkraut. *Palmen-garten* 43: 29–31.

Rasmussen, E. 1981. *Dactylorhiza foliosa. Orchideer* 2: 3–4.

Rauschert, S. 1973. Zur Nomenklatur der Farn- und Blütenpflanzen Deutschlands 3. *Feddes Repert.* 83: 645–662.

_____. 1974. Zur Nomenklatur der Farn- und Blütenpflanzen Deutschlands (IV). *Feddes Repert.* 85: 641–661.

Ravnil, V. 1972. Nekaj o problematiki orchideje *Dactylorhiza maculata* (L.) Soó s.l. *Biol. Vestn.* 20: 31–37.

_____. 1975. *Dactylorhiza maculata* (L.) Soó subsp. *transsilvanica* (Schur) Soó nova orchideja v flori slovenije. *Biol. Vestn.* 23: 53–58.

Robac, H. 1941. Norske finnesteder for *Orchis sambucina. Nytt. mag. Naturvidensk.* 81: 43–45.

Roberts, R. H. 1961a. Studies on welsh orchids.1. The variation of *Dactylorchis purpurella* (T.et T. A. Stephenson) Vermln. in North Wales. *Watsonia* 5: 23–36.

_____. 1961b. Studies on welsh orchids.II. The occurrence of *Dactylorchis majalis* (Reichenb.) Vermln. in Wales. *Watsonia* 5: 37–42.

_____. 1962. *Dactylorchis maculata* subsp. *ericetorum* × *D. traunsteineri. Proc. Bot. Soc. Brit. Isl.* 4:418.

_____. 1966. Studies on welsh orchids.III. The coexistence of some of the tetraploid species of marsh orchids. *Watsonia* 6: 260–267.

Roberts, R., and O. Gilbert. 1963. The status of *Orchis latifolia* var. *eborensis* Godfery in Yorkshire. *Watsonia* 5: 287–293.

Rodkiewicz, B., and E. Kadej. 1971. Ultrastructure of megaspore tetrad in *Orchis maculata. Bull. L'Acad. Polon. Sci. Ser. Sci. Biol.* 19: 601–604.

Rolfe, R. A. 1907. *Orchis incarnata*—*Epidendrum trachychilum*—*Lacaena bicolor*—*Bulbophyllum ericssonii. Orchid Rev.* 15: 231–234.

Sahlin, C. I. 1960. *Orchis maculata* ssp. *ericetorum* found in Torne Lappmark, northern Sweden. *Svensk Bot. Tidskr.* 54: 275–277.

_____. 1978. *Dactylorhiza wirtgenii* (Höppner) Soó, eine echte Art. *Orchidee* 29: 268–269.

_____. 1979. Information about *Dactylorhiza traunsteineri* from Romsmaren, North Uppland was mistaken. *Svensk Bot. Tidskr.* 73:396.

_____. 1980. *Dactylorhiza maculata* subsp. *ericetorum* funnen i Bohuslän. *Svensk Bot. Tidskr.* 74: 417–418.

Sarosiek, J., and E. Szymanska. 1986. Ekologiczna organizacja populacji *Dactylorhiza majalis* (Rchb.) Hunt et Summerh. z Chwaliszewa na pogorzu Walbrzyskim. *Acta Univ. Wratisl. Pr. Bot.* 33: 55–70.

Savina, G. I. 1965. Development of sexual elements in the course of fertilization in some species of *Orchis. Bot. J.* 50: 96–102 (in Russian).

Scannel, M. J. P. 1973a. *Dactylorhiza* × *kellerana* P. F. Hunt in Westmeath and east Mayo. *Irish Nat. J.* 17:426.

_____. 1973b. *Dactylorhiza traunsteineri* (Sauter) Soó in east Cork, mid Cork, Offaly, Meath, Leitrim and east Mayo. *Irish Nat. J.* 17:426.

Scharfenberg, K. 1975. *Beiträge zur Kenntnis der Sippenstruktur der Gattung Dactylorhiza Necker ex Nevski in den Bezirken Cottbus, Potsdam, Frankfurt/Oder und Neubrandenburg.* Dissertation. Humboldt Universität zu Berlin, Berlin.

———. 1977. Beiträge zur Kenntnis der Sippenstruktur der Gattung *Dactylorhiza* Necker ex Nevski in den Bezirken Cottbus, Potsdam, Frankfurt (Oder) und Neubrandenburg. *Gleditschia* 5: 65–127.

Schmitz, J. 1982. *Dactylorhiza sphagnicola* (Höppner) Soó und *D. incarnata* (L.)Soó var. *lobeli* (Vermln.)Soó im Hohen Venn. *Decheniana* 135:13.

Scheider, P. A. 1978a. Das Blassgelbe Knabenkraut (*Dactylorhiza ochroleuca*). *Z. Bund Natursch. Oberschwaben* 15: 38–40.

———. 1978b. Das Traunsteiner Knabenkraut (*Dactylorhiza traunsteineri*). *Z. Bund Natursch. Oberschwaben* 15: 40–42.

Schrenk, W. J. 1980. The sub-alpine populations of *Dactylorhiza* Necker ex Nevski: puzzle in red. *Amer. Orchid Soc.* Bull. 49: 1241–1251.

Selga, M. 1963. Morfologiski un sistematiski petijumi par Latvijas par *Dactylorchis* sugam. *Uczen. Zap. Latviisk. Univ. Biol.* 49: 77–106.

Senghas, K. 1968a. Taxonomische Ubersicht der Gattung *Dactylorhiza* Necker ex Nevski. *Jahresb. Naturw. Ver. Wuppertal* 21–22:32–67.

———. 1968b. Bestimmungsschlussel der mitteleuropaischen *Dactylorhiza*-Sippen. *Jahresb. Naturw. Ver. Wuppertal* 21–22:123–126.

Senghas, K., and H. Sundermann. 1968. Probleme der Orchideengattung *Dactylorhiza*. *Jahresb. Naturw. Ver. Wuppertal* 21–22:127–138.

Sergievskaya, L. 1929. On *Orchis latifolia* L. and *O. incarnata* L. in Western Siberia. *Syst. Not. on mat. Tomsk. Univ.* 1: 1–4 (in Russian).

Simola, L. K. 1982. Electron microscope observations on the differentiation of protocorm cells of *Dactylorhiza maculata*. *Nord. J. Bot.* 2: 125–130.

Sipkes, C. 1972. De Rietorchis (*Dactylorhiza praetermissa*) tetug op Voorne. *Levende Nat.* 75: 180–182.

———. 1979. Hybriden van *Gymnadenia* met *Dactylorhiza*. *Orchideeën* 41: 56–57.

Siwicka-Tarwidowa, H. 1934. Sur l'evolution du chondriome pendant le developpement du sac embryonnaire de l'*Orchis latifolius* L. *Acta Soc. Bot. Polon.* 11: 511–539.

Sizova, T. P., and M. G. Vachrameeva. 1984. Some aspects of mycorrhiza in *Platanthera bifolia* Rich. and *Dactylorhiza fuchsii* Soó in connection with their age state. *Vestn. Moscow Univ.* 16, Biol. 2: 27–31 (in Russian).

Sjögren, U. 1963. Tva Dactylorchishybrider. *Bot. Notis.* 116: 102–104.

Smeidt, O. 1980. The transplantation of the *Dactylorhiza baltica*. :150. In *Abstr. Rep. Conf. Orchid Conserv. and Cultivation.* Publ. Acad. Sci. Est. SSR, Tallin (in Russian).

Smith, S. E. 1966. Physiology and ecology of orchid mycorrhizal fungi with reference to seedling nutrition. *New Phytol.* 65: 488–499.

———. 1967. Carbohydrate translocation in orchid mycorrhizal fungi. *New Phytol.* 66: 371–378.

———. 1973. Asymbiotic germination of Orchid seeds on carbohydrates of fungal origin. *New Phytol.* 72: 497–499.

Soó, R. 1928. A new Himalayan Orchid. *J. Bot.* 66: 15–17.

———. 1967. Die *Dactylorhiza*-Arten und- Formen in der Flora Rumaniensis. *Rev. Roumaine Biol. Bot.* 12: 225–231.

Stelfox, A. W. 1924. The white form of *Orchis fuchsii* and *Orchis O'kellyi*. *Irish Naturalist* 33: 143–144.

Stephenson, R., and T. A. Stephenson. 1921a. *Orchis latifolia* in Britain. *J. Bot.* 59: 1–7.

———. 1921b. The forms of *Orchis maculata*. *J. Bot.* 59: 121–128.

———. 1923a. *Orchis praetermissa* Druce. *J. Bot.* 61: 65–68.

———. 1923b. The British form of *Orchis incarnata*. *J. Bot.* 61: 273–278.

———. 1923c. *Orchis fuchsii* Druce. *J. Bot.* 61: 306–309.

———. 1925. Some French March Orchids. *J. Bot.* 63: 93–97.

Stephenson, T. 1928. Les Dactylorchidees en France et en Grande-Bretagne. *Bull. Soc. Bot. Fr.* 75: 481–495.

———. 1931. Dactylorchids of North Africa. *J. Bot.* 69: 145–150, 177–180.

Stern, W. T. 1976. The nomenclature of Madeiran Orchids (*Orchis maderensis* or *Dactylorhiza foliosa*) and other Orchidaceae of Madeira. *Bol. Soc. Brot.* 49: 89–97.

Stewart, A. M. 1910. Concerning the fertilization of *Orchis maculata*. *Entomologist* 13: 106–107.

Strasburger, E. 1878. *Über Befruchtung und Zelltheilung.* Verlag Hermann Dabis, Jena.

———. 1884. *Neue Untersuchungen über den Befruchtungsvorgang bei den Phanerogamen als Grundlage für eine der Zengung.* Verlag Gustav Fischer, Jena.

Sundermann, H. 1981. *Dactylorhiza incarnata* ssp. *praetermissa* im östlichen Rheinland. *Orchidee* 32: 37–38.

Sundermann, H., and R. Wattke. 1973. Neue Beitrage zur Zytotaxonomie der Erdorchideen (*Dactylor-*

hiza, Orchis und *Serapias). Orchidee* 24: 116–118.

Suneson, S. 1951. Fynd av dikotomiskt förgrenad *Orchis maculata* i Sverige. *Bot. Notis.* 3: 274–277.

Talla, B. P. 1979. On the systematics of the genus *Dactylorhiza* (Neck.) Nevski. In *Flora and vegetation of the Latvian SSR.* Zinatne, Riga (in Russian).

Tennant, D. J. 1979. *Dactylorhiza traunsteineri* in Yorkshire. *Naturalist* 104: 9–13.

Tennant, D. J., and A. G. Kenneth. 1983. The scottish records of *Dactylorhiza traunsteineri* (Sauter)Soó. *Watsonia* 14: 415–417.

Terschuren, J., and P. Devillers. 1981. Quelques observations d'orchidées en Belgique. *Natur. Belg.* 62,11–12: 264–274.

Tichy, H. 1971. Zwischenbericht über die zytologischen Untersuchungen an *Dactylorhiza maculata* und *Dactylorhiza fuchsii. Mitt. Arbeitskr. Heim. Orch. Baden-Wurt.* 3: 28–40.

Tikhonova, M. N. 1983. About the nature of the underground organs of some representatives of the tribe Orchideae. *Bot. J.* 68: 648–652 (in Russian).

Tira, S. 1971. Monocotyledonae, Orchidaceae, Isoquercitrin from *Orchis sambucina. Phytochem.* 10: 1975–1976.

Tohda, H. 1971. Development of the embryo of *Orchis aristata. Sci. Rep. Tohoku Univ.* 4,35: 239–243.

Tolmaczov, A. I. 1973. Neue daten uber die Orchideen-verbreitung im aussersten norden eurasiens. *Acta Bot. Ac. Sci. Hung.* 19: 375–378.

Tournay, R. 1968. *Dactylorhiza maculata* (L.)Soó en Belgique. *Bull. Soc. Roy. Bot. Belg.* 101: 323–326.

Tyteca, D. 1981. Observations sur quelques *Dactylorhiza* de Belgique et du nord de la France. *Bull. Soc. Roy. Bot. Belg.* 114: 15–30.

_____ . 1986. Les orchidées des marais–2. *Reserv. Natur.* 1: 8–14.

Uphoff, W. 1979. Die Farbstoffe der gefleckten Blätter von *Orchis* und *Dactylorhiza. Die Orchidee* 30: 184–186.

Vachrameeva, M. G., and L. V. Denisova. 1980a. The dynamics of the number of coenopopulations of three species of orchids. *Vestn. Moscow Univ.* 16, *Biol.* 1: 58–62 (in Russian).

_____ . 1980b. The biology and dynamics of the number of coenopopulations of *Dactylorhiza fuchsii* Soó. :146. In *Abstr. Rep. Conf. Orchid. Conserv. and Cultivation.* Publ. Acad. Sci. Est. SSR, Tallin (in Russian).

Vaucher, C. 1966. Contribution a l'etude cytologique du genere *Dactylorhis* (Klinge)Vermeulen. *Bull. Soc. Neuchatel. Sci. Nat.* 89: 75–85.

Vermeulen, P. 1930. Komt *Orchis purpurella* (Stephenson) in Nederland voor? *Nederl. Kruidk. Arch.* 1930: 147–154.

_____ . 1968. *Dactylorchis maculata* und ihre Formen. *Jahresb. Naturw. Ver. Wuppertal* 21–22: 68–76.

_____ . 1970. Some critical remarks on the dactylorchids of Portugal. *Bol. Soc. Broter.* Ser. 2, 44: 85–98.

_____ . 1976a. Typification of *Orchis elata* Poiret. *Taxon* 25: 181–184.

_____ . 1976b. Was ist *Orchis latifolia* L.? *Acta Bot. Neerl.* 25: 371–379.

_____ . 1976c. Het geslacht Handekanskruid auf *Dactylorhiza. Orchideeën* 38: 189–192.

_____ . 1977. *Orchis latifolia* nomen rejicien dum propositum. *Taxon* 26:600.

_____ . 1978. *Dactylorhiza foliosa* (Vermeulen)Soó. *Orchideeën* 40: 29–30.

Vermoessen, P. 1911. Contribution a l'etude de l'ovule du sac embryonnaire et ia fécondation dans les angiosperm. (*Neottia ovata, O. latifolia, O. maculata, E. palustris, E. latifolia). Cellule* 27: 115–162.

Vöth, W. 1971. Knollenentwicklung und Vegetations-rhythmus von *Dactylorhiza romana* und *sambucina. Orchidee* 22: 254–256.

_____ . 1978. Biometrische Untersuchungen an *Dactylorhiza maculata* s.l. -Sippen in Niederösterreich (Orchidaceae). *Linzer Biol. Beitr.* 10: 179–215.

Vöth, W., and J. Greilhuber. 1980. Zur Karyosystematik von *Dactylorhiza maculata* s.l. und ihrer Verbreitung, Insbesondere in Neiderösterreich. *Linzer Biol. Beitr.* 12: 415–468.

Watt, L. 1909. Notes on *Orchis ericetorum* Linton and other flowering plants. *Glasgow Nat.* 1: 93–96.

Wattez, J. R. 1973. L'espéce collective *Dactylorchis incarnata* (L.)Vermeulen dans le nord la France. *Rev. Soc. Sav. Haute Normand.* 68: 37–53.

Webb, N. P. 1979. Marsh orchids on an unusual site in W. Lancs. *B.S.B.I. News* 23:26.

Weston, I. 1979. A variant of *Dactylorhiza fuchsii* (Druce)Soó in N. Lincs. *Watsonia* 12: 399–400.

Wiefelsputz, W. 1968. Uber *Dactylorhiza sphagnicola. Jahresb. Naturw. Ver. Wuppertal* 21–22: 86–95.

Wilmott, A. J. 1936. New British marsh orchids. *Proc. Linn. Soc. London.* 148: 126–130.

Wirth, W. 1975. Zur Nomenclatur von *Orchis/Dactylorhiza latifolia. Orchidee* 26: 263–270.

Zinsmeister, J. B. 1910. Eine bemerkenswerte Form des Bastardes *Orchis incarnatus × latifolius* F. Schulz: *Orchis Aschersonianus* Haussknecht. *Mitt. Bayer. Bot. Ges.* 2: 297–299.

Glossary

Agene cell. Any protodermal cell, adjacent to the guard cells and which remains in this position without dividing.

Agenous. Type of development where the stomatal meristemoid forms two guard-cells only. The stomatal complex at the end of the development is surrounded solely by agene cells. This term is applied in accordance with the origin of the cells and their position during development.

Aggregate. A group of closely related species which is named as the oldest specific epithet among species that form it. The term was introduced by Heywood in 1963.

Alloploid stabilization. Stabilization of hybrids by means of polyploidy as a result of which these hybrids between species with different genomes became capable of producing fertile seeds.

Allopolyploidy. A number of chromosomes equal to the total of both parents in hybridization between species which contain different chromosome numbers.

Alpine orogenesis. A series of orogenic events in Southern Europe and Asia during the Tertiary when the Alps were largely raised.

Aneupolyploidy. A somatic chromosome number which is not the same or even a multiple of the basic haploid number.

Anomocytic. A type of stomate in which subsidiary cells are not associated with the guard cells. The term is applied in accordance with purely morphological criteria.

Anther. The pollen-forming part of the stamen.

Anthropogenic. A factor produced by human activities.

Anticlinal. Perpendicular to the surface.

Apical meristem. A group of meristematic cells at the tip of a shoot from which all the tissues of the mature axis are ultimately formed.

Autopolyploidy. Formation a polyploid organism which has three or more sets of chromosomes, all of which come from the same species. This usually results from the doubling of chromosomes in a single individual.

Bilocular. Two-celled, or with two locules.

b.m. Bicrometer = 1/1000 of a mm, 1/1,000,000 of a m.

Bract. A modified, often much reduced leaf subtending a flower or inflorescence; morphologically a foliar organ.

Calciphilous. Plants growing on the soils containing lime; e.g. calcium carbonate, calcite, or magnesium carbonate.

Carpels. The ovule-bearing structure (megasporophyll) of a flower, regarded as a single, modified, seed-bearing leaf.

Caudicle. A slender, mealy, or elastic extension of the pollinium which is produced within the anther.

Chlorenchyma. Parenchyma cells that contains chloroplasts.

Chloroplasts. A cellular organelle in photosynthetic eukaryotes that contains chlorophyll; the site of photosynthesis.

Clavate. Club-shaped; gradually thickened toward the apex from a slender base.

Cryophilic. Cool loving, adapted to live in tundra or in polar regions.

Derivate. A divergent part of an entity; a daughter taxon evolved by divergence from its ancestral form.

Disjunct distribution. The occurence of one species in widely isolated geographical areas. Disjunction is the region between such isolated areas where the species does not occur.

Egg. A female gamete.

Ephemeroids. Perennial herbaceous plants in deserts with different underground storage organs (bulbs, tubers, etc.) which have a very short annual growth period.

Eutrophic. A body of water or marsh which is rich in organic and inorganic nutrients.

Exine. The outer wall layer of pollen grains.

Gene pool. The genetic constitution of a population.

Geophytic. Adapted to the terrestrial mode of life.

Geophytes. Plants with meristematic portions located below the soil surface, as on bulbs or rhizomes.

Hemimesogenous. Type of stomata development where one or more mesogene cells are formed by the meristemoid, incompletely surrounding the stomatal complex. The stomatal complex at the end of the development is surrounded by agene and mesogene cells. This term is applied in accordance with the origin of the cells and their position during development.

Hemimesoperigenous. Type of stomata development where both the mesogene and perigene cells are formed by the meristemoid, incompletely surrounding the stomatal complex. The stomatal complex at the end of the development is surrounded by agene, perigene and mesogene cells. This term is applied in accordance with the origin of the cells and their position during development.

Hemiperigenous. Type of stomata development when the perigene cells are formed by the meristemoid, incompletely surrounding the stomatal complex. The stomatal complex at the end of the development is surrounded by agene and perigene cells. This term is applied in accordance with to the origin of the cells and their position during development.

Hybridogenic. Originated by means of hybridization.

Hydrophilous. Water loving, growing in moist places.

Inferior ovary. An ovary that is situated below the point of insertion of the other floral organs.

Intercalary meristem. A localized meristematic region in an elongating internode; a meristem that lies between areas that are more or less mature (differentiated).

Introgressive hybridization. Genetic modification of one species by another though the intermediacy of hybrids.

Karyotype. The general appearance of the chromosome complement of an individual or a group of related individuals, with regard to their number, size, shape, etc.; usually based on observations of chromosomes in mitotic metaphase.

Lobes of stigma. Segments of lobed stigma, the portion of a carpel upon which pollen germinates.

Massula (pl. Massulae). See polyade.

Mesogene cell. Any cell derived by division of a stomatal meristemoid before it divides into the two guard cells.

Metacentric chromosome. A chromosome which has a centrally located centromere.

Middle Asia. A modern term (replacing the old name Turkistan) widely used in Soviet literature. It designates the North West regions of Central Asia which at present are within the limits of the USSR (Uzbek, Turkmen, Kazakh, Kirghiz and Tadzhik Socialist Soviet Republics).

Mucilaginous. Having the character of, or containing mucilage; being gelatinous, gummy or sticky.

Nom.invalid. Taxonomical abbreviation from Latin *"nomen invalidum,"* i.e. incorrect name.

Ontogenesis. The entire development of an organism from the zygote to maturity.

Operculum. A lid, or cap, covering the retinacula in dactylorchid flowers.

Paleogene. The span of time comprising Paleocene, Eocene and Oligocene. The Lower Tertiary. Also, corresponds to the division of rocks of respective age.

Palmate. Having lobes, veins or divisions radiating from a common point, as in palmately lobed, palmately veined or palmately compound.

Papilla (pl. Papillae). A soft, nipple-shaped protuberance, a type of trichome.

Parallel placentation. The arrangement and distribution of placentae and ovules within the ovary forming lines which are parallel to the axis of the ovary.

Parenchyma. Tissue composed of parenchymous cells.

Parenchyma cell. The most common cell type in plants; the cells are characteristically alive at maturity, usually thin-walled and exhibit a variety of sizes and shape. Functions include photosynthesis, storage, secretion, transport of water and food substances.

Parietal placentation. Placentation with ovules or placenta attached on the inner wall of the ovary.

Pectinaceus. Comblike; having closely parallel, narrow, toothlike projections.

Pedicel. The stalk of an individual flower in an inflorescence.

Periclinal. Parallel to the surface.

Perigene cell. Any daughter cell formed by one or more divisions in a protodermal cell adjacent to the guard-cells.

Philogenetic. Pertaining to the evolutionary history and relationships among a group of organisms.

Pleistocene. The epoch of the Quarternary following the Pliocene and preceeding the Holocene, also corresponds to the division of rocks of the respective age.

Pollinarium (pl. Pollinaria). The complete set of pollinia from an anther, with associated parts, retinaculum or retinacula and stipe (caudicle).

Pollinium (pl. Pollinia). A more or less compact and coherent mass of pollen (in dactylorchids consists of polyades).

Poltava flora. Term pertaining to the fossil flora which existed in the para- Tetis region about Eocene time. Made up mainly of tropical and subtropical plants.

Polyade. A packet of pollen in those genera in which the pollinium is subdivided into small packets usually connected by elastic threads.

Polytopic formation. Origin and development of a taxon in two or more separate areas.

Retinaculum (pl. Retinacula). A viscid part of the rostellum which is clearly defined and removed with the pollinia as a unit, and serving to attach the pollinia to an insect or other agent.

Rosette. A crowded, circular cluster of leaves or other organs; often in reference to a growth habit in which leaves radiate from a crown, close to the ground.

Rostellum. The tissue which separates the anther from the fertile stigma; a modified portion of stigma.

Saccate. Sacklike, deeply concave.

Sclerenchyma. A tissue composed of sclerenchyma cells, including fibers, fiber-sclereids and sclereids; functions include support and sometimes protection.

Series. A taxonomic rank usually comprising a group of closely related allopatric species.

Sessile. Without a stalk; sitting directly on its base.

s.l. Taxonomical abbreviation from Latin "*sensu lato*" i.g., in a wide sense. It means a taxon which includes taxa which sometimes are considered as independent.

s.str. Taxonomical abbreviation from Latin "*sensu stricto*" i.g., in a narrow sense. It means a taxon which includes only one taxon (including the nomenclatural type) and no other similar taxa.

Spur. A slender, tubular or sacklike projection from a flower part, usually a nectary, commonly formed by the base of the labellum.

Staminode. A sterile stamen which does not produce pollen; staminodes in orchids are variable in form.

Stenoendemic. Native or confined naturally to a particular and very restricted geographical area or region.

Sympatric. Originating in, or occupying the same geographical region; species or populations which occur close enough together to be within the range of mutual pollinating vectors.

Taxon (pl. Taxa). A taxonomic group of any rank.

Testa. The outer seed coat, which is derived from the outer integument of the ovule.

Thermophilic. Heat-loving.

Torulose excrescences. Minutely torose projections.

Trabecula (pl. Trabeculae). A rodlike part of a cell wall extending across the lumen; structure which partially or completely traverses an intercellular space.

Type section. Section which includes the type species of a genus.

Vascular bundle. A strand of vascular tissue composed of xylem, phloem and procambium.

Whorl. A circle of floral organs; e.g., stamens, petals, carpels.

Xerothermic maximum. Driest and hottest period.

Zygomorphous. Bilaterally symmetrical.

Zygomorphy. The condition of being bilaterally symmetrical.

6

Power and Passion: The Orchid in Literature*

MARTHA W. HOFFMAN LEWIS

*The literature review pertaining to this chapter was concluded in January 1987; the chapter was submitted in July 1987 and the revised version was received in October 1987.

Introduction

Orchids have been discussed extensively in scientific and horticultural literature, and their history and uses have been well documented (Reinikka, 1972; Lawler, 1984). Little has been written about their role in literature. Although Arditti (1979, 1980, 1984)[a] has collected references to orchids in science fiction, mystery and adventure stories, and Winspear (1986) has associated orchids with the "Decadent" movement of the 1890s, scholars have not discussed the role of the orchid in poetry or drama. This chapter presents a summary of the images which orchids have projected in the literature of Britain and the United States.

Before the twentieth century, orchids seldom appeared as symbols in literature. Until then orchids were thought of primarily as medicinal plants, especially aphrodisiacs (Lawler, 1984), and as such they were discussed principally in botanical, horticultural and medical literature. Except for a brief description of their use by prostitutes in the Roman novel *Satyricon* by Petronius (ca. 54–68 A.D.), orchids were not mentioned in Greek and Latin poetry, fiction or drama. Consequently they did not provide a model for floral symbolism in a literature which depended on Classical tradition.

Shakespeare did not include orchids among the flowers which he used as symbols. His reference to orchids in *Hamlet* is of interest largely because it suggests the common names given to orchids in 1602 (Ellacombe, 1884; Ames, 1948). Orchids, together with other common field flowers, made up the "fantastic garlands" gathered by the mad Ophelia before her tragic drowning. Shakespeare called them "long purples" or "dead men's fingers" and indicated that "liberal shepherds" gave them "a grosser name."

Because plant nomenclature was not scientific in Shakespeare's day, a precise identification of Ophelia's flowers is impossible. "Long purples," the name used by the Queen, refers not only to *Orchis mascula* (early Spring orchis) but also to *Lythrum salicaria* (loosestrife) and to other plants (*Oxford English Dictionary*, 1971). Both *Orchis* and loosestrife possess spikes of deep rose-purple or crimson flowers and grow near water. "Dead men's fingers" properly refers to *Orchis latifolia* or *Orchis maculata*, which have dark, hand-like tubers instead of a double root (*Oxford English Dictionary*, 1971). This name was used by chaste maidens, cold because they had not experienced hot passion. The statement that "long purples" possessed a vulgar common name supports the identification of "long purples" with a species of *Orchis*. In the herbals of the period common English names for *Orchis* and *Satyrion*, were "Stones" ("Dogs," "Fools," "Foxes," "Goats," "Hares," "Serapias," and "Sweet"), "Hares coddes," "Sweet cullions" and "Hares ballockes." In 1562 Turner (1568) called the latter name "unmanerly." An orchid described in 1597 by Gerard (1633), the Satyrion royall or Finger orchis, in Latin *Palma Christi*, seems to fit Shakespeare's description. This orchid had a spike of purple flowers, palmate roots and the same properties as dogstones (*Orchis mascula*).

"Dead men's fingers" became "Dead man's thumb" in an anonymous ballad of 1652 (*Roxburghe Ballads*, quoted by Ellacombe, 1884; Withner, 1959; *Oxford English Dictionary*, 1971), which described a love-sick maiden walking through the meadows picking "Dead Man's Thumb and Harebell blew." In this poem "Dead man's thumb" can be identified with *Orchis* because it grew near the harebell, the English hyacinth or squill, often called bluebell. These flowers were often found together in pastures and woodlands.

---

[a]In a popular rather than scholarly manner.—Ed.

The orchid appeared as a fertility charm on the tapestry known as "The Unicorn in Captivity" in the de la Rochefoucauld series, "The Hunt of the Unicorn," now in New York in The Cloisters of the Metropolitan Museum of Art. According to Medieval legend, the unicorn could be captured only by a virgin. Allegorical interpretation equated the unicorn with the risen Christ and the virgin with his mother, the Virgin Mary. By about 1500 when this French or Flemish tapestry was woven, probably as a wedding gift, the legend had been secularized so that the unicorn often represented a lover captured by his lady, in this case his bride (Freeman, 1976). Freeman called the orchis (probably *Orchis mascula*) "a potent aphrodisiac" and "*knabenkraut*" which "could ensure that a couple would have sons."

In this tapestry the unicorn rests in a circular, fenced enclosure under a pomegranate tree to which he is tethered. He resembles a small horse, but the cloven hoof, beard and spiralled horn suggest a goat. The orchis occupies a prominent position against his body beside the squill (Fig. 6-1). Although now it has become faded, dull purple/brown and indistinct in detail, when the tapestries were new, it must have gleamed crimson and immediately caught the eye. The flowers placed so near the unicorn have clearly been singled out from the background of a myriad of small flowers (Alexander and Woodward, 1941).

Orchids in Nineteenth Century England

The nineteenth century represented a period of intense interest in tropical orchids or exotics as they were commonly called. Exotic orchids were passionately collected and cultivated by aristocrats and landed gentry, and by mid-century orchid collecting rivaled horse racing, art collecting and shooting as a pastime of the rich.

Tropical orchids were very seldom mentioned in fiction before 1890, and then only in reference to the very rich. A rare instance in fiction is Bronte's (1971) description in *Jane Eyre* (1847) of a house party at which "vases of exotics bloomed on all sides" throughout the country house and "a large marble basin" which usually stood in the conservatory "surrounded by exotics" was brought into the drawing room.

In spite of the admiration of the rich, tropical orchids did not appeal to popular taste in flowers. Ruskin (1906), the foremost art critic of the century, spoke for many Victorians when he asserted that the native flowers of Europe, growing wild in fields and woodlands, were more beautiful than those cultivated in hothouses and formal gardens. For him such a flower was an expression of the beauty, symmetry, purity and perfection of God. The British naturalist Wallace (1969), in a book published in 1853 about his travels on the Amazon and Rio Negro, commented that although in the tropics one might find "grandeur and solemnity," spectacular flowers and an unusual diversity of species, the English landscape equalled in beauty and brilliant color the splendor of the tropics.

Consistent with the belief that the wild flowers of England were more beautiful than those of the tropics, nineteenth century literature included references to the native orchids. The sentimental flower books popular during the century included Orchis, "A Belle"; Bee Orchis, "Industry"; Butterfly Orchis, "Gaiety"; Fly Orchis, "Error"; Frog Ophrys, "Disgust"; Spider Ophrys, "Adroitneas"; as well as Lady's Slipper, "Capricious Beauty, Win me and Wear me" (Marsh, 1978; Lawler, 1984).[b] Although Keats and

[b]The extensive list of flowers in Marsh (1978) was compiled from lists in about 150 nineteenth century flower books.

Fig. 6-1–6-2. Orchids in literature. **1.** Detail of "The Unicorn in Captivity" Tapestry 7 of "The Hunt of the Unicorn", ca. 1500, showing the orchid and the squill or bluebell. The Metropolitan Museum of Art, The Cloisters Collection, Gift of John D. Rockefeller, Jr., 1937 (37.80.6). **2.** Detail of portrait of Joseph Chamberlain as Colonial Secretary, 1896. Portrait by Sargent. National Portrait Gallery, London.

Shelley preferred to write about the flowers of Greece, the Romantic poet Clare included orchids in the poems in which he extolled the beauties of the English countryside. In early poems written in 1821 (1935a, 1935b, 1935c, 1935e, 1935f), he called the early spring orchids cuckoos hiding their freckled pouch lips, hooked noses and spotted leaves in the woodlands. Later ("The Nightingale's Nest," 1835) he (1935d) used the name "orchis" to describe an orchid "blushing" in the woods as it listened to the "rich ecstasy" of the song which the nightingale poured forth in "luscious strain."

The Victorian poets, Tennyson (1899) in his "In Memoriam," (1850) and E. B. Browning (1900) in *Aurora Leigh* (1856), mentioned orchis. In "Stanzas Composed at Carnac" (1859) Arnold (1926b) described the old abandoned Druid stones, which were covered with gold broom, fragrant blue-bells, and "the orchis red [which] gleams everywhere." Arnold included orchis in two other poems in which he described the pastures near Oxford, "The Scholar Gipsy" and "Thyrsis." In 1853 he (1926a) wrote that the Scholar Gipsy, a student who had left Oxford two centuries before and had joined a band of gipsies who taught him their "mystery," had been seen near the Thames by maidens to whom he gave "purple orchises with spotted leaves," "dark blue-bells" and the "white anemone." In 1866 Arnold (1926c) asserted that the Scholar Gipsy still travelled the hillsides near the Thames on which once "far descried,/ High tower'd the spikes of purple orchises." By then the orchises were no longer there because they had been destroyed by "the ploughboy's team." In "The Burden of Itys," a poem written ca. 1878 during his student days, Wilde (1927) echoed Arnold's delight in the pastures near Oxford. In these idyllic fields "diadems/ Of brown bee-studded orchids . . . meant/ For Cytheraea's [Venus's] brows" hid in the reeds near the Thames while they listened to the song of the nightingale.

The orchis appeared in 1864 in *The Trial: More Links of the Daisy Chain,* one of the nearly 100 novels suitable for young minds written by Yonge (1865). In this novel Yonge compared the face of her heroine Ethel May to an orchis, which she thought resembled a grotesque, i.e., absurd and comical, "gurgoyle (*sic*) on the church tower." When Ethel vigorously contorted her face to amuse her younger brother, the boy commented that she looked like an "orchis blossom" and that he had "read of a woman with an orchidaceous face." Whereupon Ethel twisted her face even more and exclaimed, "I do pride myself on being of a high order of the grotesque."

Ruskin (1906) did not share Yonge's amusement at the bizarre shape of the orchis. He considered orchids sensual, disgusting, distorted, and imperfect. Their irregular and misshapen petals and form, so unlike the pure and perfect symmetry of the rose or poppy, suggested to him some kind of diabolical influence. He found their Greek name *orchis,* which, he thought, was "founded on some unclean or debasing association," so offensive that he proposed changing the name of the entire family to *Ophrydae,* Ophryds in English. This name, which Linnaeus had used for one group of orchids, seemed proper because it meant eyebrow in Greek "on account of their resemblance to the brow of an animal frowning, or to the overshadowing casque of a helmet."

Ruskin wrote about the Ophryds in *Proserpina* (1875–1886), a book in which he attempted to unite the offices of poet and painter and to present flowers as expressions of divine beauty. He was not a scientist; he rejected the sexuality of flowers, and he deplored the botanist's preoccupation with "obscene processes and prurient apparitions."

He divided the Ophryds into three groups: *Contorta, Satyrium* and *Aeria.* He chose the Latin name, *Contorta,* in English Wreathe-wort, because of the twisted stem of these flowers. The Classical name, *Satyrium*, seemed appropriate for a second group of Ophryds which exhibited "Satyric ugliness." He called the third group of Ophryds *Aeria* because it lived "actually in the air," supported but not nourished by "the ground, rock, or tree-trunk on which it is rooted." These Ophryds had "long been popularly known in English by the name of Air-plant."

Ruskin thought that the groups called *Contorta* and *Satyrium* represented a "special manifestation" of an evil or diabolical character. Although he admired the color of the wild "wreathe-worts" which in the spring carpeted English meadows and Alpine valleys with a rich, dark purple which contrasted with white and gold flowers, he especially disliked the group called *Satyrium*. In his opinion these Ophryds possessed "livid and unpleasant colours" and often lived in "torn and irregular ground, under alternations of unwholesome heat and shade, and among swarms of nasty insects." Not only were the stalks twisted, but one of their petals was twisted also and was extended out in the way in which "a foul jester would put out his tongue." In this group "the singular power of grotesque mimicry," which in most Ophryds seemed "playful," was "definitely degraded, and, in aspect, malicious." Ruskin thought that the lady's slipper resembled not a lady's slipper but "rather a goblin's with the gout!"

Although Ruskin conceded that aerial (i.e. epiphytic Ophryds sometimes had "gracefully fantastic forms," he considered this group very different from other plants which drew their "vital energy" from earth or water. He commented that this "tribe" had "long been noted for the resemblance of its flowers to different insects; and it has recently been proved by Mr. Darwin to be dependent on insects for its existence . . . in some cases this race of plants all but reaches the independent life of insects. It rather *settles* upon boughs than roots itself in them; half of its roots may wave in the air."

Orchids in England before World War II

The Orchid (Tanner et al., 1903), a musical comedy presented at the New Gaiety Theatre, reflected British interest in orchids. Although the play contained the combination of lovers, dance, song and burlesque characteristic of music hall productions, the central theme of the complicated plot concerned a missing orchid which Zaccary, a professional orchid hunter, had brought to Mr. Aubrey Chesterton, the Minister of Commerce, "a man of position and wealth." Zaccary sang a lyric about his pursuit of this "rare and splendid" orchid in "far Peru," where he had encountered hostile panthers, snakes, crocodiles, vampire bats, gorilla hordes[c] and bloodhounds. For weeks he had climbed "icy peaks" and even had been swallowed by a boa-constrictor. He had escaped from this monstrous snake by drawing his trowel and digging his way out.

When Zaccary met Mr. Chesterton to deliver the orchid, he discovered to his dismay that the box which had contained the orchid was empty. At this point Zaccary learned that Meakin, the gardner at the horticultural college, possessed an orchid which seemed exactly like his lost orchid. Zaccary bought this orchid from Meakin for five pounds and rushed off in triumph. In another scene Meakin told Caroline, a rich woman, whose affections he hoped to win, that his orchid was worth 800 pounds.

Mr. Chesterton, who wore an orchid buttonhole and monocle, bore a striking resemblance to the prominent statesman and cabinet minister from Birmingham, Joseph

[c]Gorillas are found only in Africa, suggesting that the songster was not well versed in apes and/or geography.—Ed.

Chamberlain[d] (1836–1914; *Play-Pictorial,* 1904a, 1904b). Chamberlain's enthusiasm for orchids was well known, and he was easily caricatured because he had made an orchid buttonhole and a monocle his hallmarks (Swinson, 1970; *Oxford English Dictionary,* 1971; Powell, 1977). Unlike other officials, Chamberlain wore an orchid at Parliament, at diplomatic meetings abroad and at university functions. Sargent painted him in 1896 when he was Colonial Secretary, formally attired in black with a prominent orchid buttonhole (Fig. 6-2).

Even though aristocrats and wealthy industrialists like Chamberlain admired the splendor of rare orchids, many people agreed with Ruskin that orchids seemed grotesque. The definition of "orchid" published in 1903 in the *Oxford English Dictionary* (1971) reflects both attitudes. Orchids were defined both as exotic flowers "now cultivated for their beauty" and as flowers which were "often remarkable for brilliancy of color or grotesqueness of form."

The adjectives "orchidaceous" and "exotic," i.e. "showy" and "foreign," characterized behavior which seemed flamboyant and immoral. During the nineteenth century most Britons disliked foreigners and especially despised the French as depraved and disgusting (Hynes, 1968). Le Gallienne (1894), a friend of Wilde who was flamboyant himself, used the adjective "orchidaceous" when he lamented the disappearance of the whole man and "the simple, old type of manhood . . . lost long since in endless orchidaceous variation."

In 1891 in "The Soul of Man under Socialism" Wilde (1982b) protested the practice of using the adjective "exotic" as a term of abuse. In so doing, he wrote, the public was exhibiting "the rage of the momentary mushroom against the immortal, entrancing, and exquisitely lovely orchid." Yet, although Wilde objected to this use of "exotic," he himself seems to have used "orchid" as a term of derision. In 1895 on the opening night of "The Importance of Being Earnest," he called the artist Beardsley "'the most monstrous of orchids'" (Wyndham, 1963). At this moment of triumph, he took the opportunity to ridicule Beardsley's dandyism and grotesque eccentricities.

During the last decade of the nineteenth century orchids were associated with Wilde (Brooke, 1950, 1981a, 1981b, 1981c; Winspear, 1986), who was called "The High Priest of the Décadents" (Thornton, 1980), and with homosexuality. Wilde's novel, *The Picture of Dorian Gray* (published in 1890/1891), was among those artistic works which the public considered orchidaceous and exotic. The *Daily Chronicle* called it "a tale spawned from the leprous literature of the French Décadents—a poisonous book, the atmosphere of which is heavy with the mephitic odours of moral and spiritual putrefaction" (quoted by Hart-Davis, 1962).

The *Picture of Dorian Gray* (1982a) contains frequent references to orchids. The young hero Dorian often bought orchids to decorate his London house and possessed a conservatory with orchids at his country estate. In an important scene in the novel Dorian was in this conservatory choosing orchids for one of his guests, the Duchess of Monmouth, to wear at dinner. His mentor in his pursuit of sensual pleasures, Lord Henry Wotton, whose wife complained that she could not afford orchids, described an orchid from Dorian's conservatory which he had chosen for his buttonhole as "a marvellous spotted thing, as effective as the seven deadly sins." Unfortunately, he thought, like other "lovely" things it had a "dreadful" name, something like *"Robinsoniana."* In the bantering conversation which followed this remark Lord Henry

[d]Chamberlain's eldest son Austen (1863–1937) was a cabinet minister and co-winner of the Nobel peace prize in 1925. His son Neville (1869–1940) was prime minister from 1937 to 1940.

suggested that in England beauty, as expressed in the orchid, was a sin. "Ugliness [was] one of the seven deadly virtues." Elsewhere in the novel Wilde called the metaphors used in a sensuous novel which became, so to speak, Dorian's Bible "as monstrous as orchids, and as subtle in color." This novel was based in part on Huysmans's novel *À rebours*. Huysmans's hero, the decadent aristocrat des Esseintes, who found true beauty in decline and decay, seemed to the Victorian public a model for Wilde himself.

Although the public identified Wilde with Lord Henry (Wilde, 1962c) and the orchid with homosexuality, Wilde himself seems not to have worn orchids. He and his aesthetic friends admired sunflowers and lilies in their student days at Oxford (Hyde, 1976). Later he wore the green carnation, a flower which distinguished homosexuals in Paris (Wyndham, 1963; Hyde, 1976; see also Wilde, 1962d).

Although Wilde and his young Oxford friends preferred flowers which had a Classical tradition like roses, lilies, hyacinths and narcissi (Wilde, 1962a, 1962b, 1962e), they occasionally wrote about orchids. A sonnet, "Heartsease and Orchid" by Percy Osborn (1893), published in *The Spirit Lamp,* an Oxford student magazine edited by Wilde's friend Lord Alfred Douglas, third son of the Marquis of Queensberry, confirms the orchid's association with homosexuality. In the poem, which is suggestive of Greek homoerotic lyrics, the orchid was contrasted with the simple garden flower, the heartsease (the pansy or cultivated violet). The "strange and rare" orchid, given by one "with a far-off look," ensnared the senses and caused the recipient to forsake "sunlight for the furnace."

"The Flowering of the Strange Orchid" (1894), a short story by Wells (1924) which reflects the influence of Wilde, provides a subtle illustration of Victorian hypocrisy regarding sex. In this story Wells gently ridiculed orchid collectors and their fantasies. Winter-Wedderburn, the hero of the tale, represented the timid bachelor collector who substituted passion for an orchid for love for a woman. The strange, gold and white orchid, which perhaps had killed its collector in the jungle, represented a beautiful, passionate woman who was attempting to seduce the bachelor. Such an orchid indeed seemed terrifying to a bachelor who was afraid of women.

Wells' story first poked sly fun at orchid collectors who were motivated by pride, love of beauty, desire for profit and the gaining of a trivial sort of immortality from the naming of a fragile flower. One might, he wrote, name it "'Johnsmithia.'" After recounting the circumstances under which the collector, Winter-Wedderburn, had acquired the orchid, he described the encounter with the plant when it finally came to blossom. When Winter-Wedderburn entered the greenhouse to see his "new darling," he became aware of a "rich, intensely sweet scent." He stopped before the "three great splashes of blossom . . . in an ecstasy of admiration. The flowers were white, with streaks of golden orange upon the petals; the heavy labellum was coiled into an intricate projection, and a wonderful bluish purple mingled there with the gold." The blossoms emitted a heavy perfume which caused him to faint, but he was saved by his female cousin-housekeeper, who found him with the tentacles of the orchid wrapped around his chin, neck and hands. Fortunately she arrived in time, and although he had lost a lot of blood, he survived. The original collector of the orchid had not been so fortunate and had died in the jungle under a mangrove tree, drained of his blood.

"The Purple Terror," a short story by White in *The Strand Magazine* (1899), presented a more complete illustration of the dangers attendant in the search for rare and deadly orchids. In this adventure story White characterized orchids as repulsive, blood-thirsty plants which lured collectors to their deaths. White described the orchids, which Cuban natives called "the devil's poppies," as enormous, deep purple blossoms with blood-red center. Like demons they seemed to wear an expression of "ferocity and cunning" on their cruel faces. They exuded "a queer, sickly fragrance . . . the perfume of a corpse."

Will Scarlett, the young American hero of the tale, who was leading a naval mission across the Cuban jungle, first saw the orchids in a wine house deep in the jungle. They had been fashioned into a wreath, "a trembling zone of purple flame," which a native dancer wore around her bare shoulders. Scarlett gazed at them eagerly because as a skilled botanist he longed "to present . . . to the horticultural world" a species which was "unknown to collectors anywhere." When the dancer extended a shell to him asking for a gift, he looked deep into her "dark liquid" eyes and asked where he might find the rare flowers (Fig. 6-3). Like most sailors who had been at sea for a month, Scarlett really was interested not in orchid collecting but in the "coquettish gleam" in the girl's "velvety" eyes. Her jealous lover recognized Scarlett's emotion and readily agreed to take him to the orchids.

Scarlett found the orchids growing like parasites on huge forest trees which formed a circle on a small plateau high in the mountains overlooking the jungle. Underneath the trees, bones of animals and men were piled in a perfect circle. As Scarlett and his men soon learned, the tendrils of the orchids, which by day were drawn up into the trees like spider webs, dropped down at night, caught unsuspecting animals, birds, and men in their snake-like embrace, killed them with their spines and flung them to the ground. The story ended happily when Scarlett and his men escaped the deadly orchids and brought the treacherous Cuban to justice. The only casualty was the ship's fierce mastiff.

Fig. 6-3. "The girl came forward extending a shell prettily." Reprinted from "The Purple Terror", 1899, *The Strand Magazine,* Vol. 18, p. 244, by F. M. White. Courtesy of the Newberry Library, Chicago.

Although White's story was primarily the tale of an encounter with a deadly jungle orchid, it contained unmistakable sexual innuendos. The dancer who wore orchids represented an enchantress who attempted to entice her victim into her lair and then destroy him.

The symbolism of the seductive woman who wore orchids seldom found expression in British literature. Shaw (1897) indicated the reason for the omission. To describe a woman as orchidaceous was to suggest that she behaved like a courtesan. In a review of a current play, "The Daughters of Babylon," by the actor, Wilson Barrett, Shaw called the behavior of the whore or daughter of Babylon "orchidaceous and flamboyant." He euphemistically named this courtesan, "the Improper Person of Babylon," in imitation of a euphemistic phrase used by Corelli, the popular writer on Biblical themes.

Shaw devoted much of his review to a discussion of Barrett's deficiencies as a playwright and criticism of the way in which he handled Scriptural language. Although he admired Barrett as actor and stage manager, he objected to his usurping the role of playwright. He suggested that Barrett would propose in his defense that in Corelli's "expert opinion," he possessed "power and passion, orchidacity and flamboyancy." Shaw showed clearly what such words meant when he criticized the actress who played the role of the courtesan: "Miss Lily Hanbury, specially engaged to be orchidaceous and flamboyant as the Improper Person of Babylon, and wholly guiltless of the least aptitude for the part, honestly gives as much physical energy to the delivery of the lines as she can, and is very like a pet lamb pretending to be a lioness." He and the rest of the audience lost all sympathy for the hero of the play when he failed to succumb to Miss Hanbury's charms and "baked in the fiery furnace." Hanbury was, of course, ill-suited for the role of the courtesan. In 1892 she had successfully played the original role of the pure and innocent Lady Windemere in *Lady Windemere's Fan,* a play which Wilde originally named *A Good Woman* (Hyde, 1982).

Bennett (1918) repeated Shaw's association of the courtesan with orchids. In *The Pretty Lady* he even invented a verb, *orchidise,* to indicate her passionate nature. The protagonist of this novel, a wealthy British aesthete, planned to set up an exiled French courtesan, the pretty lady, as his mistress in a flat. There in an environment "of taste and moderate luxury, she would be exquisite." She would live only for him and "would dream amid cushions like a cat. In the right environment she would become another being, that was to say, the same being, but orchidised."

In *The Laughter of the Gods* by the Anglo-Irish playwright Lord Dunsany (1917), rich crimson orchids symbolized the beauty and splendor surrounding a faithless city which was destined for destruction. In this play which took place at "About the time of the decadence in Babylon," the small city Thek suggested Babylon, the prosperous city which according to the Bible (Revelation 18) was destined to sink because of its sin like a millstone cast into the depths of the sea. Its kings had stolen the gold and silver vessels from the temple in Jerusalem and had failed to give glory to God.

In Dunsany's play the jungle surrounding Thek lay like a sea, purple with splendid orchids. "The orchids," said the courtiers, "that blaze on it are like Tyrian ships, all rich with purple of that wonderful fish. . . . They are like faint, beautiful songs of an unseen singer . . . temptation to some unknown sin." "They are like the diadem of some jubilant king." King Karnos, who had come to Thek because of the orchids, admired their beauty from dawn to sunset from his marble palace which reflected their "wonder" and "glory." At sunset the immortal flowers seemed to him "like a picture done by a dying painter, full of a beautiful colour."

Although the King and the courtiers were contented in Thek, the frivolous wives of the courtiers longed for the large, decadent city of Barbul-el-Sharnak, which they had left. They persuaded their husbands to attempt to trick the King into leaving Thek. The husbands, who thought that the gods no longer existed, blackmailed the Prophet, Voice-of-the-Gods, into making a false prophecy that the city would be destroyed in three days. Although he obeyed the courtiers, the prophet wept because he had betrayed the gods and had forced them to lie. He prophesied that the gods would not let this wicked deed go unpunished.

Like the courtiers, the King did not believe the prophecy. He boasted that although he himself would die some day, his city and his dynasty would endure forever. For just as long as they had "flashed their purple on the gleaming walls of Thek," so long would the orchids continue to "flash there on our immortal palace." Such arrogance did not go unpunished. At the end of the play, the doom which the prophet foretold came true. The gods who could not lie exacted vengeance on the faithless city and its king. On the third day as the sun finally set over the orchids, the jungle sank, and the city fell in ruin amid the laughter of the gods.

The ancient world described in *The Laughter of the Gods* resembled in many ways the world in which Dunsany lived. Both had lost much of their religious faith, and both had substituted material values in its place. For Dunsany, a peer of the realm, whose chief enthusiasms in addition to orchids and writing, seem to have been shooting and chess (Amory, 1972; see Dunsany, 1928), orchids symbolized the rich beauty of both worlds.

Dunsany's plays enjoyed more success in the American little theater than they did in either England or Ireland. Although *The Laughter of the Gods* was a favorite of the author, it seems not to have been performed professionally in Britain. It was, however, presented in New York and Baltimore in 1919 (Amory, 1972). This play seems to have been the Dunsany play which Lewis (1961) described in *Main Street* (1920).

During the decades following World War I, British literature continued to reflect the association of orchids with the rich and with decadence. In 1931 in "Green Thoughts" Collier (1941) retold Wells's story. Huxley (1965) in *Point Counter Point* (1928) and Maugham (1946) in *The Razor's Edge* (1944) used images of the jungle and the intrepid collector in pursuit of rare orchids to characterize the predatory nature of high society. Firbank (1949) frequently mentioned orchids in his novels about high society. In *Prancing Nigger* (1924) he even named an orchid after himself, "a dingy lilac blossom of rarity untold." Waugh (1946) in *Brideshead Revisited* described a second Lord Alfred and Wilde in Lord Sebastian Flyte and his Oxford friend Charles Ryder, who picked orchids for their buttonholes during the long, luxurious Arcadian summer of 1923 at Brideshead. In *Lady Chatterley's Lover* by Lawrence (1959) the dandy Michaelis brought lovely mauve orchids to Lady Chatterley, with whom he once had an affair. Orchids symbolized the sex which was denied Connie by her impotent husband. He thought the fine intellectual relationship of their marriage was a "real flower," but Connie knew it was an orchid, "parasitic on her tree of life" which produced "a rather shabby flower."

French and German Orchids: 1884–1921

Although attitudes towards orchids in France and Germany were similar to those in England, orchid imagery in French and German literature seems far more vivid than that found in British literature. British authors emphasized the jungle and the perils of collecting and merely suggested the sensuality of the orchid. In France, Proust stated explicitly that orchids symbolized sex and used them as symbols of courtesans and homosexuals. In Germany orchids symbolized the power of Woman to seduce and destroy her victim. German orchids also differed from British orchids because at times they appeared in dreams and grotesque phantasmagoria and seemed capable of evoking dark jungle passions and hidden impulses. The British seem to have had little interest in dreams and the dark, sexual impulses of the unconscious.

The orchids described in *À rebours* by the French novelist Huysmans (1884, translated in 1966 by Baldick) seem especially grotesque and repulsive. A *Cypripedium* and a

Cattleya were among the bizarre flowers which the hero of the novel, the Decadent Aesthete des Esseintes, purchased to relieve his boredom (*ennui*). In contrast to the artificials flowers which looked real in his previous collections, the real flowers in this new collection looked artificial.[e] They suggested the ravages of diseases like leprosy or syphilis or the multilations of amputations or flesh wounds. Des Esseintes was especially fascinated by a dark red *Cypripedium* from India, which looked as if it had been designed by a "demented draughtsman." Its lower petal, which dripped a viscous paste, resembled a clog or tidy above which the back of a human tongue had been stretched tight like tongues pictured in medical books on diseases of the throat and mouth. Two little wings of a "jujube red" like a child's toy windmill completed the picture. The *Cattleya* in his collection had a dream-like mauve color, which seemed out of place, and a disagreeable smell, like varnish, which reminded him of an unpleasant childhood memory.

Des Esseintes contemplated evolution as he looked at his collection and reflected that it had permitted Nature to create animal-like monstrosities with "vivid tints of . . . rotting flesh . . . and hideous splendors of . . . gangrened skin." Nature with the help of man had handed down through the ages the gift of syphilis. He believed that horticulturists who bred monstrous plants were the only true artists living.

In Paris, just as in London, orchids appeared in music halls. Loie Fuller's skirt or serpentine dance, which opened at the Folies Bergère in 1892, was said to resemble an orchid. This dance, which she originated in the United States, depended on the use of many floating scarves illuminated by multiple electric lights (de Morinni, 1948). In 1927 Isadora Duncan (1955) described the magic of Fuller's dancing as it appeared to her in Berlin in 1902. "Before our very eyes she turned to many coloured, shining orchids, to a wavering, flowing sea flower, and at length to a spiral-like lily, all the magic of Merlin, the sorcery of light, color, flowing form." Others described the dance as a kaleidoscope of colors and shapes. To one viewer, as she burst from the darkness, she resembled the dawn: first mauve and then lilac (Jullian, 1969, translated in 1971 by Baldick).

Fuller herself (1913) claimed that her dance resembled an orchid. She wrote in her autobiography that she had originated the dance in an obscure theater "in a small city of which the average New Yorker had hardly heard." As she moved across the stage in her flowing skirt, a cry rang out from the audience, "It's a butterfly." A second cry followed, "It's an orchid." Later in her New York debut the audience gave her an ovation: "Three cheers for the butterfly—three cheers for the orchid, the cloud, the butterfly."

Although Fuller's story seems apocryphal, it is clear that by 1913 her dance suggested an incarnation of the orchid to many people. Her performance at the Folies Bergère made her the rage of Paris, and in 1900 she had her own theater at the Paris Exposition. At first popular mostly with music hall audiences, she was later taken up by high society. She was a lesbian, who traveled with a troupe of young dancers, one of whom was named Orchidée and called a "child of nature" (de Morinni, 1948).

Perhaps the best known example in literature of a woman who resembled an orchid is Proust's courtesan Odette de Crécy, whom in *Du côté de chez Swann* (1913, translated as *Swann's Way* in 1982 by Moncrieff and Kilmartin), he called the "elegant . . . sister" of the cattleya. Odette was so closely associated with orchids that Jullian (1969, translated in 1971 by Baldick) even asserted in his study of Symbolist painters that the orchid "only entered literature thanks to Odette."

---

[e]I have heard more than once the comment that some orchids are unusual enough to be artificial.—Ed

Odette considered cattleyas, along with chrysanthemums, her favorite flowers because they looked artificial as if they had been made "of silk or satin." Although at first she pretended to be "blushing at the indecency" of a "fleshy cluster of orchids," she thought that orchids seemed "chic," "delicate" and "refined." On the evening when she and Swann, the wealthy aesthete, first agreed to become lovers, Odette was covered with cattleyas. She held a bunch in her hands; more were fastened to a swansdown plume which was covered by the lace which she wore on her head. A few more were fastened to her bodice; these came loose and as Swann helped her rearrange them, he asked to smell them to see if they were still fresh. He had never smelled cattleyas before. Later when the couple became lovers, to "do a cattleya" became synonymous with "to make love."

Proust's novel confirms the association of orchids with homosexuality. In *Sodome et Gomorrhe* (1921a, translated as *Cities of the Plain* in 1982 by Moncrieff and Kilmartin) he compared a homosexual encounter of the debauched aesthete, the Baron de Charlus, and the tailor, Jupien, to the appearance of a bumblebee which might possibly fertilize a precious and flirtatious orchid. Unfortunately because of his interest in watching the encounter, the Narrator of the incident never learned whether the bee actually succeeded in reaching the orchid.

The orchid which Proust compared to Jupien belonged to one of the few genera which produce separate male and female flowers. In spite of the fact that this orchid had "a hideous name and a horrid smell," its owner, the Duchesse de Guermantes, was "very fond" of its "charming" flowers with "their little purple velvet collars." Yet, she was afraid that this "lady" plant could "still qualify for the white flower of maidenhood" and would die as sterile as it had lived. Although she placed the orchid at an open window as often as possible and on the occasion of the meeting of Jupien and Charlus had set it in the courtyard, she did not really expect an insect bearing the proper pollen to appear and provide the services of a marriage "by proxy" (*Le côté de Guermantes 2* 1921b, translated as *The Guermantes Way* in 1982 by Moncrieff and Kilmartin).

In a lengthy discussion of homosexuality, Proust (1921a) reinforced the orchid metaphor by calling a solitary homosexual an orchid or sterile jellyfish cast up on the beach. Although such a creature might seem disgusting at first glance, "from the standpoint of natural history and aesthetics," it resembled "an exquisite blue girandole." "Are they not," Proust wrote, "with the transparent velvet of their petals, as it were the mauve orchids of the sea?"

In 1895 in his play *Erdgeist* (translated as *EarthSpirit* in 1923 by Eliot) Wedekind presented Lulu, the earth spirit of all women. Wedekind characterized this sensuous and promiscuous woman who wore orchids as the snake who was created to use her seductive charms to cause evil and death. The orchid symbolized her sexual being. She wore orchids in her hair and at the bodice of her low-cut, elegant Parisian ball gown in the final scene of *Erdgeist* in which she shot her third husband and patron, who had attacked her in a fit of jealousy. A large bouquet of "wonderful" flowers also stood on a table nearby. The attention of the audience was directed towards the bouquet when Lulu explained that the Countess Geschwitz had sent them. In response to a question about her appearance, her father, an old beggar, asked what kind of flowers she was wearing. As Lulu bent seductively, she replied, "Orchids; smell."

Although *Erdgeist* was presented in North Germany in 1897/1898 by a traveling company and had great success in Berlin in 1902/1903 under the direction of the Austrian Max Reinhardt, its sequel *Die Büchse der Pandora* (1902, translated as *Pandora's Box* in 1923 by Eliot) seemed the height of immorality. Its translation was banned in both English and

French (Eliot, 1923). In this play Lulu died as a common prostitute in London at the hands of Jack the Ripper.

In 1936 the Vienese composer, Berg (1964) based his opera *Lulu* on both of Wedekind's plays. In 1979 the complete opera was performed for the first time in Paris with Teresa Stratas in the title role. Because Lulu wore orchids in the opera, the impresario of the Paris Opera sent Stratas clusters of orchids after the performance (Sargeant, 1981).

In Prague and South Germany, orchids were characterized as grotesque and sensual creatures which inhabited a fantastic jungle world. The word "grotesque" originally referred to a Classical art style in which representations of human, animal and plant forms were distorted and interwoven in a strange and unnatural way (*Oxford English Dictionary,* 1971). The fantastic or dream world created by a grotesque sometimes was viewed as gay and amusing; at other times it seemed sinister and threatening and included an element of the demonic or Satanic (Kayser, 1957, translated in 1981 by Weisstein). Orchids, both European and tropical, readily could be called grotesque because they resembled animals, especially birds, insects and jungle snakes. Kayser considered especially grotesque "The inextricable tangle of the jungle with its ominous vitality, in which nature itself seems to have erased the difference between plants and animals."

In *Der Träumer,* a poem written ca. 1895 during his student days at Prague, Rilke (1955) compared dreams to orchids. Both dreams and orchids, he thought, were colorful and rich; out of the giant stem they drew their powers from the saps of life, gloried in the sucked up blood, rejoiced in the fleeting moment and in the next were pale and dead. For Rilke the dreamer, dreams seemed real, at times more real than the physical world in which he lived (Simenauer, 1980).

In 1905 Meyrink (Meyer) of Prague gave the name, *Orchideen: Sonderbare Geschichten* (*Orchids: Strange Stories*), to his collection of unusual and bizarre tales. These stories dealt with alchemy, witchcraft, Eastern magic and fantasy, weird dreams, murder, astronomical signs and similar wonders. The German Meyrink was fascinated by Medieval occult lore and Christian, Jewish and Oriental mystery cults (Brod, 1960).

In one grotesque "orchid" tale, *Bologneser Tränen* ("Bolognese Tears"), he (1905) characterized the orchid as a devil in disguise serving an Orchid Queen, a witch with red hair, the color of dead copper, skin with a greenish glow and hard cold eyes like those of a snake. This story related the fate of Tonio whom the Orchid Queen, Mercedes, charmed and led to destruction. In this biting satire, Meyrink demonstrated the triumph of evil in a seemingly beautiful world. Rich sensuous orchids, with which he was obviously very familiar, symbolized the deluding presence of the devil under the guise of fantastic beauty. Bolognese tears were worthless bits of spun glass which resembled women's hair, so called because they shone like the phosphorescent Bolognian stone of the alchemists. When kissed by a witch and given to her lover, they ensured not only his destruction but also, if brought into Church at a High Mass, that of the Host.

In the scene in which Tonio met Mercedes, the beautiful Creole, Mercedes sat on the veranda of the Orchid Club overlooking a dreamy lake. Faint sounds of Spanish songs drifted from the distance as a Negro servant brought her a Jasper dish containing the Bolognese Tears which she kissed and gave to a lover lying at her feet. From the ceiling garlands of splendid orchids dropped in cascades. There was *Cattleya aurea,* the Queen of immortal flowers, *Odontoglossum* and *Dendrobium* on rotted wood, and shimmering white laelias. Entangled in a mass of foliage, deep blue lycastes with their narcotic-like stupefying perfume seemed engorged with blood. Mercedes seemed half-covered by violet vandas. A fantastic black and purple speckled tongue-like flower, a Burmese *Bulbophyllum,* caught in her hair as if to whisper strange sins. The scene evoked an image of a tale from the Arabian Nights about a Sultana, who turned into an owl and flew out of the palace at full moon to eat the flesh of the dead from the graves. When a gigantic, fearful orchid with the face of a demon sprang forward from the leaves and bent on its stem towards Mercedes' hands as if laughing wickedly, the narrator of the tale realized:

> Orchids are not flowers [at all]—they are Satanic creatures—Beings who only show us the antennae of their form [and] counterfeit for us eyes, lips, tongues in a sense-deluding whirlwind of colors so that we should not suspect the dreadful viper's body which—invisible—death bringing, conceals itself in the riches of the shadows.

> (*Orchideen sind keine Blumen,—sind satanische Geschöpfe,—Wesen, die nur die Fühlhörner ihrer Gestalt uns zeigen, uns Augen, Lippen, Zungen in sinn-betörenden Farbenwirbeln vortäuschen, dass wir den scheusslichen Vipernleib nicht ahnen sollen, der sich—unsichtbar—todbringend verbirgt im Reiche der Schatten.*)

Between 1919 and 1921 a literary magazine called *Der Orchideengarten: Phantastische Blätter* (*The Orchid Garden: Fantastic Pages*) appeared in South Germany. It contained the work of a group of German authors dedicated to presenting the grotesque (Kayser, 1957, translated in 1981 by Weisstein). Art, poetry, notes and short fiction within its pages resembled Meyrink's fantastic orchids. A typical issue (1, 11: 1919) consisted of accounts of weird or supernatural events, Medieval and Eastern lore, stories about corpses, spirits and visions, poems about death and grotesque and macabre illustrations. These illustrations included not only contemporary art but also a woodcut by Weiditz (ca. 1532) and a sketch by Callot (early 17th century).

The covers of these magazines display fantastic scenes in which orchids often appear (Fig. 6–4, 6–5). Surrounding these orchids or bursting from their centers are grotesque figures of little men and women, corpses, skeletons, wizards, demons and weird animals like toads, snails, spiders, salamanders and black cats.

Perhaps the most intriguing cover is an illustration of the devil as alchemist (2, 17: 1920). The black clad figure stands before a wood fire over which has been placed a flask or retort containing a writhing, naked hermaphrodite. The alchemist holds up a beaker from which rises a black flower surrounded by a white halo and a black ring. Behind the blossom which he has distilled from the person in the flask, there is a golden cloud. The figure in the flask represents the substance which the alchemists called Hermes or Mercurius, the philosopher's stone or elixir of life. When properly "killed," i.e. fired and distilled, this substance was thought to produce the perfection of pure gold or symbolically the perfection of the human soul. Alchemists often called the powdered distillate, golden flower of air (*flos aeris aureus;* Jung, 1944, translated in 1953 by Hull). In contrast to the pure gold which had absorbed the rays of the divine sun, the diabolical orchid on the cover had developed from the fires of Hell.

One of the stories in the magazine, "*Orchideen*" ("Orchids") by Otto te Kloot (1919), illustrates clearly the sensuous and grotesque character of German orchid symbolism. In this tale sinister, carnivorous orchids grew in the primeval forest on the banks of a slimy lake. These poisonous plants had spurs like the Rider of Death and trailing plumes. They swayed sensuously in the death-hot night like the flames of a wood fire. Insects and

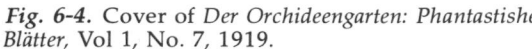

Fig. 6-4. Cover of *Der Orchideengarten: Phantastishe Blätter*, Vol 1, No. 7, 1919.

Fig. 6-5. Cover of *Der Orchideengarten: Phantastishe Blätter*, Vol 2, No. 17, 1920.

hummingbirds attracted by the heavy perfume and the fantastic colors drank from their hanging lips. By day their brilliant colors sparkled in the fiery sunshine. The blood-thirsty blooms, which resembled seductive women, had sharp teeth, claws like a panther's, and stripes of color like a tiger's. They greedily devoured both a fisherman and a seductive woman whose jet black bodies reflected the dazzling colors.

Orchids in the United States: The Nineteenth Century

During the nineteenth century, American writers occasionally mentioned the wild orchids which blossomed in their native fields and woodlands. Osgood (1841) listed *Orchis*, "A Belle"; Spider *Orphrys* (sic), "Skill," and Lady's Slipper, "Win Me and Wear Me," in her sentimental flower book. The New England poets Bryant (1969–1972) in "The Death of the Flowers" (1825) and Emerson (1904) in "Woodnotes" (1848) referred to orchis. In poems written between 1858 and 1862 Dickinson (1955a, 1955b, 1955c) rejoiced in the return of spring when "The orchis binds her feather on/ For her old lover, Don the Sun,/ Revisiting the bog!"

Thoreau (1949) included orchids among the wild flowers which he described in his *Journal*, which was not published in its entirety until 1906. To him the flowers which he saw every spring and summer in his rambles through pastures and woodlands near

Concord revealed the divine essence of Nature. "Do I not," he wrote, "live in a garden,—in paradise?"

Between 1850 and 1860 Thoreau recorded the blossoming of at least fifteen different species of wild orchids. He especially admired the delicate beauty of the great purple fringed orchis, the fragrance of lady slippers and the rich, intense red-purple of the *Pogonia, Calopogon* and *Arethusa,* whose brilliance appeared "very foreign in the midst of our plants." Thoreau thought of orchids as "fair and delicate, nymph-like" flowers which would blush if they knew men gave them names like *Calopogon* or *Pogonia* (bearded).

Thoreau was especially awe-struck when he discovered the great purple fringed orchis. In mid-June this plant raised its delicate pale-purple spike above the vegetation of the cool, shady alder swamp near Concord. Like a rare bird, he wrote, this "rare and beautiful flower, which you may never find again, perchance," enriched the wildness of the forest with its beauty. He thought it a "delicate belle of the swamp. . . . A beauty reared in the shade of a convent, who has never strayed beyond the convent bell." This proud flower, so little dependent on man's admiration, displayed its charms only to the inhabitants of the swamp. As it stood regally in the dim light, it seemed "a relic of the past as much as the arrowhead, or the tomahawk" left by the uncivilized red man who formerly inhabited these woods. Once, he too, stood wild and free, in close communion with nature. Again in late July Thoreau unexpectedly came upon the smaller purple fringed orchis, "What a surprise to detect under the dark, damp, cavernous copse, where some wild beast might fitly prowl, this splendid flower, silently standing with all its eyes on you!"

References to exotic orchids seem to have appeared in American literature for the first time in the fiction of Poe. He seems to have thought of vanilla as an aphrodisiac. In "Eleonora" (1841) he (1983a) described "the soft green grass" in the Valley of the Many-Colored Grass, a tropical paradise in which divine love reigned supreme, as "thick, . . . and vanilla-perfumed . . . besprinkled throughout with the yellow buttercup, the white daisy, the purple violet, and the ruby-red asphodel." Poe also had read about "*Epidendron,*" which he described as an orchid which grew on a tree from which it received no nourishment, "subsisting altogether upon air." In 1844 in "The Thousand-and–Second Tale of Scheherazade" he (1983d) included "*Epidendron*" among the wondrous plants seen by Sinbad the Sailor in a voyage around the world in an iron monster (a steamship). Some of these strange "vegetables . . . grew not upon any soil, but in the air; . . . others . . . moved from place to place at pleasure."

In 1838/1839 Poe (1983b, 1983c) referred to *Epidendrum* in "The Signora Psyche Zenobia" (later titled, "How to Write a Blackwood Article") and "The Scythe of Time" (later titled, "A Predicament"), two short stories which made fun of lady authors and literary magazines. In the first of the stories, Psyche Zenobia, a lady author from Philadelphia, received advice from Mr. Blackwood, the editor of the renowned literary magazine, on how to write an article for his magazine. The story, he suggested, should involve an unusual scrape and should include interesting facts and expressions which would display the author's erudition, for example this reference to an orchid: "'*The Epidendrum Flos Aeris,* of Java, bears a very beautiful flower, and will live when pulled up by the roots. The natives suspend it by a cord from the ceiling, and enjoy its fragrance for years.'"

In the story which Zenobia wrote following Mr. Blackwood's advice, Poe, in effect, compared the orchid to the hair of a dwarf Negro, Pompey, whom Zenobia had brought to Edinburgh from Philadelphia. During their climb up the narrow stairway to the belfry of a Gothic cathedral, the Negro caused Zenobia to stumble and fall headlong onto the floor of the belfry. In a rage she tore out a handful of his black "wool" and flung it among the ropes of the belfry. There it hung as if alive and standing "on end with indignation." At this point in her story Zenobia inserted the quotation about the orchid, calling it "the *happy dandy Flos Aeris* of Java."

In the United States, just as in England, the rich enthusiastically collected orchids, especially during the latter part of the century (Reinikka, 1972). In 1879 Whitman (1977) noted the beauty of the "incredible" orchids in the conservatory of the Baldwin mansion on Chestnut Street in Philadelphia. Yet, in spite of the interest in orchids, few American authors wrote about the exotic orchid. In his discussion of the orchid paintings (1871–1904) of Heade, a landscape painter of the Hudson River School, Stebbins (1975) asserted that these paintings which usually depicted sensuous orchids in a jungle setting did not appeal to popular taste in flowers. Contemporary art critics, he suggested, paid little attention to the orchid paintings because "the orchid was not considered a proper subject for art, since it carried with it an unmistakably dangerous aura of sexuality." Stebbins thought that although orchids were discussed in botanical and horticultural journals, "no American author ventured to consider the symbolism or connotations of the flower until the twentieth century."

Although Americans may not have discussed the sensuality of the orchid, Hawthorne and Melville did dare to consider the symbolism of the exotic orchid. Both men associated orchids with the rich and used this flower to symbolize the diabolical and sensual nature of man. Each had a deep sense of the evil which seemed to be continually present in the universe masquerading under the guise of beauty. Hawthorne, as a man from Salem embued with a Puritan consciousness of sin and guilt, was particularly conscious of the devil. To these novelists, the orchid symbol provided an antidote to the perpetual optimism of the Concord Transcendentalist philosophers.

Like Thoreau, Hawthorne exulted in the beauty of Concord. He thought that the Old Manse, to which he brought his bride Sophia Peabody in the summer of 1842, was a paradise on earth, a garden filled with both beautiful and useful plants. When spring returned to Concord, he begged his wife to record in her notebooks "the appearance . . . of the Arethusa, one of the delicatest, gracefullest, and in every manner sweetest of the whole race of flowers. . . . its hue is a delicate pink, of various depth of shade, and somewhat in the form of a Grecian helmet" (Hawthorne, 1972).

Hawthorne (1974) seems to have been thinking of tropical orchids when he wrote "Rappaccini's Daughter from the Writings of Aubépine" (1844), a story of an entirely different garden Paradise. Unlike the flowers of Concord, those in Rappaccini's garden in Padua were poisonous flowers which the learned physician had created to protect his daughter Beatrice from evil. This garden seemed threatening as if "savage beasts, or deadly snakes, or evil spirits" lurked in the gigantic foliage. To Beatrice's young lover the plants "seemed fierce, passionate and even unnatural . . . no longer, of God's making, but the monstrous offspring of man's depraved fancy, glowing with only an evil mockery of beauty."

One plant in the garden stood out from the others, a "magnificent" shrub with purple, gem-like blossoms which perfumed the air with a rich, spicy fragrance and cast a radiant glow on the waters still gushing from the shattered remains of a marble fountain. These brilliant purple flowers brought death to all living creatures who breathed their perfume except the lovely Beatrice. She seemed a sister to this shrub, which was born at the same hour as she, and she alone could tend it and give it a "passionate" and "intimate embrace." Her beauty seemed brilliant like the purple blossoms; her hair "glistened" like a gem, and her voice suggested deep purple and crimson hues, tropical sunsets and heavy perfumes.

Although Hawthorne did not name Beatrice's purple blossoms orchids, he made it clear in 1852 that the magic flower, which Zenobia, the heroine of *The Blithedale Romance* (1964), always wore in her "dark, glossy" hair, was an orchid. He called it an "exotic, of rare beauty, and as fresh as if the hothouse gardener had just clipt it from the stem. . . . So brilliant, so rare, so costly as it must have been, and yet enduring only for a day." It was "a hothouse flower—an outlandish flower—a flower of the tropics, such as appeared to have sprung passionately out of a soil the very weeds of which would be fervid and spicy." When Zenobia was in the city fashionably dressed, her rich flower became "cold and bright" like an exquisite jewel or a great diamond.

Zenobia was an exotic, a wealthy woman who had come to Boston from the Midwest. The exotic orchid symbolized her passionate nature. To Miles Coverdale, who narrated the story, Zenobia seemed "womanliness incarnated," so voluptuous that at times he feared to gaze at her. Although Coverdale claimed to be repelled by her sensuality, he subconsciously lusted after her. He imagined her "perfectly developed figure, in Eve's earliest garment" and believed she would be a fit subject to sit for painters or, preferably, sculptors "because the cold decorum of the marble would consist with the utmost scantiness of drapery, so that the eye might chastely be gladdened with her material perfection in its entireness."

Coverdale called Zenobia an "enchantress," a witch whose talisman was a magic flower. He suggested that she had made a pact with devil in the person of the dark, handsome magician Professor Westervelt, her lover or possibly her husband. Westervelt's gold teeth and serpent-headed cane revealed the mark of the devil.

Hawthorne thought it inevitable that a passionate woman like Zenobia would be punished. At the end of the novel Zenobia stood in the forest condemned to death as a witch in a Salem-like trial. She resembled the Zenobia of history, the Oriental queen led captive in a Roman triumph, "with her jewelled flower as the central ornament of what resembled a leafy crown or coronet." Deprived of her money and consequently unable to secure the affections of the zealot leader of the community, she stated that she would convert to Catholicism and end her life in a nunnery. She removed her magic flower, the talisman without which she could not live, and sent it to her triumphant rival, her half-sister Priscilla. Yet she did not go to a nunnery after all; unlike most witches, who died in hot fire, she drowned in the cold, dark, murky waters of the Charles River.

The Blithedale Romance caricatures the Brook Farm Utopian community in West Roxbury, Massachusetts of which Hawthorne was a member in 1841. Zenobia is thought by many critics to represent the feminist writer Margaret Fuller, of whom Hawthorne disapproved. A brilliant woman, a protégé of Emerson, she became America's first woman foreign correspondent, secretly married an Italian marchese and drowned tragically in 1850 in a shipwreck.

In 1857 Melville, Hawthorne's friend and admirer, chose the orchid to symbolize the diabolical nature of man and the power of money to corrupt. In the tragic tale of China Aster, the poor candle-maker in Marietta, Ohio, and his rich friend Orchis, a brief story interpolated into his novel, *The Confidence Man* (1984), he satirized the Transcendental philosopher who in his opinion professed Emersonian idealism but exhibited hard-headed Yankee business sense when his altruism was put to the test. This story probably is autobiographical, reflecting perhaps Melville's own experience with a loan on his farm which he could not repay. Orchis has been identified both with Hawthorne and with members of Melville's family (Branch et al., 1984).

In *The Confidence Man* Egbert, a disciple of Mark Winsome, whom scholars usually identify with Emerson, told this story to Frank, the cosmopolitan or Confidence Man. When he told the story, Egbert assumed the *persona* of Charlie, and Frank pretended to be Charlie's old friend Frank. When Frank begged Charlie for a loan, Charlie refused him, saying that loans destroyed friendship because they were business transactions requiring both security and interest. He told Frank that even if the roles were reversed, the experience of China Aster would remind him not to ask for a loan.

In this allegory Orchis, who had been a shoemaker before he had become wealthy through luck in the lottery, swaggered arrogantly into his old friend China Aster's candle shop dressed in "fine apparel," "switching" his gold-headed cane. Now "A small nabob," he urged poor honest China Aster to expand his business, "'drop this vile tallow and hold up pure spermaceti [the white, waxlike substance found in the head of the sperm whale] to the world.'" He promised to help his friend in this venture by loaning him one thousand dollars which he said he would never collect. After China Aster had yielded to the temptation and accepted the loan, Orchis departed for Europe leaving China Aster to the mercies of a hard-hearted agent. Later when he returned to Ohio, having acquired a wife and a new religion, his wife's sect of the Come-Outers, he changed his "gay" character to one which seemed dour and dyspeptic. He now insisted on repayment of the loan. Though he exhausted his wife's inheritance, China Aster could not repay the loan and in despair dropped dead on a hot July day. On his tomb was inscribed the moral of the tale: "'The root of all was a friendly loan.'"

In this tale China Aster, the humble garden and field flower, represented the man who was tragically deceived by the Confidence Man. In Greek, *aster* means *star*, and the role of the candle maker was to bring light to a dark and troubled world. *Aster* may also refer to the Latin Virgin Astraea, the goddess of Justice, who abandoned the earth during the first Golden Age and returned to Heaven. This identification would be appropriate because in China Aster's world honesty, hard work and trust did not pay.

Orchis, the colorful tropical flower prized by the rich, represented the Confidence Man. In Greek his name means *testicle*, and the role of the former shoemaker had been "to defend the understandings of men from naked contact with the substance of things." Having become rich by chance, Orchis changed into a diabolical Tempter who urged his old friend to give up his ideals and experience sensual pleasures. Then, after corrupting his friend, he abandoned him for the sake of selfish profit. In the end of the story the words of the proverb proved to be true. The lust for money not only ruined China Aster, but it caused Orchis to lose his cheerful disposition, his friendship and his friendly loan (Hoffman, 1950).

Orchids in the United States before World War II

Wealth and Status

During the first half of the twentieth century American literature reflected the close association of exotic orchids with wealth and status. Orchids were mentioned in novels and plays about high society, in Hollywood movies, and in popular crime fiction. Although American authors recognized the sexuality of the orchid, the majority avoided overt reference to this aspect of orchid symbolism. In the United States the sexy women who were compared to orchids usually were society leaders or glamorous actresses.

In 1905 Sinclair (1974) included orchids among the extravagances of the rich. In *The Jungle* he described a "huge carven bowl, with the glistening gleam of ferns and the red and purple of rare orchids, glowing from a light hidden somewhere in their midst" which stood on a table in the dining hall of the palatial mansion of a Chicago meat packer. Two other novels published in 1905, *The Orchid* by Grant and *The House of Mirth* by Wharton, associated orchids with the society of New York and Newport, Rhode Island. Wharton (1962) described this world as one in which a "long bank of orchids, suggestive . . . of a jeweler's window" decorated the dinner table at a splendid country house and "a simple country wedding" took place "in a church packed with fashion and festooned with orchids." She called this glittering environment a "little, illuminated circle in which life reached its finest efflorescence."

The orchid-like heroines of the latter novels were charming and sensuous society women. Grant's heroine, Lydia Arnold, who described herself as "an exotic," represented the "new woman" who thought for herself and rejected the role set for her by society of ideal wife and mother. This charming young woman insisted on the presence of love and passion in marriage and "sold" her daughter to her husband in a divorce settlement for two million. Neither she nor the man she really loved wished to marry without money. Grant, a Boston probate judge who had seen many divorce settlements, thoroughly disapproved of this woman, who because of her money never paid for her sins by losing her place in society. Wharton compared her heroine, Lily Bart, to a delicate orchid, shielded from the cold of winter in the hothouse where "basking in its artificially created atmosphere [it] could round the delicate curves of its petals undisturbed by the ice on the panes." In such a warm environment, Lily blossomed "like some rare flower grown for exhibition." Like an orchid which could not survive outside its expensive hothouse, Lily needed luxury and the warm security provided by wealth. Because she had no money, she devoted her sensuous charms unceasingly to the pursuit of a marriage with a wealthy man.

Other American authors associated orchids with the rich. Dos Passos (1969) frequently mentioned orchids in his novel about the twenties, *The Big Money* (1933). The heroine of *The Orchid* (1931) by Nathan was an actress in a play called *The Orchid.* She rejected the love of a wealthy married man, who sent her orchids, as immoral and decided to devote her life to the theater. In the sentimental religious novel, *White Orchids* (1935) by Hill, the white orchids which the son of a multi-millionaire sent to the girl he loved represented pure love. The father of the young hero of the hit play, *You Can't Take It With You* (1937) by Hart and Kaufman, was a staid and repressed investment broker who raised orchids at "ten thousand dollars a bulb" to relieve the tension created by Wall Street.

By 1925 orchids had become associated with the glamour and romance of motion pictures as well as with wealth. Fitzgerald (1925) compared Daisy, the heroine of *The Great Gatsby,* to a lovely movie actress, who posed romantically in the moonlight at one of Gatsby's lavish parties. This actress was "a gorgeous, scarcely human orchid of a woman who sat in state under a white-plum tree" while her motion-picture director bent over her to plant a kiss on her cheek. The scene reminded the narrator of an evening in Louisville when Gatsby had kissed Daisy in the white moonlight, and she had "blossomed for him like a flower" and created a similar "incarnation." Daisy was a golden girl, a cold, ruthless blonde, whose voice rang of money. She had often worn orchids carelessly when she was a young girl in the rich and artificial world of Louisville society.

During the thirties orchids clearly stood for quality both in Hollywood and in high society. In the film *Brother Orchid* (1940) a gangster (Edward G. Robinson) used a monastery as his hideout from a rival gang leader (Humphrey Bogart). When he became a novice, he chose the name "Brother Orchid" because to him orchids represented "class." In *A Star Is Born* (1937) when producer Oliver Niles (Adolphe Menjou) finally cancelled the contract of actor Norman Maine (Fredric March), the *Theatre Men's Guide* congratulated him with the words, "'Orchids to Niles!'" Although Maine was "finished" as a star, his wife Vicki Lester (Janet Gaynor) became a success. At the banquet at which she received the Academy award, her place was set with orchids.

In Hollywood orchids also symbolized the passion generated by the romantic jungle. *Wild Orchids* (1929), a silent film starring Greta Garbo told a stock tale of a staid business man in Java (Lewis Stone), who paid too much attention to his work and to big game hunting and not enough to his seductive wife Garbo. The wife fell in love with a handsome young Javanese Prince (Nils Asther) who possessed vast estates (Hall, 1970). Both Garbo and her Prince wore orchids in the movie (Bainbridge, 1955). Orchids also inspired passion in the movie, *Flying down to Rio* (1933), the first to star both Fred Astaire and Ginger Rogers. When his plane broke down on a jungle island, the hero, band leader Roger Bond (Gene Raymond), composed the romantic song, "Orchids in the Moonlight" (Kahn et al., 1933), for Belinha (Dolores del Rio), a beautiful Brazilian whom he was taking to Rio. Conveniently the plane was equipped with a small piano. Bond chose the title because he thought that Belinha, with whom he had fallen in love, was like an orchid. "And there's the moonlight," he added.

"Orchids in the Moonlight" provided one of the dance sequences in the movie. During the dancing Julio (Raoul Roulien), Belinha's Brazilian fiancé, told Belinha that "Orchids in the Moonlight" was "romantic music—and," he warned, "the words are romantic, too,—and dangerous. In the moonlight on a tropical island they might make any woman fall in love with any man." Then he passionately sang "Orchids in the Moonlight" to Belinha while enormous white orchids revolved in the background. Belinha promptly responded to the song and begged Julio to marry her right away. When Bond unexpectedly appeared, Belinha turned in confusion to Fred (Astaire) and danced the tango with him.

In 1933 in *The Day of the Locust* West (1969) suggested how "dangerous" orchids might be. In this novel he described a poster advertising a Tarzan movie which showed a muscular young man passionately embracing a young girl with torn clothes before a jungle backdrop in which "writhed great vines loaded with fat orchids."

Orchids appeared in crime literature in 1934 when Stout published *Fer-de-Lance*, the first of his novels about the detective Nero Wolfe (McAleer, 1977). A connoisseur of fine living, Wolfe possessed an extensive orchid collection (Table 6-1, 6-2), which he kept on the roof of his New York brownstone (Baring-Gould, 1969; Hamilton, 1971). In his passion for orchids Wolfe resembled wealthy business men. Although he employed a curator to care for his orchids, he himself spent at least four hours a day with the orchids, which he called his "concubines" (McAleer, 1977). Fleming (1963) in *On Her Majesty's Secret Service* contrasted Wolfe's taste in orchids with that of M., the bachelor retired naval officer, who in the novel was the head of the British Secret Service. On one occasion when the dashing ladies' man, James Bond, visited his superior, he found him painting an insignificant Autumn Lady's Tresses, which he had got from an "assistant to a chap called Summerhayes,[f] who's the orchid king at Kew." M. preferred this orchid to those raised by "that fat American detective who's always fiddling about with orchids, those obscene hybrids from Venezuela." After Bond expressed his admiration for Wolfe, M. grudgingly admitted that Wolfe did solve his murders.

One of Stout's stories, "Death Wears an Orchid" (1941), in hard cover "Black Orchids" (1942), introduced the black orchid. In this novel murder took place at a flower show at which black orchid hybrids were exhibited (McAleer, 1977; Vandermeulen, 1985). Black orchids also appeared in the comic strip, *Brenda Starr*. In this romantic story the mystery man, whom the glamorous, red-haired reporter married, could not live without black jungle orchids. Messick (quoted by White, 1986) who created the strip in 1940 for *The Chicago Tribune*, claimed that she "invented the black orchid."

In contrast to the beautiful orchids which Nero Wolfe loved, the orchids which Chandler (1973, 1976) described in 1939 in *The Big Sleep* (an expansion of "The Curtain," a short story which appeared in *Black Mask* in 1936) seemed sensual and repulsive. These orchids were clearly associated with the decadent rich. Chandler's attitude towards orchids reflects both his early years in England, where he received his education, and his experience in Los Angeles as an oil executive.

The orchids which Philip Marlowe, the tough, detective hero of *The Big Sleep*, described in an opening scene of the novel "grew and festered" in the hot steamy orchid house in which he interviewed his client, a rich old general. Although the general needed the orchid house to keep his body warm, he despised the orchids because he thought they were "nasty things" with flesh like men and a "perfume [which had] the rotten sweetness of a prostitute." To Marlowe the steamy orchid house resembled a dense jungle forest. The leaves of the orchids seemed "nasty" and "meaty," and the stalks resembled "the newly washed fingers of dead men." In the "unreal greenish" light, the blooms exuded a "cloying" smell "as overpowering as boiling alcohol under a blanket."

The British mystery writer Chase made use of orchid symbolism in two novels which mimicked the style of American crime fiction, *No Orchids for Miss Blandish* (1939) and its sequel *The Flesh of the Orchid* (1948). In a letter written in 1948 Chandler (1981) described *No Orchids for Miss Blandish* as "half-cent pulp writing at its worst" and sarcastically referred to Chase as "the distinguished author . . . [who] made a practice in one of his books of lifting verbatim or almost verbatim passages from my books . . ." Chase "was eventually forced to make a public apology" for this plagiarism.

No Orchids for Miss Blandish (1980) was set in Kansas City during the Pendergast era. In this novel Miss Blandish, the strikingly beautiful, red-haired daughter of a Kansas City millionaire, became an innocent victim of a brutal kidnapping and rape and then found herself unable to live without her half-witted captor. Before he met Miss Blandish, this gangster had not been interested in women and had derived sexual satisfaction from knifing his victims. When she was rescued at the end of the novel, Miss Blandish, believing that she was unable to return to her former carefree existence, committed suicide by jumping out of her hotel window.

In an essay comparing *Miss Blandish* to the traditional British detective story, Orwell (1946) deplored the brutality of the novel and the immorality of its characters, both gangsters and policemen. To him the novel, which he called a "cesspool," was dedicated to "the pursuit of power" and the victory of the strong over the weak. He accounted for

[f]The late Victor Summerhayes who was active as orchid taxonomist at Kew for many years.—Ed.

its enormous popularity in 1940 by suggesting, "It was, in fact, one of the things that helped to console people for the boredom of being bombed." Although, as far as Orwell knew, Chase had never been in the United States, so thoroughly had he assimilated the fantasies of the American gangland that many people believed that *Miss Blandish* "was an American book reissued in England."

In *The Flesh of the Orchid,* a novel set somewhere on the West Coast, Chase told the story of Miss Blandish's daughter Carol. With her brilliant red hair and green eyes she possessed her mother's extraordinary beauty; yet, she also had inherited her father's homicidal tendencies. She might go for months being sweet and lovable; then suddenly her eyes would become glassy, her muscles would tense; she would give an odd metallic laugh and like a lithe jungle cat she would attack, invariably clawing her victim's eyeballs. After her lover died at the hands of two hit men, Carol wore a scarlet orchid as symbol of her revenge. She left this flower as a warning sign for one of the hit men after she had caused the death of his partner. She sent masses of scarlet orchids to the funeral of her victim. Unlike her mother, Miss Blandish, for whom there were no orchids, Carol destroyed her enemies and secured her rightful inheritance.

Table 6-1. The Nero Wolfe orchids (Hamilton, 1971, 1984).

Orchids Mentioned by Name[a]	Name of novel and date of first publication[b]
Brassocattleya Calypso	1951, *Murder by the Book*
Brassocattleya Fournierae	1951, *Murder by the Book*
Brassocattleya Nestor	1951, *Murder by the Book*
Brassocattleya Thorntoni	1942, *Black Orchids*
Brassocattleya Thorntoni	1946, *The Silent Speaker*
Brassolaeliocattleya Truffautiana	1934, *Fer de Lance*
Cattleya Dionysus	1951, *Murder by the Book*
Cattleya dowiana aurea	1934, *Fer de Lance*
Cattleya dowiana aurea "with Nankeen yellow sepals"	1950, *Curtains for Three*
Cattleya gaskelliana alba	1959, *Plot It Yourself*
Cattleya Hassallii	1942, *Black Orchids*
Cattleya Katadin, 1923[c]	1951, *Murder by the Book*
Cattleya mossiae (also 14 varieties)	1955, *Before Midnight*
Cattleya mossiae Wageneri	1959, *Plot it Yourself*
Cattleya Peetersii	1951, *Murder by the Book*
Cattleya trianae	1936, *The Rubber Band*
Cochliodanoeliana	1957, *If Death Ever Slept*
Cymbidium Alexanderi	1934, *Fer de Lance*
Cymbidium Doris	1963, *Trio for Blunt Instruments*
Cymbidium Miranda, 1916[c]	1942, *Black Orchids*
Cypripedium lawrenceanum hyeanum	1963, *The Mother Hunt*
Cypripedium Lord Fisher	1951, *Murder by the Book*
Cypripedium Minos	1951, *Murder by the Book*
Cypripedium pubescens	1942, *Black Orchids*
Dendrobium bensoniae	1949, *The Second Confession*
Dendrobium chlorostele	1934, *Fer de Lance*
Dendrobium chrysotoxum	1961, *The Final Deduction*
Dendrobium Cybele	1951, *Murder by the Book*
Dendrobium nobile	1963, *Trio for Blunt Instruments*

[a]Of the more than 200 varieties in the 10,000 plants of Wolfe's collection, 70 are mentioned by name. Of these, 46 are species. In addition to the orchids mentioned in his collection, Wolfe desired an *Angraecum sesquipedale* (1934, *Fer de Lance*).
[b]There are 44 novels or collections of novella in which orchids are mentioned.
[c]The latest registration date is 1923; the next latest is 1916. A specific name or the parents of a cross is never mentioned.

Table 6-1. Continued.

Orchids Mentioned by Name[a]	Name of novel and date of first publication[b]
Dendrobium nobilius	1954, *The Black Mountain*
Laelia gouldiana[d]	1962, *Gambit*
Laelia purpurata	1961, *The Final Deduction*
Laeliocattleya Barbarossa	1951, *Murder by the Book*
Laeliocattleya Carmencita	1951, *Murder by the Book*
Laeliocattleya Jacquetta	1954, *The Black Mountain*
Laeliocattleya Luminosa aurea	1936, *The Red Box*
Laeliocattleya Lustre	1934, *Fer de Lance*
Laeliocattleya Lustre	1936, *The Rubber Band*
Laeliocattleya St. Gothard	1951, *Murder by the Book*
Lycaste delicatissima[e]	1960, *Too Many Clients*
Miltonia Bleuana	1966, *Death of a Doxy*
Miltonia Charlesworthii	1968, *The Father Hunt*
Miltonia hellemense	1968, *The Father Hunt*
Miltonia roezlii	1943 [sic], *(?)*
Miltonia roezlii	1961, *Homicide Trinity*
Miltonia roezlii	1964, *A Right to Die*
Miltonia roezlii alba	1953, *The Golden Spiders*
Miltonia vexillaria	1961, *The Final Deduction*
Odontioda Cooksoniae	1957, *If Death Ever Slept*
Odontoglossum aireworthi [sic][e]	1966, *Death of a Doxy*
Odontoglossum Armainvillierense	1957, *If Death Ever Slept*
Odontoglossum Crispo-Harryanum	1966, *Death of a Doxy*
Odontoglossum harryanum	1949, *The Second Confession*
Odontoglossum hellemense	1966, *Death of a Doxy*
Odontoglossum pyramus	1961, *Homicide Trinity*
Odontoglossum pyramus	1968, *The Father Hunt*
Oncidium forbesii	1951, *Murder by the Book*
Oncidium marshallianum	1961, *The Final Deduction*
Oncidium varicosum	1951, *Murder by the Book*
Oncidium varicosum	1955, *Before Midnight*
Paphiopedilum (see *Cypripedium*)	
Phalaenopsis aphrodite	1960, *Three at Wolfe's Door*
Phalaenopsis aphrodite	1964, *A Right to Die*
Phalaenopsis aphrodite	1965, *The Doorbell Rang*
Phalaenopsis aphrodite	1968, *The Father Hunt*
Phalaenopsis aphrodite sanderiana	1968, *The Father Hunt*
Phalaenopsis schilleriana	1956, *Might as Well be Dead*
Phalaenopsis stuartiana	1956, *Might as Well be Dead*
Renanthera imschootiana	1956, *And Four to Go*
Vanda coerulea	1939, *Over My Dead Body*
Vanda peetersiana	1950, *In the Best Families*
Vanda peetersiana	1956, *Might as Well be Dead*
Vanda rogersi[e]	1966, *Death of a Doxy*
Vanda sanderae [sic]	1956, *And Four to Go*
Vanda suavis	1964, *A Right to Die*
Zygopetalum crinitum	1948, *And be a Villain*

[d]*Laelia gouldiana* was used in hybridizing; the other parent is not mentioned (1956, *And Four to Go*). Another hybrid, *Laelia schroederi* × *ashworthiana* (pollen parent so far unreported) is valued at maybe a couple grand (1968, *The Father Hunt*).
[e]This orchid is "new to science."

Table 6-2. The Nero Wolfe orchids (Hamilton, 1971, 1984).

Orchids not mentioned by specific name	Name of novel and date of first publication[a]
Brassavola	1953, *The Golden Spiders*
Calanthe	1952, *Three Men Out*
Cattleya	Many references, including
	1934, *Fer de Lance*
	1936, *The Rubber Band*
	1948, *Three Doors to Death*
	1949, *Trouble in Triplicate*
	1951, *Murder by the Book*
	1958, *Champagne for One*
Cochlioda	1951, *Murder by the Book*
Coelogyne	1936, *The Red Box*[b]
	1939, *Over My Dead Body*[c]
	1958, *Champagne for One*[d]
Cymbidium	1934, *Fer de Lance*
	1936, *The Rubber Band*
Dendrobium	1934, *Fer de Lance*[e]
	1949, *Trouble in Triplicate*
	1950, *Curtains for Three*
Laeliocattleya	1936, *The Rubber Band*
	1938, *Too Many Cooks*
	1958, *Champagne for One*
Miltonia	1934, *Fer de Lance*
	1958, *Champagne for One*
Odontoglossum	Many references, including
	1934, *Fer de Lance*
	1935, *The League of Frightened Men*
	1950, *Curtains for Three*
	1955, *Before Midnight*
	1958, *Champagne for One*
	1963, *Trio for Blunt Instruments*
Oncidium	1936, *The Rubber Band*
	1963, *Trio for Blunt Instruments*
Paphiopedilum	1938, *Too Many Cooks*
Phalaenopsis	Many references, including
	1934, *Fer de Lance*
	1948, *Three Doors to Death*
	1949, *Trouble in Triplicate*
	1955, *Before Midnight*
	1958, *Champagne for One*
Renanthera	1950, *Curtains for Three*
Vanda	1942, *Black Orchids*
	1956, *And Four to Go*[f]
Zygopetalum	1950, *Curtains for Three*

[a]Orchids also are mentioned in 1938, *Some Buried Caesar;* 1940, *Where There's a Will;* 1944, *Not Quite Dead Enough;* 1947, *Too Many Women;* 1951, *Triple Jeopardy;* 1952, *Prisoner's Base;* 1954, *Three Witnesses;* 1955, *Three For the Chair;* 1969, *Death of a Dude.*
[b]*C. pandurata* was offered to Wolfe at the "quite unfriendly price" of $3000 a pair.
[c]This "enormous" orchid "with white petals and orange keels" was probably *C. cristata.*
[d]Wolfe bought a rarer species for $800 from a man in Burma.
[e]Wolfe received a hybrid of *D.* Melpomene × *findleyanum* (never registered) from a friend.
[f]For years Wolfe tried to hybridize a pink *Vanda.*

The Secret of Life

The orchid poems of Frost reflect the New England of the Transcendentalists. For him the woodlands and pastures of New Hampshire represented a paradise on earth. Throughout his life he enjoyed tramping through the wild looking for rare blossoms, especially orchids. The search for a rare orchid like the Calypso or the Purple-Fringed seemed analogous to man's journey through life, struggling courageously against obstacles but finding pleasure in a task well done. Discovery of the orchid at the end of the search revealed the ultimate secret of existence. To Frost (1969c), man seemed insignificant in the face of eternal nature. After he had spent his "little hour" on earth, the eternal woods would miss him even less than the lowly coralroot flower which the poet had picked ("On Going Unnoticed," 1925).

In "Rose Pogonias" (1913), a poem which suggests Poe's Valley of the Many Colored Grass, Frost (1969e) described a magic circle of tall trees surrounding a tiny meadow, "Sun-shaped and jewel-small," covered with grass and "A thousand orchises; . . . every second spear/ . . . tipped with wings of color." As the viewers bowed in worship in this "temple of the heat," they prayed that the mowers would spare the grass "while so confused with flowers."

In "The Quest of the Purple-Fringed" (1942), a poem first published in 1901 under the title, "The Quest of the Orchis," Frost (1969d), led by a fox's trail, found "the purple spires" of the orchis in a grove of alders. As he knelt in reverence, he counted them all, even the buds which "were pale as a ghost." Now that he had found the orchises, the poet "Said that the fall might come . . . / For summer was done," i.e., having found his prize, he was ready for death.

Like the ghostly buds of the purple-fringed, the orchises described in "Mowing" (1913) represented sexual flowers of death and rebirth (Frost, 1969b). The poet's "long scythe . . . whispered" as it cut the hay under a hot sun with "earnest love . . . / Not without feeble-pointed spikes of flowers/ (Pale orchises), and scared a bright green snake." Bacon (1975) noted the similarity of the death of the pale orchises to that of Adonis, Attis and Persephone, who died to ensure the fertility of the fields, and suggested that the orchises, like the rose pogonias and the purple-fringed, were flowers "destined for sacrifice to the harvest."

In "The Self–Seeker" (1914) Frost (1969f) described the courage and determination required of man as he labored for his eternal reward. The poem told about a man who had been injured in an industrial accident and could no longer walk through the fields in search of "forty orchids," among them the rare *Cypripedium reginae*. Nevertheless he had not given up and had trained a little girl to do his searching for him. The child brought him a Ram's Horn orchid which she had found under a beech tree on a "woodchuck's knoll." She had been careful not to pick the common Yellow and Purple Lady's Slippers and had left some of the Ram's Horn flowers to make a "seedpod for a woodchuck." Thompson (1966) considered this poem a poetic tribute to Frost's high school friend Carl Burell, who had a similar accident in 1896.

In "An Encounter" (1916) Frost (1969a) contrasted the determination of the Self–Seeker with his own half-hearted efforts to find the rare orchid. Frost was aware that he often was weak and ineffectual, easily swayed from his goal. In the poem the poet himself became entangled in a cedar swamp on a hot sultry day as he searched for the Calypso orchid. Hot, tired and sorry that he had ever left the beaten track, he looked up and saw to his surprise a telephone pole whose wires carried news to places as far distant as Montreal. Whimsically he told this "resurrected tree," "'Me? I'm not off for any-where at all./ Sometimes I wander out of beaten ways/ Half looking for the orchid Calypso.'"

"An Encounter" seems to have been based on an episode in the *Odyssey* in which Hermes, the messenger god, visited Calypso to tell her that she must send Odysseus on his homeward way. He found the shining goddess sitting at her loom before a hearth blazing with cedar wood. Meanwhile Odysseus sat by the shore weeping bitter tears because he longed for his home and his mortal wife and no longer took any interest in the goddess and her promises of immortality (Homer, ca. 750 B.C.).

Calypso, the orchid named for the immortal Greek goddess, became a symbol of eternity in "An Octopus" (1924) by Moore. In this poem Moore (1935b) described Mount Tacoma (Rainier), as a "fossil flower," an octopus of ice and snow. High on its cliffs, the sun, like acetylene, burning his shoulders white, stood the mountain goat, a "special antelope." Flowers grew on this "antique" mountain, "gentians, lady-slippers, harebells, mountain dryads,/ and 'Calypso, the goat flower—/ that greenish orchid fond of snow,'" clinging tenaciously to "glacial ledges" which only hardy mountain climbers ever reached, her chief companion the blue jay, who "knows no Greek."[g] On this eternal peak, the "antique pedestal" of the mountain goat, in the clear white solitary air of eternity (Stapleton, 1978), Calypso bloomed forever.

The Power of the Imagination

Pound and Williams differed from the majority of American authors because they saw sexuality at the core of existence and considered it the source of poetic inspiration. For them the orchid, a flower whose name meant testicle in Greek, provided an excellent symbol of this vital and procreative force.

In 1920 Pound first presented the new sexual orchid to the literary world. The orchid was a key symbol in *Hugh Selwyn Mauberley*, Pound's statement that as an artist he could no longer survive in the bloodless, enervated world of English letters which remained after the destruction of the War. To Pound this decadent world seemed desparately in need of a rebirth of the vitality of ancient Greece.

In *Mauberley* Pound (1926) combined the orchid and the iris into a floral symbolism which enabled him to convey a sexual message (Espey, 1974). In Part II of the poem he presented the poet Mauberley, who drifted for three years in a dream world "Amid aerial flowers" failing to identify "His new found orchid." He passed without seeing "The wide-banded irides/ And botticellian sprays implied/ In their diastasis." Because he failed in sexual awareness, his poetry lacked passion, and in the end he died.

Mauberley is a complicated poem in which the poet wrung every possible meaning from each image. The words "orchid" and "iris" indicated in Greek both a flower and a part of the body. "Orchid" represented both the exquisitely lovely, ethereal flower prized by the Aesthetes and the orchid of ancient Greece, "mandate/ Of Eros." "Iris" which represented both a flower, popular with the Aesthetes, and the iris of the eye suggested the seductive expression seen in the eyes of a sensuous woman.

---

[g]In later editions of her poems, Moore omitted the passage on the flowers. She stated in her note that the quoted lines in the poem were from Department of the Interior Rules and Regulations, *The National Park Portfolio* (1922).

The poem also depends on a complex Aphrodite/Venus symbolism. The phrase "wide-banded irides/ And botticellian sprays" seems to refer to Botticelli's painting, *The Birth of Venus* (ca. 1480). This favorite painting of the Aesthetes portrays the naked goddess, blown to shore by two Zephyrs on her cockle shell amid showers of roses, after her birth from the sea foam which surrounded the severed testicles of Uranus (Hesiod, ca. 700 B.C.). Botticelli, under the influence of the Neoplatonists, painted the earthly pagan goddess of love in order to depict in allegory the divine love and beauty of the Heavenly Venus or Virgin (Janson, 1977).

Pound used the orchid/iris symbolism to express the hope of a return to an earlier time in Greece when Venus or Aphrodite, the mother of Eros (Love), represented a goddess of procreation. He thought that in the twentieth century a potent male orchid, combined with a seductive female iris, could initiate a rebirth of a vital art like that of ancient Greece. Pound found the combination of orchid and iris in Chinese literature (Espey, 1974). In 1918 he commented on a Chinese girl, perhaps a priestess, who bathed in water made fragrant by boiling orchids in it, washed her hair and bound it with iris and awaited the descent of a divine lover.

The description of washing in orchid water in preparation for divine love suggests a Cambodian orchid ceremony which Frazer (1913) compared to the Druid rite in which the parasitic mistletoe was cut from the sacred oak tree. Before the Druids kindled their sacred bonfires, they cut the mistletoe at a set time of the moon with a golden sickle, not an iron knife, and caught it in a white cloth so that it might not touch the ground. In the Cambodian ritual, someone dressed in white broke the orchid from the tamarind tree at noon, placed it in an earthenware pot and then dropped it on the ground. Afterwards the orchid was made into a decoction, used either by drinking or washing, which was said to confer invulnerability.

In *Mauberley* Pound used "orchid" in a symbolic way in which the meaning of the word was not immediately obvious. He (1970) was more direct in *Canto 48* (1937) when he used the Greek word instead of an English word to describe a yellow caterpillar clambering upward, "a ball, into its orchis."

A simile in a poem written in 1940 by Auden (1976) on the occasion of the birthday of St. Cecilia, patron saint of music, recalls Pound's sexual symbolism and his association of orchid and iris with Botticelli's painting. In the poem Auden wrote, "Blonde Aphrodite rose up excited,/ Moved to delight by the melody,/ White as an orchid she rode quite naked/ In an oyster shell on top of the sea" to hear the saint play her organ on the Roman seashore.

Like his old friend Pound, Williams viewed the orchid as a symbol of the procreative sexuality which he considered basic to art. He chose this flower to symbolize sex not because of its name but because of its sexual appearance. Although he probably knew the meaning of the name "orchis" because he was a physician, he was not a student of Greek and Latin derivations. He was indebted to Pound for encouraging him to read Greek literature (in translation) and for teaching him about Greece.

Williams (1967) sincerely admired rare and splendid orchids. He wrote in his *Autobiography* (1951) that he would never forget the magnificent, rare orchids which he and his wife presented to Bob McAlmon and Winifred Ellerman (Bryher), daughter of the wealthy British shipping magnate, Sir John Ellerman, on the occasion of their wedding in 1921. At the wedding supper the guests, who included Bryher's friend, the poet, H. D. (Hilda Doolittle), and Marianne Moore, marvelled at the splendor of the orchids, and Marsden Hartley, the painter, suggested a newspaper headline, "POETS

PAWING ORCHIDS." Later Williams received a postcard signed D. H., which showed several actors "with their hands in a pot of money." He suspected that H. D. had sent the card, but when asked later, she violently denied sending it.

H. D. (1929), who had been Pound's fiancée in Pennsylvania and who had been closely associated with him in England during the years when he was writing *Mauberley*, also wrote about orchids. In "At Baia," a poem included in *Hymen* (1921), she phantasized an unfulfilled erotic dream in which she mused, "I SHOULD have thought/ in a dream you would have brought/ some lovely, perilous thing,/ orchids piled in a great sheath."

In "A Celebration" (1921), Williams (1966) described a visit to the Orchid Show. This poem suggests the theme which can be found at the base of much of his work: the legend of Kora the Grain Maiden and the cycle of the seasons in which the grain lying hidden in the earth during the winter seems dead but bursts forth to new life in the spring time. Williams felt that he, too, like the grain, descended in the winter into the dark earth, the depths of Hell, and returned to the light renewed and refreshed in the spring. For Williams the phallic orchids at the show illustrated the seasons as they revolved in their eternal circle.

As Williams described the orchids, he chose a flower to represent each month of the year. Two represented winter months: January was named for Villon, a snowy orchid which reminded him of death and the lost beauties of the past; February, a "falling spray of snowflakes . . . / a handful of dead Februaries," was named for Rafael Arévalo Martínez of Guatemala. Spring was represented by April's "full, fragile/ head of veined lavender," and summer was June's "yellow cup." There was also a "branch of blue butter-flies." August was "over-heavy," and other "russet and shiny" orchids symbolized the harvest and fall months. All of the months were there, said the poet, except March. "Ah, March—," he broke off impatiently; he had seen enough of the show, and now it was time to return home to a warm fire. In this particular spring April had been cold and disagree-able like a second March. The year was still green and immature, and the promise of spring had yet to unfold. "Time," he concluded, "is a green orchid."

In 1923 Williams (1956) associated the orchid with a vanished civilization which possessed the secret of life. In an essay published in Berlin in January, "The Destruction of Tenochtitlan: Cortez and Montezuma" (Mariani, 1981), which he later incorporated into *In the American Grain* (1925), he characterized as "orchidean" the paradisiacal beauty of America before it had been corrupted by the Spanish conquerors.

William's essay about Montezuma suggests a poem by Lawrence, published in October, 1923, in which the orchid was associated with another extinct civilization. In "Cypresses," Lawrence (1977) called the Etruscans "rare and orchid-like/ Evil yclept." In their tombs near the dark cypress trees of Tuscany, he said, "We have buried so much of the delicate magic of life." These men, he thought, who possessed the magic secret of existence, sexual knowledge, were not evil—only called evil by the Romans who had destroyed their civilization in the same way that modern mechanical America was still destroying that of Montezuma. Like Thoreau's purple fringed orchis which seemed a relic of a past era when Indians roamed the woodlands of New England, the orchid-like Etruscans belonged to a lost civilization.

Williams believed that the Negro from the African jungle also knew the magic sexual secret. In his unfinished novel, *Man Orchid*, on which he collaborated with Fred Miller in 1946, Williams chose the orchid to symbolize his sexual potency. To Williams (quoted by Mariani, 1981) the jungle flower looked "like an oversized scrotum . . . that lived on air, words, ideas . . ." The hero of the novel, Wray Douglas, as the son of a Greek father and a black mother, represented the combination of the transfiguring Apollonian vision of light and the dark Dionysiac sexual impulses which Nietzsche (1980) in *Die Geburt der Tragödie* (1872), thought was essential to the production of great art.

In the projected novel Douglas, a stuttering, ineffectual copy writer, longed to be a great trumpet player like the black performer Bunk Johnson, whose primitive jungle jazz Williams admired. Bunk's trumpet which Williams (1973) called an "autochthonous horn" resembled a magnificent orchid. "Orchids," he wrote, "grow *on* trees, flaunting . . . their complex sexual devices . . . the fluted and bulbous mechanism." In his part of the novel Miller compared Bessie Smith to an orchid and called her "vast" voice, "the voice of the tropics." In another section he asked, "Why the orchid? . . . There's the old tiresome . . . literary assumption that the Negro in America is an exotic bloom. Negro equals jungle."

In 1955 in "Asphodel, That Greeny Flower" Williams (1962a) included the Polynesian as well as the Negro among the primitive peoples who knew the magic sexual secret of life, the orchid. A black man, whom he had seen on a train deep underground in the New York subway, symbolized the Negro who held the knowledge of the magic secret. This man reminded Williams not only of his father and of his own face in the mirror, but also of all men and women of future generations. Williams was sure that the black man would know "the secret." Yet the man got off the train without revealing his knowledge. Williams called the secret a flower which had lost its "savor," a lilac painted by primitive men in prehistoric caves or "some exotic orchid/ that Herman Melville had admired/ in the/ Hawaiian jungle."

Although there are no lilacs in cave art nor orchids in Melville's tales of the South Seas, Williams used these flowers as phallic symbols of the magic secret which lay hidden in the dark of the earth. Melville (1947) in *Moby Dick* (1851) had described three royal savages, who knew the magic secret; the three harpooners, a cannibal from the South Seas, an American Indian and a Negro. The little Negro Pip also went down to the depths of the sea and saw its secrets.

In "Asphodel" Williams used the sexual orchid to symbolize the power of woman to inspire the poet. He compared Helen of Troy to a "sexual orchid that bloomed then/ sending so many/ disinterested/ men to their graves." The world would have called "those crimson petals/ spilled among the stones,/ . . . simply/ murder" if they had not inspired an eternal poem, *The Iliad*.

Williams' imagery depended on the description of Aeschylus (458 B. C.) of Helen as a blood flower which would shine forever in the memory of men and on a statement in the *Iliad* (ca. 800 B. C.) in which Helen told Hektor that Zeus had placed an evil lot upon them so that they might become subjects of song for future generations. The bloody crimson orchid symbolized the power of the whore to inspire an eternal poem.

In 1958 in *Paterson 5* Williams (1963) asserted that all women were alike, and all could inspire the poet. The pure white virgin could be found even in the whore house. He quoted an essay by Sorrentino to illustrate this point (Weaver, 1971). In his description of the whores of a Mexican border town, Sorrentino described the beauty of the snow white virgin "in the orchid stench." The encounter with the virgin/whore produced hot white passion, "brighter-white than the lights . . . white and deep as birth, deeper than death." The orchid was the potency of sex in all phases of man's life: birth, intercourse and death. Williams already had made this assertion in *Paterson 1* (1946) in a passage in which he spoke of the children of the poor who see all aspects of life from "the convolutions of the sexual orchid/ hedged by fern and honey smells," to the last moments of the dying. The sexual orchid, which in "A Celebration" represented each month of the cycle of the seasons, symbolized in *Paterson* all aspects of the similar cycle of man's life, as it revolved from birth to maturity and to death.

In his final statement about the power of the Virgin to inspire the artist, Williams chose the lady's slipper instead of the exotic orchid. The name of this orchid suggests both Venus (Latin *Cypripedium,* Venus's slipper), the earthly goddess of love, and Our Lady, the Heavenly Virgin (German, *Marienschuh*). In "The Rewaking" (1962b), a short poem which he placed at the end of his final book of poems, *Pictures from Breughel* (Mariani, 1981), three flowers closely associated with the Virgin Mary, the rose, the violet (Freeman, 1976), and the lady's slipper, symbolized the power of woman to create the sunshine of an eternal spring. In the sunshine of this eternal paradise, the poet hoped to live forever.

Orchids in Contemporary Literature

In contemporary British and American literature, orchids continue to project traditional images. They symbolize not only wealth and status, but also the "power and passion" of the exotic jungle. Orchids suggest sex today just as they have for centuries. A few modern poets like Tomlinson (1958), Christopher (1983), and Karp (1983) even have used "orchid" in its Greek sense instead of an English word.

Updike (1984) left no question about the erotic character of the American orchid. As he looked back on the formal dances of his high school days in the late 1940's, he recalled the corsages pinned on the strapless gowns of the bare shouldered girls who swirled seductively with their partners in the hot gymnasium," . . . what heats, what shadowy, intense glandular incubations came packaged with the five-dollar purchase of a baby orchid in a transparent plastic box!" How well, he thought, the florists "knew . . . the symbolic value of their folded, fragrant, fragile merchandise." In Bernstein's musical *West Side Story* (1956), which opened in New York in 1957, "black orchid" clearly symbolized sex. In preparation for a dance after the gangs' rumble, the sexy Puerto Rican girl Anita planned to "take a bubble bath all during supper; Black Orchid." She told Maria that the men fought and danced as if they had "to get rid of something, quick. . . . Too much feeling. And they get rid of it: after a fight, that brother of yours is so healthy! Definitely: Black Orchid."

In a recent collection of short vignettes entitled *The Orchid Stories,* Elmslie (1973) presented a contemporary orchid which blended images of the past with a new expression of the power of sex. In these stories, Elmslie created a surrealistic dream world of fantastic tropical orchids which he described with a frankness which would have been impossible earlier in the century. A box named "Native Innards" appeared crimson, the color of the life blood which flowed from a cut on the arm. In addition to the purple "Native Innards" orchid, it contained a dried blue and pink mottled "Locust" orchid called "Edith's Death" orchid, the "'Dog Roots Girl' orchid retrieved day after ecstasy incident" and a white frosted, artificial plastic orchid. As a final project for a "good Orchid year," Elmslie suggested the construction of "a human-sized orchid plant/ with interchangeable private parts."

Elmslie compared orchids to amusing and exciting shapes of animals and people. He spoke of women with minks and orchids. One story concerned an operetta, *Gilda Grey,* about an old actress, a silent screen star who had seen better days. "Alien Moon," the aria which she sang, contained "sweet orchids of desire to me/ Descending on skeins of wire to me." An orchid cut at midnight on Midsummer's Eve lay under the actress's pillow.

Although orchid collecting no longer is an exclusive prerogative of the rich, contemporary literature continues to reflect the association of orchids with wealth and status. In *A Coat of Varnish* by Snow (1979) "a sumptuous gleaming of orchids" surpassed all the other flowers at the simple funeral of Lady Ashbrook, whom Snow called one of the last of England's great ladies. This "lordly wreath" was the anonymous gift from her grandson's father-in-law, a Liberal politician and Labor leader from Birmingham. A key symbol in *The Little Drummer Girl* by Le Carré (1983) was a "sprig" of golden-brown orchids worth thirty pounds which a wealthy Arab sent to the actress heroine after a performance at the theater. Eva Gabor (1954), the glamorous actress from Budapest, named her autobiography *Orchids and Salami* because people thought that orchids and salami represented "the spirit of the true Eva." On one occasion her refrigerator contained only these items.

Modern stories often are about orchid collectors. Among these stories are "The Reluctant Orchid" (1954) by Clarke (1974), a story dedicated to Lord Dunsany which parodied Wells's tale of the "strange orchid," and two recent novels, *Orchids for Mother* by Latham (1977) and *Dream of Orchids* (1985) by Whitney. In Latham's novel Mother (Code name), the head of the U.S. Counter-intelligence Department, was a rather unsavory operative who raised orchids as a hobby. He always dressed in black and white and "looked like a crooked black snake in a garden of brightly colored orchids." In Whitney's novel, murder took place in an orchid house in front of orchids which seemed both violent and beautiful. Improbably the victim bled to death from a cut incurred when the collector broke a flask of seedlings. The title of another recent novel, *Blood and Orchids* by Katkov (1983), depended on the popular association of orchids with Hawaii.

Three autobiographical novels, *The Military Orchid* (1948), *A Mine of Serpents* (1949), and *The Goose Cathedral* (1950), by Brooke reflect British attitudes towards orchids. Like most Britons, Brooke associated exotic orchids with Decadence. But his life-long passion was searching for wild orchids both in his native England and in North Africa and Italy where he served during World War II. Discovery of a rare orchid always filled him with ecstatic joy and contentment.

Although most modern orchids are propagated in greenhouses, many of the references to orchids in modern literature suggest the exotic jungle. These modern jungle orchids seem sensuous, sometimes beautiful and full of life and at other times grotesque and deadly. Many modern orchids, especially those in science fiction and adventure stories are bizarre, sensual and sometimes obscene. Orchids also are characterized as delicate, fragile and feminine unlike the phallic orchids of Pound and Williams. In literature such orchids often symbolize innocent victims in a modern jungle world of crime and violence.

In his poem "Orchids" (1948) Roethke (1975) described the orchids in his father's greenhouse in Michigan as grotesque creatures which inhabited the primeval world. These orchids resembled the grotesque dream orchids of German tradition. They seemed alive and breathing, by day, seductive like the snake in Eden, "delicate as a young bird's tongue," and by night, deathly and terrifying, "devouring infants" in "mossy cradles," as they threatened to draw the poet downward toward the dark womb of earth which is the source of all life. Bleached white and pale by a sinister moon, they resembled "Soft luminescent fingers,/ Lips neither dead nor alive,/ Loose ghostly mouths/ Breathing."

Like the Transcendentalists, Roethke thought that nature was divine. He (1968a, 1968b) considered the greenhouse a "symbol for the whole of life, a womb, a heaven-on-earth," an Avalon or an Eden. To him (1968c) the flowers which his father grew were "life-symbols; indeed," he wrote in a letter, "the little-blooming rare types (not for sale) were eternity symbols." Among the eternity symbols were the rare orchids and roses in which his father specialized (Roethke, 1968d). In a notebook he commented that the greenhouse was both a jungle and a paradise (Seager, 1968).

The orchids in a poem by Plath (1981b), "The Surgeon at 2 a.m." (1961), seem victims in the nightmarish dream world created by the modern hospital. In the operating room the surgeon gazed at a body which resembled a garden. In this "purple wilderness" there was "the lung-tree," a heart which was "a red-bell-bloom" and "splendid" orchids which "spot and coil like snakes." The Surgeon was a mechanical god, substituting new pink, plastic parts for real ones.

In "Fever 103°" (1962) Plath (1981a) associated the orchid with Babylon, the sinful city, which according to the Bible, would be enveloped in Hellish flames. This orchid, like the orchids in Lord Dunsany's play, became a victim of sin, in this instance the sin of Hiroshima. In this poem Plath compared herself to a sinful whore burning in the fires of Hell. She feared that her yellow smokes would not rise and would catch in the wheel like the scarf of Isadora Duncan (Duncan, who revived the art of Greek dance, had been killed when her flowing, red scarf had caught in the wheel of the open car in which she was riding). Plath envisioned a scene of destruction in which the smokes would encircle the world, "Choking the aged and the meek,/ "The weak/ Hothouse baby in its crib,/ The ghastly orchid/ Hanging its hanging garden in the air," and radiation would kill the "devilish leopard."

Although Plath's orchid in this poem reflects Roethke's image of "devouring infants" in "mossy cradles," the phrase, "Hanging its hanging garden in the air," suggests Babylon. Plath's imagery depends on Biblical images of Babylon, the great whore clad in purple and scarlet, yellow wheels, an amber-colored cloud and a leopard-like beast who received power from Satan (Ezekiel 1, Daniel 7, Revelation 13 and 17).

A poem by Moore (1935a), "The Frigate Pelican," may have suggested the combination of orchid, leopard and Grecian dancer. In Moore's poem, too, the "red spotted" orchid was stained with innocent blood, that of natives slain by the sinful Spanish conqueror of Panama, Pizarro.[h] As the pelican flew high over the jungle, he looked down on fierce jungle creatures which seemed to be dancing by like animals on a merry-go-round "within the circular view." Among these creatures were a jaguar, "peacock-freckled small/ cats" and a fer-de-lance sleeping near "the/ spattered blood—that orchid which the native fears—." On the carousel too was "a leopard with a frantic/ face, tamed by an Artemis," wearing a spotted dress.

In *Wide Sargasso Sea* (1966) by the British novelist Rhys, the orchid symbolized a victim of sin, in this instance a victim of the evils of racism, prejudice, colonial exploitation and above all the double sexual standard for men and women. In this story Rhys contrasted the warm sensuality of the paradisiacal world of the West Indies and the cold morality of nineteenth century England, which rejected sexual passion. Rhys (1979) thought of Dominica in the West Indies, where she had been born and raised, as a paradise on earth.

[h]In later editions of her poems, Moore omitted this passage but left the note.

To her an old abandoned garden on a mountain estate belonging to her mother's family, symbolized a lost Eden. Rhys (1985a, 1985b) wrote about this garden, first in *Voyage in the Dark* (1934), an autobiographical novel about a young girl who left Dominica for a cold, dark England, and more extensively in *Wide Sargasso Sea*. She described it as wild and unkempt, a place where roses grew and tree ferns cast a green light. "Orchids flourished out of reach or for some reason not to be touched." One of the orchids was "snaky looking"; another resembled an octopus. The octopus orchid with its heavy perfume flowered two times each year, "a bell-shaped mass of white, mauve, deep purples, wonderful to see." Rioting blacks had destroyed the house on the estate, but the garden remained hidden in the jungle.

Wide Sargasso Sea (Rhys, 1985b) retold the story of Bronte's novel, *Jane Eyre*, largely from the point of view of Antoinette, the mad Creole bride of the English Rochester. As a child Antoinette had lived on the old estate and had loved the garden. In the first days of her marriage to Rochester the couple was happy, but Rochester soon became afraid of his bride, whom he compared to a golden-brown orchid, because her warm seductive beauty aroused a passion in him which he called lust. Believing she had inherited her family's insanity he rejected her love as unnatural and evil. In the end of the novel Antoinette chose to go with the cold Rochester to an empty England. There she, too, became cold and mad. After a dream in which she saw the orchids and the tree of life in flames, she set the fire in which she died.

In "Jean Rhys," (1980), a poetic tribute to Rhys after her death, the Caribbean poet, Walcott (1986), recreated Rhys's childhood world. A faded photograph showed her family seated stiffly on the veranda surrounded by a brown jungle. The yellow moon which shown on this scene had a face like that of a "feverish" child, a "malarial angel," and "the sigh of that child/ is white as an orchid/ on a crusted log/ in the bush of Dominica." The ghostly white orchid on the long dead log belonged to a lost jungle paradise in the West Indies to which the child, who would devote her life to English letters, was linked forever.

In *The Orchids* Cook (1982) characterized orchids as innocent victims of ignorance and superstition as well as symbols of the beauty which existed in a grotesque modern world. Cook described this world as "the paradise of Dorian Gray, a perfect landscape of green shade where orchids spread their petals in the crystal air." Man could survive the terror beneath this landscape only by believing in nothing or by laughing a "laughter strange as orchids growing on the moon."

The novel took place in a small South American jungle republic where a German doctor who had participated in the atrocities of World War II had found refuge after the defeat of Germany. There the doctor cultivated beautiful jungle orchids. These orchids were dying in spite of the prayers and ministrations of the peasant servant. Yet, in their decay they still were beautiful and inspired the doctor to an act of heroism.

Although the majority of references to orchids in modern literature pertains to the exotic flower, the orchid of New England, which the Transcendentalists thought divine, sometimes appears in contemporary literature. In "The Smaller Orchid," a poem first published in 1979 as "Ladies' Tresses," Clampitt (1983) rejected the sensuous, over-powering and glamorous cattleya of Proust in favor of the inconspicuous white ladies' tresses, which she "found/ flourishing in the hollows/ of a granite seashore." This "cheerful . . . down-to-earth," little orchid, which proclaimed "its authenticity,/ . . . in a powerful/ . . ./ whiff of vanilla," seemed to her to express the essence of love.

Acknowledgments

I wish to thank my sons, James Hoffman Lewis and John Andrew Lewis, without whose help my study could not have been completed. Both have aided me in the collection of data in libraries which were inaccessible to me. Their criticisms and suggestions have been invaluable. Special thanks are due my husband who has provided constant support and encouragement.

Literature Cited

Aeschylus. 458 B.C. Agamemnon, lines 1455–1460. *In* G. Murray (ed.), *Septem quae supersunt tragoediae.* 1938, rpt. 1947. Oxford University Press, London.

Alexander, E. J., and C. H. Woodward. 1941. The flora of the unicorn tapestries. *J. N.Y. Botanical Garden* 42: 105–122.

Ames, O. 1948. *Orchids in retrospect.* Botanical Museum Press, Cambridge, Mass.

Amory, M. 1972. *Biography of Lord Dunsany.* William Collins, London.

Arditti, J. 1979. Orchids in science fiction, mystery and adventure stories. *Amer. Orchid Soc. Bull.* 48: 1122–1126.

———. 1980. Orchids in science fiction, mystery and adventure stories—2—no blandishments for Miss Orchid. *Amer. Orchid Soc. Bull.* 49: 1005–1009.

———. 1984. Orchids in novels, music, parables, quotes, secrets, and odds and ends. *Orchid Rev.* 92: 373–376.

Arnold, M. 1926a. The scholar gipsy. In *The poems of Matthew Arnold 1849–1867.* Oxford University Press, Oxford, pp. 218–225.

———. 1926b. Stanzas composed at Carnac. In *The poems of Matthew Arnold 1849–1867.* Oxford University Press, Oxford, pp. 370–371.

———. 1926c. Thyrsis. In *The poems of Matthew Arnold 1849–1867.* Oxford University Press, Oxford, pp. 351–358.

Auden, W. H. 1976. Anthem for St. Cecilia's Day (for Benjamin Britten). In E. Mendelson (ed.), *Collected poems.* Random House, New York, pp. 220–221.

Bacon, H. 1975. "In-and outdoor schooling" Robert Frost and the classics. In *Robert Frost: lectures on the centennial of his birth.* Library of Congress, Washington, D.C., pp. 3–25.

Bainbridge, J. *Garbo.* 1955. Holt, Rinehart & Winston, New York.

Baring-Gould, W. S. 1969. *Nero Wolfe of West Thirty-Fifth Street.* Viking, New York.

Bennett, A. 1918. *The pretty lady.* G. H. Doran, New York.

Berg, A. 1964. *Libretto, Lulu, Oper von Alban Berg nach den Tragödien Erdgeist und Büchae der Pandora von Frank Wedekind.* Universal ed. H. E. Apostel, Vienna.

Bernstein, L., A. Laurents, and S. Sondheim. 1956. *West side story.* Random House, New York.

Branch, W., H. Parker, and H. Hayford with A. MacDougall. 1984. Historial note. In H. Hayford, H. Parker, and G. T. Tanselle (eds.), *Herman Melville, The confidence-man: his masquerade,* Northwestern-Newberry ed. of the writings of Herman Melville, vol. 10. Northwestern University Press & The Newberry Library, Evanston & Chicago, pp. 255–357.

Brod, M. 1960. *Streitbares Leben Autobiographie.* Kindler Verlag, Munich.

Bronte, C. 1971. *Jane Eyre.* W. W. Norton, New York.

Brooke, J. 1950. *The wild orchids of Britain.* T. Y. Crowell, London.

Brooke, J. 1981a. *The military orchid. In* The orchid trilogy. Penguin, Harmondsworth, England, pp. 13–107.

———. 1981b. *A mine of serpents. In* The orchid trilogy. Penguin, Harmondsworth, England, pp. 108–303.

———. 1981c. *The goose cathedral. In* The orchid trilogy. Penguin, Harmondsworth, England, pp. 304–437.

Browning, E. B. 1900. Aurora Leigh. In *The complete poetical works of Elizabeth Barrett Browning.* Houghton Mifflin, Boston, pp. 254–410.

Bryant, W. C. 1903. The death of the flowers. In *The poetical works of William Cullen Bryant.* Rpt. 1969–1972. AMS Press, New York, pp. 92–93.

Chandler, R. 1973. The curtain. In *Killer in the rain.* Ballantine Books, New York, pp. 87–127.

———. 1976. *The big sleep.* Vintage Books, New York.

———. 1981. Letter to Cleve Adams, September 4, 1948. In F. MacShane (ed.), *Selected letters of Raymond*

Chandler. Columbia Univ. Press, New York, pp. 125–127.

Chase, J. H. N. d. [1948]. *The flesh of the orchid: a continuation of no orchids for Miss Blandish.* Jarrolds Publishers, London.

_____ . 1980. *No orchids for Miss Blandish.* Penguin Books, New York.

Christopher, N. 1983. The house where Lord Rochester died. *The New Yorker.* January 24: 42.

Clampitt, A. 1983. The smaller orchid. In *The kingfisher: poems by Amy Clampitt.* Alfred A. Knopf, New York, p. 52.

Clare, J. 1935a. Cowper Green. In J. W. Tibble (ed.), *The poems of John Clare.* Vol. 1. J. M. Dent & Sons, London; E. P. Dutton, New York, pp. 174–180.

_____ . 1935b. The cross roads or the haymaker's story. In J. W. Tibble (ed.), *The poems of John Clare.* Vol. 1. J. M. Dent & Sons, London; E. P. Dutton, New York, pp. 455–462.

_____ . 1935c. May noon. In J. W. Tibble (ed.), *The poems of John Clare.* Vol. 1. J. M. Dent & Sons, London; E. P. Dutton, New York, p. 280.

_____ . 1935d. The nightingale's nest. In J. W. Tibble, *The poems of John Clare.* Vol. 2. J. M. Dent & Sons, London; E. P. Dutton, New York, pp. 213–216.

_____ . 1935e. Recollections after a ramble. In J. W. Tibble (ed.), *The poems of John Clare.* Vol. 1. J. M. Dent & Sons, London; E. P. Dutton, New York, pp. 181–188.

_____ . 1935f. The wild-flower nosegay. In J. W. Tibble (ed.), *The poems of John Clare.* Vol. 1. J. M. Dent & Sons, London; E. P. Dutton, New York, pp. 225–227.

Clarke, A. C. 1974. The reluctant orchid. In *The nine billion names of God: the best short stories of Arthur C. Clarke.* Signet, New York, pp. 184–192.

Collier, J. 1941. Green thoughts. In *Presenting moonshine: stories by John Collier.* Viking, New York, pp. 35–37.

Cook, T. H. 1982. *The orchids.* Houghton Mifflin, Boston.

de Morinni, C. 1948. Loie Fuller—the fairy of light. In P. Magriel (ed.), *Chronicles of the American dance.* Henry Holt, New York, pp. 202–220.

Dickinson, E. 1955a. All these my banners be. In T. H. Johnson (ed.), *The poems of Emily Dickinson.* 3 vols. Harvard University Press, Cambridge, no. 22.

_____ . 1955b. Some rainbow—coming from the fair. In T. H. Johnson (ed.), *The poems of Emily Dickinson.* 3 vols. Harvard University Press, Cambridge, no. 64.

_____ . 1955c. There is a flower that bees prefer. In T. H. Johnson (ed.), *The poems of Emily Dickinson.* 3 vols. Harvard University Press, Cambridge, no. 380.

Doolittle, H. 1929. At Baia. In *Collected poems of H. D.* Horace Liveright, New York, pp. 186–187.

Dos Passos, J. 1969. *The big money.* Signet, New York.

Duncan, I. 1955. *My life.* Liveright, New York.

Dunsany, E. Plunkett, Lord. 1917. The Laughter of the gods. In *Plays of gods and men by Lord Dunsany.* John W. Luce, Boston, pp. 51–129.

_____ . 1928. *The blessing of Pan.* G. P. Putnam's Sons, New York.

Ellacombe, H. N. 1884. *The plant-lore & garden-craft of Shakespeare,* 2nd ed. Satchell; Simpkin, & Marshall, London.

Eliot, S. A., Jr. 1923. *Introduction to Tragedies of sex by Frank Wedekind.* Boni & Liveright, New York, pp. vii–xxiv.

Elmslie, K. 1973. *The orchid stories.* Doubleday, Garden City, N.Y.

Emerson, R. W. 1904. Woodnotes. In *Poems by Ralph Waldo Emerson.* Houghton Mifflin, Boston, pp. 43–57.

Espey, J. 1974. *Ezra Pound's Mauberley: a study in composition.* First published in 1955. University of California Press, Berkeley.

Firbank, R. 1949. Prancing nigger. *In* Five novels. New Directions, New York, pp. 95–145.

Fitzgerald, F. S. 1925. *The great Gatsby.* Charles Scribner's Sons, New York.

Fleming, I. 1963. *On Her Majesty's secret service.* Signet, New York.

Frazer, J. G. 1913. *Balder the beautiful: the fire-festivals of Europe and the doctrine of the eternal soul.* Vol. 2. (*The golden bough: a study in magic and religion*). Macmillan, London.

Freeman, M. B. 1976. *The unicorn tapestries.* Metropolitan Museum of Art, New York.

Frost, R. 1969a. An encounter. In *The poetry of Robert Frost: the collected poems, complete and unabridged.* Holt, Rinehart & Winston, New York, p. 125.

_____ . 1969b. Mowing. In *The poetry of Robert Frost: the collected poems, complete and unabridged.* Holt, Rinehart & Winston, New York, p. 17.

_____ . 1969c. On going unnoticed. In *The poetry of Robert Frost: the collected poems, complete and unabridged.* Holt, Rinehart & Winston, New York, p. 247.

_____ . 1969d. The quest of the purple-fringed. In *The poetry of Robert Frost: the collected poems, complete and unabridged.* Holt, Rinehart & WInston, New York, pp. 342–343.

_____ . 1969e. Rose pogonias. In *The poetry of Robert Frost: the collected poems, complete and unabridged.*

Holt, Rinehart & Winston, New York, pp. 13–14.

———. 1969f. The self-seeker. In *The poetry of Robert Frost: the collected poems, complete and unabridged.* Holt, Rinehart & Winston, New York, pp. 92–101.

Fuller, L. 1913. *Fifteen years of a dancer's life with some account of her distinguished friends.* Herbert Jenkins, London.

Gabor, E. 1954. *Orchids and salami.* Doubleday, Garden City, N.Y.

Gerard(e), J. 1633. *The herball or generall historie of plantes.* T. Johnson (ed.). Islip, Norton & Whitaker, London.

Grant, R. 1905. *The orchid.* Charles Scribner's Sons, New York. Rpt. 1968. Gregg Press, Upper Saddle River, N. J.

Hall, M. 1970. Tea and the tiger, Wild orchids: the screen by Mordaunt Hall. In *The New York Times Film Reviews 1913–1968.* Vol. 1. N.Y. Times & Arno Press, New York, pp. 516–17.

Hamilton, R. M. 1971. The orchidology of Nero Wolfe. *Orchidata* 10: 133–137.

Hamilton, R. M. 1984. The orchidology of Nero Wolfe. *Canadian Orchid J.* 2: 31–38.

Hart, M., and G. S. Kaufman. 1937. *You can't take it with you.* Dramatist's Play Service, New York.

Hart-Davis, R. (ed.). 1962. *The letters of Oscar Wilde.* Harcourt, Brace & World, New York.

Hawthorne, N. 1964. The Blithedale romance. In W. Charvat, R. H. Pearce, C. M. Simpson, F. Bowers, M. Bruccoli, and L. N. Smith (eds.), *Centenary edition of the works of Nathaniel Hawthorne.* Vol. 3. Ohio State University Press, Columbus, Ohio, pp. 5–247.

———. 1972. The American notebooks. In W. Charvat, 1905–1966, R. H. Pearce, C. M. Simpson, F. Bowers, L. N. Smith, and J. Manning (eds.), *Centenary edition of the works of Nathaniel Hawthorne.* Vol. 8. C. M. Simpson (ed.). Ohio State University Press, Columbus, Ohio.

———. 1974. Rappaccini's daughter from the writings of Aubépine. In W. Charvat, 1905–1966, R. H. Pearce, C. M. Simpson, F. Bowers, L. N. Smith, J. Manning, and J. D. Crowley (eds.), *Centenary edition of the works of Nathaniel Hawthorne.* Vol. 10. Ohio State University Press, Columbus, Ohio, pp. 91–128.

Hesiod. ca. 700 B.C. *Theogony,* lines 190–198. In H. G. Evelyn-White (ed.), *Hesiod, the Homeric hymns, and Homerica.* 2nd ed. Trans. in 1936 by H. G. Evelyn-White. Loeb Classical Library. Harvard University Press, Cambridge.

Hill, G. L. 1935. *White orchids.* Grosset & Dunlap. New York.

Hoffman, D. G. 1950. Melville's "Story of China Aster." *Am. Lit.* 22: 137–149.

Homer. ca. 800 B.C. Iliad, bk. 6, lines 357–358. In D. Monro and T. Allen (eds.), *Homeri opera.* 1920. 3rd ed. Vol. 1. Oxford University Press, London.

———. ca. 750 B.C. Odyssey, bk. 5, lines 55–158. In T. W. Allen (ed.), *Homeri opera.* 1908. 2nd ed. Vol. 3. Oxford University Press, London.

Huxley, A. 1965. *Point counter point.* Harper & Row, New York.

Huysmans, J.-K. 1884. *Against nature.* Trans. in 1966 by R. Baldick. Penguin Books, New York.

Hyde, H. M. 1976. *Oscar Wilde: a biography.* Eyre Methuen, London.

———. (ed.). 1982. *The annotated Oscar Wilde: poems, fiction, plays, lectures, essays, and letters.* Clarkson N. Potter, New York.

Hynes, S. 1968. *The Edwardian turn of mind.* Princeton University Press, Princeton, New Jersey.

Janson, H. W. 1977. *History of art.* 2nd ed. Prentice-Hall & Harry N. Abrams, New York.

Jullian, P. 1969. *Dreamers of decadence: symbolist painters of the 1890's.* Trans. in 1971 by R. Baldick. Praeger Publishers, New York.

Jung, C. G. 1944. *Psychology and alchemy.* Trans. in 1953 by R. F. C. Hull. Pantheon-Bollingen Books, New York.

Kahn, G., E. Eliscu, and V. Youmans. 1933. *Orchids in the moonlight.* T. B. Harms, New York.

Karp, V. 1983. Tulips: a selected history. *The New Yorker,* October 10: 54.

Katkov, N. 1983. *Blood and orchids.* St. Martin's/Marek, New York.

Kayser, W. 1957. *The grotesque in art and literature.* Trans. in 1981 by U. Weisstein. Columbia University Press, New York.

te Kloot, O. 1919. Orchideen. Der Orchideengarten: Phantastische Blätter 1,5: 1–4.

Latham, A. 1977. *Orchids for Mother.* Little, Brown, Boston.

Lawler, L. J. 1984. Ethnobotany of the Orchidaceae. In J. Arditti (ed.), *Orchid biology: reviews and perspectives, III.* Cornell University Press, Ithaca, N.Y., pp. 27149.

Lawrence, D. H. 1959. *Lady Chatterley's lover.* Signet, New York.

———. 1977. Cypresses. In V. de Sola Pinto, and W. Roberts (eds.), *The complete poems of D. H. Lawrence.* Penguin Books, New York, pp. 295–298.

Le Carré, J. 1983. *The little drummer girl.* Alfred A. Knopf, New York.

Le Gallienne, R. 1894. Fractional humanity. In *Prose fancies.* G. P. Putnam's Sons, New York, pp. 28–34.

Lewis, S. 1961. *Main street.* Signet, New York.

McAleer, J. 1977. *Rex Stout: a biography.* Little, Brown, Boston.

Mariani, P. 1981. *William Carlos Williams: a new world naked.* McGraw-Hill, New York.

Marsh, J. 1978. *The illuminated language of flowers: illustrated by Kate Greenaway.* Holt, Rinehart & Winston, New York.

Maugham, W. S. 1946. *The razor's edge.* Pocket Books, New York.

Melville, H. 1947. *Moby Dick.* W. Thorp (ed.), Oxford University Press, New York.

———. 1984. The confidence-man: his masquerade. In H. Hayford, H. Parker, and G. T. Tanselle (eds.), *Northwestern-Newberry ed. of the writings of Herman Melville.* Vol. 10. Northwestern University Press & The Newberry Library, Evanston & Chicago.

Messick, D. 1940. *Brenda Starr.* Chicago Tribune Syndicate, Chicago.

Meyrink, G. 1905. Bologneser Tränen. In *Orchideen: Sonderbare Geschichten.* Albert Langen Verlag, Munich, pp. 77–84.

Moore, M. 1935a. The frigate pelican. In *Selected poems.* Macmillan, New York, pp. 22–25, 111 note.

———. 1935b. An octopus. In *Selected poems.* Macmillan, New York, pp. 82–89, 121 note.

Nathan, R. 1931. *The orchid.* Bobbs-Merrill, Indianapolis.

Nietzsche, F. 1980. Die Geburt der Tragödie. In G. Colli, and M. Montinari (eds.). *Sämtliche Werke.* Vol. 1. Deutscher Taschenbuch Verlag, Walter de Gruyter, Berlin, pp. 11–156.

"'The Orchid' at the Gaiety, Part 1." 1904a. *The Play-Pictorial* 4,19: 1–26.

"'The Orchid' at the Gaiety, Part 2." 1904b. *The Play-Pictorial* 4,22: 81–112.

Der Orchideengarten: Phantastische Blätter. [1919–1921]. Ed. by A. von Czibulka, H. Hofmann-Montanus, and K. H. Strobl. M. Müller & Sohn, Munich. Vols. 1–3.

Orwell, G. 1946. Raffles and Miss Blandish. In *Dickens, Dali & others: studies in popular culture.* Reynal & Hitchcock, New York, pp. 202–221.

Osborn, P. 1893. Heartsease and orchid. *The Spirit Lamp,* 3, 2, February 17: 43.

Osgood, F. S. (ed.). 1841. *The poetry of flowers and flowers of poetry: to which are added, a simple treatise on botany, with familiar examples, and a copious floral dictionary.* J. C. Riker, New York.

Oxford English dictionary. 1971. J. Murray, H. Bradley, W. A. Craigie, and C. T. Onions (eds.), compact ed. Oxford University Press, Oxford.

Petronius. ca. 54–68 A. D. *Satyricon of Petronius Arbiter.* Translated in 1913 by M. Heseltine, and revised in 1969 by E. H. Warmington. Loeb Classical Library. Harvard University Press, Cambridge; William Heinemann, London.

Plath, S. 1981a. Fever 103°. In *The collected poems.* Harper & Row, New York, pp. 231–232.

———. 1981b. The surgeon at 2 a.m. In *The collected poems.* Harper & Row, New York, pp. 170–171.

Poe, E. A. 1983a. Eleonora. In T. Mossman (ed.), *The unabridged Edgar Allan Poe.* Running Press, Philadelphia, pp. 721–726.

———. 1983b. The scythe of time. In T. Mossman (ed.), *The unabridged Edgar Allan Poe.* Running Press, Philadelphia, pp. 506–513.

———. 1983c. The Signora Psyche Zenobia. In T. Mossman (ed.), *The unabridged Edgar Allan Poe.* Running Press, Philadelphia, pp. 498–506.

———. 1983d. The thousand-and-second tale of Scheherezade. In T. Mossman (ed.), *The unabridged Edgar Allan Poe.* Running Press, Philadelphia, pp. 1012–1027.

Pound, E. 1926. Hugh Selwyn Mauberley (life and contacts). In *Personae: the collected poems of Ezra Pound.* New Directions, New York, pp. 185–204.

———. 1970. Canto 48. In *The cantos.* New Directions, New York, pp. 240–243.

Powell, J. E. 1977. *Joseph Chamberlain.* Thames & Hudson, London.

Proust, M. 1913. Swann's way. In *Remembrance of things past.* Trans. in 1982 by C. K. S. Moncrieff, and T. Kilmartin. Vol. 1. Random House, New York, pp. 3–462.

———. 1921a. Cities of the plain, part 1. In *Remembrance of things past.* Trans. in 1982 by C. K. S. Moncrieff, and T. Kilmartin. Vol. 2. Random House, New York, pp. 623–656.

———. 1921b. The Guermantes way, chap. 2. In *Remembrance of things past.* Trans. in 1982 by C. K. S. Moncrieff, and T. Kilmartin. Vol. 2. Random House, New York, pp. 358–620.

Reinikka, M. A. 1972. *A history of the orchid.* University of Miami Press, Coral Gables, Fla.

Rhys, J. 1979. *Smile please: an unfinished autobiography.* Harper & Row, New York.

———. 1985a. Voyage in the dark. In *The complete novels.* W. W. Norton, New York, pp. 1–115.

———. 1985b. Wide Sargasso Sea. In *The complete novels.* W. W. Norton, New York, pp. 463–574.

Rilke, R. M. 1955. Der Träumer. In *Sämtliche Werke.* Vol. 1. Insel-Verlag, Leipzig, pp. 36–37.

Roethke, T. 1968a. Letter to Kenneth Burke, February 27, 1945. In R. J. Mills, Jr. (ed.), *The selected letters of Theodore Roethke.* University of Washington Press, Seattle, pp. 112–114.

1968b. Letter to Babette Deutsch, January 22, 1948. In R. J. Mills, Jr. (ed.), *The selected letters of Theodore Roethke.* University of Washington Press, Seattle, pp. 139–142.

———. 1968c. Letter to Kenneth Burke, September 17, 1949. In R. J. Mills, Jr. (ed.), *The selected letters of Theodore Roethke.* University of Washington Press, Seattle, pp. 160–163.

———. 1968d. Letter to Ralph J. Mills, Jr., March 23, 1962. In R. J. Mills, Jr. (ed.), *The selected letters of Theodore Roethke.* University of Washington Press, Seattle, pp. 251–254.

_____ . 1975. Orchids. In *The collected poems of Theodore Roethke.* Doubleday, Garden City, N.Y., p. 37.

Ruskin, J. 1906. Proserpina: studies of wayside flowers, while the air was yet pure among the Alps, and in the Scotland and England which my father knew. In E. T. Cook, and A. Wedderburn (eds.). *The works of John Ruskin.* Vol. 25. George Allen, London, pp. 187–569.

Sargeant, W. 1981. Profiles: presence. *The New Yorker.* January 26: 40–60.

Seager, A. 1968. *The glass house: the life of Theodore Roethke.* McGraw-Hill, New York.

Shakespeare, W. 1936. Hamlet, Act 4, scene 7. In G. L. Kittredge (ed.), *The complete works of Shakespeare.* Ginn, Boston, pp. 1145–1193.

S[haw], G. B. 1897. Mr. Wilson Barrett as the Messiah. *The Saturday Review.* February 13: 168–170.

Simenauer, E. 1980. R. M. Rilke's dreams and his conception of dream. In F. Baron, E. Dick, and W. Maurer (eds.), *Rilke: the alchemy of alienation.* Regent's Press of Kansas, Lawrence, pp. 243–262.

Sinclair, U. 1974. *The jungle.* Robert Bentley, Cambridge.

Snow, C. P. 1979. *A coat of varnish.* Charles Scribner's Sons, New York.

S[orrentino], G. 1963. Bordertown. Quoted in W. C. Williams, *Paterson.* New Directions, New York, pp. 214–215.

Stapleton, L. 1978. *Marianne Moore: the poet's advance.* Princeton University Press, Princeton.

Stebbins, T. E., Jr. 1975. *The life and works of Martin Johnson Heade.* Yale University Press, New Haven.

Stout, R. 1934. *Fer-de-lance.* Farrar & Rinehart, New York. Cited in 1977 in J. McAleer, *Rex Stout: a biography.* Little, Brown, Boston.

_____ . 1942. Black orchids. In *Black orchids.* Farrar & Rinehart, New York. Cited in 1977 in J. McAleer, *Rex Stout: a biography.* Little, Brown, Boston.

Swinson, A. 1970. *Fredrick Sander: The orchid king: the record of a passion.* Hodder & Stoughton, London.

Tanner, J. T., A. Ross, P. Greenbach, I. Caryll, L. Monckton, and D. Godfrey. 1903. *The orchid.* Chappell, London; Boosey, New York.

Tennyson, A. 1899. In Memoriam. In *The complete poetic and dramatic works of Alfred Lord Tennyson.* Houghton Mifflin, Boston, pp. 217–259.

Thompson, L. 1966. *Robert Frost: the early years 1874–1915.* Holt, Rinehart & Winston, New York.

Thoreau, H. 1949. *The journal of Henry D. Thoreau.* Ed. by B. Torrey and F. H. Allen. 14 vols. Houghton Mifflin, Cambridge.

Thornton, R. K. R. 1980. "Decadence" in later nineteenth-century England. In I. Fletcher (ed.), *Decadence and the 1890's.* Holmes & Meier, New York, pp. 15–29.

Tomlinson, C. 1958. "Poem." In *Poems: seeing is believing.* McDowell, Obolensky, New York, p. 24.

Turner, W. 1568. *The first and second parts of the herball.* Arnold Birckman, London.

Updike, J. 1984. Personal history: a soft spring night in Shillington. *The New Yorker,* December 24: 37–57.

Vandermeulen, J. H. 1985. Nero Wolfe—orchidist extraordinaire. *Amer. Orchid Soc. Bull.* 54: 142–148.

Walcott, D. 1986. Jean Rhys. In *Collected poems 1948–1984.* Farrar, Straus & Giroux, New York, pp. 427–429.

Wallace, A. R. 1969. *A narrative of travels on the Amazon and Rio Negro, with an account of the native tribes, and observations on the climate, geology, and natural history of the Amazon valley.* Reprint of 3rd ed., 1895. Greenwood Press, New York.

Waugh, E. 1946. *Brideshead revisited: the sacred and profane memories of Captain Charles Ryder.* Little, Brown, Boston.

Weaver, M. 1971. *William Carlos Williams: the American background.* Cambridge University Press, Cambridge.

Wedekind, F. 1895. Earth-Spirit. In *Tragedies of sex,* pp. 111–216. Trans. and intro. in 1923 by S. A. Eliot, Jr. Boni & Liveright, New York.

_____ . Pandora's Box. 1902. In *Tragedies of sex,* pp. 217–304. Trans. and intro. in 1923 by S. A. Eliot, Jr. Boni & Liveright, New York.

Wells, H. G. 1924. The flowering of the strange orchid. In *The Works of H. G. Wells,* Atlantic ed. Vol. 1. T. Fisher Unwin, London, pp. 308–319.

West, N. 1969. The day of the locust. In *Miss Lonelyhearts and the day of the locust.* New Directions, New York, pp. 59–185.

Wharton, E. 1962. *The house of mirth.* Holt, Rinehart & Winston, New York.

White, F. M. 1899. The purple terror. *The Strand Magazine* 18: 242–251.

White, J. 1986. Cartoonist retired but not retiring. *Kansas City Star,* November 20: 1 C, 6 C.

Whitman, W. 1977. The first spring day on Chestnut Street, pp. 545–547, Specimen days. In *The portable Walt Whitman,* Penguin Books, New York, pp. 387–640.

Whitney, P. A. 1985. *Dream of orchids.* Doubleday, Garden City, N.Y.

Wilde, O. 1927. The burden of Itys. In *The poems of Oscar Wilde.* Boni & Liveright, New York, pp. 61–82.

_____ . 1962a. Letter to Robert Ross, May/June, 1892. In R. Hart-Davis (ed.), *The letters of Oscar Wilde.* Harcourt, Brace & World, New York, p. 314.

_____ . 1962b. Letter to Lord Alfred Douglas, January, 1893. In R. Hart-Davis (ed.), *The letters of Oscar

Wilde. Harcourt, Brace & World, New York, p. 326.

       . 1962c. Letter to Ralph Payne, February 12, 1894. In R. Hart-Davis (ed.), *The letters of Oscar Wilde.* Harcourt, Brace & World, New York, p. 352.

       . 1962d. Letter to the editor of the Pall Mall Gazette, October 1, 1894. In R. Hart-Davis (ed.), *The letters of Oscar Wilde.* Harcourt, Brace & World, New York, p. 373.

       . 1962e. Letter to Ada Leverson, May 4 or 5, 1895. In R. Hart-Davis (ed.), *The letters of Oscar Wilde.* Harcourt, Brace & World, New York, p. 395.

       . 1982a. The picture of Dorian Gray. In H. M. Hyde (ed.). *The annotated Oscar Wilde: poems, fiction, plays, lectures, essays, and letters.* Clarkson N. Potter, New York, pp. 138–253.

       . 1982b. The soul of man under socialism. In H. M. Hyde (ed.). *The annotated Oscar Wilde: poems, fiction, plays, lectures, essays, and letters.* Clarkson N. Potter, New York, pp. 398–417.

Williams, W. C. 1951. A celebration. In *The collected earlier poems.* New Directions, New York, pp. 188–190.

       . 1956. The destruction of Tenochtitlan: Cortez and Montezuma. In *In the American grain.* New Directions, New York, pp. 27–38.

       . 1962a. Asphodel, that greeny flower. In *Pictures from Brueghel and other poems: collected poems 1950–1962.* New Directions, New York, pp. 153–182.

       . 1962b. The rewaking. In *Pictures from Brueghel and other poems: collected poems 1950–1962.* New Directions, New York, p. 70.

       . 1963. *Paterson.* New Directions, New York.

       . 1967. *The autobiography of William Carlos Williams.* New Directions, New York.

       . 1973. Man orchid. In P. Mariani (ed.) A. Williams garland: petals from the Falls, 1945–1950. *Mass. Rev.* Winter: 65–148.

Winspear, S. 1986. *Les fleurs du mal"* and others: the orchid as a literary image. Orchid Rev. 94: 19–21.

Withner, C. L. (ed.). 1959. *The orchids: a scientific survey.* Ronald Press, New York.

Wyndham, V. 1963. *The sphinx and her circle: a biographical sketch of Ada Leverson 1862–1933.* André Deutsch, London.

Yonge, C. M. 1865. *The trial: more links of the daisy chain.* 2 vol. in one. D. Appleton, New York.

Additional Literature

Adams, P., and C. Nightingale. 1976. Planting time. In P. Strick (ed.). *Antigrav.* Taplinger, New York, pp. 129–143.

Allfrey, P. S. 1954. *The orchid house.* E. P. Dutton, New York.

Allred, P., and T. 1942. Orchids for Margaret. *One Act Play Magazine.* May–June: 169–191.

Auchincloss, L. 1968. *A world of profit.* Houghton Mifflin, Boston.

Ballard, J. G. 1963. Prima belladonna. In J. G. Ballard, *The four dimensional nightmare,* Penguin Books, Harmondsworth, England, pp. 83–97.

Boyd, J. 1978. *The pollinators of Eden.* Penguin Books, New York.

Clampitt, A. 1983. Imago. In *The kingfisher: poems by Amy Clampitt.* Alfred A. Knopf, New York, pp. 74–76.

Clare, J. 1935a. Dewdrops. In J. W. Tibble (ed.), *The poems of John Clare.* Vol. 2. J. M. Dent & Sons, London; E. P. Dutton, New York, pp. 426–427.

       . 1935b. I pluck summer blossoms. In J. W. Tibble (ed.), *The poems of John Clare.* Vol. 2. J. M. Dent & Sons, London; E. P. Dutton, New York. p. 428.

       . 1935c. Joys of childhood. In J. W. Tibble (ed.), *The poems of John Clare.* Vol. 2. J. M. Dent & Sons, London; E. P. Dutton, New York. p. 41–43.

Clarke, A. C. 1980. *The fountains of paradise.* Ballantine Books, New York.

Emerson, R. W. 1904. "The Adirondacs." In *Poems by Ralph Waldo Emerson.* Houghton Mifflin, Boston, pp. 159–170.

Franke, H. W. 1973. *The orchid cage.* Daw Books, New York.

Fuentes, C. 1982. *Orchids in the moonlight.* World premiere. Amer. Repertory Theatre (Harvard).

van Gulik, R. 1967a. The two beggars. In *R. von Gulik, Judge Dee at work.* Charles Scribner's Sons, New York, pp. 94–115.

       . 1967b. *Necklace and calabash.* Charles Scribner's Sons, New York.

Herburger, G. 1979. *Orchidee: Gedichte.* Hermann Luchterhand Verlag, Hagen.

Hesse, H. 1927. *Steppenwolf.* Trans. in 1969 by B. Creighton. Bantam Books, New York.

Hettinger, E. (ed.). 1970. *Springs of friendship.* Herder and Herder, New York.

Ireland, K. 1974. *Orchids hummingbirds and other poems.* Auckland University Press, Auckland, New Zealand.

King, S. 1982. *Different seasons*. Viking Press, New York.

Kipling, R. 1951. Reingelder and the German flag. In R. T. Bond (ed.), *Handbook for poisoners*. Rinehart, New York, pp. 179–182.

Kull, A. S. 1976. *Secrets of flowers*. Stephen Greene, Brattleboro, Vt.

Lawrence, D. H. 1955. The witch a la mode. In *The complete short stories*. Vol. 1. Heinemann, London, pp. 54–70.

_____ . 1955. The man who loved islands. In *The complete short stories*. Vol. 3. Heinemann, London, pp. 722–746.

Mayer, S., and T. de Zuniga. 1973. The anger of the black orchid. *D.C. Adventure Comics* 39: 1–14.

Meyer, N., and B. J. Kaplan. 1978. *Black orchid*. Bantam Books, Toronto.

Moore, M. 1935a. Marriage. In *Selected poems*. Macmillan, New York, pp. 72–81.

_____ . 1935b. People's surroundings. In *Selected poems*. Macmillan, New York, pp. 62–65.

_____ . 1935c. The plumet basilisk. In *Selected poems*. Macmillan, New York, pp. 16–21.

Neal, J. ca. 1884. *Rays from the realms of nature; or, parables of plant life*. 5th ed. Casell, Petter, Galpin, London, Paris & New York.

Perera, R. 1968. *Orchids and cacti: a miscellany, poems, a short story, two dramas*. Kularatne, Colombo, Ceylon.

Pound, E. 1926. Sennin poem by Kakuhaku. In *Personae: the collected poems of Ezra Pound*. New Directions, New York, pp. 139–140.

Proust, M. 1919. Within a budding grove. In *Remembrance of things past*. Trans. in 1982 by C. K. S. Moncrieff, and T. Kilmartin. Vol. 1. Random House, New York, pp. 465–1018.

Rilke, R. M. 1959. Die Sprache der Blumen. In *Sämtliche Werke*. Vol. 3. Insel-Verlag, Leipzig, p. 36.

Sitwell, S. 1972. *Tropicalia*. Ramsay Head, Edinburgh.

Snow, K. 1984. Gifts. In *Fifty years of American poetry. Anniversary Volume for the Academy of American Poets*. Harry N. Abrams, New York, pp. 241–242.

Stevens, W. 1972. Lulu gay. In *Opus posthumous by Stevens*. Alfred A. Knopf, New York, p. 26.

Stout, R. (E. Day). 1914. Rose Orchid. *All-Story Weekly*, March 28: 876–883. Cited in J. McAleer, *Rex Stout: a biography*. Little, Brown, Boston, pp. 142–143, 581.

Tepper, S., and R. Bennett. 1948. *Red roses for a blue lady*. Belwin-Mills, Miami.

Walcott, D. 1986. The swamp. In *Collected poems 1948–1984*. Farrar, Straus & Giroux, New York, pp. 59–60.

Wells, H. G. 1924a. Aepyornis island. In *The works of H. G. Wells*. Atlantic ed. Vol. 1. T. Fisher Unwin, London, pp. 320–336.

_____ . 1924b. The Wonderful Visit. In *The works of H. G. Wells*. Atlantic ed. Vol. 1. T. Fisher Unwin, London, pp. 119–275.

Williams, W. C. 1950. To a lovely old bitch. In *The collected later poems*. New Directions, New York, p. 74.

7

Perspectives of Tropical Orchids In Space Research*

TATYANA M. CZEREVCZENKO and IRENE V. KOSAKOVSKAYA

*The literature survey for this chapter was concluded in August 1987; the chapter was submitted in October 1987, and the revised version was received in November 1987.

Introduction

Higher plants are necessary components of the human environment. Therefore methods for the cultivation of plants in space must be developed as part of biological life-support systems for astronauts. Long before the start of space flights, Konstantin E. Tsialkovsky (Tsialkovsky, 1929) planned to introduce plants into the life-support systems for astronauts. After the first space flight of Yury Gagarin, intensive research and experimental design were directed toward the use of plants in closed artificial ecosystems. These investigations were associated with the problem of plant cultivation for oxygen production, food and phytodesign during prolonged space flight. The criteria for evaluating plants as bioregenerative components were based on the degree of adaptation to the environment of spacecraft, efficiency of biomass production and possible use as food. In addition, the plants had to have an esthetic value within the closed artificial system, because this is an important factor in increasing human efficiency (Czerevczenko et al., 1986).

We attempted to select suitable plants on the basis of the literature and the problems of phytodesign in orbital stations. Our aim was to select plants which have biological and other characteristics suitable to weightlessness and other unfavorable factors. We also wanted plants which can contribute to a cheerful state of mind and efficiency (capacity to work) of the astronauts. Long-term studies of tropical and subtropical plants introduced into protected habitats in middle latitudes indicated that tropical epiphytic orchids would be most suitable (Czerevczenko and Majko, 1983).

Materials and Methods

After preliminary screening we examined three epiphytic orchids, *Epidendrum radicans*, *Doritis pulcherrima* and *Dendrobium kingianum*. To determine whether our assumption that epiphytic species are most suitable for cultivation under prolonged space flight conditions, we also studied an equal number of terrestrial orchids, a *Paphiopedilum* hybrid, *Paphiopedilum insigne* and *Anoectohilus dawsonianus*. All species were used in the bud or flowering stage.

The orchids were grown in a specially constructed microgreenhouse "Malahit-2" made by the Botanic Institute of the Ukrainian Academy of Sciences and designed in the scientificresearch Institute "Biotechnica" in Moscow, and in the Central Republic Botanical Garden in Kiev. These growth chambers measure $45 \times 35 \times 10$ cm (Fig. 7-1). Two lamps of 1500 lux each are installed in the upper part of the chamber whereas the watering and aeration systems are at the base (Fig. 7-2). The removable front panel is made of glass-fiber plastics. We used a synthetic substrate consisting of ion exchange materials.

The system was taken into space in the spaceship "Soyus-36" and placed in the orbital station "Salut-6" on 9 April 1980. The first orchids were returned to earth after a 60-day flight and replaced by new plants. The next expedition was after 110 days in space and after 171 days all astronauts and the test system returned to earth. As a result we could investigate three different steps in the adaptation of orchids to space flight conditions.

A "Malahit-2" system was maintained on earth with the same orchids, illumination, temperature, humidity and photoperiods. The same species, grown in the greenhouse of the Central Republic Botanical Garden in Kiev, served as a control.

Fig. 7-1. Tropical orchids in space experiments. **A.** "Malahit-2" system. **B.** Planter box with *Phaphiopedilum* orchid. **C.** *Epidendrum radicans* after 171-day flight (the upper part of the plant developed in space). **D.** *Doritis pulcherrima* three years after 60-day flight.

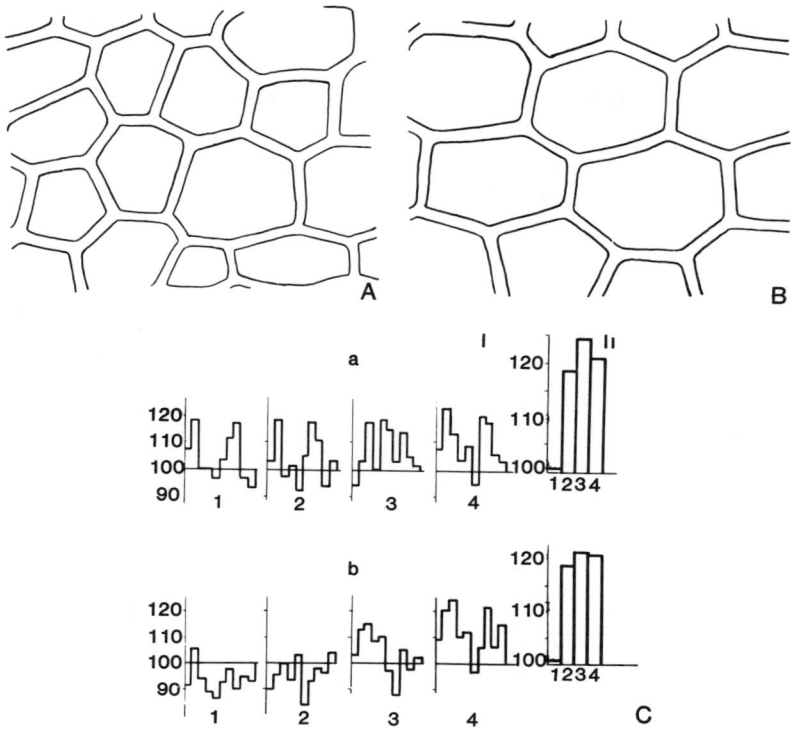

Fig. 7-2. Anatomy and phytohormone characteristic of *Epidendrum radicans.* **A.** Upper epidermis of leaf produced during space flight. **B.** Upper epidermis of leaf produced on earth. **C.** Histograms of auxin (I) and gibberellin (II) activity in vegetative parts of the plant after two (a) and four (b) months on a clinostat; 1—immediately after removal from the clinostat; 2—24 hr later; 3–48 hr later; 4—control.

During the flight astronauts Leonid Popov and Valery Rumin maintained the plants and carried out phenological observations. Biometric investigations consisted of cell size measurement with an ocular-micrometer and a microscope.

Plants of *Epindendrum radicans* were maintained for a long period (four months) on a horizontal clinostat at 3 rpm. The centrifugal force produced by the rotation of the clinostat was 5×10^{-5} g. Temperature and illumination regimes on the clinostat were the same as on board the orbital station. The activity of growth substances in the tissues of the orchids was monitored by paper cromatography and bioassay (Vlasov et al., 1979). Butanol : acetic acid : water (3:2:95,v/v/v) was used as a solvent for gibberellin chromatography; butanol : ammonia : water (30:1:6, v/v/v) was employed for auxin. The lettuce hypocotyl bioassay was utilized for gibberellin determinations and wheat coleoptile growth was used for auxin assays.

Soluble and structural proteins were extracted from the orchids' leaves by the method of Safonov (Safonov and Safonova, 1971) with some modifications (Czerevcenko et al., 1984; Kosakovskaya et al., 1984). Electrophoresis was carried out by the method of Davis (Davis, 1964) in 7.5% polyacrylamide gel under a current strength of 4 mA to each tube. Gels were stained with 0.2% Kumassi solution. The relative electrophoretic mobility of polypeptides was measured for 5–6 samples. Activity of ribulose bisphosphate carboxylase was determined by radiometrical method using Tris-HCI buffer at 30°C (Czernyadjev et al., 1975).

Results

Orchids taken to outer space endured longitudinal overloads of up to 4.5 units for 15 minutes and vibration of up to 8 units with a frequency of 1500–2000 Hz in three interperpendicular directions. Flowers and inflorescences maintained their ornamental features under these conditions, but flower longevity was reduced. Blossoms of *Doritis pulcherrima* lived only four days, those of *Paphiopedilum insigne* lasted five days, and *Epidendrum radicans* blooms remained fresh for seven days. In the greenhouse of the Botanical Garden, these flowers lived 35, 69 and 87 days respectively. The buds of *Doritis pulcherrima,* two species of *Paphiopedilum* and *Epidendrum radicans* died before opening, but growth of the plants continued.

Studies following the return to the earth showed that the different orchids varied in their response to space flight conditions (Table 7-1). The most tolerant species was *Epidendrum radicans,* which kept its ornamental characteristics and produced visible growth, leaves and aerial roots. Two lateral shoots appeared on the upper part of the main axis of the plant. However, the growth rate of *Epidendrum radicans* under space flight conditions was lower than that of the greenhouse-grown plants. Biometric and anatomical investigations of this orchid and comparison with control plants, placed in the climate chamber on (Tables 7-2, 7-3, 7-4, 7-5), demonstrated that under space flight conditions the linear and radial growth of axial organs was inhibited, and leaf size decreased.

Table 7-1. Growth of vegetative organs of orchids under conditions of space flight and on earth.

Species	Duration of flight, days	In space			On earth		
		Growth, cm	Number of		Growth, cm	Number of	
			Leaves	Aerial roots		Leaves	Aerial roots
Epidendrum radicans	171	10.2	5.6	2.3	18.7	9.9	4.2
Doritis pulcherrima	60	1.3	1.0	3.1	2.2	2.0	4.6
Dendrobium kingianum	171	0	0	—	0	3.0	—
Paphiopedilum hybrid							
Paphiopedilum insigne	Plants died after two months						
Anoectochilus dawsonianus							

Table 7-2. Biometric indices of *Epidendrum radicans* growth under space flight conditions and on earth.

Parameters	Millimeters	
	In space	On earth
Length internodes	16.2±2	20.2±1
aerial roots	48.3±6	71.2±10
Diameter axil shoots	2.4±1	3.0±0.2
aerial roots	1.7±0.06	2.5±0.2
Dimension of leaves length	44.5±3	69.2±8
width	11.3±2	13.2±2

Table 7-3. Indices of cell growth of *Epidendrum radicans* in space flight and on earth (in mμ).

Internode (in order of appearance)		Parenchyma		Sclerenhyma		Xylem veins	
		Space	Earth	Space	Earth	Space	Earth
4th,	produced before the flight	90±5	88±2	7±0.2	7±0.2	14±2	13±1
5th,	produced during the flight	85±3	90±1	6±0.5	8±0.2	11±2	14±1
6th,		77±4	88±2	4±0.1	7±0.2	13±2	14±2
7th,		79±5	87±1	7±0.2	8±0.3	14±3	15±1
8th,		77±4	87±2	10±0.3	8±0.2	13±1	15±1

Table 7-4. Indices of aerial root anatomy of *Epidendrum radicans* during space flight and on earth.

Aerial root (in order of appearance)	Velamen		Ectodermis	Parenchyma	Endodermis	Vascular tissue	
	Thickness of layer, mμ	Diameter of cells, mμ	Diameter of cells, mμ	Thickness of layer, mμ	Diameter of cells, mμ	Thickness of layer, mμ	Diameter of cells, mμ
			Space				
3rd formed on earth	208±10	55±3	49±2	608±3	31±5	110±19	34±4
4th[a]	250±12	60±4	49±2	470±14	23±4	95±12	29±3
5th[a]	154±14	50±4	43±3	372±12	21±2	110±10	22±2
6th[a]	188±8	52±2	41±4	315±20	20±2	108±10	26±6
			On earth				
3rd	220±8	56±2	48±8	598±8	33±5	115±10	33±3
4th	233±10	58±4	48±2	603±12	30±4	112±12	34±2
5th	208±12	54±2	22±4	572±3	27±3	114±15	26±6

[a]Aerial roots formed during the flight.

Table 7-5. Indices of *Epidendrum radicans* leaf anatomy in space flight and on earth.

Leaves (in order of appearance)	Thickness of lamina, mm	Number of epidermis cells on 1 mm² of leaf area		Space between veins, mμ	Stomata		
		upper	lower		Number per 1 mm² of leaf area	length, mμ	width, mμ
			In space				
6th produced before the flight	745	519±8	703±10	179	29±1	29±2	25±2
7th[a]	578	580±4	717±6	140	41±4	31±2	30±2
9th[a]	391	558±8	813±10	124	44±2	30±1	28±2
12th[a]	325	584±12	855±10	111	45±4	28±1	25±2
13th[a]	300	617±15	934±12	90	54±5	27±1	24±1
			On earth				
6th	750	525±10	708±8	184	29±1	28±1	24±3
7th	783	530±8	710±5	180	31±2	30±3	27±1
9th	790	528±12	706±5	185	28±3	27±1	24±2
12th	685	525±12	698±4	145	30±1	28±2	25±2
13th	640	580±6	720±5	140	37±3	27±1	24±1

[a]Leaves appeared during the flight.

Anatomical observations showed that the differentiation of shoot and roots tissues was nearly normal. The only differences in space were decreased cell size and considerable reduction of parenchyma tissues (Tables 7-3, 7-4). These may be the reasons why shoots and aerial roots decreased in diameter.

Space flight conditions had a more pronounced effect on leaf development in *Epidendrum radicans*. Leaves produced in space were smaller than those formed on earth. In addition, leaf thickness decreased consistently during the flight due to weak development of parenchyma tissue. The size of epidermis cells decreased also. All these lead to increased proximity of veins and a larger number of stomata per cm^2 leaf surface. The size of stomata remained nearly constant (Table 7-5).

Studies of the dynamics of accumulation and activity of endogenous gibberellins and auxins were carried out on the orchids maintained on a clinostat for four months. After two months the activity of gibberellins decreased considerably. Auxin activity levels were high initially and decreased only after four months. Within two days after terminiation of the clinostat experiment, the content and activity of gibberellins in the experimental plants increased to control level. Following 48 hours the level was somewhat higher than in the control plants. The content and activity of auxins which was reduced more slowly took longer to reach control levels.

After being returned to earth, the plants were grown in pots and placed in the greenhouse together with the controls. In some cases complete inhibition of *Epidendrum radicans* terminal shoot growth was observed. New lateral shoots appeared 55–65 days after landing and aerial roots developed on them soon thereafter. These plants grew well and did not differ from the controls.

Plants of *Dendrobium kingianum* lost their leaves during the flight, a phenomenon which does not occur in this species even during the rest period. Pseudobulbs remained alive, maintained their form and color and produced leafless shoots out their bases. Following the return to earth when grown under greenhouse conditions, the pseudobulbs of *Dendrobium kingianum* started to dry and died after 8–10 months. Growth of *Doritis pulcherrima* like that of *Epidendrum radicans* was retarded considerably during space flight. However, on the second day after landing, a new flower-bearing stem appeared from a leaf axil near the base of the main stem. In 30 days we observed a new leaf and aerial roots. The growth rate of flower-bearing stems and leaves was twice that of the control and the period from stem appearance to flowering was reduced from 98 to 45 days. The height of the new stem, the average diameter of flowers and length of peduncles were somewhat lower than in the controls. Phenorhythms of *Doritis pulcherrima* returned from the orbital station stabilized within a year and were very close to those of the controls. The data of biometric plant studies during 1980–1983 are presented in Table 6.

In 1982 we noticed that stems of the experimental plant branched unusually up to a third order of branching. Because three stems developed in quick succession, flowering continued for almost an entire year except for the period from the second half of March until May. The delicate characteristic of the inflorescence was retained years after the flight.

In 1982 and 1983 an increased number of flowers was noticed on inflorescences. Three years after the flight two so-called "children"[a] developed on the experimental plant. After removal from the parent plant, one grew and produced two flower-bearing

---

[a]In the west these would be called keikis (plural) or keiki (singular)—Ed.

Table 7-6. Effects of 60-day space flight on growth and development of *Doritis pulcherrima.*

Year	Height of plant, cm	Leaves Number	Length, cm	Aerial roots Number	Length, cm	Length of stem, cm	Length of peduncle, cm	Number	diameter, mm	Time from budding to anthesis, days
						In space				
1980	4.4	7.0	7.6	7.0	4.5	6.8	2.4	6	32	45
1981	4.4	3.0	7.5	8.0	4.5	8.7	2.9	11	31	57
1982	4.8	8.0	7.6	8.0	5.0	16.4	3.0	20	34	79
1983	7.9	9.0	8.1	11.0	5.8	28.6	3.2	25	32	87
						On earth				
1980	4.4	8.4	7.5	8.2	5.5	18.2	3.1	17	36	92
1981	4.9	8.8	7.4	9.3	5.5	17.6	3.0	18	34	88
1982	7.6	8.9	7.7	9.4	5.7	17.1	3.1	17	34	97
1983	7.6	8.7	7.4	8.2	5.5	16.9	3.0	16	35	94

Table 7-7. Relative electrophoretic mobility of soluble and structural proteins from epiphytic orchids.

Soluble proteins					Structural proteins				
Epidendrum radicans			*Doritis pulcherrima*		*Epidendrum radicans*			*Doritis pulcherrima*	
1[a]	2[a]	3[a]	1[a]	3[a]	1[a]	2[a]	3[a]	1[a]	3[a]
—	0.01	—	—	—	0.01	—	—	—	—
0.03	0.03	0.03	0.03	0.03	0.03	0.03	0.03	0.03	0.03
0.05	0.05	0.05	—	0.05	0.05	0.05	0.05	0.06	0.05
—	0.08	0.08	0.08	0.08	—	0.08	0.08	0.08	0.08
—	—	—	—	—	0.11	0.12	0.11	0.12	0.12
—	0.14	—	0.13	—	0.13	—	—	—	—
—	—	—	—	—	0.15	—	0.16	—	0.16
—	0.17	—	0.17	0.18	0.18	—	—	—	0.18
—	—	—	—	—	0.23	0.20	0.24	—	0.20
—	—	—	0.23	0.22	—	0.38	—	—	—
0.26	0.25	0.26	0.26	0.26	—	0.45	—	—	—
—	—	—	0.29	0.29	—	0.53	—	—	—
0.32	0.32	0.33	—	0.34	—	0.63	—	—	—
—	—	—	—	—	—	0.74	—	—	—
0.38	0.40	0.37	—	—					
—	—	0.50	0.48	—					
0.55	0.53	0.55	0.55	—					
0.58	0.58	0.58	—	0.59					
—	0.63	0.61	0.60	0.63					
0.70	—	—	0.70	—					
0.79	0.79	—	—	—					
0.85	—	—	—	—					
—	0.90	—	—	—					

[a]1, control (greenhouse on earth); 2, prolonged space flight; 3, 12 months in a greenhouse after return to earth.

Table 7-8. Carboxylase activity of ribulose bisphosphate carboxylase from leaves of epiphytic orchids.

Species	Activity in mE/mg of protein		
	Greenhouse	Prolonged space flight	12 months in a greenhouse after return to earth
Doritis pulcherrima	83.1	80.2	141.7
Epidendrum radicans	126.4	126.4	130.8

stems each year. Because on the length of their axes these inflorescences are larger and more pliable than the control.

Terrestrial orchids could not endure prolonged space flight and died.

The substantial hardiness of epiphytic orchids under conditions of prolonged space flight was confirmed by: 1) qualitative and quantitative determinations of protein content and 2) carboxylase activity measurements of the key enzyme associated with photosynthesis and photorespiration, ribulose bisphosphate carboxylase-oxygenase (RuBPCase). Space flight affects the composition and content of soluble and structural proteins in orchids' leaves (Table 7-7). An increase in the number of rapidly moving soluble and structural proteins was detected in *Epidendrum radicans*. New polypeptides appeared under stress during space flight conditions. Similar changes occurred in the leaves of *Doritis pulcherrima*. Studies of the spectra of soluble and structural proteins in orchids' leaves after 12 months of cultivation in a greenhouse on earth showed that initial values were restored completely.

Epidendrum radicans and *Doritis pulcherrima* were characterized by stable levels of carboxylase activity of RuBPCase. The data pertaining to carboxylase activity of the enzyme from *Doritis pulcherrima* plants grown in a greenhouse after the flight are particularly interesting. A two-fold increase of carboxylase activity of RuBPCase was recorded in *Doritis pulcherrima* after the return to earth and culture in the greenhouse. This enzyme was more active in the "child", and its activity was equal to 167.9 mE/mg of protein (Table 7-8).

Discussion

An understanding of plant growth and development under space flight conditions is very important now, because it can be indicative of how plants will adapt to future space greenhouses. That is why the main thrust of our research was to study growth and development of plants under space flight conditions and to determine the response of the hormones and protein systems to these circumstances. We also tried to analyze the after-effects of prolonged space flight conditions on the growth and development of orchids. Phytodesign intended to create simple comforts for humans was yet another aim of our work.

During the first attempts to grow higher angiosperms in space ships, the plants did not reach the reproductive stage. Studies of seedlings growth and development of several agricultural plants during space flight indicate that there are no visible changes during the initial stages of growth. However, after some time, the growth is retarded and the plants died (Merkis, 1976; Merkis and Laurinavichus, 1980).

In 1981 *Arabidopsis thaliana* plants maintained on an agar medium under sterile and hermetic conditions on board an orbital station flowered for the first time (Korydum and Chernyaeva, 1982). In 1982 fruits of *Arabidopsis thaliana* were obtained in space in the "Phyton" apparatus (Merkis and Laurinavichus, 1983). Basic changes in metabolism, structural and functional organization of plant cells during space flight was observed by many workers (Sytnik et al., 1982; Korydum and Sytnik, 1983).

We studied tropical epiphytic orchids. Our long experiment during 1980–1981 on board the space ship "Soyuz-36" and in the orbital station "Salut-6" was successful. We assumed then that an important biological characteristic of epiphytic orchids is a reduced gravitropic response and that this would be important under conditions of weightlessness in space. Roots of epiphytic orchids attach and grow in many positions and direction on tree bark, forks and hollows. We also considered the fact that many epiphytic orchids grow on poor substrates, and have shallow roots in humus layers which are not deep. Furthermore, many epiphytic orchids endure drought very well and can survive without watering for two or three weeks[b]. This is due to their pseudobulbs (thickened stems); fleshy leaves which accumulate water and nutrient reserves, and thickened cuticles on leaves and stems. The optimal temperatures for many orchids are similar to the comfort range for humans.

Flowers of many tropical orchids are very ornamental and live for long periods. For example, *Cattleya* flowers last two weeks, *Cymbidiums* blooms can live for up to four months and *Phaelenopsis* or *Epidendrum* blossoms remain alive as much as 6 months. Even cut flowers of orchids remain fresh for a long time. Thus, even if orchids could not grow in orbital stations, it would be possible to use cut flowers to decorate the surroundings of astronauts.

The fact that orchid pollen is not released when shaken because it is in pollinia, was also important in the selection of orchids for closed areas in space. This eliminates the possibility of allergic reactions. To test for this, the Problem Oncology Institute of the Ukrainian Academy of Sciences tested extracts from generative and vegetative organs of the orchids we studied. This work showed that these species do not affect even persons which are sensitive to the pollen of other plants. To avoid other negative reactions, we selected species which despite their high ornamental value produce no fragrance.

The results of our investigations showed that the epiphytic orchids *Epidendrum radicans, Doritis pulcherrima* and *Dendrobium kingianum* remained alive during prolonged space flights. This is due to their reduced gravitropic sensitivity and limited survival requirements. These species can survive for long periods without watering and on a poor medium. The xeromorphic structure of these epiphytic orchids is one of the reasons for this.

Our tests also showed that not all epiphytic orchids can endure prolonged space flight. This is due to the biological characteristics and the development of each species. Those that have rest periods as, for example, *Dendrobium kingianum,* have transitional periods characterized by significant changes in growth regulators. The content of inhibitors in particular increased sharply and the activity of growth stimulators was reduced considerably (Kefeli, 1974). To simulate space flight in a model system, we grew plants on a clinostat and studied the activity of endogenous growth regulators. On the basis of these studies we assume a negative influence of space flight conditions on auxin and gibberellin synthesis and this in turn inhibits cell extension. Rapid restoration of phytohormone activity after returning the plant to normal conditions leads to normalization of growth processes and even to their intensification, as was observed in *Doritis pulcherrima.* It is quite possible that gibberellin deficiency in plants on board of the space ship is the main reason of the absence of flowering (Chajlahyan, 1974).

The death of *Dendrobium kingianum* plants after their return to earth and cultivation in a greenhouse indicates that the conditions of prolonged space flight lead to serious irreversible damage to the metabolic processes of this species. The heavy growth and intensive flowering of *Doritis pulcherrima* under the influence of prolonged space flight conditions is of considerable interest for subsequent investigations of the metabolism of this species. It is also important to develop methods for maintaining the new post-flight characteristics.

[b]Or longer—Ed.

Our leaf protein studies show that most of the qualitative and quantitative changes in soluble and structural proteins are reversible. *Epidendrum radicans* and *Doritis pulcherrima* are characterized by more intensive changes in protein synthesis under the effect of extreme conditions and this may be one reason for their hardiness (see also Czerevczenko et al., 1984). These species showed stable activity of RuBPCase, and this too may be a reason for their tolerance. The sharp rise of carboxylase activity in the enzyme from *Doritis pulcherrima* following the return to earth and particularly the data for "child" growth, testify to significant changes in the physiological state of the plant, caused by space flight conditions.

Experiments with cut orchid flowers are also interesting. In June 1982 a cut inflorescences of *Dendrobium phalaenopsis* inserted in a special test tube filled with water and placed in a cellophane package, were sent to the orbital station which had an international crew on board. These flowers retained a fresh appearance 1–1,5 months under standard conditions. The inflorescences survived the stress associated with putting them in orbit very well and the flowers remained fresh during the period of expedition—10 days. This experiment shows that cut orchids can be used successfully in the phytodesign of space aircraft. Reports from the Space Flight Control Center note that astronauts Alexander Berezovoy and Valentin Lebedev were particularly glad to receive mail and the bouquet of beautiful orchids. Astronaut Leonid Popov said several times that living plants played a major role in maintaining the positive mood of the crew.

Altogether our studies regarding the influence of prolonged space flight on tropical orchids indicate that epiphytic species are very hardy and characterized by stable process of growth, development, and protein synthesis system activity and content of phytohormones and photosynthetic apparatus. Most adaptable to the conditions of prolonged space flight were *Epidendrum radicans* and *Doritis pulcherrima*.

Our results show that tropical epiphytic orchids can be used successfully as a model for studying 1) growth characteristics and development under conditions of space flight, 2) physiological changes of plants under stress, and 3) phytodesign of orbital stations.

Literature Cited

Chailahyan, M. H. 1974. New data to undergrounding hormonal conception of flowering. In: *Growth and Hormonal Regulation in Plants*. Irkutsk. USSR. 207–219.

Czerevczenko, T. M., T. K. Majko, V. B. Bogatir and I. V. Kosakovskaya. 1986. Perspectives of tropical orchids in space investigations. In: *Space Biology and Biotechnology*. Kiev. USSR. 41–54.

_____ . V. V. Shmigovskaya and I. V. Kosakovskaya. 1984. Effects of prolonged dynamic weightlessness on the orchid proteins. *Reports of Ukr. Acad. Sci.* 5: 78–80.

_____ . and T. K. Majko. 1983. Some results of weightlessness effects on epiphytic orchids growth investigations. *Vestnik of the Ukr. Acad. Sci.* 1: 31–35.

Chernyadjev, I. I., I. V. Terehova and N. G. Doman. 1975. Effects of pH on the speed of CO_2 fixation and activity of some photosynthetic enzymes of *Spirulina*. *Plant Physiology* (USSR). 22: 903–909.

Davis, B. J. 1964. Disc electrophoresis. II. Method and application to human serum protein. *Ann. N.Y. Acad. Sci.* 121: 404–427.

Kefely, V. I. 1974. *Nature inhibitors and phytohormones*. Moscos. Nauka. 252p.

Korydum, E. L. and K. M. Sytnik. 1983. Perspectives of genital organ formation in *Arabidopsis thaliana L.* under specific conditions. *Adv. Space Res.* 3247–250.

_____ . and I. I. Chernjaeva. 1982. Features of *Arabidopsis thaliana L.* generative organ formation under space flight conditions. *Reports of Ukr. Acad. Sci.* 8: 69–73.

Kosakovskaya, I. V., V. V. Shmigovskaya and I. I. Chernyadjev. 1984. Biochemical characteristics of proteins from orchids. *Ukr. Bot. J.* 41: 51–54.

Merkis, A. I. and R. S. Laurinavichus. 1983. The whole cycle of individual development of *Arabidopsis thaliana* L. on the board of orbital station "Salut-7". *Reports of Acad. Sci. USSR.* 272: 509–512.

_____. 1980. The growth and development of plants in the weightlessness. In: *Regulation of Growth and Nutrition of Plants.* Vilnus. USSR. 54–72.

_____. 1976. The role of weightlessness in plant growth. In: *Problems of Space Biology: Gravitation and Organisms.* Moscow. Nauka. 146–173.

Safonov, V. I., and M. T. Safonova. 1971. Protein investigation by electrophoresis in polyacrilamide gel. In: *Biochemical Methods in Plant Physiology.* Moscow. Nauka. 118–136.

Sytnik, K. M., E. L. Korydum, and N. A. Belyavskaya. 1982. Ultrastructure of meristemic and root tissues of seedling under space flight conditions. *Reports of Ukr. Acad. Sci.* 6: 78–80.

Tsialkovsky, K. E. 1929. *Rocket space trains.* From the works of Konstantin E. Tsialkovsky. Book II.

Vlasov, P. V., V. V. Mazin, and R. H. Turezkaya. 1979. Complex method for the nature growth regulators identification. *Plant Physiology* (USSR). 26: 628–640.

APPENDIX

Flowering Months of Orchid Species Under Cultivation*

ROBERT M. HAMILTON

*The survey of the literature pertaining to this appendix was completed in December 1987; it was submitted and accepted in January 1988.

Introduction

This list contains the names of orchid species with their exact flowering months recorded over the past 150 years or more in the northern hemisphere which means mainly the middle belt of that area. With the synonyms given in the preliminary listing it provides a key to virtually every species ever grown in the United States, Great Britain, Germany, France, Canada, Switzerland with a few from other countries. It is designed to meet the needs of serious amateurs and hobbyists, to help with problems in identification, cultivation, collection-building and even spelling.

In the main section, tabular listings of species are arranged so that across the top appear the abbreviations for the months of the year and under them appear the numbers representing the incidences of flowering. Each time a plant was reported as flowering a tally was made under the specified month. Records of flowering in native tropical locations were not included. Where a record of flowering mentioned more than one plant in a display,—the variables being expressed as "a few" or "several" or "a lot", up to such sizable quantities as "a table-full" or "fifty" (or whatever)—it was represented by a number ranging from one to five in the tallying. These "weighted" numbers are useful to exercise arbitrary control over exceptional flowering incidences. This rise and fall of incidences is the bell curve or gaussian curve of events. Without the use of weighted numbers, it can be distorted by one highly exceptional number. In this list the highest numbers across a line show the peak months of flowering or the top of the bell curve.

A bell curve exists for most of the species listed, especially the widely-grown ones. Many exceptions to it, however, can be found for a variety of reasons. In many cases there were not enough incidences reported to establish a bell curve, assuming there should be one. In other cases, individual species can flower for many months without stopping, but not always in the season so that where a number of reports are combined, the flowering will register across the line. This characteristic should make those species all the more attractive to hobbyists. Some plants have two flowering peaks a year, among them *Cymbidium bicolor, Encyclia vitellina, Meiracyllium wendlandii, Oncidium crispum, Trichopilia nobilis* and others, although in some cases there may have been some confusion of two species over varying periods of time.

Another variation in the flowering of species is what may be called the "June slump". In many frequently-flowering species there is a decrease in flowering in June although there is no reduction in the number of orchid shows as there is in July and August. Many such species can be mentioned: *Angraecum eichlerianum, A. falcatum, Broughtonia sanguinea, Bulbophyllum falcatum* (to name only the first ones in a long list). Flowering records kept at Kew in the 1970's show a similar slump. The reasons for the drop are not clear.

Varieties of species have been largely excluded but those which flowered five times or more are listed separately. Otherwise, the data were included with incidences for the main type of a species. There are about 550 varieties in the file which did not reach the minimal number of five. The record shows that they flower at or about the same time as the main type, although there are instances where the "alba" forms flower later.

Names which could not be verified in *Index Londinensis, Index Kewensis* or elsewhere were excluded. There were over 100 of them.

In the preliminary list of synonyms which was compiled for this list only, names of some genera are shown in juxtaposition to other generic names without the use of an equal sign, such as "*Bothriochilus Coelia*" or "*Camerotis Micropera*". This shows the listing will be found under the second name. I do not presume to take responsibility for such "synonymy" because I am not qualified to state that there is any "equality" involved. Similarly, at the species level where equal signs are used ("*Abola radiata = Caucaea radiata*") they are to be taken as arrow signs leading the reader to the place used here but not because I determined its proper place in the taxonomic system. This list is not an authority in any way, except for flowering incidence. Also, in the list of "synonyms" there are entries ("*Aganisia cyanea × Acacallis cyanea*") where the specific epithet is not repeated but is to be taken for granted. Where this happens the Latin gender of the specific epithet may have to be changed to agree with the genus as in *Angraecum bilobum × Aerangis biloba*. These changes are supplied in the main text.

As the series is entitled "Orchid biology, reviews and perspectives," this may be an appropriate place to trace briefly the historical growth in the numbers of species grown in the northern greenhouses from the earliest times. Interest in the cultivation of species was catered to by the publication of a number of comprehensive manuals and guides which provided descriptive and cultural information on the available species. Interest in new species never abated and demand for them, except in wartime, has been constant and the size of the manuals has usually increased.

We can trace the growth by counting the numbers of genera and species in half a dozen of the most famous guides. The first, *A Manual of Orchidaceous Plants,* by James Veitch and Son (London, 1887–1894) listed 110 genera and described 1740 species. The second, Williams' *The Orchid Grower's Manual,* 7th edition (London, 1894) showed an increase to 129 genera but a drop to 1,548 species. However, it included over 900 supplementary or brief descriptions, mainly of varieties. The next big compendium is *Sanders' orchid guide* (St. Albans, 1901) actually a more compact treatment but which still increased the count of genera to 132 and the species to 2,083. Varieties also were very much a feature of this work. The numbers continued to grow. The new *Sanders' orchid guide revised (1927) edition.* (St. Albans) listed 159 genera and 2,388 species.

About twenty-five years later the Royal Horticultural Society published its great *Dictionary of Gardening* (4 vols., Oxford, 1951; a supplementary volume published later contains no orchids) which raised the figure for genera to 255 (in spite of the compiler's practice of lumping many genera together) and the number of species to 3,216, the highest count up to now. Incidentally, this publication is the most valuable for tracking down orchids of the past.

The next large work, which brings us up to recent times, is A. D. Hawkes' *Encyclopaedia of Cultivated Orchids.* (London, 1965). It includes, contrary to the title, a large number of genera which the author admits have probably never been seen in cultivation, being terrestrials. Eliminating those, the number of genera "in cultivation" reaches 402, a sizable increase over the previous offering. The number of species, however, is only 2,192, a surprising drop from the previous 3,216 and explains why the book is so frequently found wanting. The next and last of the great guides is *The Manual of Cultivated Orchid Species* (Cambridge, Mass., 1981; later revised) by Bechtel, Cribb and Launert, which shows a sharp decrease in the numbers of both genera, 217, and species, 967. One reason for this may have been the inclusion of colored photographs of the flowers of the species described in this book. Still, a valuable feature for the searcher is the expert listing of 1,444 synonyms, a high count indeed. In 100 years since 1887 the count has risen from 110 to 519 for genera and from 1,740 to 5,594 for species, as represented in this list, and presumably those figures will continue to increase.

The long time span covered by this list made it necessary to find current names of genera and species for many entries. It is not difficult to chose new names for "obsolete" ones if they have some measure of currency. However, it is more difficult to choose between names that are "out-of-date" to the expert but still favored by the hobbyists, growers and the editor of the authoritative but anachronistic *Sander's List of Orchid Hybrids*. Regardless of the policy followed, whatever choices are made they are not going to please all users of any comprehensive list. The hope expressed recently (*Florida Orchidist*, December 1987, 143) that we should "all look forward to the day when names of our beauties won't be changing every time another scientist publishes a monograph," is not likely to be realized in the near future.

In fact, the opposite is happening. The situation in the genus *Epidendrum* is a good example of how new generic names are proliferating. Robert L. Dressler [*Orchidea* (Mex.) May 1984, 291–298] reviewed a number of them. About a dozen new ones have been more or less adopted. He said that "bad biology" has persisted in orchid classification because of the "great number of orchids and the very limited number of botanists who have dedicated themselves to studying them. In other words, we sometimes grasp at straws in an effort to find some semblance of order in this large and complex group." Nevertheless, eleven generic names have found their way into this list. *Encyclia, Dimerandra, Jacquiniella, Oerstedella, Neowilliamsia* and *Diothonea* are among those he considers valid. Some of the others are considered questionable at best, but no more should be accepted until additional research is carried out on the whole complex of *Epidendrum*.

Another example from among the larger genera, which seem to be the targets of the "splitters", is *Dendrobium*. In 1981, Brieger, a leading taxonomist, divided them into 26 separate genera, a lead I fortunately did not follow. This was called "a rather revolutionary re-arrangement" by Gunnar Seidenfaden (Orchid genera in Thailand XII—*Dendrobium* Sw.—*Opera botanica* 83, 1985, 7). Like Dressler, he suggested that very deep and broad studies of all the species of *Dendrobium* must be undertaken before changes are made. One other taxonomist did publish a paper accepting Brieger's arrangement, an act which Seidenfaden terms "irresponsible and most regrettable", and suggests that editors of journals should have the right to declare certain material as "not published"— in effect, to remove it from the record. So, it looks as if things are stirring in *Dendrobium*.

One more example of the pitfalls that await the innocent: new names are always appearing in the genus *Odontoglossum*. First, in 1982 all the *Odontoglossum* taxa in Central America were split off from the South American ones and many new names were advocated. *Odontoglossum cervantesii* and its dozen or so lovely relatives were declared to be *Leucoglossum* Then a year later the author decided that the new name should not be *Leucoglossum* but *Cymbiglossum*. In 1984 it was changed again, this time to *Lemboglossum* which was the name I chose for this list [Orquidea (Mex.) 1984, 351]. Fortunately, I bought a copy of Rogers McVaugh's new book *Flora Novo-Galicia, a descriptive account of the vascular plants of Western Mexico; volume 16 Orchidaceae* (Ann Arbor, 1985) which was described in the pages of *Orquidea* (Mex.) as "the best orchid flora yet produced for any part of the Americas" and in it on page 70 I found that Lemboglossum is declared to be a superfluous name, and *Cymbiglossum* the correct name. Therefore, I changed all the entries and cross-references back again. How long this name will remain valid is anybody's guess. I know that the four species in my greenhouse now can be considered as members of a distinct group, all with a markedly boat-, or prow-, shaped lip.

Similar examples can be given in *Bulbophyllum/Cirrhopetalum, Catasetum, Oncidium*, and other general. The fact that choices had to be made for generic and specific entries in this list does not mean that I have delusions about it being a definitive listing.

Sources for compiling data for this list have been many and varied. They consist of both printed and non-printed materials. In fact, everything has been grist for the mill: periodicals, books, catalogues, herbarium lists, show lists, personal correspondence, circulated checklists, etc. A bibliography of all sources would look well in a doctoral dissertation but would not be of much value to users of this list. The printed materials begin with a periodical which was begun in 1841, *The Gardeners's Chronicle* (London), followed by *L'Orchidophile* (Paris, etc., 1881–1895), *Le Journal des Orchidees* Bruxelles, 1890–1897), *The Orchid Album* (London, 1892–1897), *Lindenia* (Gand, etc., 1885–1906), *The Orchid Review.* (London, etc., 1893 to date), *The American Orchid Society Bulletin* (Cambridge, Mass., etc., 1931 to date), *The Orchid Digest* (California, 1951–1987), *The Florida Orchidist* (Florida, 1958–1987), *Orchidata* (New York, 1961–1980), *Die Orchidee* (Frankfurt, etc., 1966–1987) and many others, some of which were made available to me by Dr. J. Arditti, in whose library I spent several productive months.

Printed awards lists include the *American Orchid Society Awards Quarterly* (Cambridge, Mass., etc., 1978–1987) and its predecessors, dating from 1932. Similar lists issued by the Cymbidium Society, the South Florida Orchid Society and others were used. English, German, Japanese, Swiss and Canadian awards lists, some separately and some garnered from Elinor Yocom's comprehensive compilations going back to the 1850's were also searched. Yocom's *Parades* covered *Sarcanthinae, Paphiopedilum, Oncidium,* the *Cattleya alliance, Other subtribes,* plus a supplement (Naples, Florida, 1978–1980, 6 vols.).

I have made constant use of reference works written by outstanding authors and dealing with orchids from a geographical area: Ames, Ball, Dockrill, Dunsterville and Garay, Garay alone, Hamer, Holttum, the *Icones plantarum tropicarum,* Luer, McVaugh, Pabst and Dungs, Piers, Pradham, Quisumbing, Schlecheter (New Guinea), Schweinfurth, Schultes, Seidenfaden, Seidenfaden and Smitinand, Stewart and Hennessy, Williams (several with this name), Williamson, and others, well known to orchidists. I have also used constantly treatises dealing with a single genus such as *Angraecum, Cattleya* (bifoliate), *Dendrobium, Encyclia, Epidendrum, Lycaste, Masdevallia, Oncidium,* (Varigata), *Paphiopedilum, Pleione, Sarcanthinae, Stelis* and several others, always wishing I could afford to buy more of them.

The non-printed sources include private and personal compilations prepared by both individuals and institutions. The late Dr. George C. Kennedy gave me a list of 130 pages with flowering times of 4,000 or more species in his greenhouse. Mrs. Rebecca T. Northen provided flowering times of 600 or more species which flowered in her greenhouses in Wyoming and California. Dr. Phillip Cribb provided me with a massive list of species flowering in Kew in the 1970's. (This list is a part of the Kew record. In the early 1900's, 32 listings of "New orchids at Kew" with months of flowering appeared in the pages of the *Kew Bulletin*). Russell Vernon supplied the flowering records of the Wheeler Orchid Collection and Species Bank at Ball State University, Indiana. A similar listing from the Royal Botanic Garden in Edinburgh provided many new entries, including 11 new genera. Dr. Carl Withner gave me access to his large library and working collection of flower slides.

In addition to those large items, I received additions in varying numbers from a large circle of friends and correspondents, including Noble Bashor, Roger Beck, Dr. Hilda Belman, Iris Cohen, Denis Duveen, Dr. J. A. Fowlie, Howard Gunn, Fred Hillerman, Irene Kothuber, John L. Leonard, Harold S. Levinson, John L. Mickel, Mike Millar, Jim E.

Russell, Dr. Yoneo Sagawa, Richard Snow, Dr. W. L. Stern, Carol Turlow, John S. Wemesfelder, Deric M. Wenzler, Dr. Howard P. Wood, Dr. Patrick Woods, Elinor S. Yocom and others.

The first edition of this list was published under the title *When does it flower? (Orchids in the USA),* (Richmond, B.C., 1977). A second edition was published in 1986 with the subtitle *Orchid species in the greenhouse since 1881.* The present list has extended the coverage back about forty years and forward to the end of 1987. Twenty-two new genera, about 300 new species and several thousand new flowering incidences have been added.

R. M. H.

Abbreviations and Signs

Abbreviations and Signs
Ag — August
also — the flowering data have been distributed erroneously in the past to more than one species
Ap — April
Cont. — continued
De — December
Fe — February
Fma. — form, a taxonomic category below variety
Hort. — horticultural name or hybrid
Hyb. — Hybrid
Ja — January
Jn — June
Jy — July
Mr — March
My — May
N.H. — natural hybrid
Nat. Hyb. — natural hybrid
No — November
Oc — October
Se — September
ssp. — subspecies
var. — variety
SIGNS: × — hybrid, or "crossed with" another plant
+ — data are distributed among more than one name
? — an authority stated this plant was once confused with another

Note for readers in the Southern Hemisphere: the names of the months in the north can be inverted like this to correspond to their seasons:

: Ja	: Fe	: Mr	: Ap	: My	: Jn	: Jy	: Ag	: Se	: Oc	: No	: De
: Jy	: Ag	: Se	: Oc	: No	: De	: Ja	: Fe	: Mr	: Ap	: My	: Jn

Synonyms*

Abola
radiata = Caucaea

Acampe
longifolia = ridiga
wightiana = praemorsa

Acineta
colossus = rhubyana
humboldtii = superba

Acropera
loddigesii = Gongora galeata

Aerangis
colum-cygni = compta
grantii = kotschyana
pumilio = also hyaloides
rhodosticta = luteoalba var.

Aerides
affine = multiflora
ballantineanum var. aureum = odorata
dayana = odorata
expansum = falcata
falcatum var. houlettianum = houlletiana
godefroyana = multiflora
japonica = Sedirea
mitrata = Seidenfedenia
racemiferum = Cleisostoma
roseum = multiflora
sanderiana = lawrenceae var.
schroederi = odorata
suavissimum = odorata

Aganisea
cyanea = Acacallis
tricolor = Warrea warreana

Amesiella
philippinense = Angraecum

Angraecum
arcuatum = Cyrtorchis
arnoldianum = eichlerianum
articulatum = Aerangis
bicaudatum = Tridactyle
bilobum = Aerangis
brongniartianum = eburneum
caudatum = Plectrelminthus

chailluanum = Cyrtorchis
citratum = also Aerangis
distichum = Mystacidium
eburneum var. giryamae = also giryamae
falcatum = Neofinetia
humblotii = leonis
hyaloides = Aerangis
imerinensis = Aeranthes
modestum = Aerangis
moloneyi = Calyptrochilum christyanum
mooreanum = Aerangis
rhodostictum = Aerangis luteoalba
rothschildianum = Eurychone
stylosum = Aerangis
virens = superbum

Anguloa
eburnea = uniflora
imbricata = Calyptrochilum

Ania Tania

Anoectochilus
dawsonianus = Ludisia discolor
discolor = Ludisia
elwesii = Odontochilus
lowii = Dossinia
ordianus = Ludisia discolor var. dawsoniana
petola = Macodes
veitchianus = Macodes petola

Anota
violacea = Rhynchostylis gigantea

Ansellia
africana confusa = africana
confusa = africana
confuša var. lutea = africana
congoensis = gigantea
lutea = gigantea var.

Arachnanthe
bilinguis = Armodorum labrosum

Arachnis
bilinguis = Armodorum labrosum
labrosa = Armodorum labrosum
lowii = Dimorphorchis
rohaniana = Dimorphorchis

*Since there is no single opinion, or reference work, regarding orchid nomenclature Mr. Hamilton has compiled this list of synonyms to avoid duplicate listings in the appendix.—Ed.

Armodorum
  siamense = also *Aerides larpentae*

Arundina
  bambusifolia = *graminifolia*

Ascocentrum
  hendersonianum = Dyakia

Aspasia
  epidendroides var. *principissa* = *principissa*
  pusilla = *Cischweinfia*

Barlia
  longibracteata = *Himantoglossum*

Batemannia
  peruviana = *colleyi*
  wallisii = *Huntleya*

Bifrenaria
  aurantiaca = *Rudolfiella*
  bicornaria = *Rudolfiella*
  fuerstenbergiana = also *inodora*
  hadwenii = *Scuticaria*
  harrisoniae var. *pubigera* = *pubigera*

Bletia
  hyacinthina = *Bletilla striata*
  pallida = *purpurea*
  tuberculosa = *Gastorchis*
  verecunda = *purpurea*

Bolusiella
  maudae = *Angraecum*

Bothriochilus
  Coelia

Brachtia
  verruculifera = *andina*

Brassavola
  amazonica = *martiana*
  digbyana = *Rhyncholaelia*
  fragrans = also *perrinii, tuberculata*
  glauca = *Rhyncholaelia*
  lineata = *acaulis*
  perrinii = also *tuberculata*
  subulifolia = *cordata*

Brassia
  allenii = *Ada*
  antherotes = *arcuigera*
  chlorops = *Ada*
  glumacea = *Ada*

  guttata = *maculata*
  keiliana = *Ada*
  lewesii = *caudata*
  ocanensis = *Ada*
  rhizomatosa = *arcuigera*
  spathacea = *Ada ocanensis*
  wrayae = *maculata*

Broughtonia
  cubensis = *Laeliopsis*
  domingensis = *Laeliopsis*
  lilacina = *Laeliopsis domingensis*

Bulbophyllum
  amesianum = *cumingii*
  andersonii = also *lepidum*
  balfourianum = *macrobulbon*
  bicolor = *Sunipia*
  bootanensis = *spathulatum*
  bootanoides = *frostii*
  breviscapum = *lasiochilum*
  confurtum = *scabratum*
  densiflorum = *cariniflorum*
  dichromum = *Monomeria*
  ecornutum = *helenae*
  galbinum = *uniflorum*
  griffithianum = *lepidum*
  henshallii = *lobbii*
  koordersii = *weberi*
  kusukuensis = *affine*
  lobbii var. *colossus* = *lobbii*
  miniatum = also *flaviflorum*
  nigripetalum = *secundum*
  papillosum = *thaiorum*
  pechei = *cupreum*
  pobeguinii = *congolanum*
  radiatum = *laxiflorum*
  reinwardtii = *uniflorum*
  rhizophoreti = *purpurascens*
  siamense = *lobbii*
  tentaculigerum = *sandersonii*
  transarisanense = *pectinatum*
  winckleri = *schlechteri*

Burlingtonia
  candida = *Rodriguezia*
  decora = *Rodriguezia*
  fragrans = *Rodriguezia bracteata*
Calanthe
  amamiana = *discolor*
  elmeri = *rubens*
  furcata = *triplicata*
  japonica = *alismaefolia*
  kintaroi = *okinawaensis*
  kirishinensis = *arustulifera*
  liukiuensis = *lyroglossa*

longicalcarata = *masuca*
natalensis = *sylvatica*
sieboldi = *striata*

Calypso
californica = *bulbosa*

Camaridium
ochroleucum = *Maxillaria camaridii*

Camarotis
Micropera

Campylocentrum
tuerckheimii = *scheidii*

Capanemia
uliginosa = *superflua*

Catasetum
appendiculatum = *barbatum*
bungarothii = *pileatum*
ciliatum = *discolor*
claesianum = discolor
darwinianum = *callosum*
dilectum = *Dressleria*
eburneum = *Dressleria*
garnettianum = *barbatum*
imperiale = *splendens*
labiatum = *splendens*
luciani = *splendens*
obrienianum = *splendens*
oerstedii = *maculatum*
platyglossum = *expansum*
roseum = *Clowesia*
rostratum = *maculatum*
russellianum = *Clowesia*
saccatum var. *tenebrosum* = *tenebrosum*
scurra = *Clowesia warscewitzii*
sodiroi = *macroglossum*
suave = *Dressleria*
thylaciochilum = *Clowesia*
tridentatum = *macrocarpum*
trifidum = *cernuum*
warscewiczii = *Clowesia*

Cattleya
gigas = *warscewiczii*
granulosa var. *schofieldiana* = *schofieldiana*
harrisoniae = *loddigesii* var.
harrisoniana = *loddigesii*
leopoldii = *guttata*
leopoldii alba = *guttata alba*
nobilior = *walkeriana* var. *nobilior*
Pachecoi = Nat. Hyb.
patinii = *skinneri*

prinzii = *amethystoglossa*
quadricolor = *chocoensis*
sincora = *Laelia sincorana*
speciosissima = *lueddemanniana*

Cattleyopsis
guaensis = *lindenii*
northropiorum = *lindenii*

Centropetalum
Fernandezia

Cephalanthera
pallens = *damasonianum*
xipophyllum = *longifolia*

Ceratostylis
rubra = *retisquama*

Chelonistele
imbricata = *Pholidota pallida*
perakensis = *Coelogyne*
sulphurea = *Coelogyne*

Chondrorhyncha
amazonica = *Zygosepalum lindeniae*
costaricensis = *Kefersteinia*
discolor = *Cochleanthes*
fimbriata = *flaveola*
lactea = *Kefersteinia*
lindeni = *Zygosepalum*
wailesiana = *Cochleanthes*

Chysis
lemminghei = *aurea*
tricostata = *laevis*

Cirrhaea
viridipurpurea = *dependens*

Cirrhopetalum
Bulbophyllum
africanum = *B. longiflorum*
amesianum = *B. cumingii*
appendiculatum = *B. putidum*
breviscapum = *B. lasiochilum*
brunnescens = *B. brienianum*
campanulatum = *B. auratum*
collettii = *B. wendlandianum*
concinnum = *B. pulchellum*
cornutum = *B. helenae*
fascinator = *B. putidum*
flavesepalum = *B. retusiusculum*
gamosepalum = *B. lepidum*
griffithianum = *b. lepidum*
mannii = *B. delicatescens*

mandulum = B. taeniophyllum
obrienianum = B. brienianum
psittacoides = B. gracilimum
refractum = B. wallichii
siamense = B. lepidum
stramineum = B. vaginatum
tenuicaule = B. lepidum
thouarsii = B. longiflorum
wallichii = B. retusiusculum

Cleisostoma
kunstleri = arietinum
lanatum = Cleisomeria
micranthum = Smitinandia
peninsularis = tenuifolium
pugioniformis = subulatum
racimifer = subulatum
secundus = subulatum
teres = simondii
termissus = discolor
wendlandiana = Pomatocalpa

Cochleanthes
wendlandii = Zygopetalum

Cochlioda
sanguinea = Symphyglossum

Coelia
baueriana = triptera

Coelogyne
brunnea = fuscescens
cinnamomea = also trinervis
conferta = nitida
elegans = huettneriana
graminifolia = viscosa
humilis = Pleione
imbricata = Pholidota pallida
lagenaria = Pleione praecox
maculata = Pleione
ocellata = nitida
ochracea = nitida
pachybulbon = trinervis
rhodeana = trinervis
rossiana = trinervis
stenophylla = cinnamomea
uniflora = also Panisea
virescens = also brachyptera
wallichiana = Pleione praecox

Colax
Pabstia

Comparettia
rosea = falcata

Coryanthes
maculata = speciosa

Corybas
trilobus = also Corysanthes

Crybe
rosea = Bletia purpurea

Cryptophoranthus
acaulis = Pleurothallis tribuloides

Cyclopogon
Beadlea

Cycnoches
aurea = egertonianum
warscewiczii = chlorochilon

Cymbidium
albuciflorum = madidum
aspidistrifolium = lancifolium
atropurpureum = finlaysonianum
elegans = Cyperorchis
formosum = goeringii
forrestii = goeringii
gracillimum = goeringii
grandiflorum = hookerianum
gyokuchin = ensifolium
hoosai = sinense
mastersii = Cyperorchis
munronianum = ensifolium
oiwakense = faberi
pendulum = finlaysonianum
pubescens = bicolor
pulcherrimum = dayanum
pumilum = floribundum
purpureo-hiemale = kanran
rubigemmum = ensifolium
sanderi = insigne var. sanderi, + parishii var.
    sanderi
simonsianum = dayanum
simulans = aloifolium
tortisepalum = goeringii
virens = goeringii
virescens = goeringii
wilsonii = iridioides

Cynosorchis
Cynorkis

Cypripedium
calceolus var. parviflorum = parviflorum
petri = Paphiopedilum
planipetalum = calceolus var.
sanderianum = Paphiopedilum

spectabile = reginae
yatabeanum = guttatum

Cyrtochilum
exasperatum = Oncidium
macranthum = Oncidium

Cyrtoglossis
gracilipes = Mormolyca

Cyrtopera
woodfordii = Eulophia alta

Cyrtorchis
bistorta = ringens

Cystorchis
Cyrtorchis

Dactylorhiza
maderensis = foliosa

Dendrobium
acuminatum = Epigeneium
amoenum = aphyllum
andersonii = draconis
aurantiacum = Bulbophyllum
aureum = heterocarpum
bancroftianum = speciosum var.
bensoniae = signatum
biggibum = phalaenopsis
boxallii = gratiosissimum
bursigerum = gracilicaule
cariniferum = williamsianum
chloroleucum = subflavidum
chlorops = barbatulum
ciliatum = rupicola
coelogyne = Epigeneium
coerulescens = nobile
crassinode = pendulum
cupreum = moschatum var.
cuthbertsonii = also sophronites
cymbidioides = Epigeneium
dalhousieanum = pulchellum
densiflorum = also thrysiflorum
eburneum = draconis
elongatum = gracilicaule
erythroglossum = falconeri
fairfaxii = teretifolium
foelschii = canaliculatum
fragrans = sarmentosum
fusiforme = ruppianum
goldiei = also superbiens
haniffi = tortile
hedyosmum = scabrilingue
imperatrix = gouldii

jamesianum = infundibulum var.
japonicum = monifilforme
jenkensii = aggregatum
lawanum = crepidatum
leucorhodum = anosmum
lindleyi = aggregatum
lineale = gouldii
linguella = hercoglossum
lyonii = Epigeneium
macfarlanei = johnsoniae
macranthum = anosmum
macrophyllum = anosmum
monile = monifilforme
mortii = also beckleri
nakaharaei = also Epigeneium
nodatum = aphrodite
ophioglossoides = Pleurothallis
pallens = Flickingeria
paxtonii = chrysoglossum
pierardii = aphyllum
polyphlebium = rhodopterygium
praestans = also forbesii
puniceum = Alamania
roseum = crepidatum
rotundatum = Epigeneium
rumphianum = minax
sanguineum = Broughtonia
schroederianum = thyrsiflorum
secundum = gracilacaule
sophronitis = cuthbertsonii
strebloceras = tangerinum
striatum = Bulbophyllum
striolatum = beckleri
suavissimum = chrysotoxum
superbum = anosmum
takahashi = ovipositoriferum
tigrinum = spectabile
toffti = nindii
tosaense = stricklandianum
triadenium = mutabile
undulatum = discolor
veratrifolium = gouldii

Dendrochilum
saccolabium = Acoridium

Diacrium
bicornutum = Caularthron

Dichaea
verrucosa = muricata

Dilomilis
montana = Octadesmia

Dinema
polybulbon = Encyclia

Dipteranthus
  alleniana = *Zygostates*

Disa
  grandiflora = *uniflora*

Doritis
  buyssoniana = *pulcherrima* var.
  esmeralda = *pulcherrima*
  wightii = *Kingidium deliciosum*

Dracula also *Dryadella, Masdevallia*
  gaskelliana = *erythrocaete*

Elleanthus
  capitatus = *sphaerocephalus*

Encyclia
  acularis = *bractescens*
  atropurpurea = *cordigera*
  bifida = *cordigera*
  bulbosa = also *inversa*
  capartianum = *osmantha*
  ciliare = *Epidendrum*
  confusa = *baculus*
  dickinsonianum = *guatemalensis*
  incumbens = *aromatica*
  ionophlebium = *chacaoensis*
  kennedyi = *adenocaula*
  linearis = *luteorosea*
  nemorale = *adenocaula*
  papillosa = also *adenocarpon*
  pastoris = *venosa*
  pentotis = *baculus*
  variegata = *vespa*
  virens = *belizensis*

Ephemerantha also
  Flickingeria

Epidendrum
  ambiguum = *Encyclia*
  arachnoglossum = *secundum*
  atropurpureum = *Encyclia cordigera*
  aurantiacum = *Cattleya*
  auritum = *Nidema boothii*
  barbeyanum = *Neolehmannia*
  bicornutum = *Caularthron*
  boothii = *Nidema*
  brachyglossum = *Neocogniauxia monophylla*
  carinatum = *eustirum*
  centradenium = *Oerstedella*
  cepiforme = *Encyclia candollei*
  chinense = *Barkeria*
  cristobalense = *laucheanum*
  christi = *Encyclia vespa*

claesianum = *chioneum*
clavatum = *purpurascens*
cobanense = *Jacquiniella*
condylochilum = *Encyclia livida*
costaricensis = *oerstedii*
deamii = *Encyclia deamii*
deltoglossum = *Kalopternix*
dickinsonianum = *Encyclia guatemalensis*
difforme = also *Neolehmannia*
diguetti = *Encyclia tripunctata*
discolor = *nocturnum*
doeringii = *Encyclia cordigera*
elongatum = *secundum*
endresii = *Oerstedella*
equitans = *Jacquiniella equitantifolia*
equitantifolium = *Jacquiniella*
exasperatum = *Oerstedella*
falcatum, also *parkinsonianum*
flabellatum = *candollei*
floribundum = *paniculatum*
fuscatum = *anceps*
gladiatum = *juergensenii*
glumaceum = *Encyclia*
graminifolium = *Octomeria*
guttatum = *Encyclia maculosa*
helleri = *Encyclia gracile*
ibaguense = *radicans*
inversum = *Encyclia bulbosa*
lacustre = *obesum*
lambeauanum = *Neolehmannia porpax*
laterale = *rousseauae*
latifolium = *carpophorum*
latilabre = *Neolehmannia difformis*
lindleyanum = *Barkeria*
longipetalum = *Encyclia alata*
macrochilum = *Encyclia cordigera*
magnificum = *arbuscula*
mathewsii = *Neolehmannia porpax*
medusae = *Nanodes*
montana = *Octadesmia*
morsenii = *strobiliferum*
moyobambae = *coronatum*
myodes = *polyanthum*
nemorale = *Encyclia adenocaula*
ottonis = *Nidema*
parkinsonianum, also *falcatum*
peraltense = *Encyclia oncidioides*
physodes = *Physinga*
plicatum = *Encyclia*
porpax = *Neolehmannia*
pristes = *radicans*
pumila = *Oerstedella*
ramonense = *Encyclia ceratistes*
schlechterianum = *Nanodes discolor*
secundum = also *elongatum*
skinneri = *Barkeria*

sophronitis = *Kalopternix*
stenopetalum = *Dimerandra emarginata*
subpatens = *coronatum*
tesselatum = *deamii*
tigrinum = *Encyclia vespa*
trachychilum = *Encyclia ambigua*
umbellatum = *Neolehmannia difformis*
vanneriana = *Barkeria lindleyana*
variegatum = *Encyclia vespa*
verrucosum = *Encyclia adenocaula* +
  Oerstedella verrucosa
violaceum = *Cattleya*
virens = *Encyclia belizensis*
wallisii = *Oerstedella*
widgrenii = *Encyclia papilio*

Epigeneium
coelogyne = also *amplum*

Eria
aeridostachya = *robusta*
convallarioides = *spicata*
fragrans = *javanica*
glabra = *ovata* var. *retroflexa*
hypomelana = *amica*
kingii = *ridleyi*
lanata = *flava* var.
langbianensis = *globifera*
longispica = *latifolia*
saccata = *saccifera*
stellata = *javanica*

Eriopsis
werckeleyi = *biloba*

Erythrodes
maculata = *Platythelys*
querceticola = *Platythelys*

Euanthe
sanderiana = *Vanda*

Eulophia
cristata = *purpurata*
gigantea = *Lissochilus*
krebsii = *paivaeana*
ledienii = *Oeceoclades*
lurida = *Graphorkis*
maculata = *Oeceoclades*
paniculata = *Oeceoclades*
peetersii = *Eulophiella roempleriana*
phillipsae = *Eulophiella roempleriana*
saundersiana = *Oeceoclades*
virens = *epidendrae*

Eulophidium
maculatum = *Oeceoclades*

Eulophiella
hamelinii = *roempleriana*
peetersiana = *roempleriana*

Finetia
falcata = *Neofinetia*

Flickingeria
kelsallii = *angustifolia*

Gastrochilus
odoratus = *Haraella retrocalla*
somai = *japonicus*

Gastrodia
bigibbum = *Gastrochilus*

Gongora
citrina = *truncata*
galeata = *flavida*
leucochila = also *quinquenervis*
nigrita = *quinquenervis*
odoratissima = *quinquenervis*
tricolor = *quinquenervis*

Goodyera
dawsonianus = *Ludisia discolor* var.
discolor = *Ludisia*
gardneri = *utriculata*
japonica = *schlechtendaliana*
lagenophora = *superba*

Habenaria
ciliaris = *Platanthera*
columbea = *lindleyana*
geniculata = *dentata*
goodyeroides = *Peristylus*
iantha = *Brachycorythis obcordata*
lacera = *Platanthera*
longicalcarata = *longicorniculata*
militaris = *rhodocheila*
odontopetala = *floribunda*
radiata = *Pecteilis*
susannae = *Pecteilis*
viridis = *Coeloglossum*

Haemaria
dawsoniana = *Ludisia discolor* var.
discolor = *Ludisia*

Harrisella
porrecta = *Campylocentrum*

Hartwegia
Nageliella

Hexadesmia
fasciculata = ? Scaphyglottis lindenianum

Hexalectris
mexicana = grandiflora

Hormidium
tripterum = Encyclia pygmaea

Houlletia
chrysantha = wallisii
landsbergii = tigrina

Hygrochilus
parishii = Vandopsis

Ione
intermedia = Sunipia
paleacea = Sunipia
scariosa = racemosa
siamensis = racemosa

Ionopsis
paniculata = utricularioides

Kefersteinia
lamellosa = Pescatorea
lojae = Chondrorhyncha

Kingiella
decumbens = Kingidium
taeniale = Kingidium

Laelia also Schomburgkia
acuminata = rubescens
boothiana = lobata
cowanii = flava
crispilabia = mantiqueirae
grandiflora = speciosa
kautskyi = esperitosantensis
majalis = speciosa
monophylla = Neocogniauxia
ostermayeri = lucasiana
praestans = pumila
rupestris = crispata
superbiens = Schomburgkia
undulata = Schomburgkia

Lanium
colombianum = microphyllum

Lemboglossum
Cymbiglossum

Leochilus
pulchella = Oncidium waluewa
pygmaeus = Dignathe

Leptotes
paranaensis = unicolor
serrulata = bicolor

Lindleyella
aurantiaca = Rudolfiella

Liparis
chloroxantha = stricklandiana
elata = nervosa
longipes = veridiflora
neoguiniensis = caespitosa
prainii = caespitosa
rufina = nervosa
tabularis = atrosanguinea
taiwaniana = stricklandiana

Lissochilus
arenarius = Eulophia cucullata
micrantha = Eulophia stenophylla
purpuratus = Eulophia
speciosa = Eulophia

Listrostachys
arcuata = Crytorchis
caudata = Plectrelminthus
chailluana = Crytorchis
forcipata = Podangis
kindtiana = Angraecum
obrienianum = Angraecum
pellucida = Diaphananthe
whytei = Angraecum

Lockhartia
chocoensis = micrantha
robusta = oerstedii
verrucosa = oerstedii

Lueddemannia
sanderiana = Lacaena bicolor

Luisia
indivisa = brachystachys
megasepala = teres

Lycaste
gigantea = longipetala
lawrenceana = candida
longisepala = schilleriana
measuresiana = macrophylla ssp.
micheliana = crinita
peruviana = fimbriata
plana = macrophylla
rossiana = cruenta (?)
rossyi = ciliata
strobellii = ciliata
suaveolens = aromatica

tetragona = Bifrenaria
virginalis = skinneri

Lycomormium
elatum = squalidum

Macradenia
modesta = brassavolae

Macroclinium also Megaclinium, Notylia

Malaxis
ensiformis = Oberonia
rheedii = Liparis
stenostachys = Oberonia myriantha

Marsupiaria
iridifolia = Maxillaria valenzuelana

Masdevallia also Dracula, Dryadella
acrochordonia = ephippium
anchorifera = Scaphosepalum
benedictii = Dracula
bruchmuelleri = coriacea
chimaera = Dracula
crossii = racemosa
ellipes = civilis
fragrans = civilis
fulvescens = schroederiana
gargantua = elephanticeps
gibberosa = Scaphosepalum
gracilenta = Cryptophoranthus
grandiflora = ignea
haematosticta = civilis
harryana = coccinea
horrida = erinacea
houtteana = Dracula
huebneri = Trisetella
inflata = corniculata
leontoglossa = civilis
lindeni = coccinea
ludibunda = estradae
militaris = ignea
muscosa = Porroglossum echidnum
myriostigma = floribunda
ochracea = coriacea
ochthodes = Scaphosepalum
platyrachis = Pleurothallis pfavii
porcilliceps = civilis
roezlii = Dracula chimaera
sceptrum = schlimii
shuttleworthii = caudata
trichaete = gemmata
tridactylites = Triaristella
trochilus = ephippium
vespertilio = Dracula
zebrina = Dryadella

Maxillaria
acutipetala = rufescens
amparoana = brunnea
atropurpurea = Bifrenaria
boothii = Nidema
dichroma = elegantula
divaricata = cerifera
fractiflexa = ecuadorensis
henchmanii = variabilis
hirtzii = grandiflora
houtteana = curtipes
leptosepala = setigera
lindeniana = meleagris
murrilliana = marginata
nasalis = nasuta
nervosa = divaricata
ochroleuca = camaridii
pallidiflora = Xylobium
plebeja = ferdinandiana
punctata = gracilis
punctostriata = hematoglossa
purpurea = conferta
ringens = also brunnea
rupestris = picta
sanguineolenta = miniata
scabrilinguis = Xylobium variegatum
triangularis = elatior
yzabalana = brunnea, + ringens

Megaclinium
bicolor = Macroclinium
elegantulum = Bulbophyllum

Meiracyllium
gemma = wendlandii

Menadenium
ballii = Zygosepalum
labiosum = Zygosepalum
rostratum = Zygosepalum labiosum

Mesadenella
esmeraldae = cuspidata

Mesospinidium
sanguineaum = Symphyglossum

Micropera
pallida = apiculata
purpurea = rostrata

Microstylis also Malaxis
bella = Liparis rheedii
scottii = Malaxis calophylla

Miltonia
anceps = flava

clowesii = *Oncidium*
cuneata = *Oncidium*
endresii = *Miltonioides warscewiczii*
fuscata = *Oncidium*
laevis = *Miltonioides*
roezlii = *Miltoniopsis*
russelliana = *Oncidium*
schroederiana = *Miltonioides*
stellata = *flavescens*
vexillaria = *Miltoniopsis*
warscewiczii = *Miltonioides*

Mormodes
flavida = *buccinator*
histrio = *lineata*
wendlandii = *colossus*

Mormolyca
lineolata = *ringens*

Myrmecophila
Schomburgkia

Mystacidium
aporoides = *Angraecum*

Nanodes
mantinii = *Epidendrum*
mathewsii = *Neolehmannia porpax*
schlechterianum = *Epidendrum congestum*

Neomoorea
wallissii = *irrorata*

Nephelaphyllum
grandiflorum = *Tainia wrayana*

Notylia
augustilancea = *barkeri*
bicolor = *Macroclinium*
bipartita = *barkeri*
cordesii = *Macroclinium*
lexarzana = *Macroclinium*
mirabilis = *Macroclinium*
multiflora = *barkeri*
norae = *mirabilis*
tridachne = *barkeri*
trisepala = *barkeri*
wullschlaegeliana = *Macroclinium*
xyphophorus = *Megaclinium manabinum*

Oberonia
emarginata = *micrantha*
tahitensis = *iridifolia*

Odontochilus
discolor = *Ludista*

Odontoglossum
alexandrae = *crispum*
anceps = *Osmoglossum dubium*
angustatum = *ramosissimum*
apterum = *Cymbiglossum*
aspersum = *humeanum* (Nat. Hyb.)
bictoniense = *Cymbiglossum*
brevifolium = *Otoglossum*
cervantesii = *Cymbiglossum*
chiriquense = *Otoglossum*
citrosmum = *Cuitlauzina pendula*
confusum = *Miltonioides*
convallarioides = *Osmoglossum*
cordatum = *Cymbiglossum*
coronarium = *Otoglossum*
dayanum = *praestans*
dubium = *Osmoglossum*
egertonii = *Osmoglossum*
ehrenbergii = *Cymbiglossum*
floribundum = *auropurpureum*
galeottianum = *Cymbiglossum*
gloriosum = *odoratum*
grande = *Rossioglossum*
hastilabium = *Oncidium*
hortensiae = *Cymbiglossum*
hrubyanum = *cirrhosum*
× *humeanum* = *Cymbiglossum rossii*
hystrix = *luteopurpureum*
insleayi = *Rossioglossum*
karwinskii = *Miltonioides*
krameri = *Ticoglossum*
laevis = *Miltonioides*
liliiflorum = *ramosissimum* var.
londesboroughianum = *Mesoglossum*
maculatum = *Cymbiglossum*
majale = *Cymbiglossum*
oerstedii = *Ticoglossum*
pendulum = *Cuitlauzina*
platycheilum = *Cymbiglossum majale*
pulchellum = *Osmoglossum*
purum = *wallisii*
pygmaeum = *Rhynchostele*
reichenheimii = *Miltonioides*
rossii = *Cymbiglossum*
schleiperianum = *Rossioglossum*
schroederianum = *Miltonioides*
splendens = *Rossioglossum*
stellatum = *Cymbiglossum*
stenoglossum = *Miltonioides*
tigroides = *Solenidiopsis*
uroskinneri = *Cymbiglossum*
williamsianum = *Rossioglossum*
wyattianum = *harryanum*

Odontorrhynchus
ghillanyi = *Thelychista*

Oeonia
  polystachya = Oeoniella

Oncidium
  acrobotyrum = harrisonianum
  aemulum = superbiens
  alboviolasceum = incurvum
  aloisii = planilabre
  altissimum = luridum
  aureum = Odontoglossum
  bicolor = martianum
  bidens = Brassia
  brienianum = widgrenii
  brunlesianum = Baptistonia echinata
  bryalophotum = heteranthum
  caloglossum = pectorale (Nat.hyb.?)
  candidum = Miltonia
  carderi = orgyale
  confusum = ensatum, also Miltonioides
  corynephorum = volubile
  cosymbephorum = luridum, + altissimum
  dichromum = Odontoglossum aureum
  digitatum = leucochilum
  dimorphum = trulliferum
  echinatum = Baptistonia
  ghiesbreghtianum = Mexicoa
  glaziovii = cebolleta
  glossomystax = Psygmorchis
  gracillimum = cogniauxianum
  guatemalense = oliganthum
  guianense = also desertorum
  haematochilum = Nat. Hyb.
  hastilabium = Miltonioides
  helicanthum = ascendens
  hieroglyphicum = ansiferum
  hrubyanum = lietzei
  iridifolium = Psygmorchis pusilla
  jacquinianum = altissimum
  jamesonii = cultratum
  janierense = longipes
  johnianum = barbatum
  kramerianum = Psychopsis
  laeve = Miltonioides laevis
  larkiinianum = pectorale
  leopardianum = tigratum
  leopoldianum = volubile
  longifolium = cebolleta
  luridum = also altissimum; guttatum
  macropterum = micropogon
  montanum = pirarense
  oerstedii = carthagenense
  ornithocephaloides = trulliferum
  panduriferum = carthagenense
  papilio = Psychopsis
  pardinum = Odontoglossum
  pardothyrsus = planilabre
  pauciflorum = Miltonioides

  peruvianum = Brassia
  pinnifera = Oerstedella
  polycladium = baueri
  pseudo-schumannianum = Oerstedella
  pseudo-wallisii = Oerstedella
  pumilum = Psygmorchis pumilio
  pusillum = Psygmorchis
  reichenheimii = Miltonioides
  reisii = ciliatum
  retemeyerianum = also oestlundianum
  rupestre = excavatum
  sanderae = Psychopsis
  scansor = globuliferum
  schumannianum = Oerstedella
  schweinfurthianum = Oerstedella
  sprucei = cebolleta
  staceyi = wittii
  stenostalix = martianum
  suave = reflexum
  suttonii = reflexum
  titania = Psygmorchis gnoma
  trilingue = kienastianum
  undulatum = carthagenense
  unguiculatum = tigrinum var.
  unicorne = longicornu
  warneri = Mexicoa ghiesbreghtiana
  weltonii = fuscatum
  zonatus = heteranthum

Orchis
  foliosa = Habenaria alata
  hircinum = Himantoglossum
  longibracteata = Himantoglossum

Ornithidium
  Maxillaria

Ornithocephalus
  grandiflorus = Dipteranthus
  inflexus = gladiatus
  reitzii = myrticola
  tripteris = gladiatus

Ornithochilus
  fuscus = difformis

Osmoglossum
  anceps = dubium

Pabstia
  puydtii = jugosa

Pachystoma
  ancistrochilus

Paphiopedilum
  affine = gratrixianum

amabile = bullenianum
bodegonii = glanduliferum
boxallii = villosum
celebense = bullenianum var.
chamberlainianum = victoria regina; see
    liemianum
chiwuanum = hirsutissimum
curtisii = superbiens
curtisii var. sanderae = superbiens var.
    sanderae
dianthum = parishii
elliotianum = rothschildianum
esquirolei = hirsutissimum
fowleyi = hennisianum var.
gardineri = glanduliferum
johorensis = bullenianum
keyesianum = concolor
laevigatum = philippinense
leucochilum = godefroyae var.
linii = bullenianum
moquetteanum = glaucophyllum var.
niveum var. angthong = × angthong
petri = dayanum
poyntzianum = appletonianum
praestans = glanduliferum
purpurascens = javanicum
robinsonii = bullenianum var.
roebelinii = philippinense
schmidtianum = callosum
sublaeve = barbatum var.
virens = javanicum
volonteanum = hookerae var.
wilhelminiae = glanduliferum

Pelexia
maculata = laxa

Peristylus
veridis = Coeloglossum

Pescatorea
roezlii = wallisii

Phaius
blumei = tankervilliae
bracteosus = flavus
grandifolius = tankervilliae
maculatus = flavus
tuberculatus = Gastorchis tuberculosa
wallichii = tankervilliae
woodfordii = flavus
zollingeri = amboinensis

Phalaenopsis
boxallii = mannii
buyssoniana = Doritis pulcherrima
decumbens = parishii

delicata = intermedia var. portei (Nat. Hyb.)
denevei = Paraphalaenopsis
esmeralda = Doritis pulcherrima
grandiflora = amabilis
parishii var. lobbii = lobbii
psilantha = amboinensis
regnieriana = Doritis
rimestadiana = amabilis var.
rosea = equestris
serpentilingua = Paraphalaenopsis
tetraspis = speciosa var.
zebrina = sumatrana

Pholidota
conchoidea = imbricata
grandis = ventricosa

Phragmipedium
caudatum = lindenii
hincksianum = longifolium
macrochilum = grande var. (Nat. Hyb.)
schomburgkianum = klotzchianum
schroederae = Hort. Hyb.
warscewiczii = lindenii

Physosiphon
guatemalensis = tubatus
herzogii = Pleurothallis aurantiolateritia
lindleyi = also tubatus
loddigesii = tubatus
moorei = tubatus

Physurus
ortgiesii = Erythrodes calophylla
querceticola = Platythelys
validus = Erythrodes

Pilumna
Trichopilia
nobilis = Trichopilia fragrans

Platanthera
susannae = Pecteilis

Platyclinis
Dendrochilum

Platystele
dunstervillei = ornata

Pleione
birmanica = praecox
formosana = also bulbocodioides
formosana var. nivea = bulbocodioides var.
    formosana
lagenaria = praecox, also Nat. Hyb.
pogonioides = bulbocodioides var.

pricei = bulbocodioides var.
reichenbachiana = praecox
speciosa = bulbocodioides
wallichiana = praecox var.

Pleurothallis
acostaei = phyllocardioides
acrisepala = brighamii
astrophora = Lepanthopsis
atropurpurea = Cryptophoranthus
barberiana = aristata
bidentula = saundersiana
bifalcis = segoviensis
biflora = orbicularis
biglandulosa = grobyi
broadwayi = foliata
caespitosa = luteola
calyptrosepala = segregatifolia
cardium = undulata
chamensis = casapensis
crocea = glumacea
cuneifolia = hypnicola
diaphana = Octomeria
diffusa = revoluta
dryadum = grobyi
foliosa = Gomesa
ghiesbreghtiana = quadrifida
hamata = crenata
hispida = Dressleria
kraenzliniana = panduripetala
lamprophylla = dolichopus
lepanthiformis = ciliaris
leptopetala = discoidea
lilacina = recurva
linguifera = lansbergii
loncophylla = hystrix
longicaulis = auriculata
longisepala = miqueliana
longissima = quadrifida
macrophyta = aphthosa
maculata = recurva
mantiquyrana = Pleurobotyrum
marginalis = grobyi
marginata = uniflora
microphylla = grobyi
mirabilis = Pabstiella
modestiflora = obovata
ophiocephala = Restrepiella
ornata = scheidii
ospinae = Restrepia antennifera
penduliflora = revoluta
peduncularis = aphthosa
peraltensis = blaisdellii
pfavii = endotrachys
picta = grobyi; pubescens
platyrachis = endotrachys
platysemos = barbacenensis

platystachys = tricarinata
plumosa = lanceana
prorepens = Barbosella
puberula = Restrepiella ophiocephala
pyrsodes = fulgens
raymondii = Myoxanthus reymondii
repens = ascendans
riograndensis = pubescens
roezlii = restrepioides
rotundata = orbiculata
rusupinata = resupinata
scapha = biserrula
schlechteriana = cardiothallis
semipellucida = revoluta
serripetala = Myoxanthus
smithiana = pubescens
stenopetala = sclerophylla
teretifolia = Cryptophoranthus atropurpurea
truxillensis = pubescens
umbrosa = uniflora
vaginata = imrayi
villosa = ciliaris
vinosa = saundersiana
vittata = pubescens
wendlandiana = ruscifolia
xanthophthalma = Restrepia

Podangis
forcipata = dactyloceras

Pogonia
scottii = Nervilia aragoana

Polyrrhiza
lindenii = Polyradicion

Polystachya
bracteosa = affinis
bulbophylloides = Genyorchis pumila
cerea = foliosa
clavata = foliosa
galeata = also *cucullata*
grandiflora = cucullata
luteola = also *concreta*
mauritiana = also *concreta*
minor = foliosa
minuta = concreta
repens = Stolzia
rufinula = odorata
ruwensoriensis = lindblomii
shega = vaginata
tessellata = also *concreta*
tricruris = concreta
uganda = lindblomii

Ponera
australis = striata

Porroglossum
muscosum = echidnum

Prescottia
plantaginifolia = plantaginea

Promenaea
citrina = xanthina
paulensis = rollisonii

Ptychogyne
flexuosa = Coelogyne

Reichenbachanthus
modestus = reflexus

Renanthera
bilinguis = Armodorum labrosum
histrimona = Ellanthera
lowii = Dimorphorchis
moscifera = Arachnis

Restrepia
dentata = aspasicensium
leopardina = guttulata
maculata = guttulata
peduncularis = Pleurothallis
xanthophthalma = muscifera

Rhipidoglossum
rutilum = Diaphananthe

Rhynchostylis
densiflora = gigantea

Ritaia
Ceratostylis

Robiquetia
paniculata = succisa

Rodriguezia
crispa = Gomesa
fragrans = venusta
gomesioides = Rodrigueziella
lindeni = pubescens
recurva = Gomesa
secunda = lanceolata
teuscheri = lehmannii

Rudolfiella
saxicola = Bifrenaria

Saccolabium
acutifolium = Gastrochilus
ampullaceum = Ascocentrum
bellinum = Gastrochilus

bigibbum = Gastrochilus
blumei = Rhynchostylis retusa
brevifolium = Robiquetia
calcaratum = Cleisostoma tridentatus
calceolare = Gastrochilus intermedius
cerinum = Robiquetia
curvifolium = Ascocentrum
dasypogon = Gastrochilus
giganteum = Rhynchostylis
gracile = Robiquetia
guttatum = Rhynchostylis retusa
hendersonianum = Ascocenda + Malleola
    penangiana
insectiferum = Malleola
longicalcaratum = Robiquetia pachyphyllum
micranthum = Smitinandia
obtusifolium = Uncifera
paniculatum = Cleisostoma; + Aerides
    ringens
papillosum = Acampe
parviflorum = Angraecopsis
praemorsum = Acampe; + Rhynchostylis
    retusa var.
purpureum = Ascoglossum calopterum
    quisumbingii = Tuberolabium kotoense (?)
rubescens = Aerides
trichromum = Cleisocentron
tridentatum = Cleisostoma
violaceum = Rhynchostylis gigantea

Sarcanthus
acutifolium = Gastrochilus
bicornis = Cleisostoma
halophilus = Cleisostoma
kunstleri = Cleisostoma arietinum
longifolius = Cleisostoma
pachyfolium = Cleisostoma
pachyphyllus = Cleisostoma
pallidus = Cleisostoma racemiferum
pendulatum = Cleisostoma
peninsularis = Cleisostoma tenuifolium
racemifer = Cleisostoma
recurvus = Cleisostoma
robustus = Robiquetia spathulata
strongyloides = Cleisostoma
subulatus = Cleisostoma
termissus = Cleisostoma
uraiensis = Cleisostoma

Sarcochilus
appendiculatus = Pteroceras
divitifolorus = Rhinerrhiza
luniferus = Chilochista
mannii = Micropera
pygmaeus = Thrixspermum
saruwatarii = Thrixspermum
segawai = Chilochista

suaveolens = *Petroceras*
unguiculatus = *pallidus*

Sarcoglottis
orbiculata = *rosulata*
picta = *acaulis*
rufescens = *ventricosa*

Sarcopodium
acuminatum = *Epigeneium*
coelogyne = *Epigeneium amplum*
cymbidioides = *Epigeneium*
elongatum = *Epigeneium*
lyonii = *Epigeneium*
triflorum = *Epigeneium*

Scaphosepalum
violaceum = *Cladobium*

Scaphyglottis
behrii = *graminifolia*
confusa = *Pachystele minuta*
crurigera = *Hexadesmia*
cuneata = *prolifera*
leucantha = *graminifolia*
lindeniana = *Hexadesmia fasciculata*
livida = *Pachystele dubia*
reedii = *Hexadesmia sessilis*
tenuis = *Hexadesmia sessilis*
unguiculata = *longicaulis*
violacea = *Cladobium*

Schlimia
trifida = *alpina*

Schoenorchis
hainanensis = *gemmata*
manipurensis = *fragrans*

Schomburgkia
brysiana var. *thomsoniana* = *thomsoniana*
exaltata = *tibicinis*
moyabambae = *Laelia*
violacea = *undulata*

Seraphyta
difusa = *Epidendrum*
multiflora = *Epidendrum diffusum*

Serapias
congesta = *Beadlea*

Sigmatogyne
Panisea

Sigmatostalix
lunata = *picta*

racemifera = *picturatissima*
radicans = *Ornithophora*

Smitinandia
ambikianum = *Schoenorchis fragrans*

Sobralia
dichotoma = *Cattleya*
holfordii = *macrantha* var.
lindeni = *pulcherrima*
panamensis = *fenzliana*

Sophronitis
grandiflora = *coccinea*
violacea = *Sophronitella*

Spathoglottis
fortunei = *pubescens*

Spiranthes
acaulis = *Sarcoglottis*
aestivalis = *lucida*
aurantiaca = *Stenorrhynchus*
australis = *sinensis*, + *lancea*
autumnalis = *spiralis*
cernua var. *odorata* = *odorata*
cinnabarinus = *Dichromanthus*
colorata = *Stenorrhynchos speciosum*
elata = *Beadlea*
gracilis = *lacera*
hamata = *Pelexia*
lanceolata = *Sacoila*
nutans = *Stenorrhynchos*
polyantha = *Mesadenus*
rufescens = *Sarcoglottis ventricosa*
speciosa = *Stenorrhynchos*
weberbaueri = *Pelexia*

Stanhopea
amesiae = *lowii* var.
anfracta = *wardii*
aurea = *wardii*
bucephalus = *oculata*
convoluta = *tricornis*
eburnea = *grandiflora*
graveolens = *connata* (?); + *lietzei*
hoppii = *jenishiana*
inodora = *lietzei*
negroviolacea = *tigrina*
radiosa = *saccata*
rodigasiana = *Embreea*
venusta = *wardii*

Stauropsis
fasciata = *Trichoglottis*
gigantea = *Vandopsis*
guibertii = *Trichoglottis*

lissochiloides = Vandopsis
marriottiana = Vanda parishii var.
philippinensis = Trichoglottis
undulata = Vanda
warocqueana = Vandopsis

Stelis
binotii = aprica
cascajalensis = superbiens
chamaestelis = Apatostelis
ciliaris = Apatostelis
fragrans = pauciflora
grossilabris = Apatostelis
hymenantha = catharinensis
inaequalis = Apatostelis
inaequisepala = papaquerensis
leucopogon = superbiens
littoralis = argentata
macrochlamis = megantha
mexopous = gemma
micrantha = aprica
miersii = minutiflora
mucronata = pauciflora
nexipous = gemma
omalosantha = pauciflora
ophioglossoides = Pleurothallis
rodriguesii = aprica
rubens = Apatostelis
rufobrunnea = Apatostelis
simacoensis = virens
triseta = biserrula
viridipurpurea = papaquerensis

Stenocoryne
aureofulva = Bifrenaria
secunda = Bifrenaria aureofulva

Stenorrhynchos
aphyllus = Sacoila lanceolatus
cinnabarinus = Dicromanthus
coccineus = Sacoila lanceolatus
lanceolatum = Sacoila
navarrnsis = Coccineorchis
standleyi = Coccineorchis

Stereochilus
bicuspidatus = Cleisostoma aspersum

Sturmia
wagnerii = Liparis

Symphyglossum
roseum = Cochlioda

Telipogon
angustifolia = nervosus
dendriticus = andicola

wallissii = bruchmuelleri

Tetramicra
bicolor = Leptotes

Theodorea
gomezoides = Rodrigueziella

Triarstella
reichenbachii = Masdevallia

Trias
grandiflora = Bulbophyllum

Trichocentrum
albopurpureum = albococcineum
panamense = capistratum

Trichoceros
armillatus = antennifer
parviflorus = antennifer

Trichoglottis
brachiata = also philippinensis var.
calcarata = Oeceoclades

Trichopilia
backhousiana = fragrans
coccinea = marginata
dasyandra = Cischweinfia
lehmanii = fragrans
nobilis = fragrans
powelii = maculata
sanguinolenta = Helcia
subulata = Leucohyle
wageneri = fragrans

Trichosma
suavis = Eria coronaria

Trichotosia
elongata = Eria
pulvinata = Eria
rufinula = Eria
velutina = Eria

Trigonidium
spathulatum = egertonianum

Tuberolabium
quisumbingii = also kotoense

Uncifera
maxillaleonis = Cleisomeria lanatus

Vanda
batemani = Vandopsis lissochiloides

boxallii = *lamellata* var.
gigantea = *Vandopsis*
lissochiloides = *Vandopsis*
lowii = *Dimorphorchis*
parishii = *Vandopsis*
roxburgii = *tessellata*
suavis = *tricolor* var.
teretifolia = *Cleisostoma*
testacea = *parviflora*
vipani = *denisoniana*

Vandopsis
guibertii = *Trichoglottis*
luchuensis = *Trichoglottis ionosma*

Vanilla
articulata = *barbellata*
fragrans = *planifolia*

Waluewa
Leochilus

Warmingia
arminii = *eugenii*

Warrea
tricolor = *warreana*

Warscewicziella
discolor = *Cochleanthes*
flabelliformis = *Cochleanthes*
lindeni = *Chondrorhyncha;* + *Cochleanthes amazonica*
marginata = *Chondrorhyncha*
wailesiana = *Cochleanthes*
wendlandi = *Chondrorhyncha aromatica*
velata = *Chondrorhyncha*

Xylobium
scabrilingue = *variegatum*
squalens = *variegatum*

Zygopetalum
ballii = *Zygosepalum*
binoti = *Neogardneria*
burtii = *Huntleya*
coeruleum = *crinitum*
discolor = *Cochleanthes*
gramineum = *Kefersteinia*
jorisianum = *Mendoncella*
lindeni = *Zygosepalum*
mosenianum = *pedicellatum*
murrayanum = *Neogardneria*
proteroelanum = *triste*
rhombilabium = *Huntleya heteroclita*
rostratum = *Zygosepalum labiosum*

Flowering Months of Species Under Cultivation

	Ja	Fe	Mr	Ap	My	Jn	Jy	Ag	Se	Oc	No	De
Acacallis												
cyanea			2	6	5	5	6	2	6	1	1	1
Acampe												
dentata											1	1
multiflora								1		1		
ochracea												1
pachyglossa			1				3		3	1	1	
papillosa	3									21	20	5
praemorsa				1		2						
rigida			1			1			1	1	2	
Acanthephippium												
bicolor				2	3	2	2					
curtisii				1	1							
javanicum						1	1	2	4	2		2
mantinianum				2	3	4						
papuanum								1				
splendidum								1	2			
striatum					4	2	3					
sylhetense				7	6	4	3	1				
yamamotoi							1					
Aceras												
anthropophora						3		1				
Acianthus												
exsertus				1								
fornicatus									1			
Acineta												
barkeri						1	6	3	3	1		
chrysantha			1			1	4	4	8	7		1
densa					2		1	6	5	4	2	
erythroxantha								1				
hrubyana							1	3				
moorei											1	
sella-turcica								1				
superba			1	6	6	12	6	8	2	1	1	
Acoridium												
curranii			3									
graminifolium	1	4	6	1								
pumilum	3	4	3									
saccolabium	5	2	1									1
tenellum	1	2	5	2	1							
Acostaea												
costaricensis	1	1	2	2	1				1		1	2
pleurothalloides	1		2	3	1		1		1			
Acriopsis												
indica	1											
javanica			1	1	1						1	
nelsoniana											1	

	Ja	Fe	Mr	Ap	My	Jn	Jy	Ag	Se	Oc	No	De
Ada												
allenii					1	1			3	2	5	2
aurantiaca	16	30	67	53	20	1						1
chlorops	3	1	1	1	3	3				1	2	3
elegantula				1	1	2	2	1	2		1	
glumacea			1							1	2	1
keiliana			1	4	3	8	1	4	2	2		
lehmannii							1	1				
ocanensis	1	1			2		1	1				1
Aerangis												
aporoides				1								
appendiculata						1						
articulata			2	1	2		2	4	9	4	4	1
biloba	4	1	1	1				2	1	11	12	6
brachycarpa				1		1			2	3		
calantha										3		
calligera	3							1		1	3	6
citrata		5	7	1	3	5	14	8	1	2	3	2
clavigera	1									2	5	4
compta				1					3		3	4
confusa	1		1				1		3	2		1
coriacea	2	3				3	2	2	3	3	2	1
cryptodon	3	1							2	2	3	1
curnowiana			2	1	1		1	1		2	2	
decaryana	1										1	1
ellisii	1	1	1				1		6	4	5	1
fastuosa	2	3	15	12	3							
flabellifolia				1		1	2	4		4	3	
friesiorum	2	1	4	3	1	2		1	3	5	5	
fuscata	1							1				
hyaloides	3	8	1									
jacksonii				1								
kirkii									4	4		1
kotschyana					1	2	1	4	5	3	4	
laurentii											1	
luteo-alba	2	5	15	19	5	1	4	8	7	9	2	7
—var. *rhodosticta*	2	2	5	6	1	1			1	1	2	1
macrocentra				1								
malmquistiana var.												
venusta									1			
modesta		1	5	5	2		1					
mooreana	2		1									
mystacidii				3		2	1	5	5	2	3	3
platyphylla										1	5	
pumilio	3	9	1									
roseocalcarata										1		
scottii										1		
somalensis	1			1	1							2
stylosa	1	2	3	12	7		1	2	4	1		1
thompsonii				2				1				1
ugandensis				2	3		3	6	4	4	7	1
umbonata				1	1	1						
venosa											1	
verdickyi							1	1	1		1	

	Ja	Fe	Mr	Ap	My	Jn	Jy	Ag	Se	Oc	No	De
Aeranthes												
albidiflora											1	
antennifera								1	2	1		
arachnites	2				1	5	4	1	3	2	2	1
caudata								2	3			
denticulata	1	3										1
dentiens					3	1	1					
erectiflora									1			
filipes						1	1	1	2			
grandiflora				1	1	11	30	12	9	4	2	
henricii	1	1							1	4	2	2
imerinensis	1					2	6	8	7	2	2	1
longipes				1		1	1	1	1			
modestum			4	2	2	3						
moratii								2	2	1		1
neoperrieri				3	1	1	2	1	1	1	1	
nidus					1	2	2					
orthopoda							1					
peyrotii						1	1	1				
ramosa		3	1	2	3	4	9	10	7	7	5	4
robusta							1					
sambironoensis	1											
zygopetaloides									1			
Aeranthus												
carpophorus						1						
Aerides												
augustiana									1			
biloba										1		
crassifolium			5	6	14	7	6					
crispum				1	14	3	4					
cylindricum	1	2	1					1	1			
emericii				1								
falcata				1	12	23	14	2	1			
fieldingii		3	1	8	41	24	10	3	1		4	3
flabellata				1	2	3	5	1				
friesiorum										1		
houlettiana		1	8	8	27	13	10	5	1		1	
hughii				1								
huttoni			1				1		1			
jarckiana	4	9	2		1					1		
larpentae					1	1						
lawrenceae	2					5	2	15	17	17	9	2
—var. *sanderiana*	2			2			2	9	2	3	2	
leeanum					3	1				1	1	
lobbii				1	5	6	2	1				
longicalcarata			1		1			1				
longicornu							3			2	1	
maculosum			1	1	1	5	1	2			1	
micholitzii				1	2							
multiflora		2	1	4	42	42	38	4				1
odorata		1	2	2	23	47	48	22	13	10	3	1
—var. *alba*						5	5	1	2	1		
—var. *bicuspidata*						1		4	4	1		

	Ja	Fe	Mr	Ap	My	Jn	Jy	Ag	Se	Oc	No	De
ortgiesiana	1											
pachyphylla						1						
pallida						1						
platychila			1									
quinquivulnera	4	2			1	1	5	6	7	3	2	
radicosa	2					2	2					1
—var. *alba*	2					2			1	1	2	1
ringens					2	1	2					
rubescens			2									
savageana					3	1						
siamense					1	1						
thibautiana						1			1			
vandara	6	10	22	7	4					2		
virens	1	1	1	3	16	5	6					
williamsii					1							
Aganisia												
ionoptera								4	2	1	1	1
pulchella											1	
Aglossorrhyncha												
viridis						1						
Agrostophyllum												
brevipes										1		
lampongense									2			
majus				1					1			
occidentale								1				
uniflorum												
Alamania												
punicea			1		1	5	2	1		1		
Altensteinia												
fimbriata	1											
matthewsii										2		
Amblostoma												
armeniaca							1	3	6	1	1	
cernua	1											1
tridactylum	8	4	4	1		1				1	3	4
Amitostigma												
gracile				1		1	1					
keiskei				1		1						
Amparoa												
beloglossa										1	2	
costaricensis								2				
Anacamptis												
pyramidalis					1							
Ancistrochilus												
rothschildianus	6	2	1				1				1	
thompsonianus			1	1	1		1	16	13	13	3	
Ancistrorhynchus												
capitatus	3				1					2	3	3
cephalotes	4	3										

	Ja	Fe	Mr	Ap	My	Jn	Jy	Ag	Se	Oc	No	De
clandestinus	5		1						2	3	5	1
metteniae											1	
ovatus	1	3		1						1		
recurvis							1	1				
refractus	2			1				1	1			
tenuicaulis											2	
Angraecopsis												
amaniensis			1	1								3
breviloba												1
gracillima			1		4	1					1	
parviflora					1							
tenerrima							3					1
Angraecum												
acutipetalum									2			
andersonii												1
angustum							1					
aporoides	3	1		2			1	2		1	2	2
appendiculoides	1											
arachnites	2		1	2	1							
augusti							2					
bicallosum						3	2	1	2	1		
birrimense								1	1			
bistortum		1								1	1	
bosseri	1	1										1
breve		1										
buyssonii				1					1		2	
calceolus				2	5	6	5	10	6	2	1	
caricifolium							1					
chevalieri	4							2		3	2	1
chloranthum							1					
citratum	4	10	17	4	2		1		1	2		
comorense								4	7	4	2	
compactum	1	1	3	4	5	10	4	2	1		1	
compressicaule	1											1
conchiferum						1	1					
cucullatum			1	1	1							
cultriforme	1		1		1		1	1	2		1	
dasycarpum	1								1		1	
dendrobiopsis						1	1	1	2	1	1	
didieri			1	3	1	2	2	1	1	1		
dives										2		
eburneum	44	36	8	2	1	2	1	1	2	12	26	26
—var. *giryamae*	3	1								1	3	4
—var. *longicalcar*										2	5	
—var. *superbum*	5	2					2	3	1	3	6	4
egertonii									1			
eichlerianum	1	2		3		1	8	5	10	16	8	10
elephantium	2	2										2
ellisii			1	1					5	7		
equitans			1	4	2							
erectum		1	1	1	1							
expansum					1	1		1	1		1	
filicornu							1		2	1		1
filiforme									1			

	Ja	Fe	Mr	Ap	My	Jn	Jy	Ag	Se	Oc	No	De
fimbriatum											1	
florulentum				1	4	1						
forcipatum							1	2				
fournierianum						2						
germinyanum			1	3	3	1	1	2		3		
giryamae	15	10	1	2			1	1			4	9
gracile			1									
gracilipes	3		1					1		6	5	5
henriquesianum										1	1	
hildebrandtii		2	3							1	1	1
humberti	1	1									1	1
ichneumoneum				1					1	2		
infundibularum	2	1		1	3	2	6	2	5	7	9	5
kindtianum								2				
kotschii							2		1	1	2	
leonis	3	8	13	14	13	3	1	1	3	2	4	8
longicalcaratum						1			1	1	2	2
magdalenae				3	7	8	8	6	4	1		
mahavavense				1	1	1						
maudae	1								1			
mauritanium										6	1	
maxillarioides	2										2	3
metallicum				1								
mirabile	1	1				1			2			2
mitrata	1	1	3	1				1			1	
montanum											1	
monteirei											1	1
musculiferum				1								
nasutum												2
obesum			1			2	1	1	1			
o-brienianum							1	1				
odoratissimum		1	1							1	1	1
pauciramosum		1		1	1							
pectinatum								1	1		1	
pellucidum		1								1	2	2
penzigianum				2	3	1						
pertusum			2	1		1		1		1	1	2
philippinense	12	20	14					1		1		2
picturatense							1	1	1	1	1	
porrigens			1									
praestans								1	2	2		1
protensum									2	2	1	
pseudodidieri				1								
pseudofilicornu					2	2	2	4				
pungens			1								1	
ramosum			1	1	4	1	1		1	2	1	
recurvum		1							3	5	2	
reygaerti									1			
rhynchoglossum	1											
rutenbergianum					1	2	1	6	4	1	1	
sacciferum									1			
saccolabioides					1							
sambiranoense						1	1					
sanderianum				4	8	10	2			1		
scottianum			1	2	4	6	13	21	17	13	3	4

	Ja	Fe	Mr	Ap	My	Jn	Jy	Ag	Se	Oc	No	De
sesquipedale	64	43	34	26	21					1	10	14
sororium						1	1	2	2	1		
squamatum								1	1			
stella-africae	3											
stolzii	1	1							1	1	3	2
striatum						1	1	1		1		
suarezense	1											
subulatum	3	1	2	4		1			2	4		1
superbum	11	9	2							1	3	4
teretifolium			2	7	2	1	1	1				
tridactylites								1				
triendatum					1							
triquetrum						1	1	1				
viguieri			3	8	1			1				
whytei								2				
xylopus								1				
Anguloa												
brevilabris	1		1		1	1	7	2	1			
cliftonii	2	1	1		4	18	28	10	4	3	1	
clowesii		2	3	4	74	41	21	7	4	1		
hohenlohii					1	1						
rückeri			1	2	23	18	17	10	2			
uniflora			4	3	4	11	15	9	5	2	3	
virginalis				1	2	4	6	4	2	1		3
Anoectochilus												
cincinnus					1		1		1			
formosanus										1		
hispida								1				
intermedius							1			1		
marmorata							1					
regalis		1	1				1	1				
reinwardtii							1					
rollinsoni					1		1	1				
roxburghii	1				1	1	1				2	1
setaceus				1			4			1		
sikkimensis	1				1	1		1		2	1	
Ansellia												
africana	7	13	28	28	34	18	11	4			3	8
concolor	2											
gigantea	3	5	6	9	6		5	4	1	1		
—var. *nilotica*			1	5	6		4	2	3	1	1	2
humilis	1				1						1	
nilotica	5	1	2		7	4	8	2	4	2	5	4
Anthogonium												
gracile							1	3	4	1		
Apatostelis												
braccata					6	2	1					
chamaestelis		1										
ciliaris		1	2	2	1							
grossilabris						1						
inaequalis	1											
latipetala	7	9	2							1	3	5

	Ja	Fe	Mr	Ap	My	Jn	Jy	Ag	Se	Oc	No	De
muscosa					1	1						
rubens						1					1	
rufobrunnea					1				1			
Appendicula												
bifaria						1	1					
calcarata												1
cornuta	2	2			1							2
elegans	1		1	1	1	1	1		1		2	2
lewisii										1		
pendula								1	2	1		1
reflexa								1		1		1
rubens		1	5									
Arachnis												
annamensis				1								
cathcartii	4	14	8						1			1
clarkei		1						1	3	2	2	4
flos-aëris		1			2	1	5	2	1	2	2	3
moscifera		1			2	2	3					
Argrostophyllum												
khasianum									1			
Armodorum												
labrosum				1	1		3	2				
siamensis			1	1								
Arpophyllum												
alpinum	1		1	1								1
cardinale				1								
giganteum	6	10	14	18	10	1						
spicatum	3	4	3	10	8	2	2	1	1	2	2	1
Artorima												
erubescens	2	1				1					2	6
Arundina												
chinensis										2	3	
graminifolia			3	1	1	1		4	3		1	2	1
Ascocentrum												
ampullaceum	3	11	13	34	36	18	5	2				
aurantiacum	1	1		2								
curvifolium	1	4	4	12	21	9	5	2				
micranthum				1								
miniatum	5	3	10	14	21	13	8	3	2	1	2	8
pumilum	1			1		1					4	3
Ascoglossum												
calopterum	2	5	2	2			1		1			
purpureum			1									
Aspasia												
lunata		1	1	4	5	9	4	1	3			
principissa	3	6	11	8	11	8						1
variegata		1									1	
Aulosepalum												
hemichrea		1										

	Ja	Fe	Mr	Ap	My	Jn	Jy	Ag	Se	Oc	No	De
Baptistonia												
echinata	1	3	3	2	2				1	1	1	
Barbosella												
australis								1	1	1		
caespitifica						1					1	
circinata				1								
cucullata		1	1	1	1							
dolichoriza			1									
dusenii									1	1		
fuscata												1
gardneri							2	1				
handroi	1				1			2				
microphylla								1				
miersii						1						
monstrabilis										1		
prorepens				1	1							
Barkeria												
barkeriola	1	1					1	3	1	2	3	4
chinensis	2	2	1	2							1	2
cyclotella					3					3	6	2
dorotheae	1			2							1	2
elegans	5	3			2				2	2	2	1
hagsateri		1										
halbingeri				2	2	3	4	1				
lindleyana	2				2	4			1	10	16	6
melanocaulon	4	2										2
naevosa	1	2	2	5	2							
palmeri	6	1										3
scandens									1	3	3	2
shoemakeri	1	3					1			3	1	
skinneri	8	2		1		2			4	8	8	8
spectabilis	1		1	11	14	8	7	2	4	10	3	3
uniflora										3	2	
Barlia												
robertiana		1		1								
Bartholina												
pectinata						1	1					
Batemannia												
colleyii		1	4							1		
Beadlea												
argyrifolius				4	5	2	1					
congesta	4	9	12	4	1							1
elata	15	11	13	6	2	1	2	1				4
elegans	3	4	6									3
longibracteata				1								
Beclardia												
macrostachya		1										
Beloglottis												
costaricensis			3	4	3							
Biermannia												
bimaculata							1					

	Ja	Fe	Mr	Ap	My	Jn	Jy	Ag	Se	Oc	No	De
Bifrenaria												
atropurpurea			3	2	3	3	1				1	1
aureofulva						2	1	2	1	4	4	1
fuerstenbergiana					4							
harrisoniae		3	22	56	57	6	3	2				
—var. *alba*				4	6	1						
inodora		1		3	5	1	1					
melanopoda				2	4		1				1	
pubigera			1	2	5	1						
racemosa	1		1		1	1				1		1
saxicola				4	4	1						
secunda		1	1			1	2	2	1	3		1
tetragona				1	1	5	2	5	3		1	
tyrianthina		1	1	2	12	7	5					
—*alba*			1	3	1							
villosula				1								
vitellina	1			1	2	4	6	1				
wendlandiana							1			1		
Bletia												
catenulata				2	4	1	1	1	4			
florida					1	3	2	3				
patula		1					1					
purpurata							1	1				
purpurea	3	5	10	12	5	6	7	3	4	5	2	3
shepherdii			1	2	6	8	2	1				
Bletilla												
chinensis						1						
striata	10	5	9	4	5	4	1	1		1	3	4
Bollea												
coelestis					1	3	5	6	1	1		
hemixantha					1	1		1				
lalindei		1		1	1	1	11	7	3		1	2
lawrenceana				2	1		1	1				
patinii			1		3				1			
pulvinaris					1	1			1	1	1	
schroderiana			2	1							1	
violacea	1		1	1	3			1		1	2	3
Bolusiella												
imbricata		4	1				1		2	5	2	3	3
Bonatea												
cassidea			1	1								1
speciosa		1	2	2			1			1		1	1
steudneri									1			
ugandae											1	
Brachycorythis												
kalbreyeri				4		6		1	3			
obcordata								2				
pleistophylla				1								
Brachtia												
andina	1			1						2	1	2
glumacea					1							

	Ja	Fe	Mr	Ap	My	Jn	Jy	Ag	Se	Oc	No	De
Brachypeza												
archytas									1			
Brassavola												
acaulis	2	1			3	3	3	1				
ceboletta	1	2	1	3	5	4	3	2	2	5	2	2
cordata	7	6	6	2			7	7	7	7	13	9
cucullata	1		1	1	3	5	10	12	15	11	8	7
flagellaris		1		2				1	2			
fragrans					2	1	1		1	1	1	1
martiana	3	7	9	2	6	1	1	5	3	2		3
multiflora						1	2	1				
nodosa	11	13	7	4	9	9	19	35	36	48	29	14
—ssp. *grandiflora*	2	3						2	2	3	3	2
perrinii	1	3	9	11	9	6	17	6	6	4	2	1
revoluta		2		2	1						1	
rhopalorhachis							1					
tuberculata			1	1	2	10	10	4		2	1	
venosa									1			
Brassia												
arachnoides					3	1	1					
arcuigera		1	2	6	4	5		1	2	2		3
bicolor								1				
bidens	3					2					1	1
brachiata	1	1	2	19	20	7	9	25	11	3		
caudata	1	3	2	8	8	14	15	13	6	2	1	1
chloroleuca	1											
filomenoi						1	1					
forgetiana							1	1				2
gireoudiana		1	7	4	12	10	7	2	2	2		
lanceana		2		1		2	2	5	7	2	3	
lawrenceana		2		1	6	4	5	1	5	5	3	
—var. *longissima*					1	3	6	2	2	4	1	
longissima		1		3	11	12	12	9	10	7	8	
maculata		1	3	7	14	21	9	5	3	2	1	
mexicana	2				3	6	3					1
neglecta				1			1					
peruviana												2
picturata			1	1		1	1	1			1	1
signata						1	1		1	1		
thyrsodes							1					
verrucosa		2	3	1	11	20	8	2				
wageneri				1			1	1	1			
warscewiczii	2									2	3	
Bromheadia												
aporoides		1	1	1								
finlaysoniana					1							
Broughtonia												
negrilensis	3	5	4	4	1	1						2
sanguinea	2	1	8	14	38	20	33	14	7	5	4	4
Brownleea												
coerulea										1		

	Ja	Fe	Mr	Ap	My	Jn	Jy	Ag	Se	Oc	No	De
Bulbophyllum												
adenambon						1	1	3	3	1		
affine						1	2	2				
africanum											1	
alticolum					1							
ambrosia	5	3	1								1	3
amplebracteatum						1						
anceps						3	1					
andersonii							1	3	5	2		
antennatum				2		1						
ariel				1								
arnoldianum							1	1				
atropurpureum		1										
aurantiacum						2	1					
auratum	1	1	1	1	4	2	1		2	3		
auricomum	1	1								1	1	1
auriflorum			1									
baileyi							2	1				
barbatum		1	2									
barbigerum	3	4	11	9	54	21	24	11	10	9	1	1
becquaertii		2		1	1	1	1		3		2	
—var. *brachyanthum*	2	3	1	2	1	1	1					1
biflorum						3	5	2	1	1		
binnendijkii					5	1	1	1			1	
bisetum									2	1		
blepharistes	1											2
blumei				1								
bowkettae			1									
brachypetalum						1						
bracteatum				1								
bracteolatum			1	1								
brevistylidium										1		
brienianum				3	2		2	1		2	9	1
bufo			2	7	10		2	1				
buntingii				1								
caespitosum	1	1	1	2		1		1	3	2	4	1
calamarium					1	1	1	3	2	4	3	
careyanum	6	5	3	1					1	6	19	3
cariniflorum						3	4	4	2			
cauliflorum							1	1	1			
chaunobulbon		1										
cheiri				2		1						
chinense							1					
claptonense					2							
clarkeanum	1	1		1			1					
clavatum	1	1	1	1	1						1	
cochleatum	2										1	
cocoinum							4		2	2	1	
colubrinum										1		
comosum	4	7	1								1	1
concinnum		1			1					1		
congolanum	1			1	2						1	
cornosum	1											
cornutum	1	1	1	1		1	1	1			1	1
crassipes	2	1	1			1	1		6	6	8	1

	Ja	Fe	Mr	Ap	My	Jn	Jy	Ag	Se	Oc	No	De
cruciatum											1	
cumingii			1		3	8	4	2	4			
cupreum		5	4	2					2	1	14	5
curranii								1	1	1		
cylindraceum								3			2	
dalatensis			2	1	2	1				1	1	1
dayanum	6	6	2	3	5	1	1		1	2	2	2
dearei	2			2	2	5	8	10	5	9	1	
delitescens									4	2	2	
densifolium							1	2	1			
dependens											1	1
digoelense								1	1	1		
dispersum							1					
distans		1	1		2			3	3	4	2	2
ebulbum			1	1	1	2	1	1			1	1
echinolabium									1			1
efogi								1				
elassonotum								1	1	2	3	2
elatum							1		2	1	5	
elegantulum				1	3		1					
elliae	1	3	1									
elongatum				1								
encephalodes			1									
erchelli						1	1					
ericsonii			1	1	2		3		1	2	3	
erubescens												1
erythrostachyum					1							
exaltatum								2				
falcatum	1	3	17	16	10		1	1	2			
fimbriatum		1	1	2	1							
flavidum	1											
flaviflorum		1	3	2	2			1				1
fletcherianum	5	5	4	4	6						1	
foveatum			1									
fritillariiflorum						2	2		1			
frostii					3	3	4					
fusco-purpureum						1						
fuscum			1	2								
garupinum				1								
gibbosum	7	4	4	3	4	3	5	2	2	3	3	5
giganteum						1						
glutinosum					1						1	1
godseffianum	1			1	4	6	4	1	2	4	2	3
gracillimum	5	1	3	2	3	4	3	4	3	5	5	4
grandiflorum		1	2	1	2	1	4	14	20	22	7	3
graveolens					1							
gravidum	1											
guamense												1
guttulatum	2		5		2	3	3	7	10	5	1	1
gymnopus			1									
habropus							1					
hahlianum			1									
hamadryas			1		1							1
hamelinii								1				
helenae	1		1	3		5	5	1	1		3	

	Ja	Fe	Mr	Ap	My	Jn	Jy	Ag	Se	Oc	No	De
hirtum	3								2	7	8	5
imschootianum						2	1					
inflatum				2	6	3	3					
intertextum	1				1						1	1
intricatum			1	1						1	1	1
ipanemensis	1	2										
kewense			1	1	1							
kindtianum					2	1		1	1	1	1	
lamprobulbum										1	2	
lasiochilum	2		1	1	1	1	1	2	1	2	6	2
laxiflorum				1		1		1				
lemniscatoides	1				2		1	2		1	4	1
lemniscatum	1				1						1	1
leopardinum					1	1	2	4				
lepidum	2	2	3	6	11	8	9	7	2	4	5	3
lilacinum	1		1							2	2	1
linearilabium				1					1			
lobbii	2	1	2	10	43	35	44	13	5		2	3
longiflorum	1	2	1		3	3	3	1	1	2	1	1
longiscapum									1			
longisepalum					1		4	3	1			
longissimum			1	4	2					6	6	5
macphersonii									1		2	1
macraei							1				1	
macranthum						8	4	5	1	1	1	
macrobulbum						6	1	8	2			1
maculosum						1				1	1	1
makoyanum	2		3	3	3	2	2	2	3	2	4	4
mandibulare	1	2	2		1	1	2			1	6	3
masonii						1						
mastersianum	1	7	7	7	4	2	3	2	4	7	1	2
maximum	1	1	3	2					3	2	1	1
medusae	8	5	3					2	3	16	22	14
—var. *album*	1							1		2		2
melanorrachis		2		1	4							
micholitzii	2				1	1	2	1	6	5	3	1
micropetalum	1											
miniatum				1			1	2	6	5	7	
minutum	2				2			1				1
mirum		3	2		1		1	1	3	2	4	1
modestum							1					
morphologorum			1	1		1						
multiflorum	1			1	1	2	1		1		1	
mutabile									1			
mysorense			1							1	1	
neilgherrense	1		1					1		2	2	3
nigrescens						1	2	1				
nitidum						2	1	1	3	1	1	
nudiscapum						5	1		1	2	1	
nutans						3						
nyassae	1										1	1
obrienianum						1				1	1	
occultum				1						1		
odoratum											1	
odoratissimum				1		2	1	3	2	1	2	

	Ja	Fe	Mr	Ap	My	Jn	Jy	Ag	Se	Oc	No	De
oreonastes		3	3	4	1			1			1	1
ornatissimum	1	3			1		4	1	10	28	4	3
orthoglossum		2			4	5			1			
patens					3	3	12	4	1			
pavimentatum				1							1	
pectinatum					1	1						
peltopus										1		1
penicillium	5	1	2	4	4	1						
pentastichum					1							
phaeopogon							2	2	2	2		
phalaenopsis								1				
picturatum	4	21	42	13	11	7	5	3	2	4	2	3
platyrhachis	1		1		3							1
plumulum			1		2	1						
polyblepharon								1	1			
porphyroglossum										1		
protractum							2					
pulchellum									1	1		1
pulchrum			3	1	2	9	16	11	1	1	2	1
purpurascens				1			6					
purpureorachis	4	4	9	10	10	1		2		2	2	1
pusillum			1									
putidum	1	2	2	9	5	2	1	4	14	25	10	5
pygmaeum						2						
quadratum		1	2									
ramosum							1					
raui											3	
recurvum		1								2		1
retusiusculum		1				1			1	1	1	4
rhodoglossum			1									
rhodoleucum				1								
rigidum									1		2	
robustum	2	1		3	5	9	9	4				
rothschildianum		1	1	2	1			6	16	28	13	1
roxburghii			1	5	3	4	3	1	1	4	4	2
rufinum		1		1	1	1			2	7	3	3
saltatorium	4	1				1				1		
sanderianum							3					
sandersonii				1	1		1	1				
saurocephalum				4	6	4	5				1	
scabratum								1				
schinzianum	2										3	3
schlechteri												1
secundum		1		2	1						1	
seychellarum										2		
sichyobulbon	2		1	1	1		1	1			1	
sikkimensis								1	2			
sillemianum			4	5	3							
spathulatum			1				1		1			
striatum											2	1
suavissimum		1	3									
taeniophyllum		1					1			2	2	
thaiorum							1	3				
thomsonii											1	1
trachyanthum						1	2	1	1			

304 APPENDIX

	Ja	Fe	Mr	Ap	My	Jn	Jy	Ag	Se	Oc	No	De
tremulum			1	3	4	9	2	1	1			
tripudians					1							
triste			4	6	9	4	2	1	1			
tseanum			1			1						
umbellatum	3			1	1	4	7	6	6	6	3	4
uniflorum	2	1		2	6	6	1	2	1	2		
vaginatum			1		1	2	3	2	3	4		1
velutinum					1	4	1					
verrucirhachis				1	1							
virescens			2		1	5	4	7	8		2	
vitiense							1	1	2	3	4	4
vulcanicum				1								
wallichii	1								4	9	6	4
watsonianum	1	5	2							1		
weberi				1								
weddellii										1		
weinthallii										2		
wendlandianum	1	4	8	17	38	9	1		2	2	1	
Cadetia												
ceratostyloides	2	1	3	2			1	1	2	3	3	2
chamaephytum			1	1		1				1		
chionantha				2				1		2	2	
dischorensis				1	1		1	1				1
hispida			1		1	1		1	2	2	4	1
quinqueloba											1	
taylori			2	2	2	2	3	1	1	1	2	3
Caladenia												
alba							1					
clavigera				1								
deformis			1									
Calanthe												
alismaefolia			1	1		1	1	3				
alpina var.												
schlecteri					1	1						
angusta				1	1							
angustifolia			1					3		4		3
argenteo-striata					2				1			
arisanensis												1
aristulifera				2	1	1						
biloba									1	1		
brevicolumna						1	2					
bungoana					1	1						
cardioglossa	3	2										9
ceceliae									1			
chrysantha											2	
densiflora									3			
discolor			2	9	2							
gracilis var. *venusta*									1	1		
× *harrissii* Hort.	17									10	30	19
hattori							1	1	1			
hizen			1									
hololeuca								1	1	1		
izu-insularis				4	1	1						

	Ja	Fe	Mr	Ap	My	Jn	Jy	Ag	Se	Oc	No	De
labrosa	1										1	
lyroglossa				1	1							
masuca				1	2	1	5	5	2	1	4	1
mexicana			1							1	1	
micrantha							1			1		
nipponica			1	1	1	1						
oblonceolata				1	1							
oculata var. *rubra*	1											
okinawensis				2	1	2	3	7		1	1	
plantaginea	1											
pleiochroma							1	1				
reflexa							1	3	2	1		
regnieri	5	11	15	1	3						1	1
rosea	5	2									2	5
rubens		3	7	4	2					1		1
sanderiana	1	1	3	1	1	1		4	2	1		
striata		2	7	4	1							
sylvatica								2	1			
takane (Nat. Hyb.)			1									
textori				1	1			2				
tricarinata			1	1	1		1					
triplicata	4	3	4	8	5	3	5	7	4	3	1	2
venusta				1								
veratrifolia				6	28	7	9	5	7	3	4	1
versicolor											1	1
vestita	23	18	7	2		1			1	6	11	25
—var. *rubro-oculata*	1	4								1	3	7
violacea								1	1			
Calochilus												
robertsonii		1										
Calopogon												
barbatus				1		1						
Caluera												
vulpina				1								
Calymmanthera												
major						1						
Calypso												
bulbosa			8	1	2							
Calyptrochilum												
christyanum			1		2	7	4	3		3	1	1
emarginatum				2						1		
imbricatum										1		
Campylocentrum												
constanzense			1									
fasciola											1	
hasslerianum	1											
micranthum		1		3	1	2	1					
monteverdi	1											
porrectum								1	2	4	1	
schiedii			1						1			

	Ja	Fe	Mr	Ap	My	Jn	Jy	Ag	Se	Oc	No	De
Capanemia												
angustilabia			1									
australis					1	2					1	1
micromera	4	4	1	1	2	1						1
superflua				2	17	16	1	1	1	1	1	
thereziae		2										
virginalis						1						
Catasetum												
apertum								1				
atratum			1					3	3		1	
aurantiaca			1						1	1		
barbatum	6	5	4	1				1			3	3
bicolor						1					1	
callosum	1						2	7	4	12	3	3
cernuum				2	9	1	1					
christyanum	1		1	1			3		1	4	4	1
cliftonii						3	2	3	1	5	1	
cornutum var. darwinianum											1	
cristatum		1			2	1						
discolor	6	5	5	1	1	1		3	2	6	4	1
expansum		2	2		1	1	3	1	4	3	2	
fimbriatum		1	1		1	2	2	18	10	14	4	6
glaucoglossum									1	1		
globiflorum							1		1	1		
gnomus	1		2			4	1	1	4	3	6	1
hookeri				1			1	1	1			
horichiana							1					
imschootianum									1	1	1	
integerrimum					1	3	5	6	8	10	4	2
laminatum					1					1		
lemosii	1			1								
longifolium											1	
luridum									1	1	2	
macrocarpum	8	3	3	4	5	2	9	11	10	21	13	11
maculatum	2	1			3	7	6	6	11	11	7	7
microglossum		1					2	3	4	2		
naso			1				1			1		
ochraceum							2	2	1	1		
pendulum								1	2			
pileatum	3	4	7	1	5	5	6	18	12	24	21	8
—var. *aurantiacum*				1					1		3	
—var. *aureum*	1								1	1	4	
planiceps						4	2	2	2			
poriferum					1	1						
pulchrum			1	2								
punctatum								1				
purum								1	1	1	2	2
randii			1							2		
reflexum								1				
rodigasianum					2		1					
rondonense							2					
saccatum	2	3	2	4	1	4	5	5	4	10	5	7
sanguineum										1		

	Ja	Fe	Mr	Ap	My	Jn	Jy	Ag	Se	Oc	No	De
speciosum				1								
splendens				1	1			1	2	8	7	
streptocarpum											1	
tabulare					1	3	1	3		1		3
tenebrosum			5	6	11	9	5	2	2	4		
triodon									1	1		
trulla				2	1	2	2	5	4	4	1	
trulliferum		1										
tubulare var. *rugosum*									1			
violascens								1				
viridiflavum	1						3	9	7	5	4	1
Cattleya												
aclandiae		1	4	13	30	15	15	11	9	3		
amethystoglossa	4	38	34	22	4	1				2		4
araguaiensis						1	4	2				
aurantiaca	10	35	53	30	17	2	1			4		
bicolor	1		1				3	30	64	40	12	
—var. *coerulea*									3	4		
—var. *grossii*				1			2	8	10	3	2	
bowringiana	2							2	31	184	127	10
—var. *splendens*									3	3	1	
brasiliensis				1						1		
brownii								1		3	5	
chocoensis	8	4	1							2	3	5
—var. *alba*	4	8	2								1	2
deckeri	1	1	1			1		1		2	3	2
dolosa				2		6	4		1	1	1	
dormaniana						1	1	1	1	5	15	10
dowiana				1	3	4	13	30	20	33	16	2
—var. *alba*									2	4	1	
—var. *aurea*		1	1	2	2	3	12	43	51	113	84	7
eldorado	1	1				3	25	25	19	5	1	1
—var. *alba*		1				1	6	2	3	3		
elongata								1	9	5		
forbesii	1	1	3	8	27	11	23	15	9	17	8	2
gaskelliana			1	3	2	8	15	102	66	61	14	2	
—*alba*			1	1		2	7	40	51	38	10		1
granulosa		6	6	6	10	20	41	26	25	8	7	1
guatemalensis	1	16	42	28	7	2						
—var. *alba*		1	3	1								
guttata	1	1	4	3	2	11	28	23	21	11	3	1
—var. *alba*							6	3	1			
—var. *leopoldii*			3	1	1	3	6	9	4		1	1
—var. *prinzii*			1					3	1			
intermedia	3	8	23	31	59	8	1	14	4	1	1	
—*alba*		2	10	43	63	15	8	4	4	5	1	
—fma. *aquinii*		6	4	7	15	3				1	1	
—var. *coerulea*					8	5						
iricolor			3	7	5							
jenmanii	1	1							1	1	1	4
labiata	4	3		1		1	7	26	91	526	454	79
—fma. *alba*	1	1				1		2	3	53	98	9
—fma. *coerulea*										6	7	
lawrenceana			2	8	74	48	3					

	Ja	Fe	Mr	Ap	My	Jn	Jy	Ag	Se	Oc	No	De
loddigesii	16	11	12	9	8	12	26	50	42	33	15	12
—var. *alba*		1		3		5	10	1	16	9	4	
—var. *harrisoniae*	1	2	1		1	5	15	20	19	5	2	1
—var. *violacea*						4	3	3				
lueddemanniana	4	10	25	20	8	6	9	13	13	3		
—*alba*		1	3		1				2	2		
luteola	3	3		1	8	5		3	2	22	17	7
maxima	1	6			1	1	2	6	14	25	25	9
mendelii	1	2	15	165	556	298	114	10	1			1
—var. *alba*				6	9	8	1					
mossiae	1	4	12	64	722	526	118	6				
—var. *alba*					31	55	18	2	1			
—var. *arnoldiana*					10	10	2					
—var. *reineckiana*				2	81	90	32					
—var. *wageneri*	1			1	85	112	62	2	1			
percivaliana	59	43	9	1					1	2	2	20
—var. *alba*	7	3	1								1	2
porphyroglossa	1			1	3	2						
rex					2	20	5					
schilleriana		1	9	32	78	15	6	4	3	2	2	
schofieldiana					2	7	11	7	7			
schroederae	4	17	169	299	160	13	1	2				
—var. *alba*	1	1	8	21	22	1						
skinneri	3	39	48	72	164	22			1	4	4	3
—var. *alba*		3	16	22	116	6	1	2			2	
—var. *autumnalis*	2									1	4	
trianaei	177	493	385	85	11	2	1	6	1	2	7	25
—var. *alba*	30	51	39	10	1	1					1	3
velutina					1	1	4	23	11	2	1	
× *venosa* (Nat. Hyb.)							1	4	3	1		
violacea			1	4	8	4	23	17	3	5	5	2
—var. *alba*					1	2	3	2	1			
walkeriana	8	8	4	3	11	17	1			3	11	11
—var. *alba*		1	3	6	2	1					1	1
—var. *nobilior*	3			1	9	1	1					
warneri			3	2	45	49	13	4	1	1		1
—var. *alba*		1	1		6	2	5					
warscewiczii	3	5	7	4	38	155	310	82	19	32	6	1
—var. *Frau M. B.*							7	19	7	3		
× *whitei* (Nat. Hyb.)						1	4	2	3			
× *wolteriana* Hort.					3	1						
Cattleyopsis												
acunae					1							
cubensis	1	2	2		1							
lindenii		1			3	3	6	1				
ortgiesiana		4	2	1	1							
Caucaea												
radiata	1						1			1		
Caularthron												
bicornutum	1	9	9	24	43	11	2					
bilamellatum					2	5						
Centrogenium												
setaceum				1								

	Ja	Fe	Mr	Ap	My	Jn	Jy	Ag	Se	Oc	No	De
Centroglossa												
macroceras			1									
Cephalanthera												
damasonianum				1	1							
longifolia				1								
rubra			1				1					
Cephalantheropsis												
tricarinata				1								
Ceratostylis												
eriaeoides	2	2	1				1					
himaliaca					1	1						
philippinensis	1	3	3									
retisquama		1				3	3	5	10	15	12	7
senelis			1									
simplex						1						
subulata	4	3	3	2	2	1	1	2	1	5	7	3
Chaetocephala												
lonchophylla									1	1	1	
punctata	2								1	2	4	1
Chamaeangis												
hariotiana		1	3	3	2							
hildebrandtii			2	3								
odoratissima	2	1		1	3	6	4	1				2
oligantha												1
pobeguinii					1							
vesicata	1		1	1	1	2		1	1		1	1
Chaubardiella												
chasmatochila									1			
tigrina									1		1	1
Chelonanthera												
clypeata			2									
Chiloschista												
lunifera	3	12	4	5	11	5	3	2		2		
segawai	1	2	4									
usneoides			1	4	7	1	1					
Chilopogon												
distichum						1						
Chondrorhyncha												
albicans				1		1			1			
amabilis									1			
aromatica					2	1	7	8	3	2		
bicolor	1		1	2	3	1	1		1			1
caloglossa					1							
chestertonii		2	2	8	11	2	1	7	7	1	2	
flaveola	4	2	1	2	2	3	2	6	3	2	2	1
helleri						1	3	2	2			
lipscombii				1							1	2
lojae	1			1	3			2	1			1
marginata	3			1		3	2	2	5	7	2	5

	Ja	Fe	Mr	Ap	My	Jn	Jy	Ag	Se	Oc	No	De
reichenbachiana				1	1				1	1		1
stenoides						1						
velastigui						1						
velata	1						1	1	1	2	1	1
Chrysoglossum												
cyrtopetalum				1								
Chysis												
aurea		2	3	7	12	13	10	17	3	1		
bractescens		3	10	35	24	17	2	3	1	1		
bruennowiana												1
costaricensis						1	1		1			
laevis			1	3	4	6	5	4	1	1	1	1
maculata												1
Chytroglossa												
aurata				1	2							
marileoniae				1								
Cirrhaea												
dependens						2	6	4		1		
longiracemosa							1					
saccata				2		2	1	1				
warreana				1				1				
Cischweinfia												
dasyandra					1	1	3	3	1	2		1
pachysandra					1							
platychila					2							
pusilla					1	1		1	1	2		2
Cladobium												
violaceum	7	5	8	7	1		1		1	1		1
Cleisocentron												
pallens								1	4	2		
trichromum				1	1		1	2	1			
Cleisomeria												
lanatus						1	1		1			
Cleisostoma												
appendiculatum									1			
arietinum							8	3	1			
aspersum					1						1	
bicorne										2		1
crassifolium					1	1						
dichroanthum					1	1		1			2	
discolor				1		1						
filiforme							2	1	3			
halophilum										1		
longifolius				1								
lowii						1						
pachyfolium					1							
pachyphyllus				1								
pallidus							1	3	2	1		
paniculatum				1	1	1	1	1				
parishii						1						

	Ja	Fe	Mr	Ap	My	Jn	Jy	Ag	Se	Oc	No	De
pendulata						1						
racemiferum	1							4	4	7	5	2
ramosum				1								
recurvus								1				
rostratum								1	1	1		
simondii				1	1						1	
strongyloides										1	1	
subulatum	1					1	2	2	4	6	3	3
tenuifolium							1	2			1	1
teretifolium									2		1	
termissus				1								
tridentatus		1										2
uraiensis							1					
williamsoni						1	1	1				
Clowesia												
dodsoniana								1	1	1		
glaucoglossa							1	1				
rosea	5	7	5	1							1	5
russelliana						3	7	25	31	8	4	
thylaciochila					2	4	8	3				
warczewitzii	4	5	7	4	1	1	2	2		5	2	2
Coccineorchis												
navarrensis	1	3	3								1	3
standleyi	2	1									1	
Cochleanthes												
aromatica				1			1	2	4	1	1	
discolor			3	8	27	20	11		5	5	3	
flabelliformis			1	1	1	1		2	2	1	2	
heteroclita											1	
marginata			1						1			
rhombilabia						1		2		1		
wailesiana			1		4	2	4	7	7	6	2	
Cochlioda												
beyrodtiana				1	2							
noezliana	1	6	7	21	100	53	54	7	1	3	1	2
rosea	6	7	10	9	9	6	5	1		1	4	3
vulcanica	6	8	10	9	4	3	5	4	6	9	7	8
Coelia												
bella	11	3			1			1			1	12
guatemalensis							1					
macrostachya		2	1		1	2	3	5	9	3		2
triptera	1	4	10	6	2							1
Coeliopsis												
hyacinthosma	1	2			1					3	5	1
Coeloglossum												
viride						2						
Coelogyne												
asperata	2	1	2		8	8	5	1		1		2
assamica		1								2	2	1
barbata			1	1					2	11	14	8

	Ja	Fe	Mr	Ap	My	Jn	Jy	Ag	Se	Oc	No	De
beccarii				1			2		2			
bella							2	1	1			
bilammelata	1	2	2	1	3	2	1	1	1	2	2	1
brachyptera			3	9	11	7	1					
breviscapa		1	4	1	2							
× *burfordiense* Hort.					2	3	1	1				
calcicola					4	1						
carinata					2	2						
chloroptera				1	1							
cinnamomea												3
corrugata		1			1	2	2	2	3		1	1
corymbosa		3	6	7								
crassifolia			1									
cristata	58	116	122	21	7		1				1	7
—*alba*		10	33	8	2							
—var. *hololeuca*		1	7	1								
—var. *lemoniana*	3	11	12	2								
cumingii		1	1	1			2	2		1		
cuprea			2									
dayana		1	3	6	65	30	12	3	1	5	1	
dulitensis									1	1		
elata		6	5	4	4	1						
fimbriata	7	2						1	9	21	27	13
flaccida	11	23	35	11	3		1	1				1
flavida				1	5	4	1					
flexuosa		1	1	2	1							
foerstermannii							1	2				
fragrans			2	5	8	1		2	2			
fuliginosa	5	3						1	6	23	13	5
fuscescens	1									1	7	4
—var. *brunnea*									2	2	4	
gardneriana		1	1								5	2
glandulosa			3									
huettneriana	1	1	10	6	2	1	1				1	1
—var. *lactea*	1			3			1					1
integerrima		1	1		3	2						
× *intermedia* Hort.	5	13	9	4								
javanica		2										
lactea			1	4	2	1						
lamellata							4	3	5	1		
lawrenceana		1	26	34	10	1	1		1			
lentiginosa	10	3	2	4	2	1					1	4
longipes						1						
marmorata							1	1				
massangeana	4	5	13	14	17	25	20	19	12	14	28	11
meyeriana			1		1	2	3	3	2	1		
media	1											5
membranifolia					1							
merrillii											1	1
micholitziana					2	1	1	3	6			
miniata		3	1	1					1	2	4	3
mooreana	32	21	18	15	30	8	15	18	12	31	49	28
mossiae		4	5	1								1
multiflora						1						
nervosa		1			1	2		2	4	3	2	

	Ja	Fe	Mr	Ap	My	Jn	Jy	Ag	Se	Oc	No	De
nitida			4	24	33	52	4		7	6	5	
odoratissima						1	1					
ovalis		2	2	1					6	22	10	1
pandurata	2		10	15	58	38	24	6	4	4	2	2
parishii				7	5	22	3					
peltastes			1		2	1						
perakensis		2	1					1				
pholidotoides					1							
prolifera		1	1		1		1					
pulchella				21	3	1						
punctulata				1								
rhabdobulbon	1	1	1									
rochussenii											2	1
rumphii					2		1					
sanderae			14	11		4	6	2		2	1	
schilleriana					4	1						
sparsa	5	25	27	3	2							
speciosa	7	6	14	6	12	8	13	13	21	19	22	9
—var. *alba*	4	6	7	2	3	4	2	4	1	6	10	6
—var. *albicans*	3						1	3	5	4	3	2
stenochila									1			
stricta	5	4	1	1	1	2				1		3
suaveolens					1	4						
sulphurea	3	5	2	1		1	2	2		3	5	6
sumatrana			1									
swaniana				2	2	4	3	3	3	1	2	1
tenompokensis										1		
testacea						2						
thailandica			1									
tomentosa				2	13	16	3					
trinervis	13	1	1	1	3					1	21	20
uniflora		1	2	6	10	6	6	3		2	2	
valida					3							
veitchii		2	1					3	7	11	5	
venusta		2	1	3	2							
virescens				1	1	1						
viscosa	12	7	3	2	2	2					1	1
yunnanensis					1							
Collabium												
nebulosum	1										1	
Comparettia												
coccinea	2				1			5	2	3	4	1
cryptocera												1
falcata	5	4	8	3	7	4	10	6	2	3	3	2
macroplectron	12	8	7	2	2	3		3	6	6	5	6
speciosa	3	2	2	1			3	3	6	4	8	2
Constantia												
cipoensis	1									6	7	
Corallorhiza												
maculata						1						
Coryanthes												
albertinae						1						

	Ja	Fe	Mr	Ap	My	Jn	Jy	Ag	Se	Oc	No	De
balfouriana	1											
hunteriana										2		
leucocorys						2	1					
macrantha					3	2	1	2			1	
mastersii											1	
punctata				1								
sanderi								1				
speciosa	1		1	5	1	6	4	3	3	2	1	
trifoliata							1					
wolfii					1							
Corybas												
orbiculatus			1									
rivularis		1	1									
trilobus			1	2								
Corysanthes												
trilobus				4								
Cottonia												
macrostachya				2	3	2	2	2	2	2	1	1
Cranichis												
muscosa	1	1										
Cryptanthemis												
oblongifolius											2	
Cryptarrhena												
lunata								1	2	2	3	
Cryptocentrum												
calcaratum										1		
gracilipes					1							
gracillimum	2		1	2	2	1	1	2	2	4	5	3
jamesonii											2	1
latifolium					1	1	1					
lehmannii									1			
Cryptochilus												
luteus								1	2			
sanguineus				1	7	10	4	1		1		
Cryptophoranthus												
atropurpureus								1	3	3	3	1
auriculatus	1											
dayanus						1	3	4	5	2	2	2
gracilentus							1					
hypodiscus									1			
lehmanni					1		1	1	1			
longifolius										1		
maculatus											1	1
oblongifolius										3	3	1
Cryptopus												
elatus		1		3	4	1	1					
Cryptostylis												
arachnites	2	2								3		

	Ja	Fe	Mr	Ap	My	Jn	Jy	Ag	Se	Oc	No	De
leptochila							1				1	
ovata				1								
subulata							1					
Cuitlauzina												
pendula			3	16	94	50	25	8				
—var. *alba*					15	1	1	1				
Cycnoches												
chlorochilon	12	12	4	2		2	12	30	41	43	25	14
cooperi	2											
densiflorum										2		
egertonianum	1				2	4	9	18	21	15	7	1
esperitosantense								1		1		
guttulatum										2		
haagii	1						2	2	1	3	2	
lehmanii				1	1				3	1	1	1
loddigesii		1	1			4	5	9	13	10	4	2
maculatum							2	4	12	3	3	2
pentadactylon	3	3	1	2	1	3	1	2	2	3	3	3
peruviana		1					4	2	9	10		
stelliferum							1	2	2	2		
ventricosum	2	3	2	1	1		2	6	9	8	3	4
—var. *warscewiczii*	1	1	1	1								1
Cymbidiella												
flabellata		1	3	1	1	1						
humblotii				5	1	2	2					
rhodochila		1	1	1	21	11	1			1		
Cymbidium												
aloifolium		3	8	16	10	8	9	4				
bicolor	1	1			4	5	2		2	6	5	1
canaliculatum	1	1	4	6	1							
—var. *sparkesii*	4	2	11	3	5		1	1	2		1	1
chloranthum		1		2		2		1			3	1
cyperifolium	1		1							2	5	1
dayanum						1		3	5	10	11	6
devonianum	4	5	36	48	52	2						1
eburneum	4	16	45	19	6				1			
ensifolium		1	1		3	5	5	11	5	4	3	1
erythrostylum	1	1							11	32	27	2
faberi	2	2	6				1	1				
finlaysonianum			1		2	3	5	16	8	5		
floribundum			4	7	5	1						
giganteum	6								1	10	30	17
goeringii	3	8	31	1			1		1		1	2
hookerianum	6	24	18	5	1					1	2	3
huttoni					6	4	5					
hymatodes									1			
× *i'ansonii* Hort.			3	9	5		2					
insigne	3	10	23	15	23							
—var. *sanderi*	1	4	4	3	1							
iridioides	3	2									2	
kanran	1	1					1	1	2	1	2	5
lancifolium	2		2	2	7	5	6	4	7	5		1

	Ja	Fe	Mr	Ap	My	Jn	Jy	Ag	Se	Oc	No	De
longifolium	3								1	3	7	5
lowianum	2	6	35	66	133	18	5				1	1
—var. *concolor*		3	8	17	47	4	1					
madidum		2	1	8	8	7	1	2	2			1
papuanum	1											
parishii		5	1	2	2		1					
—var. *sanderae*			3	3	5							
pendulum			1	7	6	1	1					
schroederi				2	1	1						
sinense	10	6	12						1	2	1	3
soshin								1				
suave					1							
suavissimum							4	5	3			
tigrinum			2	11	31	6	5				1	
traceyanum	37	14	3							22	83	45
tsukengensis	2											
whiteae												1
Cymbiglossum												
apterum	2	1	4	5	6	4	2		1	1	1	
bictoniense	24	24	17	6	2	3	11	11	23	32	29	29
—var. *album*	1					2	2	11	12	7	3	1
cervantesii	11	20	31	32	13	3			1	4	4	5
—var. *roseum*		1	2	2	1	1						
cordatum	6	7	14	12	51	37	26	2	5	5	4	5
ehrenbergii						1	3	1	1	1	1	
galeottianum						4	3	2				
hortensiae		1	2	1	2							
× *humeanum* Nat. Hyb.	5	5	8	5	2					1	5	2
maculatum	9	21	19	13	13	2	3	5		4	3	4
majale		2	4	9	13	5	4		1		2	
rossii	46	45	55	34	9	4	8	9	9	12	27	24
—var. *majus*	13	13	13	7	2	1	1	4	3	3	6	4
stellatum	10	15	10	9	10	6	3	1	2	2	1	7
uroskinneri	11	5	9	7	15	10	21	27	21	15	10	7
—var. *album*	3		1		3	1	7	6	8	3	1	1
Cynorkis												
angustipetala									2			
compacta	2		3									
fastigiata					1	1			1			
gibbosa						1	2					
grandiflora	2	1					4			1	1	
kassneriana	1											
× *kewensis* Hort.		1	3	2								1
lowiana	3	4		1				1		1	2	2
purpurascens				1					1		1	1
ringens				1								
saundersiana											1	
uncata										1	3	4
uncinata				1				1				
Cyperorchis												
elegans	2	1	1							7	15	2
mastersii	1	1		1						4	15	11
—var. *album*	1									1	2	2

	Ja	Fe	Mr	Ap	My	Jn	Jy	Ag	Se	Oc	No	De
Cypripedium												
acaule			3	4	22							
arietinum		1			9							
calceolus			1	5	15	2						
—var. pubescens			1	6	2							
californicum				1	4	1	1					
candidum				2	5	1						
cordigerum						1						
debile			1	2	2							
formosanum			2	3	1							
guttatum							1					
henryi			2									
irapianum						1						
japonicum			1	1	4							
kentuckiense				3								
macranthum					23	6						
montanum				1	12							
parviflorum					14	1						
pubescens				1	22	2						
rebunense			1									
reginae			5	3	26	11	9					
speciosum				1								
tibeticum					2	1						
Cyrtidium												
rhomoglossum									2	2	1	
Cyrtochilum												
filipes					1							
xanthodon			1								1	
Cyrtopodium												
andersonii		1	3	8	4	7	4	3	1	1		
cristatum		1										
falcilobium			1									
gigas			1	1								
paniculatum				1								
paranaense					1							
punctatum		8	15	18	21	4	1	1				
virescens					1							
Cyrtorchis												
arcuata	2		2	2	8	5	2	13	17	7	6	1
aschersonii									1	2	3	4
brownii										2		
chailluana			1				2	2	4	6	7	1
crassifolia									1	1		
hamata					1				2			
monteiroae	1	1			1							
praetermissa	2						1		1	1	2	3
ringens	2	4										
Dactylorhiza												
elata					2	3	1					
foliosa					1	2	2					
incarnata					2							
majalis							1					

	Ja	Fe	Mr	Ap	My	Jn	Jy	Ag	Se	Oc	No	De
praetermissa					1							
purpurella							1					
romana			1									
sambucina					1							
Dendrobium												
aberrans	1	3	1	1	1		1					1
acerosum			1		1		1				1	1
acinaciforme			1	1	1				1			
adae	2	1	2	2								
aduncum				2	7	7	3	2	1	1	1	1
aemulum	5	11	4									
affine	1	2			2	1	2	1	2	1	3	1
aggregatum	4	12	43	34	20	3	6	1	1			
—var. *jenkinsii*	1	1	6	9	10		2					1
—var. *majus*	1	2	11	11	6	1		1				
agrostophyllum	1	3	1							1	1	
alaticaulinum					1		1				1	
albosanguineum				1	8	2						
alexandrae											1	1
alpestre									1			
amboinense					1							
amethystoglossum	2	9	13	1	4		2					
amphigenyum		1					1		2			
amplum									1	5	2	1
anacrophyllum		1										
anceps	3	1	4	3	2		1			1	1	1
anosmum	3	28	58	24	18	15	7	4	2	6	4	5
—var. *album*			4	3								
—var. *dearei*			11	2								
antennatum	1	1	1	1	5	4	2					
apertum								1			1	
aphrodite			1	2	3					1		
aphyllum	3	36	44	45	41	12	10	3	2	1		1
—var. *album*				3	1				1			
aqueum	1	2						2	1	2	1	
arachnites	3	2	2	4	24	6	3	1	1			1
arcuatum		1					1	1				
armeniacum		1										
ashworthiae	2	2	6	1	1							
asperifolium							1		2			
aspidorhinum		1										
atropurpureum						1						
atroviolaceum	7	23	32	45	52	9	6		3	1	1	2
attenuatum									1	1	1	1
aurantiaco-purpureum			2									
aurantiroseum	2	4	2		1	2		1	2			
bairdianum						1	1	1				
barbatulum	2	8	7	5	3		1					
batanense	3		1						1		1	1
beckleri		6	8	8	3	1			1	3		1
bellatulum	5	4	12	9	4	2	2	3	2	3	2	
bicameratum						2	7	6	2			
bicaudatum					1				1		1	
bifalce										3		

	Ja	Fe	Mr	Ap	My	Jn	Jy	Ag	Se	Oc	No	De
bifarium		1	1	1	1	1	1					
bilobum	2	2	5	2	2	1	2	2	1	2	2	1
bismarckiense		1								1		
bolbiflorum							1	1				
bracrophyllum				1								
bracteosum				1	1	3	4	5	5	2	2	1
brassii	2	1	1			1	1					
brevicaule		1	1	1	2	1	1	2	2		1	1
bronckhartii				7	7	1	1	1				
brymerianum	2	8	45	38	15	2	2		1		1	
bulbophylloides	1									1		
bullenianum		2	1		1	1	5	2		1	1	1
calcaratum	1											
canaliculatum			7	7	10	8	3			1	2	1	1
candidum			1	1	1	5	3	2		1	2	
capillipes			3	6	16	3	1			1		
capituliflorum	2	5	6	2	1						1	2
carinatum				1	1							
cathcartii				1	1	1						
chameleon				1			1					
chloropterum				1	1	1					1	
chordiforme			1									
chrysanthum				4	6	7	10	17	15	12	13	2
chryseum			1	3	1							
chrysocrepis					1		2	1				
chrysoglossum		1			2		1		1	1	1	
chrysotoxum		4	22	55	69	43	12	1	1	1	1	
—var. *suavissimum*			1	2	2	2	4	2	2	1		
chrysotropis								2	1	2		
clavatum				1	1	8	4	2	2			
compactum		1					1	1		2		
conanthum						1						
crepidatum			1	7	17	17	3		1			1
cretaceum		2	2	3	2							
crispilinguum				1	1			1	1	1	1	
cruentum			3	1	1	3	2	1	1			
crumenatum			3		5	4	4	3	4			
cruttwellii						1	1	1				
crystallinum				2	3	11	14	6	3	1	1	
cucumerinum			1		3	1	1	1	2			
cumulatum	2	1			1	2	1		1	3	4	1
cunninghamii	2				6	3	2	1				
curtisii	1		1									1
curviflorum							1					
cuthbertsonii	11	10	4	10	7	16	22	15	15	11	13	5
cyananthum			1		1							
cyanocentrum	1		1	1		1	1		2		2	
d'albertisii	1	3		1	3	3	5				1	
dearei	2	1	6	7	42	27	37	23	19	14	17	1
dekockii	1	1	1			2		1		1	2	
delacourii						1	3	3	3			
delicatulum	2	3	3	1	1		1	1	1		2	
delicatum Nat. Hyb.	8	15	25	2					1		2	
denneanum							2					
densiflorum			3	26	53	31	27	18	3	1		

	Ja	Fe	Mr	Ap	My	Jn	Jy	Ag	Se	Oc	No	De
denudans							1		2	2	1	
devonianum			2	15	23	31	13	3				
dichaeoides	1	1	1					2	1		1	1
dichromum				2								
dicuphum	1		2				1			1		
dillonianum											1	
discolor	4	8	22	5	8	6	6	7	3	5	4	5
—var. broomfieldii			5	3	1							
distichum	1	2	2	2	3	3	2	1		1		
dixanthum	1	1	4	9	15	3		1				
draconis	1	1		3	5	4	6	2	1	1		
dryadum			2	3	6	4	3	4	1	1	2	
endocharis		1										
engae	1											
epidendropsis	1		1						1		1	
equitans	1		1	1	2	1	1		1			1
eriaeflorum								1	3	2	4	
eriopexis										1		
erythroglossum			1				1	1				
eximium					1							
fairchildae									1			
falconeri	1	1	3	10	21	8	5					
falcorostrum			4	2			1					
fantasticum		2	2								1	
farmeri	3	5	10	26	20	15	8					
fimbriatum	6	5	18	19	14	3	1	1	1			3
—var. oculatum	1	4	19	21	12	5	3	1				
findlayanum	3	8	20	12	3	1						1
finisterrae	1	1		2	1		1	1				
flammula		2		1		1						
flaviflorum						1	5	3				
fleckeri				1	3							
forbesii	3							2	1	1	2	4
formosum			3	3	12	6	7	7	30	22	15	3
—var. giganteum		2	3	5		6	7	5	6	12	39	10	3
friedericksianum				1	4	2	2					
fulgidum				1								
fuscescens		1	1							1		
fytcheanum			2				1					
gibsonii				2	3	8	10	2	1			
giganteum				1	1							
glomeratum	1		1		1	5	4	3	3		2	1
glomeriflorum			1			1						
glumaceum		1	8	2								
—var. validum	2	3	2									
goldfinchii	1						1		2			
goldiei		1	1		1	2	1			3	3	2
gordoni							1			1	1	
gouldii	5	7	4	7	10	14	7	4	2	3	1	3
gracile		1										
gracilicaule	10	20	24	13	8	8	10	7	7	2	4	2
gracillimum	2	2										
graminifolium				1	1							
gratiotissimum			5	8	5	1		2				
gratrixianum										1		

	Ja	Fe	Mr	Ap	My	Jn	Jy	Ag	Se	Oc	No	De
griffithianum			2		1	5	1	1				
grimesii	1											
guerreroi	1	1			1						1	
guerrotii										1		
guibertii								1				
habbemense											1	
harveyanum		1	1	9								
hasseltii								2		1		
helix						2	2	2				1
hellwigianum	1	3	1	1	1	1	1	2	1	4	5	1
herbaceum	1								1	1		
hercoglossum				3	14	9	7	5	1	1	2	1
heterocarpum	20	22	20	6	2			3	3	12	9	11
heteroglossum											2	
heyneanum				1	1		1					
hildebrandii	2	4	6	10	8		1					
hodgkinsoni		1	1									1
hookerianum					3		2	2	3	1	1	
hughii					1							
inauditum										1		
indivisum							1	2	2	2	1	1
infundibulum	2	9	42	44	30	12	4	1	2	1		2
—var. *jamesianum*	5	7	22	32	36	2	1	1				1
inobulbon						1						
insigne			1		2				1			
ionoglossum							1					
jerdonianum		1			5	3						
johannis	1		2	1	2	1	1				1	
johnsoniae	4	3	5	3	2	5	3	1		3	4	5
junceum						1		1	1	2		
karoense								1				
kestevenii		3										
kingianum	12	40	86	15	11	1						
—var. *album*	5	10	15	6	1							1
laciniosum								2	1	2		
laevifolium	1	1				3	1	1				1
lamellatum	1	1			1	1	1			1		1
lasianthera			1			2	1	2	1			
lasioglossum				2								
latifolium					2		1					
lawesii	1		3	1	4	3	5	8	3	3	3	6
× *leeanum* Nat. Hyb.	1	1			1		1			1	1	
leonis	1			1		3	1		1	1		
leucocyanum	1											1
leucolophotum						1						
lichenastrum	1	3	5	4	3	2	2	2	1	2	2	2
—var. *prenticei*		1	4	5	4	2	2			1		
linawianum		1	1									
lineale			1				1		1			
linguiforme	4	11	19	12	1	2	1			1		
litorale								1	1			
lituiflorum			2	6	11	6	3	1	1			1
loddigesii			3	7	18	12	5		1			
longicolle						1		1	1	1	1	1
longicornu	6	1	2		1	1	4	8	5	8	10	7

	Ja	Fe	Mr	Ap	My	Jn	Jy	Ag	Se	Oc	No	De
lowii	1	2		1	2	3	5	1	1	2		
luteolum		3	2	1	4	1						
mabelae gammie							1	1	1			
maccarthiae				2	4	1	6	4	4			1
macraei			1	1			3	3				
macrogenion	1						1	1				
macropus		2	2									
macrostachyum				2		5	7	2		1		
madonnae	1											
margaritaceum	1					1	4	2	1	1		
mayakei							1	1		1	1	
mayandyi							3	3		1		
mearnsii			1									
melianthum							1					
microbulbon	1											1
minax		1	1	2	3	3	3	1			1	1
minjemense				1								
mirbelianum	1									1		
miserum			1									
miyakei	1		5				3	1		2	1	1
mohlianum		2	3	2	2		1					
moniliforme	3	6	12	7	7	4	2	2				1
monophyllum		1	1		1		1			1		
monticolum							3	3				
moorei						1		1		2	1	2
mortii												1
moschatum				1	16	22	28	7	1	1	1	
—var. *cupreum*					1	2	2	3		1		
muricatum								1	1			
musciferum			1	1				1	1			
mutabile		1			2	3	4	1	2	3		
nakaharai								1		1	2	1
nardoides			1			1		1		2		
nebularum	2	1	1	1			2			1	2	
nindii							3	3	2		1	
nobile	55	141	297	130	49	5	5	3	1	1	4	3
—var. *album*	2	21	22	8	1							
—var. *cooksonianum*	3	13	25	10	2							
—var. *nobilius*	3	20	39	16	4							
—var. *sanderianum*	1	8	1	1				1				
—var. *virginale*	6	52	92	111	16	5	1				1	1
nudum					1	1						
nutans					2			1	1	1		
o'brienianum			2	1	1		2					
ochreatum		1	10	6	6	3		2		1		
oexillarium			1									
olivaceum	1											
ophioglossum		1				1		1				
orecharis				1			1	1	1			
otaguroanum							1					
ovatum									1	1	1	
ovipositoriferum						2		1				
pachystele							1					
palpebrae				3	1	1		1			4	
panduratum							1					

	Ja	Fe	Mr	Ap	My	Jn	Jy	Ag	Se	Oc	No	De
papilio	1			1	2	3	1			2		
papilionaceum							1					
parcifolium				1	1							
parcum			1	1								
parishii			1	5	8	40	20	10	6			
pauciflorum						1						
peguanum										1	1	
pendulum	8	25	25	14	6				1	2	1	1
—var. album		4	10	4								
—var. barberianum		1	2	2								
pentapterum	1	2	1	2	1	3	2	2	3	2	2	1
petiolatum			1		1	1	1	1				
phalaenopsis	25	17	21	14	34	17	19	41	132	266	215	75
—album	2				1		1	1	13	17	29	3
—var. compactum				1		1	1	16	16	12	5	
—var. hololeucum	1	1				1	1	1	6	11	9	2
—var. schroederianum	1						1	3	6	45	17	2
—var. schroederianum album	1							1	5	4	6	
philippinense						1						
phlox	2		1	1		1	3		2	2		
pitcherianum	1	1		1								
platycaulon			1						1		1	1
platygastrium					1					1		1
plicatile								1				
polysema	2	2		2					2		2	3
porphyrochilum	1	1										1
porphyroglossum	1											
praestans				3	1							
prasinum	2	3	1				1	4	1	1	2	4
prenticei		1		1								
primulinum	1	16	25	21	19	5	2	1			1	
pseudoconanthum				1		1						
pseudofrigidum				1	1							
pseudoglomeratum				1								
pseudotokai								1				
pugioniforme				3	5	1						
pulchellum			4	10	23	55	24	14	2	2		
—var. luteum					1	7	8		1			
pulchrum			1	1				1			1	
pulvilliferum			1									
pumilum			1	1	1					1	1	1
punamense					1							
purpureum	2	4	8	6	4	4	4	1	2	4	3	
putnami	1										2	
pycnostachyum				1	2							
pygmaeum	1										1	1
quinquecostatum				1		1						
racemosum	2											
ramosum					1	1						
raphiotes							1	2	1			
regium					2	3	5	21	8	1	4	
revolutum				1	4	4	5	5	5	1		
rhodocentrum					3			1	1			
rhodopterygium Nat. Hyb.				1	1	3	4	4				

	Ja	Fe	Mr	Ap	My	Jn	Jy	Ag	Se	Oc	No	De
rhodostoma Hort.				1	1	4	3	1	1	1	2	
rhodostictum			2	1	4	1			2	1		
rhytidothece			2	4	2	3	1	1	1	1	4	1
rigidifolium					1							
rigidum	3	2	3		1	1				2	1	1
roseipes				2			1					
ruckeri		1		2	1							
ruginosum	1											
rupestre										1		
rupicola							15	14	9	8	1	
ruppianum	4	6	11	6	1			1				
salaccense				1								
sanderae	1	1	4	8	6	11	13	15	8	6	5	1
sanguinolentum	2		1		1			6	6	3	2	1
sarmentosum		1										
scabrilingue	1	1	5	1	1	1	1			1		
schneiderae									4	2		
schuetzei	2	4			6	1			2			
schulleri			3			2						
seemannii	1	1					2					2
seidenfadenium							1					
senile	3	4	3	8	9	2				1		
serratilabium											1	
signatum			3	4	5	49	10	4				
sladei						1	1					
smilliae		1	3		2	1	1	2		2		
spatella					1							
spathaceum					1	1						
spathulatum									1			
specio-kingianum Nat. Hyb.				1								
speciossimum			1			1	6	2				
speciosum	13	21	20	4	1							4
—var. *bancroftianum*	1	6	5	2	1							
—var. *hillii*	3	3	3									
spectabile	4	2	3	1	3		1				2	1
spectatissimum						1						
sphegidoglossum						1						
stratiotes			3		2	3	4	3			2		1
stricklandianum	1	1	1	1	3							
strongylanthum						1			1			
stuartii							1					
stuposum							3			1		
subacaule				2	1		1	2	1			
subclausum	3	2		2	1		1	2		2	3	
subflavidum		1										1
subserratum		2	5	2	6	1	1	1		2	2	1
subulatum					1							
subuliferum	2			1	1	1						
suffusum	1	1			1							
sulcatum				1	4					1		
sulphureum	2	1	2	1	2	2		2	1	2	2	
superbiens Nat. Hab.	5	4	11	6	7	7	7	8	8	18	19	4
tangerinum			1	1		1	1	2	1			1
taretifolium						1						

	Ja	Fe	Mr	Ap	My	Jn	Jy	Ag	Se	Oc	No	De
tarthenium										1		
taurinum				2	5	2			4	4	1	
tenuissimum			1	2								
teretifolium	1	3	11	2	1	1	2	2	1	1	1	
terminale		1	1		1			1	1	1		
terrestre							1					1
tetragonum	9	10	17	9	3	2	2	1				3
—var. *giganteum*	3	4	1							1		4
theionanthum	1			2			1	2		1	2	
thyrsiflorum	1	4	34	82	149	37	23	4	1	2		
tipuliferum					1							
tixieri		1		1		1		1	1	1		1
topaziacum			1	3		1	5		1	3		
torresae				2		1	4	1		1		1
tortile		1	4	5	4	3	1					
trachyrhizum												1
transparens	1		1	8	13	1	2					
treacherianum		2										2
treubii						1						
triflorum	2		2	1	1	2		1		1	1	2
trigonopus		2	2	5	3	1		1				
trinervium	1				1	1	1	1	1	1	2	1
triviale							1	1				
uncatum	2		1									1
uncinatum	2	5	3	2	5	3		2	1	1	1	1
unicum	1	2	5	6	7	1						
uniflorum							1	3	1	1		
velutinum		1	5	1	3		1		1			
vexillarium	3	3	3	3		3				1	7	
victoriae-reginae	3		5	16	60	30	22	14	15	17	15	4
violascens							1					
violaceoflavens										1		
violaceum	1	1	1	1	2	3	1	2	1	1	1	3
virgineum		1	2								1	
wardianum	25	40	137	63	20				1		2	1
—var. *album*	1	4	17	3	1							
warianum							1	1		1	1	
wassellii							1				1	
wattianum	1											
wattii	1	1	1	1					1			1
wiganiae		1										
williamsianum	2	1	4	9	10	9	3	1	3		1	1
williamsonii		2	7	2	1							1
wilsoni			1									
woodsii											1	
xanthophlebium									2			
Dendrochilum												
abbreviatum					4	1	1					
anomalum	1	2	1									
arachnites	3	5	2									
bartonii			1		4	2	2	1			1	
bicallosum	2	2										
cobbianum	6	12	5		2	1	1	3	2	26	35	15
cornutum					7	4	2			1		

	Ja	Fe	Mr	Ap	My	Jn	Jy	Ag	Se	Oc	No	De
cucumerinum											1	
filiformis			5	1		1	16	81	37	11	9	7
formosanum												1
glumaceum	34	86	64	13	5	1		1	1	7	7	4
—var. *validum*	5	9	7	1								
latifolium			2	1	3	22	18	3	1	1	2	4
longifolium	7	3	1		1	3	1	3	1	2	3	3
magnum								1	3	2		
mearnsii			1	1								
odoratum								3				
uncatum	9	9	1	1	1						6	10
Dendrophylax												
barrettiae						1	1		1	1		
fawcettii							2		1			
funalis			1	2	1	1	4	1	2			1
varius							1	2	1			
Diaphananthe												
adoxa											2	
bidens						1		2	1		1	
bilobata										1		
fragrantissima			1	2								1
kamerunensis											1	
pellucida	12	5	3						1		1	5
pulchella	5			1				1		2		
rutila	1	2	5		2	2			1	3	3	2
xanthopollinia				1	1			1				
Dichaea												
ancoraelabia			1									
australis				1								
ciliolata										1		
glauca					1	1	3	2	1			
graminoides	2	1	2	2	1	1	2	2	3	2	2	1
histrio					2	1	2	1				
latifolia	1											
morrissii									2			
muricata			1	1	2	3	1	1	2	4	4	3
neglecta						1		1	1	1		
panamensis		2		1	1			2		1		
picta			1		1				2	3	1	1
trachycarpa					1	1						
trulla					1					1		
Dichromanthus												
cinnabarinus		1							1			
Dignathe												
pygmaeus		2	1							1		2
Dimerandra												
emarginata	1		2	1			2	1	1	4	2	1
Dimorphorchis												
lowii	2							7	8	6	2	
rohaniana								1		2		

	Ja	Fe	Mr	Ap	My	Jn	Jy	Ag	Se	Oc	No	De
Diplocaulobium												
chrysoglossum				1								
dichotropis				1								
fariniferum			1		1	1	2	1	1			
guttulatum								1				
iboense				1	1		1	1				
jadunae									1			
macrobulbon					2	1	1	2				
mekynosepalum				1		1						
phalangium			1		1		1				1	
pulvilliferum			1									
regale							1					
tipula		1										
Diplocentrum												
recurvum					2		1	2				
Diplomeris												
hirsuta						1	1		2			
Diploprora												
championii				2	1		1					
Dipodium												
ensifolium							1					
pictum										1		
Dipteranthus												
cornigera					1							
grandiflorus				3	14	11	6		1			
pellicidus		1										
planifolius		1		3	6		1	2				1
pustulatus			1									
Disa												
cardinalis								1				
chrysostachya				2								
cornuta						1		1				
ferruginea			1									
incarnata	1		1									
lacera												
—var. multifida		2	1									
lugens					1							
marlothii			1									
nervosa									1			
polygonoides									5	1		
pulchra											2	1
racemosa					2	1						
sagittalis				4	1	3		2				
tripetaloides				1		3	1					
uniflora				2		2	12	136	199	8	2	2
venosa					2							
Disperis												
fanniniae								1				
Diuris												
longifolia			2	1	1							
maculata			3		1							

	Ja	Fe	Mr	Ap	My	Jn	Jy	Ag	Se	Oc	No	De
Domingoa												
haematochila				2	1		1	1				
hymenodes		1		8	6	1		1	1	1		
nodosa					2	3				1		
Doritis												
chiliatum											1	
pulcherrima	3		1	2	2	4	22	43	69	64	33	11
—var. *alba*							1	1	1	1	4	4
—var. *buyssoniana*						1	1	5	9	7	5	1
taenialis				2		1					1	1
Dossinia												
lowii								1				
marmorata						2	9	1		1		
Dracula												
andreettae						1		1	1	1	1	1
astuta					1	1	1	2			1	
bella	4	3	4	8	14	8	7	5	7	6	4	3
benedictii			1		4	1						
berthae				1								
callifera			1	3	2							
carderi		1	3		5	7	6	6	3	2	1	1
chestertonii			4	2	1	2	2					
chimaera	4	9	11	12	26	19	20	16	20	12	11	3
—var. *wallisii*			1		1	2		4				
cochliops		1										
cordobae									1			
deltoidea								1				
deorsa					1							
diabola					1				1			
dodsonii											2	
erythrocaete	2	1						3	3	1	2	1
fuliginosa				1								
gigas					1							
gorgona		2			2							
hawleyi			1									
hirtzii						1						
houtteana	1		3	17	28	8	1					
lemurella					1							
lotax					1				1			
mopsus	1	1	2									
ophioceps				1								
parapusilla					1							
pettarina						1			1			
platycrater								1				
platyglossa						1					1	1
polyphemus					1				1			
posadorum											1	
psitticina			1	1								
radiosa				1								
robledorum			2	2	1							
roezlii						1	3	2	2			
simia	1											
soderoi		2	1	1	1							

	Ja	Fe	Mr	Ap	My	Jn	Jy	Ag	Se	Oc	No	De
trinema		2	3		1			4	1	1	2	1
troglodytes		1		3					1		1	
vampira			1	1	2			1		1	2	
velutina			1	1	1	1		1				
vespertillo	2								1	1	1	
vlad-tepes					1							
wallisii					1							
woolwardii						1						
Dresslerella												
pilosissima						1						
stellaris			2						1			
Dressleria												
dilecta			1	1	3	2	7	3			1	2
eburnea						1			1	1		
hispida										2		
suavis				2		2	1					
Dryadella												
albicans	1	1										2
edwallii				6	12				1			
lilliputiana	1	1	2		2				1			1
obrieniana			4	5	9	2			2	2		
simula		1	2	6	9	4	4	1	1	4	2	1
—var. *obrieniana*	2	2	3	7	1				1	1	2	2
trigonopetalla												1
zebrina		1	13	1	2					1		
Drymoanthus												
adversus					1	1				1	1	
minutus						1	1					
Dyakia												
hendersoniana	1					3	7	4	6	2	2	
Earina												
autumnalis	3	2	2	1	1	1						
mucronata	1	1		1	1	1	2	1	1	2		
suaveolens	1							1				
Eggelingia												
ligulifolia	1	2				1	1		1		1	
Elleanthus												
aurantiacus					1							
brasiliensis									1			
caricoides											1	
cephalotus			1			1						
curtii							1				1	
graminifolius												1
hymenophorus										1	1	1
linifolius	1											1
longibracteatus			1	1		1						
sphaerocephalus				1	1	1	1					
teotepecensis								1				
trilobatus					1	1						

	Ja	Fe	Mr	Ap	My	Jn	Jy	Ag	Se	Oc	No	De
Eltroplectris												
calcarata	1	2	1									
roseo-alba								1				
Embreea												
rodigasiana							1	5				
Encyclia												
abbreviata			1		1							
adenocarpon			1	1	3	8	7	5	1			
adenocaula		1	2	5	15	23	47	10	1			
advena			2			2			1	1		
aenicta				1	4	11	3	3	1			
alata	2	2	6	12	21	38	25	13	7	7	1	1
allemanii	2	2	1	1			2	2				
allemanoides	1	4	1			1			1			
amanda						1						
ambigua				1	4	9	11	5				
angustilabia				2								
aromatica	1	3	3	14	32	20	9	3	3	3	4	1
aspersa											1	1
atrorubena		1					1			3		
baculus	2			2	13	27	15	3		1		
belizensis				4	11	20	25	4	1			
—ssp. *belizensis*					1	1	6	4	1			
bicamerata	1	4	3	1							2	
bipapulare						2			2			
boothiana		3	2		2	1	3	1	1		3	
brachiata	1	2		1	1							
bracteata			1		1		2	5		3	3	
bractescens	1	4	13	17	13	7	4					
brassavolae	2	1	2	1	2	6	19	31	9	6	3	1
brymeriana				1								
bulbosa	1					2	1		1	4	10	3
caetensis			1									
calamaria	3				2	1					4	3
campylostalix			1	2	5	8	5	1				
candollei		3	3	11	13	9	9	3	1			
ceratistes			2			3	2	2	1			
cerinum		1										
chacaoensis			3	2	8	7	10	6	5	2	1	
chondylobulbon	1	1	1		1			2	3	8	5	2
citrina		1	15	52	122	43	18	4	1	4		
cochleata	22	19	20	16	18	25	27	22	16	31	19	14
concolor	1		1	1	1	2						
cordigera	1	14	28	44	70	34	16	7	2	7	2	
—var. *alba*		3	4	3								
—var. *rosea*	1	1	4	3	16		1	1				
crassilabia		1		1				1			1	
cretacea				1								1
cyanocolumna				2								
deamii							3	3	1			
dichroma		1	1	3	4	3	2	5	3	3	7	1
diota	1	1		2	7	5	1	2		1	1	
—var. *atrorubens*		1						1	1	4		1
distantiflora							1	1				

	Ja	Fe	Mr	Ap	My	Jn	Jy	Ag	Se	Oc	No	De
diurna						1						
duveenii					1	1						
ensiformis				1								
fausta			1						2	1		
flabellifera				1	1							
fragrans	14	9	5	10	19	19	20	22	11	13	20	13
fucata						1						
garcianum	4		1	1			1					1
ghiesbreghtiana			1	8	8	3	2					
glauca				1	3	1	2	2				
glumacea		1		2	2				1	1	1	
gracile	1	3		1	2	5	4					
granitica					1	2	1					
gravida	1	1		1	1							
guatemalensis				1	5	21	11	3				
hanburyi			4	5	8	7	6	1				
hartwegii						1						
hastata				2	8	1						
howardii						2	1		1	1		
huejuquillensis							1	1	1			
inaguaensis							1					
inversa	1	1					1	2	2	9	12	4
ionosma					3							
kienastii				1								
lancifolia			2	1	2	3	5	3			1	1
leucantha									1			
leuchochilum	1	1	1	3	6	3			1			
limbata				2	1	2						
linearifolioides					1							
linkiana			4	5	16	2	1	1	1			
livida			3	4	6	6	8	6	4	2	3	2
longifolia						4	2					
luteorosea				2	7		1					
maculosa		2	1	4		2						1
magnispatha		2								1		1
mariae			1	1	8	30	42	4	1			
megalantha								5	4			
meliosma			1	5	5	6	1					
michuacana		1	2		3	3	3	2	1			
microbulbon		1	2	1	7	1						
microcharis	2											
mooreana				1	6	4	4	6				
nematocaulon				1	2	5	6	3				
obpiribulbon										1	1	1
ochracea	2		1	3	3	3	3	6	2	2	2	
odoratissima	2	4	2		5	3	2	1	2			2
oestlundii				1		5	7	4	1			
oncidioides	1	2	2		2	8	6	3				
osmantha			1		2	1		2	2	1		
pachyantha				1			2					
panthera		2	1	1	3				1			
papilio		1						1	1			
papillosa					1	2	1					
patens	7	2							1	1	1	1
pauciflora				1	1				1	1		

	Ja	Fe	Mr	Ap	My	Jn	Jy	Ag	Se	Oc	No	De
phoenicea					1	4	5	1	2			
plicata						1	4	7	2			1
pollardiana				1	1	5	1	1	1			
polybulbon	35	25	7	2	2	2	2	1	1	1	4	12
—var. *album*	3	4										
pringlei			1		1		1	1				
prismatocarpa					19	50	61	23	13	3	1	
profusa						3						
pseudopygmaea	1	2	1							1	1	1
pterocarpa		1	1		1	2	3	3	1	2		
punctifera				1								1
pygmaea	5	4	1					1		2	3	2
radiata	1	3	2	4	12	16	35	39	20	16	4	1
rhombilabia				1								
rhynchophora		2		1		3	5	9	4		1	
rueckerae									1	4	4	
rufa			1	2	5	2	1	1				
sceptra	3	3	4	4	5	6	3	3	2	4	4	
selligera		2	5	6	10	2	6					
semiaperta		1		3								
serroniana	1		2						1			
sima	1	1										
spatella					2	9	1	1				
spondiada			1	1	1							
stenopetala	6	2	4	6	2	3						3
subulatifolia		1	1	3		1						1
tampensis	1	5	2	1	5	26	28	8	1	5	7	
—var. *alba*					2	4	2					1
tarumana						1	1	2				
tenuissima		2	2	5	2							
trachycarpa						1	4	2	1			
tripunctata			3	11	7	6	1	2			1	
truncata		1	1	3	5			1		2		
tuerckheimii			2	1			1					
vagans					1	2	1	1				
varicosa	1	3	11	6	5	4	1				2	1
vellozoana					1							
venosa				1	3	7	2	3	1			
vespa	5	3	3	3	17	8	14	18	15	13	12	15
virgata	1		8	3	5	2	2					
vitellina	7	3	4	5	63	44	70	46	46	108	86	20
—var. *majus*	3	2	1		4	7	10	14	7	11	7	4
voluta					1		5	4				
xipheres			2	1	4	9	1	2				
Ephemerantha												
angustifolia								1				
Epiblastus												
auriculatus						1	1	1	1	1		1
lancipetalus	1	4	3	1	2							
Epidanthus												
paranthicus					2							1
Epidendropsis												
flexuossimum					2	1			1	1	1	1

	Ja	Fe	Mr	Ap	My	Jn	Jy	Ag	Se	Oc	No	De
Epidendrum												
acutifolium						2	2	2	1			
alabastrialatum							1					
amethystinum					1							
amethystoglossum			1									
amplexicaule	1											
anceps	2		3		5	5	2	1		2		2
anisatum		1	1	1								1
apaganum								1				
arbuscula	2	2	1	3	8	4	4	1	1	1		
argentinense					1							
armeniacum			1	1	3	2		1	4	5	4	1
atacazoicum					1							
bagnense					1		1	1				
bahamense				2	3				1	1		
blepheroclinium								1				
brevifolium							1					
burtonii			2	4	1							
campylostalix		1	1	2	5	6	3	1	1			
capricornu		2	1			1						
cardiochilum	2	1					1					
carolii	3						1	2			4	3
carpophorum	2	2	5	4	5	4	3	2	2	2	1	2
centropetalum	1	1		1								1
cerinum		1										
chimborazoensis	3	6										
chioneum	1				1							
chitagense					1							
chloe			1									
chlorops		1										
ciliare	25	18	8	5	10	6	7	15	16	24	13	26
cinnabarinum			1	1	4	3	10	4	1			
clowesii	1	2	1			1						1
cnemidophorum	1	2	4							1		
cogniauxii								1	1	1	1	
collare						1						
compressum										1		
congestum		2	1			1			1		1	1
conopseum	1	2		1			2	3	5	6	3	2
cooperianum	4				3						1	2
coriifolium	4	2	3	1	2	1	6	2	5	7	6	3
coronatum	1	2	1	1	7	7	16	8		2	1	2
cornucopus		1										
costatum	1	1	1				2	1		1		
criniferum	4	2		1		1	1					
cristatum				3	6	6	4	2	1	1		
cyperifolium						1						
dayanum										1		
densiflorum		2	3	4	5	1	2	1	2	5	2	1
denticulatum		1	2									
dichotomum	2									2	2	1
difforme	3	3	6	5	5	10	11	9	9	8	6	2
diffusum	2		2				1	2	12	14	5	4
discoidale	1											
domingensis				1								

	Ja	Fe	Mr	Ap	My	Jn	Jy	Ag	Se	Oc	No	De
dunnii	1											
durangense	1			1				1				1
eburneum		2							2	3		
ekmanii			1									
ellipsophyllum	1	1	1		1		1	1		2	2	2
ellipticum	1	1	4	1	5	1	1	2		4	3	3
ellisii		1		2	2							
erubescens	3	3										2
eustirum	1									3	4	1
evectum	1	1	2	1	1							
exaltatum		1										
eximium	2		2	5	3							1
falcatum	3	4	2	6	14	8	8	4	4	2	1	
faustum										1		1
ferrugineum										4	4	1
fimbriatum	1		1		3	2	1		1		1	1
fournierianum								1				
friederici-guilielmi					4	2	1					
gasteriferum				1	1							
geminiflorum							1			2		
gomezii											1	1
harrisoniae	1	2	1				1	4	1			
hartii			2		1		1		1	1		
hermannianum							1					
heterodoxum				1								
hewlettianum						1						
hodgeanum							5	1	1		1	1
hondurense					1		9					
huebneri	2	1	2	1	1		3	3	2	2	1	
humidicola	1		1									
ilense	3					1	2	3	1	2	2	2
imatophyllum		2		1	1							
incomptum											1	
ionodesme						1						
isochilum				1								
isomerum									1			
jamaicense						1	2	1				
juergensenii	2	3	2	1	1		2					
kewense		2										
kraënzlinii	1	1	8	5			2	1				2
krugii		1	1	2				2	2			
lacertinum				1	2	1						
lanipes						2			1	1	1	
latilabre						1	1			1		
latisegmentum									1			
laucheanum	3			1	1	1	1	2	5	3	4	4
ledifolium	1	1	1	1		2		1	1	1	3	
leucanthum							1					
lindenii		2										
liontianum		1					1					
lockhartioides					1							
longicolle	2			1				1	1	1	1	
longispathum	1	1	1	1			1	1	1		2	2
mantinii						2	1		1	1		
marmoratum		2	1	1				1	2	2	1	

	Ja	Fe	Mr	Ap	My	Jn	Jy	Ag	Se	Oc	No	De
megalanthum			1	1			1	1				
microtos								3				
mirabile	1	1	1	1		1	1		2	1	3	3
miserrimum	1				1					2		
nagelii										2		
neogaliciense											1	
neoporpax										1		
nitens	1	1							1	2		1
nocturnum	11	12	6	11	8	3	6	5	5	16	18	12
nubium	1											
nutans	4	2	3	2	1			2		1		2
oaxacanum		1		1		1				1		1
obesum	1	1			2			1			1	1
obrienianum Nat. Hyb.	4	7	9	6	24	6	3	2		1		4
octomerioides	2											
odoratissimum	6	3										
oerstedii	4		2	1			4	6	3	1	2	4
olivaceum					1				1	2		
orbiculatum			1									
organense					2	5	2	1				
orpetianum			1									
osmanthum						3		1		2	1	
pallens										1		
paniculatum	6	3	10	7	2	2	1	6	7	9	6	7
parkinsonianum	1	4	2	8	8	7	13	7	4	2	1	
patens			1		2	6	3				1	
pendulum				1								
pfavii	1		1			1	3	4	1	1	2	3
platychilum	1			1						1		
polyanthum	2	1	1	2	2	4	1	1	3	4	4	2
porphyreum		1			1	1				1		
propinquum	1	1								1	1	
pseudepidendrum	2	3	15	7	11	8	2		1		1	1
pseudohuey-catenangense		1	1		1		1					
pseudopygmaeum												1
pubiflorum							1					
pugioniforme				1	2	5						1
purpurascens						1	3	7	1			
purum	1							2	4		2	1
puteum				1								
quinquepartitum		1										
radicans	5	42	30	29	49	16	13	10	5	9	7	6
radioferens	2	2										
ramosum		1						1	1	3	1	
raniferum				1	1	4	1	2				
repens										2	1	1
rigidum	4	4	3	2	2	4	9	5	3	3	3	3
rivulare				1	2		1		1			
rousseauae		1				3	1			1		
rowleyi				1	1							
rufum					1							
ruizianum								1				
saxatile					3	2	2	1		2		
schlimii				1								

	Ja	Fe	Mr	Ap	My	Jn	Jy	Ag	Se	Oc	No	De
schomburgkii					3	5		3	1		1	
scriptum			1	1				1	1	2	1	1
sculptum			1		5	2				1		
scutellum				1								
scytocladium				1								
secundum	22	24	32	30	37	19	31	23	23	29	17	18
serpens												1
simulacrum									1			
sobraloides		1										
speciosum										1		
spondiadum			1		2							
stamfordianum	18	24	33	20	9	4						2
stenocarpum			1									
steinbachianum	1							1				
strobiliferum	1				1						1	2
subaquilum		1			1							
subpurum					2	2	2	2			1	
superpositum								1	3	4		
sylvettei			2									
teretifolium	1			1								
tipuloideum			1									
tortipetalum	1		1		1		1		1		1	
trachypus				2						1		
trialatum	1											1
trianguliferum							1		2			
tricolor										1		
tunguraguae				1								
turialvae	3									1		1
vesicatum		1			2			4	3	1	2	1
viviparum	3			1								1
warasii						1						
warscewiczii								4				
wightii		2	1									
xanthinum		3	7	1	4	4	1	2	1	3	3	2
Epigeneium												
acuminatum				1	1	48	22	8	8	3	4	
amplum						1		1	1	5	8	
coelogyne	2	1							1	12	14	6
cymbidioides	11	7	10	7	5	2	1		1	1	5	6
elongatum	1		1						1			1
lyonii				2	1	16	7	10	1			
nakaharaei								1			1	
rotundatum				2	1							
triflorum	9	6	5	5	4	1				2	3	6
Epipactis												
gigantea						1	2		1			
thunberghii							1					
Epipogium												
roseum					1							
Epipogon												
aphyllum									1			

	Ja	Fe	Mr	Ap	My	Jn	Jy	Ag	Se	Oc	No	De
Eria												
acervata						3	5	4				
albidotomentosa			1	1	2					1		
amica			1		3	4	1	1		1		1	1
apertifolia								1				
barbarossa									1	1	1	1
barbata			1				1			1		
bicolor	1		1						2	1		
bicristata										1		
biflora			1	1	2			1	2		1	
braccata							1		1	1		
bractescens				3	2	3	1		1		1	
brownei									1			
citrina						1		2				
clarkei						1						
confusa			1	2	1		1	1				
congesta							3					
cooperi	1								2	1		
corneri							1	1				
coronaria	2	1	4	1			1	2	2	14	18	11
dasyphylla						1	1	1				
densa		1	1				1					
densiflora			1			1				1		
elegans								1	4	3	3	1
elongata		1				1	1					1
erecta		1	2	3								
excavata				1		3	3	4	2	1		
extinctoria					6							
feddeana						1						
ferox										1		
ferruginea	1	1	3	4	2	3	5	1	1	1		1
flava	6	6	4	3	3		1	1	1		1	
flavescens				1								
floribunda	3	1	4	4	3	2	2	6	5	4	3	
globifera	5	6	1								1	
graminifolia								1				
hindei										1		
hyacinthoides	2	2				4	6	3	7	4	6	4
imitans	1											
inornata				1								
javanica	7	5	10	5	3	4	5	18	17	10	4	5
kajewskii	1	1										
labianensis												
—var. major			1									
lactibracteata						1						
laniceps			1	1								
latifolia					1			2	1			
lobata		1										
longifolia										1		
luchuensis										1		
marginata			2		1	1					1	
merrillii										1		
micholitzii								1			1	
micrantha			1	1	1			1	1	4	2	
monophylla								2			1	

	Ja	Fe	Mr	Ap	My	Jn	Jy	Ag	Se	Oc	No	De
monostachya				1								
myristicaeformis									1			
mysorensis								1				
nutans										1		
obesa	1	1	6	5			1		2			
odoronia					2			1				
ornata			1	1	11	3	2					
ovata				1			1					
pachystachya							2					
paniculata	1	1		3							1	2
pannea	1			4	10	2	4					
pubescens			2	4	2			1	1			
pudica											1	2
pulvinata											1	
pumila					1		1		1			
queenslandica					1		2					
ramuana		1										
rhynchostyloides							5	8	1	1	3	1
ridleyi					2							
rigida						1						
rimanni	1			1								
robusta			1	1			1					
rosea	6	9	2			1						
rufinula				1				2		5	4	
saccifera												1
sessileflora	3	2					1			2	2	1
sicaria			1	1		2	1					
spicata		2	1	1	6	5	5	3	1			
stricta	2	2	2		1							1
tricolor	1											
undiculia								4				
velutina	1	1					1	4	5	9	5	
vestita					1			2	1	1		
vittata	2	1										
xanthocheila		1		1								
Eriochilus												
cucullatus										1		
Eriopsis												
biloba			3	3	3	6	2	1	2	1	2	
rutidobulbon		2		2	5	6	1	2			1	
Erycina												
diaphana	6	5	2	3								1
echinata	1	3	5	3	2				1			1
Erythrodes												
calophylla					1							
kuczynskii				1				2	4	2	4	
ovatilabia										1		
picta			1	1								
valida	1											
Esmeralda												
cathcartii				1	1			1	1			

	Ja	Fe	Mr	Ap	My	Jn	Jy	Ag	Se	Oc	No	De
Eucosia												
papuana				1								
Eulophia												
alta		2		1					2	4		1
andamenensis				1	7	4	2					
burkei					1	2	1					
caffra					1		1		1			
coleae					1							
cucullata				1								
decaryana							1					
ecalcarata				1								
ensata								1	1			
epidendrae	1	1	1									
euglossa					1	1	2	3	1	1		
gracilis		1	2		4	3	2	2	1			
graminea						2	1			1		
guineensis		2	4	3	10	4	1	5	3	2		1
horsfallii			2									
keithei				4	7	6	2					
leachii						1	3					
leonensis				1								
lindleyana				2								
lubbersiana				1		1	1					
macra	5	4	1									1
macrostachya											1	
mannii							1	1				
megistophylla												1
nuda						2	2					
orthoplectra									1	1		1
paivaeana			1	12	3	1	4	1	5	9	8	
plantagenia							1					
porphyroglossa				2	3							
pulchra		1	1		1	2	1					
purpurata			1	1	2							
quartiniana			3	4	7	3	1					
speciosa				3	6		1		2			
squalida					1			1		1		
stenophylla			1				1	2				
streptopetala	2			2	4		1	1	1	1	1	2
stricta				1								
taitensis					1	1	1					
tristis			1									
Eulophiella												
elizabethae	1		13	23	2						1	
longtalli			1									
perrieri	1			3	1							
roempleriana	3	5	9	4	9	8	7	1	1		1	
Eurychone												
rothschildiana	1		1	1	1	1	5	11	6	3	2	1
Eurystyles												
actinosophila											1	
cotyledon										1		

	Ja	Fe	Mr	Ap	My	Jn	Jy	Ag	Se	Oc	No	De
Fernandezia												
maculata	1							2				
sanguinea					1							
Flickingeria												
angustifolia				1								
comata								1				
fimbriata	1		1	2			1		1	1	2	
fugax							3					
hesperis							3					
pallens		1	1									
plicatile				2			1			1		
Galeandra												
barbata		1										
batemanii	1					1	2	2	2	1	1	
baueri	1					1	2	3	4	2	2	1
claesii							1					
devoniana	2	5	5	5	4	4	5	3	1	2	1	
dives								1				
lucustris	1			2	1		3	3				
lagoensis							1	1				
minax	1		1	2			1	1			1	3
nivalis	1		2		1				2	2		
pubicentrum	2	1	1	1	1		1					
stangeana					1							
Galeola												
javanica											2	
Galeottia												
fimbriata	1				1		1				1	
grandiflora				2	3	1						
Gastorchis												
humblotii								2	3			
tuberculosa	1	3	6	2								
Gastrochilus												
acutifolius	1	2	3	2	2		1	1	7	17	21	6
bellinus	24	28	14	4	3	1	1	1			2	3
biggibus								2	1	2	1	
calceolaris	2	3	6	3	1			2	7	9		
dasypogon		1				1	1	2	1	3	18	2
fuscopunctatus						1	1	1				
inconspicuus							3	3				
japonicus					1			2	3	3		
pechei					1	1	1	1				
Geesinkorchis												
phaiostele										1		
Genyorchis												
pumila	1			1	3	2	1					
Geodorum												
candidum						1						
citrinum					1	3	1	1				
densiflorum			1	1			1					

	Ja	Fe	Mr	Ap	My	Jn	Jy	Ag	Se	Oc	No	De
duperreanum					1		1					
nutans			1									
pictum							1					
purpureum							1					
Glomera												
rugulosa				1								
Glossodia												
major						1						
Glossorhyncha												
adenandroides						1					1	
citrina						1						
torricellensis			1			1						
Gomesa												
barkeri	6	2								1		5
binotii												1
crispa	8	2	8	2	1	1	7	4	6	9	8	15
foliosa			1		1							
glaziovii	1											
laxiflora							1					
planifolia	6	6	1			1	1	6	4			4
recurva	2	5	2	1	1	1	1	3	5	4	4	11
sessilis				1		1						
verboonenii							1			1	1	
Gomphicis												
viscosa									1			
Gongora												
armeniaca	1	2	1			6	7	2	2	3	2	
aromatica			1									
atropurpurea	1	4	1	2	5	4	4	3	2	2	1	1
bufonia			1		6	6	3					
cassidea			1				1	2				
claviodora										1		
cornuta											1	1
flavida	1			1	1	6	12	13	9	8	3	3
gratulabunda						3						1
grossa						1			2			
leucochila			1	1	1	1						
maculata	3	5	6	7	6	10	3	3	5	3	3	2
portentosa					2	2						
quinquenervis	1	1	8	10	16	10	12	12	8	4	2	3
quintuplinerva											1	
saccata			1			2						
sanderiana						2	1					
scaphephorus		1			2	3	1	3	2	1		
stenoglossa										1	1	1
tracyana		1	1	2								
truncata	1	4	10	6	1	2	5	3	2			
unicolor										1		
viridi-purpurea							1					
Goodyera												
bifida										1		

	Ja	Fe	Mr	Ap	My	Jn	Jy	Ag	Se	Oc	No	De
daibuzanensis									1	1	1	
foliosa									1			
hispida									2			
oblongifera									1			
oblongifolia		1				1	2	1				
procera		1		1			1					
pubescens		1				1	1					
rollinsonii							1	1	1			
rubicunda	1	1		1	1		1					1
schlechtendaliana	1									1	1	
striata			2									
velutina											1	1
viridiflora					1						1	1
Govenia												
capitata					1							
liliacea					1							
superba					3	2						
tequilana					1							
tingens										1		
utriculata											1	1
Grammangis												
ellisii					2	10	10	10	2	2	1	
fallax						1	1					
Grammatophyllum												
elegans				3	1	2	3				1	
measuresianum	1		1	1	3	7	2					
multiflorum				1		1						
papuanum					1							
rumphianum				1	3	5	3	2	1			
scriptum			1	4	7	9	8	2	2			
speciosum						1	5	5				
wallisii											1	
Graphorkis												
lurida	4	2	2	2				1				1
scripta				1	1	1	1					
Grobya												
amherstii		1					1	1	2	1	1	
bibrachiata										1	1	
fascifera		1										
galeata	1						1	2		5	4	3
Gymnadenia												
conopsea							2					
Habenaria												
alata					1	2	3	4				
arietina											1	
bonatea				1								
bractescens											1	
carnea						2	2	10	5	6	1	
cinnabarina			1				1	1		1		
dentata								1	2	1		
dilatata							1	1				

	Ja	Fe	Mr	Ap	My	Jn	Jy	Ag	Se	Oc	No	De
floribunda	1											
gabonensis									4	1		
hyacinthosma			1									
loerzingii								1				
longicorniculata								1	1	2		
josephensis						1	2	1		2		
leonensis										2	4	1
lindleyana										1	1	
lucida								1				
lugardii										1		
macrandra							1					
marmorophylla		2	1							1	2	
medioflexa										1		
plantaginea								3	3			
procera								6	8	1		
quinqueseta								1	1	1		
rariflora								1				
repens										1		
rhodocheila					6	6	15	5	17	32	6	3
roebelenii	3		1							4	1	1
splendens	2											
ugandensis	2										1	
xantholeuca								3				
Hagsatera												
brachycolumna							1					
rosilloi										1		
Haraella												
odorata	1					3	5	7	9	9	8	3
retrocalla	1											
Hartwegia												
purpurea								1				
Helcia												
sanguinolenta	8	7			2		1	1	1	3	4	3
Helleriella												
guerrerensis										1		
Hellerorchis												
gomezoides					1							
Hemipilia												
amethystina							2	1				
calophylla						1	1		1			
cordifolia						1						
Herminium												
angustifolium										1		
Herschelia												
graminifolia				1								
Hexadesmia												
bidentata				1								
crurigera			3	1	2	6	7	4				
dunstervillei					2	1						1

	Ja	Fe	Mr	Ap	My	Jn	Jy	Ag	Se	Oc	No	De
fasciculata			1	4	1							
fusiformis					1	1						
hondurensis			1									
jimenezii				1								
lindeniana	1		2		2							
micrantha					3	1	1					
pulchella							1					
sessilis			2	2	3	1						
Hexalectris												
grandiflora						1						
Hexisea												
bidentata	13	9	10	7	3	4	3		2	6	1	5
imbricata	6	2	2	2					2	1	1	2
reflexa			1	1								
Himantoglossum												
hircinum					3			1				
longibracteatum			2	2	1							
Hintonella												
mexicana	2			2								
Holcoglossum												
kimballianum									2			
quasipinifolium				5	1	1	1					1
Holothrix												
orthoceras				1								
Homalopetalum												
pumilio					1	2	2	3	5	2	2	1
Houlletia												
brocklehurstiana				1			3	4	7	4	3	3
clava												1
lowiana								1				
odoratissima	1	2		1	5	1		3	1			1
sanderi			4		1		1			1		3
tigrina		1	1		1	1		1	2	1		
vittata		1						1	1	1		
wallisii						1	1	1	4			
Huntleya												
albidofulva			2									
burtii			1	6	5	1	4	6	4	5	3	
fasciata				2	1			1				
heteroclita					1			2	5	2	2	
lucida							1	1				
meleagris	1	2	5	4	2	7	8	10	2	2	2	
wallisii					1	2						
Hyalosema												
tricanaliferum					1	1	1					
Hybochilus												
inconspicuus			1		1	1						
Ione												
racemosa					1							

	Ja	Fe	Mr	Ap	My	Jn	Jy	Ag	Se	Oc	No	De
Ionopsis												
satyrioides				1	1	2	1	2			1	
utricularioides	4	14	7	13	10	7	6	5	7	6	9	5
Ipsea												
speciosa	1	5	2									
Isabelia												
pulchella	1										7	3
virginalis											13	4
Isochilus												
amparoanus						2	1	1	1	1	1	1
aurantiacus		1	1	1	2	1						2
carnosiflorus										1		1
linearis	1		1			2	1	4	4	1	2	2
major	3			1	3	3	3			2	6	2
Isotria												
medeoloides					2							
verticillata				6								
Jacquiniella												
cobanensis				1	2		2	1				
equitantifolia	5	1				2	1			1		2
globosa	1		7	2	1	2	2	2	2	4	2	
leucomelana	1					1	1	2	2	1		
teretifolia			1					1	1	2		1
Jumellea												
amplifolia	1	1	1									
anjouanensis			1		2	1	2	1	1	1		
arachnantha			2	2	1	1						
arborescens						2	3	1	1	1		
comorensis	7	6	5	3	6	6	5	4	3	6	6	5
confusa	2	1	1	1	1	1	1	4	1		3	2
erecta							1	1				
flavescens	5	2	1	2	6	2	2	1	1	4	1	3
filicornoides	1							1		1	2	2
gracilipes	2	1	5	2	3	2						1
hyalina	1											
ibityana			1	1	1		1	1				
lignosa			1									
linearpetala			1	1								
major		1	1								1	
marjejiensis	1	2	1		1	1		1	2	2	2	1
maxillarioides	1					1	1	1	1			
pachyceras									1			
pandurata	1	2	1		1							
papagensis										1	1	
punctata			1									
recta									2	1		
rigida						1	2	2	1			2
sagittata	4	1	5	5	2						3	5
teretifolia						1	2	2	1	1		
zaratananae			1									

	Ja	Fe	Mr	Ap	My	Jn	Jy	Ag	Se	Oc	No	De
Kalimpongia												
narajitii				1	3							
Kalopternix												
deltoglossus								1				
sophronitis			2		2	1	1	5		1		
Kefersteinia												
costaricensis	1	1	1		1	1	1		1	1	1	
deflexipetala									1			
elegans						1						
graminea		2	1	3	2	3	3	2	3		2	
lacerata			1			1			1			1
lactea								2	1	1	2	
laminata									2			
lindneri								1	1	1		
microcharis									2			
mystacina								2	3			
sanguinolenta			1			2			1	1		
tahiensis											1	
tolimensis	1	1	2	3	3	1	3	2	1	2		
Kegeliella												
houtteana								1				
kupperi										2		
Kingidium												
decumbens							2	1				
deliciosum			1				1	9	11	5	6	4	1
philippinensis								1	4	3	2	1	1
taenialis		1		2	8	5		1				
Koellensteinia												
eburnea												1
graminea	2	3	3	1	3	2					2	1
ionoptera										1		
tricolor								3	2	3	1	3	1
Lacaena												
bicolor						2	5	1				
spectabilis						3						
Laelia												
albida	17	5	1					3	1	10	12	12
anceps	295	238	14	2		1	2		2	19	27	128
—var. *hillii*	23	1	1									1
—var. *sanderiana*	40	13										5
—var. *schroederiana*	10	10	2								1	3
anceps alba	102	65	5	1						3	4	13
—var. *sanderiana*	23	5	1							1	1	3
angereri				1	1	1	1					
autumnalis	42	2						1	1	16	19	34
—var. *alba*	6									1	6	12
bahaiensis				1	3	2						
bancalaria				2	2							
blumenscheinii	4	4				1						
bradei					1			2	1	2		
briegeri		2		1	4	4						

	Ja	Fe	Mr	Ap	My	Jn	Jy	Ag	Se	Oc	No	De
cinnabarina	5	10	24	18	27	8	4	4	1		1	1
crispa		2	2		1	3	19	26	7	1		
crispata	1	7	3	1		1				5		
dayana	1	1	1	1	2	1	2	4	11	18	7	
—var. coerulea									2	6		
dickinsonii								1	1		1	
endsfeldzii		1		1								1
esalqueana			1		1	1	2		2	1		
espirito-santensis							1					
fidelensis						1	3	1				
flava	5	17	29	12	4	2	1	5	4	1		
fournieri	1				1			1		1		
furfuracea	2	1	2				1		3	5	5	3
ghillanyi					1		1					
gloedeniana	1	1	2	1								1
gouldiana	67	13							2	3	19	62
gracilis										1		
grandis			1	2	15	6	3		1			
harpophylla	6	46	43	19	4			1	1			1
itambana				1	1	1		1				
jongheana	6	16	60	15	1		1		1			
kettieana		1			2							
lilliputiana				2				1				
lobata				13	13	5						
longipes					1	1	1		2	4	1	
lucasiana		1				4	1	3	2	1	1	1
lundii	7	8	1									1
—var. regnellii	1	5										
mantiqueirae	2	4	2	2	2	1	1	1				3
milleri	1			7	26	5	4	1	3	1	1	1
montana Not pub.	2		1								1	4
moyobambae	1		1									1
oweniae		1			1			1				1
perrinii									6	53	28	
pfisteri				2	3	3						
pumila	5	8	7	2	1			9	38	125	78	11
—var. alba		1							5	27	5	2
—var. dayana								3	4	1		
—var. praestans	1	5		1				2	10	16	11	3
purpurata				1	34	452	184	23	5	3	7	1
—var. alba					2	20	10	1				
—var. carnea				1	12	10		2				
—var. werckhauseri				1	4	3						
reginae				1	4	2				1		1
rubescens	13	20	10	4	3				1	4	12	19
—var. alba	2										4	1
—var. aurea									1	1	1	
schroederi						2	4	2				
sincorana				2	6	11	4			2	1	
speciosa				1	4	27	22	9	1		1	
—var. alba						3	1	1				
tenebrosa		3	2	3	48	130	40	5	5	7	3	1
tereticaulis										1		
xanthina		2			5	1	16	9	5	1	2	
xanthotropis									2	1	3	

	Ja	Fe	Mr	Ap	My	Jn	Jy	Ag	Se	Oc	No	De
Laeliopsis												
domingensis	1	1	1	5	13	11	3	4			1	1
Lanium												
avicola					2		1		4	5	6	2
berkeleyi			1								1	1
microphyllum	1	1	5		1						1	
Lankesterella												
ceracifolia	1										1	
orthantha					1							
serensis				1								
Leochilus												
ampliflorus			1	1	1					2		
carinatus					1	3	2	1	1		1	
herbaceus										1		
johnstonii		1	2									
labiatus			1		1		2					2
oncidioides	6	9	7	3	1						1	5
scriptus	1	1		1	4	1		1				1
Lepanthes												
appendiculata					1							
asoma				1								
brevispatha										1		
brownii							1					
byfieldii		2			1							
calodictyon		3			1							
caprimulgus				1							2	
chiriquensis			1									
cochlearifolia					1							
cryptus		1										
deformis				1								
disticha							1					
divaricata		1				1				1		
dodiana				1								
ejecta			1									
elata											1	
elliptica	1	1										
erepsis			1									
escobariana	1	4	2	2	1							
eumecaulon												
felis	1				5		2					
gargantula			1	1								
grandiflora						1						
hirsuta												2
horrida		1										
hubeinii										1		
interio-rubra					1							
mephistopheles											1	
multiflora		1										
mystax				1	1							
obtusa					1				1			
odobenella				1								
ovalis			2	2	1	2	2	2	1	5	3	2

	Ja	Fe	Mr	Ap	My	Jn	Jy	Ag	Se	Oc	No	De
pecunialis			1									
pulchella		1										
quadrata										1		
rauhii										1		
rotundifolia				1	1		1					
samacensis					1							
sanguinea		1	1	1	1				1			
seegeri										1		
selenipetala			1									
simplex					2							
talpinaria				1								
tridentata		1	1	1								
trilobata			1									
turialvae					2							
urbaniana	1											
wageneri		1	1	1								
woodiana	1	2										1
wullschlaegelii			1					1				
xenos				1								
Lepanthopsis												
acuminata				1								
astrophora	2	7	5	3	1	1	1	2	1	4	1	1
blepharanthes	1	1		1								1
constanzensis			2						1	2	1	
dodii		1	1									
floripecten				2		1					1	1
hotteana	2		1		1					1	1	
melanantha		1										
microlepanthes					1		2	1		2		
serrulata										1	1	
vinacea										2		
zacuapensis												1
Leptotes												
bicolor	5	21	48	33	34	3	4		1			1
paulensis			1									
tenuis								2				
unicolor	2	2	1			1		1	1	1	7	12
Leucohyle												
braziliensis								1	1	1		
subulata		1	2			1	2		1	1		
Liparis												
astrosanguinea				1		1						
bistriata											1	
bituberculata		1	1									
bootanensis										3	1	
bowkeri									1			
breviscapa				1								
caespitosa	1			1		4	9	1				1
chlorophrys								1				
coelogynoides							1					
condylobulbon	1	1									8	3
cordifolia											1	

	Ja	Fe	Mr	Ap	My	Jn	Jy	Ag	Se	Oc	No	De
cruenta					1							
cuneilabris									1			
deisteli				1								
elegans											3	
epiphytica											1	1
finisterrae			2									
formosana					1							
fulgens											1	
gibbosa		2	1	2	2	2	3	3		3		
grandiflora											1	
grossa											1	1
horsfallii			5				1					
javanica								1				
keitaoensis										2		1
laevis									2	1		
latifolia							1					
lilifolia					3							
loeselii							1					
macrantha		1	1	1	2		1		1		3	
makinoana		1										
monophylla							1					
nervosa		2	4	3	4		3	3	4	1		
nugentae			1	3	4	1	1		1			
persimilis	1		1						1		2	
plantaginea						1	2	1				1
reflexa					2			1	2	2	1	
rheedii				2			2	1	1			
rhodochila	1						2		1			
rizalensis						2					1	3
sasakii				1								
stricklandiana	11	2									2	9
sutepensis							1					
tricallosa			1	1						1		
ugandae							1					
vexillifera											2	
viridiflora	9	1	1						6	19	19	9
wageneri										1	4	3
Lissochilus												
giganteus						1			4			
krebsii			1		2							
parviflorus					2							
streptopetalus					4							
stylites					4	1						
Listera												
australis	1											
ovata					1		1					
Listrostachys												
pertusa	1	1	3	1						1	2	
vesicata					1	1	1				1	1
Lockhartia												
acuta			1	1		2	1				1	1
amoena		1	1	1	1		1			2		
elegans		1								1		

	Ja	Fe	Mr	Ap	My	Jn	Jy	Ag	Se	Oc	No	De
hercodonta	1	3	4	1		3	2	2	3	2	3	4
imbricata	1	3	6	7	4	1	4	2	2	2	3	2
lunifera	1	3	7	5	5	7	5	7	7	5	4	1
micrantha	3	1	5	4	4	1	2			4	4	4
obtusata					2	1	1					
oerstedii			3	2	8	12	7	4	2	6	5	4
pallida		3		1		1						
parthenocomas											1	
parthenoglossa									1	1		
pittieri					1				1	1	1	
serra	2							2	2		2	3
Ludisia												
discolor	26	39	16	9	8		6	3	6	7	9	17
—var. *dawsoniana*	7	6					2	1	1		1	4
Lueddemannia												
densa									1			
pescatorei				1	1	2	2					
triloba					1		1				1	
Luisia												
amesiana					1	5	1					
birchea				1								
botanensis				1	1							
brachystachys			1	4	4	1		1				
cantharis				1								
filiformis								1				
inconspicua				1	4	4	1	1				
jonesii			1	1		2	3					1
primulina						1						
psyche							2					
teres				1	1	1						
teretifolia	1	3	5	2	3	2	5	3	1	4		
thailandica						2	2	1		1		
trichorhiza		1		3	3							
tristis				1								
volucris					1	1						
zeylanica		1	3	4								
zollingeri						1						
Lycaste												
aromatica	2	8	15	19	78	34	22	9	5	3	3	1
balsamea							1					
barringtoniae		1		3	6	6	2	2				
bradeorum					1		1	2	3			2
brevispatha	3	5	5	11	8	7	2	1				
campbellii				2		3						
candida	1		1	8	11	2	1	1	3	3		1
ciliata	5	3	1			1		2	1	1	3	3
cinnabarina		1										
cochleata				1	4	7	1			3		
consobrina				2	3	4	3	3	3			
costata	5	8		2	2	1	2	1	1	2	2	3
crinita		1	3	3	4	2	1	2				
cruenta	5	18	17	13	24	21	13	6	2	11	13	9
denningiana						1	2	5	5	2		1

	Ja	Fe	Mr	Ap	My	Jn	Jy	Ag	Se	Oc	No	De
deppei	2	1	4	13	52	43	36	12	5	3	2	2
dowiana	1	2	5		4	6		3	1	2	2	
dyeriana			1	1		1	2					
fimbriata	4	3	1	1	4	2	1	1		1	3	1
fulvescens	1	2	3	1	4							
lanipes	5	1		2	2	1			1	1		
lasioglossa	21	20	6	2	3				1	2	6	9
lata	1	1										1
leucantha	1		1		5	4	14	8	7	6	8	4
linguella		1										
locusta		1	1	1	21	11	2		2			
longiscapa	1		1						1	2		
macrobulbon	4	2	4	2	2		5			2	3	
macrophylla	6	13	11	6	20	6	5	5	5	6	4	3
—var. *alba*										1	2	2
—ssp. *measuresiana*	1	4					2			1	1	1
mathiasiae			2									
mesochlaena	2	3	1								1	
powellii			2				1	5	1	2	2	
reichenbachii				1								
rossiana										1		
saccata				1	2	1	2	1				
schilleriana	2	4	18	16	14	1	2		1	4	1	1
skinneri	125	230	246	145	73	7	2	12	10	29	57	49
—*alba*	38	75	63	39	22	2	2	2	6	10	21	10
—var. *armeniaca*	3	2	1	1	1							1
—var. *hellemensis*	2	2	1	4	3							
sulphurea						2	2					
tricolor				1	13	11	9	1	1			
—var. *alba*								5	4			
trifoliata	1		1	2		1	3	1			1	
xytriophora		1	10	6	1	8	3	1	4	1	1	
Lycomormium												
squalidum						1	1	2				
Macodes												
javanica		1										
petola	1	1	1	1	6	2	7	2	1	1		
sanderiana		2			2	1				1	1	
Macradenia												
brassavolae											1	
lutescens	1	1							1	1	2	1
multiflora			1	2	1	1		1	2		1	
paraensis							1					
tridentata		2										
Macroclinium												
bicolor	3	2	1	3			1	2	2	8	2	1
cordesii				1								
lexarzanum					1							
mirabile						1					1	
wullschlaegelianum						3		2				1
Malaxis												
acuminata							3					

	Ja	Fe	Mr	Ap	My	Jn	Jy	Ag	Se	Oc	No	De
allanii				1	1							
binabayensis											1	1
brachycaulos				2				1				
brachyrrhynchos					1							
calophylla					1	12	1	1				
carnosa								1				
commelinifolia		1	3	3	3	5	2	3	3	3	2	2
congesta				1								
diploceros			1									
discolor									1			
fastigiata							1					
khasianus						1	2	2		1		
laevis						1						
latifolia					1	6	4	4	3			
latisepala									1			
lunata									1			
macrochila					4							
metallica			1	1	2		1	2				
monophyllos							1					
oculata										1		
quaifei									1			
reniloba					2							
scottii					2	1	2					
streptopetala							1					
taurina	2	1								1	3	4
unifolia				1								
versicolor							1					
wallichii					1							
xanthochila								1				
Malleola												
dentifera										1		
insectifera										3		
penangiana								1	3			
Masdevallia												
abbreviata	2	1			1						3	1
aenigma						1				1		
albicans	1											
allenii									1			
amabilis	4	1	2	3	1	2	2	5	3		4	4
amaluzae					1	2						
amanda			1		1	1	1					
ampullacea											1	
angulata	3	4	2	1		2		2	1	8	7	5
angulifera		1			2		2		2	4	2	
anisomorpho				1	1							
antioquiensis			1	1	1		1					
aphanes	2	1										
arangoi		1										
aristata		1		1	1							
arminii			3	12	3				2			
aspera						1	1	1				
asterotricha					1							
atropurpurea		1			1	1	2		1	4	4	
attenuata	1		3	1	2			1	4	1	2	

	Ja	Fe	Mr	Ap	My	Jn	Jy	Ag	Se	Oc	No	De
audax								1				
aureopurpurea	1					1	1					1
ayabacana	1		3									
barlaeana	1	1				2		1	2	2	5	4
bicolor		1	1	1				1			1	
bonplandii	2	1		1	1	3	4	3	2		3	2
bottae									1			
brachyura				1								
buccinator				2								
buchtienii						1						
burbidgeana									1			
burfordiensis		1			1		1				1	
cacodes									1			
caesia									1			
caloptera	5	6	4	4	3	2	2	1		3	4	2
calura	1	1			9	10	18	2	5	4	2	1
campyloglossa					1		5	1		1		1
canaliculata								1				1
cardiantha					1	1	1			1	2	
carruthersiana		1										
casta					1							
caudata	5	4	39	20	18	4	3	1		2	1	3
caudivolvula				2			1	1			1	
chaetostoma	3	1										
chaparensis				2	1		1					
chaucharuago					1							
chestertonii				3	1	1	1	1				
chiquindensis						1	1			2		
chontalensis				2	1	4	3	3	3	4	1	2
cinnamomea	2				1						1	
citronella			1									
civilis	10	5	12	16	8	7	5	2	7	8	10	5
coccinea	4	1	10	43	98	72	44	18	15	9	8	4
—var. *alba*				2	2	6	3	2		1		1
—var. *lindenii*										3	2	
—var. *rosea*					3	3	1			1	1	
—var. *xanthina*				1	2	4	1					
coesia				1								
collina											1	
colossus						2	2				1	
constricta				1								
coriacea	1		1	3	8	16	13	8	6			2
corniculata				2	2	1	5			4	5	2
cucullata	4	5	5	2	6	2	1		1	3	4	2
cupularis	3					1				2		3
curlei				1								
cyclotegal									1			
datura					1	1						
davisii	1	1	1	2	1	4	1	2		2	2	1
decumana						4						
deformis			3	5	2	4				1		1
delfinia					1							
demissa						2	4	3				
deorsa	3	3	6	7	6	2	4	1		1	2	
diantha										1	1	

	Ja	Fe	Mr	Ap	My	Jn	Jy	Ag	Se	Oc	No	De
discolor						2						
don-quijote				1								
ecaudata	3					1				2	5	8
echidna						1		2				
echo			4	1	1	1	1					
edwallii			1	3	3	1						
elegans		1										
elephanticeps	5	12	13	3	2	1	5	3	7	3	4	6
encephala			1	1								
ephippium		2	3	5	15	3	6	3	3	2	4	1
erinacea	2			1	5	4	8	3		2		1
estradae	3		4	7	11	4	1	1	2	4	1	2
falcago			1									
×*falcata* Nat. Hyb.		1		2	2							
filamentosa			1	2								
floribunda		2	2	2	4	3	6	7	12	10	7	3
forgetiana		2	2	3	1							
fractiflexa							1	2				
garcia				1								
gemmata				1	8	10	5	3	2	3		1
gilbertoi										3	3	
glandulosa	1										1	1
guianensis				2								
guterrezii							1		1	2	2	3
guttulata	1	1	1		1	2	2	2	1	1	1	
herradurae								2	1		1	
heteroptera		1	2	1	2	1		1		1	1	
hieroglyphica	1				4	2					1	1
hortensis		1										
huari											1	1
humilis						1						
hurraz			3									
hymenantha							3	2				
hystrix		2										
ignea	10	11	18	33	56	20	10	4	6	1	7	7
impostor	1	1	1	1	1	1	1	1	1	1	1	1
infracta			1	4	13	14	15	7	2	2	3	1
—var. *purpurea*		1	1	1	3	2	2	1		2	1	
—var. *lutea*		4	1	1	1	1	1					
instar	1				2					3	2	
ionocharis	1				1	1		2	1	1		
iricolor	1			1				1				
kuhniorum		4										
lamprotyria					2	1						
laucheana	1	1								8	4	7
lehmannii					1				1			
lepida								1	2	1	7	
leucantha												1
lilliputiana			1		1						1	
limax		2	2								2	
lineolata				1								
lintricula								1				
livingstoneana	3		1	1	1							1
lychniphora							1	1				
lyndiniphora?			1									

	Ja	Fe	Mr	Ap	My	Jn	Jy	Ag	Se	Oc	No	De
macrura	8	7	4	5	2	2	3	2	7	9	13	6
maculata		1	2		1	3	5	2	5	1	1	
maloi	1											
malox					2	1						
marginella	1	1	1		2		1	1				
mastodon					1			1				
meirax					1	1						
mejiana					1						2	2
melanopus	4	3		2	1		1		1	2	3	5
melanoxantha			2	1	3	2	3		1	3	1	1
mendozae	1		1								1	1
mezae												1
minuta	1	2	2		1	1		1		2		1
misasii		1										
mollosus			1							1		
monogana										1		
mooreana	1		2								2	2
nidifica	3		1	9	3		5	1	2	6	4	2
norops			2									
noto-siberica			1		3							
nycteriana				2	1		2	1	1			
o'brieniana					1	14	5					
ocalli								1				
ocanensis												1
odontocera		3		1								
oligantha	1											
ophioglossa					1	1	1	1	1	2	1	
oreas											1	
ortalis				1								
ortgiesiana										1		1
ova-avis												1
pachyantha		1		2							1	3
pachyura	7	2		2	3		1				5	3
paisbambae										1		
paivaeana		2	1	1	3	1				1		1
pallida	1	1	1	1	1					3	2	
panguiensis											1	
paranaensis							1					
pardina				1								
patriciana				1								
patula				1	1							
pelicaniceps					1							
peristeria	3	1	3	6	11	10	13	6	7	2	1	2
persicina										2	2	
peruviana	1		1									
phoenix										1		
picturata	2	5									1	1
pinocchio						1						
polysticta	16	11	1	1	1	1	1		1	1	7	5
porphyrea		1										
prodigiosa		1		3	2	3	3		1	1	2	1
prosartema				1								
pteroglossa						1						1
pumila	1	1										
purpurella	3							1		2		

	Ja	Fe	Mr	Ap	My	Jn	Jy	Ag	Se	Oc	No	De
pygmaea	1											2
pyxis	1	1	1	1	1	1	1	1	1	1	1	1
racemosa				1	1	1	2		1	1		
radiosa			1	1	1	2	5	4	2	1	1	
rechingeriana			1									
reichenbachiana	3	3		2	9	10	8	3	1	1	2	4
replicata	1		2									
rigens	1	1	1	1	1	1	1	1	1	1	1	1
rimarima alba		2	1									
rodolfoi	1											
rolfeana			1		7	12	8		1	2	1	2
rosea	5	2	1	1	13	2						3
rubiginosa											1	
rufescens												1
saltatrix	1				3	1	1		1	3	4	
sanctae-fidae			1		1							
santae-inesae	1	2	1	1	1	2	2	1	1	2	1	1
scabrilinguis			1									
schlimii		2	4	7	12	5	5	3	1	4	3	2
schmidt-mummii										1		
schroederiana	46	42	26	11	5	1	2		1		2	10
scobina					1							
selenites											1	
setacea		1	1									
simula	2	3	4	5	12	6	3	3	1	2	2	2
—var. *o'brieniana*		2	1	2	4	2						
spilantha					1							
stenorhynchos			2	1								2
striatella	3				1					1		1
strobelii	1									1	3	6
strumifera						3						
stumpflei					1							
susanae									1	1		
tenuissima								1				
tobosa	1	3										1
tonduzii												1
torta	2		2	2	2	1	1		1	4	1	3
tovarensis	58	27	7	4	4	2			2	8	33	70
triangularis	1	1	4	1	2	1	2	4	4	6	7	4
triaristella		2	1	8	25	6	11	4	4	4	6	1
tricarinata		1										
tridens										2		
triglochin						1						
trigonopetala	3											
tubuliflora	1	1	1							4	2	1
tubulosa			1		1							
uniflora	1	2		2	2	4	1	1				
urceolaris						1						
urosalpinx				1							1	
veitchiana	5	6	8	18	81	11	9	9	13	8	15	12
—fma. *grandiflora*		1	1	6	9	3	1			1		1
velifera	2			2		4	1	2	2	1	1	2
venezuelana			2									
ventricosa					1	1	1			2	1	
ventricularis	1	1	1	4	3				1	3	2	

	Ja	Fe	Mr	Ap	My	Jn	Jy	Ag	Se	Oc	No	De
venusta				1	2							
virgo-cuencae					1							
wageneriana		2	1	4	7	12	5	1	5	2	2	5
weberbaueri		1	1		1	2		2	2	2	2	
welischii					1							
wendlandiana					2				1	1		
whiteana			1				1					1
woolwardiae			1	2								
wurdackii				4						1	2	
xanthina			4	2	1	3				2		1
xipheres					1	2		2		1		
Maxillaria												
aciantha										2	1	1
acicularis				2	1							
acuminata		1										
alba		1					1	1	1	1		
amazonica	1	1							1	1	1	
angustisegmenta	1											
arachnidiflora							2					
arachnites	2	4	1	1								
arbuscula		1										
bicolor						1						
brunnea	1		1							2	1	
caespitosa	1				2	1				1	1	2
callichroma	1	2	1			2				1		
camaridii	1		3	4	5	3	2	1	9	6	4	1
candida												1
capularis							1					
cepula		1										
cerifera	1	2	2			1	2					
chartacifolia	1		1								1	1
chrysantha	4	2		1								
cobanensis					1	2						
coccinea	5	4	4	2	3	4	1	1	5	5	1	4
cogniauxiana			1	1							2	
conferta									2			
confusa								1				
consanguinea	1									1	3	3
crassifolia	3	2	2	3	4	2	2	2	1	1	5	3
crocea		1						1				1
ctenostachya											1	
cucullata		2	2	2	4	3			3	10	10	7 : 5
curtipes		4	6	7	14	16	11	2				1
dendrobioides											1	
densa	26	26	11	2	1				1		1	4
desvauxiana	1						1	1		2		2
discolor	1					1	1	2	3	6	2	2
eburnea	1	2							1		1	1 : 1
echinophyta				2	1							
ecuadorensis				1	1	1	1					
elatior	5	17	13	8	3					2		5
elegantula	5	1					1		1	2	5	1
equitans								1				
ferdinandiana	1	1	5	5	1	1			1			

	Ja	Fe	Mr	Ap	My	Jn	Jy	Ag	Se	Oc	No	De
flava			3	3	2							
fletcheriana			3	3	10	3						
fragrans						1						
friedrichsthalii	2	1			1	1	1					1
fucata					1	2	1	4	1			
fulgens	1								1	2	6	7
galeata			1									
gracilis	2				3				1		1	7
grandiflora	4		1	3	3		3	6	3	3	11	4
harrisoniae				1								
hedwigae		1										
hematoglossa	2								4	15	7	5
heterophylla			1					1				1
histrionica											1	2
horichii	1										1	1
huebschii	3					1	2	1			1	2
inaudita	2											1
jenischiana	2						1			4		1
juergensii	2	2	9	4	1		1					
lancifolia										1		
lawrenceana			4						1			
lepidota	3	5	14	10	6	1	4	7	2	8	5	3
leucaimata							1	1				
lindleyana				1								
longipetiolata											1	1
longisepala	1	1		1			2	1	3	4	4	
longissima					1			1		2	2	1
lutea	1	2	3	2	2	2	2	2	1	2	1	2
luteoalba	7	8	15	18	21	4	11	3	1		2	2
macrura	2	1									1	1
maculata									1			
madida				1								
mapiriensis				4	3	3	3	2				
marginata							2					1
meleagris	3	1	1	2	7	12	11	1	8	16	5	2
meridensis						1						
miniata	1	3	1				1	1			1	
minuta			3	2	2	1						
mirabilis		1									1	
molitor						1						
monocantha								2				
mooreana											1	
multiflora											1	
nagelii				2	1		1					
nasuta							1		3	2		1
neglecta	2						·			1	1	1
nigrescens	6	1	3	1	12	6	4	7	7	7	13	3
oceophylla										2		
ochracea						1						
pachyneura		1									1	
pachyphylla			1								1	
parkeri	2		2		1			1	1	2	2	2
parva		1										
phoenicanthera	1										7	10
picta	9	10	9	3		1	5	1		11	24	20

	Ja	Fe	Mr	Ap	My	Jn	Jy	Ag	Se	Oc	No	De
porphyrostyle	7	15	5	4	2	1					3	3
porrecta	4	3						1				
praestans			1	7	12	10	3	1			1	
prolifera										1		
pterocarpa					1							
pulchra					1							
pulla			3	2	3	1		1	1	1	3	3
pumila		4	2	2	2		1		1			
reichenheimiana	2					1					2	
rhombea						3	6	4	5	5	2	1
ringens										1	2	
rufescens	7	4	11	7	9	13	23	11	15	21	13	13
sanderiana	3	7	13	32	70	20	6	1				
sanguinea	2	14	9	5	6	1						
scurrilis						1	1					
seidelii		2	2								2	1
setigera	2	1	2	1							6	6
sophronitis	12	4	2	2	3	4	3	4	2	4	14	7
spaetifica						1						
splendens										1		
stenophylla				1						3	3	2
striata			1					5	7	4		
strobelii					1	2	2					
tenuifolia	3	4	12	22	79	42	22	3				
triloris		1	1	1				1				1
trinitatis	2											2
turneri	1	1	1	3		1						
ubatubana								1	1			
uncata	5	3	1	3	1		1	1	1	3	1	2
vagans						1						
valenzuelana	9	3	6	1	4	2	6	1	6	6	6	2
variabilis	16	19	36	27	18	11	5	6	4	9	14	16
—var. *villosa*	1	3	2	3	2	1	1					
venusta	2	1				2	7	7	1	2	2	2
vernicosa			1	3	3	1	1	1				
vestita												3
villosa	1	2			1	2			1	3	4	1
vitelliniflora		2	3	9	8		1	1				
witsenioides								1				
Mediocalcar												
agathodaemonis							1					
bifolium		1			1		1	1			1	
monticola			1									
pygmaeum										1	1	
sepikanum	1	1				1	1					
uniflorum							1					
versteegii								1			1	
Megaclinium												
bicolor	3	2	1	3			1	1	1	6	1	1
manabinum						1	4	5	8	2	2	1
Meiracyllium												
trinasutum				1	2	8	4	4	6	1		
wendlandii	2	2	3	7	7	2	3	1		2	6	7

	Ja	Fe	Mr	Ap	My	Jn	Jy	Ag	Se	Oc	No	De
Mendoncella												
fimbriata							1					
grandiflora			1	1	2	3	1	1				
jorisiana				1						1	1	
negrensis					1				3	3		
Mesadenella												
cuspidata								1				
petensis			2									
Mesadenus												
polyanthus				1								
Mesoglossum												
londesboroughianum	1									1	5	1
Mesospinidium												
incantans			1				1	1				1
Mexicoa												
ghiesbreghtiana	1	9	17	24	22	4	2	2		1		
Microcoelia												
amaniensis				1								
caespitosa		1									1	
corallina					1							
dahomeensis											1	
exilis		1					2	1	2	2		1
guyoniana				2	2	5				2	1	
megalorrhiza							1					
obovata					1							
stolzii					1	1						
Micropera												
apiculata							2	2				2
mannii								1	1	1		
obtusa					2	1			1	2		
rostrata					1		1		2	2		
Miltonia												
candida	1			1		3	4	10	18	15	5	
flava	1											
flavescens			1	10	19	21	12	5	14	4	4	
× *leucoglossa* Nat. Hyb.									2			
regnellii						1	1	6	23	38	14	2
—var. *alba*						2	4	1		2		
spectabilis				2	5	26	13	7	26	21	13	1
—var. *moreliana*								6	40	69	35	6
Miltonioides												
confusa					1			1				
hastilabium	1		1	3	20	4	3	5	1	2		
karwinskii					1		1					
laevis			1	4	8	24	9	6	3	2		2
pauciflora					1	1						
reichenheimii	3	1	7	7	10	10	2					1
schroederiana	3	1	1	1	0	2	7	24	8	6	2	4
stenoglossa		1	2		3	1	4	2	2		1	1

	Ja	Fe	Mr	Ap	My	Jn	Jy	Ag	Se	Oc	No	De
warscewiczii	20	26	38	19	9		5	10	5	15	17	20
—*alba*				2	4	1						
Miltoniopsis												
phalaenopsis	3	1	9	12	30	13	7	5	9	4	6	
roezlii	3	9	22	27	38	15	13	19	12	16	6	3
—var. *alba*	1	1	4	5	16	4	8	8	2	1	5	1
santanaei					1	2	1					
vexillaria	5	4	19	103	499	308	167	69	26	31	14	8
—var. *alba*	2	4		5	13	10	8	3		1	1	
Mischobulbon												
cordifolium				1		1						
scapigerum					1							
Mobilabium												
hamatum				1								
Monomeria												
barbata	3									1	1	1
dichroma			3	1								
Mormodes												
aromatica			1			4	3	3	3	1	1	
atropurpurea		1	1						1			
badia	5	4									2	4
buccinator	3	6	5	3		1	1		1	7	6	3
cartonii	1	2										
cogniauxii	3								2		3	1
colossus	7	12	6				2					5
dayana												1
ephippilabia		2										
estradae			1									
fractiflexa								1				
gigantea	1		1								3	1
hookeri	1	1	1									1
horichii	1	2	4									
ignea	4	3	5	1							3	2
—var. *albascens*	1	2									1	1
lawrenceana	1	1	2	1							2	4
lentiginosa										1		
lineata	7	10	5	1		2				1	3	9
luxata					2		1	7		1		
maculata						1	2	3	1	1		
oberlanderiana		1	1							1		2
oceloteoides							1					
oenantha				1								
pabstiana				1								
pardina	1	2	2	1	1	3	7	3	2	1	2	1
punctata	1						1					
ramirezii										1		
rolfeana	1	1	2							1		1
saccata						1						
sanguineoclaustra												1
schultzei												2
sinuata			1							3	1	2
skinneri				1		1	1					

	Ja	Fe	Mr	Ap	My	Jn	Jy	Ag	Se	Oc	No	De
stenoglossa									1			
tezontle	1	1									1	2
tigrina		1	1					1		1	1	
uncia					1	1	1					
unicolor				1			1	1				
variabile			1		1		1	2				
vernixia										1		2
warscewiczii												1
Mormolyca												
gracilipes	1		2	3	4	1						
peruviana	1											
ringens	9	15	15	11	6	3	3	7	6	9	7	5
Myoxanthus												
reymondii	5		1		1		1			3	5	5
serripetalus		1			1	1					1	1
Mystacidium												
acrobotryum					1							
aliciae							2		1			
caffrum		2			1							
capense				4	3	10	7	3	2	1	1	1
distichum	9	1	1	3	2	4	4	6	10	20	19	11
millarii							1	1	2			
venosum	1						1	1	1	1	3	3
Nageliella												
angustifolia				1	2	9	4	3		1		
purpurea				1	9	27	32	21	5	3		
Nanodes												
discolor		1	7	2	8	5	3	1		5		1
lankesteri					1							
medusae	1	3	7	9	32	31	33	8	3	7	3	2
Neobathiea												
filicornu		2	5	1	1							
perrieri	1	1							2	2	1	2
Neobenthamia												
gracilis	5	2	2	2	1	3	5	6	7	9	6	4
Neocogniauxia												
hexaptera					3	1	4	9	3		1	
monophylla					1	1	17	27	20	11	4	1
Neodryas												
herzogii				1								
rhodoneura		2		1	1		1		2			1
Neofinetia												
falcata		1			6	18	18	17	5	5	1	1
Neogardneria												
binoti											1	
murrayana	2	1				1	1				3	2
Neogyne												
gardneriana			1									1

	Ja	Fe	Mr	Ap	My	Jn	Jy	Ag	Se	Oc	No	De
Neokoehleria												
paniculata	1											
Neolauchia												
pulchella	1									2	15	7
Neolehmannia												
apagana	1											
barbeyana					1					1	1	
difformis	3	3	7	6	7	4	10	5	3	8		1
porpax	2					2	4	19	18	10	14	8
Neomoorea												
irrorata			5	18	8	8	2	2			1	
Neotinea												
maculata				1								
Neottia												
nidus-avis						7	1					
Neowilliamsia												
wercklei									1			
Nephelaphyllum												
beccarii						1						
cordiofolium					1							
latilabrum			1								1	
pulchrum			1			6	6	9	3	1	1	1
Nephrangis												
filiformis	1											
Nervilla												
acuminata				1								
aragoana		1								1		
discolor				1		1						
fuerstenbergiana				1				1				
plicata				1	1							
Nidema												
boothii	3	2	3	6	10	6	8	1	3	3	3	5
ottonis								1	3	3	1	
Nigritella												
angustifolia					1							
nigra						1	1					
Notylia												
albida									1			
barkeri	3	7	11	5	8	3	5	1	2	3	2	1
buchtienii						1						1
bungerothii				1	2	1				1	1	
longispicata					1			3	1			
manabina						1						
orbicularis					1					1		
panamensis				1	1							
punctata					1							
rhombilabia				1		1	1	1				
sagittifera			1					2				

	Ja	Fe	Mr	Ap	My	Jn	Jy	Ag	Se	Oc	No	De
Oberonia												
acaulis								2	3	3	2	
disticha		1		1				1				
ensiformis											1	1
falcata						1						
iridifolia									2	4	1	1
japonica				1							1	
micrantha				1	1							
muelleriana					1							
myriantha		1							1	1		
pachyrachis										1		
pectinata			1									
rufilabris				1								
semifimbriata								1				
Octadesmia												
montana			1			1						
Octarrhena												
angraecoides								1				
condensata			1			1						
Octomeria												
albopurpurea					1				1		1	
alboviolacea		1		1								
arcuata						1			1	1	1	
bauerii				1						2		
brevifolia		1		2	3	3	2	2	2	1	6	3	3
concolor										1	1	
crassifolia										1		2
diaphana			1			8	1	1	1	2	1	
erosilabia											2	
eumecocaulon				1								
geraensis											1	
gracilis					1					1		
graminifolia												1
grandiflora		1			2	3		1		4	6		1
juncifolia				1								
linearifolia						1	1	1				
lithophylla								1			5	2	
loddigesii		1											1
nana								1				
oxycheila											1	
rhodoglossa			1									
robusta		1								1	2	2	1
stellaris										1			1
steyermarkii												2	
supraglauca					1							1	1
surinamensis									2			
tricolor					1							
iridentata													1
umbonulata												1
Odontochilus												
elwesii					1							
inabai		1										

	Ja	Fe	Mr	Ap	My	Jn	Jy	Ag	Se	Oc	No	De
Odontoglossum												
× *amabile* Nat. Hyb.	12	5	14	12	17	9	8	1	3	11	10	7
armatum								1				
aspidorhinum		1					2	6	1			
astranthum						1	1	1				
aureum	2		3	1	1				1		1	1
auriculum					1							
auropurpureum		1								2		
blandum	2	2	4	1	1		1		1		1	1
calodryas	1	1	1		1							
candidulum				1	1							
cariniferum	3	3	2		3		2	4	4	5	5	4
cirrhosum		3	15	18	29	23	2			1	5	2
claviceps			1									
constrictum		1	5				1	1	2	1	2	2
× *coradinei* Nat. Hyb.			1		1	3						
crinitum			3		2			1				
crispum	224	288	501	668	1560	505	162	90	127	216	216	161
—var. *album*		1		3	9	1		1				1
—var. *premier*	3	4	7	6	13	3	5	2	2	1	3	1
—var. *xanthotes*	12	5	12	29	48	14	6	18	12	20	16	7
cristatum	2	3	3	2	2	1	2	3	1	1		
crocidipterum								1				1
cruentum			1	1			1					
dipterum				1								
dormanianum											2	1
edwardii	3	8	18	18	12					1		
elegans			2	1		2	1					
× *eximium* Hort.	9	2	1	2	3	4		4			2	2
expansum					1							
facetum			1									
flavescens					1						1	
funis				1								
hallii	14	18	16	27	46	9	2			3	3	5
harryanum	1	7	11	3	25	16	26	25	18	16	7	2
hennisii	1								1			
hunnewellianum	2	2	4	5	9	2		3				
ioplocon	1				1		1					1
kegeljani		1			1	2		1				1
lindenii	1	1	1	2	2	1	2	1	1	1		
lindleyanum	2		1	4	5	1	2	2	1	1	2	
longipes		1							1	1	1	1
luteo-purpureum	1	9	31	34	59	19	9	2				1
madrense			1					2	3	4	2	
marginellum					2							
maxillare			2					2	7	5	2	
megalophium				1								
mirandum	1		4	2							2	
multistellare		1		1						1		
myanthum		1		1								1
naevium	2	6	6	7	14	7	1	1	2			
nebulosum	4	1	6	9	17	6	6	4	3	3	1	2
nevadense	4	3	1	1	4							1
odoratum	2	1	6	7	8	3		1	1	1	3	3
pachecoi							1					

	Ja	Fe	Mr	Ap	My	Jn	Jy	Ag	Se	Oc	No	De
pardinum	6	1	1	3	2	1	2	2	2	4		2
peruviense						1						
pescatorei	20	25	58	90	146	39	43	19	16	10	17	6
—*alba*		2		7	4	2	3					
polyxanthum		6	4	12	45	3		2				1
praenitens					1							
praestans	1		1					1			3	
prasinum						1						
pusillum	1											
ramosissimum	1	4	5	13	16	1	2	2	1	1	1	1
ramulosum					1							
retusum		3	3	1	1							
ringens	1			1								
sapphiratum						1						
sceptrum	1	7	5	9	19	4			1			1
schillerianum		1	2	2	1		1	1				
spilotanthum										1	1	
subuligerum				2								
trilobum			5	3	1		4	1			2	
tripudians	1	4		3	10	2	2	1		7	2	2
triumphans	3	11	55	81	61	7	1	1	2	2	3	1
virgulatum	1		1	1			1					
vuylstekeanum				1	2		1					
wageneri								1				
wallisii						3	5	3	1	2	1	1
weirii				1			1			1		
wilckeanum				1							1	
Oeceoclades												
calcarata						2	2					
cordilinophylla								3	4	2		
decaryana							1					
gracillima								1				
ledienii						1	3	2	1	4		
lubbersiana					2	1						
maculata	2				1	1	2	5	9	10	15	10
paniculata					2	2						
pulchra									1	1		
roseovariegata	7	3	1									4
saundersiana	1	5	14	15	9	2			1	3	4	3
Oeonia												
elliotii												1
oncidiflora			2							2		1
Oeoniella												
pellucida		1										
polystachya		7	11	6	1					2	4	4
Oerstedella												
centradenia	2	8	5									
endresii	9	29	23	22	19	3	2		1	2	1	1
exasperata			1									
pinnifera			1	2	3		2					
pseudo-schumanniana	1		3		1	2						
pseudo-wallisii			3	3	1	1		1	1		1	

	Ja	Fe	Mr	Ap	My	Jn	Jy	Ag	Se	Oc	No	De
pumila	2	3	2		1							
schumannianum	1	2		4	3	1	1		1	2		1
schweinfurthianum						1			1			
verrucosa							1	1				
wallisii	7	10	11	16	17	3	2		1	3		1
Oncidium												
abortivum		1	1	2	1	1	3	4	4	2	1	1
acrochordonia	1											
aequinoctiale			1	1	1							
alcicorne								1				
altissimum		12	19	33	33	7	9	17	11	5	1	1
amictum							1					
ampliatum		23	15	20	35	5	3	1	1	1		
—fma. *majus*	1	6	16	10	5	3	2					
andigenum								1				
andreetiana		3										
annulare					1							
ansiferum	1	3	2	1	4	1	5	3	2		1	1
anthocrene	1	3		1							1	1
antioquiense				1								
apiculatum										1		
arizajulianum	1	1	1	4	3	1						
ascendens	2	4	11	7	2	1					1	1
asparagoides							1	2	2	1	1	1
aureum	3			1	2					2	2	
auriferum				1		4		1				
aurisasinorum	4	2	2	1							5	9
bahamense		1	3	8	4	3					1	1
ballii									1			
barbatum	3	2	2	6	4			2	5	4	2	1
batemanianum		3	6	6	3		2	5	4	1		
baueri	1	6	6	8	4	2	4	2			2	1
berenyce										1		
bicallosum	6	2						3	5	29	35	13
bifolium		2	4	6	1	1	3	1	1	1	1	1
blanchetii		1	1			3	5	2	2		3	
bolivianense	3	4			1							1
boothianum					1	1	2	3				1
brachyandrum			2	6	6	12	5	2				
bracteatum						1	1		2	2	2	2
brevelabrum												1
brunnipetalum									1			
cabagrae	1	2	2	4		1				1	2	2
cajamarcae										1	1	1
calanthum					1							
caldense							2					
calochilum	1	1	7	9	15	11	3	2	1			1
caminiophorum					1							
cardiochilum										1	1	
carthagenense	1	2	7	7	11	6	18	22	19	14	9	2
castaneum					1							
cavendishianum	25	36	29	13	8			1	1	4	4	5
caymanense				1		1		2				
cebolleta	21	15	14	14	12	5	3	4	2	4	7	3

	Ja	Fe	Mr	Ap	My	Jn	Jy	Ag	Se	Oc	No	De
cheirophorum	47	30	4	1	2	1	2	1	3	18	43	27
chimborazoënsis		1		2								
chrysodipterum		2	2	1	1							
chrysomorphum									1			
chrysothyrsus										1		
ciliatum		1							1	1	1	
cimiciferum		4		1			1					5
citrinum							2	1		1	1	
claesianum				1	2	2	2					
clowesii	1					1	2	7	45	29	8	3
cocciferum	1			2					1		1	1
cogniauxianum						1			1	1		1
compressicaulis		1	4	2	2		1	1				
concolor			34	81	97	11	5	4	5	1	1	
cornigerum		3		2	9	2	1	1	1	2		
crispum	5	1	1	2	17	13	15	8	10	18	12	4
—var. *grandiflorum*			1	2	1	1	1	3	3	2		
crista-galli	2	1	1	1	1			1		1	1	1
cruciatum		1		2	1	2	1	1				
cruciferum					1	1						
cucullatum	6	14	13	11	23	4	7	4	3	2	5	3
cultratum	1				2	1	1					1
cuneata	2	7	14	7								
cuneilabium											1	1
curtum			2		1	3	5	1	2		2	
dactylopterum										1		1
dasystyle		1	2			1	5	4	2		2	
dayanum	2			1							1	
desertorum	1		4	7			5	3	1	2		
—var. *alborubrum*				1		1	1	8	1	2	1	
diceratum			1					1				
dicromaticum				2								
diodon		1										1
disciferum						1			1			
divaricatum	2	1			7	7	7	2	1	1	1	1
donianum		1	1	1	1					1		
durangense		1							1	1		1
ebrachiatum	3	2	1									
edwallii	1		2	3	1				1		1	
enderianum					1			1		5	5	
endocharis	1	2	1								1	
ensatum	5	4	6	2		4						3
estradae					1							
exasperatum								2	2			
excavatum	3	4	4	3			2	5	5	8	6	6
falcipetalum	2		3	1	2	1	1		1	3	1	1
fasciculatum							4	1	7	1		1
fimbriatum			1	3	2	3	1				1	
flavovirens									1	1	2	4
flexuosum	2	1	7	4	13	8	17	24	15	7	8	4
floridianum		2			1		3	2	1			
forbesii	7	2	1	8	4	2	5	32	65	88	78	20
formosissimum										1	1	1
fuscans					1	2	2				2	1
fuscatum		1	2		1		1					

	Ja	Fe	Mr	Ap	My	Jn	Jy	Ag	Se	Oc	No	De
fuscopetalum			2									
galeottianum							1					
gardneri	2	2	3	8	34	12	21	8	5	6	3	4
gargantua												
gauntlettii									2			2
globuliferum					1	1	3	3	4	4	4	1
gracile					1	1		1	2			
graminifolium	1	3	3	6	2	1	2					1
gravesianum		1	1		1				2	5	3	1
guianense	1		2	1	2	1						
guttatum		3	1	3	1	2	1	1				
gyriferum	1			1		3		1		1	1	1
× *haematochilum* N. H.	2	4	4	2	2		1	3	9	5	6	5
haitiense				1	7	2	1					
harrisonianum	1	1		5	12	14	19	9	8	4	4	
hastatum		3	5	6	24	18	11	1				
henekenii	1	1	1	7	13	10	3		1	1	1	1
henrici gustavi			1									
heteranthum	2	1	1	2	1		2	1	3	2		2
hians			1			1	1	1				
hintonii			1	1	7	9	2	3	2			
hookeri			1			2		1	2	3	4	
hydrophilum						1	1	1			1	
hyphaematicum	7	4	2	3	2	3	1		2			2
incurvum	4	3	3	3	4	1	15	32	50	33	17	6
—var. *album*	1	1					1	7	23	20	6	3
insculptum			1		2	1	1	1				1
ntermedium			2					1				
ionopterum									1			
isopterum								1				1
isthmii	1	1		1	1	2						
jamaicense				1								
jonesianum	1	2	4	4		5	8	30	17	9	3	1
kennedyi											2	
kienastianum											1	
lamelligerum	3	1	2	3	4	1			3		1	
lanceanum	1	1	1	2	16	18	43	49	45	33	15	1
lankesteri			1	1	1						1	
lentiginosum	1			1								
lepidum					1	1				1		
leucochilum	6	11	12	23	56	23	39	13	6	1	6	7
liebmannii	3	1							1	4	3	5
lieboldii		1					1	4	3	3	1	
lietzei			1	2	4		1		1	3	7	1
lindenii						1	1					
loefgrenii			1		1							
longicornu	1		1		10	6	8	4	3	1	1	
longipes	1	1	2	7	9	10	10	11	9	8	27	7
loxense		1	2	1								1
lucasianum			1	3						1		
lucayanum		1	2	2	4	2	5	6	3	2	2	1
luridum	2	1	6	1	1	1	2	3			1	1
luteum					2					1		
macranthum	6	5	8	5	31	32	51	8	5	15	17	9
—var. *nanum*		1	1				1	2	1	1		

	Ja	Fe	Mr	Ap	My	Jn	Jy	Ag	Se	Oc	No	De
macronix						6	1	2			4	
macropetalum	5	14		1	1			1				1
macropus		1										
maculatum	16	27	20	13	16	3	3	2	4	2	1	14
maizifolium						1			1	1	1	3
margalefii	1	1										1
marshallianum		2	1	56	157	20	5	4	9	4	5	1
martianum			1				1	1			1	
meirax				3	1	2	4	3	1	1		
meliosmum				1								
mentigerum				1					2			
microchilum		1				1	3	7	25	9	3	
micropogon		4	1		1		1	4	3	2	3	2
microxiphium			1	3								
millianum		2										
mimeticum	1	1		1	1					1	1	
moirianum									1			
monachicum		2		3	11	3	1					
morenoi				3	6	9	6	1		1	2	1
muelleri					1							
nanum	1	1	1	2	2	1		4	3	2	2	2
nebulosum	2		1		2	1		1		2	1	2
nigratum					3			1				
nubigenum	1	3	1	7	6	3		1			1	2
oblongatum	3	1			1	2	4	5	18	16	5	1
obryzatum		2	3	6	1			2	1	1	1	4
ochmatochilum				4	2	1				1		1
octhodes												1
oestlundianum				1	1	2	2	2	1			
oliganthum	1	1		1				2	1	1	1	1
olivaceum	4	7	3	4	6	2	7	2	1	2		4
onustum	2	4	6	7	5	7	2	4	9	13	10	8
orbatum						1						
orgyale		2		1			2	1		1		
onithopodon					1							
ornithorhynchum	26	15	2	2	2		4	8	18	68	44	40
—var. *album*		1						3	4	19	10	7
orthostates	1	1	3				1	1	3	4	2	
osmentii		1			1	3	2		1			
ottonis		2	8	2								1
panamense					4	1	2					1
panduratum									3	2		1
paranaense			1			1						1
paranapiacabense										1	1	1
parviflorum	1				1							1
pastasae					1							
pectorale					4	1	2				1	1
peliograma						1						
pergameneum										2	1	1
phalaenopsis	2	5	15	8	4	2	2			1	2	4
phymatochilum					12	35	20	5	2	1	3	
pictum												1
picturatum	1							1				
pirarense	1			2			1	1	5	1		
pittieri							1	1		1		

	Ja	Fe	Mr	Ap	My	Jn	Jy	Ag	Se	Oc	No	De
plagianthum				1			1		1		1	1
planilabre						1		1	3	3	2	2
pollardii										1		
polyadenium				2						1	2	
porrigens					1		1					
powellii	2	2	3	1	1	1			1	1		1
praetextum				1	3		9	4	2	7	13	4
prionochilum				1	2		2					
pubes		3	8	11	13	3	3	3	5	2		
pulchellum	4	2	7	23	64	17	4	3	5		1	3
pulvinatum	4	3	1	2	3	14	11	2	5	6	6	5
punctatum					1				1			
quadrilobum			2	1	3		2		1			
raniferum	3					1	2	2	2		5	
reflexum	4	4	2			2		2	2	1	2	2
reichenbachii							1					
retemeyerianum		1		1	3	1	2	4	3	1		
rhinoceros				2	1							
rhodostictum	2				3	1						
riograndense			1									
robustissimum						4	1			2	1	1
roraimense					1							
russellianum	1								1			3
rusticum				1	1							
saltabundum			1	1					1			1
sarcodes	1	1	25	33	50	14	15	1	2	3		
sasseri			3	2	2	1						
sawyeri			1	1								
scandens					3	1						
schillerianum								1				
schlimii					2		2		1			
schmidtianum	4	1									1	2
schroederianum	3	1	1			2	6	24	8	5	1	2
serratum	3	2	4	2	3	4	3	2	1	1	5	1
sessile				2								
sphacelatum	1	13	26	42	90	25	16	1	2	3		1
sphegiferum	1				9	3	3		1	2	1	1
spilopterum	2	2	3	2	3		2	4	4	5	2	
splendidum	54	122	54	5	1			1	4	10	8	12
stanleyi									1			
stelligerum		2	1	1								
stenoglossum					1	1	1					
stenotis	4	2		2		1				1	1	6
stipitatum	2	13	9	1		1						1
stramineum	1	4	16	24	15	2	3					
strobelii	1						1	1				
subobscurum					1	1	1		1	1		
superbiens	1	2	8	8	17	5	1	2		3	1	
suscephalum			1	1		1	1					1
sylvestre				2	4	2		2				
tectum		1										
tenue						1				1		
tenuipes										1	1	
teres				1								
tetracopis					1	1						

	Ja	Fe	Mr	Ap	My	Jn	Jy	Ag	Se	Oc	No	De
tetrapetalum	1	2	3	2	5	4	3	3	3	1		
tetraskeledion							1					
tetrotis				4				2	1	1	1	
tigratum		1	1	2	1	2			1	1	1	1
tigrinum	26	8	2	3	1		2	6	18	43	60	35
tigrinum var. *unguiculatum*	3	2	4							2	3	3
tonduzii		1		1			2	1				
trichodes								1		1	2	
tricolor		1										1
trifurcatum				1								
trilobum					1							
tripterygium			1			1						
triquetrum		2	4	2	7	9	11	11	7	8	3	1
trulliferum			1	1		1		5	6	5	5	1
tuërckheimii								3				
turpe										1		
unicolor									1		1	
uniflorum					5	10	3	1		1	4	4
urophyllum		1		2	3	1	1	1				
valueva										1		
varicosum	4	2	3	4	10	4	13	20	46	96	84	37
—var. *rogersii*	7	6	2	6	12	3	3	10	37	59	96	18
variegatum	3	7	8	7	10	2	3	6	6	5	2	4
velutinum			2									
vernixium			1	2								
viperinum		3	2	3	2	1	3				1	
volubile							1		1	3		
volvox						1						
waluewa		1			1	1	2		1	2	3	1
warmingii	1			1								
warscewiczii	3	4	3	1	1	2		1			1	3
welteri				1								
wentworthianum		1				7	12	26	15	5	5	1
widgrenii				1	2					1		
wittii		1	1	1			1	4	17	9	1	1
wydleri	1			3		2						1
zappii				1						1		
zebrinum								1	1	1		
Ophrys												
apifera						1	3	5				
arachnites					2							
aranifera					2							
atlantica					1							
atrata			4									
bertolonii				1								
fuciflora						1						
fusca			3	1								
holoserica			1									
lutea			2	4	1							
muscifera					3							
scolopax			1	2	2							
speculum			1	2								
sphegodes			2									

	Ja	Fe	Mr	Ap	My	Jn	Jy	Ag	Se	Oc	No	De
tenthredinifera			3		1	1						
vernixia			1		1							
Orchis												
anatolica				1								
aranifera					1							
cretica				1								
fusca				1		4						
holoserica				1								
italica					2	2						
joo-iokiana							1					
lactea				1								
latifolia						5	8					
laxiflora				1								
longicornu				1	1	1						
lutea				3								
maculata						4	2	7				
mascula				1	2	4		1				
militaris						4						
monophylla								1				
morio					1	3		1				
papilionacea					4	4						
provincialis					2							
pyramidalis						1		2				
quadripunctata				1								
sambucina						1						
sphegodes				1								
tridentata					1	1						
ustulata						1						
Orleanesia												
maculata						1	2					
pradei					1		1		1			
Ornithocephalus												
bicornis	2	5	4	2	1	1	3	3	3	3	1	1
bonplandi						1						
bryostachyus											1	1
chloroleucus									1			
cochleariformis		1	3	1	3				1			
gladiatus				3	1	4	4	2	12	4	3	2
iridifolius	1	1	3	1		4	9	4	3	2	4	1
kruegeri				1								
myrticola								1	4			
powellii					1							
pustulatus		1	1	1				2				
Ornithochilus												
difformis					1	4	8	9	2	1		
taenialis		1	1						1			
Ornithophora												
radicans	1					2	3	13	26	17	9	3
Osmoglossum												
convallarioides			2	1	1	3		1				
dubium					1	1	1	1				

	Ja	Fe	Mr	Ap	My	Jn	Jy	Ag	Se	Oc	No	De
egertonii		2	2	1		1	1		1			1
pulchellum	31	39	46	16	10	4	3	3			2	8
Otochilus												
alba	1										1	
fusca	4					1						
porrecta					1	2					3	1
Otoglossum												
brevifolium		2	4	1	1			1				
chiriquense	4	5	5	4	6	6	5	4	1		1	2
Otostylis												
lepida								1				
Pabstia												
jugosa	4	2	6	4	8	4	9	3	2	2		
triptera								1				
viridis							5	3	2			
Pabstiella												
mirabilis	9	5	2	1		1						
Pachystele												
dubia	2	5	1	1							2	4
minuta				1								
Palmorchis												
trilobulata									1			
Palumbina												
candida				1	2	11	8	2	1			
Panisea												
apiculata				1								
pantlingii										1		
uniflora	1	2	6	10	6	6	3		2	2		
Paphinia												
cristata	1	1			1	3	12	7	9	5	7	2
grandiflora				1				1		1		
lindeniana							1					
Paphiopedilum												
acmodontum	2	3	17	30	22	8	1	4			2	
adductum			1		2	1		2	2	1	2	2
× *angthong* Nat. Hyb.			3	3	7	3	8	4	4	5	3	1
appletonianum	15	11	20	8	3	1	1			4	5	9
argus	12	21	36	31	25	6			1	1	3	2
armeniacum	8	20	19	6	3					2	3	7
barbatum	11	12	22	38	119	26	40	21	9	13	15	18
—var. *sublaeve*	4	7	4	3	7	3	1			1	2	4
bellatulum	10	4	12	54	220	93	46	14	20	32	14	7
—var. *album*	3		1	3	28	16	2	1	2	5	3	2
bougainvilleanum							1		4	2	3	2
—var. *celebense*		1	1		2	1						
bullenianum	9	18	12	6	8	4	1			1	2	3
—var. *linii*	2	2	3		1						2	
—var. *robinsonii*	1	3	3	3	2		1			1		

	Ja	Fe	Mr	Ap	My	Jn	Jy	Ag	Se	Oc	No	De
callosum	24	22	33	28	60	48	26	22	10	14	15	20
—var. *sanderae*	1	5	6	6	101	42	37	14	4	4	2	3
charlesworthii	11	3	2	1		1	8	23	40	74	46	20
ciliolare	8	10	23	26	32	24	10	4	3	6	4	11
concolor	8	13	14	13	37	31	44	32	33	16	4	14
—var. *hennisianum*		1			2		1	1	2	3	2	
—var. *regnierii*					4	1	1	2				
dayanum	4	6	12	9	13	9	17	6	2	2	4	7
delenatii	4	20	82	39	28	3					1	3
druryi		1	1	6	20	5	3	1	1			
emersonii				7	5	2						
exul	1	8	10	12	25	5				1	2	1
fairrieanum	46	36	30	4	3	4	4	7	100	256	142	66
—var. *giganteum*			2	1					2	3	5	5
glandulifereum	3	3	9	7	9	15	9	10	8	5	1	3
glaucophyllum	6	8	13	9	18	24	13	9	11	9	12	6
—var. *moquetteanum*	1	3	2	3	3	3	3	2	1	3	4	2
godefroyae	2		2	3	18	30	38	24	21	11	10	
—var. *leucochilum*	2		1	2	18	22	43	16	17	6	1	
gratrixianum	7	2	2	1			1		1	5	3	4
haynaldianum	7	10	23	18	10	1	4	7	6	5	5	4
hennisianum	1	2	7	13	16	8	2	1		1		
—var. *fowleyi*		2	8	2	1							
hirsutissimum	7	14	60	59	64	16	12	2		1	2	1
hookerae	4	3	6	7	20	22	11	3				
—var. *volonteanum*	1		1	2	3	4	1					
insigne	191	76	58	15	5	2	2	2	19	122	454	456
—'Harefield Hall'	45	8	7	3					3	35	154	149
—var. *Sanderae*	64	21	11	3	2		1	3	27	125	320	152
—var. *sanderianum*	10	4						2		10	64	26
javanicum	5	6	3	7	13	3	6	5	8	6	8	7
kolopakingii			1	1								
lawrenceanum	8	3	9	28	74	52	36	16	16	13	9	5
—var. *hyeanum*			3	8	40	18	11	5	2	4	3	
liemianum	1	2		1	1	2			2	2	1	
lowii	4	6	8	9	22	6	6	4	3	3	3	
malipoense	2	2	2	1								1
mastersianum	1	4	27	25	39	5	4	2			3	1
micranthum	3	10	14	12	3	1		2	1			
niveum	8	7	15	36	160	88	98	24	28	14	11	4
papuanum			4	1			2		1		3	
parishii		1	1	4	12	32	48	21	9	3	5	
philippinense	1	4	12	27	34	32	19	11	6			
primulinum		4	4	7	8	6	1	2	2		1	3
—var. *purpurascens*				1	2							2
purpuratum	9	1	3				1	9	15	46	21	15
randsii				1	2	2	1					
rothschildianum	2	16	41	41	79	35	26	12	8	7	2	1
sanderianum	1		3	3	7	1		3	2	4	7	
stonei	1	5	4	6	16	23	22	7	1	2	3	2
—var. *platytaenium*					2	3	1	2				
sukhakulii	19	21	21	12	9	7	12	18	23	22	18	7
supardii							1					
superbiens	9	4	10	20	74	98	96	24	11	5	5	5
—var. *sanderae*					11	27	18	9	2	2		2

	Ja	Fe	Mr	Ap	My	Jn	Jy	Ag	Se	Oc	No	De
tonsum	10	7	11	9	9	5	8	7	13	19	24	13
urbanianum	8	7	11	4	2	1				2	1	1
venustum	62	30	34	10	11	1	1	2	1	10	14	46
—*album*	3	1	1					1			3	4
victoria-mariae			3		3			1	1	4	2	2
victoria-regina	8	9	20	17	40	22	15	4	10	20	11	10
villosum	30	62	64	35	12	5	2		3	3	8	10
—var. *aureum*	9	8	2	1	2						2	1
—var. *boxallii*	7	12	14	13	14	7	2				1	2
violascens	3	2	2	4	2		2			1		3
wardii	12	3	3	1	2		2		3	1	3	8
wentworthianum	1	1										
wolterianum	17	11	14	1	1	1				1	3	7
Papperitzia												
leiboldii				1		1			2		1	
Paradisanthus												
bahiense												1
micranthus		1	1				1	1	1	2	1	2
Paraphalaenopsis												
denevei		1		2	4	7	3	3	1			
labukensis				1								
laycockii			1	1	1			1				
serpentilingua		2		1	1		1					
Pecteilis												
gigantea									3			
radiata				4				2	4	1		
sagarikii								3	3	2		
susannae							1	4	5	5	4	3
Pelantantheria												
ctenoglossa			1									1
insectifera										2	2	1
Pelexia												
hamata				1								
laxa				2	4	1	1					
olivacea					1							
weberbaueri			1									
Peristeria												
aspersa						2		1	1	1		
cerina								1				
elata				1			6	14	17	13	6	
guttata								1				
lindenii											1	1
pendula	2	1	2	2	1				1	1		
Peristylus												
goodyeroides							1					
Pescatorea												
cerina			1	2	3	11	22	8	7	5	5	4	4
cochlearis	1								1		1	1
dayana				2	1	1	3	1	2	4	3	
klabochorum	1	1	4	3	3	7	1	2	9	4	5	

	Ja	Fe	Mr	Ap	My	Jn	Jy	Ag	Se	Oc	No	De
lamellosa					1	1		1				
lehmanni			4	5		3	3	3	1	1	3	3
wallisii			2			2	1		5		1	3
Phaius												
amboinensis			1					1		2		1
bicolor				1	1	4	3					
callosus											2	1
cooperi	2							2				
flavus	4	6	8	5	1		1	3		1		1
francoisii								3	2	1		
gravesianum				1								
humblotii						5	5	6	5	1	1	
lutens					1							
mishmensis	1						1	1			1	2
paucifloris	1							2				
pulchellus			2	3	2	2						
sanderianus				3	3	5	3	1	1			
schlechteri								1				
simulans			2	2	3							
somai				1								
tankervilleae	10	42	64	32	16	5	1	1		2	2	2
Phalaenopsis												
amabilis	50	48	55	47	182	78	117	20	16	22	26	16
—var. *rimestadiana*			3			1	1	1	1	1		1
amboinensis	8	8	6	5	9	7	5	7	8	7	5	2
aphrodite	7	7	8	4	1	1						1
celebensis	2						2	1		2	4	2
cochlearis				1	2	1	1	1				
corningiana					3	8	2	2	2			
cornu-cervi	1	3	1	4	8	10	18	24	14	15	6	4
—var. *picta*		2	1	1	1	1		2	1	1		
equestris	3	11	13	12	8	4	2	7	13	14	13	3
—var. *rosea*		1	2		3			3	1	1	1	
fasciata		1			2	2	5	8	9	5	1	1
fimbriata				4	1	5	1		1	1		1
flavus								1	1	1		
fuscata					2	2	5	2	2			
gigantea	1	3	1	3	1		2	8	11	7	1	1
hieroglyphica						1	1	1	4	4	1	1
intermedia	2	3	6	3	5	2	3	3	1	2	1	2
javanica	1		1	1	1				2			
kunstleri				1	1		3					
× *leucorrhoda*	2		6	2	2			1				
lindenii	4				1	4	3	9	10	7	7	4
lobbii	2	3	10	1	3	1						
lowii									4	1		
lueddemanniana	5	6	30	20	42	25	17	10	9	10	5	3
—var. *ochracea*	1	3					2	3				2
—var. *hieroglyphica*							1	7	15	20	8	2
—var. *pulchra*				1	4	1	2	2	4			
maculata							2	3		1		
mannii	5	5	14	15	11	5	4	1				
mariae	1	3	3	1	6	7	3	2	1	1		
micholitzii				1								1

	Ja	Fe	Mr	Ap	My	Jn	Jy	Ag	Se	Oc	No	De
pallens	1	2	6	1					1	1	6	6
pantherina					1	3						
parishii	3	11	21	10	4	1	2	1	1		1	1
pulchra					3		1	1	1			
sanderiana	8	5	7	4	12	3	6	5	6	2	1	2
schilleriana	58	133	69	27	8	1	2	1		3	12	8
speciosa	1				5	6	2		2	1		
—var. *tetraspis*				3	7							
stuartiana	21	44	66	19	11		1	3	1		1	2
sumatrana		1	2	4	20	12	8	1	1	1	1	
venosa								1	1	3	3	
violacea		1	8	3	9	10	36	32	36	27	8	
violacea (Borneo)						2		4	7	6		
violacea (Malaysia)					2		1		3	2	1	
viridis					1							
Pholidota												
articulata			1		3	9	9	1	2	3		1
cantonensis			1									
carnea	1	2		1				1				2
chinensis	1	2	8	12	7							
clemensii												1
convallariae				2		2				1		
crotalina								1				
griffithii					3	3						
imbricata	2			2	11	1		1	3	14	4	4
longibulba									1			
obovata						1	1					
pallida			2		7	8	8	5	2	7	1	2
parviflora						1						
protracta											1	
ventricosa			13	8	2							
Phragmipedium												
besseae				1	1	2		1		1	1	
boissierianum	2	3	4	2	1		1	1		4	1	4
caricinum	2	5	5	4	2	4	5	2	3			1
czerwiakowianum	1		1	1						1		
ecuadorense	1	1			2	1	1	1	2			1
exstaminodeum						1	1					
hartwegii				1	4	2	4	2	2	2	2	2
klotzscheanum		1		1			1	1	1	2	2	2
lindenii	2	9	21	42	61	29	23	7	5	2	1	6
lindleyanum	2	2	1	2	2	1		1	1		2	3
longifolium	12	9	10	8	8	11	13	13	10	18	16	15
—var. *hartwegii*	1	2	1	2	2	2	1	1	3	2	1	2
—var. *roezlii*	6	2		1	3	2	4	6	6	7	7	5
pearcei	5	3	3	4	9	8	5	5	2	3	3	6
reticulatum								1		1	2	
sargentianum		1	4	1	3	5	1	1	1	1	1	
schlimii	6	7	8	6	5	5	3	5	10	22	19	15
vittatum							1		1			
wallisii	1		1	1			1				1	
Phreatia												
collina	1	1			2	7	1	5	2	4		

	Ja	Fe	Mr	Ap	My	Jn	Jy	Ag	Se	Oc	No	De
macrophylla							3					
robusta			1									
samoensis							1			1		
stenophylla			1									
stenostachya					1	2	1					
sulcata					1							
Phymatidium												
delicatulum			1			2		1	2	1	1	1	1
limae					1							
myrtophilum								2				
tillandsioides				1		2	13	5	1		2	1
Physinga												
physodes	2		1						1		1	1
Physosiphon												
costaricensis						2	1					
lansbergii		2	3		2							
lindleyi	1		1	3	3	2	2					
pubescens	1				3	1	1					1
spiralis			1									
tubatus	1	3	14	15	30	33	26	13	8	5	1	
Physothallis												
harlingii	2	1	1		2	2	1		3	5	4	2
Piperia												
unalascensis							1					
Platanthera												
bifolia					2	1						
ciliaris								1			1	
clavigera										1		
fimbriata						1						
lacera						1						
montana					2							
nivea									1			
orbiculata							1					
Platyrhiza												
quadricolor				1								
Platystele												
compacta								1		2		1
lancilabris		1		2	2			1		1	1	
misera	1		2			1		1	1		1	
ornata			2	2	5		3	3	1		1	
ovatilabia										1		
propinqua			1		1							
rauhii										1		
stenostachya	1	3			2	2	2	1	5	4	4	4
taylori										1		
Platythelys												
maculata	1											1
querceticola							1	1	1	1		

	Ja	Fe	Mr	Ap	My	Jn	Jy	Ag	Se	Oc	No	De
Plectorrhiza												
tridentata				1								
Plectrelminthus												
caudatus	1					2	2	2	2	4	4	1
Plectrophora												
alata			2	2	2	1	1	1	1			
cultrifolia				1	1		2	1	3	1		
Pleione												
bulbocodioides	3	15	90	22	13							
—var. *alba*		1	2	2	6							
—var. *pricei*		2	30	12	2							
coronaria				3	1							
forrestii				3	1	1						
formosana	4	16	9	95	18	7						
hookeriana				1	3	4						
humilis	5	3	3	3	1			1	1	2	3	1
× *lagenaria* Nat. Hyb.										1	1	1
limprichtii				4	3	3						
maculata									1	7	17	5
—*alba*										1	8	
praecox						1	1	2	9	52	43	4
—var. *wallichiana*											3	5
yunnanensis		6	12	8	3							
Pleurobotyrum												
mantiquyrana												1
Pleurothallis												
abjecta							1					
acestrophylla											1	
allenii							1		1	3	6	2
alligatorifera	1											
alpina					1							
amparoana	1	1	1	3	1	2	2				1	1
angustilabia					1							
antonensis			1									
aphthosa	4	3	6		5	1			2	1	7	3
appendiculata									1			
arcuata											1	
aribuloides				1	3	2		1				
arietina	1	1	3	3	3	1						1
aristata	1		2			1						
aristocratica		3	1		1				1			
ascendens	1											
attenuata									2	3		
aurantiolateritia		1			2	1	2	3				
auriculata					1							2
australis					1							
avenacea				1								
barbacenensis			1		1							
barboselloides				1								
barbulata	2		2	1	1	1			1			
bicarinata	1			2	2		1				1	1
birchenallii			1	8	7	2	1		3		3	

	Ja	Fe	Mr	Ap	My	Jn	Jy	Ag	Se	Oc	No	De
biserulla	3	3	4	2	1		2	2	1	4		5
bivalvis	2		2	2	2	1				1		4
blaisdellii			3	3					1	2	3	1
breviscapa	2									1	1	
brighamii	1	1		1	1	1		1	2	1	1	4
cabellensis		1	1	1	3	3	2	1	1	1	1	
cactantha										1		
caespitosifolia										1		
calyptrostele		1	2	2			1	1	2	1	3	
cardiantha	3	3	1	1	1	1				4	1	1
cardiostola	1	2	4	5	3		2	3	4	3	5	4
cardiothallis			2		1	2	1	1	1	1	8	4
carioi					1			1				1
carnosa										1	1	
casapensis	3	1			1				5	5	3	2
ceratothallis	2		1						3	5	4	2
cercinata					1							
cestrochila											1	
chrysantha											1	
ciliaris		4	2	1	2		1	1		2		1
circumplexa	2	6	5	3			3	1	3	1	3	4
cochleata												1
conanthera										1	1	
concolor			1									
convallaria										1		
correllii		1										1
corticicola		1										
costaricensis	2		1	1	2		1	2	3	3	3	1
crenata								1				
crocodiliceps			1						1	2		
cucullata							1		1			
cypripedioides				1					2			
dayana												1
delicatula	1	2										
dentipetala		1	2						2	5		
depauperata					1	2						
dioniae	1									1	2	1
discoidea	6	5	6	10	10	4	5	7	8	15	12	4
dolichopus	3	4	3	2	3	4	1		1	1	5	5
dolichorizo							1					
dressleri										2		
dussenii									1			
edwallii					1							
elachopus	1	2	3	2	1		1	1	2	4	3	2
endotrachys	4	2	3	5	5	2	2	4	3	6	4	3
eumecocaulon										1	2	
flexuosa			3			1						
floribunda					1							
foliata				1	4	4	3		1			
fulgens	1	1	2	2	1	1	1	1	1	1	1	2
fuscata					1							
gacayana											1	
gardneri					1							
gelida	1	2	1	1	2	1	1	1		2	2	1
glandulosa										1		

	Ja	Fe	Mr	Ap	My	Jn	Jy	Ag	Se	Oc	No	De
glumacea				1								
gracillima		1										
grandis	1								1	1		
gratiosa	1	2									1	2
grobyi	1	5	18	22	16	9	7	13	10	3	4	
halbingeriana									1			
handroi					1				1			
hastata					1							
helenae				1								
hemirhoda	1		3	3	3		2	1	5	3		2
hians							1			1		1
hieroglyphica			1	2			1		1			
hintonii										1		
hirsuta		1		2	5	4	3	1	1			
hitchcockii							2					
horichii			1					1				
hypnicola	1	1	1	1				2	2	2		4
hystrix									1			
immersa	4	8	10	6	1	1		2	4		6	8
imperialis	1											
imrayi				1								
inflata						1						
insignis			1	1								
ionantha	2	3	4	4	3						2	2
janetiae	1	2										
johnsonii							1		1			
kegelii				1								
lanceana						1		1	1	3	1	1
lanceola	1											1
lancipetala				1	3	1	2					
lansbergii	1	1	2	4					1	1	3	
lateritia								1	1	5	2	
laucheana			1	1					1	1	1	
leontoglossa			1	3						1		
leptophylla			2	1								
leptotefolia											2	3
leucantha		1	1		1		1		2	2	1	1
lilijae	1		1		1		1		1		1	
linearifolia	1			5			1					
linguifera			1			1	1	1	1		2	1
liporangis												1
listerophera								1	1	1		
longicornu		1										
longipedicellata	2	2	1	2	2	4				2	2	1
longispicata								1	1	1		
loranthophylla									3	2		
luteola										2	1	
macroblepharis	1	1	2	1	3	1	5	1	1		1	
macrocarpa					2							
macrophylla			1									
macropoda									1			1
malachantha					1		2	1			2	
matudiana		1										
microphyta				1	2							
miersii							1					

	Ja	Fe	Mr	Ap	My	Jn	Jy	Ag	Se	Oc	No	De
minutalis					1		2	1				1
miqueliana					1		1			3	1	
monocardia	3	4	7	5	4	4	2	6	5	10	5	3
monstrabilis								1				
mornicola							1			1		
mystax									1			
nervosa										1		
nipterothallis												1
niveoglobula	1	1	1		2	1	1		1		1	
northenae	1		1		1		1		1		1	
oblanceolata			1									
obovata									1	2	1	
obscura				1	1							
ochreata	2							3	4	2	2	1
octomerioides			2	1	2						1	
ophiantha												1
ophiglossoides	1	2	1	5	10	8	4	3	8	3	3	
orbicularis		2	1		1		1	1	3	5	5	2
ovatilabia												1
pabstii		2	1									
pacayana			1									
pachyglossa								2		2	1	3
palliolata	2									1	1	1
panduripetala							1				1	1
pansamalae	1									2	1	1
pantasmoides				1								
parvifolia										1		
pectinata							1					
peregrina				1								
pergrata		1										
pernambucensis												1
pertusa	1	1				1	1	1	2	1	1	
phalangifera	2	1	1							1	1	
phyllocardioides										1		
pidax	1											
platystylis									1			1
pluriracemosa	3	1									1	3
podoglossa								2				
powelii										1	1	2
pringlei					1	1		1	1		1	
procumbens	1					1	2		1			
prolifera	1	1	3	2	2	1	3	4	4	1	2	
pruinosa	1		1	1						1		1
pterophora		2		1	3	4						
pubescens					3	6	15	5	2	1	6	
pulchella		1			2			3	2	4	6	2
pulcherrima	1							1				
punctulata	3		1								1	3
purpureo-violacea				1	1							
quadrifida	11	9	10	9	10	8	5		2	7	8	7
racemiflora	2	1	1	2					1	1	4	3
ramosa	1											1
recurva				2	2	1	1	3	1	3	9	3
restrepioides	21	25	16		1					1	2	7
resupinata			1			1			1	1	1	

	Ja	Fe	Mr	Ap	My	Jn	Jy	Ag	Se	Oc	No	De
revoluta		2		4	2	5						
rhombipetala		1										
rowleei				1							1	
rubens					1	2	3	2		1		
ruberrima							1					
rubescens				1								
rupestris						1	5	6	1			
ruscifolia	1	1			2	1	2	1	1	1	4	6
saccata				1							1	
sanderiana			1	1							1	
sanguinea				1								
saundersiana			1					2	1	2	3	
saurocephala			1			4	1					
schaidii	3	5	7	10	10	4		1	1	1	1	1
sclerophylla		1	3		1	3	6		3	9	12	1
segoviensis	3	6	6	2	1	1		1	2	1	1	
segregatifolia		2	4	5			1		1	1	1	
semperflorens		1										
sertularioides										3	1	
sibatensis	2											
sicaria												2
sigmaodea		1										
sonderiana							2	7	5			
stellis		1	2	2								
stenocardium			2	1					1	3		
stenophylla							1					
stenosepala				1								
strupifolia					1						1	1
talpinaria	2	4					1				2	
teletifolium				1	1							
teres						1	1	2	2	2		
tonduzii		1	2						2			
trianaei										1		
tribuloides			2	6	8	13	10	7	2	2	1	1
tricarinata		1	1				1					
tridentata	7	5	3	5	3	1	1	3	4	7	5	4
trifida					1							
truncata	1	2		1							1	2
tuerckheimii				1	2	1	3	3	9	3	4	2
undulata	1	1	1				1	1	3	4	4	6
uniflora		1	1	1					1	1	2	1
velaticaulis	3		1		2			1	8	9	7	1
viduata				1	1							
warmingii							1					
ypirangae		1										
yucatenensis							1					
Plocoglottis												
bicallosum	1	1										
javanica	2											
lowii						1						
Podangis												
dactyloceras			2		2	3	4	4	1	1	1	2

	Ja	Fe	Mr	Ap	My	Jn	Jy	Ag	Se	Oc	No	De
Podochilus												
cultratus				1								
falcatus								1				
microphyllus								1				
Pogonia												
ophioglossoides					2							
Polycycnis												
barbata			1		2	3	3	2	2	1		
breviloba								1	1		1	
charlesworthii								1				
gratiosa							2	1				
lehmannii							1	6	1			
muscifera						1	1	3	2	1		
surinamensis					1		1					
tortuosa									1	1		
Polyradicion												
lindenii		3	2		1	4	4	1				
Polyrrhiza												
sallei			1	1								
zambesiaca					1							
Polystachya												
aconitiflora		4	3	1	3	1	3	2	4	2	3	1
acridolens								1	3	3	4	2
adansoniae	3		1	1		1	2		1	1	4	2
affinis			4	11	9	11	15	7	2	1	1	1
—var. *nana*	1	3	2	1	1						1	
albescens ssp.												
imbricata	1	1	2		1	1	3	1	1	1	2	1
anceps						1	4	1	1	1		
bella	6	2	7	3	1	1	2		2	3	1	4
bennettiana	1						4	4	2	2		1
bicarinata									2			
bicolor	2											
brassii							2	1				
buchananii									1		1	
caloglossa	1	2	5	4	3	3	2	1	1	2	2	1
campyloglossa		3	1		1	1	2	2	1	1	1	1
concreta	5	7		1	2		2	2	6	14	8	5
coriscencis												1
costaricensis					1	1	1					
cucullata							2		2	1	1	
cultriformis	6	2	5	3	8	5	8	6	8	3	4	4
dendrobiflora							1					
dolichophylla							3	5	3	8	2	
elaticaulis									1			
estrellensis									1	1		1
eurychila				1	1							
extinctoria	1							2	1		3	1
fallax	4	4	3	1	5	5	4	3	1	2	1	2
flavescens	1										1	
flexuosa						1	1	1		1	1	
foliosa	1	1		1	1				2	4	1	1

	Ja	Fe	Mr	Ap	My	Jn	Jy	Ag	Se	Oc	No	De
fulvilabia	1							2				
fusiformis	1					1		1	1		2	2
galeata	4	3	2	2	2	1	3	4	4	13	14	6
golungensis	2	1		1	1	2					1	2
haroldiana				1	1							
hastata		1	2							2	1	
hislopii					2	1						
inconspicua					1	2				1	2	
isochiloides		1						1				
jenmanii									1	1	1	
johnstonii					1	1		1		1		
latilabris	1			1	2							
laurentii			1			1					1	
lawrenceana					1	3	4					
laxiflora	9	2	5	4	3	2	7	5	5	9	10	7
leonensis							2	3	2			
leucorhoda		1		1	1	1	2			1		
lindblomii	3	1	1						1		1	
lineata									1			
lutea				2								
luteola	1	1			1	1	2	2	2	1	1	
lutescens				1	1	1						
malilaënsis							1	1	2	1		
masayensis	2							1				
mauritiana	6	3	2					1	2	5	7	6
melliodora							1		1			
meyeri					1	2	3	1				
minima							4	1				
mukantaensis	2	1	2		1						2	4
mystacioides				1				1			1	1
nyanzensis	1						1	1			3	2
odorata	4	2	3	1			1	6	6	9	7	4
—var. *odorata*	2								1	2	7	4
—var. *trilepidis*								1	2	5	7	1
ottoniana					6	2		1		1		1
paniculata	3	1	7	14	10	2	1	3	4	7	6	5
parva		1										
polychaete				1	1							
praecipitis					1							
puberula	4								1	4	5	3
pubescens	12	9	14	7	12	3	4	2	1	3	6	6
purpurea							1					
ramulosa									1	2		1
reflexa								1	1			
rhodoptera				2			1			1		1
sandersonii					1					1		
serpentina		1	3	2				2	1	2		
seticaulis										1		
setifera							1					
simplex						1			2	2		
spatella	1											
stauroglossa	1	4	1									
steudneri	2						1					
stricta		2								1	3	3
stuhlmannii	1											

	Ja	Fe	Mr	Ap	My	Jn	Jy	Ag	Se	Oc	No	De
suaveolens			2					1				
subdiphylla	1											
subulata				3	1							
tessellata	1	2	2	4	1				2	6	8	3
transvaalensis								1	1			
uluguruensis		1						1	1			
undulata							1	1	1			
vaginata				1			1					
villosa							1		1			1
virginea				1								
vulcanica			4	5	8	7	6	2	3	3	3	1
zambesiaca			1	1	4	2	3	1	1			
—var. *hislopii*					1						3	3
Polystele												
stenostachya											1	
Pomatocalpa												
bicolor				1				1	1			
brachybotrya			1	2								
kunstleri								1				
marsupiale										1		
spicatum				1					1			
wendlandorum					1							
Ponera												
equitantifolia											1	
glomerata			1					1				
graminea					1							
graminifolia									1	2	1	
juncifolia					1	1						
longipetala				1								
prolifera										1	1	
striata		1	2							1	3	1
subquadrilabia										1		
Ponerorchis												
graminifolia					1			3				
Ponthieva												
brenesii								1				
maculata		2	1	5	1	3	1					
racemosa		3	8	10	1					1	3	
ventricosa										1	1	
Porpax												
meirax												2
reticulata		1										
Porroglossum												
amethystinum			2	4	8	7	4	1	1	1	1	
echidnum		1	4	3	3	9	21	26	5	7	4	3
eduardii							1					
meridionale				4								
mordax						1				1		
rodrigoi			1		1					2		

	Ja	Fe	Mr	Ap	My	Jn	Jy	Ag	Se	Oc	No	De
Prescottia												
oligantha			5	1								
plantaginea		5	3	2	1							
rodeiensis			4	5	1		1					
stachyodes				2		1				1	2	
tubulosa											1	
Promenaea												
guttata						1						
lentigenosa											1	1
microptera					1	2		1				
ovatiloba			1								1	
paranaensis						2	2	2	1			
rollesonii						1	2	2	1		1	
stapelioides					3	10	34	10	7			
xanthina			2	8	31	43	33	7	2	3	3	2
Pseudolaelia												
corcovadensis			1								1	
vellozicola			1									1
Psychilis												
dodii				4								
macconnelliae				1	1							
Psychopsis												
kramerianum	5	9	24	14	25	18	18	19	18	9	15	8
limminghii			1	1		6	6	3	3	3	2	
papilio	8	13	21	26	54	20	40	34	42	26	26	13
sanderae	2	1					5	2	3	2		
Psygmorchis												
glossomystax						1		2		1		
gnoma			1	1								
pumilio	2	4	2	15	25	15	13	4	4	3	2	2
pusilla	3	5	3	5	4	5	6	6	7	4	3	5
Pteroceras												
appendiculatum									1	3	2	1
spathipetalum										1		
suaveolens					1							
Pterostylis												
banksii			1	1								
baptistii				1			1				1	1
concinna	1	2	1		1		1				2	1
curta			1	3							1	
decurva												1
hamata						1		1	1			
ingens	1											
longifolia			1			1						
nutans	1	2	1				1		2	2	1	1
obtusa						1	1	1		1		
pedunculata	1	4	3			1						
robusta				1					1			

	Ja	Fe	Mr	Ap	My	Jn	Jy	Ag	Se	Oc	No	De
Quekettia												
jenmani						1						
microscopica			1									
Rangaeris												
amaniensis	1	1		2	1	1	2	6	4	4	2	3
brachyceras			1		1					1	6	2
longicaudata		2										
muscicola	4	1						2	2	3	5	2
rhipsalisocia								2	1			
Reichenbachanthus												
reflexus	1					1		1				
Renanthera												
coccinea		10	8	3	3	1	1	1	2	5	2	1
elongata											1	
imschootiana	6	20	48	72	195	79	46	5	3	1		1
isosepala												1
matutina	1	2				2	2	3	4	2	3	
monachica	1	9	13	4	10	3	2	3	2			
philippinensis									1	1	2	
pulchella						2						
storiei			1			3	7	12	6	4	3	
Renantherella												
histrionica							2					
Restrepia												
antennifera	3	2	6	2	3	2	4	3	4	6	7	6
aspasacensium	1			2					2	1		1
brachypus				1							1	1
chocoensis				1								
dodsonii					1					1	1	
ecuadorensis		1								2		
elegans	4	6	5	7	10	6	9	9	2	2	2	1
erythroxantha	1	1	1	1						2	3	1
falkenbergii										2		
filamentosa				2	1	1					2	
guttata				2						1	2	3
guttulata	6	9	3	7	7	6	5	4	2	8	3	
hemsleyana	2	2		1						1		
lankesterii				2				1			1	1
lansbergii										1		
leontoglossa					1							
muscifera			1	5	4				1	2	3	3
nittorhyncha											1	1
pandurata			3	1							1	
pelyx		1										
sanguinea	1	3	1	1	1		1		3	3	2	4
striata	13	9	10	5	4	1	1	5	2	3	8	7
subserrata								1				
teagui						1						
trichoglossa					1	6	2			1	2	
wageneri						3	2	1	1	2	1	

	Ja	Fe	Mr	Ap	My	Jn	Jy	Ag	Se	Oc	No	De
Restrepiella												
ophiocephala	10	11	9	7	4			1		4	6	10
Restrepiopsis												
powersii			1									
Rhinerrhiza												
divitiflora			1		1							
Rhipidoglossum												
kamerunense										1		
xanthopollinium			1									
Rhyncholaelia												
digbyana	2	10	2	10	47	43	53	3	1	3	1	1
glauca	26	37	17	1								
Rhynchostylis												
coelestis				1	4	8	12	17	8	1	1	1
gigantea	75	80	23	6	7	1	3		3	1		15
—var. *alba*	5	2	1					1	1			2
—var. *petotiana*	9	4	2								1	3
—var. *sagarik*		6	2									
retusa	2	2	2	5	32	41	59	33	13	10	3	
violacea		2	2			1	1	1				
Ridleyella												
paniculata	1	1										
Robiquetia												
brevifolia										1		
cerina	1			1								
compressa	1		1						1		2	1
flexa					1							
fuerstenbergiana											1	
gracilis						1						
merrillii		1										
mimus	1											1
mooreana	4	2	2									3
pachyphylla				1	2	2	1	1				
pantherina			1		3		1				1	1
spathulata				1	3		2	1	1			
succisa										1		
wassellii				1		2	1	1				
Rodriguezia												
bahiensis				1			1		1	1		
batemanii	1	1	2		1				1	2	3	
bracteata			1	1	3	1	1	2	2	4	1	3
caloplectron							1					
candida							1	1	1	5	1	
decora	3	2	1		2	2	3	1	1	12	5	8
granadensis		1						1	1			1
lanceolata	2	6	10	3	3	2	1	9	11	14	11	9
—*alba*	2	4	3		1		2	6	1	2	4	1
leeana		1										
lehmannii	1	1	5		1	1				1	1	1
obtusifolia							1					

	Ja	Fe	Mr	Ap	My	Jn	Jy	Ag	Se	Oc	No	De
pubescens			1				5	3			3	
refracta							2					
rigida										1		1
strobellii				2			1					
venusta			1	3	11	17	12	2	9	3		1
Rodrigueziella												
gomezoides					1	1	1	4	6		2	1
Rodrigueziopsis												
antillensis						2			1		1	1
eleutherosepala	1	1	1		1				2	3		
eliae					1							
microphyta									2			
Rossioglossum												
grande	7	6	1	3		4	11	50	149	208	76	18
—var. *aureum*									4	19	10	
insleayi	12	9	4	2			2	1	2	6	8	4
—var. *aureum*		2					2	1			3	
—var. *splendens*							1		1	5	2	2
schlieperianum				2	3	16	62	32	3	2	1	1
—fma. *citrinum*						1	9		1			
splendens			2	1	1			1	3	7	2	2
williamsianum						6	35	28				
Rudolfiella												
aurantiaca				3		2	3	4	3	1		
bicornaria					1			1				
picta							1					
Saccoglossum												
papuanum											1	
verrucosum										1		
Sacoila												
lanceolata		1	1	2								
Sanderella												
discolor		1	1									
Sarcochilus												
australis								1				
berkeleyi				2	1							
ceciliae						3	3	6	5	2	2	
chrysanthus							1					
dilatatus							1					
falcatus			3	3	2	1			2		1	
fitzgeraldii	1	11	21	5	4	1						
hartmannii	3	9	18	13	6	2		1		1		
hillii					1							
longicalcarus							1	1				
olivaceous	1		1									1
pallidus						1		2	1			
roseus		1					1					
teres	1											
Sarcoglottis												
acaulis	7	7	10	9	5	2	6	9	5	2	3	1

	Ja	Fe	Mr	Ap	My	Jn	Jy	Ag	Se	Oc	No	De
biflora			2									
grandiflora				4	10	3						
herzogii												1
homologastra					1							
metallica	1	1										
rosulata				1	1							
sceptrodes		2		1								
ventricosa					1		3	5				
Sarcoglyphis												
mirabilis						1						
Sarcorhynchus												
bilobatus							1	1				
Satyrium												
carneum								1				
coriifolium				3	2		6	3				
longicauda										1		
membranaceum							1	2	3			
nepalense		2								1		
princeps				1				1				
sphaerocarpum									1			
Saundersia												
mirabilis				1								
Sauroglossum												
nitidum		2	4	3	1							
Scaphosepalum												
anchoriferum					1	3		1			1	1
antenniferum	1	1	1		2		1	2	2		2	1
clavellatum										1		
endresianum				4		1		1			2	
escobarianum				2	1							
gibberosum		2	1	2	1	3				1	2	
lima	1		1		2		1		1		1	
microdactylum		2										
ochthodes	18	12	11	21	18	13	15	17	17	23	19	22
ovulare											1	
pulvinare	3	1	1	1	1	1	1	2	1	1	1	1
punctatum				1		2	6	2	2	4	4	2
rapax			1									
reversum				1	1							
standleyi	1		1		1		1		1		1	
swertiaefolium			2	2	2	2	3		2	1	2	2
verrucosum	4	5	5	7	8	7	5	7	4	9	4	4
Scaphyglottis												
amethystina			1	3	6	8	4	1				
bergeriana				1	1							
cogniauxiae	1											
graminifolia			3	2	1				1	1	1	1
hondurensis	2	1										
huebneri		1										
lindenianum					2							
longicaulis				1								

	Ja	Fe	Mr	Ap	My	Jn	Jy	Ag	Se	Oc	No	De
modesta	1				1		1		2	2	1	1
prolifera			3	2	1				3	9	4	
Scelochilus												
langlassei				1								
latipetalus							1					
ottonis				1								1
pichinchae						1						
variegatus		1		1								
Schlimia												
alpina						1		1	2			
Schoenorchis												
densiflora	1	1	1									
fragans					3	5	5	3				
gemmata			3			5	2					
herklotziana										1		
juncifolia								1		2	1	
micrantha	1			1								
Schomburgkia												
chionodora											1	4
crispa			5	4	2	2	1	2	5			1
galeottiana						1			1	3	4	2
humboldtii				2				1		1		
lueddemannii			4	5	5	1						
lyonsii			1	3				2	4	1		
rosea			1	2		1			1			
splendida			2	1	2	1			1			1
superbiens	10	12	13	4					1		2	2	3
thomsoniana				1	1	4	4	6	1			
tibicinis			3	6	9	19	6	4	2			
undulata		4	15	23	5	1					1	3
vellozicola												2
wallisii						3	2	2	3			
weberbauriana	4	1										
wendlandii			3	4	1							
Scuticaria												
dodgsoni							2					
hadwenii				3	4	10	3	4	1	1		
irwiniana					1							
kautskyi								2			1	
mooreana	1					2						2
salesiana					2	2						
steelii	2	3	3	2	9	2	2	3	1	3	2	3
strictifolia			1			1						
Sedirea												
japonica				2	1	1	1					
Seidenfadenia												
mitrata			1	3	3	7	4	1				
Serapias												
cordigera				1	2	1						
lingua			1	1	3	4						

	Ja	Fe	Mr	Ap	My	Jn	Jy	Ag	Se	Oc	No	De
neglecta				2								
occultata					1							
vomercea				1								
Sievekingia												
fimbriata						1	1	1				
peruviana									1	1		
rhonhofiae				1							1	1
suavis	2		1	1		1	1	1				
Sigmatostalix												
adamsii	1						1	1	1		1	1
amazonica	1	1	2		2	1					1	
aurosanguinea				1					1			
bicallosa				1	1							
brachycion								1			1	
crescentilabia				1	1					1		
cuculligera				1				1				
eliae					1		2	1	1			
graminea			2	1	2	3	1				1	1
guatemalensis	3		2	2	3	1	3	3	2	5	5	3
huebnerii				2	1					1		
hymenantha	1		1		2			4	2			
lehmanniana					1							
pandurata				1					2			
peruviana				1	2	2				1		
picta	1		1	1	2					2		2
picturatissima										2		1
Sirhookera												
lanceolata											1	
Smitinandia												
micrantha			1	3	7	3	1		1			
Sobennikoffia												
humbertiana						1		1	1	1	1	
robusta						1	6	1	1			
Sobralia												
cattleya						1			1			
charlesworthii			1			1	1					
cliftoniae				2		1						
decora									2	1		
fenzliana			1									
leucoxantha						1	3	2				
lindleyana				1	1							
lowii								4	3	1	1	1
lucasiana				3	5	6	14	1				
luteola			1									
macrantha	4	3	4	4	29	29	29	10	3	7	4	1
—var. *alba*					8	12	13	2				
—var. *kienastiana*					2	20	12					
—var. *nana*			2			1	2	2				
mucronata							1	1		1	1	
powellii									1			
pulcherrima									1		1	2

	Ja	Fe	Mr	Ap	My	Jn	Jy	Ag	Se	Oc	No	De
ruckeri				1		3						
sanderiana								2	5	3	2	1	
sessilis			2	2	2	1	1	1	1			
virginalis						1						
wilsoniana				1	4	3	3	1				
xantholeuca						2	6	32	18	5	2	
Solenangis												
aphylla				1								
clavata											1	
scandens								1				
Solenidiopsis												
tigroides				2								
Solenidium												
lunatum			1									
racemosum									2			
Sophronitella												
violacea	8	5	2			2	1				1	10
Sophronitis												
acuensis			1							2	3	1
brevipedunculata										5	8	2
cernua	6	3	4	1		1		1	4	26	28	16
coccinea	82	109	176	74	41	6	19	19	15	36	57	58
—var. *rosea*	3			1						1	1	4
lowii	2		2	1						1		
mantiqueirae		2	8									2
pterocarpa										3	1	
rosea	4	3								1	3	7
wittigiana	2	5									2	4
Spathoglottis												
affinis	1								1		1	2
altigena								2			1	
aurea			1	6		15	1	1		2		1	
eburnea											1	
edinensis									1		2	
grandifolia		1										
hardingiana											2	
ixioides							1					
kimballiana				1		3	1				1		
lobii	1		2	1	2	1				1		1
longifolia										1		1
parsonsii					1							
petri		2	1	1	1	3	2	1	1			
plicata	3	4	3	1	1	5	11	8	2	3	3	4
portus-finschii		1										
pubescens								5	3	4	2	
rivularis									1			
vieillardii					5	1	2	2	1	2	1	1
Sphyrarhynchus												
schliebenii				3	3					2		

	Ja	Fe	Mr	Ap	My	Jn	Jy	Ag	Se	Oc	No	De
Sphyrastylis												
escobariana				1				1				
Spiranthes												
cernua	2	1	1	2	2	1				1	6	2
gutturosa	1	1										
lacera		1			1							1
laciniata		1				1		1		1		
lancea	3	2	2			1						2
lucida						1	1					
odorata	2		2	1		1				5	5	6
praecox					1							
sinensis			2	1	1	1	2		1			
spiralis alba	1											
vernalis				1								
Stanhopea												
annulata								1	1	1		1
bolivariense					1	3	1	1				
candida									1	2	1	
cirrhata					2			2	1	2	1	
connata		2			3			1	3	1		
costaricensis					1	6	10	1	7			
devoniensis					1		4		1		1	
ecornuta					2	2	2	7	2	2		
embreei				1				1				
florida					1	1					1	
fregeana					1		1	1				
frymirei							1					
gibbosa						2						
grandiflora	1	1	4	2	1	2	4	7	7	11	7	1
guttulata				1		1	2	4	1		1	
hasseloviana								1				
hernandezii							4	3	1	2		1
impressa				1					1			
insignis					3	2	8	7	7	2	3	
intermedia					1		1	1	1	1		
lietzei					1	3	12	17	6	6	1	1
lewesii							1					
lowii								2		1	1	
—var. amesiana		1		1	3	1	2	1	2		1	
maculosa							1		1			
madiouxiana						1						
martiana					2	2	3	3	2		1	
moliana				1			1					
nigripes	1							2	1	1		
novogaliciana							1					
oculata		1	2		2	8	16	29	24	17	4	
ospinae						1	1					
panamense								2	1			
peruviana					1	1	2	2	2			
platyceras					1	1	1	3	2	1		
pulla								1		1	2	
reichenbachiana		1						1				1
ruckeri								3		1		1

	Ja	Fe	Mr	Ap	My	Jn	Jy	Ag	Se	Oc	No	De
saccata					3	5	8	9	3	4	1	
shuttleworthii			1			1		2	1			
stevensonii							1	1				
tigrina					4	9	54	22	10	5		
tricornis		1				1	1	3	2	2	2	2
wardii	1	1	2	1	2	10	27	24	30	20	12	6
warscewicziana							2	2	2			
Staurochilus												
ionosma				1								
micrantha			1									
Stelis												
aemula				1								
alba	1					1		1			1	1
aprica			4	5	3	1	1				2	4
argentata	1	2		6	6	1	7	5	8	6	6	2
bidentata			1	1				1	1			
biserrula					5			3	2	3	2	
bractescens						1						
catharinensis	2	1							3	5	6	3
chihobensis	1	5			2							
cucculata		3	1	1	1							
curvicarina					1							
despectans									3	4	1	
discolor								1				
ekmanii	1											
fraterna							1	3	2			
gemma				2						3		
guatemalensis								2	1	1		
guianensis									1	3	4	3
longipetiolata						1	1					
lutea	2	5	2	2	3	1		1				3
major				1								
maxima		1										
microchila			1					2				
minutiflora						1		1				
muscifera			1	2	2	2				2		
papaquerensis			1	2								
parvula					3							
pauciflora	5	5	7	5	4	1	2	3	4	7	10	5
peliochyla						1	1	2	1			
porschiana		1										
prolifera					1							
pubescens	2				1				2	4	3	1
purpurascens				1				1	1			
semperflorens		1		1			1					
storkii	3	4	3	1	4	4	4	3	2	2	3	1
superbiens	1		4	3	2	1	2	6		3	2	
transversalis											1	
tricardium			1		1							
trigoniflorum										2	3	1
tristyla				1	3	1	1	1				2
virens								1				
wercklei				1								

	Ja	Fe	Mr	Ap	My	Jn	Jy	Ag	Se	Oc	No	De
Stellilabium												
astroglossum				1								
minutiflorum										1		
Stenia												
pallida				1	3	1	2	5	2	2	3	3
saccata								1		1		
Stenoglossum												
coryophorum				1								
Stenoglottis												
fimbriata				1	2	1	1	4	4	6	6	2
longifolia		7			9	2	1	10	25	60	46	5
woodii			3			1	1				1	
Stenorrhynchos												
aurantiacum								1	1	2	1	
nutans		5	7	7						1	3	11
speciosum		6	6	5							2	5
Stereochilus												
hirtus						3	2					
ringens								1				
Stolzia												
repens							1		2		1	
Sunipia												
bicolor									2		1	1
intermedia											1	
paleacea											2	
racemosa		1										
Symphyglossum												
sanguineum		1	1	4	7	11	4	8	6	5	1	
Systeloglossum												
costaricencis					1							
Taeniophyllum												
crepidiforme										1		
filiforme								1				
formosanum					1					1		
Tainia												
hongkongensis				2	1							
hookeriana		6	10	6	1	1						
latifolia		2	1									
laxiflora				1								
minor												1
penangiana	5	4										
shimadai				1				1				
speciosa						1	1					
wrayana				1	1	1						
Tapeinoglossum												
centrosemiflorum					2			1				

	Ja	Fe	Mr	Ap	My	Jn	Jy	Ag	Se	Oc	No	De
Telipogon												
ampliflora			1									
andicola						1						
biolleyi						1						
bruchmuelleri			1	2				1	1			1
croesus	1	1									1	
falcatum								1				
gnomus					1							
gracilipes			1									
hemimelas	1											
kalbreyerianus			1	1								
latifolius			1									
nervosus		1	1	1	1		1				1	
pulcher				1			1			1	1	
radiatus		1										
Tetramicra												
bulbosa		1	4	1	1							
canaliculata						2	2	1	1	1		
ekmannii				1								
elegans		1	1	1				1				
parviflora					1							
urbaniana				2								
Teuscheria												
cornucopia									1			
horichiana										1		
pickiana								1				
Thecostele												
alata				1	1		2	1				
secunda				1								
Thelasis												
capitata										1		
carinata								1	1			
longiflora						1						
micrantha								1				
Thelymitra												
aristata								1	1			
canaliculata		1						2				
longifolia											1	
pauciflora											1	
Thelyschista												
ghillanyi											1	1
Thrixspermum												
acuminatissimum										2		
arachnites								2	1	3	1	
elongatum		2							1			
formosanum				1		1				2		1
hystrix				1						1		
japonicum				1								
leucarachne									1	1	1	
pygmaeum		1										
saruwatarii	1	1	2									

	Ja	Fe	Mr	Ap	My	Jn	Jy	Ag	Se	Oc	No	De
Thunia												
alba				4	20	10	14	2				
bensoniae	1				11	16	6	2	1	1	1	1
brymeriana				1	3	2	2					
candidissima						1						
marshalliana					28	43	9	4				
pulchra								2				
venosa					3	2		3	2			
winniana					1	2	3					
Ticoglossum												
krameri	4	1			1	1	3	11	6	11	6	4
—v. album									1	1	2	2
oerstedii	2	5	14	12	10		2	1	1	1	1	
Trevoria												
chloris									1			
Triaristella												
dressleri		1	1								1	1
tridactylites				1	1							
Trias												
disciflora								2	1	2	1	
intermedia						1						
picta	2	9	6	4	1					1		3
Trichocentrum												
albococcineum			2	1			2	2	7	2		2
calcaratum				1								
caloceras		1										
candidum							1	3	1	3	3	1
capistratum	5	3	2	1	3					3	3	3
fuscum	1	1								3	1	1
hoegei						1	1	2				
iridifolium									1			
maculatum	2	1	1						1			2
panduratum				1								
pfavii	3	3	5							3	3	6
porphyrio	1						1	1				2
pulchrum						1		2	1	1		
purpureum									1			
tigrinum	2	1	3	4	4	8	4	3	1	1	1	
Trichoceros												
antennifer	1	1		1	1	1	4	5	8	10	6	5
breviracema			1	2	2	1	1					
muralis				1	1		1	2	2	7	2	2
platyceros											1	
Trichoglottis												
brachiata				1			2	2		5	3	1
breviraceme				2								
dawsoniana					1	1	3					
fasciata				1	2	1	1			1		
guibertii			1	2			2					
intermedia				1								
ionosma			2				2		1			

	Ja	Fe	Mr	Ap	My	Jn	Jy	Ag	Se	Oc	No	De
joyceana			1	1								
lissochiloides								1	3			
lowkeriana						1					1	
luzonensis				1								
misera				1	2		1		2	3	1	
pantherina					1	1						
papuana		1	3	3								
phillippinensis								2	2		4	
—var. *brachiata*									2	6	3	1
pusilla			1									
rosea	2			2						1	1	
sagarikii					1	1						
wenzellii			2		1							1
Trichopilia												
albida										1		
brevis	1							2			2	2
crispa			1		9	7	2					
elegans	1										1	1
fragrans	7	4	8	17	28	13	9	9	9	16	8	
galeottiana					2	7	8	3			2	
× *gouldii* Nat. Hyb.	1	2							1	7	3	1
hennisiana			1	7	4	2	1					
laxa	1		1		2			1		3	1	3
leucoxantha					2	1						
maculata					2						1	
marginata	1		2	7	31	17	11	4	3		5	1
oicophylax			1	1	1	1		2	1	1	1	1
rostrata					1			1	1	1	1	
suavis	14	23	42	30	27	6	5	1		1	7	10
tortilis	2	2	11	20	24	18	11	2	1	1	2	
turialbae	1						1	4	1	1		1
variabilis				1								
Trichosalpinx												
farrago				1								
Tridactyle												
anthomaniaca					1	2						
armeniaca					1							
bicaudata	2	1	1	4	2	1			1			
fusifera					3	3	3					
gentilii		1										
lepidota								2				
teretifolia								1				
tricuspis	1	2				1	1					
tridactylites	1	2		2	5	3	10	5	5	7	2	
tridentata		1										
wakefieldii				1								
Trigonidium												
acuminatum							1		2	1	2	
egertonianum	5	6	4	4	4	1	1	1	1	1	3	3
grande									1			
lankesterii				1								
macranthum				1								

	Ja	Fe	Mr	Ap	My	Jn	Jy	Ag	Se	Oc	No	De
obtusum			2	1		3	2	5	2	2		
riopalenquense												1
tenue			1				1	1				
Trisetella												
huebneri		1							1			2
tridactylites									1	1		
Trizeuxis												
falcata				1								
Tropidia												
angulosa									2	2		
curculigoides							2	2			2	
Tuberolabium												
kotoense	6										5	2
quisumbingii				1	1	1			1	1	1	
Tylostylis												
discolor	1											
Uncifera												
obtusifolia		1	2	1								
Vanda												
alpina			2	2	7	3		2		1		
amesiana	35	18	14	2		2				2	4	13
bensonii			2	6	6	10	2	4	1			1
brunnea				1				1		2	1	
coerulea	18	5	13	5	17	18	39	103	133	179	260	90
coerulescens	1		12	26	31	8	3					1
—var.*boxalli*				3	2							
concolor					1	1				1	1	
cristata			2	12	25	45	21	6	3	2		1
dearei				2			2	2	1	2		
denisoniana			2	9	8	16	5	7		2	2	1
furva				2	3	2						
hookeriana			2	3	3	3	5	7	3			
insignis		1	2		3		1	3	4	6	3	
kimballiana							3	5	26	43	23	
lamellata	2	3		1	2	1	1	1	1	2	2	1
—var. *boxalli*				1	1		1			1	4	4
laotica	1	1	2	1	1							2
lawrenceana						1						
limbata					3		1					
luzonica							3		6	13	9	2
merrillii		2		1				4	5	3	4	4
parviflora				2	3	4	3	3			2	
pumila					4	5	1	3				
roeblingiana						1	12	9	4			
sanderiana	15	14	3	6	4	5	18	25	51	90	49	28
—var. *alba*			1				1	1	2	7	3	1
spathulata		1							1		1	
stangeana		1	2	4	7	5	4			4	1	1
teres			8	5	42	233	91	13	3	3	1	1
—*alba*			10		2	10	1	2	1		1	2
tessellata			2		4	10	6	4	3	4		

	Ja	Fe	Mr	Ap	My	Jn	Jy	Ag	Se	Oc	No	De
tricolor	8	7	20	41	50	20	20	14	16	10	8	6
—var. insignis		1	1	2	2	2	1	2	3		1	
—var. planilabris				1	3		1	1				
—var. purpurea				2	1	2	2	2				
—var. suavis	9	8	27	48	50	11	17	7	9	9	9	5
—var. veitchii	2	2	4	2	2	2	1					
tricuspidata						1						
undulata				1	1							
watsonii	16	17	6	2							3	1
Vandopsis												
gigantea	2	18	5	3	4		1					1
lissochiloides				1		4	6	14	11	3	3	2
parishii			1	3	11	21	7	13	4	1		
—var. marriottiana			2	3	8	3						
undulata			2	1	1	1	1	1				1
warocqueana												1
Vanilla												
barbellata			2	1								
imperialis				1		3	3					
phaeantha			1									
planifolia			3	3	4	3	1	1	2	1	1	1
pompona			2		1	1						
Warmingia												
elegans							1	1	1		1	
eugenii						1	2	4	1			1
Warrea												
bidentata			1							1		
costaricensis	1									1	1	1
warreana			1					2	2	1	4	2
Warscewiczella												
ionoleuca					2	1						
lipscombiae	1		1									
paludosa	1											
sanderiana										1	1	
Xylobium												
bractescens									1	1	1	1
citronum											1	
colleyi							1		2	1	1	
corrugatum			1								1	
elatum							1					
elongatum	1		1							2	3	1
foveatum	1	3			1		1	2	4	1	2	
hyacinthinum				1						2		
latilabium					2							1
leontoglossum	3	5	2		1		1			1		2
pallidiflorum	1								1	1	2	1
palmifolium	1		1						1	2	2	1
peruvianum									1			
tuerckheimii							1	1	1			
variegatum	4	2	3	1	12	2	2	1	1	3	5	6

	Ja	Fe	Mr	Ap	My	Jn	Jy	Ag	Se	Oc	No	De
Ypsilopus												
graminifolius			1									
longifolius										1		2
Zeuxine												
oblonga	1											
strateumatica	6	3										5
Zootrophion												
atropurpureum										2		
dayanum											2	
dodsonii									1			
Zygopetalum												
brachypetalum	3	1			1	1						1
burkei								1	1	1		1
crinitum	3	9	12	10	7	3	3	4	3	2	7	2
graminifolium				1			1					
grandiflorum					2		1					
intermedium	19	9	2						2	3	7	8
mackayi	26	17	11	2			3	4	6	13	53	43
maxillare		2			2	1	1	7	23	5	1	1
pedicellatum											1	
perrenoudi Hort.			1		3							
reginae					1							
sellowii								1				
triste			1	1					1			
wendlandii				2	2		1	2	1	9	1	1
Zygosepalum												
ballii		2			1	1						1
labiosum	5	2	1	2	11	2	2	3	7	3	6	5
lindeniae			1	1			3	2	1	2		2
Zygostates												
alleniana				1	4				1	1		
cornuta				1					1			
grandiflora					3	2	2					
lunata				2	1		1	4	1		1	
pustulata				1		1	2	1				1

Orchid Biology: Reviews and Perspectives, **volume 1, 1977**

1. A Personal View of Orchids
   Richard E. Holttum
2. Fossil History of the Orchidaceae
   Rudolf Schmid and Marvin J. Schmid
3. Orchids in Rumphius' *Herbarium Amboinense*
   Hendrik C. D. de Wit
4. The Distribution and Chemistry of Alkaloids in the Orchidaceae
   Michael B. Slaytor
5. Anthocyanins of the Orchidaceae: Distribution, Heredity, Functions, Synthesis, and Localization
   Joseph Arditti and Michael H. Fisch
6. Vitamin Requirements and Metabolism in Orchids
   Joseph Arditti and Charles R. Harrison
7. Variations in Clonal Propagation
   Thavorn Vajrabhaya
Appendix: Clonal Propagation of Orchids by Means of Tissue Culture—A Manual
   Joseph Arditti

Orchid Biology: Reviews and Perspectives, **volume II, 1982**

1. Auyán-tepui: Reminiscences of an Orchid Search
   G. C. K. Dunsterville and E. Dunsterville
2. A General Review of the Orchid Flora of China
   Chen Sing-chi and Tang Tsin
3. Orchid Mycorrhiza
   Geoffrey Hadley
4. The Biology of Orchids and Euglossine Bees
   Norris H. Williams
5. Carbon Fixation in Orchids
   Popuri Nageswara Avadhani, Chong Jin Goh, Adisheshappa Nagaraja Rao, and Joseph Arditti
6. Mineral Nutrition of Orchids
   Hugh A. Poole and Thomas J. Sheehan
7. Flower Induction and Physiology in Orchids
   Chong Jin Goh, Michael S. Strauss, and Joseph Arditti
Appendix: Orchid Seed Germination and Seedling Culture—A Manual
   Joseph Arditti, Mark A. Clements, Gertrud Fast, Geoffrey Hadley, Goro Nishimura, and Robert Ernst

Orchid Biology: Reviews and Perspectives, **volume III, 1984**

1. Orchids: Their Innocent Past, Their Promising Yet Perilous Future
   Rebecca Tyson Northen
2. Ethnobotany of the Orchidaceae
   Leonard J. Lawler

Orchid Biology: Reviews and Perspectives, **volume IV, 1987**

INDEX OF PERSONS

Where only one name is given in the text, initials and/or last names were added whenever possible by the editor/indexer to facilitate identification. Two brackets, [ ], indicate that initials and/or last names were not added. Initials may not have been added for 1) individuals usually referred to in the literature by one name only (i.e., Aeschylus, Homer, Confucius, Darwin, etc.), and 2) for characters in works of fiction for whom only one name is mentioned or used. Boldface numerals indicate illustrations of or by that person. The computer program used for the preparation of this index is *Utilities for Writers*, originally written by Kevin J. Hackett in 1983–1984 and updated by Ling Shao and Hanny Suryadharma in 1989–1990. All were computer science majors at UCI.

INDEX OF ORGANISM NAMES

This index includes the names of orchids and all other organisms mentioned in chapters 1–7. Names from the Appendix are not included because they already appear therein in alphabetical order. Scientific names are italicized (e.g., *Vanda suavis*). All others, including orchid names used as symbols and/or in literary works and/or applied to fictional characters (Chapter 6) are in roman type. Taxonomic groupings above the generic level are in capital letters (ORCHIDACEAE, for example). Illustrations are designated with **boldface** numerals (84 for text entries vs. **84** for an illustration, for instance). The tables in chapters 3–6 were scanned with an Apple™ scanner attached to a Macintosh™ IIX computer and converted into ASCII files with the Omnipage™ program. These files were then "translated" into IBM™ format, edited with the WordStar™ 5.5c word processor in the document mode, combined with a file containing organism names from the text of chapters 1–7 and converted to non-document form. This file, which contained 89 kilobytes (50 kilobytes from the scanned tables and the rest from the text), was sorted (and reduced to 68 kilobytes because multiple entries are combined in the process) into an index with the Indexer which is part of *Utilities for Writers* first written in 1983–1984 by Kevin J. Hackett and revised in 1989–1990 by Ling Shao and Hanny Suryadharma (all computer science majors at UCI). Mr. Steve Okura of the Microcomputer Services Group, University of California, Irvine, was very helpful with the scanning.

SUBJECT INDEX

Boldface numerals indicate illustrations. Glossaries were scanned and incorporated in this index in the same manner as plant names, which were taken from tables for the Index of Organism Names. This index was prepared with the indexing program used for the other two indices.